CONDUCTIVE ADHESIVES FOR ELECTRONICS PACKAGING

CONDUCTIVE ADHESIVES FOR ELECTRONICS PACKAGING

Edited

by

Johan Liu

ELECTROCHEMICAL PUBLICATIONS LTD
1999

ELECTROCHEMICAL PUBLICATIONS LTD
Asahi House, Church Road, Port Erin,
Isle of Man, British Isles

©

Electrochemical Publications Ltd
1999

ISBN 0 901150 37 1

DISCLAIMER

We believe the information provided in this work is reliable and useful, but it is furnished without warranty of any kind from the publisher, editor or authors. Readers should make their own determination of the suitability or completeness of any of the material included for specific purposes and adopt any safety, health, and other precautions as may be deemed necessary by the user. No licence under any patent or other proprietary right is granted or to be inferred from the provision of the information herein.

Typeset by Electrochemical Publications Ltd, Port Erin, Isle of Man, British Isles
Printed by Arrowsmith, Bristol, England

PREFACE

During recent years, I have been focusing my research work on conductive adhesive joining for various electronics packaging applications. However, in order to promote the use of conductive adhesives on a large scale, I realise that the knowledge must be transferred to a wider range of electronics production engineers, designers and decision makers. Therefore, together with Rolf Jansson, TeknikCentrum, Norrköping, Sweden, I started to organise professional courses in electronics packaging using conductive adhesives. In this context, we recognised the need for a book on conductive adhesives in electronics packaging where state-of-the-art knowledge is comprehensively summarised.

Conductive adhesives have been used for electronics packaging applications for decades in hybrid, die-attach and display assembly. During the past decade a growing interest has been noticed from the electronics industry in other kinds of electronics packaging applications. In my opinion, it is the toxicity and environmental incompatibility of the lead in tin-lead solders that triggered the greater interest from the outset. However, as the technology and development progress, it is realised that conductive adhesives can offer the following additional potential advantages:

— fine-pitch capability especially when using anisotropic conductive adhesives (ACAs) for flip-chip;
— elimination of underfilling with ACA bonding;
— low temperature processing capability;
— flexible and simple processing and thereby low cost.

Hence, a lot of research work has recently been focused on surface mount and flip-chip applications. This book is an effort to consider conductive adhesive joining technology as a science and an art. It is organised in the following way:

Chapter 1 serves as an introduction to the conductive adhesives that are useful for electronics packaging applications. Chapters 2 to 7 deal with fundamental and design issues, and joining processes of conductive adhesive materials. In Chapter 2, materials aspects of UV-curable conductive adhesive are outlined. Two volume manufacturing processes utilising in-line UV and off-line thermal cure are described. Fundamental aspects of electrical conduction and its relationship to the microstructure of isotropic conductive adhesives (ICAs) are elaborated in Chapter 3. Various electrical conduction mechanisms and the influence of the microstructure of the conducting filler on such mechanisms are described. In Chapter 4 models are presented to treat electrical shortings and ACA fluid flow behaviour during curing. The necessary time for the ACA film or paste to be squeezed out between the substrate and bump is given for both unbumped and bumped die. Curing mechanisms of ICAs and models based on DSC measurement designed to predict curing degree are discussed in Chapter 5. These models are a useful tool for obtaining the appropriate temperature and period of time required to guarantee full cure. Chapter 6 describes the electrical resistance-pressure relationship for ACAs. The selection and development of solder-filled metal fillers are given in Chapter 7. Theory and experimental evidence are discussed for the selection of solder-filled ACA and the matching bonding surfaces. It is shown that, for solder-filled ACAs, the best bonding surfaces are solder-based molten surfaces.

Various applications related to conductive adhesives joining technologies are given in Chapters 8 to 16. Applications of ACA and ACF for flip-chip and surface mount applications are discussed in Chapters 8, 9 and 10. Chapters 8 and 9 provide a summary of state-of-the-art ACA flip-chip joining technology. Conductive adhesive flip-chip joining technology will be, in my opinion, the most feasible next large application area as it offers potential for low cost, high reliability and fine-pitch capability. It can cope with extremely fine pitch (70-125 μm). In Chapter 9, a system consideration (from the manufacturability viewpoint) for the use of conductive adhesives is given, including various solutions involving ACA/ACF bonding. It is shown that ACA paste technology for fine pitch flip-chip assembly together with mixed soldering technology may offer potential cost and reliability advantages for future fine pitch flip-chip applications (for interconnections with less than 150 μm pitch). Some promising test results on ACF flip-chip on Al surface are given in Chapter 10. However, long-term reliability and mechanism issues must be investigated further before this interconnection technology can be used in practice. The reliability and failure mechanisms of ICAs for surface mount applications are discussed in Chapter 11. An overview of the use of non-conductive adhesives for surface mount applications is covered in Chapter 12 and a considerable amount of reliability data is given in this chapter. In the following two chapters, the use of conductive adhesives for die-attach applications is elaborated. While Chapter 13 focuses on thermal conduction mechanisms and stress-strain patterns in high power die-attach applications, the reliability data for this process are given in Chapter 14. Chapter 15 gives an overview of the display interconnection technology and applications based on conductive adhesive joining. In Chapter 16, an example and idea are given for the use of conductive adhesives for microsystem applications. Finally, the last two chapters deal with the health and environmental aspects of the use of conductive adhesives in relation to solder based technology.

This book presents state-of-the-art conductive adhesive joining technology in various electronics packaging applications. It is an invaluable reference book for design, production and quality engineers, decision makers and research scientists who may be engaged or have an interest in electronics packaging research and development using conductive adhesive joining technology.

Professor Johan Liu, PhD
Senior Member IEEE
Göteborg, Sweden
December 1998

ACKNOWLEDGEMENTS

I would like to take this opportunity to thank all the contributors to this book. A short biography of each contributor can be found after the contents list. Without their contribution and enthusiasm, it would not have been possible to complete this book. I would also like to thank IEEE, their transactions part A and B as well as their conferences (Electronic Components and Technology Conferences, ECTC), the American Institute of Physics and its *Journal of Physics*, Wiley Publications, ISHM and its proceedings, and the *Journal of Adhesion Science and Technology* for the use of some of their figures in the present book.

I would also like to thank the many participants in my consortium research programmes including 'Techniques for better adhesive joints (TBL)', 'Solderless Multi-Chip Modules', the currently ongoing 'Solderless Flip-Chip', The National Swedish Board for Technical Development (NUTEK) and Nordisk Industrifond (NI) who have sponsored me in my endeavour to contribute to worldwide conductive adhesive research work. Specifically, I would like to mention the following persons who have served as referees for the book: Robert Lindgren, Alfa Laval Automation; Mikael Andersson, Ericsson Telecom; Jens Hansson, Mydata Automation, Sweden; Arun Chaudhuri, Delco Electronics; Michael Zwolinski, Delphi Packard Systems, USA; Charles Lin, Gul Technologies, Singapore; Gerhard Liebing and Volker Brielmann, Robert Bosch; Bela Rösner, Thomson Multimedia, Germany; Jannick Guinet, Schneider Electric, France; and Kenichi Suzuki, Namics, and Hiroaki Takezawa, Matsushita Electric, Japan.

In this context, I would also like to acknowledge the co-operation of Hans Danielsson, Mikroelektronikkonsult AB, Sweden, who introduced me to the electronics conductive adhesive research area in Sweden, and Kåre Gustafsson, Ericsson Components, who has continuously encouraged and supported me to continue the conductive adhesive research work. I also wish to take this opportunity to thank Mr Rolf Jansson, TeknikCentrum, for his encouragement during the preparation of this book. I am also grateful to Mousumi Chaudhuri, Kokomo, Indianapolis, USA, who helped me edit a significant part of the text.

In addition, I would like to acknowledge IVF for allowing me to work in this interesting and fascinating field.

Finally, I would like to dedicate this book to my most sacrificing parents and family and wish them good health, and to my wife Christine and my daughters Lilian and Natalie, who have given me many free weekends and holidays to finish editing this book.

CONTENTS

CHAPTER THREE

Conduction Mechanisms and Microstructure Development in Isotropic, Electrically Conductive Adhesives

CHAPTER FOUR

Models to Determine Guidelines for the Anisotropic Conducting Adhesives Joining Process

CHAPTER FIVE

Curing of Isotropic Electrically Conductive Adhesives

CHAPTER SIX

Contact Reliability Modelling and Material Behaviour of Conductive Adhesives under Thermomechanical Loads

CHAPTER SEVEN

Design and Modelling of Solder-filled ACAs for Flip-chip and Flexible Circuit Applications

CHAPTER EIGHT

Recent Advances and Evaluation of Anisotropically Conductive Adhesives for Microelectronics Assembly

CHAPTER NINE

Manufacturability, Reliability and Failure Mechanisms in Conductive Adhesive Joining for Flip-chip and Surface Mount Applications

CHAPTER TEN

Anisotropic Conductive Adhesive Films for Flip-chip Interconnection

CHAPTER ELEVEN

Reliability of Electrically Conductive Adhesive Joints in Surface Mount Applications

CHAPTER TWELVE

Electrically Conductive Joints using Non-conductive Adhesives (NCAs) in Surface Mount Applications

CHAPTER THIRTEEN

Use of Conductive Adhesives as Die-attach for Power Electronics Applications

CHAPTER FOURTEEN

Replacing Solder with Isotropically Conductive Adhesives in Die Bonding of Power Semiconductors

CHAPTER FIFTEEN

Overview of Conductive Adhesive Interconnection Technologies for Display Applications

CHAPTER SIXTEEN

Integration of Microsystems using Flip-chip Technologies and Adhesives

CHAPTER SEVENTEEN

Adhesives and Health Hazards

CHAPTER EIGHTEEN

Health and Environmental Aspects of Conductive Adhesives — The Use of Lead-based Alloys compared with Adhesives

BIOGRAPHIES

THE CONTRIBUTORS *(in alphabetical order)*

Maja Amskov graduated with an MScEE degree from the Technical University of Denmark in 1995. She worked previously on optimisation of PECVD processes for NKT Research Center, and anodic thin film wafer to wafer bonding for Brüel & Kjær, and is currently employed by DELTA Danish Electronics, Light & Acoustics as a research engineer.

Ann-Beth Antonsson graduated with an MSc in chemical engineering from Chalmers University, Gothenburg, in 1979. In 1991, she was awarded a PhD at the Royal Institute of Technology, Stockholm. From 1980-1983 she was project leader at the Swedish Environmental Research Institute (IVL), where she has also been Section Manager since 1983, and Vice Director of Environmental Technology since 1993. In addition, she was Research Officer with the Swedish Work Environment Fund from December 1984 to April 1985. Dr Antonsson's fields of specialisation are: chemical health hazards; control strategies for improving the chemical working environment; the working environment in small companies; the integration of working and outdoor environments; and internal control of the working environment.

Andreas Bauer received his diploma in physics from the University of Stuttgart, Germany, in 1991 with a diploma thesis on charge separation in thin organic films for application as photovoltaic cells. From 1991 to 1996, he was with the Centrum für Mikroverbindungstechnik in der Elektronik (CEM) in Neumünster, Germany, where he worked as a project manager on several projects concerned with adhesive bonding, micro application of adhesives and wire bonding. His scientific work in this period was primarily focused on conductive adhesive joints with non-conductive adhesive. In July 1996, he joined the Microwave Department of Daimler-Benz Aerospace AG in Ulm, Germany, as technologist for micro- and millimetre-wave circuit assembly.

Heiner Bayer studied chemistry at the Ludwig Maximilian University, Munich, and received his PhD (natural sciences) in 1979. He joined the Corporate Research and Development department of Siemens AG,

Munich, in 1980. His main activities involved liquid resin chemistry for electrical and electronic applications, and his special work fields at present are UV curable epoxy systems as adhesives and encapsulants for microelectronic and optoelectronic assemblies to develop automated mass production.

Are Bjorneklett received his Master's degree in solid state physics from the Norwegian Institute of Technology in 1988. He joined SINTEF in Oslo working on research projects within thermal design and analysis of electronics, cooling systems based on boiling liquids and electronic materials including adhesives. He was awarded his PhD degree in 1993 for fundamental studies of plasma spray deposition of ceramic materials as a substrate for power electronics. He spent one year at the European Space Research and Technology Centre in Nordwijk, The Netherlands, from 1993 to 1994 working on thermal analysis and reliability aspects of spacecraft power electronics systems. From 1994 he has been with Ericsson Components AB in Stockholm working on physical modelling of failure mechanisms associated with electronics packaging, thermal measurement techniques, analysis of moisture effects in outdoor electronics and optimisation of production processes.

Helene Carlsson obtained her MSc in chemical engineering from Lund Institute of Technology in 1990. From 1990-1994, she was occupational hygienist at the Swedish Environmental Research Institute, focusing on chemical health hazards, measuring techniques, and occupational hygiene in small companies. Her areas of special interest were: curing adhesives, degreasing, metal surface finishing, plastic recycling, and occupational hygiene in life cycle analysis. From 1994-1996, Ms Carlsson was Assistant to the Technical Attaché at the Swedish Embassy in Bonn, with environment and energy as her main areas of interest. Since 1996, she has been Secretary on the National Committee on Agenda 21.

Thomas Gesang received his diploma in physics on synthesis, growth and characterisation of ternary semiconductors for application in photovoltaics and for the emission of spin polarised electrons from Konstanz University in 1987. After his graduation, he obtained a post in the optics group of Cambridge Consultants Ltd in Cambridge, UK, where he developed optical systems and coating processes for ink jet printer production. In 1989, he joined the adhesive bonding group of the Fraunhofer Society in the research institute in Bremen, Germany. His main occupation was project work and management in fundamental research on adhesion as well as in adhesive applications in electronics and micro systems. In parallel to his employment, in 1996 he received a PhD from Dortmund University for a thesis on fundamental aspects of adhesion and ultrathin polymer films.

Henrik L. Hvims graduated in 1980 from the Technical University of Copenhagen, and for two years worked for the Danish Defence Research Establishment. In 1982 he joined Motorola working as a research scientist in microelectronic interconnection technologies. In 1985 he started, and became project manager of, a Nordic Polymer Thick-film interconnection project.

In 1989 Mr Hvims joined DELTA Danish Electronics, Light & Acoustics (the former ElektronikCentralen), where he has managed several projects including PTF, TAB, and Green Tape multilayer techniques. During the last six years, he has been responsible for a number of research projects within the field of conductive adhesive joining techniques for electronics packaging. In 1990 he started the major Danish electrically conductive adhesive research project and in 1992 the international Nordic conductive adhesive research project, NORAD. He is heavily involved in the national research project, 'MicrosystemCentret (MSC)', responsible for flip-chip combined with conductive adhesives and adhesives for assembly and encapsulation. He is now engaged in several thematic networks on 'Adhesives in Electronics', both Nordic and European.

Mr Hvims has contributed a number of international articles and papers published at international conferences. He holds patents for HF thick-film interconnection circuits.

Henrik Hvims is a professional member of IEEE and ISHM, and has been a board member of ISHM-Nordic since 1985. He is also a member of the technical committee of Adhesives in Electronics conferences, the technical committee of Polymer Electronics Packaging conferences, and the programme committee of the EuPac conferences.

Professor Jorma Kivilahti received a DrTech degree in physical metallurgy and materials science from Helsinki University of Technology (HUT) in 1976. After a few years of research and development work in industry he returned to HUT, where he heads the laboratory of Materials and Manufacturing Technology in Electronics. Currently his research and development work involves new electronic materials and assembly technologies. In his scientific research the emphasis is on physical and chemical compatibility issues and their relation to the reliability of high density interconnections. He is a member of IEEE and ISHM-Nordic.

Helge Kristiansen received his Master's and PhD degrees in physics from the University of Oslo, Norway, in 1988 and 1996 respectively. Since completing his Master's degree, he has been with the Center for Industrial Research, now SINTEF. He has worked mainly with adhesive technology in electronics and thermal management. He currently holds a part-time position at the University of Oslo. Dr Kristiansen is the author of more than 30 articles and papers within the field of electronics packaging.

Li Li is currently a process development engineer at Motorola Advanced Interconnect Systems Laboratory, Tempe, AZ, working on low-cost flip-chip interconnect. She received BS and MS degrees in material science and engineering from the University of Science and Technology, Beijing, China, and a PhD degree in electrical engineering from Binghamton University, Binghamton, NY. She worked at Motorola Corporate Manufacturing Research Center on advanced flip chip on board encapsulant materials, and on conductive adhesive research both at IVF, Sweden, and CMRC. Dr Li is the first Motorola-IEEE/CPMT graduate fellowship winner for research in electronic packaging.

Johan Liu received his Master's degree in materials science and engineering from the Royal Institute of Technology, Stockholm, Sweden, in 1984. He also received his PhD there in 1989 in the area of rapid solidification technology. He has been with IVF since 1989. As a member of the management team for the IVF Electronics Packaging Research Division, he is a team leader for the interconnection and encapsulation technology group at IVF and runs a number of multi-client research programmes including conductive adhesive joining, chip on board and lead-free solders. He is also an adjunct professor in electronics packaging at Chalmers University of Technology, Gothenburg, Sweden.

Dr Liu serves as the European editor of the *Journal of Electronics Manufacturing*, vice chairman of the technical committee of the international conference on 'Adhesives in Electronics', member of the international programme liaison committee for the Interpack´97 Conference, European liaison chair for the AmericanVLSI Computer and System Packaging Workshop, and general chair of the first IEEE International Symposium on Polymeric Electronics Packaging. He is a senior member of IEEE, a member of ISHM, The Institute of Welding and Materials Research Society. He also chairs the IEEE CPMT Sweden Chapter. He has given a number of invited papers and tutorials at international conferences in the area of conductive adhesive joining technology. He has twice been guest editor for the *Journal of Electronics Manufacturing*. He has received a number of awards for his work on conductive adhesives in electronics packaging. He received the best paper award'96 from the IEEE *Transactions of CPMT*, Part B: Advanced Packaging, for a paper entitled 'Anisotropically conductive adhesive flip-chip bonding on rigid and flexible printed circuit substrates'.

Samjid H. Mannan received BA degree in physics from Oxford University, UK, in 1988 and a PhD degree in theoretical elementary particle physics from Southampton University, UK, in 1991. After working as a Research Assistant at Salford University and Loughborough University in the area of electronics interconnection (solder paste and ACAs), he is currently working in the area of electronics manufacturing as a Research Fellow at Loughborough University. He is a Chartered Physicist, a Member of the Institute of Physics and the author of over 20 scientific papers.

James E. Morris is a Professor of Electrical Engineering in the T. J. Watson School of Engineering and Applied Science of the State University of New York at Binghamton, USA. His BSc and MSc degrees are from the University of Auckland, New Zealand, with 1st Class Honours in physics, and his PhD in electrical engineering is from the University of Saskatchewan, Canada. He was the first Director of Binghamton's Institute for Research in Electronics Packaging, and served for six years as EE Department Chairman. Professor Morris has been Treasurer of the IEEE Components, Packaging, and Manufacturing Technology (CPMT) Society since 1991, and has been Guest Editor for three Special Sections on Electrically Conductive Adhesives in the IEEE *Transactions on CPMT*. He serves on the ECTC Program Committees for Materials &

Processing, and Education, and on the International Advisory Committees for the Adhesives in Electronics Manufacturing and the Polymers in Electronics Conference series. He edited three volumes of the Electronics Packaging Forum monograph series (VNR/IEEE), and is currently developing an electronics packaging text. His current research activities include the electrical conduction mechanisms in discontinuous thin metal films (a continuing interest for nearly 30 years) and nanoelectronic devices, electrically conductive adhesives, and electrical performance modelling in packaging

Adebayo Oliyinka Ogunjimi received a PhD degree at Loughborough University, UK. After graduating, he has worked as a Post-doctoral Research Associate at both Loughborough and at CALCE EPRC and is currently working at PERA International Ltd. He has been employed in electronics manufacturing research and development since 1990 and has taken part in projects in surface mount technology including the use of conducting adhesives, both isotropic and anisotropic, as replacements for solder in electronics interconnection. He has undertaken research in the physics of Failure approach to Electronics Reliability. His experience includes manufacturing process modelling and design evaluation using classical theory and finite element analysis.

Outi Rusanen received her Master's degree in electrical engineering from the University of Oulu in 1988. Since graduating, she has worked as a research scientist with VTT Electronics and has concentrated on bare die joining and encapsulation techniques. She has been researching the use of isotropically conductive adhesives for the past five years and has written and co-authored several publications on the topic. She has also prepared her licenciate thesis on adhesive die bonding of power components.

Petri Savolainen received a Doctor of technology degree in materials science in 1996 from Helsinki University of Technology. His field of study was anisotropic electrically conductive adhesives, especially solder-filled adhesives, for display and flip-chip applications. Currently, he is at Nokia Research Center where his work concentrates on new component packaging solutions and high-density printed wiring boards. He is a member of IEEE-CPMT and IMAPS-Nordic.

Kenzo Takemura is currently a Research Scientist, Tsukuba Research Laboratory of Hitachi Chemical Co. Ltd. He has been employed by Hitachi Chemical since 1983. He has been responsible for developing anisotropic conductive adhesive films for flip-chip technologies(chip on glass, chip on board). He has also worked on thin film technologies for electroluminescent displays and printed circuit boards. He received his BS in Physics from Science University of Tokyo.

Itsuo Watanabe is currently a Senior Research Scientist, Tsukuba Research Laboratory of Hitachi Chemical Co. Ltd. He has been employed by Hitachi Chemical since 1982. He has been responsible for developing anisotropic conductive adhesive films for flat panel displays and flip-chip technologies (chip on glass, chip on board). He had been a visiting scientist of Massachusetts Institute of Technology (Department of Materials Science and Engineering) from 1987 to 1989. He has also studied conducting polymers, organic optical recording materials and polymeric materials for optical communication. He received his BS and MS degrees in chemistry from Utsunomiya University and PhD in polymer science from Kyoto University. His doctoral research was concerned with syntheses, thin film formation, electrical and optical characteristics of conducting polymers.

Helle Westphal has been the Head of Department of Consumer Health and Toxicology with the Danish Toxicology Centre since 1995. She received her MSc in pharmacy from the Royal Danish School of Pharmacy. (Postgraduate education in toxicology). Since 1990 she has been a consultant with the Danish Toxicology Centre (DTC) in the Department of Biology within the field of general toxicology — the use of chemistry in relation to biological issues. Ms Westphal has specialised in health aspects of industrial handling of chemicals/materials in general, in life cycle assessments and in regulatory affairs in Denmark and the EU. Since 1992, she has specialised in assessment of the environmental impacts of the use of conductive adhesives within the electronics industry.

Key fields of activity have included joint venture projects on cleaner technology, e.g., in the electronics industry, health evaluations of polymeric materials as medical equipment, food packages, tap water installations etc., and environmental joint venture projects in the former Soviet Union, especially Belarus.

David C. Whalley received BSc and MPhil degrees from Loughborough University, UK. Since then he has been involved in research into electronics interconnection reliability, the use of engineering analysis techniques both in electronic product design and in process simulation, and on new electronics interconnection technologies such as conducting adhesives. He has worked as an engineer both at Loughborough University and at Lucas Industries' Advanced Engineering Centre, Solihull, Birmingham, before being appointed in 1990 as lecturer in Processes for Electronic Manufacture within Loughborough University's Department of Manufacturing Engineering. He is the author of over 60 papers and reports in the areas of electronics manufacturing processes and interconnection technology, and electronic thermal design.

David J. Williams received a BSc degree from UMIST and PhD degree from Cambridge University, UK. He has been Professor of Manufacturing Processes in Loughborough University since January 1989. He was head of the Department of Manufacturing Engineering from 1991 to 1995. His present research focuses on the resolution of problems within electronics manufacturing. This research includes work at the process engineering science level, understanding of the interaction between process understanding and design for manufacture (encompassing take-back), and business globalisation. This follows a number of years of control oriented work in CIM. Before taking up his present post he was a

Lecturer in Manufacturing Engineering and Design in the Engineering Department, Cambridge, UK, and worked for Metal Box and GKN. He has published three books and more than 200 papers and contributions to books in the area of manufacturing. He is Editor-in-Chief of the *International Journal of Computer Integrated Manufacturing* and *Journal of Electronics Manufacturing*, and is an active consultant to the manufacturing industry and various governments.

C. P. Wong received a BS degree in chemistry from Purdue University, and a PhD degree in organic/inorganic chemistry from Pennsylvania State University. After his doctoral study, he was awarded two years as a postdoctoral scholar with Nobel Laureate Professor Henry Taube at Stanford University, where he conducted studies on electron transfer and reaction mechanism of metallocomplexes. He was the first person to synthesise the first known lanthanide and actinide porphyrin complexes which represent a breakthrough in metalloporphyrin chemistry.

Dr Wong joined AT&T Bell Laboratories in 1977 as a member of the technical staff. He has been involved with the research and development of polymeric materials (inorganic and organic) for electronic applications. He became a senior member of the technical staff in 1982, a distinguished member of the technical staff in 1987, and an AT&T Bell Laboratories Fellow in 1992.

Currently, Dr Wong is also a Program Manager of the AT&T Moisture Sensitive Components R&D Project, a cross company R&D effort in obtaining Moisture Insensitive Components by addressing the Materials, Processes and Reliability Issues. His research interests lie in the fields of polymeric materials, high Tc ceramics, materials reaction mechanism, IC encapsulation, in particular hermetic equivalent plastic packaging, electronic manufacturing packaging processes, interfacial adhesions, PWB, SMT assembly and components reliability. He is one of the pioneers who demonstrated the use of silicone gel as a device encapsulant to achieve reliability without hermeticity in plastic IC packaging.

Dr Wong received the Best Paper Award in 1981 at the International Society for Hybrids and Microelectronics Annual Meeting, AT&T Engineering Research Center Technical Achievement Award in 1983, the AT&T Bell Laboratories Distinguished Technical Staff Award in 1987, a 1992 AT&T Bell Laboratories Fellow Award, the IEEE Components, Packaging and Manufacturing Technology (CPMT) Society Outstanding Paper Awards in 1990, 1991 and 1994, the IEEE-CPMT Society Board of Governors Distinguished Service Award in 1991, the IEEE Technical Activities Board (TAB) Distinguished Service Award in 1994, and the 1995 IEEE CPMT Society's Outstanding Sustained Technical Contributions Award (the highest Society honour). He holds over 35 US patents, numerous international patents, has published over 90 technical papers and 100 key-notes and presentations in the related area. He was the editor and an author of the Academic Press text book on 'Polymers for Electronic and Photonic Applications' in 1993, and is an Associate Editor of the IEEE *Transactions on Components, Hybrids and Manufacturing Technology* (1995-).

Dr Wong is a Fellow of the IEEE and AT&T Bell Labs, and a member of the Sigma Xi, Phi Lambda Upsilon, National Honorary Chemical Society, and Materials Research Society. He was programme chairman of the IEEE 39th Electronic Components Conference in 1989, and general chairman of the 41st Electronic Components and Technology Conference in 1991. He was elected to the Board of Governors of the IEEE-CHMT Society from 1987-1989, served as the IEEE-Components, Hybrids and Manufacturing Technology Society technical vice president (1990 and 1991), and president of the IEEE-CHMT Society (1992 and 1993). He currently chairs the IEEE Technical Activities Board, Steering Committee on Design and Manufacturing Engineering (1995-).

Chao-pin Yeh received his PhD degree from the School of Mechanical Engineering at Georgia Institute of Technology in 1992. Since graduating, he was employed at the High-performance Packaging Division at IBM-Endicott for one and half years before joining Motorola in April 1993. Since 1993, he has been a department manager at the System & Component Simulation Center (SCSC), Corporate Global Software Division, Motorola, Inc. His department is responsible for the development of advanced reliability, mechanical, and RF simulation and modelling solutions to portable electronic communication products, components, and interconnect technologies (Flip Chip, BGA, CSP, Fine Pitch QFP, High Density Interconnects, MCM, MEMS, etc.). Dr Yeh's research interests encompass finite element modelling, reliability prediction methodologies, design optimisation, design tool integration and concurrent engineering with an emphasis on electronic packaging applications. He has authored or co-authored more than 70 conference papers and technical reports.

Chapter 1

INTRODUCTION TO CONDUCTIVE ADHESIVE JOINING TECHNOLOGY

KEN GILLEO

Alpha Metals — Electronic Polymers, Rhode Island, USA

1.1 INTRODUCTION

Adhesives may be the oldest joining material used by civilisation. Early man used mud and clay as binders for dwelling construction; ancient Egyptians made animal hide glue for assembling furniture; Native Americans (American-Indians) used amber for enhancing the strength of spears. The early and wide-ranging applications for adhesives are a testimony to their compatibility and versatility. Even now, it is the extraordinary versatility and unmatched compatibility that make adhesives so important. However, today, there is a newer and even more important attribute that makes adhesives essential to modern civilisation: our ability to synthesise and customise them, thus improving on nature.

It is no wonder that adhesives play a major rôle in electronics. In fact, the electronics industry has grown so dependent on synthetic polymer-based adhesives that most of our modern electronic products would be impossible without them. This book examines one very important category of electronic adhesives: conductive adhesives. This introductory chapter is intended to give the reader the essentials of polymer-based adhesives in order to better understand the chapters that follow. For the specialist already familiar with adhesive principles, it is hoped that some new and interesting facts are also provided.

Conductive adhesives represent an intrinsically clean, simple and logical solution for all kinds of electrical interconnect challenges. Adhesives not only provide a 'lead-free', 'no clean' alternative to solder; these highly compatible materials also offer viable answers to problems where solder is totally inadequate. However, is conductive adhesive technology really the right choice for today's high density interconnects and our ever-increasing environmental problems? This chapter will give you the basic concepts needed to understand and appreciate the wide variety of materials to be discussed. The chapters that follow will give the detailed information to let you make your own conclusion. Authors around the world from industry, academia, private organisations, research consortia and government laboratories have contributed to this world class book on an important emerging technology.

The writers have pointed out both strengths and weaknesses of the various electronic adhesives to provide a balance of information. It is their hope that potential users will adopt the technology for applications where the benefits are strong and that problem-solvers among the readers will want to help improve materials. This emerging branch of science and applied technology could ultimately become the successor to metallurgical solders because of its extraordinary versatility and ability to be custom-engineered. Breakthroughs in the field of intrinsically conductive polymers (ICPs) that recently brought us the polymer transistor may yield exciting new adhesive products in the future. Adhesives alone, of all the established interconnect methods, offer the best options for product recycling and reclamation that will become essential in the not too distant future.

1.2   ADHESIVE TYPES

First, the chapter will address the various adhesive types and then examine the materials typically used. There is a number of polymer-based bonding agents, or conductive adhesives, employed in the electronics field. The most common materials are the die attach adhesives which are used to bond bare silicon die to lead frames as part of the packaging process. Billions of IC chips are packaged in this way. These materials are called isotropic conductors since electrical conductivities are equal in all directions.

There is another important class of bonding agents with unidirectional conductivity, called anisotropic. These anisotropic bonding agents are experiencing significant growth since they are well suited for very fine pitch bonding and solve basic interconnect problems associated with the widely used flat panel displays. Non-conductive adhesives are also used to create electrical junctions which may seem like a paradox. The common scheme employed is to mate component conductors and circuit pads using the non-conductive adhesive as the means of producing force on the opposing junctions. Each of these adhesive types will be covered in more detail in the following sections.

1.2.1   Isotropic Conductive Adhesives

Isotropic conductive adhesives produce approximately equal electrical conductivity in all directions. They are typified by the silver-filled epoxies originally used for die attach, but now modified for component assembly. Epoxies have been the workhorse polymers of electronics due to their ease of use, the availability of hundreds of resin-hardener combinations, balanced properties and generally superior bonding properties.

Since die attach adhesives had relatively reliable electrical conductivity, they were the obvious starting point for component assembly conductive adhesives.

Pioneers in the polymer thick film (PTF) field experimented with various die attach adhesives as a substitute for solder several decades ago. Since conductive adhesives do not wick on to wires and terminations or form fillets as does solder, these materials worked poorly with feed-through component devices. The advent of surface mount technology (SMT) provided an excellent form factor for adhesives. Once SMT became established, conductive adhesives were developed for this application since materials did not have to wick and fillet or flow into holes, as was the case for feed-through device wave soldering. Assembly adhesives only needed to be dispensed on to circuits and form reasonably reliable electromechanical junctions with components placed in the paste. The SMT form factor, which produced the desired butt joint, was the ideal packaging change needed to boost conductive adhesive technology.

One problem with using the unmodified die attach adhesive for assembly was the long duration and high temperature curing requirements. Many materials required more than one hour cure schedules at processing temperatures of 150°C to over 200°C. This precluded their use on low-cost polyester substrates, the most obvious target for adhesives since soldering was not viable due to its higher temperature processing. The long cure schedule, even if the high temperatures could be handled, was not competitive with solder processing. During the 1980s, new materials started to appear specifically designed as bonding agents for polymer thick film circuitry.

Fast cure systems were designed with cure cycles that could be achieved with IR reflow ovens set at lower temperature profiles. This meant that the conductive adhesive could be run on a surface mount line without modification or adding equipment. The increasing popularity was also a big boost for PTF bonding since there was no practical way of using conductive adhesives on wave soldering lines. The 1980s saw the successful commercialisation of conductive adhesive assembly.

Another problem that appears to be resolved was that of junction instability. Even though very stable adhesives became available, the junction between the component and circuit often showed a large increase in resistance after temperature and humidity ageing. The result is thought to be the formation of insulative oxide on the component leads and circuit conductors. Oxidation of the circuit conductors can be solved in various ways such as adding gold flash plating. However, since most SMT component terminations are finished with tin-lead solder, this presented a greater problem. Junction stable adhesives were eventually developed that were compatible with standard solder-finished components, although mechanisms are uncertain. One material, called Poly-Solder, is thought to be stable with oxidising surfaces because of small conductive particles that penetrate oxide. The mechanism has been studied by IVF and Chalmers University, both in Gothenburg, Sweden. The information is provided in later chapters.

Oxide-reducing hardeners, such as anhydrides and carboxy acids, have also shown promise for improving junction stability. Several studies have confirmed that conductive adhesives are reasonably stable under 85% RH/ 85°C on soldered surfaces.

Not only were new, low temperature thermosets introduced, but various thermoplastics isotropic conductive adhesives were commercialised. The thermoplastics could be applied as solvent-containing pastes, dried to solids and then melted for assembly. The thermoplastics conductive adhesives, much more akin to solders, have been referred to as 'organic solders'. Unlike the thermosets that change chemically during curing, the thermoplastics can be re-melted for repair. Bonding is much faster with the hot melts since heating is only used to bring the material to the melting point, not to induce chemical reaction. A negative characteristic of most thermoplastics is lower strength and porosity caused by entrapped solvent. Much more work can be, should be and is being done in the thermoplastic adhesive area.

1.2.2   Bi-directional Anisotropic Conductive Adhesives

As implied, bi-directional adhesives effectively have conductivity paths in two directions. The first bi-directional conductors were not adhesives at all, but interposer strips that required continuous external force. The products are also called elastomeric conductors or pads. One of the earliest products consisted of a stack-up of silicone rubber and carbon-filled elastomer sheets. These were then sliced vertically through the stack to produce the familiar black and clear striped pad commonly referred to as a 'zebra strip'. True adhesive materials evolved with similar constructions of conductive/non-conductive stripes. These bi-directional anisotropic adhesives are available in films as rolls and strips. Most use thermoplastics and are typically used for connections to flat panel displays, especially liquid crystal displays (LCDs). One of the most popular product families is made by Nippon Graphite Co. Ltd of Japan. The product is sold under the Elform brand name in the United States.

Another version of the self-adhering interconnect cable is the now defunct ScotchLink tape from 3M Co. The product consisted of parallel conductors coated with hot melt insulators. Small conductive spheres of silver were embedded in the dielectric but they were not in contact with the parallel conductors which, incidentally, were made of metallised silver. The product was supplied in rolls of different pitch. A length was cut from the roll and heat bonded to the two interconnect sites. Two hard boards, for example, could be interconnected with ScotchLink tape. The concept was innovative and appears to have been unique since the adhesive served as an insulator, unlike the zebra strip style where conductors could be shorted out. The implementation, however, produced limitations. The use of thin silver as the conductor limited current and invited silver migration. The product was finally withdrawn from the market but a re-engineered version has recently become available.

1.2.3   Unidirectional Anisotropic Conductive Adhesives

The next evolution of interposer bonding materials was the introduction of unidirectional products although the concept actually goes back several decades. There was a serious need for an interconnect material that did not require parallel alignment and one that would also be capable of finer pitch than the strip products. The solution is remarkably simple, perhaps so simple that it was overlooked several times. The basic idea is to disperse conductive particles in a dielectric adhesive. The loading is kept low enough so that the material is not made conductive by contact between particles (allowing it to remain an insulator in its plane). It is a little like making a conductive adhesive without enough conductor. Conductor loading levels are typically much lower for isotropics and range from 10-40% by volume, but with many exceptions. When the adhesive is interposed between two sets of conductors, application of heat and pressure cause inter-plane connections (Z-axis) to be made.

The invention and rediscovery of the anisotropic concept are quite interesting. During the early 1980s, several companies, most notably Sheldahl in the United States and Sony in Japan, were attempting to connect difficult materials. While the Japanese worked on the LCD interconnect problem, Sheldahl, Amp and other flexible circuit manufacturers attacked the flex interconnect issue. IBM Corporation had presented a significant challenge with their Quiet Writer typewriter program. The printing head was made of tungsten metal but it needed to be connected to a flexible circuit made of copper. After many attempts to solve the mating problem by classical means, Sheldahl and Amp simultaneously hit on the idea of using polymer materials. Both companies produced PTF membrane switches at that time, so it was logical to investigate this area of technology. Meanwhile Sony began offering limited samples of an interconnect film made with oriented carbon fibres. In many ways, the product was similar to the zebra strip since the fibres were oriented in parallel. Yet, the fibres were so short that alignment was not critical. The US companies quickly realised that the conductors should be spherically-shaped metals. By 1985, both Sheldahl and Amp had produced reasonably good anisotropic conductive adhesives based on silver particles. The author chose the simpler term, Z-axis adhesive, to describe the product. This was a name which caught on quickly after the product was described in the trade literature. A search of patents, however, will show that the anisotropic electrical concept was conceived in the 1950s and developed more extensively in the next several decades.

Today, anisotropic adhesives are available in just about every form and type ranging from liquids to dry films and from thermosets to thermoplastics. Considerable work has gone on in many laboratories to better exploit the fascinating concept of unidirectional conductivity. Much work has been devoted to the polymer binder. Many materials have hybrid properties of thermoplastic and thermosets combined. Both thermoplastics, noted for fast processing, and thermosets, for higher temperature performance, are in use today. Research today is focused on the conductive particles, of which perhaps a dozen basic types are under study. In this book, several of the chapters deal with research on anisotropic adhesives. Details regarding performance and failure mechanisms are also given.

1.2.4 Patterned Anisotropic Conductive Adhesives

Most anisotropic conductive adhesives employ a random dispersion of conductive particles because this is easy to do. More recently, adhesive films with patterns of conductors have been introduced by several companies.

All are based on a bondable dielectric continuous film, but with different types of conductors. One approach, called GAZA for Grid Array Z-Axis, employs columns of isotropic conductive adhesive arranged in a grid pattern. The conductive adhesive can be patterned by printing methods with the dielectric film cast as the last operation. Alternatively, holes may be formed in a dielectric sheet and filled with conductive adhesive. Good results have been shown but the difficulty in manufacturing such materials at low cost has limited the technology. The patterned adhesive concept would seem to have benefits in many applications and further work is warranted.

1.2.5   Non-conductive Adhesives

Although it may sound like a paradox, non-conductive adhesives can be used to provide electrical interconnects. The materials are used to create mechanical tension which creates force between opposing conductors. The adhesive, of course, must form an insulation barrier between contact interfaces. This is accomplished by selective application of adhesive or, more commonly, by applying enough force to displace adhesive from between electrical contact areas. The method has been claimed to be successful for circuit-to-circuit mating, circuit-to-LCD and bare die to circuit connections. Gold contacts are preferred because of their ability to form low ohmic contacts with minimum force.

Work by the DELTA (formerly Elektronik Centralen) and other laboratories has shown that non-conductive adhesive film could be used to mate LCDs to circuits with reliability equal to that of the anisotropic conductive materials. More actual contact area is achieved with the non-conductive adhesive since the entire conductor trace makes contact instead of random particle connections created with the anisotropic materials. Work carried out primarily in Japan has shown that bare ICs can be reliably connected to circuit boards with non-conductive adhesives. Japanese workers have reported a process where gold bumped die are bonded to glass circuits using UV cured non-conductive adhesive. The circuit board is coated with a layer of adhesive, the die is pressed against the circuit pads, and radiation cures the adhesive from the circuit side. Pressure prior to curing squeezes adhesive out of the contact areas. The polymerisation of the adhesive causes shrinkage which exerts force on the junctions to produce a mechanical compression connection. Some products have been in commercial use for several years although long-term failure due to polymer relaxation has been reported.

1.3   MATERIALS

Polymer-based conductive adhesives reside in the province of the chemist and material scientist. Virtually all of the polymers used in conductive adhesives today are synthetic materials designed to provide the right characteristics for printing, stencilling and other industrial dispensing methods. The seemingly simple conductive adhesives are actually very complicated mixtures of customised ingredients. The custom-crafted polymer materials and special inorganic fillers allow adhesives to be used with standard industrial processes, effectively and efficiently. Material application and bonding for many types of conductive adhesives can be practised on the same equipment used for soldering because the chemistry has been tailored to fit the infrastructure.

Solders are inherently conductive but polymers are not. This would seem to make them a very poor choice since all but a few structures are excellent insulators. However, one very narrow class of polymers is electrically conductive polymers. These are generally called ICPs for intrinsically conductive polymers. ICPs do not yet have the required physical and chemical properties to make them as practical as adhesives. The great strides being made in the field of intrinsically conductive polymers, like the recent announcement of the polymer transistor, suggest that ICPs will eventually be used for adhesives. Today's conductive adhesive formulators are forced to use non-conductive polymers at this point in time.

The task of converting a very good insulator to a conductor, however, is solved rather easily. Polymers readily accept fillers which modify most of their properties. Conductive adhesives are therefore produced by adding the right fillers. All commercial conductive adhesives are made with a non-conductive binder that is loaded with fillers having the desired electrical characteristics. Conductive adhesives are actually composites of polymer binders and fillers, making them very different from the other common class of joining materials, metallurgical solders. The requirement of fillers to achieve electrical conductivity might seem a disadvantage since solders are naturally conductive. Actually, the use of conductive fillers in a non-conductive binder results in an interesting and valuable attribute for adhesives. Electrical properties are independent of most of the other characteristics. We will see why this is a positive factor next.

Since adhesives achieve conductivity by means of fillers, electrical properties can be adjusted independently of properties provided by the binder, such as mechanical. Adhesives, unlike solders, have electrical and mechanical properties that can be adjusted and tuned independently to a large degree. The polymer binder can be modified to achieve the required application characteristics and bond strength. The filler can be selected to provide the desired electrical attributes, including directional conductivity, a feature not available in solders. There is, of course, some interaction between filler and binder. Nevertheless, to a large extent, electrical and mechanical adhesive properties are independent. It is best to view conductive adhesives as a complex composite where filler, binder and additives can be selected to provide formulations having a very wide range of useful properties. Basic polymer types used as adhesive binders will be briefly examined next.

1.3.1 Polymer Binders for Conductive Adhesives

Polymers are commonly classified as either thermoplastics — typically able to be melted or softened with heat, or thermosets — which resist melting and cannot be re-shaped. A few of the very high temperature thermoplastics, like polyimides, actually decompose before reaching their melting points.

Adhesive binders can be of either type, and each system is very different especially in terms of storage and processing. The function of the binder in an adhesive is actually manifold. First, the monomer or pre-polymer binder, in the case of thermosets, must provide the right handling characteristics before hardening by polymerisation. Viscosity must be in the right range for the application method employed. The addition of solvent is usually avoided for polymerisable systems and the pre-polymers (unpolymerised ingredients) should be low enough in viscosity to provide a dispensability after the solid ingredients have been added. Some thermoset monomers and oligomers are solids, and solvents or liquid co-reactants must be used to provide the needed viscosity. However, modern resins, hardeners and catalysts can be low viscosity fluids that allow substantial amounts of fillers to be added. All thermoplastic adhesive pastes contain solvents.

1.3.2   Thermoplastics

Thermoplastics are a class of polymers that are capable of being heated to a specific melting point or melting range without significantly altering their intrinsic properties. The thermoplastics are also called remeltables and hot melts. Repeated melting does not change their basic properties although changes in crystallinity can occur which affect secondary characteristics like tensile strength. Very high melting thermoplastics may oxidise or otherwise degrade when attempts are made to melt them, however. The typically linear molecular structure of thermoplastics allows these materials to melt and flow, unlike thermoset materials that will not melt or only soften slightly at high temperatures. Thermoplastics for adhesives must remain solid at their maximum use temperature. Pressure-sensitive materials are an exception since these products remain in a pseudo-solid form during application and use. Thermoplastic adhesives are available in film form and in solvent solution pastes. Solvents are used to convert solid thermoplastic polymers to dispensable liquid pastes. The polymer must have the appropriate solubility characteristics and solvent release properties to be commercially useful. Rheology and surface chemistry are also important factors in needle dispensing, printing and stencilling. Thermoplastic adhesives can be cast and dried by the manufacturer and supplied to the end-user as film, tape or pre-forms. The solid form, exemplified by some of the Z-axis adhesives, is mechanically positioned and bonded by applying heat and pressure. Thousands of thermoplastic resins are commercially available that are based on perhaps less than 20 distinctive polymer types. Variations in MW, additives and alloys account for the large number of products.

1.3.3   Thermosets

Thermosets are crosslinked polymers and generally have an extensive three-dimensional molecular structure. Crosslinks are chemical bonds occurring between polymer chains that prevent substantial movement even at elevated temperatures. The 3-D structure results in a material that cannot melt although some degree of softening may occur at high temperatures. The softening or deformation point may be at a temperature where thermal degradation occurs. Thermoplastics do not have inter-chain crosslinks, and individual polymer chains will begin to slip and flow (melting) as the temperature is increased. The unmodified thermosets are usually hard, strong polymers, making them ideal binders for many types of adhesives. Solubility is very limited so that it is impractical to make a useful solution with a thermoset. However, the availability of liquid thermoset precursors — resins, catalysts, hardeners and modifiers — makes solutions unnecessary. The thermoset precursors can be single molecular unit reactive materials or low molecular weight polymers, called oligomers, that can be further polymerised to hard structures. Many of the pre-polymer ingredients, which include monomers, oligomers and generally reactive components, are liquids requiring no solvents. These solventless systems are ideal from an environmental point of view since there are no emissions during application or curing. Adhesives are also improved if solvent can be avoided, since the possibility of solvent bubbles and voids is eliminated.

1.3.4   Thermoset vs Thermoplastic

Thermoplastic-based adhesives have the important advantage of fast processing and easy rework. No chemical reactions occur during application processing. Heat is applied to cause a change in physical state, typically the transition from solid form to a flowable phase. This takes a short time, perhaps less than a second. Thermoset systems undergo true chemical reactions which require several minutes to hours. Thermosets usually have a limited shelf life or pot life for those materials that must be catalysed before use. The thermoplastic binder remains remeltable. This means that it will soften or melt if heated to a high enough temperature. Thermoplastics are therefore somewhat limited in service temperature performance. Thermoplastics also have a tendency to flow under the application of force. This is referred to as cold flow or creep. The cross-linked thermosets, however, resist deformation and are much more mechanically stable. The thermoplastics also tend to form weaker adhesive bonds. The thermosets typically start off as low molecular weight liquids that can wet out a surface for more complete bonding. The thermoset adhesive can also react with various surfaces to form strong chemical bonds. The thermosets generally form stronger bonds that are more durable. The superior properties of thermosets compared with thermoplastics offset the handling inconvenience and greater control requirements.

Although room temperature cure thermosets are commercially available, they are not latent and begin to react when the catalyst or hardener is added. Two-part, fast cure epoxies are a good example. A useful adhesive must have a reasonable working life, usually eight hours. Some lower temperature thermosets are already catalysed and must be kept frozen to prevent them from hardening prematurely. There are a few latent thermoset systems with reasonably low curing schedules. Thermoplastics, especially the solid films, have almost infinite shelf life and are stored at room temperature.

Thermoset epoxies are by far the most common conductive adhesive binders and have found use since the early 1950s. Wolfson describes epoxy-silver compositions for use as die attach and replacing solder in the early 1950s. The patent literature abounds with examples of epoxy adhesives filled with silver. In the mid-70s, NASA extensively studied conductive epoxies for use in aerospace electronics. Numerous other articles have appeared which describe the properties and performance of conductive epoxy systems as bonding agents for components, especially surface mount types, and the chapters that follow will contain many references. Silver-epoxy can be considered the base line for isotropic conductive adhesives used for component assembly.

1.3.5   Radiation Curable Systems

Radiation curing is essentially polymerisation induced by electromagnetic, beta (electron particles) or nuclear radiation. The source used in the printed circuit industry is almost exclusively high intensity ultra-violet radiation.

Energetic photons cause monomers to react with one another, typically through the action of a photoinitiator. Radiation is absorbed by the photoinitiator, causing it to release polymerisation initiating species, such as free radicals. Some initiators rearrange to a high energy state and react directly with monomers. Once the initial reaction takes place, the reacted monomer remains active so that it goes on to react with a second monomer. The process continues until most of the monomer is utilised or the active species are consumed or deactivated.

Although radiation cured conductive adhesives have been studied as far back as the 1970s, there has been a renewed interest. Adhesives that are highly filled with opaque materials, like silver, are poor candidates for radiation cure systems. The popularisation of low filler and no filler adhesives, the anisotropic and non-conductive, respectively, have increased the use of radiation curing. The filler levels in most anisotropic adhesives permit photons to travel through and induce curing. The unfilled materials, of course, present no problem.

The next section will deal with the all-important filler, which determines the basic type of adhesive and contributes most of the electrical characteristics to the composite.

1.3.6   Conductive Fillers

1.3.6.1   SILVER-BASED CONDUCTORS

Silver is by far the most commonly used conductive filler for isotropic conductive adhesives. This would seem at first a poor choice because of cost and electrochemical activity. However, silver is totally unique among the affordable metals. Its most important feature is the high conductivity of the oxide. This means that there is almost no change in conductivity as silver particles oxidise. Copper, which would appear to be the logical choice, produces adhesives that become non-conductive after exposure to heat and humidity. The use of a non-oxidising metal, like gold, is cost prohibitive. Actually, better conduction is achieved with silver than with gold because of the next important attribute. Silver particles are easy to form and to fabricate into ideal shapes. Silver can be precipitated into a wide range of controllable sizes and shapes. This means that precisely the right sizes of particles can be produced for use as is, or for milling into fine flakes. It is even possible to precipitate silver into particles so thin that they are translucent.

Optimum silver-based adhesives are obtained by blending the right balance of flakes and particles. Flakes provide improved conductivity by allowing maximum contact. The goal is to allow the flake-like particles to overlap one another like so many flagstones. The resulting voids caused by the overlapping can be filled with the small spherical particles. More sophisticated systems have optimised particle geometries which attempt to maximise metal contact. Conductive adhesives are generally compared to tin-lead solder and equal conductivity has been obtained although most adhesives are 2 to 4 times more resistive. The reason for this is that the silver particles are coated with oxide, surface agents and some amount of binder. This means that a gap between particles results in increased electrical resistance. The gap produces tunnelling electrons that have a higher threshold and also produce more electrical noise.

1.3.6.2   COPPER

Attempts to use copper in inks and adhesives have been under way for many decades. Some of the earliest printed circuit processes used copper powder with adhesive binder. The challenge for copper-based adhesives is that of inhibiting oxidation under heat and humidity conditions. Copper oxidises so quickly that oxide will form unless chemical inhibitors are present. The binder cannot be expected to exclude oxygen since polymers are permeable to gases. Since copper readily forms stable complexes with nitrogen-bases, like benzotriazole and imidazole, the complexing approach has been widely used to reduce oxidation. Azole-treated copper improves the stability of copper adhesives, but not enough for many applications. Over-plating with metals such as silver has given some improvement in stability, although once again it is not enough for many applications. A third approach has been to add solder powder to the adhesive mix. While this approach has merit and improves stability, the product has many of the drawbacks of soldering since the final structure is basically a metallurgical, solder joint.

1.3.6.3   NICKEL

Nickel metal oxidises slowly and is an important ingredient in stainless steel alloys. Nickel's ability to resist oxidation allows the metal to be used to make somewhat stable conductive inks. However, nickel is a hard, poorly malleable metal that limits the ability to make flake in an optimised size and shape. Isotropic nickel adhesives, therefore, have a much higher resistance than silver-based products, up to 2 orders of magnitude higher. However, nickel has found use in anisotropic conductive adhesives where spherical particles are commonly used. Nickel can be made into spheres of virtually any size, and a wide range of powders is available with narrow size distributions. Nickel can also be easily plated with electroless gold to provide even more oxidation resistance.

1.3.6.4   CARBON

Carbon is an extremely inert element occurring in several allotropic forms, including diamond and graphite. The two forms of interest here are graphite, a grey-black platelet form, and carbon black, a jet-black amorphous structure. Both are electrically conductive and are used in making electronic materials. Carbon-based adhesives are only used in special applications because of their poor conductivity: up to 3 orders of magnitude lower than for silver. Some calculators have been built that use carbon-based adhesives simultaneously as the ink to form the circuit.

1.3.6.5   METAL-COATED PARTICLES

A large number of metal-plated conductive particles have been described and produced. The materials can be divided into two broad categories, metal core and non-conductive core. Both types of particles are used in anisotropic conductive adhesives today. The various types of plated particles are often designed for specific characteristics and end uses although the original intent was to reduce cost.

Silver, nickel and gold plating on non-metals are the most common types of filler product. Silver was one of the first metals used because of the simple plating processes available and the metal's ability to remain conductive in an oxidising environment. Non-conductors, like glass spheres, can be silver-plated and have been commercially available for some time.

More recently, plating on plastic spheres has become popular because of useful attributes. Plated plastic particles have lower densities and therefore are less prone to settling. Some plastic spheres can deform under pressure to make better contact with bonding surfaces. The preferred metal finishes for anisotropic conductive adhesive particles are nickel, gold and gold over nickel.

1.4   APPLICATIONS FOR CONDUCTIVE ADHESIVES

Conductive adhesives dominate only one or two niche markets at this time. Die attach adhesives quickly replaced metallurgical connections many decades ago and are unlikely to be displaced in the future. Anisotropic conductive adhesive films are now the dominant means for connecting flat panel displays. What other areas are practical markets for conductive adhesives?

It must first be recognised that solder is the *de facto* joining material of the electronics industry. Adhesives are always compared with tin-lead solder in every application. Only when there are significant benefits for adhesives, do end-users seriously evaluate these materials. The cost of qualifying a new material and moving it into production is considerable. There must be a significant pay-off before most companies will make a change. Many companies find the favourable environmental attributes of adhesives interesting, but not a reason to make a change unless lead is banned. Companies will test adhesives as a future alternative, should the need arise, but do not really contemplate a switch. In today's market, conductive adhesives must provide a better solution, improve performance, reduce cost or increase productivity to sell. What are the advantages of conductive adhesives and what are the limitations compared with solder?

Adhesives have a significant processing advantage over solder, which exposes components and circuits to harsh temperature conditions. In fact, the packaging and circuit industries have had to work much harder because of the thermal shock of soldering and their products are accordingly more costly.

Adhesives process under mild conditions and allow virtually every circuit substrate and component to be bonded without harmful effects. Which applications benefit from lower temperature processing? Polyester-based flexible circuitry and moulded circuits are obvious applications. Heat stabilised polyester film, common in the membrane switch and low-cost flex circuit industries, needs to be processed below 150°C. Most isotropic conductive adhesives can be cured in reasonable times at 130-140°C, making them ideal for switches and other low-cost thermoplastic-based products. The low-cost flexible circuit industry has already started to embrace adhesives for SMT assembly enthusiastically and the trend will continue. However, only a small part of that large market has adopted adhesive assembly at this juncture.

Another important attribute of conductive adhesives is their ability to handle very fine pitch. Both isotropic and anisotropic conductive adhesives can assemble flip chips. Flip chip on organic board is a relatively new area if one considers that the technology was developed in the 1960s. Many companies are evaluating flip chips and attempting to define the joining materials and processes as the old C4 method is discarded. All types of adhesives — isotropic, non-conductive and the several types of anisotropics — can be used here. This is an excellent area for research and development and one that is already proven. Smart card flip chips are being assembled with anisotropic adhesives. Isotropic conductive adhesives are being used to bond flip chips for several applications in the United States, Japan and other countries. The finished assemblies have passed qualifications and moved into the commercial sector.

Conductive adhesives excel at solving incompatibility problems. Highly dissimilar adherents can be bonded where solder does not work. Adhesives bond readily to glass and vacuum deposited conductors while solder either will not wet or will leach off conductors. This makes conductive adhesives the best choice for nearly all flat panel displays. Anisotropic adhesives are now in use for bonding flex circuits and TAB devices to panels, but direct component attach is also enjoying success. One needs to ask what other areas of assembly have incompatibility problems that adhesives can address.

The circuit construction and assembly areas should not be ignored since adhesives are moving in as layer-to-layer connections. Sometimes called interposers, films of various anisotropic conductive adhesives are being used to make superior multilayer circuits. More recently, patterned array interposers have attracted interest for circuit layer assembly. As the circuit industry moves to higher density and the cost of drilling very small holes increases, the need for new kinds of interposer conductive adhesives will grow. This is an exciting area with huge volumes that should be seriously considered.

1.5   FUTURE POSSIBILITIES

Conductive adhesives for component assembly, including flip chips, are truly an embryonic technology. Although conductive adhesives are not really new, dedicated efforts to tailor properties towards assembly use have only begun in earnest in recent times. All of the classes of adhesives described can be greatly improved even without major breakthroughs. The authors of this book hope to provide the information that will advance interest in the field and inspire others to join in developing and expanding conductive adhesive technology. Let's now review ICPs, an unusual class of organic materials. These conduct electricity and breakthroughs here could have important ramifications for adhesives, circuitry and maybe even semiconductors.

1.5.1   Intrinsically Conductive Polymers (ICPs)

The polymer chemist has long sought to use conducting polymers to create the electrical pathways and interconnects for electronics. Intrinsically, conductive polymers could offer many advantages if only their chemical and mechanical properties were similar to those of modern plastics. A highly conductive mouldable or printable material would open up so many new horizons. The moulded polymer circuit would probably replace etched copper. Fine 'wires' could be extruded or spun like today's polymer fibres. Ultra-fine line circuitry would be possible as conductive polymers become an enabling technology for new products. Component assembly would simply involve pressing the device to the circuit while heating. Repair and disassembly would be equally as easy. Unfortunately, the ideal conductive polymer has as yet been elusive.

A large number of intrinsically conductive polymers have been produced and described over the past twenty years. Two basic types of conducting polymers exist. They are ionic and the more common electronically conducting variety based on extensive conjugated p-electron systems. The most common electronically conducting polymers are based on polyacetylene, polyaniline, and polypyrrole. A few of these materials have been commercialised for such end applications as battery electrodes. Doped polyacetylene has been pushed to a conductivity level of nearly 70% for copper metal. This is significantly higher than any values for metal-filled PTF conductors, which are still an order of magnitude higher in resistance than copper. In fact, polyacetylene is more conductive than copper on a mass unit basis. Why have ICPs not moved ahead in the electronics area?

Intrinsically, conductive polymers lack ease of processability and chemical stability. The materials can not be injection moulded, thermoformed or extruded in most cases. Processes are typically tedious and difficult, such as moulding powder under vacuum and very high pressures. The doped materials are relatively inflexible, behaving more like inorganic materials than polymers. Some modified materials can be dissolved and cast from solvents, but conductivity is usually sacrificed. The more significant problem is instability in air. The majority of materials oxidise and lose conductivity under ambient conditions. The degradation is accelerated by heat and humidity. Until the instability problem is solved, ICPs will not find any significant use in printed circuits. Substantial development will be required. Yet the recent announcement of a functional polymer transistor, based on ICPs, is encouraging.

1.5.2   Polymer Bonding

It is to be hoped that this brief tour through the world of polymer-based conductive adhesives has piqued the reader's interest. Perhaps you will wish to play a rôle in developing, applying and advancing the concept of Polymer Electronics. If so, you are in the right place at the right time. The Polymer Electronics concept has been most assuredly demonstrated and many basic applications have been successfully commercialised, but the best is yet to come. Immense opportunities exist for new materials development.

Successful creation of intrinsically conductive polymers, for example, will boost Polymer Electronics to a new level of performance and manufacturing simplicity. Later, fabrication of molecules that become selectively conductive in response to 'light' beams will bring the era of photolithography to Polymer Electronics. A new field of circuit technology will emerge based on conversion chemistry. The advent of conversion-fabricated circuitry will represent the final step in the long march in electronic circuit-making progress: subtractive to additive to conversion. So, if you are a material scientist or technologist, electronic polymers should represent a major challenge and opportunity for you. The information age, where electronics multiplies brain power, will continue to advance and require improved performance, greater manufacturability, materials and processes that are completely safe for the environment and its inhabitants.

On the process side of the equation, new methods will continue to evolve. It is notable that many of the most recent electronic assembly innovations are the result of developments in electronic polymer materials. Ultra-fine pitch bonding, for example, has been made practical by progress in anisotropic conductive adhesives. Today, nearly all liquid crystal displays (LCDs) are interconnected to circuitry using these polymer based interconnects. Rapid progress in eliminating toxic lead-based solder is the result of 'solderless' bonding processes made possible by new polymer bonding agents. A new multilayer concept, where double-sided circuits were assembled into stress-free, high yield multilayer structures, was recently developed based on anisotropic conductive polymer films. The versatility and the newness of electronic polymer materials open up a wealth of opportunities for the creative process developer. So, if you have a special talent for conceptualising new manufacturing methods and processes, Polymer Electronics is an area to consider.

The ultimate goal in developing new materials and processes is for the application of new products which serve needs. Today's important challenge for conductive adhesives is to apply this technology appropriately, effectively and efficiently to present needs. Although dozens of applications in computers, telecom, medical electronics and consumer products have been successfully reduced to practice, we have only scratched the surface. There are thousands of potential applications waiting to be discovered and developed using Polymer Electronics at its present level. Many of these applications already exist as traditional circuit and assembly methods. A large number of products are being manufactured in ways that are much less cost-effective than could be achieved with conductive adhesives. The challenge then, for the designer, applications engineer, new product developer or the inventor, is to match needs with the attributes of Polymer Electronics technology. The new product innovator has the additional challenge of pulling the technology along, by finding needs that must push the materials and the processes to new levels. If you are an applications specialist or a new product innovator, the rate of progress and the final level of advancement for Polymer Electronics rest with you. You must drive this emerging technology by winning designs today — designs that push the state-of-the-art for tomorrow.

The last, but perhaps the most important, challenge is directed towards the environmentalist. We have for so long ignored the concerns and pleas of those who would protect the environment when there was a conflict of interest with our business goals. We have all too often written off the environmentalist as an unrealistic reactionary and out of step with progress. In the last decade we have been made sadly aware of the correctness of many views held by environmental advocates. The total electronics industry has been one of the great abusers of the earth in countless ways. Action took place only when the likelihood of catastrophic damage to the earth was publicised. The threat of ozone depletion and the increased risk of skin cancer brought world action against those industries responsible, particularly electronic assemblers using CFCs. Equally threatening activities, principally the use of toxic metals and chemicals, must be remedied soon. Worse yet is the incorporation of toxic materials into products. Incorporation of lead, today's most insidious poison, must be stopped when it is practical. Polymer Electronics offers a solution.

Chapter 2

CATIONIC CURE OF EPOXY RESINS AND UV OPTIONS FOR CONDUCTIVE ADHESIVES

HEINER BAYER
Siemens AG, Munich, Germany

2.1   INTRODUCTION

This chapter presents some insight into the chemistry of special epoxy resin systems, designed to be filled with metal particles and thus to produce useful thermosetting conductive adhesives. Very fast resin cure is achieved by acid catalysed cationic processes. First, an overview is given of cationic polymerisation of epoxy resins to clarify the difference between cationic crosslinking and other cure mechanisms of epoxides. Cycloaliphatic epoxides, together with polyols and several other ingredients, provide room temperature storable one-component systems.

Besides storage stability at ambient temperature, there are two UV cure options that are promising with regard to applications in electronics manufacturing: Dual Cure and PASI systems. The former offers the possibility of alternative/simultaneous cure by UV and thermal treatment, and is important for partial areas of the resins that are not sufficiently reached by UV irradiation. The latter, pre-assembly irradiation, offers the possibility to trigger the cure of a resin after it has been applied to one 'partner' of an assembly. For a short period of time the adhesive remains liquid and tacky and the components can be adjusted; the adhesive then cures at fairly low temperatures.

When using cationically curable matrix resins, the properties of conductive adhesives can be tailored similarly to those of conventional products. The usability of the new systems has been proven in several application examples that include the die bonding of semiconductor chips, the assembly of piezoelectric ceramic arrays and the screen printing of conductive leads.

2.2   ADVANTAGES OF UV CURABILITY

There are several important chemical mechanisms that can be used for crosslinking in thermosetting materials and which can be effected by UV light. Some of these involve photochemistry in every reaction step; some are only induced by UV light, and ground state chemistry subsequently provides the growth of molecules.[1] In the latter category, a possible further distinction is whether the photoreaction leads to radicals or ions as effective starter species.[2] Radicals will induce processes of the radical chain type, e.g., with acrylates, and of the radical addition type, e.g., with thiol-olefin systems, but these mechanisms are not addressed in this chapter. The second important starter species is reactive ions. In fact, acid catalysed, cationic polymerisation and copolyaddition with hydroxyl compounds constitute the chemical platform of the work referred to in this chapter (Figure 2.1).

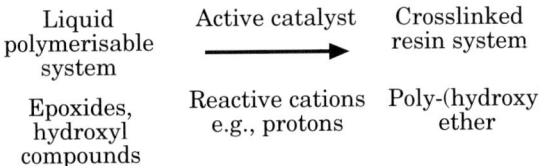

Fig. 2.1 General chemical platform.

One might question, at this stage, the unique advantage of UV curable resins: UV initiation is a means to overcome the restrictions of thermally activated exothermic reactions. According to Arrhenius' law, the speed of a chemical reaction is enhanced by temperature or *vice versa* — a reaction that is fast at a reasonably elevated temperature will also take place at room temperature, although more slowly. This is valid also when an efficient catalyst is present. The catalysed reaction will, of course, have its own temperature dependence of reaction rate and will be considerably faster than the uncatalysed one or will take place at considerably lower temperatures. However, storage stability is unlikely to be found in a straightforward polymerising system.

The difference between catalysed and uncatalysed reactions can be so great that the latter will not take place at noticeable speed or will be easily quenched by some concurrent reaction. This is the point at which the major advantage of UV initiation comes to the fore. Fast reactions are triggered by liberating an effective catalyst (Figure 2.2) to make use of the chemical energy that is locked up — in this case, in the strained three-membered epoxy ring. The photochemistry is decoupled from the Arrhenius type ground state reaction, and very fast resin systems are obtained, which can be even faster than mere heating up of an assembly or an oven.

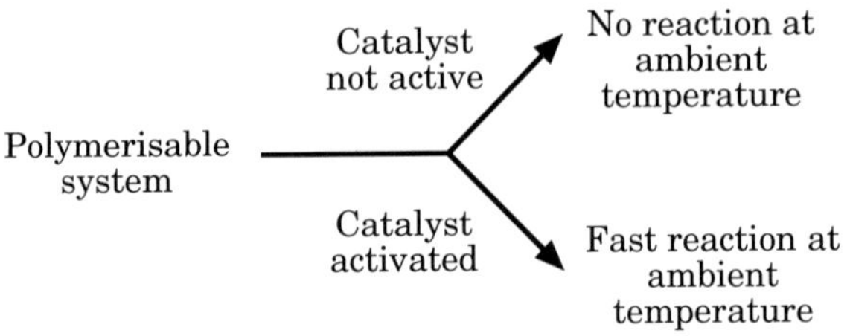

Fig. 2.2 UV initiated curing.

The resin will in some cases warm up itself, which is the case with many fast curing resin systems, not only UV curables. This leads to the second principal advantage — fast low-temperature cure, which can normally be achieved only by mixing two chemical components. UV cure may be an alternative solution, if heat sensitive substrates have to be taken into account, or if the production equipment for accurate placing of parts does not allow heating.

The special attraction of the UV curable systems is reinforced by the almost unlimited potlife which is equal to shelflife. This is true without exception for mixtures that contain only a UV sensitive catalyst and are protected from light, but can also be realised with latent thermally activated catalysts (see Sections 2.5 and 2.7). Stable properties, e.g., flow behaviour, can be essential for a precise reproducible application. In addition, long worklife is certainly a means of reducing waste and, with expensive resin systems like precious metal filled systems, also reduces cost.

There are several further arguments in favour of UV curable resins, which tend to play a minor rôle in the context of conductive adhesives, such as being free of solvents, spare energy, place and time. A summary of the aspects mentioned above, namely

— safely stored chemical power and thus stable applicability of one-component systems over long periods of time and
— light-triggered high speed cure without additional heating

should make such systems very promising for easy integration of reactive resin processing into automated production lines.

2.3   CATIONIC EPOXY CHEMISTRY

The matrix resins addressed in this chapter consist primarily of epoxy compounds which polymerise according to a cationic mechanism. A polyether is built up in a fast reaction as soon as an effective catalyst, e.g., a strong acid with non-nucleophilic anion, is present (Figure 2.3).

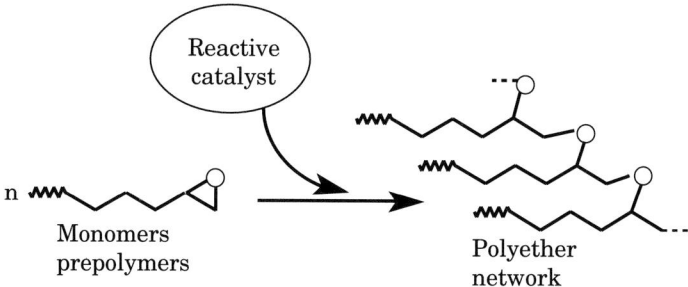

Fig. 2.3 Polymerisation of epoxides.

The uncatalysed polymerisation of cycloaliphatic epoxy compounds — though exothermic with more than 50 kJ/mole — does not take place at ambient temperature. Moreover, it is scarcely catalysed by substances like bases or onium salts, which makes it easier, compared with glycidyl ethers, to formulate storage stable mixtures. Sometimes aliphatic or cycloaliphatic resins are even stabilised by the addition of small quantities of alkaline compounds like potassium hydroxide.

When a cationic species E^+ — the simplest representative being a proton H^+ — is present for electrophilic attack of the epoxide ring, a very fast reaction starts, which can be written as a consequence of ring activation/ opening and attack of the cation on the next epoxide (activated chain end mechanism, Figure 2.4).

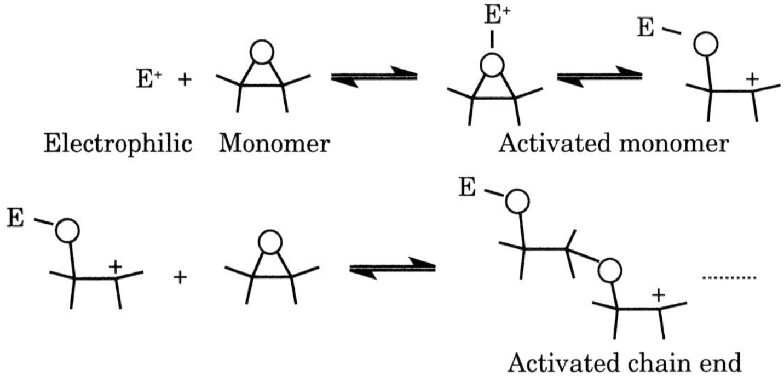

Electrophilic   Monomer   Activated monomer

Activated chain end

Fig. 2.4 Active chain end mechanism.

The epoxy compounds which are used as ingredients are of medium to rather low viscosity. Typical examples are the workhorse of cationic chemistry, namely 3,4-epoxycyclohexylmethyl-3',4'-epoxycyclohexane carboxylate and a more flexible molecule from a similar family of compounds, namely bis(epoxycyclohexylmethyl) adipate. The third example, shown in Figure 2.5, namely vinylcyclohexane oxide, will perhaps be regarded as on the borderline of what can be tolerated in terms of health and safety of workers, and burden on workplace and environment. It has the strong unpleasant odour of unsaturated organic compounds.

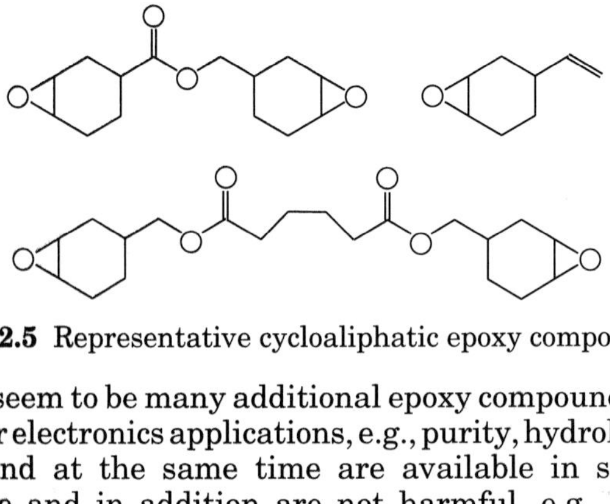

Fig. 2.5 Representative cycloaliphatic epoxy compounds.

There do not seem to be many additional epoxy compounds that fulfill the requirements for electronics applications, e.g., purity, hydrolytic and thermal stability etc., and at the same time are available in stable form at a reasonable price and in addition are not harmful, e.g., explosive, toxic, carcinogenic, mutagenic, strongly irritant etc. In Figure 2.6 two groups of compounds are represented, namely epoxidised unsaturated glycerides like soya bean oil and epoxidised long chain aliphatic olefins like dodecene oxide.

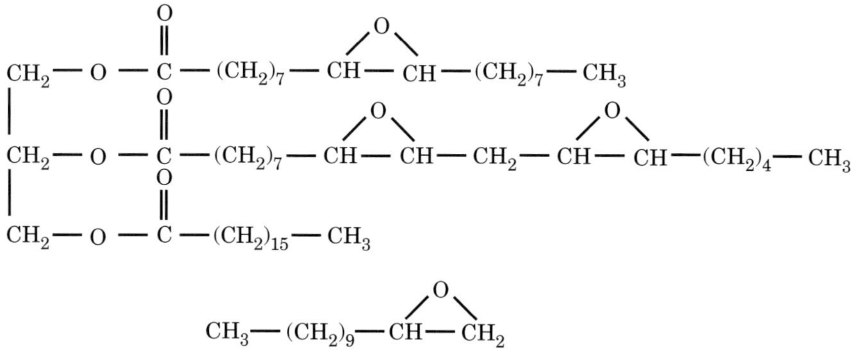

$$CH_2-O-\overset{\overset{\displaystyle O}{\|}}{C}-(CH_2)_7-CH\overset{O}{\underset{\diagdown}{\diagup}}CH-(CH_2)_7-CH_3$$

$$CH_2-O-\overset{\overset{\displaystyle O}{\|}}{C}-(CH_2)_7-CH\overset{O}{\underset{\diagdown}{\diagup}}CH-CH_2-CH\overset{O}{\underset{\diagdown}{\diagup}}CH-(CH_2)_4-CH_3$$

$$CH_2-O-\overset{\overset{\displaystyle O}{\|}}{C}-(CH_2)_{15}-CH_3$$

$$CH_3-(CH_2)_9-CH\overset{O}{\underset{\diagdown}{\diagup}}CH_2$$

Fig. 2.6 Representative aliphatic epoxy compounds.

It is pertinent to include some remarks on glycidylether resins, which in principle can also be used for the chemistry described here, but are not favoured, and are sometimes not even suitable. At least, they tend to be more sluggish in reaction behaviour[3] as they are less nucleophilic, yet, in spite of that, storage stability can be a problem in the presence of basic and salt-like compounds. Probably the best known examples are the diglycidyl ethers of bisphenol A and of butane diol (Figure 2.7).

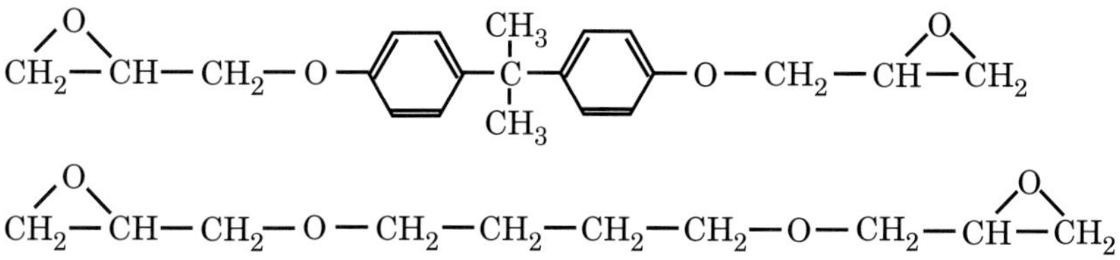

$$CH_2\overset{O}{\underset{\diagdown}{\diagup}}CH-CH_2-O-\!\!\!\bigcirc\!\!\!-\overset{\overset{\displaystyle CH_3}{|}}{\underset{\underset{\displaystyle CH_3}{|}}{C}}-\!\!\!\bigcirc\!\!\!-O-CH_2-CH\overset{O}{\underset{\diagdown}{\diagup}}CH_2$$

$$CH_2\overset{O}{\underset{\diagdown}{\diagup}}CH-CH_2-O-CH_2-CH_2-CH_2-CH_2-O-CH_2-CH\overset{O}{\underset{\diagdown}{\diagup}}CH_2$$

Fig. 2.7 Representative glycidylether compounds.

In epichlorohydrin derived epoxy resins there is always a residual amount of chlorine compounds. This may become serious when glycidyl ether resins of low viscosity have to be formulated, and when these resins are used for insulation purposes. Halogenides are known to cause problems on account of their corrosive potential, especially in highly accelerated moisture/temperature testing. Whether this is really troublesome in conductive resin systems has long been a subject of discussion. It does, however, seem to have been proven that silver migration is related to the halogen content of the resin matrix.[4]

With glycidylethers like those in Figure 2.7 and several other derivatives of polyphenols and polyalcohols, storage stable mixtures are currently formulated as heterogeneous suspensions, with the curing agents being insoluble solids like amides or dicyandiimide derivatives. Other epoxy cure mechanisms result in mixtures that are not stable at room temperature, including base catalysed polymerisation. Anhydride hardeners are moisture sensitive and can thus produce acids, which will give rise to different properties of cured products. Polyamines additionally suffer from carbamate production with carbon dioxide, sometimes appearing as a white crusty substance at the surface of the hardener. Generally, the application properties (e.g., viscosity, rate of reaction) and end properties (glass temperature, adhesion, moisture stability) of these resin systems depend to a large extent on the proper conditions of the curing agent and the exact mixing ratio.

One way out of the dilemma — mixing expenditure/risk or long cure cycles at elevated temperatures — is to freeze the ready mixed two-component systems at the resin vendor's premises. However, the resulting products incur some additional logistics, transport and storage costs as the low temperatures have to be maintained and controlled. Another way is to speed up the reaction of very slow resins by going to even higher temperatures. But what is sometimes called snap cure has its limitations with materials and production equipment, and the cooling down may impart stress to substrates and adhesive joints.

Cycloaliphatic resins and glycidylethers should not be used together as there is suspicion of carcinogenic potential.[5] Unfortunately, there do not seem to be any more recent results available on this topic, but epoxy chemistry with low molecular weight compounds will always have some relevance to metabolic chemistry. Certainly, the residual impurities of epichlorohydrin should be excluded, as this is a known carcinogenic substance.

2.4   THE POLYOL COMPONENT

The second reaction that is normally involved in cationic epoxy resins is copolyaddition with hydroxyl compounds. These will act as chain terminators if they are monofunctional, but will connect polyether chains by ß-hydroxy-ether linkages if they are difunctional (Figure 2.8), or will even help to build up a three-dimensional network if their functionality is three or more.

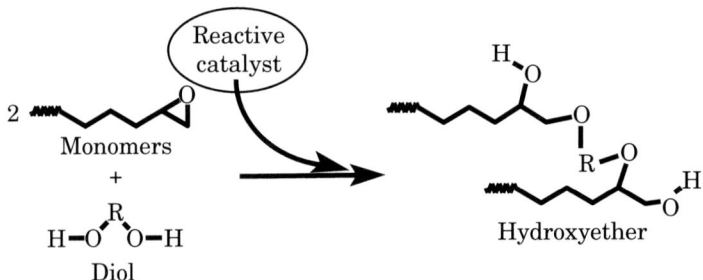

Fig. 2.8 Copolymerisation of epoxides with diols.

Compared with the polymer which would evolve from pure epoxy compounds (see Figure 2.3), the network density is considerably lower. The effect of widening by the flexible polyol chain is magnified by the fact that the epoxy groups become monofunctional and therefore diepoxides no longer deliver crosslinks. Monoepoxides in the presence of mono- and difunctional alcohols will result in some low molecular weight material, which in many cases is not desirable.

The reaction scheme for epoxy compounds (activated chain end mechanism, Figure 2.4) is to be expanded for cases where an alcohol reacts with either the activated monomer or the activated chain end. The loss of a proton leads to an ether chain or chain end. The proton acts as a new electrophile (E+ = H+) and will subsequently activate a new monomer (activated monomer mechanism, Figure 2.9).

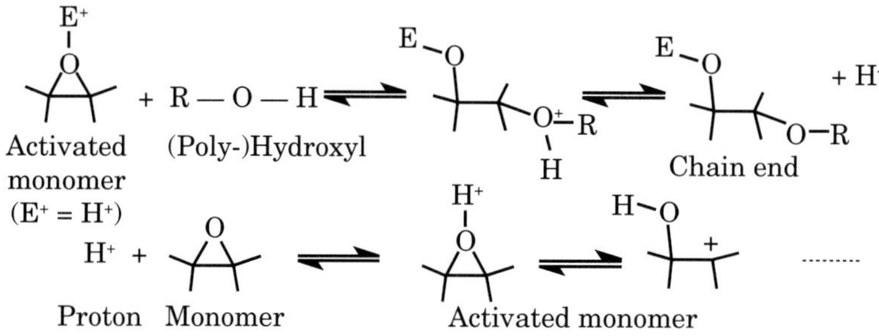

Fig. 2.9 Activated monomer mechanism.

Polyol components offer a wide latitude for formulations and to some extent their rôle can be compared with the one they play in polyurethane chemistry. The major difference is their negligible reactivity at room temperature and one must be more aware of the competitive homopolymerisation of epoxide that will lead to an unreacted proportion of original hydoxyl groups. Examples of useful compounds are polyether and polyester polyols [6] derived from glycols, triols etc., but also the parent polyols themselves. In Figure 2.10 trimethylol propane is shown beside two slightly more exotic, yet commercially available polyols, namely 3(4),8(9)-bis(hydroxymethyl)tricyclo-[5.2.1.0²,⁶] decane and bisethoxylated bisphenol A.

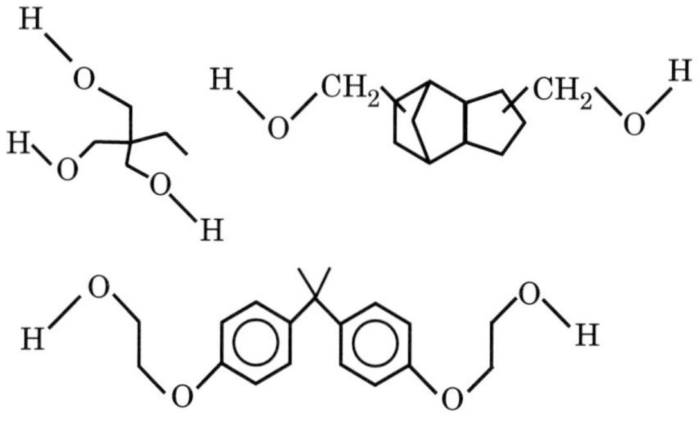

Fig. 2.10 Representative polyol compounds.

For the formulation of technically useful resins, several additives can be mentioned. Among these are substances that influence flow behaviour and surface tension, like finely dispersed silica, which can additionally be surface modified, or fluorinated resins like Modaflow (Brenntag AG) or FC 430 (3M Company), and substances that improve adhesion especially at high temperatures and with thermal cycling, such as functional alcanolates of silicon, titanium or zirconium. There can also be ingredients that are present merely to minimise shrinkage. In the simplest case these are thermoplastic or mineral powders which dilute the functional resin part. The reactivity of all of these must be analysed critically in terms of influence on the mechanistic sequences outlined.

2.5   INITIATORS FOR CATIONIC CHEMISTRY

It is evident that the essential ingredients for one-component systems are the initiators. Effective catalytic and/or initiating species must be generated from precursors which are stable at room temperature in the dark. The principle is to start with salt-like yet soluble compounds which consist of a cation that is not active towards epoxide or hydroxyl compounds and an anion that has the capability to keep a growing cationic chain alive and not collapse with it, in other words that is not nucleophilic.

Established compounds of this type are triarylsulphonium salts,[7] e.g., diphenyl-4-thiophenoxyphenyl-sulphonium hexafluoroantimonate (Figure 2.11), which is supposed to be the main component of a commercial photoinitiator (Cyracure UVI 6974, Union Carbide Corporation).

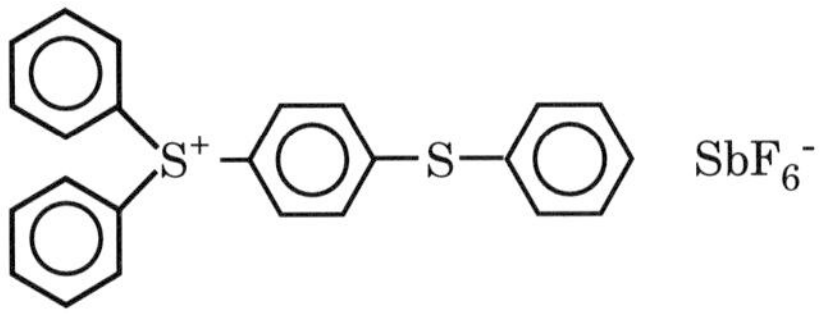

Fig. 2.11 Representative triarylsulphonium salt.

Cycloaliphatic epoxides can be formulated with this to result in fast UV curable systems. The photochemistry is actually still much faster than the ground state thermoset chemistry, so that, e.g., the beam of a UV laser, which moves at many metres per second, can effectively liberate the catalyst. The generation of protons from triarylsulphonium salts can be explained according to the simplified diagram in Figure 2.12.

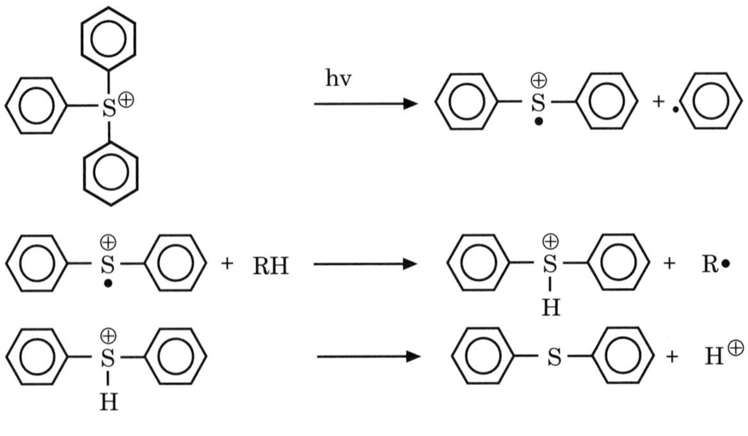

Fig. 2.12 Acid formation from triarylsulphonium salts.

Another commercial photoinitiator which is useful in the context of cationic curing[8] is cyclopentadienyl-isopropylbenzene iron (1+) hexafluorophosphate (Irgacure 261, Ciba Geigy AG). In many cases, this is combined with perylene as a photosensitiser and with organic peroxides like cumol hydroperoxide as an accelerator (Figure 2.13).

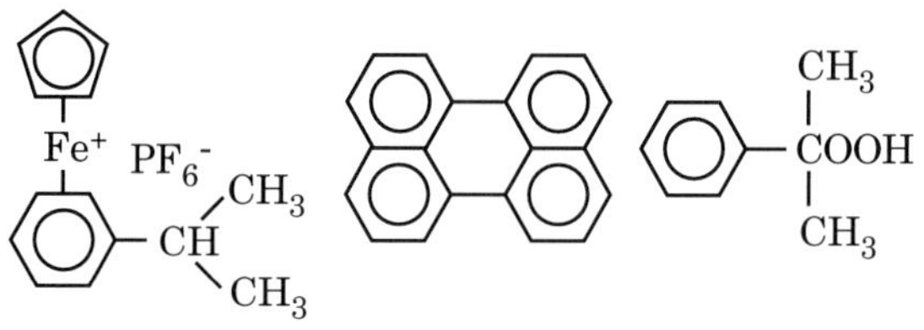

Fig. 2.13 Ferrocene type photoinitator system.

It is sensitive to UV light of longer wavelength up to visible light and seems to be effective for slowing down certain resin systems and is therefore useful in special cases. One of these is the pre-assembly irradiation technique which will be introduced later in this chapter.

Now a sort of somersault is to be performed regarding what has been said in the section on advantages of UV curing. The principle of liberating strongly catalysing species can, with only a small loss of thermal or storage stability, be extended to a few thermally sensitive substances. One of these was found to be especially useful, namely benzylthiolanium hexafluoroantimonate[9] (Figure 2.14).

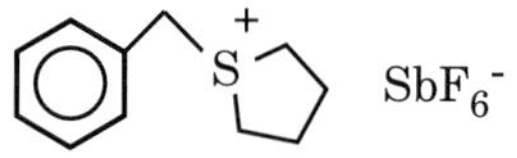

Fig. 2.14 Thermal initiator.

It is possible to produce formulations with this compound which are stable for half a year and more at room temperature. The mechanism which seems to be favourable for storage stability is monomolecular decay, but there is doubt as to whether it occurs in its pure form in real resin systems or whether it is at least assisted by nucleophilic attack of surrounding molecules (Figure 2.15).

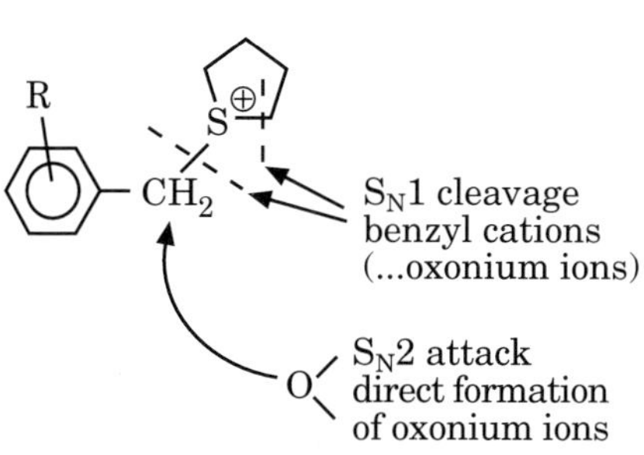

Fig. 2.15 Decay of thiolanium salts.

It has been observed that long-term stability of these mixtures can be disturbed by impurities, but can also be enhanced by adding basic compounds like ethanolamines.[10]

2.6 CONDUCTIVE FILLERS

There is still one important aspect of resin systems that has not been addressed in this chapter — the conductivity necessary for the electrical functioning of the material. The matrix resin systems described are good insulators when properly cured. There are efforts to bring metallic parts so close that there is electrical contact without any contribution by the adhesive,[11] but in most cases there will be metallic or metallised particles to form conductive paths.

When the possibility is given to shortcircuit two parts by single conductive particles of the adhesive, because of narrow distances and the right particle size, it depends on the area and probability as to whether a useful joint results. Such situations are generally classed as anisotropic conductive adhesive joining and are treated elsewhere in this book. Otherwise the filler has to be added in appropriate proportions to reach and exceed the percolation threshold, which means that on average every conductive particle is in contact with more than two others and a network of electrical paths connects the two parts that are to be joined.

Suitable conductive fillers can be of different materials, shape and size, and the percolation threshold will be reached with different proportions of fillers. Most of the results described in this chapter were obtained with fairly conventional silver flakes (e.g., products from Degussa AG or Chemet Corporation). The upper limiting factors of filler degree are flow behaviour, mechanical properties and adhesion, and ultimately the price of the resin system.

The initiator system and the growing chains may interfere with the conductive particles which are an imminent substrate (see also comments at the end of Section 2.10). This can be demonstrated by differential scanning calorimetry (DSC), which will be dealt with in more detail later. The enthalpy of reaction during the heating of a sample is considerably reduced and the onset of the reaction is shifted to a higher temperature. In some cases there is no proper cure at all. However, there are some powders that perform better than others with regard to UV curability and electrical conductivity. One can conclude that processing aids and coatings can have an influence on the precious metal powders. It is known from different experiments that alkaline compounds interfere severely with cationic polymerisation.

2.7 DUAL CURE ADHESIVE SYSTEMS

In reactive resin systems, which are electrically conductive because of dispersed metallic or metallised particles, UV curing must be assisted by a thermal cure for two reasons: First, there is an inherent lack of transparency caused by the metal particles above the percolation threshold. Secondly, in most applications non-transparent or at least partially non-transparent substrates will be bonded.

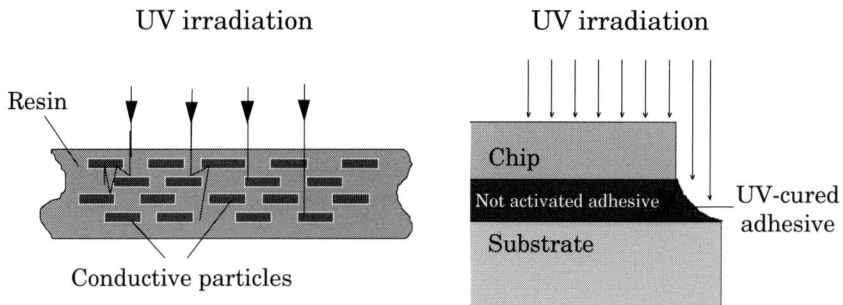

Fig. 2.16 Need for thermal cure.

In these applications only a spandrel of the resin can be cured by light. However, in many cases it is sufficient to shorten the time considerably for the process step of precise adjustment and fixation, for example using an optical pattern recognition system.[12] The rest of the resin will be cured in a thermal bake, but the parts will no longer move.

As has been indicated in the section on initiators, for dual cure applications a combination of two initiators has been developed.[10] This consists of a well known photoinitiator, namely a mixed triarylsulphonium hexafluoroantimonate whose photoinitiator efficiency is fairly well established, [7] and for thermal curing it contains a benzyl thiolanium salt.[9] The combination has been used successfully for unfilled resin systems and for systems that were highly filled with transparent fillers like silica powder. [13] Through curing of metal filled resin systems with these initiators can be achieved in layers of 20-50 μm by mere UV irradiation. The parts of the resin that are not, or not sufficiently, irradiated can be cured thermally (Figure 2.17).

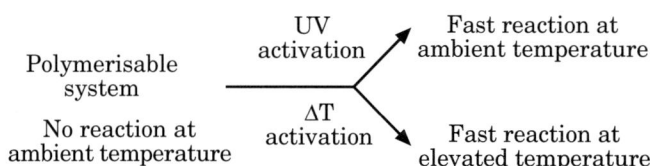

Fig. 2.17 Dual cure systems.

The special feature of the dual cure system is that the materials properties of UV and thermally cured parts are exactly the same, as the same ground state chemistry is taking place. The system should be differentiated from mixed mechanism systems, which contain components with a different chemistry for fast fixation and for postcure.

The reactivity of thermosetting resin systems can be analysed most conveniently by differential scanning calorimetry (DSC), which measures the specific heat of a sample and, as deviation from a linear course, the heat of a chemical reaction. From analysis of the dual cure system an enthalpy of

82 J/g is evolved in a conventional thermal scan (Figure 2.18, lower curve). After the resin has been baked for 30 minutes at 130°C a rest of 4.5 J/g can be found (Figure 2.18, upper curve).

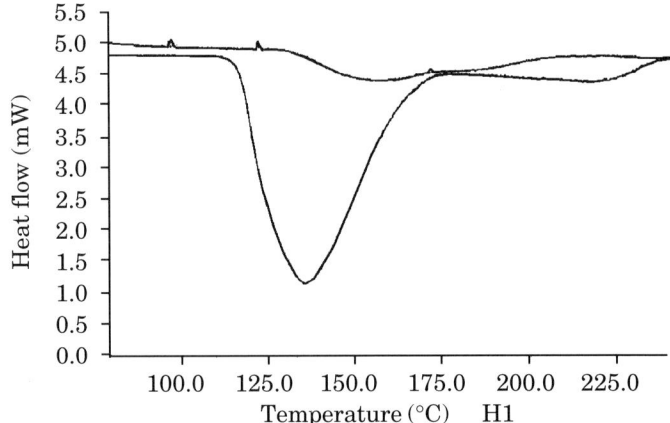

Dual cure — Conductive adhesive

Fig. 2.18 DSC scans of a dual cure system.

During irradiation in a UV-DSC accessory it can be seen that under isothermal conditions the reaction peaks after 5 seconds (Figure 2.19, the time in the picture including 0.5 minute before the lamp is switched on) and an enthalpy of 55 J/g occurs within one minute.

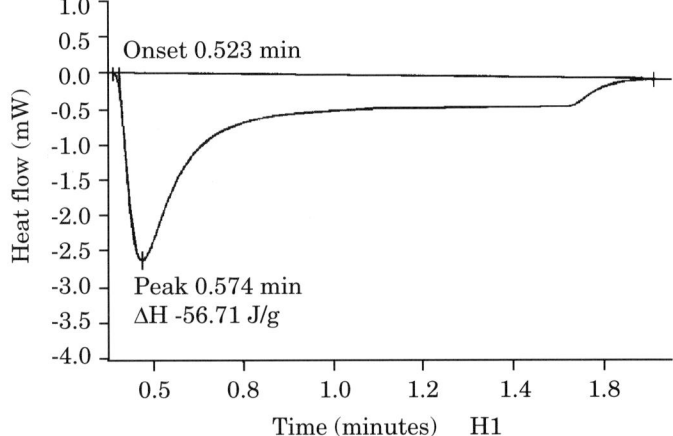

UV curing. 30mW/cm²

Fig. 2.19 UV-DSC, isothermal scan of a dual cure system.

Irradiation for longer than one minute does not make much sense, besides perhaps raising the temperature of the assembly under the production lamp. The remainder of the crosslinking chemistry is preferably achieved by a short post-bake. The resin in this example has a glass transition temperature of about 110°C. If it is essential to ensure that 100% conversion is achieved, one should postcure the UV cured area for some minutes at around that temperature. It is a general recommendation for thermosetting resins that the finally applied cure temperature should be not much lower than the possible glass transition temperature. The postcure temperature of UV cured resin parts is often reached coincidentally in some later process step. Thus, the curing conditions for the Dual Cure System are:

— Step 1: UV irradiation (several seconds up to minutes)
— Step 2: thermal cure for the final state (5 min at T = Tg)
— Step 3: thermal cure for non-irradiated parts (e.g., 1 h /130°C).

After Step 1 the parts can be handled and Step 3 can be combined with some later process step. Step 2 is only necessary if there is no Step 3 within a few hours of UV irradiation.

2.8   PRE-ASSEMBLY IRRADIATION TECHNIQUE

It has been stated that UV curing is a method for fast, ambient temperature curing of one-component systems, and it was mentioned that the photochemistry is much faster than ground state chemistry. It is possible to slow down the latter deliberately and thus a separation of fast photochemistry from a delayed response of the ground state chemistry on the time-scale can lead to useful processes.[12,14] This technique is known as PASI (pre-assembly irradiation), which means that the resin is applied to one part and then irradiated for a few seconds. With a proper choice of resin ingredients, there is a time of a further several seconds up to minutes or even hours, which can be fine-tuned by the skilled resin formulator, until the resin becomes crosslinked and the parts can no longer be moved for adjustment.

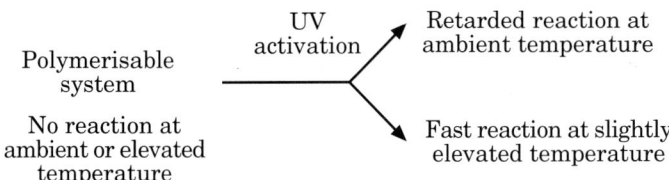

Fig. 2.20 Pre-assembly irradiation (PASI) system.

In PASI systems a commercial photoinitiator, namely cyclopentadiene-isopropylbenzene iron hexafluorophosphate,[8] can be used to advantage. However, other photoinitators can also be combined with proper formulated resin systems which contain moderating ingredients. It is clear that radical processes are not suited to PASI techniques for two reasons. First, the ground state chemistry is too fast and, secondly, it is not a living polymerisation. Sometimes mixed mechanism systems are described as 'activated resins'. Generally, these systems contain different chemistry for UV induced processes and subsequent thermal reactions.

In DSC experiments with PASI systems it can be seen that there is no reaction at all during a temperature scan, if there is no irradiation (upper curve in Figure 2.21).

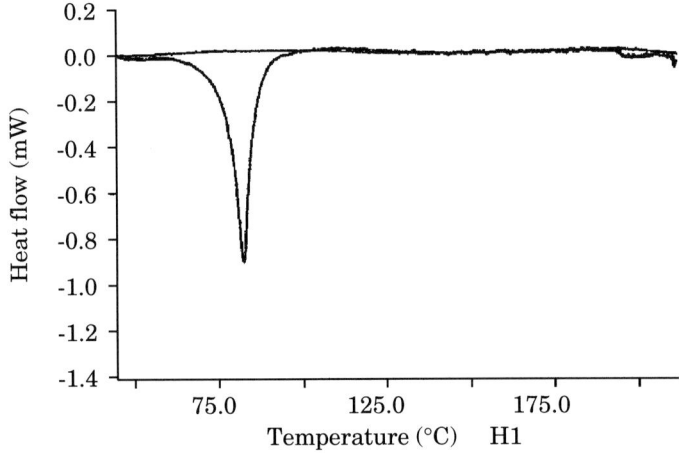

Fig. 2.21 DSC scans of a PASI system.

However, there is a fast reaction that peaks at about 80°C, if the resin has been activated for 30 seconds (lower curve in Figure 2.21). This means that the irradiated resin may well be cured at this temperature.

The PASI technique is suited to somewhat thicker layers for which thermal initiation is not indicated because of the vicinity of heat-sensitive components. It is essential to irradiate most of the applied adhesive to a certain extent, and sometimes a gentle movement of the joint to stir the applied resin may be indicated. Without any influence from light the adhesives are storage stable and will not even cure at elevated temperatures as the dual cure systems do. However, when they are exposed to their appropriate dose of light, they will cure very rapidly at ambient or only slightly elevated temperatures. Thus, the curing conditions for an exemplary PASI system are:

— Step 1: UV activation (a few seconds)
— Step 2: assembly time (several seconds up to several minutes)
— Step 3: low temperature cure (e.g., 15 min/80°C)
— Step 4: post cure (e.g., 15 min at T = Tg).

As with dual cure systems, Step 3 can be combined with some later process step. Step 3 and Step 4 will only be separated in specific cases.

2.9   ADHESIVE PROPERTIES

Since the conductive resin formulations show no chemical reactivity at room temperature, their rheology is stable over periods of half a year and longer. This makes them ideally suited to automated applications, and in production lines potlife will not be an issue. The formulator can influence viscosity, thixotropy and flow limit by filler type and percentage and by additives as long as these do not disturb the cationic cure or light penetration. The application technique can be dispensing, screen/stencil printing or pin/ tampon transfer. An exemplary adhesive has a viscosity of 20-30 Pas, some thixotropy and a low flow limit.

Cure cycles have been dealt with above. The cured resin properties are similar to those of established epoxy resin systems. The glass transition temperature depends on the composition. If one starts from pure cycloaliphatic epoxy compounds, it is possible to reach a Tg of 200°C and a very high modulus. The resins will be rather brittle and have elongations at break below 3%. More flexible types of epoxy and especially polyols decrease the Tg, so that one can arrive at room temperature and below. Then one has a rubbery material with low to medium modulus, and elongations at break that can be as high as 15%.

Stress in adhesive joints is one of the themes commonly discussed. It has its origin in chemical shrinkage and in the mismatch of coefficients of thermal expansion, and can slightly decrease due to some creep relaxation. The resins described here show no significant difference from other epoxies, which means a comparatively low shrinkage but a high modulus in the glassy state. Advantageous may be the low temperature cure, which shifts the stress-free state to lower temperatures.

Water uptake is normally measured as weight gain in relation to total weight. It may be considered as not very constructive to start with the statement that filler content makes a major contribution to water uptake; there is its contribution to total weight and a metal is one of the most effective water barriers. Attention must be paid to the type and amount of polyol, if water uptake is an issue.

The electrical performance depends on the filler type and proportion and is comparable to that of conventional conductive adhesives and also to soldered joints.[4] From four-point measurements, 500-5000 1/Ωcm was obtained. For PASI resins the values are somewhat lower and can go down to 200 1/Ωcm.

The thermal conductivity was measured as 1.8 W/mK according to DIN 52 612. From the performance of microelectronics chips it was concluded that the thermal transfer is as efficient as with solder joints because of the smaller gaps produced with adhesives.[15]

The mechanical strength of adhesive joints depends mostly on the substrates and can be rather high. In the test under DIN 53 283 conditions values for shear strength of 14-17 N/mm², steel on steel, were found. For gold to gold joints the values seem to be even higher, but were not tested under standardised conditions. Cationically cured epoxies show remarkably good adhesion to many thermoplastic materials, including high performance plastics like PPS and LCP.

2.10   APPLICATION EXAMPLES

Several examples can be given to demonstrate the versatility of applications that can benefit from UV cure options for conductive adhesives.[15] One of the common applications is die attach of semiconductor chips. In some special examples it is necessary to have very thin layers of adhesive for good electrical and thermal contact. The printer bar of a high speed LED printer (Figure 2.22) carries almost 100 LED array chips that have to be very accurately positioned. The chip surfaces should be adjusted to within a tolerance of 2 µm with one another.

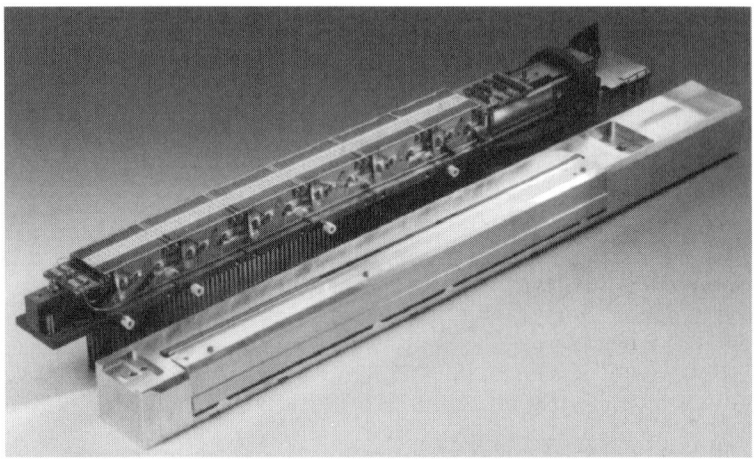

Fig. 2.22 Printer bar of a LED high speed printer.

In fact, these chips are currently mostly soldered,[12] but in future adhesive attachment will be used. Figure 2.23 shows the cross-section of such an adhesive contact between chip and heat sink. The space between the two gold surfaces is about 8 µm in this example.

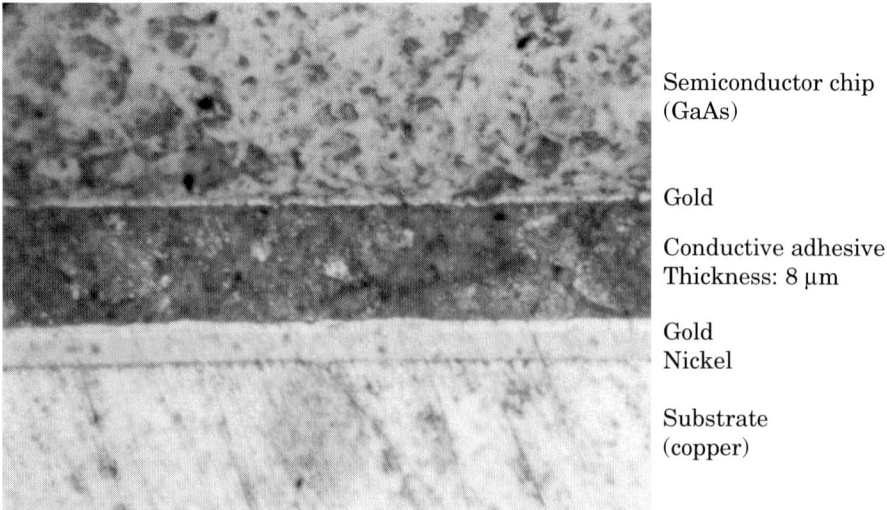

Semiconductor chip
(GaAs)

Gold

Conductive adhesive
Thickness: 8 µm

Gold
Nickel

Substrate
(copper)

Fig. 2.23 Cross-section of an adhesive joint.

For the formulation commercially available fine silver flakes in about 75% by weight were used. The resin was stamped in 27 dots per chip and the LED adjusted and pressed down with a load of about 100 g. After proper curing it takes almost 40 kg to push off the semiconductor chip of 2 mm x 6 mm in the shear tester.

The second example deals with conductive assembly of piezoelectric materials. Figure 2.24 shows a piezoceramic array that has been sawn out from one piece, which produces rather high mechanical stress on the single elements that are only held by the conductive adhesive. One element has dimensions of about 200 µm x 200 µm x 350 µm.

Piezo-ceramic

Conductive
adhesive
(PASI)

US-backing

Fig. 2.24 Piezoceramic array.

The substrate is a backing material which serves for ultrasonic attenuation and is laminated to a polyimide printed circuit board for the electrical contacts of the piezo elements; the flex circuit is hidden below the paper plane. The thermal sensitivity arises from the ceramic material which must not be heated to temperatures near its Curie point during adhesive cure. Thus, a fast and low temperature assembly process using a PASI system is indicated.

There are many other examples of temperature-sensitive substrates, like solder that must not re-melt and thermoplastics where one must stay below Tg or below melting temperature. This leads to the third application that is presented here. Figure 2.25 shows conductive leads that have been produced

Substrate
(ABS)

Lower
circuit

Dielectric

Upper
circuit

Line width
1 mm

Fig. 2.25 Screen printed leads.

by UV cured resins in a fast process free of solvents. This application works well with PASI and dual cure systems.

The conductive leads were screen printed on to commodity plastics like polystyrene or ABS with restricted thermal stability.[16] After passing a UV processor for a few seconds the first conductive structure can be overprinted by the dielectric (the dark square in the picture), which is also UV cured and conceals and insulates the lower structure except for the contact in the centre of the picture, through which upper and lower circuit are connected. A screenprinted conductive line of 1 cm length, 1 mm width and 20 μm thickness has a resistance of 5 Ω. In this application the UV curable thermosetting epoxy is an alternative to systems with thermoplastic binders or acrylate based resins, and offers better temperature stability and superior adhesion.

At the end of this chapter there should be a short comment on a possible restriction of the application of cationic curable resin systems. In principle, we are dealing with a living polymerisation. But this can be severely disturbed by basic or nucleophilic substances like amines, hydroxides, halogen ions etc. There were indications of cure inhibition on substrates that can be considered as alkaline; some polyamides, a few types of glass, e.g., cheap microscope slides, and several printed circuit boards, which were supposed to have an alkaline finish for copper conservation. The effect can range from a slimy interfacial layer and poor adhesion to the total inhibition of the cure reaction. There were also some silver powders that were found to be harmful for the cationic curing of epoxides, but fortunately there were also some that could be used without problems.

2.11 SUMMARY

UV cure options that have earlier been shown to work with mineral filled resins[13] and for fixation of electronic components for soldering[14] have been extended to electrically conductive resin systems. The cure chemistry is different from most conventional thermosetting systems and uses cationic epoxy chemistry, i.e., polymerisation and copolymerisation with polyols. The solvent-free, room temperature stable, one-component resins offer two types of attractive cure cycles, Dual Cure and the PASI technique. Therefore, it becomes possible to have automated application and fast online curing with handling systems that would be disturbed by heat and with temperature-sensitive materials like ferroelectrics, low melting solders and thermoplastics.

REFERENCES

1 Rabek, J. F., 'Mechanisms of Photophysical Processes and Photochemical Reactions in Polymers', John Wiley, Chichester (1987).

2 Pappas, S. P., ed.,'UV Curing: Science and Technology', **Vol. 1**, Stamford Technology Marketing, Norwalk, CT (1978).

3 Lohse, F. and Zweifel, H., 'Photocrosslinking of Epoxy Resins', *Advanced Polymer Science*, No. 78, pp. 61-81 (1986).

4 Orthmann, K., 'Elektrische und mechanische Eigenschaften von Leitklebungen im Vergleich zu Lötungen bei der Leiterplattentechnik', Adhäsion Buchreihe, H. Vogel Verlag, München (1991).

5   Bentley, Ph., Bieri, F. Kuster, H., *et al.*, 'Hydrolysis of Bisphenol A Diglycidylether by Epoxide Hydrolases in Cytosolic and Microsomal Fractions of Mouse Liver and Skin: Inhibition by Bis epoxycyclopentylether and the Effects upon the Covalent Binding to Mouse Skin DNA', *Carcinogenesis*, No. 10, pp. 321-327 (1989).

6   Koleske, J. V., 'Copolymerization and Properties of Cationic, Ultraviolet Light-Cured Cycloaliphatic Epoxide Systems', *Polymer Paint & Colour Journal*, No. 179, pp. 796-804 (1989).

7   Crivello, J. V., 'Cationic Polymerization Iodonium and Sulfonium Salt Photoinitiators', *Polymer Science*, No. 62, pp. 2-48 (1984).

8   Lohse, F. and Zweifel, H., 'Photoinitiated Cationic Polymerization of Epoxides with Iron Arene Complexes', *Journal of Radiation Curing*, No. 13, pp. 26-32 (1986).

9   Morio, K. Murase, H. Tsuchiya, H. and Endo, T., 'Thermoinitiated Cationic Polymerization of Epoxy Resins by Sulfonium Salts', *Journal of Applied Polymer Science*, **Vol. 32**, pp. 5727-5732 (1986).

10 Stapp, B., Schön, L., Bayer, H. and Hoffmann M., 'Photo- and Thermoinitiated Curing of Epoxy Resins by Sulfonium Salts', *Angewandte Makromolekulare Chemie*, No. 209, pp. 197-212 (1993).

11 Gesang, T., Bauer, A., Schäfer, H. and Overdiek, H., 'Conductive Adhesive Joints with Non-filled Adhesives for Surface Mount Technology', Proceedings Adhesives in Electronics '96, pp. 365-368, Stockholm (1996).

12 Bayer, H. and Lehner, B., 'Chipfixierung mit hoher Positioniergenauigkeit. UV-härtbare Montageklebstoffe', *Adhäsion*, **Vol. 34**, pp. 13-16 (1990).

13 Bayer, H. and Lehner, B., 'UV-Induced Polymerization of Highly Filled Epoxy Resins in Microelectronics', ACS Symposium Series, No. 417, Chapter 29, pp. 412-425 (1990).

14 Wanek, E. and Koran, P., 'Neues lichttechnisches Kleben für die Oberflächenmontage', *Adhäsion*, **Vol. 33**, pp. 22-25 (1989).

15 Bayer, H. and Hekele, W., 'UV Cure Options for Conductive Resin Systems', Proceedings Adhesives in Electronics '96, pp. 38-42, Stockholm (1996).

16 Schestak, W., Dissertation, Munich (1995).

Chapter 3

CONDUCTION MECHANISMS AND MICROSTRUCTURE DEVELOPMENT IN ISOTROPIC, ELECTRICALLY CONDUCTIVE ADHESIVES

JAMES E. MORRIS

State University of New York at Binghamton, New York, USA

3.1 INTRODUCTION

Metal-loaded epoxies (or other polymers) are conventionally used for electromagnetic interference (EMI) shielding in electronics packaging, e.g., in gasket seals of cabinets. However, for this application, the metal loading is relatively light since only high frequency conduction is required, where gaps between metal particles are effectively short-circuited. The application intended for the materials to be considered in this chapter is the direct replacement of solder in solder mount technology (SMT), flip-chip bumping, and even pin-through-hole (PTH) assembly. The solder replacement goal imposes the dual requirements of low impedance from dc to operational frequencies and mechanical attachment strength. Obviously, electrical conduction is provided by the metal content, and high conductivity requires high metallic content. Similarly, it is the epoxy that provides the mechanical adhesion, and adhesive strength conversely favours low metallic content.

Figure 3.1 shows the form of the transition from high to low resistance as metal loading, p, is progressively increased. The transition at $p = p_c$, the critical load value, is typically abrupt, as shown. Practical isotropic electrically conductive adhesives (ECAs) are usually manufactured with p sufficiently greater than p_c to guarantee low resistance with allowance for manufacturing tolerances. The shape of the curve and the value of p_c for various idealised conditions are predictable by percolation theory, to be outlined briefly below.

The metal in an isotropic conductive adhesive (ICA) is dispersed randomly, and it therefore conducts equally well in all three axis directions. It is also implicit in this statement that the dimensions of the ICA sample in question exceed those of the individual metal particles sufficiently for statistical

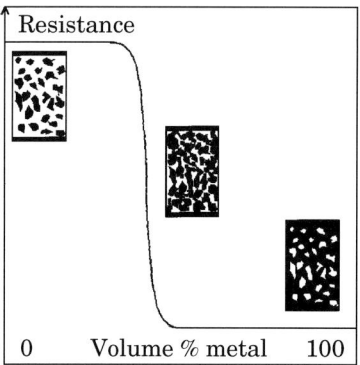

Fig. 3.1 Generalised percolation curve showing the abrupt drop in resistance at the percolation threshold.

averaging to be valid. As a result, ICAs may be deposited only where electrical connection is actually required, in contrast to the anisotropic conductive adhesive (ACA) ECA variant covered elsewhere in this book. For ACAs p << p_c and thicknesses in the conduction direction (the 'z' direction, hence 'z-axis adhesives') are on the order of particulate size.

It is worth noting at the outset that current commercial ICA pastes overwhelmingly use silver (Ag) flakes as the metallic component. However, other materials and particle shapes have been used in the past, and may return in the future. Consequently, the treatment here will emphasise the implications of theory for flakes, but will not entirely disregard other geometries, particularly in the case of spherical particles where traditional percolation theory is directly applicable. Most of this chapter will be concerned with the process of electrical conduction through the metal-epoxy matrix. This will require knowledge of the mechanism of electron transfer between metal particles and understanding of the characteristics of percolation in random media. The complete picture also includes the electrode interface (Figure 3.2) which is generally the focus of long-term reliability studies in high humidity.

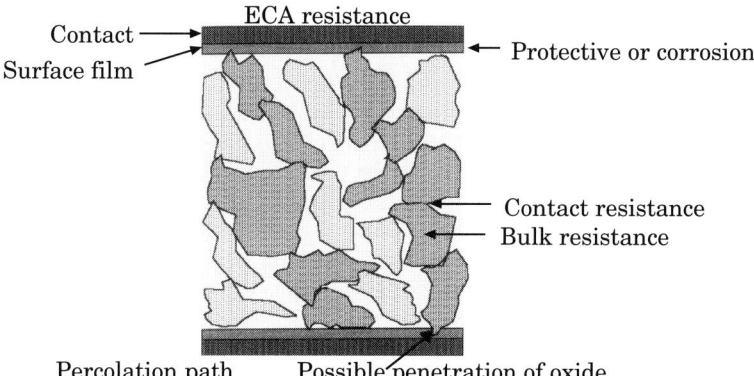

Fig. 3.2 Electrical resistance elements in commercial flake filler ICAs.

3.2   ICA STRUCTURES

There is also an economic consideration in the choice of metal particulate geometry, especially if noble metals are to be used, e.g., for reasons of stability. Some alternatives will be considered here from an intuitive standpoint.

(a) Mono-sized spheres: This can be taken as the basic case. Figure 3.3 illustrates the cases of both $p < p_c$ and $p > p_c$, (V and V_c in the figure) with the insulating phase also shown as roughly spherical particles. The situations of large and small metal particles are contrasted, and clearly p_c is much lower for the small particle case.

(b) Bi-modal spheres: The point of Figure 3.3 is that the smaller particles can fit in to gaps between large ones, and that a bi-modal distribution of metal particles can also reduce the effective p_c. Many current commercial ICAs take advantage of this effect, with bi-modal distributions of metal flake dimensions to improve the electrical connectivity at a given metal load.

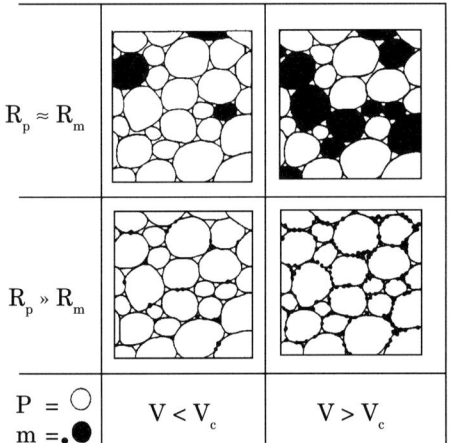

Fig. 3.3 Illustrative metal/polymer spherical particle systems.[1] Large and small metal particles above and below the percolation thresholds. (Courtesy of *Journal of Applied Physics*)

(c) Coated spheres: If one considers a conducting metal sphere system ($p > p_c$), and replaces each sphere with a metal-coated insulating sphere, then clearly the connectivity is maintained (albeit with a lower effective system conductance) at a reduced metal loading, and at reduced cost.

(d) Flakes: An important parameter in the metal particle connectivity is the surface to volume ratio. For the mono-sized cases above, if equal metallic loadings are assumed for the large and small spheres, then:

$$N.4/3.\pi\ R^3 = n.4/3.\pi\ r^3 \tag{3.1}$$

where N and n are the particle densities, and the ratio of surface areas is:

$$n.4\pi.r^2\ /\ N.4\pi.R^2 = R\ /\ r \tag{3.2}$$

in the small spheres' favour, accounting for the lower p_c values. The surface to volume ratio of a sphere is fixed, but very high values can be achieved in practice with flakes, which one can treat as discs. For a given metal proportion, p, and flake radius, the density of flakes must increase as their thickness, t, is decreased. In the limit of zero thickness, one can envisage an infinite number of flakes guaranteeing electrical continuity at p = 0! Commercial ICAs with silver flakes are pictured in Figure 3.4,[2,3] which also illustrates bi-modal size distributions.

(a)   (b)

(c)   (d)

Fig. 3.4 Scanning electron micrographs of ICA flakes, showing surface alignment effects and bi-modal size distributions.[2,3] (a) 4,000x, (b) 1,200x, (c) 800x, (d) 1,200x.

(e) Rods: A similar result is possible with the metal particles in the form of rods. Table 3.1 includes the rod in a summary of these surface to volume

Table 3.1

Surface-to-volume Ratios for Idealised Particle Shapes

	Large spheres *Radius = R*	*Small spheres* *Radius = r*	*Flakes (discs)* *Radius = R* *Thickness = t*	*Rods* *Radius = r* *Length = L*
S/V ratio	3/R	3/r	$2/R + 2/t \approx 2/t$	$2/L + 2/r \approx 2/r$
Example: R = 10 μm, r = 1 μm	S/V = 0.3 μm^{-1}	S/V = 3.0 μm^{-1}	S/V = 2.2 μm^{-1} for t = 1 μm	S/V = 2.2 μm^{-1} for L = 10 μm

effects. However, the primary interest in rods as a form of metal filler is in their potential for alignment, for example by a magnetic field during processing. Aligned particles achieve electrical conduction in the direction of the alignment at metallic filler levels less than predicted for random orientations, permitting better mechanical adhesion (see Section 3.9(i) below).

(f) Materials: Material selection is based on many factors, with electrical conductivity or resistivity being only one. The electrical resistivity of all practical polymer adhesives is sufficiently high to be considered infinite in all theoretical treatments. Polymer resistivity is not therefore a factor in adhesive selection. Since a specified ICA conductivity must be achieved at the minimum possible metallic loading, only the lower resistivity metals are viable candidates. Silver is the current material of choice. Gold might show greater stability, but is considerably more expensive, and is therefore more likely to be seen as coatings on insulating (polymer) particles. There is interest in the potential of the greater electrical conductivity of copper, but also concern about oxidation. Interest in nickel is driven by interest in its magnetic properties, rather than in its electrical conductivity, but commercial nickel ECAs are available.

(g) Spikes: Some ECA manufacturers have successfully manufactured spherical particles with sharp surface projections (i.e., spikes) — the so-called 'chestnut' structure. These are designed to penetrate possible oxide coatings on other particles or at the contacts. Flakes tend to have jagged edges which can provide essentially the same effect (Figure 3.4). These properties are inherently difficult to model.

(h) Alignment: Figure 3.4 also demonstrates a very evident particle alignment effect at the surfaces. It is not clear whether the alignment is a property of the air interface (and therefore a fundamental, universal property), whether it is a settling effect (and therefore a function of viscosity) or whether it is the result of the stencil deposition process. Whichever is the case, clearly the alignment will affect the electrical properties, and must be included when appropriate in any modelling.

(i) Fusible links: In the discussion above, it has been tacitly assumed that the contacts between conductive particles are 'passive', i.e., that the contact is mechanical and static. In some recently developed materials, the particle may have a coating that is designed to melt during processing and fuse with the coating of an adjacent contacted particle. The surface tension of the coating material may be sufficient to achieve a degree of realignment between the particles, in which case the system could no longer be considered random. Examples of such systems would include the many polymer/solder ECAs under study for flip-chip attachment,[4] tin-coated nickel particles (and variants)[5] and solder-coated glass or polymer beads.

(j) Porous metal: The porous conductive particle system is another recently developed one that does not lend itself readily to modelling by standard percolation theory, although adaptation should be straightforward. In this system, the inter-connected conductive 'particles' are themselves made up of percolating systems of smaller metallic particles (Figure 3.5).[6]

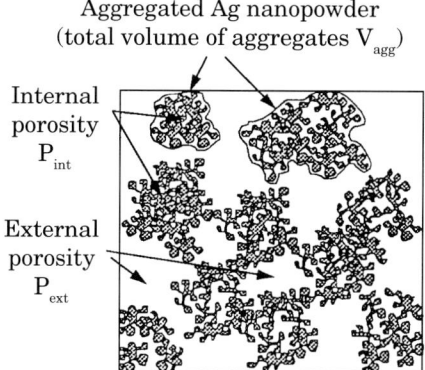

Fig. 3.5 Porous conductive particles.[6]

In consideration of the conduction modelling described below, it is important to keep in mind the differences between the real systems described above and the idealised ones to be employed in the models. The purpose of modelling such systems is to verify that one does indeed fully understand the physical processes involved, in this case the electrical conduction mechanisms, by comparison of experiment (the real world) and theory (the numerical model). The model development has not yet progressed to the point of quantitative agreement with real structures, but it can confirm that qualitative trends are understood within the model's idealisation framework.

3.3   MICROSTRUCTURAL CURE EFFECTS

It has been shown that a simple first order equation can model the polymer cure process sufficiently to predict the 100% cure point, where the ICA resistance is experimentally found to drop to its final full-cure value (Figure 3.6).[2,7]

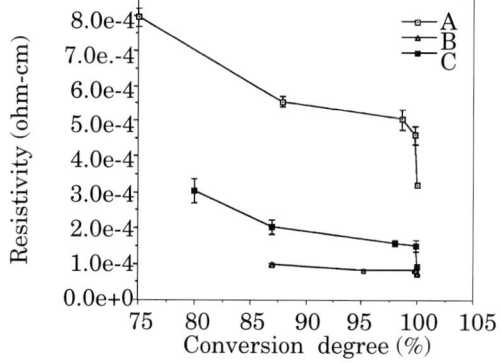

Fig. 3.6 Variation of ICA resistivity with theoretical degree of cure calculated from the first-order model.[2,7]

If it is assumed that the rate of reaction is directly proportional to the proportion of unreacted components remaining in the system, then the rate of cure, α, is given by:

$$d\alpha/dt = \kappa (1 - \alpha) \tag{3.3}$$

where κ is a temperature dependent rate constant, assumed to be of the form:

$$\kappa = A \exp - (E / kT) \tag{3.4}$$

where A and E (the thermal activation energy of the reaction) are constants, T is the absolute temperature, and k is Boltzmann's constant (1.38×10^{-23}J/K). The degree of cure at time t can then be expressed as:

$$\alpha = 1 - \exp - \kappa t. \tag{3.5}$$

A and E can be found experimentally for a given polymer from differential scanning calorimetry data.

A second-order model:

$$d\alpha / dt = \kappa (1 - \alpha)^2 \tag{3.6}$$

leads to:

$$\alpha = 1 - (1 + \kappa t)^{-1}. \tag{3.7}$$

This second-order model and a composite auto-catalysed model of the form:

$$d\alpha / dt = (\kappa_1 + \kappa_2 \alpha^m) (1 - \alpha)^n \tag{3.8}$$

both predict greater probabilities of incomplete cure with manufacturers' suggested cure schedules than the first-order model, which also predicts inadequate curing in many cases.[2,7,8]

The cure process produces a shrinkage of the polymer matrix, which exerts a pressure on the conductive particles, forcing them into closer contact. The contact area, A_c, between two particles is related to the contact force, F, by:

$$A_c = F / H \xi \tag{3.9}$$

where H is the contact 'hardness' (approximately 2.5×10^8 N/m² at room temperature for silver-silver contacts[2]), and $0.2 < \xi < 1.0$ with $\xi \sim 0.7$ for most systems.[9] However, it is not obvious in a complex two-phase material how the force is related to either the internal pressure or the external shrinkage, and there is essentially no information on either in any case.

3.4   METAL PARTICLE IMPEDANCE

(a) DC Resistance:

The dc resistivity of a metal is proportional to the electronic mean free path, λ, where:

$$\lambda^{-1} = \lambda_{bulk}^{-1} + \lambda_{grain}^{-1} + \lambda_{impurity}^{-1} + \lambda_{thk}^{-1} \tag{3.10}$$

and λ_{bulk} represents the mean free path restriction in the infinite, pure bulk material due to (thermal) lattice phonon scattering of electrons. Mean free paths in the silver grains will be less than the bulk value in practice due to finite grain sizes, λ_{grain}, and unavoidable impurities, $\lambda_{impurity}$, but there is no evidence to suggest that the differences should be significant. λ_{thk} represents the mean free path restriction due to diffuse scattering from the rough edges of a thin sample, e.g., in a thin film, but observable particle thicknesses are on the order of 1 μm (1,000 nm), which is much greater than the tens of nm mean free paths in typical metals at room temperature. So λ_{thk} is also unlikely to figure significantly in the effective particle value for λ, which can be taken as λ_{bulk} to a first approximation. Note that phonon scattering increases with temperature, decreasing λ, and leading to the positive temperature coefficient of resistance (TCR), α_{bulk}, typical of metals. (The other mechanisms of λ restriction are essentially temperature independent.)

Note that the thickness limitation on mean free path lengths may indeed be a significant consideration in the case of coated particles, if the thin-film coating thickness becomes comparable to the mean free path of the material itself. In these cases, the grain dimensions are also usually much less than in the bulk, so $\lambda < \lambda_{bulk}$, resistivity $\rho > \rho_{bulk}$, and $\alpha < \alpha_{bulk}$, due to the dual effects of both λ_{thk} and λ_{grain}.

(b) AC impedance:

For the ac impedance, one must include the self-inductance of the conductor at low frequencies, and the skin effect at higher values. The self-inductance, L_{self}, comes from the magnetic field associated with the current itself; this field is also linked by the conductor. The inductance has two components:

$$L_{self} = L_{int} + L_{ext}, \qquad (3.11)$$

where L_{ext} is associated with the magnetic field outside the conductor, which depends only on the total current carried (and not on its internal distribution), and L_{int} which represents the contribution from the magnetic field inside (Figure 3.7).

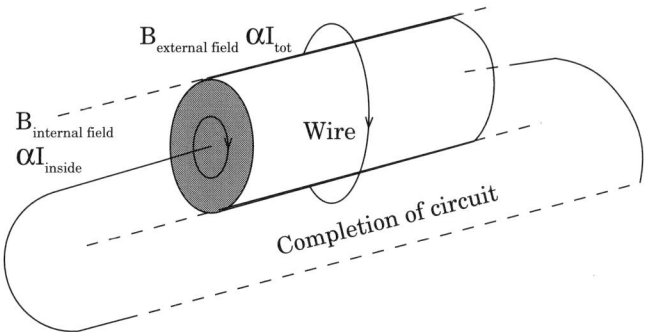

Fig. 3.7 Magnetic field lines associated with current in a conductor. Note the origins of internal and external self inductances.

As the frequency, $\omega/2\pi$, increases, the internal reactance, $X_{int} = \omega L_{int}$, also increases. The current will find the path of least impedance. This will then lead to the skin effect where the high frequency current crowds to the outer edges of the conductor. Thus it trades off the reduction in X_{int} against the resultant increase in resistance, R. At sufficiently high frequencies, the current is confined to a skin depth, δ, which can be much less than the conductor dimensions (thickness or diameter, etc.), as shown in Figure 3.8(a), with the net effect that:

$$R \to R_s = \omega L_i = \rho / \delta = (\omega\mu\rho/2)^{1/2} \qquad (3.12)$$

where $\mu \approx \mu_0 = 4\pi \times 10^{-7}$ H/m and $\delta = (\omega\mu/2\rho)^{-1/2}$, and:

$$L_{int} \to L_i. \qquad (3.13)$$

(Note that the units of the skin effect resistance, R_s, and reactance, $X_i = \omega L_i$, are ohms/square of surface area; to find the values in ohms one must multiply by the ratio of conductor length to cross-section perimeter.)

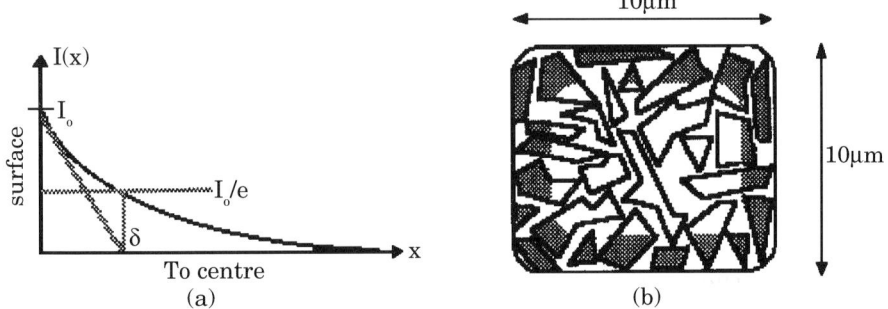

Fig. 3.8 Distribution of current with skin effect ($\rho_{Ag} \sim 4$ μm at 100 MHz) in (a) conductor, (b) ICA.

As frequency increases and the skin effect develops, the current will tend to concentrate on the outsides of the outer conductive filaments (Figure 3.8(b)). However, the situation is complicated by the possibility of very large differences in the lengths of parallel conductive paths.

3.5   INTERPARTICULATE IMPEDANCES

(a) Constriction resistance[2,9]
One can model the contact point between two conductors as a circle of radius, a, with the equipotentials forming a system of ellipsoids:

$$\frac{x^2}{a^2 + \mu} + \frac{y^2}{a^2 + \mu} + \frac{z^2}{\mu} = 1 \qquad (3.14)$$

where μ is the characteristic parameter of the equipotential ellipsoidal system shown with orthogonal field lines in Figure 3.9(a). There is a similarity between the current flow geometry shown and the electrostatic case. The electrostatic charge on the surface A_c (Figure 3.9(b)) is given by:

$$Q = \frac{1}{4\pi} \int_{A_c} \left| \frac{\partial \varphi}{\partial n} \right| dA_c \tag{3.15}$$

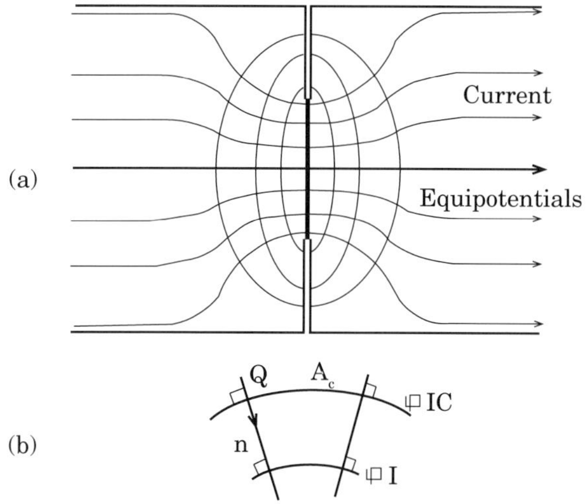

Fig. 3.9 (a) Ellipsoidal equipotentials system and field lines for 'long' circular constriction resistance contact; (b) capacitance/resistance element.[9]

With the electrostatic capacitance between the plates being $C = Q / | \varphi_c - \varphi_1 |$, and the current between them:

$$I = \frac{1}{\rho} \int_{A_c} \left| \frac{\partial \varphi}{\partial n} dA_c \right| \tag{3.16}$$

the resistance of the element is $R_{c1} = | \varphi_c - \varphi_1 | / I = \rho / 4\pi\, C$. For the ellipsoidal equipotential system, the capacitance between the ellipsoid μ and the contact circle ($\mu = 0$, $z = 0$) is:

$$C_\mu = \left[\int_0^\mu \frac{\mu^{-\frac{1}{2}} d\mu}{a^2 + \mu} \right]^{-1} \tag{3.17}$$

and the constriction resistance on one side of the contact is therefore $R_\mu = \rho / 4\pi\, C_\mu$, i.e., with the substitution $\mu = w^2$:

$$R_\mu = \frac{\rho}{2\pi} \int_0^w \frac{dw}{a^2 + w^2} = \frac{\rho}{2\pi a} \operatorname{arctg} \frac{\sqrt{\mu}}{a} \tag{3.18}$$

For a long constriction, $\mu \rightarrow \infty$ and $R_u \rightarrow \rho/4a$, giving the total constriction resistance including both sides of the contact to be:

$$R_c = \rho / 2a \qquad (3.19)$$

In the case under consideration, the constrictions will almost never be 'long' but the arc tangent varies much more slowly than μ. Therefore, it may be a reasonable approximation as well as convenient.

The TCR for the constriction resistance would appear to be the same as for the bulk metal, but this conclusion is only valid for a $\gg \lambda$, so that ρ is unchanged in the vicinity of the contact. In the ICA case, this may not be so, and the effective value of ρ will increase for a $\leq \lambda$ with a reduction in the TCR associated with the constriction.

Holm[9] shows that there is an increased inductance associated with the constriction resistance, but that it is approximately equal to the internal inductance of a length of conductor equal to the contact circle diameter. Since this dimension will be much less than those of the conducting particles, this effect may be neglected. Skin effects can similarly be neglected in comparison with those in the bulk of the conducting particle, since the constriction current is already confined by the geometry.

(b) Thermionic emission

Current can actually flow across thin insulating films separating the conducting particles without requiring direct metal-to-metal contact. Electronic conduction in traditional insulators is possible if electrons have sufficient thermal energy to reach the conduction band, viewing the insulator in more familiar terms as a wide band-gap semiconductor. Conduction across the insulator takes place by thermionic emission, with current density, J, given by the Richardson-Dushman equation:

$$J = AT^2 \exp{-\frac{\phi_0}{kT}} \qquad (3.20)$$

where the barrier height $\phi_0 = \psi - \chi$ is defined in Figure 3.10(a), and $A = 1.2 \times 10^6$ A/m^2. Figure 3.10(b) illustrates net current flow $J = J^+ - J^-$ with the application of an electrical field.

At high fields, one would expect to observe the non-ohmic behaviour predicted by the Schottky effect (Figure 3.10(c)). An electron having reached a distance, x, from the metal surface experiences a restoring force $q /4\pi\varepsilon (2x)^2$ (where q is the electronic charge 1.6×10^{-19} C, ε is the dielectric constant, $8.85 \times 10^{-12}\, \varepsilon_r$ F/m, and ε_r is the relative dielectric constant) due to the positive image charge left behind at -x. So the potential barrier at the metal surface actually has the form $\phi(x) = \phi_0 - q^2/16\pi\varepsilon x - qFx$ with applied field F included. The effective barrier is the maximum of $\phi(x)$ at $x^2 = q / 16\pi\varepsilon F$, i.e.:

$$\phi = \phi_0 - q(qF/16\pi\varepsilon)^{1/2} \qquad (3.21)$$

Poole-Frenkel emission of an electron from a localised trap-site produces a similar form of field dependence (Figure 3.10(d)).[10]

If the separation between the metal electrodes is very small, the ideal barrier height ϕ_0 is reduced by image effects. An electron, x, from the electrode in a gap of width, s (Figure 3.10(e)), has an image charge x below the surface of the near electrode, and another (s − x) below the surface of the far electrode. Each of these has an image charge in the opposite electrode, and each of these image charges has an image also, etc. So there are two infinite series of image charges, each element of which exerts a force on the electron in the gap. Following a similar theoretical treatment to the Schottky effect above, one obtains a quadratic barrier shape:

$$\phi(x) \approx \phi_0 - 0.575 \ln_e 2 \; (q^2/4\pi\varepsilon s) \, / \, ((x/s)(1 - x/s)) \tag{3.22}$$

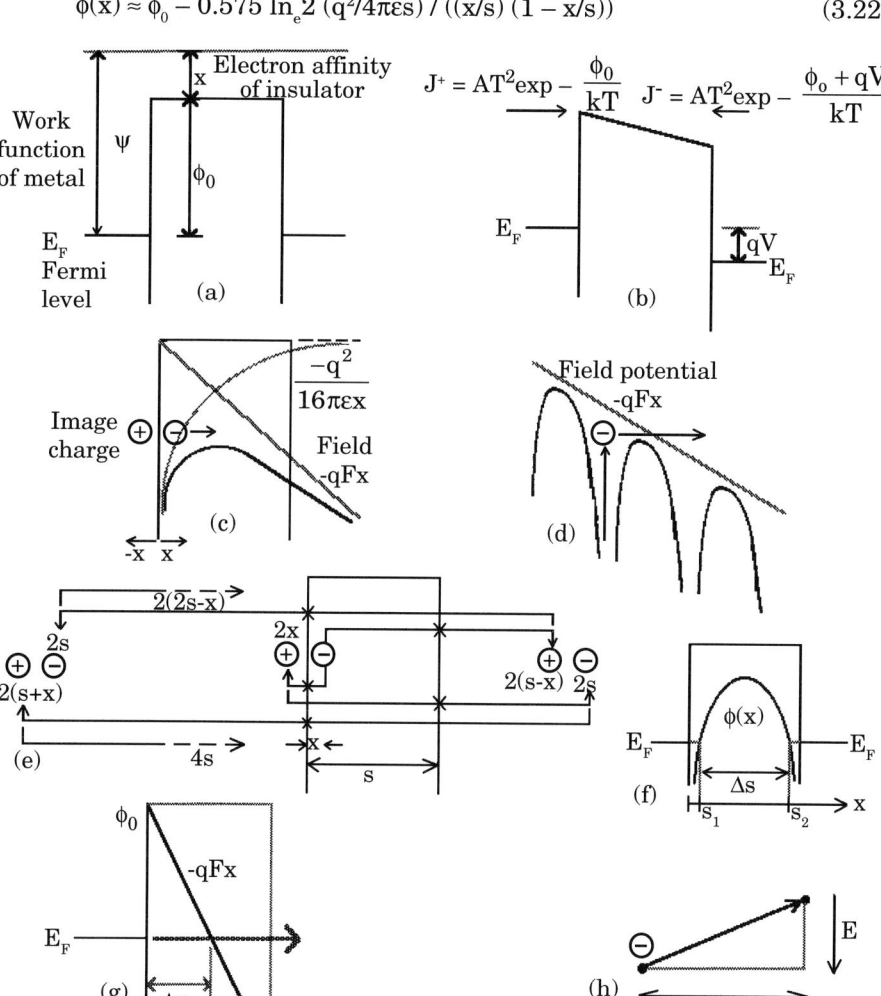

Fig. 3.10 Electron energy diagrams for (a) thermionic emission, (b) net current flow, and (c) Poole-Frenkel emission from a trap, (d) Schottky effect, (e) image effect, (f) potential barrier and electron tunnelling, and (g) Fowler-Nordheim emission, and (h) variable range hopping.

as shown in Figure 3.10(f), with the reduced barrier height (in eV):

$$\phi = \phi_0 - 2.3/\varepsilon_r \, s \tag{3.23}$$

(s in nm).[10,11]

(c) Electron tunnelling

If the barrier width (i.e., particle separation) is sufficiently small, electron transport may take place by quantum-mechanical electron tunnelling through the barrier, rather than by thermionic emission over it. Standard textbook derivations of the probability of electron transmission through the barrier are usually based on the idealised barrier of Figure 3.10(a), but at the small electrode separations necessary for significant tunnelling currents, image effect barrier reduction meets the requirements for the more physically practical WKB approximation,[10,11] which leads to the expression for current density, J, at applied voltage, V,[11,12]

$$J(V,T) = \frac{4\pi mq}{h^3 B^2} \frac{(\pi BkT)}{\sin(\pi BkT)} \cdot \exp - A\phi^{\frac{1}{2}} (1 - \exp - BqV) \tag{3.24}$$

where $B = A/2\phi^{1/2}$, $A = (4\pi/h)(2m^*)^{1/2}\Delta s$, m^* is the effective electron mass, and the effective barrier height is:

$$\phi = \Delta s^{-1} \int_{s_1}^{s_2} \phi(x) dx \tag{3.25}$$

where $\Delta s = (s_1 - s_2)$ is the effective barrier width at the Fermi level, E_F. For low fields, the unit area tunnelling resistance becomes:[10]

$$\rho_t = \frac{h^3 B}{4\pi mq^2} \frac{\sin(\pi BkT)}{\pi BkT} \exp A\phi^{\frac{1}{2}} \tag{3.26}$$

At very high fields, the Fowler-Nordheim effect may be observed,[13,14] with the effective tunnelling width $\Delta s = (\phi_0 - E_F / q)/F$ (Figure 3.10(g)) determined by the applied field, F.

(d) Other conduction mechanisms

(i) Various polymers exhibit variable range hopping conduction, where an electron tunnels to an available localised higher energy state distance s and energy E away (Figure 3.10(h)).[15] The combined tunnelling probability is proportional to $\exp - (\alpha s + E/kT)$, which yields a hopping conductivity for 3D materials of the form $\sigma = \sigma_0 \exp - (T_0 / T)^{1/4}$.

(ii) Space charge limited conduction[10,13] is characterised by current density variation with applied field: $J \propto F^2$.

(e) Surface films

Metals in general may be expected to be coated with a surface oxide film. Conduction through nominally insulating surface films follows the mechanisms described above for the polymer. For many of the metals of interest here (and especially for silver and tin), the oxide and sulphide (which is often observed on silver) are degenerate semiconductors. Figure 3.11 shows the band structures of (a) an intrinsic semiconductor (or insulator depending on the size of the band gap E_C - E_V), (b) an n-type extrinsic/doped semiconductor and (c) a higher conductivity, degenerate (heavily doped) n^+ material. For the conductive oxides, (e.g., Ag_2O/AgO), the 'doping' comes from non-stoichiometry and defects, and as such varies tremendously with individual preparations, environment, etc. So there is little useful information available in the literature on 'typical' parameters for the verification of theory by experiment. But in general terms, the position of the Fermi level within the conduction band ($E_F > E_C$) is directly analogous to metallic band structures, and there is only weak dependence of the electronic carrier density on temperature, with the thermal (phonon) component of mean free path limitation being dominated by temperature independent impurity and defect scattering.

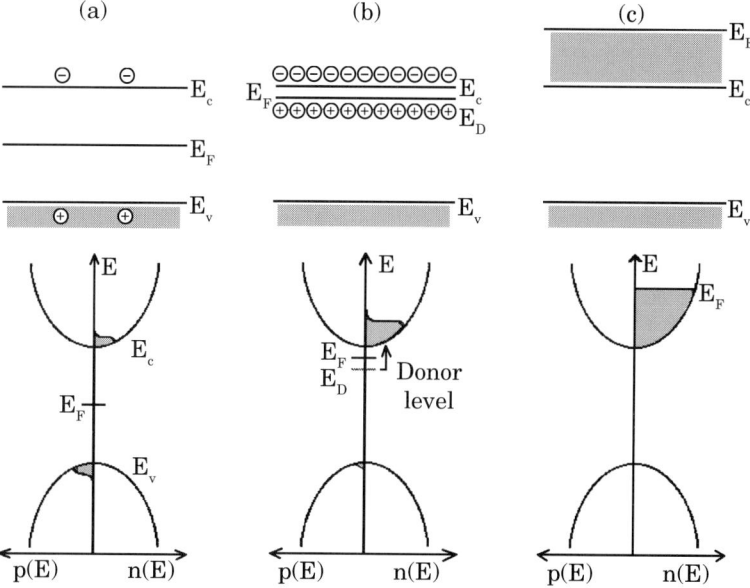

Fig. 3.11 Band diagram for (a) intrinsic semiconductor, (b) an n-type extrinsic/ doped semiconductor, and (c) an n+ degenerate semiconductor.

(f) Dielectric loss

Dielectric loss mechanisms show up at characteristic high frequencies, with ionic and polarisation resonances at around 10^{13} and 10^{15} Hz respectively,[13,14] but Debye (dipole) relaxation can occur at very low frequencies where it might be expected to be observable in ICAs. These are not strictly conduction mechanisms, but they would show up as a real component in complex impedance measurements. The complex dielectric constant is $\varepsilon(\omega) = \varepsilon'(\omega) + i\,\varepsilon''(\omega)$, where:

$$\varepsilon'(\omega) = \varepsilon_\infty + \frac{\varepsilon_s - \varepsilon_\infty}{1 + \omega^2 \tau_m^2} \tag{3.27}$$

$$\varepsilon''(\omega) = (\varepsilon_s - \varepsilon_\infty)\frac{\omega \tau_m}{1 + \omega^2 \tau_m^2} \tag{3.28}$$

with the imaginary term representing the loss mechanism, and where the terms are defined in Figure 3.12(a). In practice, the relaxation time constants are typically distributed and the responses are better characterised by Cole-Cole plots (illustrated in Figure 3.12(b) for the basic, single time constant case).

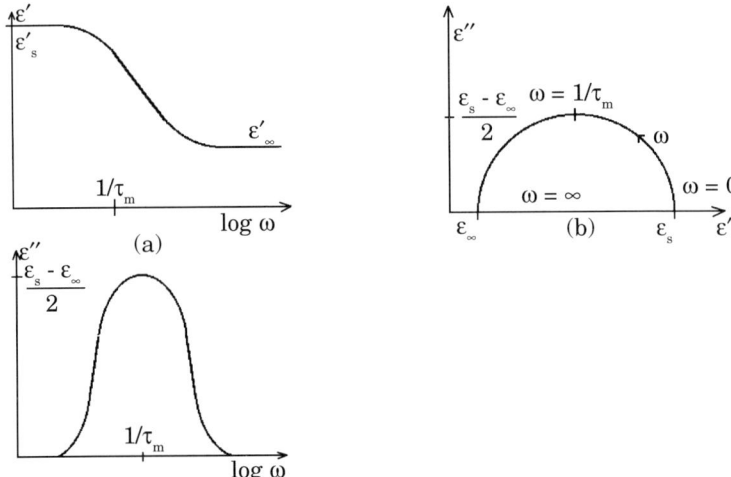

Fig. 3.12 Frequency dependence of ideal (Debye) dielectric loss; (a) real and imaginary dielectric constant versus frequency, (b) complex frequency plane (Cole-Cole) plot.

(g) Capacitance

If there are insulating gaps between particles, whether oxide or polymer, one would expect these (and mechanisms (b) to (f) above) to be short circuited at high frequencies by inter-particulate capacitances. The frequency response of a particle-gap combination is shown in Figure 3.13. Obviously, such a measurement permits the separation of the particulate

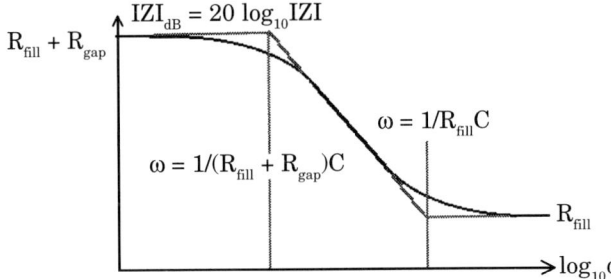

Fig. 3.13 Ideal impedance roll-off with frequency for inter-particulate capacitances.

and gap resistances, although distributed parameters in a complex series-parallel system would make interpretation more ambiguous than in this simple example.

Summary: The point of the brief review above is that the combination of conductivity measurements as functions of field, frequency and temperature is conventionally used in materials studies to identify conduction mechanisms.

3.6   ICA CONTACT EFFECTS

The electronic transfer from contact pad to percolating filler matrix involves the same physical principles as conduction between the particles themselves. If there is direct metallic contact, there is probably constriction resistance, but in this case on only one side of the contact. Also, if there is intervening polymer or oxide, etc., the same range of conduction mechanisms covered above for inter-particulate conduction would again apply.

However, if the conduction mechanism at the contacts is indeed fundamentally the same as between particles, then its variation with time and temperature as the contacts (or some specific contact materials) oxidise under elevated temperatures and humidity can provide additional information on its physics. If, for example, the transport mechanism is by electron tunnelling, and the oxidation rate is diffusion (supply) limited, $\log R = \alpha_1 \Delta s = \alpha_2 t^{1/2}$, where α_1, α_2 are constants, a relationship which should be relatively readily verified. The point here is that the inter-particulate resistances in the filler matrix are inseparable from the intra-particulate metallic properties, but that the interfacial contact resistance can be readily isolated. If the oxidation rate is rate limited, the variation would be linear in t; and other comparable relationships with t can be determined for thermionic emission, for example (or for a transition from tunnelling to thermionic as Δs increases).

Similarly, determination of the thermal variation of the interfacial resistance would provide information on the conduction process uncontaminated by the dominance of metallic properties.

3.7   PERCOLATION THEORY

The percolation process provides the second element required for the modelling of ICA conduction.

The theory has applicability to all transport processes in random media, (e.g., electrons in amorphous thin films, or water in porous rocks), and is developed by the generalised relationships that emerge from multiple Monte Carlo computer simulations of specific systems. Two simple examples illustrate some basic concepts in Figure 3.14.[16] Figure 3.14(a) is an example of a practical, experimental system, while Figure 3.14(b) represents a simple theoretical model in which bonds (connections) are successively severed at random to model the variation of the resistance. Note that it would require multiple random runs to establish the average critical threshold, p_c, shown. The experimental example is a three-dimensional random, close packed 'site' percolation system, with each site defined as conducting or insulating. The theoretical example is a 'bond' percolation system based on a simple cubic lattice, but limited here to two dimensions. The differences and equivalence between the site and bond formulations are demonstrated in the example of Figure 3.15.[16] An example of a site percolation simulation is presented in

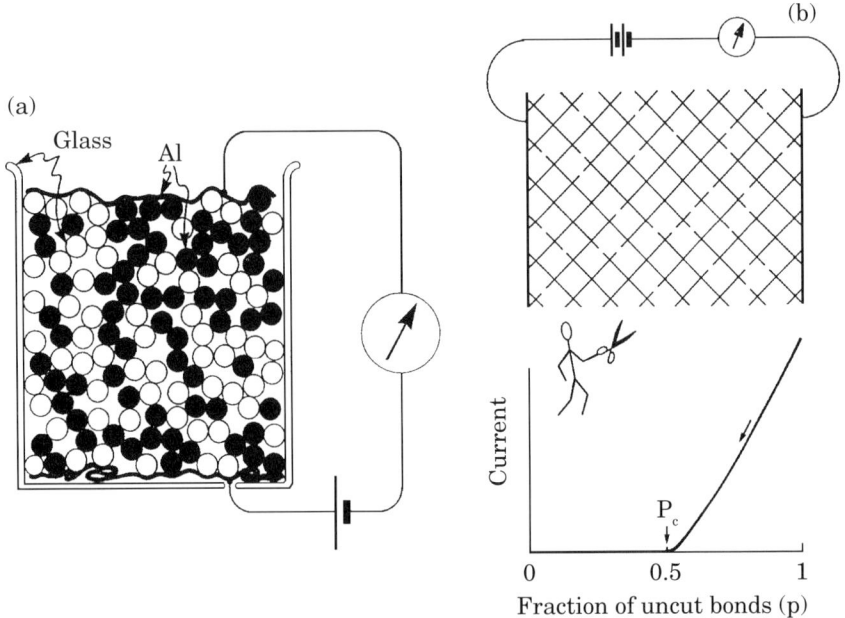

Fig. 3.14 Percolation concepts: (a) experimental — conduction in metal/glass ball mixtures; (b) simulation — modelling by cutting links.[16] (Courtesy of Wiley)

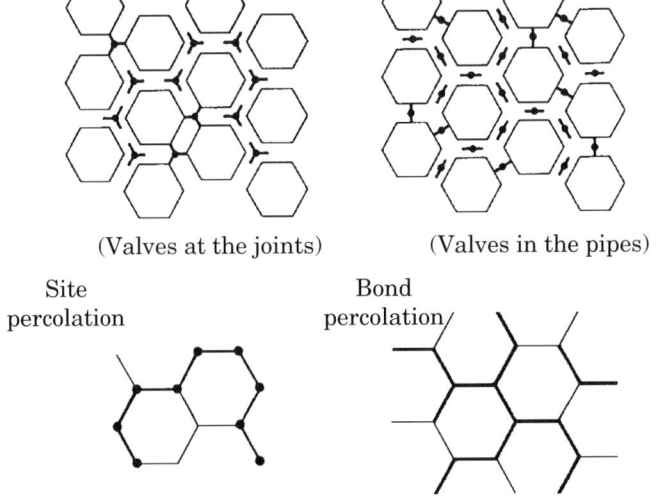

Fig. 3.15 The difference between bond and site percolation models and their essential equivalence.[16] (Courtesy of Wiley)

in Figure 3.16, where conduction across the 2-D sample is predicted for
0.5 < p < 0.6. The cluster that extends from contact to contact is referred to
as 'infinite', and consists of the 'backbone' sites which carry current and
'dead-ends' that do not contribute to conduction. The backbone contains
critical and non-critical sites, critical meaning that current would go to zero
if the site were removed.

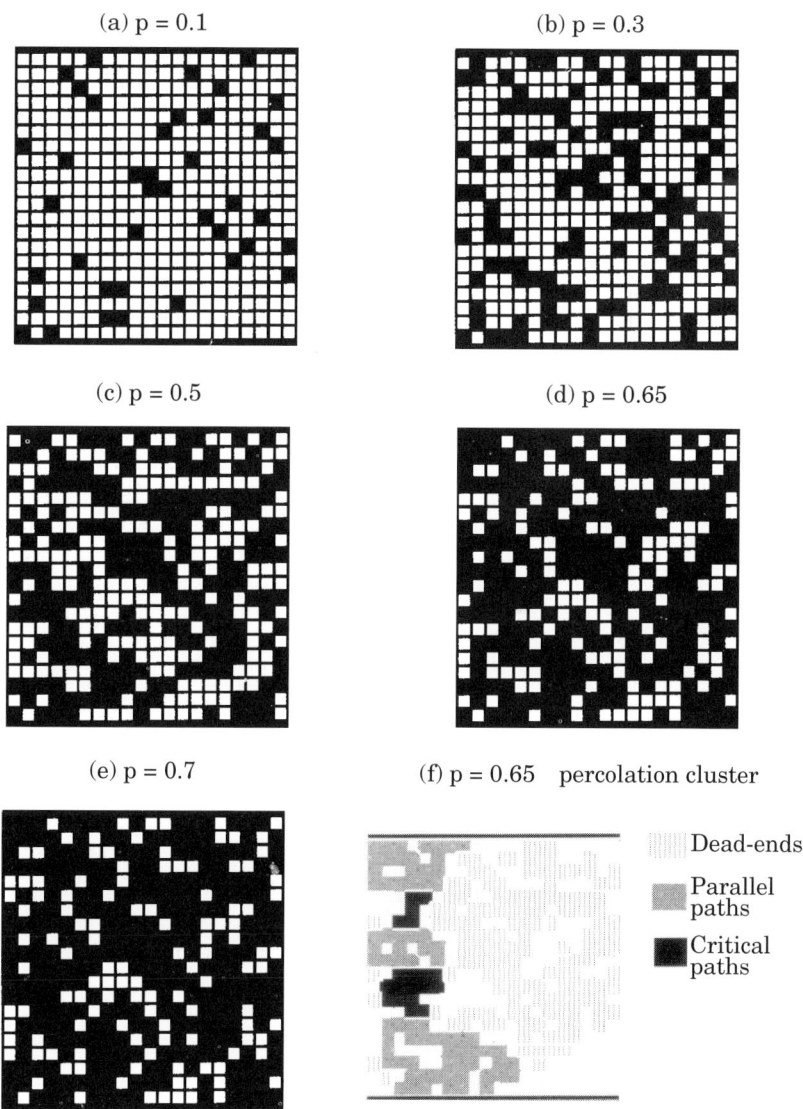

Fig. 3.16 Development of site percolation in a random 20 x 20 square lattice array:
(a) p = 0.1, (b) p = 0.3, (c) p = 0.5, (d) p = 0.65 > p_c, (e) p = 0.7, (f) the percolating cluster
in (d) with critical, parallel and dead-end paths identified.[17]

The larger the system scale, the less variation is encountered in practice
between the critical percolation thresholds determined from successive

Monte Carlo simulations, as shown in Figure 3.17.[16] Critical percolation thresholds are tabulated for the standard underlying lattices in Table 3.2.[16,18]

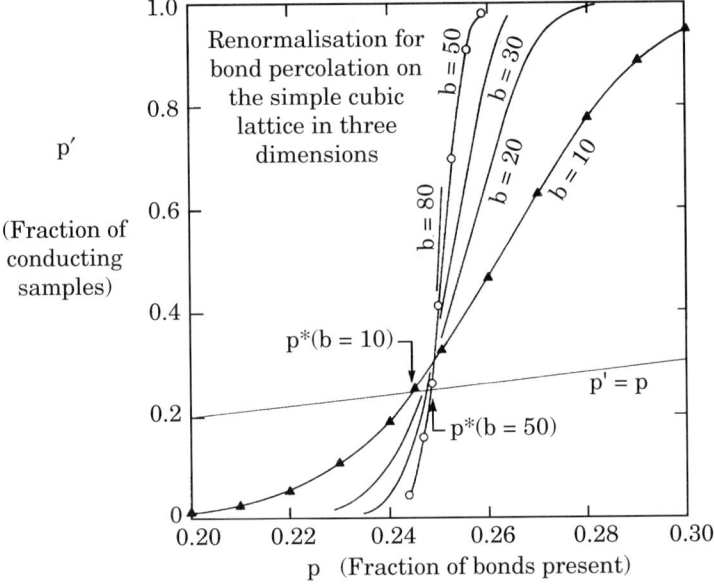

Fig. 3.17 The proportion of computer simulations which yield a percolation cluster for a given fraction of possible bonds present (bond percolation formulation), and the variation with sample size b x b x b. The transition is sharper (more reproducible) with larger sample size (normalised to bond dimension).[16] (Courtesy of Wiley)

Table 3.2

Critical Percolation Thresholds

		Bond			Site	
Lattice type	z^*	p_c	zp_c	ϕ_m^{**}	p_c	$\phi_m p_c$
2-D						
triangular	6	0.347	2.08	0.907	0.500	0.450
square	4	0.500	2.00	0.785	0.593	0.470
kagome	4	0.450	1.80	0.680	0.653	0.440
honeycomb	3	0.653	1.96	0.605	0.698	0.420
			2.0±0.2			45±0.030
3-D						
fcc	12	0.119	1.43	0.741	0.198	0.147
bcc	8	0.179	1.43	0.680	0.245	0.167
sc	6	0.247	1.48	0.524	0.311	0.163
diamond	4	0.338	1.55	0.340	0.428	0.146
rcp***	-	-	-	0.637	0.270	0.160
			1.5±0.1			0.16±0.02

*z: coordination number; **ϕ_m: filling factor; ***rcp: random close packed

In most applied studies of percolation systems, the purpose is to elucidate behaviour close to $p = p_c$, (and in the ICA case, for $p \geq p_c$), and so the 'experimentally' determined (i.e., simulated) variations of some critical parameters near (or at) p_c are listed in Table 3.3.[16] $P(p)$ and $\sigma(p)$ are the percolation probability and conductivity of the percolation path ($p \geq p_c$) respectively, $S_{av}(p)$ and $l_{av}(p)$ are the average cluster size (number of connected sites or bonds) and conduction path length through the cluster (correlation length) respectively (averaged over all clusters for $p \leq p_c$, and over all but the infinite cluster for $p \geq p_c$), and $n(S)$, $l(S)$ are the distributions of cluster size and correlation length at $p = p_c$.

Table 3.3

Parameter Behaviour near the Percolation Threshold[16]

| | | | | | Value of Exponent | |
					2-D	3-D
$p<p_c$:						
	$S_{av}(p)$	$\sim$	$(p_c - p)^{-\gamma}$	γ	2.4	1.7
	$l_{av}(p)$	$\sim$	$(p_c - p)^{-\nu}$	ν	1.35	0.85
$p = p_c$:						
	$n(S)$	$\sim$	$S^{-\tau}$	τ	2.06	2.2
	$l(S)$	$\sim$	$S^{1/f}$	f	1.9	2.6
$p>p_c$:						
	$P(p)$	$\sim$	$(p - p_c)^{\beta}$	β	0.14	0.40
	$\sigma(p)$	$\sim$	$(p - p_c)^{t}$	t	1.1	1.65

According to percolation theory, the low frequency ac conductivity of the system is determined by the (polarisation) properties of the inter-cluster dielectric, but the high frequency behaviour is a function of the percolating cluster. At frequencies greater than ω_l, where the electron diffusion length over time $(\omega_l/2\pi)^{-1}$ is the correlation length l, $R \propto \omega^{-x}$ and $C \propto \omega^{-y}$ where $x + y = 1$.

It is important in the ICA application context to recognise the implicit normalisation in basic percolation theory. The universal constants develop for large systems much greater than the site (particle) dimensions, and the sites themselves are of uniform size (although there are studies of distributed systems) and isotropic shape (square/cube or circle/sphere). Realistic ICA modelling must include system dimensions of the order of the particle (site) sizes, distributed site sizes and orientations, and irregular particle shapes. Eventually these requirements will be met by the representation of particles (i.e., flakes) by pre-determined blocks of sites. In the meantime it is sufficient to note that the percolation threshold and its divergence vary with system dimensions (as they decrease towards the particle size) and aspect ratio. Intuitively, a short system is more favourable for percolative conduction ($p_c \ll p_{c0}$) than cubic ($p_c = p_{c0}$) or long ones ($p_c \gg p_{c0}$). Thus, one can expect to see size effects unless all system dimensions are much greater than the correlation length.

3.8 THEORETICAL MODELLING

Wei and Sancaktar developed an analytical model for the percolation process, with two empirical parameters, m and C. These represent, respectively, the average number of interparticulate contacts made by each particle and the effective conduction path length multiplication factor that accounts for the meandering of percolation paths. These constants were then found by repeated Monte Carlo computer simulations.[19,20]

The resistance in the x direction, R_x, is related to the resistivity, ρ_x, and the average resistance, r_x, of k_x parallel paths, by:

$$R_x = \rho_x \frac{L_x}{L_y L_z} = \frac{r_x}{k_x} \qquad (3.29)$$

where L_x, L_y, L_z, are the sample dimensions, and:

$$r_x \approx \frac{C_x L_x}{D} R_s \qquad (3.30)$$

where R_s is the inter-particulate resistance. The subscript on C covers the possibility of the 'meander factor' varying with direction, e.g., because of dimensions approaching (spherical) particle diameter, D. Although Wei and Sancaktar assume the intra-particulate resistance to be negligible, it would be a trivial matter to include it in the model. For N_t particles in the sample, there are a total of mN_t particle-to-particle contacts, and for the necessary two per particle along the percolation paths:

$$mN_t = 2(k_x \frac{C_x L_x}{D} + k_y \frac{C_y L_y}{D} + k_z \frac{C_z L_z}{D}) \qquad (3.31)$$

N_t can be related to the volume fraction, f, of filler particles by:

$$f = N_t \frac{4\pi}{3}(\frac{D}{2})^3 \ / \ L_x L_y L_z \qquad (3.32)$$

With the simplifying assumption of isotropic properties, the equations above reduce to:

$$\rho = \frac{C^2 \pi D R_2}{mf} \qquad (3.33)$$

The variations of C and m with f, as found by simulation, are shown in Figure 3.18 and Figure 3.19. The 2D result emphasises the increased effective path lengths when material dimensions shrink towards the particle sizes.

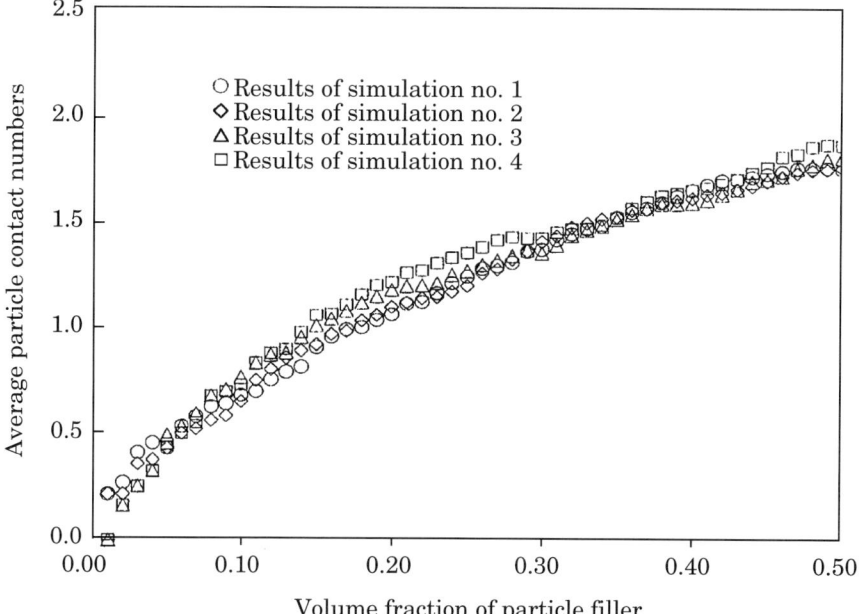

Fig. 3.18 Conductive path factors in 2D and 3D by computer simulation.[19,20] (Courtesy of IEEE)

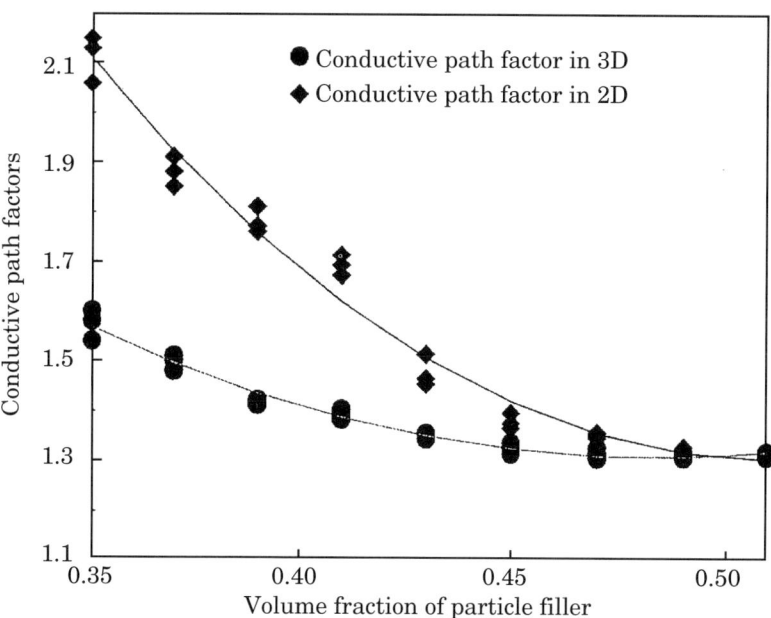

Fig. 3.19 Average number of contacts per particle by simulation.[19,20] (Courtesy of IEEE)

Ruschau *et al.*[17] focused on the issue of the variation of resistivity with sample dimensions, also with spherical particles. They defined two geometric parameters: one, $G = A/L$ to characterise the sample with electrodes of area A and separation L, and the other $\Gamma = t/D$ to characterise the particle dimension D in terms of sample (or film) thickness, t. The 2D simulations were run on a square lattice, with the results shown in Figure 3.20. Note that Γ must approach 100 before the critical volume fraction will tend to

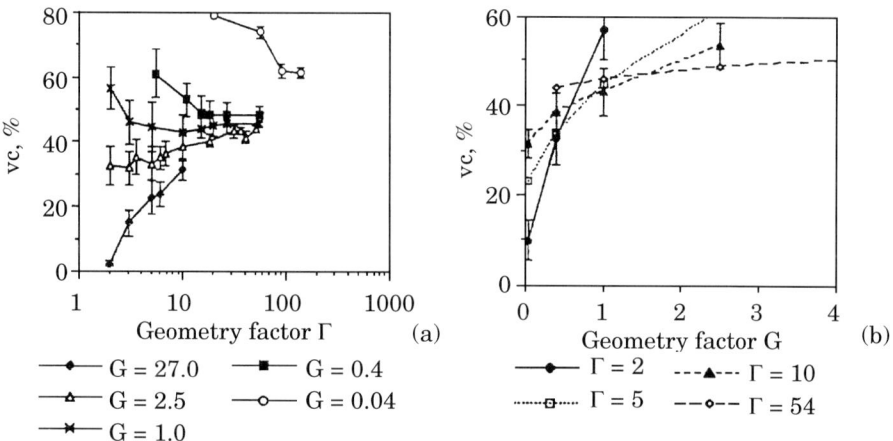

Fig. 3.20 Critical volume fraction for 2D percolation by computer simulation: variations with sample geometric factors G(cm) and Γ.[18] (Courtesy of *Journal of Applied Physics*)

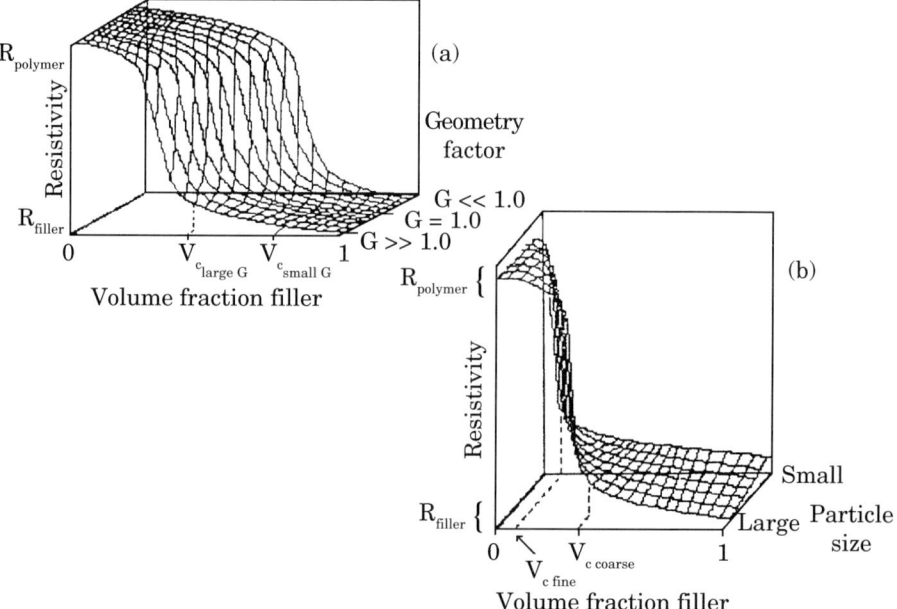

Fig. 3.21 Qualitative picture of the variation of the percolation curve with (a) sample geometry and (b) particle size.[18] (Courtesy of *Journal of Applied Physics*)

the theoretical 2D square lattice value of 47%. The general forms of the shifts in the percolation curve with geometric effects are shown in Figure 3.21.

Li and Morris have run both 2D[2,21] and 3D[2,22] simulations which include intra- and inter-particle resistances. In this work the particles are rectangular on a square/cubic lattice (Figure 3.22), and constrained to orientations along the x, y and z axes. The matrix geometries used are intended to match practical ICA contact pad dimensions, so a 2 x 2 x 1 block in a 60 x 60 x 30

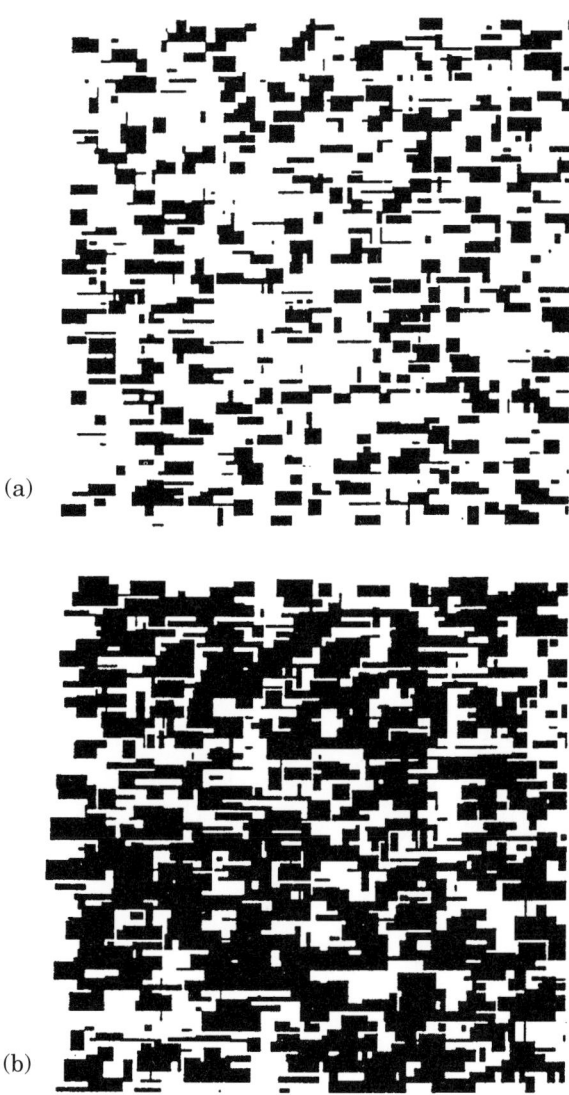

(a)

(b)

Fig. 3.22 Rectangular particle computer simulation (2D picture): (a) p< p_c (b) p > p_c.[2,21]

matrix in Figure 3.23, for example, can be interpreted as a 2 μm x 2 μm x 1 μm particle in a contact of 60 μm x 60 μm electrode area and 30 μm thickness. The size effect here is due to localised reductions in metal content within one particle dimension of the contacts. Both uniform and distributed particle sizes are used in the simulations; the distributions for the nominal sizes

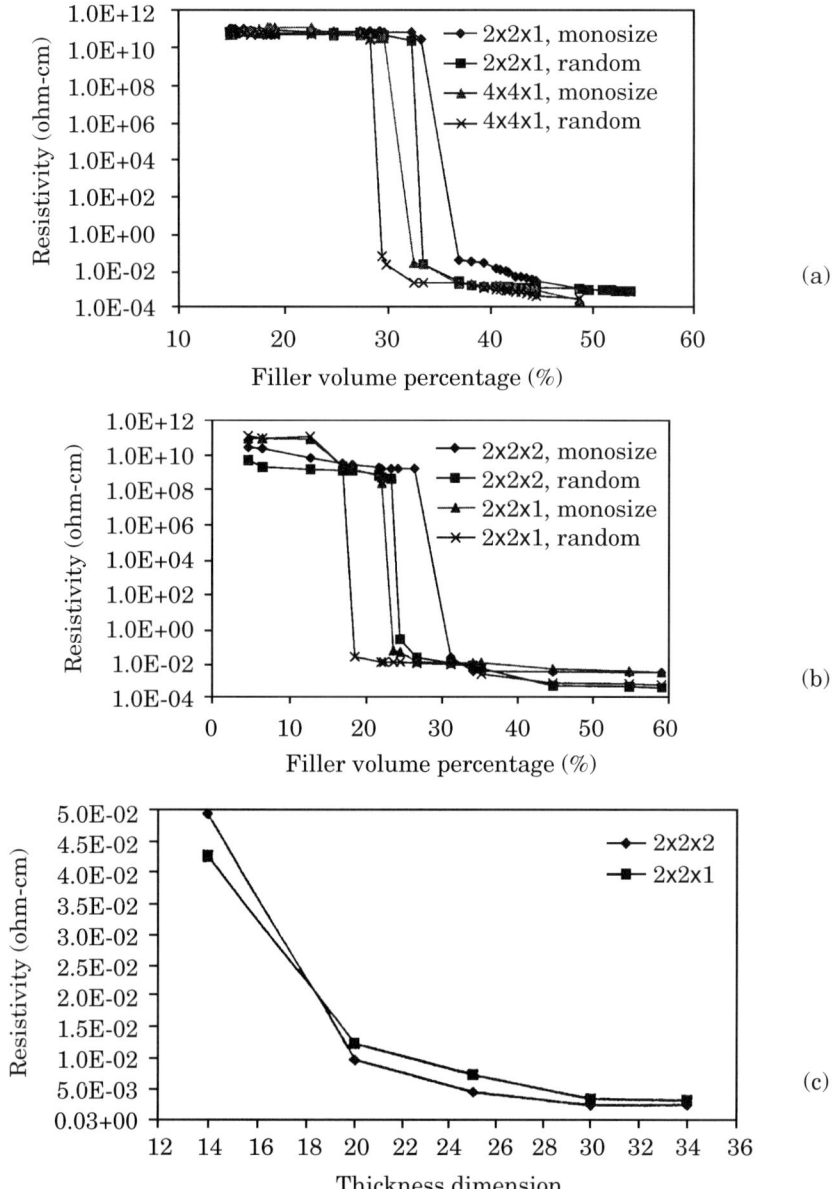

Fig. 3.23 3D simulations with monosized and distributed sized rectangular particles: effect of sample thickness in direction of conduction. Percolation curves for matrix sizes (a) 60 x 60 x 20; (b) 60 x 60 x 30; (c) effect of thickness at 36% vol. filler.[22]

quoted are shown in Figure 3.24. Examples of varying the Monte Carlo seed are shown in Figure 3.25. These are useful to give a physical view of the sort of variation one might expect among different samples of identical specification, and, as one would expect, the variations are greatest at the

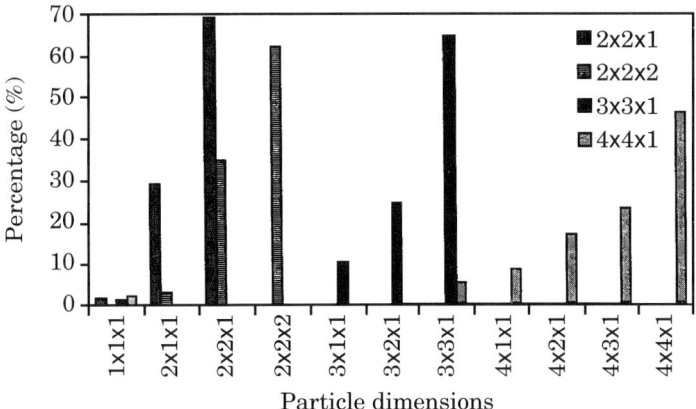

Fig. 3.24 Particle size distributions for nominal sizes given in Figures 3.23, 3.25 and 3.26.[22]

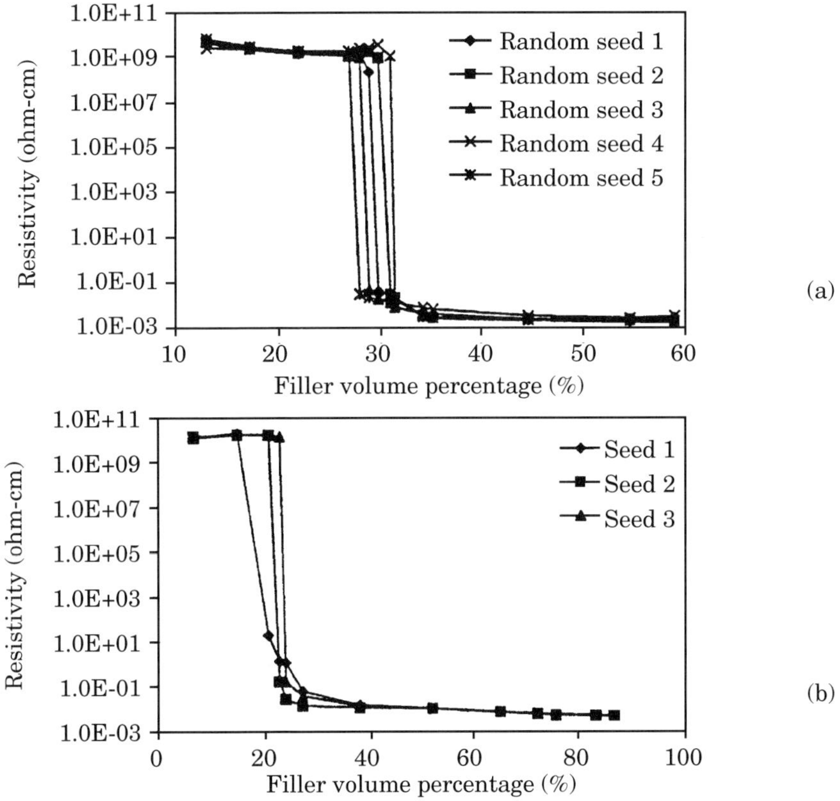

(a)

(b)

Fig. 3.25 Percolation curve variations with multiple 60 x 60 x 30 simulation runs: (a) 2 x 2 x 2 monosized particles; (b) 4 x 4 x 1 random distribution.[22]

percolation threshold. This is why practical ICAs must carry a worst-case filler load beyond the nominal or average threshold value. Figure 3.26 shows the resistance effect of surface particle alignment, as described in Section 3.2(h) above; the resistance increase is as anticipated.

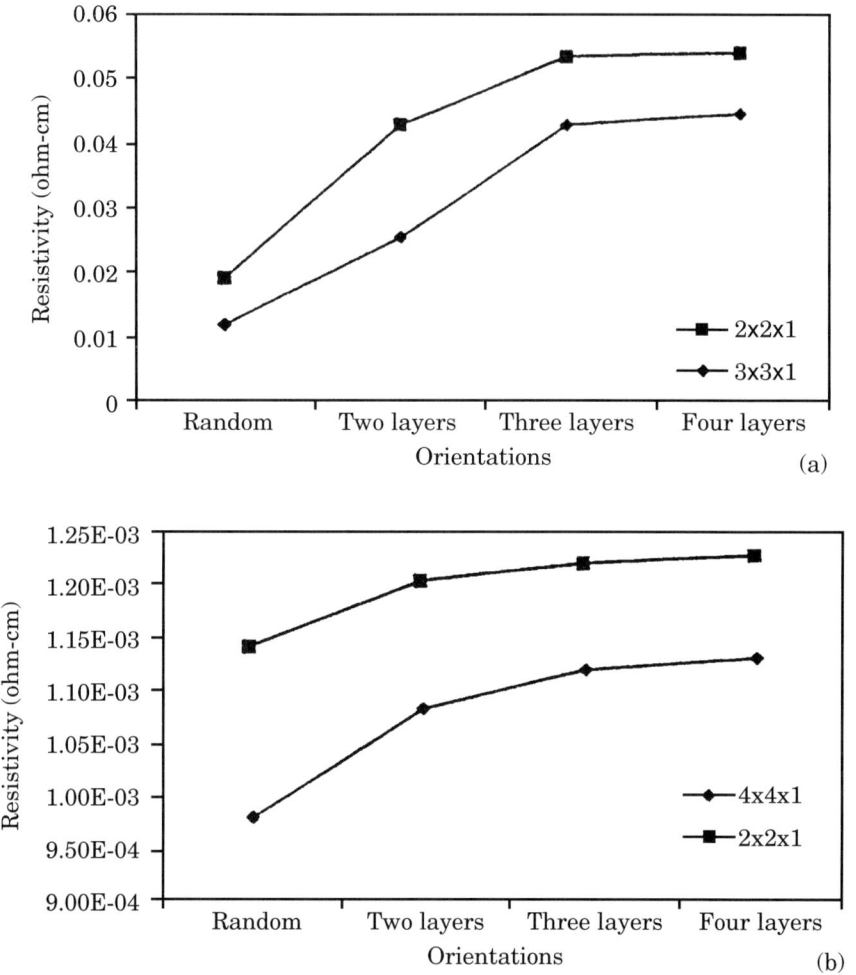

Fig. 3.26 The effect of surface orientation of particles: (a) 60 x 60 x 30 matrix, 31% vol. monosized fillers; (b) 72 x 72 x 30 matrix, 40% vol. random sized fillers.[22]

3.9   **EXPERIMENTAL STUDIES**

(a) Measurement techniques

The reader is alerted to the fact that there are several different measurement geometries in common use, and that each has potential systematic errors which must be kept in mind. The 'contact' configuration of Figure 3.27(a) is the most applicable to the actual intended material use. However, accurate measurement of small changes and differences in the already very small resistances is very difficult, even with micro-ohm resolution instruments. One commonly adopted technique is to print a long 'track' (Figure 3.27(b)) so the measured resistance can be increased by two or three orders of magnitude. Then, there are several problems in relating the data to the intended application. The measured 'contact' resistivity would be less than that of a 'bulk' sample (all dimensions >> particles), and the 'track' resistivity larger, both effects being due to the thickness, t, being less than 100 times the particle dimensions. In addition, surface alignment effects will increase the resistance of the 'contact' structure, and tend to decrease it for the 'track'. An alternative approach to increase the measured resistance is to 'daisy chain' multiple 'contacts', as in Figure 3.27(c). Now, the data are averaged and one cannot tell, for example, if a measured resistance change is a genuine trend, or the result of one element's aberrant behaviour. One must know the total interconnection resistance accurately, and be sure that any variation in it (particularly if it can change under test cycling) is much less than the total of the 'contact' elements. A similar issue exists with the use of nominal '0Ω' resistors to measure only two 'contacts' at a time (Figure 3.27(d)).

The author is not aware of anyone so far employing impedance transformers to increase the resistance measurement range (Figure 3.27(e)), a standard technique in other fields.

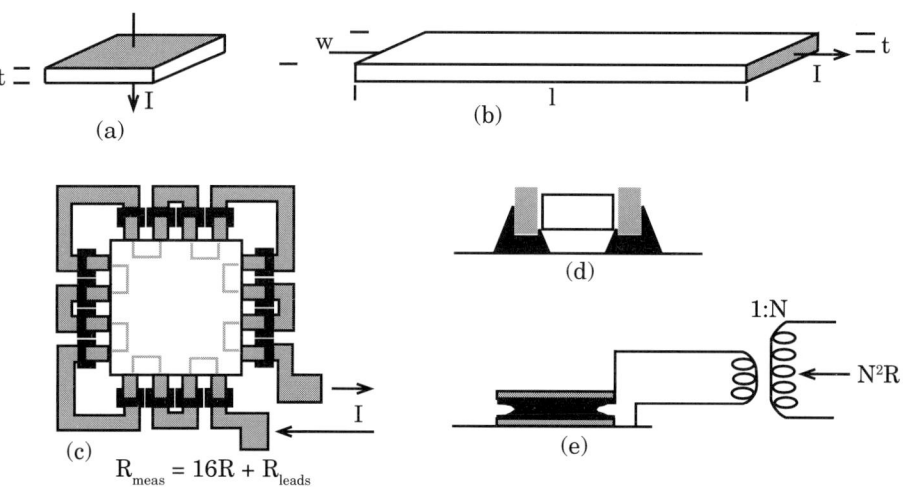

Fig. 3.27 Common test geometries: (a) 'contact' $t \ll l, w$, (b) 'track' $t \ll w \ll l$, (c) daisy chain, (d) '0Ω' resistor, (e) impedance transformer.

With the measurement of very small resistances, the use of the four-terminal technique is mandatory to eliminate the inadvertent inclusion of lead and contact impedances, etc. The concept is illustrated in Figure 3.28(a); ideally the voltmeter resistance is infinite, but the practical limit that it greatly exceeds the sample impedance is readily met. Many commercial meters offer such a measurement option, or the functional Kelvin probe equivalent (Figure 3.28(b)), which unfortunately does not eliminate the electrode interface impedance. Single 'contact' measurements are often made on the structures shown in Figure 3.28(c),[5,23] which are inherent Kelvin probes. Separation of the electrode interface impedance is achievable with the 'track' configuration of Figure 3.28(d), by combination of the four- and 'three-terminal' measurements.[8,24]

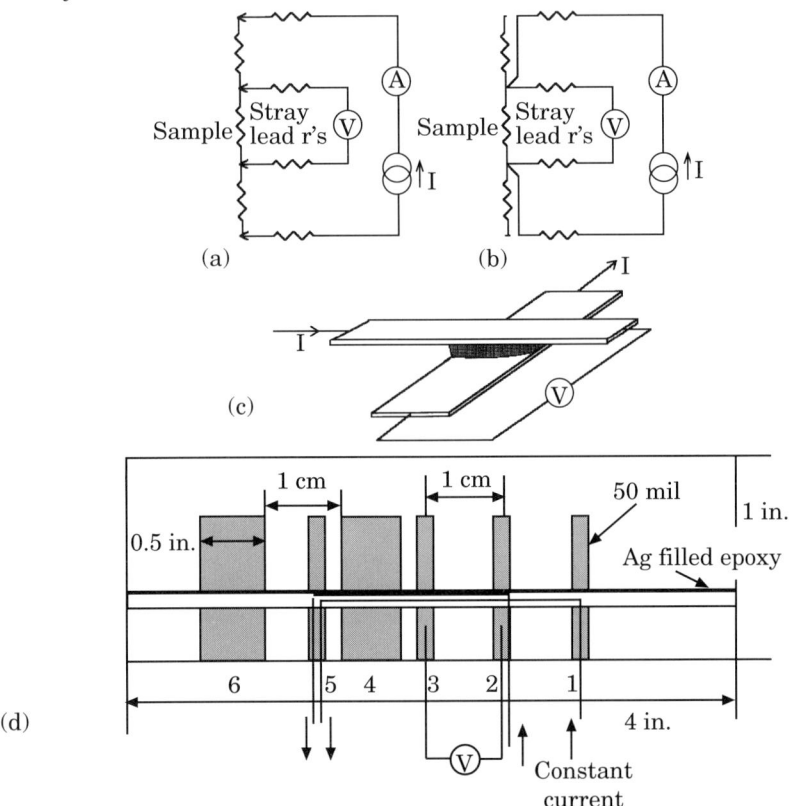

Fig. 3.28 Four-point probe configurations: (a) basic concept, (b) Kelvin probe, (c) 'contact' configuration,[5,23] (d) 'track' configuration.[8]

(b) Percolation thresholds

Figure 3.29 shows some measured percolation threshold curves for a variety of systems,[2,18,25,26-27] with the common factor that the thresholds (for spherical/powder particles in all cases) appear fairly consistently at about 40 vol.% filler. The 5 μm Ni powder samples for Figure 3.29(b) have also been tested at frequencies from 100 Hz to 10 MHz, and demonstrate clear capacitive short circuiting of inter-particulate gaps below the percolation threshold.[27,28] No such result has been reported above the threshold, although the ac experiments by Kim *et al.*[3] reported below were originally designed to pursue just such an effect. The implication is that the particles in materials far enough above threshold to function as contacts are not separated by high resistances. For example, if the gap conductance in commercial cured ICAs is by tunnelling, the tunnelling resistance must be much less than the particle resistance. Note the expected threshold drops for both flakes and small particles (the 'segregated' structure corresponding to $R_p \gg R_m$ in Figure 3.3).

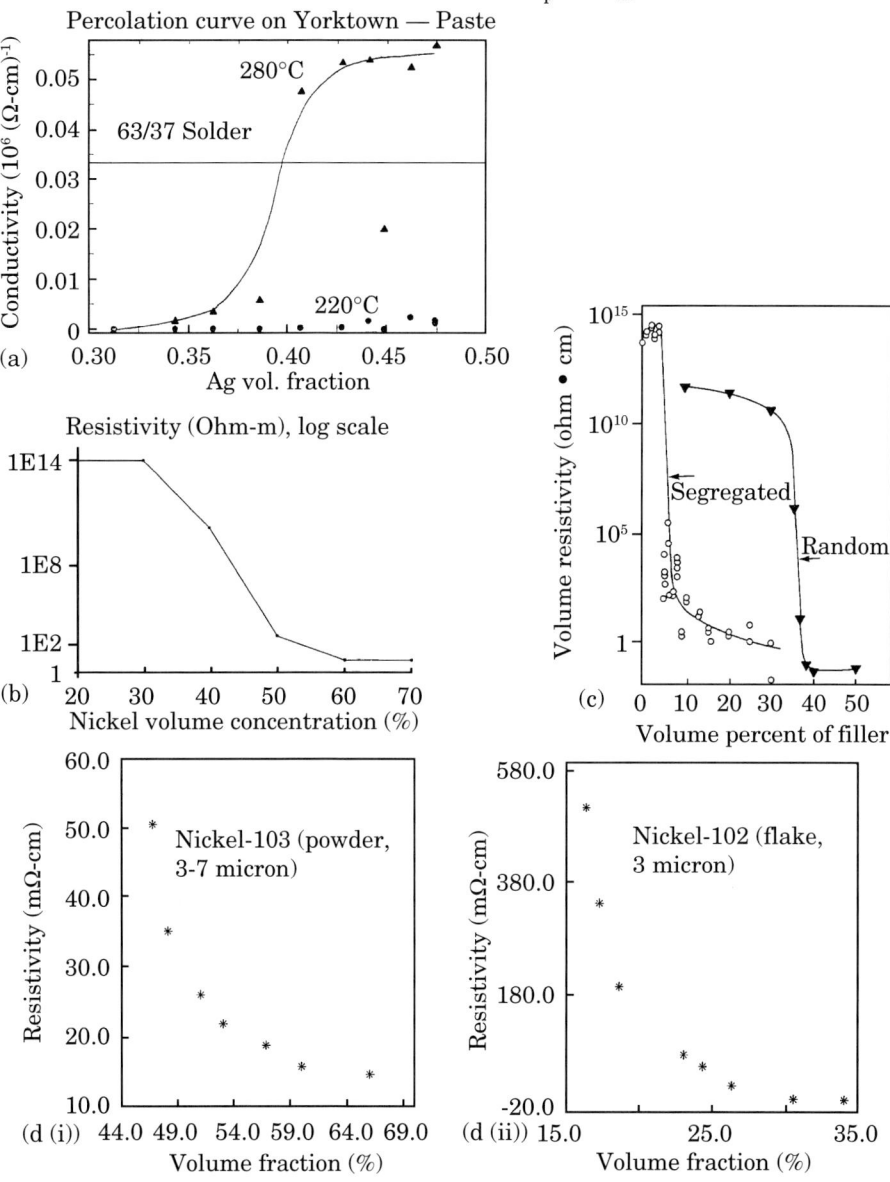

Fig. 3.29 Experimental percolation curves for spherical particle materials. (Note the approx. 40% critical vol. fraction). (a) 5 μm particles, effect of cure temperature (220 and 280°C), optimum conductivity exceeds that of solder.[23] (Courtesy of *Journal of Applied Physics*) (b) 5 μm Ni powder.[2,3,25] (c) Random and segregated match $R_m \approx R_p$ and $R_m \ll R_p$ in Fig. 3.3.[1] (Courtesy of *Journal of Applied Physics*) (d) Comparison of Ni spheres and flakes.[19] (Courtesy of Wei, Cockson University)

(c) Non-ohmic effects

The point was made above that many of the possible conduction mechanisms for electron transport between particles, particularly those that involve physical conduction by an intervening polymer film, display various high field non-ohmic effects. No non-ohmic effects have been reported; indeed, some papers specifically cite ohmic behaviour to high currents.[23] If such a mechanism operates between particles, its effective resistance must be much less than particle resistances for the requisite field effects to be masked.

(d) Temperature coefficient of resistance

Most of the inter-particulate conduction mechanisms also possess signature thermal characteristics, all with at least a weakly negative TCR. Reported TCRs are typically positive but less than that of the filler metal. No ICAs have been reported as possessing negative TCRs.

Examples of the thermal variation of resistance are presented in Figure 3.30.[2,3] The hysteresis observed in Figure 3.30(b) is not unusual.[29] The TCR values determined in these experiments, all with silver flake filled materials, ranged from 3.5 to 3.9 x 10^{-3}/°C, very similar to quoted values of 3.8 to 4.1 x 10^{-3}/°C for silver itself. Other silver systems data give TCRs of 3.0 x 10^{-3}/°C[23], 1.8-2.9 x 10^{-3}/°C[2], 2.4 x 10^{-3}/°C[2,8] and 0.8-0.9 x 10^{-3}/°C[29]. These results clearly suggest that the system filler resistance cannot be neglected, and indeed that it could be the primary resistive component.

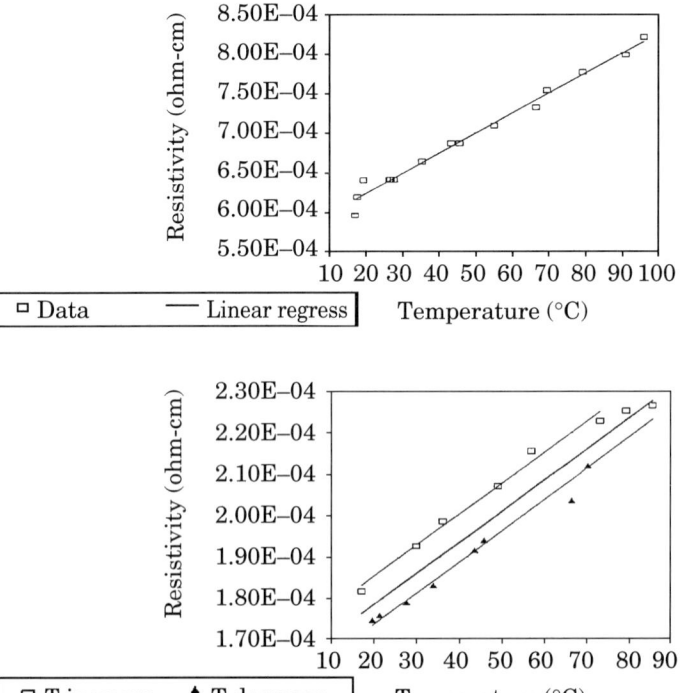

Fig. 3.30 Two examples of resistivity versus temperature for silver filler in (a) a thermoset polymer, and (b) a thermoplastic.[2,3]

If the inter-particulate TCRs were known, the composite TCR results would enable the partition of observed resistances between inter- and intra- components, but unfortunately this is not yet the case. If the inter-particulate conduction is by tunnelling, such a partition would be possible with the assumption of an effectively zero tunnel effect TCR. Further development of the constriction resistance model is required to include the effects of mean free path limitation for relatively small contact points. However, at values observed in practice, (e.g., 50-100 nm,[22] 200 nm[21] diameters), the TCR would probably be very similar to the bulk value, even for the smaller areas. It is worth noting that the TCR does indeed decrease with particle contact areas,[22] but this result is consistent with both tunnelling and constriction.

If one assumes that the inter-particulate TCR is at least very small, and approximates it by zero, then the partitioning may be achieved. In the TCR data above, a TCR close to that of silver would imply negligible inter-particulate resistance,[2,3,29] with the contrary conclusion for a small TCR.[29] The most extensive measurements of the thermal variation of resistance have been made on the porous metal system,[6] unfortunately not easily generalised to the more common flakes. In these results, the thermal variation was fitted to theory from 10 K to 325 K, but the imperfect match required adjustment of the Debye temperature fitting parameter. Thus, it suggested that the residual resistance is not completely independent of temperature.

Although an inconclusive exercise, it is interesting to put some tentative numbers to the resistances. For a 10 μm long silver flake of width 10 μm and thickness 1 μm, the resistance is 0.016 Ω, while the constriction resistance of a 100 nm diameter contact is 0.16 Ω, i.e., ten times higher. The ratios of the composite TCR to that of silver can be expressed in terms of the ratios of gap and silver flake resistances and TCRs, $\zeta_R = R_{gap} / R_{Ag} = 10$ and $\zeta_\alpha = TCR_{gap} / TCR_{Ag}$, by:

$$\frac{TCR}{TCR_{Ag}} = \frac{1 + \zeta_R \zeta_\alpha}{1 + \zeta_R} \tag{3.34}$$

For the ICA TCR to be half that of silver's, for example, the constriction TCR must be 0.45 times that of silver. This seems low, but not impossible.

For tunnelling, and the zero TCR approximation, the same ICA TCR requires $R_{gap} = R_{Ag}$, which would be met by a 3.7 nm 1 eV barrier of the same contact area. This also seems reasonable.

There is a reasonably consistent trend in the relationship between ICA TCRs and resistivities (Table 3.4), but the data have too many independent variables (polymer type, flake sizes, etc.) to expect perfect consistency. Nevertheless, comparison with the equation above does not lead to any obvious conclusion.

Table 3.4
TCR and Resistivity Trends in Silver Flake ICAs[2,3,8,23,29]

TCR/TCR_{Ag}	0.95-1.03	0.85-0.92	0.73-0.79	0.71-0.76	0.59-0.63	0.44-0.47	0.20-0.24
ρ_{ICA}/ρ_{Ag}	20	~100	100	100	72	220	10,000

At present, tunnelling and constriction are the two mechanisms receiving most attention. The electrical properties of a degenerate semiconductor surface layer are much more difficult to predict, and there is no independent evidence of the existence of such layers, even if they seem highly probable. The reasonably linear TCR plots do not support any of the thermally activated mechanisms.

(e) Skin effect

High frequency results are presented in Figure 3.31.[2,3] The form of the data matches the skin effect theory. The absolute values of skin effect resistance and inductance match to within 10% once the external inductive component is subtracted out, suggesting that at least 90% of the material resistance in this example is attributable to metallic resistivity. (This material also displayed the closest TCR to bulk silver's above.) In a percolation system, this result might appear surprising, since one would expect some significant increases in resistance as the current distribution moves towards the outer edges of the material, effectively abandoning the minimum resistance dc percolation path. The fact that there is little deviation from the ideal result only serves to emphasise that the commercial ICAs are filled well beyond the critical threshold, and that multiple comparable paths exist within the material.

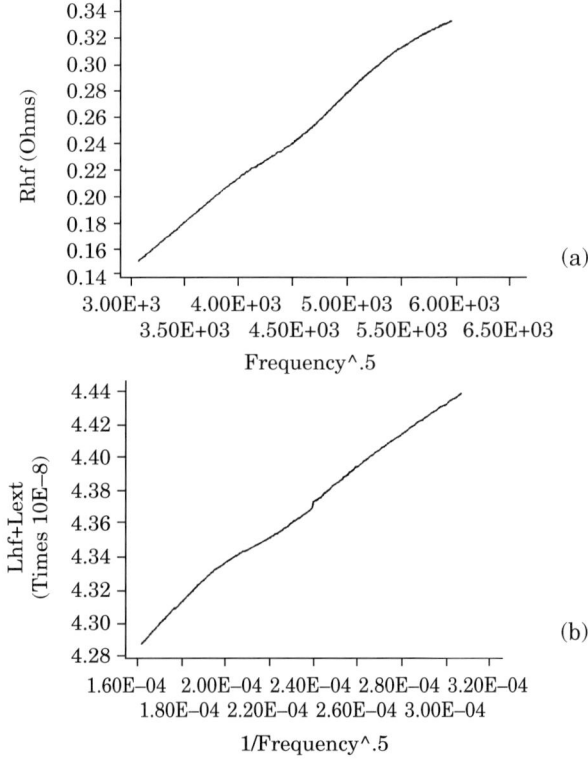

Fig. 3.31 Skin effect in a silver filled ICA: (a) R *vs* freq$^{1/2}$, (b) L *vs* freq.$^{-1/2}$ (References 2,3)

(f) Pressure

Wei and Sancaktar[30] matched the pressure dependent resistance of a 9 μm diameter nickel powder matrix (with air as the dielectric) to a theory based on the same two particle contact mechanisms assumed to apply here, i.e., a combination of constriction and tunnel resistances. The match is good (Figure 3.32), but the fitting parameters are not specified, and no conclusion is stated as to which is the dominant mechanism.

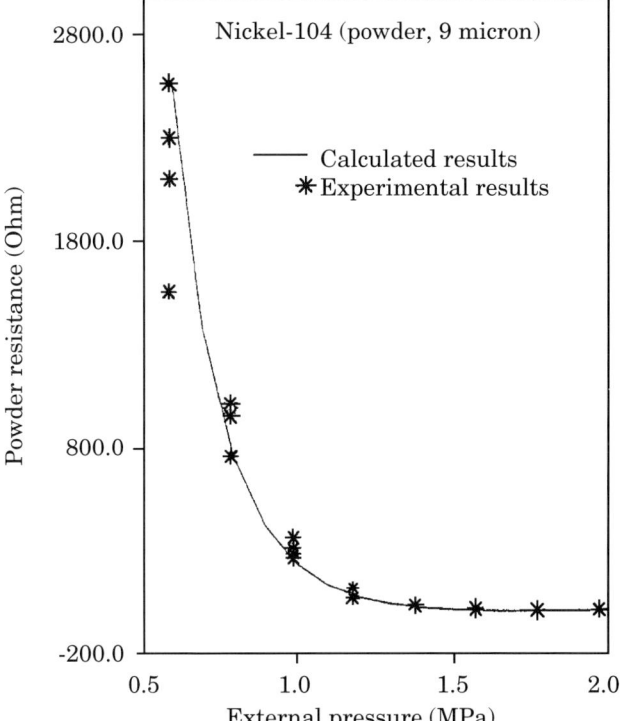

Fig. 3.32 The effect of external pressure on Ni powder resistance.[19,30] (Courtesy of IMAPS, USA)

The difficulties of directly correlating resistances with the internal pressures in cured ICAs via the theoretical pressure dependence of particle contact areas will be obvious. The author is unaware of any successful attempts to do so.

(g) Sample size effects

Much of the simulation effort has gone into the prediction of resistivity dependence on small sample dimensions, i.e., as they approach particle sizes. The prediction is that the percolation threshold and post-percolation resistance both decrease with dimensional decreases in the direction of conduction, and that both increase if the direction of shrinkage is perpendicular to current flow. Qualitative agreement with prediction is demonstrated in Figure 3.33[17] and Figure 3.34.[18,19]

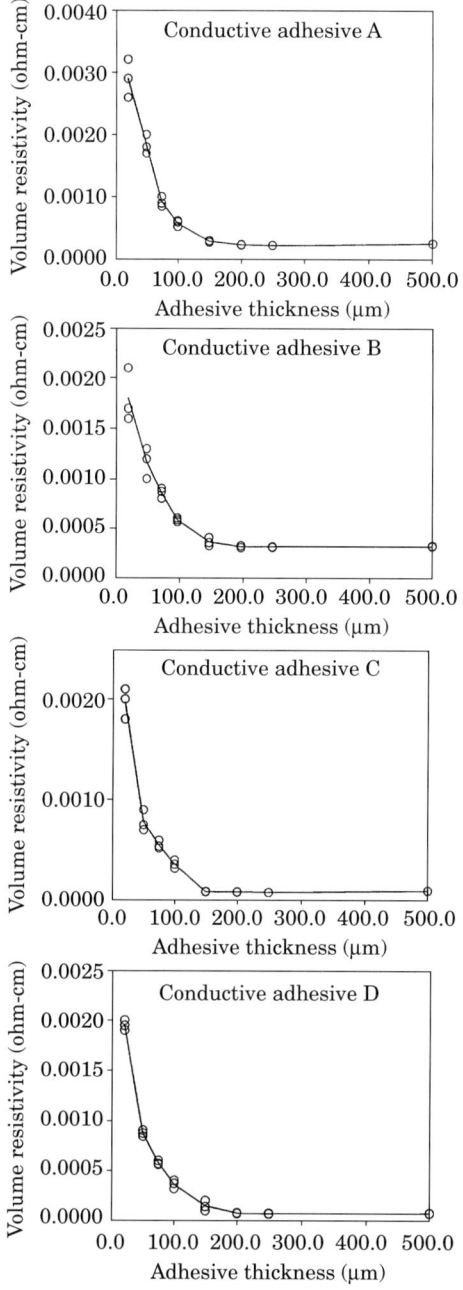

Fig. 3.33 The effect of 'track' thickness on resistivity for four materials. Note the greater data dispersion with different samples as thickness decreases.[19,20]
(Courtesy of Wei, Cockson University)

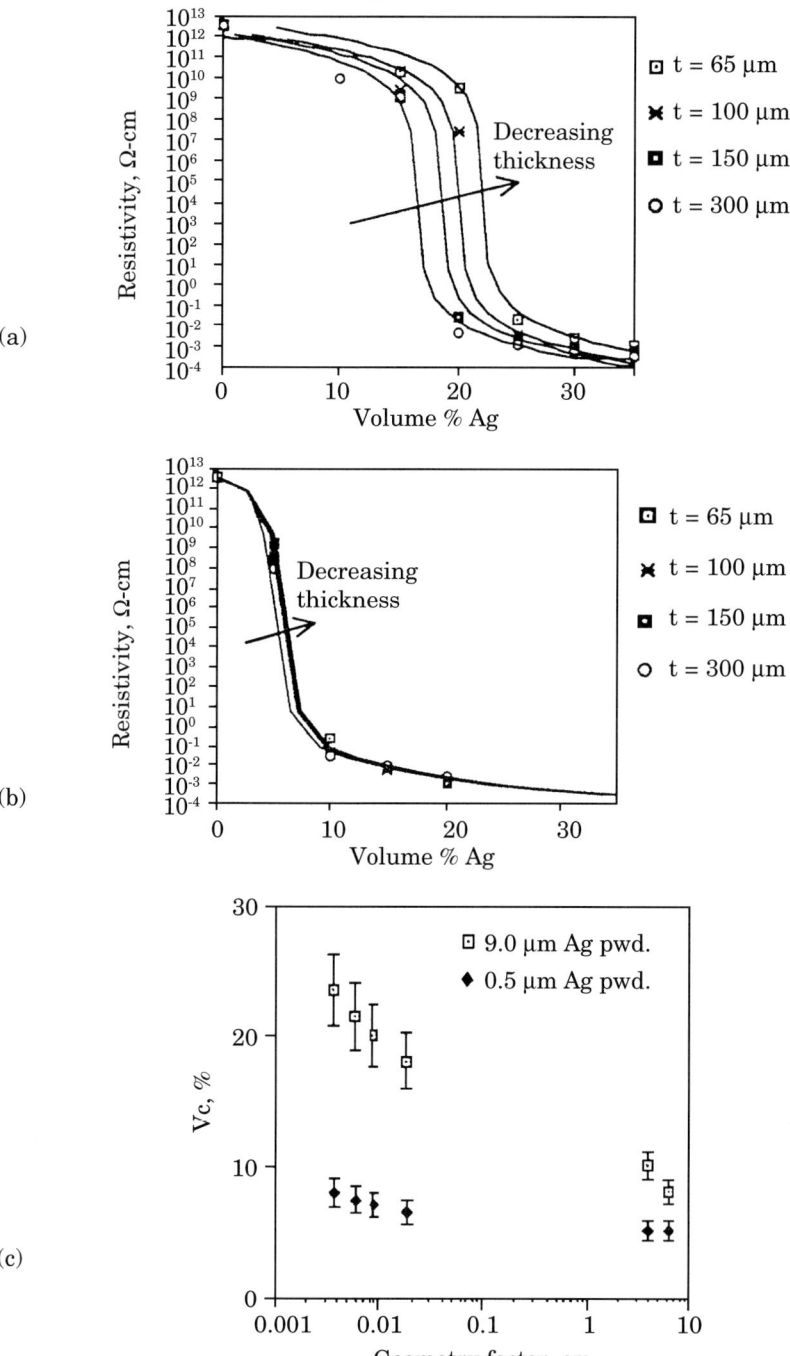

Fig. 3.34 Percolation curves for (a) 9 μm and (b) 5 μm Ag powders in silicone rubber 'tracks'; data are re-plotted in (c) in terms of the critical volume fraction and sample geometry G.[18] (Courtesy of *Journal of Applied Physics*)

(h) Cure and anneal resistances

Examples of the resistance changes observed during the cure itself are shown in Figure 3.35. There are generally three discernible stages to the process: initial packing of the filler particles as the material viscosity increases, followed by gelation (the major resistance drop), and vitrification.[2,6,24] The orders of magnitude dynamic resistance range is certainly consistent with tunnelling between particles, but additional data (e.g., ac measurements) are required before this conclusion can be drawn and other mechanisms rejected.

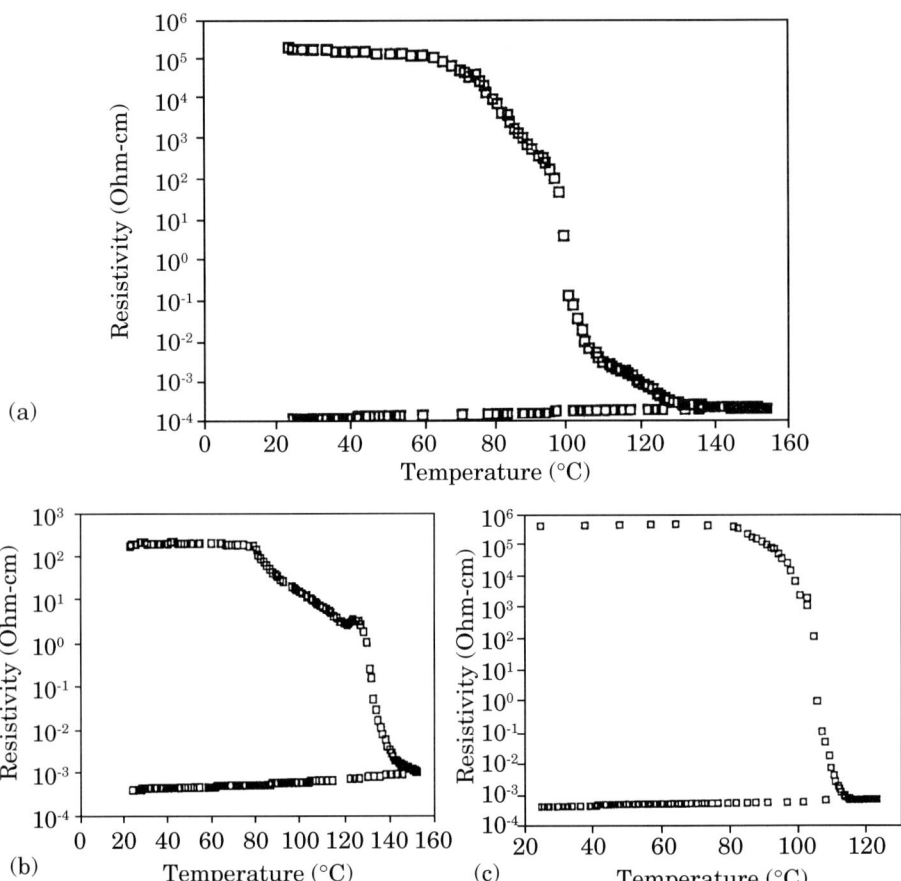

Fig. 3.35 ICA resistivity changes during cure for three materials.[2,24]

Figure 3.36 shows the resistance decrease often observed with thermal cycling up to the cure temperature following completion of the manufacturer's recommended cure schedule; this effect is usually attributed to incomplete initial cure. If the cure temperature is exceeded, the resistance may fluctuate, usually increasing, but with occasional abrupt jumps and decreases (Figure 3.37).[29] The abrupt changes suggest particle motion in the ICA and the make-and-break of percolation chains.

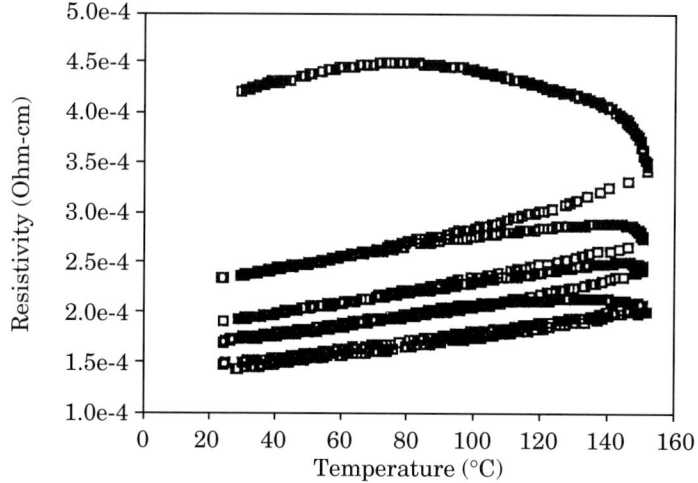

Fig. 3.36 Resistance decreases following nominal cure.[1,24]

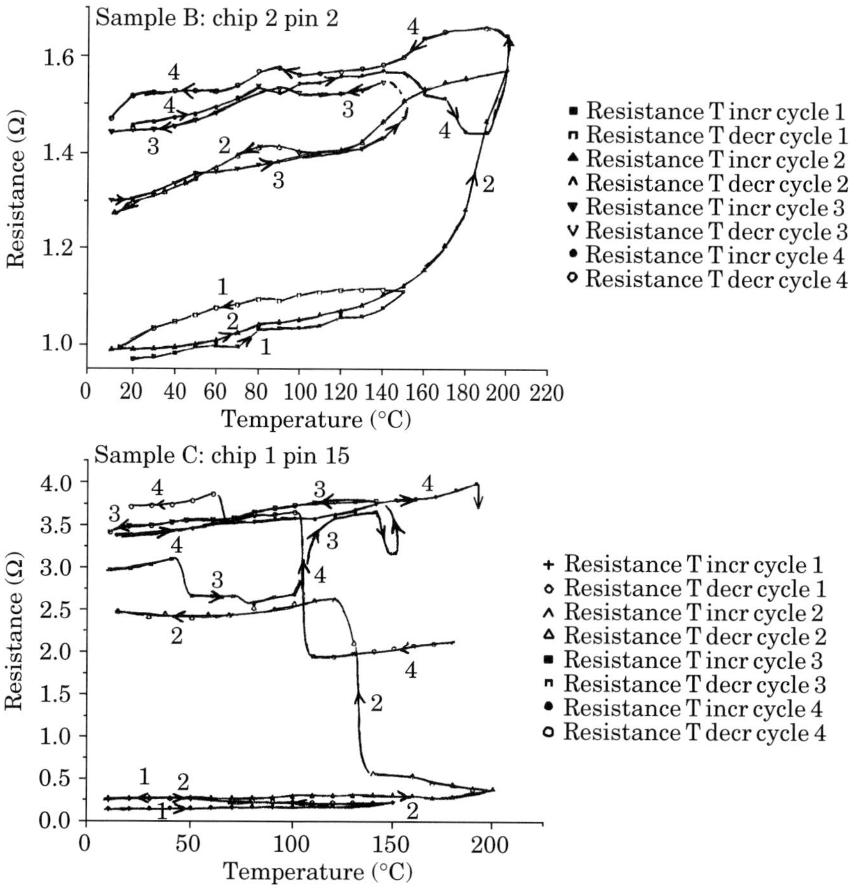

Sample B: chip 2 pin 2

- Resistance T incr cycle 1
- Resistance T decr cycle 1
- Resistance T incr cycle 2
- Resistance T decr cycle 2
- Resistance T incr cycle 3
- Resistance T decr cycle 3
- Resistance T incr cycle 4
- Resistance T decr cycle 4

Sample C: chip 1 pin 15

+ Resistance T incr cycle 1
- Resistance T decr cycle 1
- Resistance T incr cycle 2
- Resistance T decr cycle 2
- Resistance T incr cycle 3
- Resistance T decr cycle 3
- Resistance T incr cycle 4
- Resistance T decr cycle 4

Fig. 3.37 Resistance increases with thermal treatments exceeding the cure temperature.[29]

85% humidity test data[2,24] for the increase in electrode contact resistance are re-plotted in Figure 3.38. The interpretation in terms of oxidation/corrosion of the electrode metallisation should yield a linear variation of $\log R$ versus time or $(\text{time})^{1/2}$. This depends on whether the process is rate or supply (transport) limited, if the conduction process is by tunnelling. Given the complex nature of parallel contacts at this interface, the plot appears to support the model. AC data for the interface under these conditions would be most interesting.

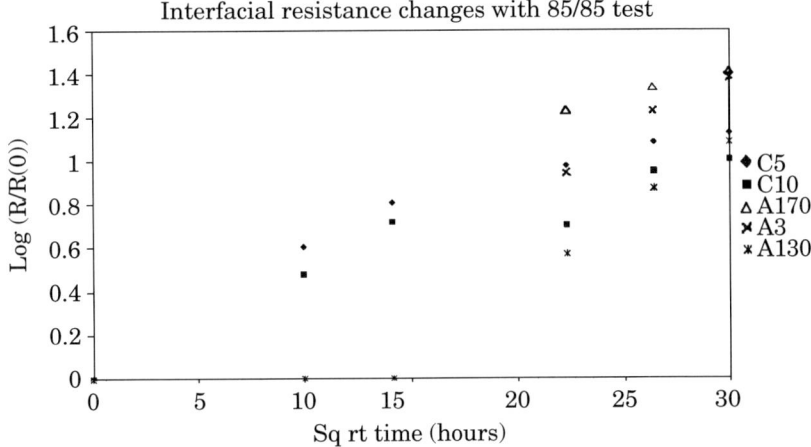

Fig. 3.38 Resistance increases attributed to coppper electrode corrosion in 85% relative humidity at 85°C.[2,24]

(i) Magnetic field alignment

The application of a magnetic field during cure of an ICA employing a nickel filament filler produces a lower resistance material[31] at low filler loads by alignment of the filaments into well connected and separated chains (Figure 3.39). This material should be much more readily modelled from electron micrographs than the conventional silver flake material, and could be useful in the future determination of the inter-particulate mechanism.

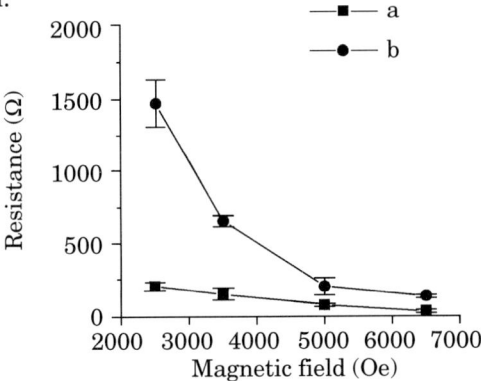

Fig. 3.39 Directional resistance of anisotropic material as a function of applied magnetic field. 10% vol. Ni filaments, (a) with 10% HCl pre-treatment, and (b) without.[31] (Courtesy of *Journal of Adhesion and Adhesives*)

3.10 CONCLUSIONS

The ultimate purpose in studying the ICA conduction mechanisms is that greater understanding will yield greater control of the development of improved materials. However, it cannot yet be said that the conduction mechanisms are even reasonably well understood. TCR results indicate that filler resistance is a significant component of the total, but even this tentative conclusion cannot be confirmed without resolving the primary issue: what is the electron transport mechanism between filler particles. In the absence of any non-ohmic effects to suggest otherwise, the bulk polymer conduction mechanisms can be disregarded (but experimental studies should continue to seek contrary evidence). The degenerate semiconductor film on the particles has not been found, although it has been expected and sought. Any theoretical model of such a film would necessarily be largely empirical given the absence of well-defined material parameters. This leaves the two primary candidates in the literature: tunnelling and contact constriction. If tunnelling, then material reproducibility suggests that there is some self-regulating mechanism to set a constant thin barrier, somewhat like the automatic establishment of well-defined native oxide thicknesses on aluminium. If constriction, the constriction resistance model requires refinement to include the reduction of electronic mean free paths.

The simulations agree qualitatively with experimental trends, but the purpose of simulation — to verify *full* understanding of the physical process — requires quantitative agreement. One part of the move in this direction is the continued development of the models towards commercial ICA structures (flakes). However, the alternative approach of experimental verification of what the current models are capable of doing accurately, i.e., spherical particle percolation, would be equally constructive. More effective simulation requires more confidence in the inter-particle conduction mechanism, however, for either.

This is the goal of the experimental studies — to deduce the mechanism from measurement of multiple electrical properties. Possibly if one can establish the transport mechanism from electrode to filler particle, one can extrapolate that result to the particles themselves. Possibly going beyond normal test temperature limits may show up non-linearities in the TCR indicative of a non-metallic process. No reports have appeared of resistance variations under mechanical stress — a fairly obvious experiment given the sensitivity of tunnelling to dimensional changes. The conclusion here is that there remains much to be done in the area of relatively obvious experiments to pin down the inter-particle conduction process.

3.11 ACKNOWLEDGMENTS

The author is grateful to Dr Liu for the opportunity to contribute this chapter. Writing such a review always provides new perspectives on the material as familiar papers are re-considered. It is hoped that the experience is as rewarding for the reader as it has been for the author. Thanks also go to Dr Li Li for her critical review of the manuscript's first draft. Finally, the chapter was written while on leave at the Zentrum für Mikrotechnologien, Technische Universität Chemnitz-Zwickau, and the author wishes to thank

Prof. Dr-Ing. Gessner and the faculty and staff there for their assistance and support.

REFERENCES

1 Kusy, R. P., 'Influence of Particle Size Ratio on the Continuity of Aggregates', *Journal of Applied Physics*, **Vol. 48**, No. 12, pp. 5301-5305 (1977).
2 Li Li, 'Basic and Applied Studies of Electrically Conductive Adhesives', PhD dissertation, State University of New York at Binghamton (1995).
3 Kim, H., Li, L., Lizzul, C., Sacolick, I. and Morris, J. E., 'Processing, Structural, and Electrical Properties of Electrically Conductive Adhesives', *IEEE Transactions on Components, Hybrids, and Manufacturing Technology*, **Vol. CHMT-16**, No. 8, pp. 843-851, December (1993).
4 Puhakka, K., Kulojarvi, K., Savolainen, P. and Kivilahti, J., 'Bonding Flexible Circuits and Flip Chips with Solder-filled Z-adhesives, Non-conductive Adhesives and Fusible Coatings', Proceedings Second International Conference on Adhesive Joining and Coating Technology in Electronics Manufacturing, Stockholm, pp. 285-291, June (1996).
5 Kang, S. K., Rai, R. and Purushothaman, S., 'Development of High Conductivity Lead (Pb)-free Conducting Adhesives', Proceedings 46th IEEE Electronic Components and Technology Conference, Orlando, FL, May (1996).
6 Kottaus, S., Haug, R., Schaefer, H. and Guenther, B., 'Investigation of Isotropically Conductive Adhesives filled with Aggregates of Nano-sized Ag Particles', and Guenther, B. and Schaefer, H., 'Porous Metal Powders for Conductive Adhesives', Proceedings Second International Conference on Adhesive Joining and Coating Technology in Electronics Manufacturing, Stockholm, pp. 14-17 & 55-59, June (1996). Kotthaus, S., Guenther, B. H., Haug, R. and Schaefer, H., 'Study of Isotropically Conductive Bondings Filled with Aggregates of Nano-sized Ag Particles,' *IEEE Transactions on Components, Packaging, and Manufacturing Technology: Part A*, **Vol. 20**, No. 1, pp. 15-20, March (1997).
7 Li, L. and Morris, J. E., 'Curing of Isotropic Electrically Conductive Adhesives', Chapter 5 of this volume.
8 Klosterman, D., Li, L. and Morris, J. E., 'Materials Characterization, Conduction Development, and Curing Effects on Reliability of Isotropically Conductive Adhesives', Proceedings 46th IEEE Electronic Components and Technology Conference, Orlando, FL, pp. 571-577, May (1996). *IEEE Transactions on Components, Packaging, and Manufacturing Technology: Part A*, **Vol. 20**, No. 1, pp. 23-31, March (1998).
9 Holm, R., 'Electric Contacts, Theory and Applications', Springer-Verlag, Berlin (1967).
10 Hill, R. M., 'Single Carrier Transport in Thin Dielectric Films', *Thin Solid Films*, **Vol. 1**, pp. 39-68 (1967).
11 Simmonds, J. G., *Journal of Applied Physics*, **Vol. 34**, pp. 1793-1803 and pp. 2581-2590 (1963), **Vol. 35**, pp. 2472-2481 and pp. 2655-2658 (1964).
12 Morris, J. E. and Coutts, T. J., 'Electrical Conduction in Discontinuous Thin Metal Films — A Discussion', *Thin Solid Films*, **Vol. 47**, pp. 3-65 (1977).
13 Pollack, S. R. and Sectchik, J. A., 'Electrical Transport through Insulating Thin Films', in 'Applied Solid State', **Vol. 1**, R. Wolfe, ed., Academic Press (1969).
14 Azaroff, L. and Brophy, J. J., 'Electronic Processes in Materials', McGraw-Hill, New York (1963).
15 Isihara, A., 'Condensed Matter Physics', Oxford Press (1991).
16 Zallen, R., 'The Physics of Amorphous Solids', Chapter 4, Wiley, New York (1983).
17 Smilauer, P., 'Thin Metal Films and Percolation Theory', *Contemporary Physics*, **Vol. 32**, No. 2, pp. 89-102 (1991).
18 Ruschau, G. R., Yoshikawa, S. and Newnham, R. E., 'Percolation Constraints in the Use of Conductor-Filled Polymers for Interconnects', Proceedings 42nd IEEE Electronic Components and Technology Conference, Atlanta, GA, pp. 481-487, May (1992); Ruschau, G. R., *Journal of Applied Physics*, **Vol. 72**, pp. 953-959 (1992).

19 Wei, Y., 'Electronically Conductive Adhesives: Conduction Mechanisms, Mechanical Behavior, and Durability', PhD dissertation, Clarkson University (1995).

20 Wei, Y. and Sancaktar, E., 'Dependence of Electrical Conduction on Film Thickness of Conductive Adhesives', Proceedings 45th IEEE Conference on Electronic Components and Technology, Las Vegas, NV, pp. 701-706 (1995).

21 Li, L. and Morris, J. E., 'Electrical Conduction Models for Isotropically Conductive Adhesives', *Journal of Electronics Manufacturing*, **Vol. 5**, No. 4, pp. 289-296, December (1995).

22 Li, L. and Morris, J. E., 'Electrical Conduction Models for Isotropically Conductive Adhesive Joints', Proceedings Second International Conference on Adhesive Joining and Coating Technology in Electronics Manufacturing, Stockholm, pp. 126-132, June (1996). *IEEE Transactions on Components, Packaging, and Manufacturing Technology: Part A*, **Vol. 20**, No. 1, pp. 3-8, March (1997).

23 Saraf, R. F., Roldan, J. M., Jagannathan, R., Sambucetti, C., Marino, J. and Jahnes, C., 'Polymer/metal Composite for Interconnection Technology', Proceedings 45th IEEE Conference on Electronic Components and Technology, Las Vegas, NV, pp. 1051-1053, May (1995).

24 Klosterman, D. and Li, L., 'Conduction and Microstructure Development in Ag-filled Epoxies', *Journal of Electronics Manufacturing*, **Vol. 5**, No. 4, pp. 277-287, December (1995).

25 Kim, H., 'Impedance Measurement of Conductive Adhesives', MSEE thesis, State University of New York at Binghamton (1992).

26 Kusy, R. P., in 'Metal Filled Polymers', S. K. Bjattacharya, ed., Marcel Dekker, New York (1986).

27 Sancaktar, E. and Wei, Y., 'The Effect of Pressure on the Initial Establishment of Conductive Paths in Electronically Conductive Adhesives', *Journal of Adhesion Science and Technology,* **Vol. 10**, No. 11, pp. 1221-1235 (1996).

28 Kim, H., unpublished data (1992).

29 Youssof, S., Feng, X., Lee, C., Oakley, E. and Morris, J. E., 'The Electrical and Mechanical Properties of Electrically Conductive Adhesives in Pin-through-hole Applications', Proceedings Second International Conference on Adhesive Joining and Coating Technology in Electronics Manufacturing, Stockholm, pp. 18-29, June (1996). *Journal of Electronics Manufacturing*, **Vol. 6**, No. 3, pp. 219-230, September (1996).

30 Wei, Y. and Sancaktar, E., 'A Pressure Dependent Conduction Model for Electronically Conductive Adhesives', ISHM'95 Proceedings, pp. 231-236 (1995).

31 Sancaktar, E. and Dilsiz, N., 'Anisotropic Alignment of Nickel Particles in Magnetic Field for Electrically Conductive Adhesives Applications', *Journal of Adhesion Science and Technology,* **Vol. 11**, No. 2, pp. 155-166 (1997).

Chapter 4

MODELS TO DETERMINE GUIDELINES FOR THE ANISOTROPIC CONDUCTING ADHESIVES JOINING PROCESS

SAMJID H. MANNAN, DAVID J. WILLIAMS, DAVID C. WHALLEY and ADEBAYO O. OGUNJIMI

Department of Manufacturing Engineering, Loughborough University, UK

4.1   INTRODUCTION

The aim of this chapter is to describe how recent research can be used to save the manufacturing engineer valuable time and effort during the setting up of an ACA process. This research has helped identify the important materials and process factors and the models discussed show how the process parameters are inter-related. Similarly, models can show the adhesive manufacturer ways to improve the adhesive formulation in order to obtain better results. The focus is on building a model to describe the flow of the adhesive resin and the conducting particles during the assembly process, and the probabilities of open circuits and shorts due to the random distribution of conducting particles.

The models outlined relate in the first instance to geometries typical of flip-chip attach (bumped or unbumped), but the ideas and models are applicable to other technologies such as SMT. This chapter deals with the type of ACA which contains a randomly dispersed conducting particle in an insulating fluid. Typically the fluid phase, on solidification, provides the adhesion between component and substrate although in some cases the conducting particle may help form the mechanical bond as well.[1] During the course of processing such a material, some of the fluid must be squeezed out from beneath the component, leaving behind some conducting particles trapped between the conducting pads on the component and the lands on the substrate (Figure 4.1).

As pressure and heat are applied, the adhesive film softens and begins to flow. The first stage of flow is designated flow type I, and occurs around the individual pads and bumps on the chip and substrate, as shown in Figure 4.2.

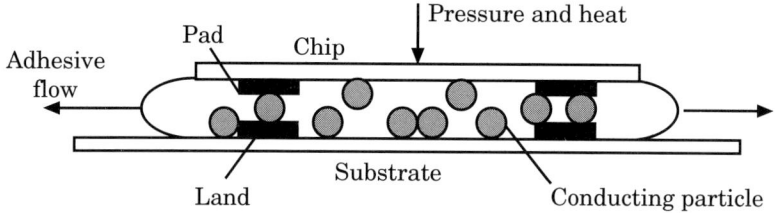

Fig. 4.1 Compression of an anisotropic conducting adhesive.

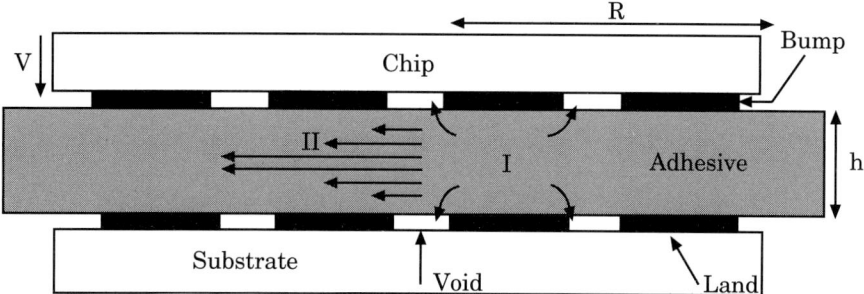

Fig. 4.2 Description of Type I flow around the lands/pads, and type II flow out of the gap.

If the adhesive film is sufficiently thick, the voids will be completely filled and then type II flow will commence, expelling the adhesive from under the flip chip to the edges. This is examined further in Section 4.3.2. During this second flow stage appreciable changes in the volume fraction of conducting particles could in principle occur, since the particles and fluid will not be expelled at the same rate. Also during this stage, the particles will be compressed between the lands and chip bumps or pads.

If the adhesive is thermosetting, as opposed to thermoplastic, the material will be curing as it flows. The flow stage must, however, be complete before the adhesive has significantly hardened as otherwise the flow will be incomplete, leading to open circuits. This entails a more restrictive range of pressures and temperatures for themosetting adhesives than for thermoplastic ones.

After the adhesive has been expelled, the assembly will cool down. Differing coefficients of thermal expansion between the chip and substrate will lead to residual stresses. Additionally the adhesive itself will shrink upon cooling, leading to residual stresses which should help to compress the conducting particles still further. Finite element models of the residual stresses between chip and substrate have been reported elsewhere.[2] The main conclusion of these studies is that the maximum stress will lie one quarter of the distance from the edge of the chip along the diagonal, and that the thinner the bond line, the higher the stress.

The final joint conductivity will be determined by the average number of particles on each pad, the amount of compression of each of the particles, and the variation in these two quantities for individual pads. The distribution of particles between pads will determine the probabilities of bridging.

The optimum process conditions and adhesive should result in the following:

— large numbers of particles on the pads to ensure that the chances of open connections are negligible;
— particle densities in the gap between neighbouring lands to be low enough to ensure that the chances of electrical shorts are negligible;
— fast process times — preferably seconds rather than minutes;
— reliable and uniform connection resistances that do not change appreciably under environmental stresses such as extremes of temperature.

Obviously the probability of opens can be minimised by increasing the number of particles in the adhesive while the probability of shorts can similarly be minimised by decreasing the number of particles to zero! Models which allow an appropriate compromise to be made between the often conflicting process requirements will be outlined. To this end, the last part of the chapter looks at mathematical models which can be used to describe shorts and opens, while the first part looks at the process of squeezing out the adhesive.

During the lifetime of the joint, localised and global temperature variations will occur, perhaps leading to chemical changes in the adhesive. Additionally moisture will be absorbed, leading to volume changes in the adhesive as well as possible oxidation of the conducting surfaces. These post-assembly issues will not be addressed here, and interested readers are encouraged to consult the relevant chapters of this book for further details. The study begins with the construction of a simple analytical model that is relevant to the flow of adhesive out of the thin gap between chip and substrate.

4.2   A SIMPLE MODEL OF FLUID FLOW DURING ASSEMBLY

4.2.1   Navier-Stokes Equations

The flow of the adhesive out beneath the flip chip during processing is a complex process. It depends on both the intrinsic properties of the ACA and the geometry of the chip and the substrate. By geometry we mean the size and shape of the chip, the height and shape of the chip bumps, and the height and shape of the lands on the substrate, as well as any features on the substrate or chip which might influence the fluid flow; in the case of an unbumped flip chip this includes features only 1 µm or so in height. Clearly, to model this complexity in one go would be a daunting task. Instead it will be modelled in stages, starting with the simplest configuration as shown in Figure 4.3. The effects of surface features such as chip bumps and substrate lands will then be added in as shown in Figure 4.2, and how the properties of the ACA influence the fluid flow will then be discussed.

The simplest flow properties that one can ascribe to a fluid are Newtonian fluid properties. To consider what this means, consider Figure 4.4 which shows a fluid between two parallel infinite plates, while a stress, τ_{xy}, is applied to the top plate and the bottom plate is held fixed. The applied stress will result in motion of the top plate at a velocity V. If the plates are at a

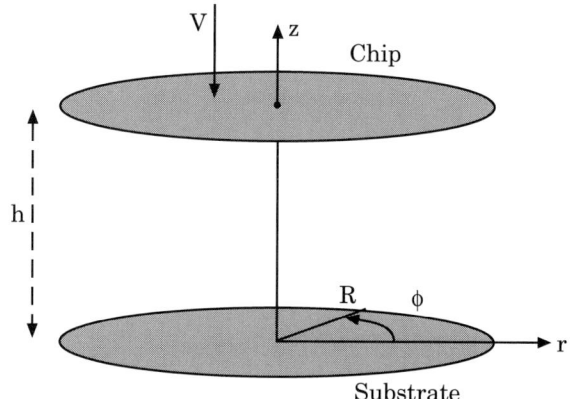

Fig. 4.3 Cylindrical co-ordinate system.

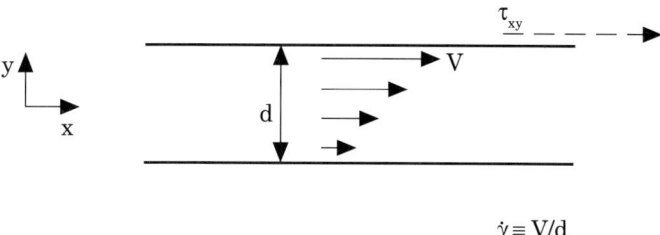

$$\dot\gamma \equiv V/d$$

Fig. 4.4 Definition of shear rate and shear stress.

distance d apart, it is useful to define the *strain rate, (γ)*, as the ratio of V to d:

$$\dot\gamma \equiv \frac{V}{d} \tag{4.1}$$

Experimental observation tells us that, for a wide range of liquids, the stress is proportional to the strain rate. A fluid that obeys this relationship is termed Newtonian, and the constant of proportionality is defined as the *viscosity*, η:

$$\tau_{xy} = \eta\dot\gamma \tag{4.2}$$

The equations of motion for a fluid can be written generically as:

$$\frac{\partial}{\partial t}(\rho v_i) = -\frac{\partial \Pi_{ij}}{\partial x_j} \tag{4.3}$$

where ρ is the fluid density, v_i is the component of fluid velocity in the i direction of a rectilinear co-ordinate system, Π_{ij} is momentum density flux tensor, and the summation convention for repeated indices applies. Π_{ij} can be written:

$$\Pi_{ij} = p\delta_{ij} + \rho v_i v_j + \eta\left(\frac{\partial v_i}{\partial x_j} + \frac{\partial v_j}{\partial x_i}\right) \tag{4.4}$$

where the first term on the right represents pressure, the second term represents momentum flow due to fluid transport and the third term is the generalisation of Equation (4.2) written in tensor form. Substituting Equation (4.4) into Equation (4.3) leads to the Navier-Stokes equations of motions, a full derivation of which may be found in textbooks on fluid dynamics.[3] For the present purposes, it is useful to solve the Navier-Stokes equations in cylindrical co-ordinates, r, ϕ, z, (see Figure 4.3) whence we obtain:

$$\rho\left(\frac{\partial v_r}{\partial t} + (v \bullet \mathrm{grad})v_r - \frac{v_\phi^2}{r}\right) = -\frac{\partial p}{\partial r} + \eta\left(\nabla^2 v_r - \frac{2}{r^2}\frac{\partial v_\phi}{\partial \phi} - \frac{v_r}{r^2}\right) \tag{4.5}$$

$$\rho\left(\frac{\partial v_\phi}{\partial t} + (v \bullet \mathrm{grad})v_\phi + \frac{v_r v_\phi}{r}\right) = -\frac{1}{r}\frac{\partial p}{\partial \phi} + \eta\left(\nabla^2 v_\phi + \frac{2}{r^2}\frac{\partial v_r}{\partial \phi} - \frac{v_\phi}{r^2}\right) \tag{4.6}$$

$$\rho\left(\frac{\partial v_z}{\partial t} + (v \bullet \mathrm{grad})v_z\right) = -\frac{\partial p}{\partial z} + \eta\nabla^2 v_z \tag{4.7}$$

where the functions $(v \bullet \mathrm{grad})$ and Δ^2 are defined as follows:

$$(v \bullet \mathrm{grad})f \equiv v_r\frac{\partial f}{\partial r} + \frac{v_\phi}{r}\frac{\partial f}{\partial \phi} + v_z\frac{\partial f}{\partial z} \tag{4.8}$$

and

$$\nabla^2 f \equiv \frac{1}{r}\frac{\partial}{\partial r}\left(r\frac{\partial f}{\partial r}\right) + \frac{1}{r^2}\frac{\partial^2 f}{\partial \phi^2} + \frac{\partial^2 f}{\partial z^2} \tag{4.9}$$

Equations (4.5) to (4.9) together with the boundary conditions and the equation of continuity determine the fluid flow. The equation of continuity for an incompressible fluid simply states that the total flux of fluid into any given volume fixed in space is zero (i.e., the fluid that leaves the volume is replaced by the fluid that enters it).

4.2.2   Stefan's Equation

Now that a full set of equations describing fluid flow has been obtained, it is time to apply them to a simplified situation as shown in Figure 4.3, which depicts fluid being squeezed out between a lower fixed surface, and an upper disk which is being moved downwards at a velocity V. We are interested in the force that must be applied to the upper plate to maintain this velocity and this relationship is described as Stefan's equation.[4]

Considerable simplification to Equations (4.5) to (4.9) now occurs as the fact that the problem is radially symmetric means that all terms involving v_ϕ or a partial derivative with respect to ϕ can be set to zero. All the terms on the left of Equations (4.5) to (4.7) can also be set to zero because we are in the low Reynold's number regime;[3] physically this means that the inertial forces are negligible compared with the viscous forces and the condition that must be satisfied to allow us to drop these terms is as follows:

$$Re \equiv \frac{\rho l u}{\eta} << 1 \tag{4.10}$$

where l is a typical length scale of the problem and u a typical velocity; during flip-chip assembly velocities are typically measured in microns per second while the largest available length scale is the chip size, measured in millimetres; putting ρ equal to $10^4\,kg/m^3$ and η equal to 100 Pa.s, we obtain Re of about 10^{-7}. Thus Equations (4.5) and (4.7) become:

$$\eta\left(\nabla^2 v_r - \frac{v_r}{r^2}\right) = \frac{\partial p}{\partial r} \tag{4.11}$$

$$\eta \nabla^2 v_z = \frac{\partial p}{\partial z} \tag{4.12}$$

while Equation (4.6) is satisfied identically. The next step to be taken in order to solve these equations is to recognise that, if $R >> h$, then those terms involving gradients of v_r in the z direction would dominate over the other terms on the left of Equations (4.11) and (4.12) leading to:

$$\eta\frac{\partial^2 v_r}{\partial z^2} = \frac{\partial p}{\partial r} \tag{4.13}$$

and

$$0 = \frac{1}{\rho}\frac{\partial p}{\partial z} \tag{4.14}$$

This latter means that the pressure is a function of r only and hence the partial differential on the right of Equation (4.13) can be replaced by a total differential:

$$\eta\frac{\partial^2 v_r}{\partial z^2} = \frac{dp}{dr} \tag{4.15}$$

This is the equation that must be solved subject to the boundary conditions relevant to Figure 4.3:

$$v_r = v_z = 0 \text{ at } z = 0 \tag{4.16}$$

$$v_r = 0, v_z = -V \text{ at } z = h \tag{4.17}$$

$$p = 0 \text{ at } r = R \tag{4.18}$$

This last boundary condition has been chosen to simplify the maths as only pressure differences influence the dynamics. Equation (4.15) can be solved by integrating twice with respect to z, and the solution which obeys boundary conditions Equations (4.16) and (4.17) with respect to v_r is given by:

$$v_r = \frac{1}{2\eta} z(z-h) \frac{dp}{dr} \tag{4.19}$$

The continuity equation will now be applied. If we take a cylindrical volume of radius r, as shown in Figure 4.5, the continuity equation states that the total flux of fluid entering the control volume through the top of the cylinder is equal to the total flux leaving the volume through the side:

$$\pi r^2 V - 2\pi r \int_0^h v_r dz \tag{4.20}$$

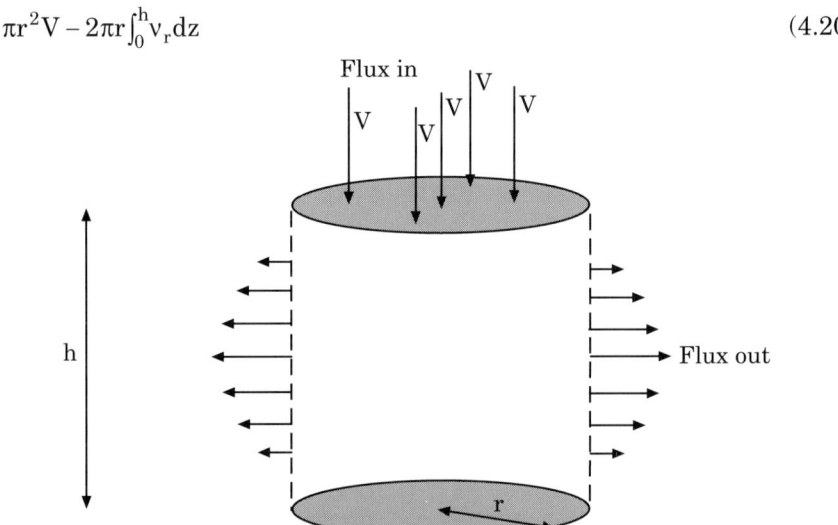

Fig. 4.5 Illustration of the equation of continuity for a cylindrical volume of height h, and radius r.

Substituting Equation (4.19) into Equation (4.20) we obtain:

$$Vr = \frac{1}{\eta} \frac{dp}{dr} \int_0^h z(z-h) dz = \frac{-1}{6\eta} \frac{dp}{dr} h^3 \tag{4.21}$$

Equation (4.21) is a first order differential equation for p which can be solved by integrating with respect to r, subject to the boundary condition, Equation (4.18), and has the solution:

$$p = \frac{3\eta V(R^2 - r^{2)}}{h^3} \tag{4.22}$$

Finally we can integrate Equation (4.22) over the area of the disk to find the force resisting the motion:

$$F = \int_0^R 2\pi r p dr = \frac{3}{2}\frac{\eta V\pi R^4}{h^3} \tag{4.23}$$

which is Stefan's equation. In this form Equation (4.23) is of limited use; it is of more interest to know the time required to squeeze the disks to a distance h apart starting from a distance h_0. To do this we note that Equation (4.23) is a first order differential equation for h(t):

$$\frac{dh}{dt} = -\frac{2Fh^3}{3\eta\pi R^4} \tag{4.24}$$

from which can be found the solution for the processing time, t_p:

$$t_p = \frac{3}{4}\frac{\eta\pi R^4}{F}\left(\frac{1}{h^2} - \frac{1}{h_0^2}\right) \tag{4.25}$$

This equation can be used as a guide for calculation of the assembly time of a flip chip, as long as the chip size (R), applied force (F), adhesive viscosity (η), initial film thickness (h_0) and final film thickness (taken to be the conducting particle diameter) are known. The derivation of Equation (4.25) has made many simplifying assumptions, such as having a circular, unbumped chip, a Newtonian fluid ACA, and assuming that the film thickness is much smaller than the chip size. In the following sections we shall show how these assumptions may be relaxed, but as a quick guide to the processing times and conditions Equation (4.25) has the advantage of simplicity.

Before we leave Stefan's equation it is worth pointing out that both the pressure distribution (Equation (4.22)) and the velocity distribution (Equation (4.19)) have been derived as stepping stones towards the final goal of Equation (4.25). The result for the pressure distribution is particularly interesting; if we combine Equations (4.22) and (4.23), we obtain:

$$p = \frac{2F}{\pi R^2}\left(1 - \frac{r^2}{R^2}\right) \tag{4.26}$$

so that the pressure distribution is seen to reach a maximum of twice the nominal pressure $(F/\pi R^2)$ under the centre of the chip, and fall off parabolically towards the edge. This finding is of use when considering the possible deformation of organic (and particularly flex) substrates during processing. Indeed, a finite element model of the deformation of the substrate with the pressure distribution of Equation (4.26) showed that the substrate could be compressed by 1-2 μm under the centre of the chip. Ceramic substrates undergo negligible deformation.

4.3   REFINEMENTS TO THE BASIC MODEL

In the preceding section we have derived an expression for the flow of adhesive out between a flat substrate and a flat, circular chip surface. The adhesive has been assumed to flow as a Newtonian fluid, and conditions of constant temperature and force have been assumed. We shall now remove some of these assumptions so that the model resembles the actual assembly process.

4.3.1   The Scott Equation

The adhesive fluid in an ACA is unlikely to be Newtonian in character; many polymer melts and solutions display shear thinning as the shear rate is increased over a wide range, and can be characterised as power law fluids:

$$\tau_{xy} = \eta_0 (\dot{\gamma})^n \tag{4.27}$$

where η_0 is termed the consistency and n the power law index. For a Newtonian fluid $n = 1$ and η_0 becomes the viscosity of the fluid, η (cf. Equation (4.2)). Starting from Equation (4.3), with the momentum flux tensor, Π_{ij}, now depending on shear rate via Equation (4.27) instead of Equation (4.2), we can derive an analogue of Stefan's equation which is termed the Scott equation[5] (see, e.g., Reference 6 for a simple derivation):

$$\frac{dh}{dt} = -\frac{n}{2n+1}\left(\frac{F(n+3)h^{2n+1}}{2\pi\eta_0 R^{n+3}}\right)^{1/n} \tag{4.28}$$

It is easily shown that Equation (4.28) reduces to Equation (4.24) in the case that $n = 1$. As with Stefan's equation, the Scott equation is a first-order differential equation for the gap height, $h(t)$, and can be solved to find the process time for reducing the gap height from h_0 to h_1:

$$t_p = \frac{2n+1}{n+1}\left(\frac{2\pi\eta_0 R^{n+3}}{F(n+3)h_0^{n+1}}\right)^{1/n}\left(\left(\frac{h_0}{h_1}\right)^{\frac{n+1}{n}} - 1\right) \tag{4.29}$$

Equation (4.28) can also be solved numerically if the dependence of viscosity on temperature is known, and the temperature is ramped up as the adhesive is squeezed. Similarly, if the force is ramped up, Equation (4.28) can be solved numerically, and if the force is ramped up at a constant ramp rate, then an analytical solution of Equation (4.28) is easily found.[7] Of particular interest is the case when the adhesive viscosity dependence on temperature may be characterised as follows:

$$\eta_0 = \eta_{00} e^{-b(T-T_0)} \qquad\qquad (4.30)$$

where b and η_{00} are constants, and T_0 is an arbitrary reference temperature. Equation (4.30) is used in conjunction with Equation (4.27) to define the viscosity. The form of Equation (4.30) has been shown[8] to approximate some ACAs over the temperature range of interest during processing even though it is not an exact fit. The advantage of using this form of the viscosity dependence on temperature is that Equation (4.28) can be solved analytically to give the following result for the processing time, given that the temperature is ramped up from T_0 at a constant ramp rate, k:

$$t_p = \frac{n}{bk} \ln\left(1 + \frac{bk}{n}\xi\right) \qquad\qquad (4.31)$$

where ξ is defined as the processing time at constant temperature, T_0, and hence can be calculated from Equation (4.29) with η_0 set equal to η_{00}. It is worth noting that, at a sufficiently high ramp rate, the processing time scales as ln(k)/k while, if the ramp rate is sufficiently low, then the processing time is independent of the ramp rate. The case where the temperature is ramped up to a certain temperature and thereafter held constant can also be solved[7] in a similar manner.

It should be noted that a power law model might not be sufficient to describe a particular adhesive. There are, however, many solutions to the squeeze film flow of a fluid between two disks that assume different viscosity models, and one of these may then be suitable. The flow might also not be describable purely in terms of viscous effects, but possibly by combined viscous and elastic effects (viscoelasticity). ACAs have been measured for their visco-elastic response[8] and it was found that, if the adhesive was completely squeezed out in less than 1 s, then viscoelastic effects may become important, but not otherwise. Again the interested reader is urged to consult the considerable literature on squeeze film flow of viscoelastic fluids.[6,9,10]

4.3.2   The Effects of Non-flat Surfaces

So far we have assumed that the substrate and the lands are completely flat. In general this will not be the case, and the models have to be modified. Initially when pressure is applied to the chip, the adhesive will flow around the pads, and this is labelled type I flow in Figure 4.2. Type II flow occurs once the voids are filled and is a flow out from the centre of the chip to the edges. It should be noted that, if only type I flow occurs, the required force will be much less than if type II flow occurs. Equation (4.29) can be used to estimate the time taken for type I flow, but with the bump radius replacing the chip radius, and the force per bump replacing the total force applied. To see when type I or type II flow occurs consider Figure 4.6.

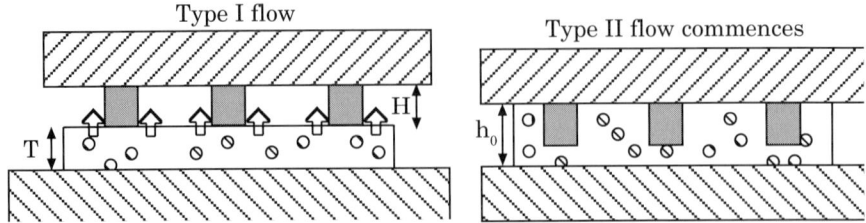

Fig. 4.6 Transition between flow Type I and Type II.

The most likely scenario is that both type I and type II flow occur, and in this case, we can estimate the value of h_0 as being the gap between chip and substrate at which the voids are filled. This value can be estimated by calculating the volume of fluid displaced by the pads/bumps as they penetrate into the fluid, assuming that type II flow is not significant at this stage: the original volume of fluid between the chip and substrate is equal to the volume of fluid in the voids added to the volume of fluid between pads and bumps:

$$TA = HA(1 - \zeta) + (h_0 - H)A \tag{4.32}$$

where A is the chip area, T is the original film thickness, H is the combined land + bump height, ζ is the fraction of land/bump area to chip area, and h_0 is the gap between chip and substrate at which type II flow begins:

$$h_0 = T + \zeta H \tag{4.33}$$

Type II flow is not desirable as it both increases the process time, and also increases the likelihood of opens as discussed below. However, if there is no type II flow at all, then the space between the chip and substrate is not completely filled, and this will weaken the strength of the adhesive bond between chip and substrate, and the presence of voids is probably undesirable from a reliability viewpoint. Therefore the best solution is to adjust the thickness of the adhesive layer so that only a minimum of type II flow occurs, just sufficient to expel any entrapped air.

The flow around the pads also has an influence on the probability of particles forming conducting chains of particles between adjacent pads to form shorts, and on the probability of the particles being swept off the pad altogether to form opens. Detailed models on shorts and opens can be found elsewhere[7,12,13] based on statistical methods. Here it is sufficient to remark that CFD has been very useful in determining the flow of fluid around the bumps. The CFD predictions have been tested against experimentally observed flows (observed by bonding the chips to glass) and good agreement has been found.[8]

Figure 4.7 shows the pattern of fluid flow around a bumped flip-chip device and flat substrate (typical of COG type assemblies). Points of interest include the sluggish flow at the corner of the chip and the resulting difference in flow patterns around the pads in these two regions. The stronger the flow over the pads, the greater is the chance that particles will be swept off the pads, so that the pads at the corners will have a smaller probability of opens. Another way of reducing the probability of opens is to ensure that the viscosity of the adhesive is minimised during the flow, as this will reduce the viscous drag on the conducting particles due to the surrounding fluids relative to mechanical friction keeping them on the pads. This could be done for example by processing at higher temperatures[7] (e.g., by reducing the loading force during the chip while the temperature is ramping up).

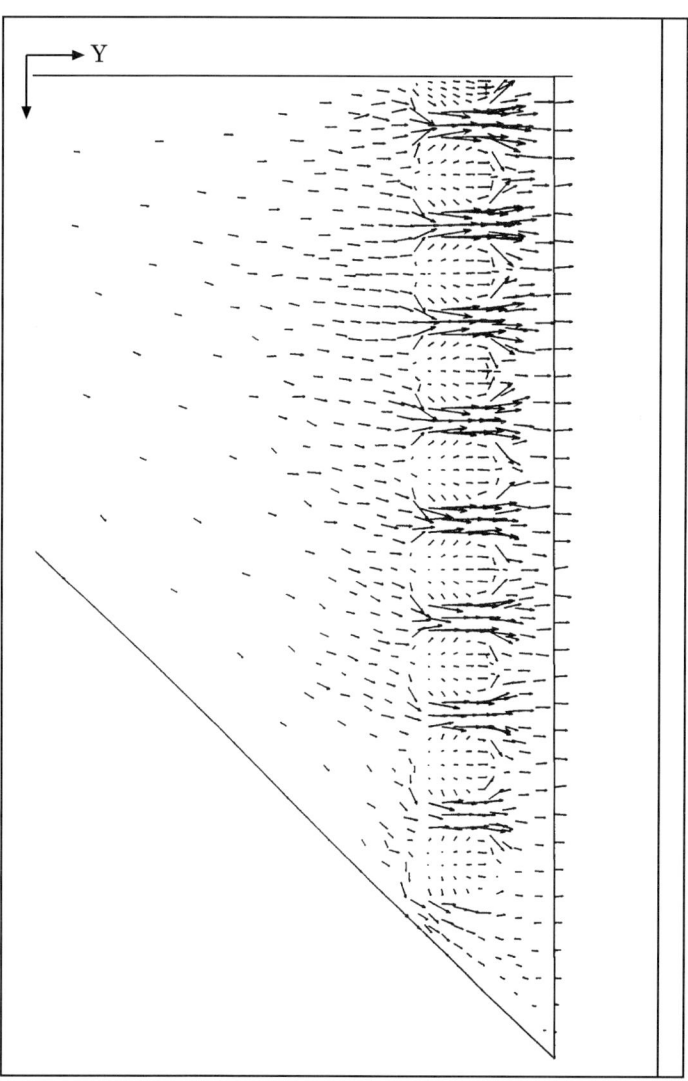

Fig. 4.7 Flow of adhesive under a square chip seen in plan view with the plane being parallel to the chip surface and 5 microns from it.

4.3.3   Model Verification

The experimental investigation in Loughborough has two main strands — *materials investigation* wherein the properties of both commercially available and development ACA materials have been examined[7] and *process screening* wherein the effects of processing temperature, pressure, substrate material and ACA type on process yield and post process reliability have been studied.[11] Materials properties which have been investigated include conducting particle size, shape and composition, adhesive resin dielectric strength and onset of cure, ACA conduction characteristics and rheology, and substrate pad shape and height variations. The results of process screening experiments have been used to determine the relative importance of pressure, time adhesive type etc. and the results of that programme are still being analysed.

The focus will now shift to the aspects of the experimental investigation that are of particular relevance to verifying the flow model introduced in the previous sections. The model can be used to predict when the chip pads and lands will eventually make electrical contact. In order to test the models it is necessary to build an apparatus which is capable of monitoring resistances through the joints during processing. Such an arrangement is shown in Figure 4.8.

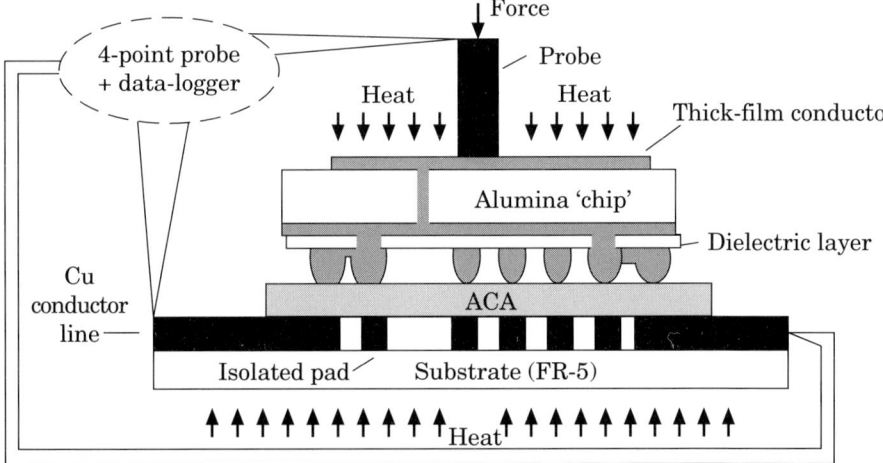

Fig. 4.8 Schematic of test rig enabling joint resistance measurements during processing.

The principal features of this test rig are the ability to apply heat at varying temperature ramp rates to both faces of the chip, the ability to apply load to the chip and to ramp the load up in a controlled manner, and the ability to measure the resistance of 16 selected joints during processing. This latter was achieved by using a ceramic test piece instead of silicon, with via holes connecting the bumps to the probe so that the resistances of each joint can be measured independently of the others. The rig can also be used to measure the resistance of daisy-chained silicon chips, but now the resistance of groups of pads is measured, and the number of groups that can be measured is reduced to eight because there is no electrical connection to the backside of the chip (and hence of the 16 connections on the substrate, eight are needed for input current and eight for output current).

A typical graph of resistance versus time using a thermoplastic ACA and an organic (FR-5) substrate is shown in Figure 4.9. Of particular note is that the time taken for electrical connection to be made and the temperature at which this occurred (also shown in Figure 4.9) agree closely with the model predictions of Equation (4.31). The details of the rheological measurements made in order to obtain the parameters relating to viscosity in Equation (4.31) are given in Reference 8, but one experiment on the ACA to find viscosity versus shear rate, and one to find viscosity versus temperature are the minimum number of experiments that must be performed in order to obtain a prediction for the process time.

Figure 4.9 also shows that in this case all the connections were made almost simultaneously. This tells us that the pads and bumps were relatively uniform in height, and that no wedge was formed, with the pads on one side touching down before those on the opposite corner. This is in part due to careful design of the probe to apply the force at a point rather than over the whole of the chip which invariably results in a wedge being formed.

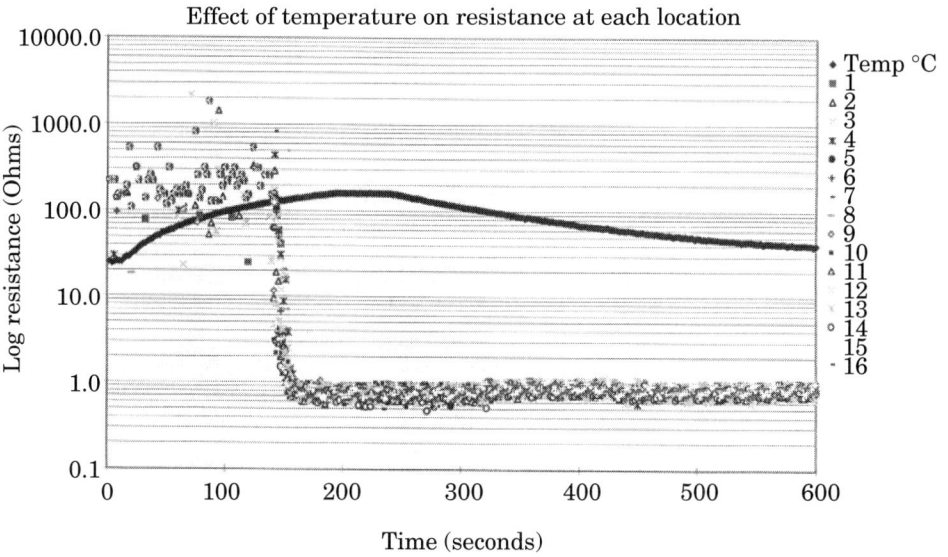

Fig. 4.9 Graph showing resistance and temperature *vs* time for chemically etched copper tracks or organic substrate.

Figure 4.10 shows another graph of resistance versus time, but in this case it is observed that the pads do not make simultaneous contact with the substrate. This is because of non-uniformities in height between the printed thick film (silver palladium ink) pads on the ceramic substrate and also because of the domed shape of these same pads. The processing yield on this type of substrate was found to be lower than on the organic substrates, confirming that thick film printed substrates must be monitored extremely carefully for pad height variations and shape.

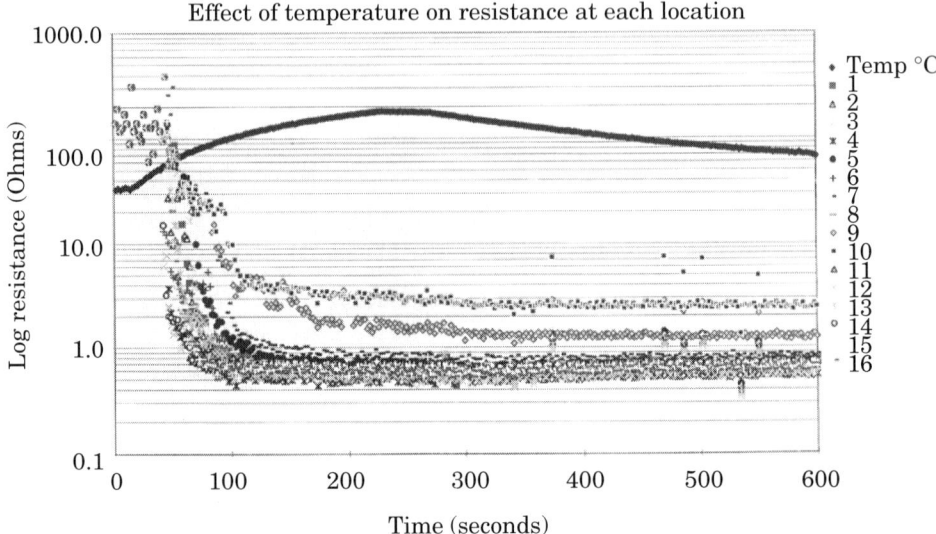

Fig. 4.10 Graph showing resistance and temperature *vs* time for thick-film printed pads on ceramic substrates.

4.4   OPENS AND BRIDGING BETWEEN PADS

In this section analytical models of bridging and shorting developed at Loughborough University will be discussed. These should be taken as complementary to the Monte-Carlo type computer models generated by Li *et al.*[12] A fundamental assumption common to both approaches is that the particles are randomly distributed in the adhesive matrix.

4.4.1   Opens

The probability of an open connection on any single pad may be small but, when it is considered that a typical component may have an excess of 100 pads, it becomes clear that for high volume production the probability of opens should be in the parts per million range for an acceptable overall yield. The number of particles on the pad can, in the first instance, be assumed to obey the Poisson distribution:

$$P(n) = \frac{e^{-\mu}\mu^n}{n!} \tag{4.34}$$

where n is the number of particles, μ is the average number of particles on the pad and P(n) is the probability of finding n particles on the pad. The value of μ can be estimated by using a transparent material in place of the substrate and counting the number of particles per pad after processing. This method, however, assumes that the replacement of the chip surface by the flat transparent surface has negligible effect on the flows of adhesive and particles. If the initial volume fraction of particles (f) is known as well as the particle radius (r), then μ is given by the volume of conducting particles between pad and land (2rAf) divided by the volume of a single particle ($4\pi r^3/3$):

$$\mu = \frac{3Af}{2\pi r^2} \tag{4.35}$$

where A is the pad area. This approach also has a flaw in that the initial volume fraction of particles will not necessarily be equal to the final volume fraction after the flow has been completed, but both experimental results and calculations show the effect to be a small one in most circumstances ($\delta f/f \sim 10\%$), so we shall take f to equal the final volume fraction of particles as well. Thus for a value of f of 10%, 250 micron square pads and a particle diameter of 10 microns, we would expect a value of μ around 120. The probability of an open in this case is:

$$P(0) = e^{-\mu} = e^{-\frac{3Af}{2\pi r^2}} = 10^{-52} \tag{4.36}$$

which is astronomically small. With the same adhesive and 50 micron square pads, μ becomes 4.8 and P(0) becomes 0.008 which is certainly too large. A value for μ of 13 is sufficient to ensure that the number of open drops below 6 sigma levels.

Equation (4.34) does not take into account the crowding effect of particles; it is only valid in the limit of f<<1, but in practice, this condition is usually satisfied well enough to make Equation (4.36) valid. The Poisson distribution has been established experimentally for 100 micron square pads at f = 10% by observing the numbers of particles on pads optically through glass.

If a more accurate distribution of particle numbers on the pad is required, taking into account the effects of particle crowding, then the Binomial distribution may be used:[13,14]

$$P(n) = C_n^N (1-s)^{N-n} s^n \tag{4.37}$$

valid for n≤N, where N is the maximum number of particles that can be contained in an area A, C_n^N is the binomial coefficient and s = f/f_m where f_m is the volume fraction corresponding to maximum packing (f_m = 0.6 for spheres hexagonally packed in the plane). In the limit that f<<1, Equations (4.36) and (4.37) give identical results for P(0).

If Equations (4.36) or (4.37) are to be used to calculate the distribution of resistances expected in a typical ACA joint, it should be remembered that the conductivity is not simply proportional to the number of particles present but in general will vary according to the type of particle. For example, assuming hard spheres and softer, plastic deforming lands and spheres, the joint contact resistivity (ρ) has been estimated[15] as:

$$\rho = \frac{A\rho_B \left[\sqrt{\frac{6\pi n\kappa}{\sigma A}} - \frac{1}{R_B} \right]}{4\pi n R_B} \tag{4.38}$$

where ρ_B is the resistivity of the sphere material, n is the number of contacts within the contact area A, κ is the shear yield stress on a single contact sphere of radius R_B, and σ is the pressure applied to the joint. For 25 micron radius Ni alloy particles with A = 0.1 mm^2, κ = 1 GPa, ρ_B = 6.1 x 10^{-8} Ωm and σ = 1 MPa, we obtain joint conductivities of 4 x 10^5 Ω^{-1}m^{-1} with 50 conducting particles and 1 x 10^5 Ω^{-1}m^{-1} for 2 particles.

4.4.2   Bridging

The probability of bridging between pads must now be addressed. For adhesives which have the conducting particles dispersed throughout the whole volume, the likely cause of bridging will be via the sides of the pads/ lands (Figure 4.11):

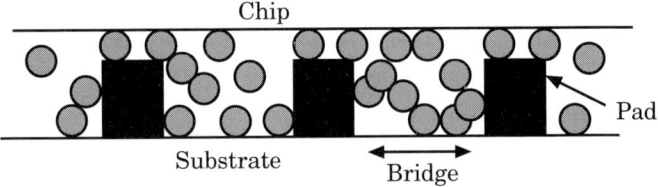

Fig. 4.11 Bridging mechanism with the conducting particles dispersed through the whole volume.

For adhesives where the particles are initially confined to a reduced volume, the bridges are likely to be completely due to particle-particle contact (Figure 4.12):

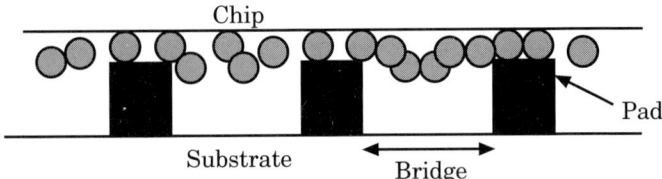

Fig. 4.12 Bridging mechanism with the conducting particles confined to a thin layer.

In the former case we may make a rough estimate of bridging densities by dividing up the volume between the pads into cubes, with sides the same length as the particle diameter, and assuming that, if a chain of such cubes linking one pad to the next is fully occupied by particles, then a bridge has been formed (Figure 4.13):

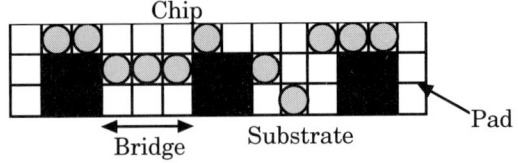

Fig. 4.13 Bridging in a model where the particles can take up restricted positions wholly inside boxes.

In taking this representation of the bridging process, clearly simplifications have been made, which we will address later. It is, however, now a simple matter to calculate bridging probabilities. If k boxes are filled out of a total of N, then the volume fraction of particles is:

$$f = \frac{k \frac{4}{3} \pi r^3}{N(2r)^3} \tag{4.39}$$

Thus the probability that any single box is occupied (k/N) is given by:

$$\frac{k}{N} = \frac{6f}{\pi} \tag{4.40}$$

In the limit that $f \to 0$, only the shortest chains will contribute to bridging and hence the probability of bridging between any two pads, p, will be determined by the number of boxes that can be fitted on to the side of a single pad and by $(6f/\pi)^q$ where q is the lowest number of particles needed to bridge the gap (q is equal to 3 in Figure 4.13). For a pad of length l, height h, and a spacing d between pads, (l, h, d>>r) we can estimate the probability of bridging in this model to be given by:

$$p = 1 - \left(1 - \left(\frac{6f}{\pi}\right)^{\frac{d}{2r}}\right)^{\frac{hl}{4r^2}} \tag{4.41}$$

where the term inside the large brackets denotes the probability that bridging does not occur on a given path, and this probability is raised to the number of possible paths present to obtain the probability that bridging does not occur on all possible paths. The last step is to subtract from 1 to obtain the probability that at least one path contains a bridge.

Although this equation can be used to estimate bridging probabilities, it is only an upper limit because the particles are not constrained to sit exactly within any particular box: Equation (4.41) gives the probability that a line of boxes from one pad to the next will all contain a given particle centre, but not necessarily the whole particle, and hence bridging may not occur; Equation (4.41) is therefore an upper limit on bridging probabilities (in the limit that $f \to 0$). Thus if it predicts bridging in any situation, bridging may not occur, while if bridging is not predicted, then it will not occur.

Next let us consider the situation depicted in Figure 4.12 where the particles are effectively confined to two dimensions. This situation has been modelled,[13] and the probabilities of bridges with 2 particles, 3 particles.... n+1 particles has been calculated as a function of the gap between pads. The result for the probability of forming an n+1 particle chain, P(n+1) is:

$$p(n) = 1 - \left(1 - (1 - e^{-4f})^n \left(\frac{\theta}{\pi}\right)^n\right)^N \tag{4.42}$$

where f is the volume fraction of particles, N is equal to the number of particles expected in an area A; A = ld; N = 2rAf/(volume of 1 sphere), where l is the length of the terminations and d is the distance between terminations, and θ is the maximum angle between contacting spheres at which contact between adjacent terminations is still possible; d = 2r(1 + ncosθ). See Figure 4.14.

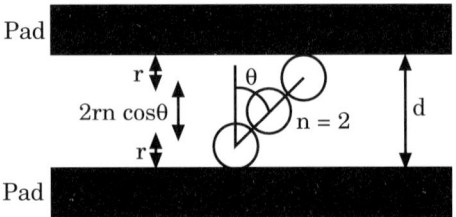

Fig. 4.14 Limiting condition under which shorting can occur for an n+1 particle short (n=2 in this example).

The assumptions in this model are that l>>d and that the probability of two particles being in contact is given by $1 - e^{-4f}$ (Reference 13) which follows from the assumption that particle positions are statistically independent of each other. The extension of this model to three dimensions is straightforward by replacing the fraction (θ/π) by an equivalent solid angle fraction; $(1 - cosθ)/2$, replacing e^{-4f} by e^{-8f}, and N becomes AHf/(volume of one sphere), when the pad/land heights, H, are large compared with d. If the latter condition is not satisfied, then the three-dimensional analogue of Equation (4.42) is still approximately valid as both the solid angle required for a short to form, and the solid angle available to each neighbour will decrease as a particle approaches either the chip or substrate surfaces.

Figure 4.15 illustrates the probability of opens for 50 micron square pads separated by 50 micron gaps (l = d = 50 microns), pad heights, H, of 30 microns

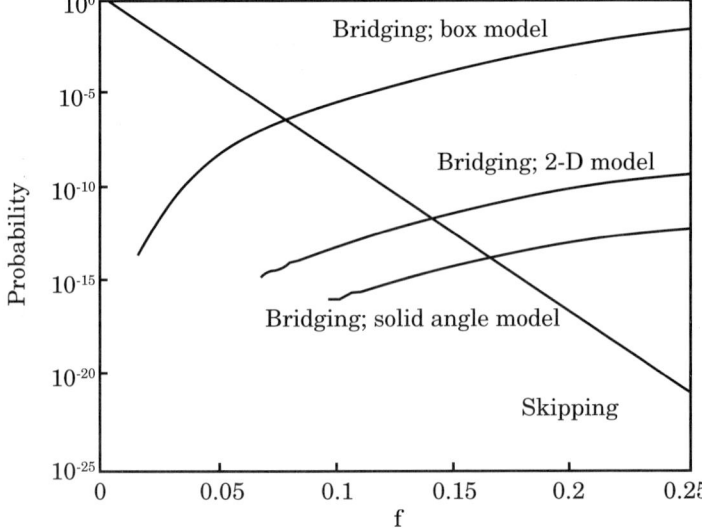

Fig. 4.15 Probability of particles bridging gap as a function of volume fraction.

for various volume fractions, f, and fixed particle radius of 2.5 microns. Also shown are the probabilities of bridging using the box model; Equation (4.41), the two-dimensional case; Equation (4.42) and the 3-D analogue of Equation (4.42). It is clear that Equation (4.41) is a gross overestimate of the probability of bridging, while the case in which particles are confined completely to 2-D is worse than the 3-D case (so that completely flat chips and substrates are not good from the viewpoint of bridging). The optimum volume fraction for this geometry is seen to lie between 7% and 15%, probably closer to 15% as the angular models are expected to be more accurate.

One aspect that has not been considered is that the particles may not actually have to be in contact for shorting to occur; if the gap between particles and the adjacent pads is small enough, dielectric breakdown may occur leading to short circuits. The limit at which this occurs must be tested for experimentally, and can then be incorporated into the models by replacing the particle radius, r, by an equivalent shorting radius, r_s, where dielectric breakdown between particles will occur when the particle centres are $2r_s$ apart.

4.5   SUMMARY

In this chapter we have attempted to show how a model of fluid flow for the adhesive in an ACA can be constructed, starting from the basic equations of fluid flow, and how this model can be used to guide the choice of materials and substrates. In particular, the relationship between process time, process geometry, chip size, adhesive rheology, temperature and applied pressure has been delineated. The use of CFD to study fluid flow in complex geometries has been described, and the influence of some of the major processing variables on opens formation has been discussed. The experimental set-up used to verify the models has been explained together with some of the capabilities and advantages of this arrangement. We have also presented formulae relating the probabilities of bridging and opens as a function of particle volume fraction, radius and pad geometry, which may be of use in determining process limits for a given adhesive, and also the changes that must be made to a particular pad geometry in order to provide the optimum balance between probabilities of opens and shorts.

4.6   ACKNOWLEDGEMENTS

The authors acknowledge the support of the Engineering and Physical Sciences Research Council (EPSRC) and a consortium of industrial partners: Cooksons Technology Centre and their associated company Alpha Metals Advanced Products, Design 2 Distribution Ltd, Eltek Semiconductors Ltd, IBM (UK) Ltd, Lucas Electronics, Mitel Telecom and Rolls-Royce plc.

REFERENCES

1   Kivilahti, J., 'Development of Solder-filled Uniaxially Conducting Adhesives', Proceedings Adhesives in Electronics 1994, Berlin (1994).

2   Whalley, D. C., Williams, D. J., Ogunjimi, A. O., Boyle, O. A. and Goward, J. M., 'A Comparison of the Behaviour of Isotropic and Anisotropic Conducting Adhesives',

PED-Vol. 65/EEP-Vol. 5, *Manufacturing Aspects in Electronics Packaging*, ASME 1993, pp. 81-91 (1993).

3   Landau, L. D. and Lifshitz, E. M., 'Fluid Mechanics', Pergamon Press (1959).

4   Stefan, J., *Akad. Wiss. Math. Natur.*, **Vol. 69**, p. 713 (1874).

5   Scott, J. R., *Transactions Inst. Rubber Ind.*, **Vol. 7**, p. 169 (1931).

6   Leider, P. J. and Bird, B., 'Squeezing Flow between Parallel Disks', *Ind. Eng. Chem. Fundam.*, **Vol. 13**, p. 336 (1974).

7   Mannan, S. H., Williams, D. J. and Whalley, D. C., 'Some Optimum Anisotropic Conductive Adhesives Properties for Flip Chip Interconnection', *Journal of Materials Science: Materials in Electronics*, **Vol. 8**, pp. 223-231 (1997).

8   Mannan, S. H., Whalley, D. C., Ogunjimi, A. O. and Williams, D. J., 'Modelling of the Initial Stages of the Anisotropic Adhesive Joint Assembly Process', Proceedings Japan International Electronic Manufacturing Symposium, Omiya, pp. 142-145 (1995).

9   McClelland, M. A. and Finlayson, B. A., 'Squeezing Flow of Elastic Fluids', *Journal of Non-Newtonian Fluid Mechanics*, **Vol. 13**, pp. 181-201 (1983).

10 Shirodkar, P., Bravo, A. and Middleman, S., 'Lubrication Flows in Viscoelastic Liquids. 3. Approach of Parallel Surfaces Subject to Constant Loading', *Ind. Eng. Chem. Fundam.* **Vol. 21**, pp. 434-437 (1982).

11 Ogunjimi, A. O., Mannan, S. H., Whalley, D. C. and Williams, D. J., 'Assembly of Planar Array Components using Anisotropic Conducting Adhesives — A Benchmark Study', Proceedings Adhesives in Electronics, Stockholm, pp. 270-284, June (1996).

12 Li, L. and Morris, J. E., 'Structure and Selection Models for Anisotropic Conductive Adhesive Films', Proceedings Adhesives in Electronics 1994, Berlin (1994).

13 Williams, D. J. and Whalley, D. C., 'The Effects of Conducting Particle Distribution on the Behaviour of Anisotropic Conducting Adhesives: Non-uniform Conductivity and Shorting between Connections', *Journal of Electronics Manufacturing*, **Vol. 3**, pp. 85-94 (1993).

14 Herczynski, R., 'Distribution Function for Random Distribution of Spheres', *Nature*, **Vol. 255**, pp. 540-541 (1975).

15 Williams, D. J., Whalley, D. C., Boyle, O. A. and Ogunjimi, A. O., 'Anisotropic Conducting Adhesives for Electronic Interconnection', *Soldering & Surface Mount Technology*, No.14, pp. 4-8 (1993).

Chapter 5

CURING OF ISOTROPIC ELECTRICALLY CONDUCTIVE ADHESIVES

LI LI
Motorola Semiconductor Products Sector,
Tempe, Arizona, USA

JAMES E. MORRIS
State University of New York at Binghamton, New York, USA

5.1   INTRODUCTION

The development of electrically conductive adhesives (ECAs) for solder replacement in the electronics assembly industry has been driven primarily by environmental pressures. The materials are lead-free and require no post-process CFC cleaning. As further motivation, there is promise of a reduction in total printed circuit board (PCB) manufacturing steps and hence a cheaper product. In principle, ECAs should also yield finer pitch limits than solder.[1] Most commercial isotropic ECA products currently consist of silver flakes in an epoxy resin, and achieve satisfactory electrical properties (with joint resistances typically an order higher than those of solder) at the expense of mechanical attachment reliability. The trade-off between electrical and mechanical properties is the subject of continued research.

The thermal cure process is critical to develop the ultimate electrical and mechanical properties of ECAs. Prior conduction studies[2,3] show that the metallic contacts between silver flakes are established during cure. Therefore, it is important to understand the reliability performance of these materials with different degrees of cure, and what happens during processing, to be able to guarantee reproducible, effective cure schedules.

The purpose of the work reported here was to assess the effectiveness of manufacturers' specified cure schedules, based on simple cure models, and to relate degree of cure to electrical properties. In addition, the electrical resistivities in 85°C/85%RH (relative humidity) are related to the material cure kinetics.

5.2   ADHESIVE CURE

(a) The curing process

Epoxy is the common matrix material used for conductive adhesives. The three materials selected for the experimental study described here are all silver-filled epoxy systems. The curing of an epoxy is complex in that several steps are involved.[4] The chemistry of cure begins with the formation and linear growth of the polymer chain that soon begins to branch, and then to cross-link. As the reaction proceeds, the molecular weight increases rapidly, and eventually chains become linked together into networks of 'infinite' molecular weight. This sudden and irreversible transformation from a viscous liquid to an elastic gel marks the first appearance of the 'infinite network'. Gelation typically occurs at between 55 and 80% conversion, and does not inhibit further curing. Beyond the gel point, the reaction continues, with substantial increase in cross-link density, towards the formation of one infinite network, and its ultimate physical properties.

Polymer gelation has been described by percolation theory.[5] If the polymer reaction time is below, but close to, a characteristic time t_g, then branched polymers form a viscous solution, usually called a 'sol'. These branched polymers are large but finite clusters of monomers. When the reaction time is larger than t_g, a very large solid network of connected monomers appears that is usually called a chemical 'gel'. The characteristic time t_g is called the gelation time, and the point at which the 'gel' network appears for the first time is called the 'gel' point (GP). Experimental studies of sol-gel transitions usually proceed by measuring the time evolution of the rheological or mechanical properties (e.g., viscosity or elastic modulus) during the chemical reaction leading to gelation. An important problem in polymerisation and gelation is the determination of the GP, and its relation to the process condition of the materials. The GP depends on the functionality of the polymer. Percolation thresholds decrease with increasing coordination numbers, which are the analogue of polymer functionality. Thus, polymers with cross-links of high functionality gel very early.

Vitrification is another phenomenon of the growing chains or network. This transformation from a viscous liquid or elastic gel to a glass begins to occur as the glass transition temperature of these growing chains or network becomes coincidental with the cure temperature. Further curing in the glassy state is extremely slow and, for all practical purposes, vitrification brings an abrupt halt to curing. The onset of vitrification causes a shift from chemical control of the reaction to diffusion control, and may be observed by a gradual decay of the reaction rate.[4]

A time-temperature-transformation (TTT) diagram of curing is shown in Figure 5.1.[6] On the diagram the time to gelation and the time to vitrification are plotted as functions of the isothermal cure temperature. At temperatures below the glass transition temperature of the unreacted resin or resin mixture (T_{c0} in Figure 5.1), reaction is confined to the solid state and is therefore very slow to occur. T_{c0} serves to define storage temperatures for unreacted resins. Between T_{c0} and $T_{c, gel}$ the liquid resin will react until its continuously rising transition temperature becomes coincidental with the cure temperature, at which stage vitrification will commence, and the reaction becomes diffusion controlled and is eventually quenched when vitrification is complete. $T_{c, gel}$ is the cure temperature at which vitrification and gelation occur simultaneously.

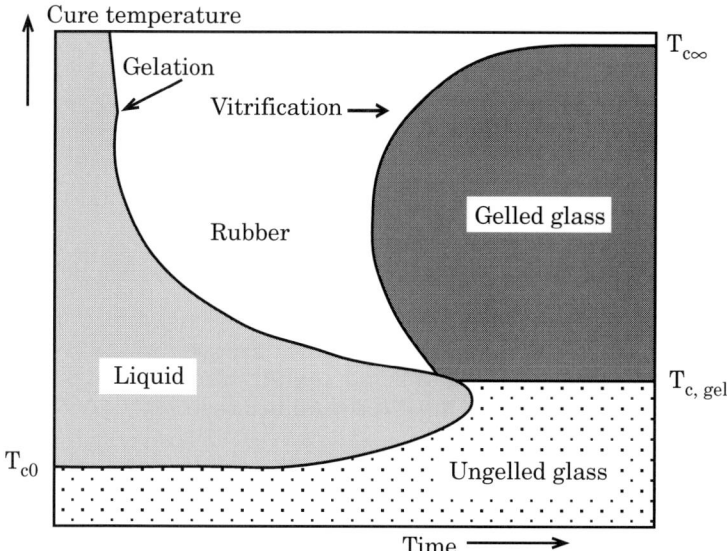

Fig. 5.1 TTT diagram showing the four material states encountered during cure: liquid, rubber, ungelled glass, and gelled glass.[6]

Between $T_{c, gel}$ and $T_{c\infty}$, gelation precedes vitrification, and a cross-linked rubbery network forms and grows until its glass transition temperature coincides with the cure temperature, and the reaction becomes quenched. Above $T_{c\infty}$, the minimum cure temperature required to achieve full and complete cure, the epoxy resin remains in the rubbery state after gelation. To achieve complete cure, and to develop ultimate properties, necessitates the avoidance of vitrification during cure. To cross-link an epoxy resin completely, it is necessary to cure above the cure temperature of the fully cured polymer network ($T_{c\infty}$). For the Shell Epon 828 (epoxies of the diglycidyl ether of bisphenol-A type) reacted with Du Pont PACM-20 (bis(*p*-aminocyclohexyl)methane,[6] the T_{c0} is around -20°C, $T_{c, gel}$ 10°C, and $T_{c\infty}$ 165°C. This is similar to the adhesive systems studied here, which have the bisphenol-A type of resins and amine curing agents.

(b) Cure models
   All kinetic studies start with the basic rate equation that relates the rate of conversion, $d\alpha/dt$, at constant temperature to some function of the concentration of reactants $f(\alpha)$ through a rate constant k:

$$d\alpha / dt = kf(\alpha) \tag{5.1}$$

Epoxy curing can be divided into two general categories: nth-order and auto-catalysed:

(i) For nth-order kinetics, the rate of conversion is proportional to the concentration of material which has yet to react: $f(\alpha) = (1-\alpha)^n$, where α is the degree of conversion.

(ii) Cure reactions which reach a maximum reaction rate at 30-40% of full cure, can be characterised by the auto-catalysed kinetics equation: $f(\alpha) = \alpha^m (1-\alpha)^n$, where m is also a reaction order.

In the usual manner, the temperature dependence (for both models) is assumed to reside in the rate constant through an Arrhenius relationship given by:

$$k = A \exp(-E/RT) \tag{5.2}$$

where E is an activation energy, R the gas constant, T the absolute temperature, and A the pre-exponential or frequency factor. The curing reaction of most thermosets can be adequately described in terms of these simple chemical models, assuming the chemical reactions are controlling the rate of cure.

Application of the cure model to the materials used in the experimental section requires parameters determined by differential scanning calorimetry (DSC). The peak exothermic temperature (T_p) in the dynamic DSC run varies in a predictable manner with the heating rate (ϕ). The DSC studies discussed below determine T_p at different heating rates. Methods for distilling the activation energy E and pre-exponential A have been devised. A simple, usable and accurate relationship between activation energy E, heating rate ϕ, and peak exothermic temperature T_p is based on a difference method.[7] Combining Equations (5.1) and (5.2):

$$d\alpha/dt = f(\alpha)A\exp[-E/RT] \tag{5.3}$$

Integration of this equation proceeds as follows:

$$\int_0^{\alpha_p} \frac{d\alpha}{f(\alpha)} = A\int_{t_o}^{t_p} e^{-E/RT}dt = \frac{A}{\phi}\int_{T_0}^{T_P} e^{-E/RT}dT \approx \frac{A}{\phi}\int_0^{T_P} e^{-E/RT}dT \approx \frac{AE}{\phi R}p(E/RT_p) \tag{5.4}$$

Values for the function $p(E/RT_p)$ were tabulated,[8] where:

$$\log p(E/RT_p) \approx -2.315 - 0.4567E/RT_p \tag{5.5}$$

for $20 < E/RT_p < 60$. It has been observed that the extent of reaction at the peak exotherm α_p is constant and independent of heating rate. Therefore, the first integral in Equation (5.4) is a constant, and the following relationship is obtained:[4]

$$E \approx \frac{-R}{0.4567}\frac{\Delta \log \phi}{\Delta(1/T_P)} \tag{5.6}$$

From the peak reaction temperature as a function of the heating rate, the activation energy can be obtained. A useful and accurate expression for the frequency factor, A, for nth-order reactions was derived[9] as:

$$A = \frac{\phi E \exp[E / RT_P]}{RT_P^2 [n(1-\alpha_P)^{n-1}]} \approx \frac{\phi E \exp[E / RT_P]}{RT_P^2} \qquad (5.7)$$

The factor $n(1-\alpha_P)^{n-1} \approx 1$ for first-order reactions, and is only 2-4% greater than unity for an nth-order epoxy cure reaction. (The treatment of A for auto-catalysed reactions is not included here.) Using ϕ, T_p, and the resulting E from Equation (5.6), the pre-exponential factor A can be obtained through Equation (5.7). The rate constant k at (constant) temperature, T, can then be calculated from Equation (5.2) with these values of E and A, permitting the determination of $\alpha(t)$.

5.3   EXPERIMENTAL RESULTS

(a) Test materials
   Three commercially available isotropic electrically conductive adhesives were selected based on previous experimental reliability results.[10] They are all silver-loaded epoxies, in the one-component versions. These materials were also chosen primarily because of their relatively fast cure times (3 to 10 minutes) which meet the cycle time requirements of existing SMT processes. Table 5.1 lists the material components as identified in the vendors' material safety data sheets. Relevant physical data are provided in Table 5.2.

Table 5.1

Components of the Adhesives Used (all in wt. %)

Adhesive A	Adhesive B	Adhesive C
Silver flake (73-75%)	Silver flake (74-84%)	Silver flake (<85%)
	Epoxy resin X (6-10%)	
	Epoxy resin Y (6-10%)	Rubber modified epoxy resin (1-10%)
	Epoxy hardener (3-4%)	Diglycidylether of bisphenol F (5-15%)
Bisphenol A-epichlorohydrin polymer (18-22%)	Gamma butryolactone (1-2%) solvent	1, 4-bis (2, 3-epoxypropoxy) butane (1-5%)

Table 5.2

Physical and Rheological Properties of the Adhesives

Adhesives	Volume Resistivity	Glass Transition Temperature	Viscosity (Kcps)	Cure Schedules
A	1×10^{-3} Ω-cm	$T_g > 80°$	310-350	120°C, 10 min
B	$1\text{-}3 \times 10^{-4}$ Ω-cm	$T_g = 90°C$	150-200	150°C, 5 min
C	3×10^{-4} Ω-cm	$T_g = 80°C$	73	150°C, 3 min

Fundamental material characterisations were conducted on these materials, including thermal analysis (DSC, thermomechanical analysis (TMA), and thermo-gravimetric analysis (TGA)), rheological, and dynamic mechanical analyses. Microstructural investigations (scanning electron microscopy (SEM), environmental SEM (ESEM), transmission electron microscopy (TEM), and Auger) were performed to identify the silver flakes' size, distributions, and contact morphologies. These analyses were related to the cure process and electrical conduction mechanisms of ICAs; detailed results can be found in Reference 2.

Microstructure development during cure was studied with a hot stage in an ESEM to relate morphological changes to changes in resistance. No significant structural changes or silver flake movements were noticed during cure, although Adhesive C is observed to shrink by about 1.5% at the gelation temperature.[2] The conduction development was accompanied by breakage and decomposition of the tarnish (organic thin layers which cover the silver flake surface), and by the enlargement of the contact area between silver flakes by thermal stress and shrinkage during the epoxy cure.

(b) Differential Scanning Calorimetry (DSC)

A Du Pont 912 DSC[11] was used in this study. Dynamic DSC studies were performed on the uncured ICAs, ramping the temperature from 25°C to 250°C at ramp rates of 10°C/minute and 6°C/minute. From these runs the onset of cure and the exothermic heat released were determined. The samples were nominally 10 to 15 mg in weight. A typical dynamic DSC curve is shown in Figure 5.2(a) with onset reaction temperature, exothermic peak temperature, and the heat released for a 10°C/minute ramp rate. The average data (eight samples) and their standard deviations (STDEV) of the onset, peak temperature, and heat release for the two ramp rates are listed for each material in Table 5.3. In addition to the dynamic runs, isothermal runs as a function of time were performed by initialising the start temperature at the manufacturer's specified cure temperature. Adhesive A was held at 120°C, while Adhesives B and C were held at 150°C. A representative isothermal DSC curve is shown in Figure 5.2(b). The averaged results and standard deviations (STDEV) are listed in Table 5.4. Cure time comparisons were determined from these runs.

Table 5.3

DSC Experimental Results with Different Ramp Rates

Materials	Ramp Rate $\phi = 10°C/minute$			Ramp Rate $\phi = 6°C/minute$		
	Onset Temp. (°C)	Peak Temp. T_p (°C)	Heat Released (J/g)	Onset Temp. (°C)	Peak Temp. T_p (°C)	Heat Released (J/g)
Adhesive	111.35	123.91	82.79	102.28	114.71	98.92
A STDEV	0.68	0.91	6.09	0.014	0.16	0.64
Adhesive	130.31	139.06	68.81	122.18	130.15	76.9
B STDEV	0.69	0.31	3.61	0.078	0.078	3.08
Adhesive	134.2	142.13	73.34	124.49	132.11	83.18
C STDEV	0.44	0.20	5.59	0.66	0.21	1.47

Table 5.4

DSC Experimental Results with Isothermal Runs

Materials	Onset Time (minutes)	Peak Time (minutes)	Heat Released (J/g)
Adhesive A	0.26	1.45	119.1
	STDEV = 0.028	STDEV = 0.014	STDEV = 14.35
Adhesive B	0.47	0.86	75.38
	STDEV = 0.044	STDEV = 0.047	STDEV = 7.89
Adhesive C	0.39	1.15	91.37
	STDEV = 0.007	STDEV = 0.014	STDEV = 7.17

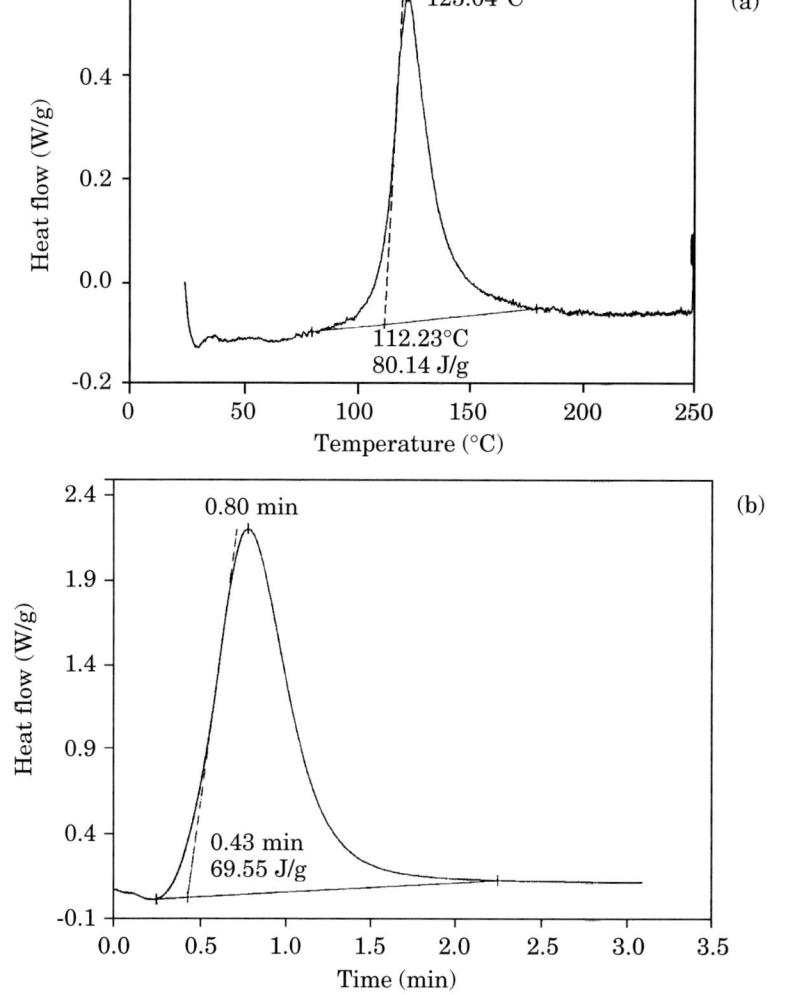

Fig. 5.2 Examples of DSC curves (Adhesive B); (a) dynamic (10°C/min. ramp); (b) isothermal.

Adhesive A has the lowest onset and peak temperatures at both 6 and 10°C/minute ramp rates. Lowering the ramp rate to 6°C/minute lowers both the onset and peak temperatures by 10°C. The cure kinetics can be calculated from the peak temperatures (T_p) at different heating rates (ϕ) of these dynamic DSC runs. The cure time can be estimated from the exothermic peak width. Adhesives A, B and C peak widths are 10, 4 and 5 minutes, respectively, at 10°C/minute. For the isothermal runs, the time for the exothermic peak to level off is 9 minutes for Adhesive A (120°C), 2 minutes for Adhesive B (150°C), and 3 minutes for Adhesive C (150°C). Adhesive B has a 5-minute recommended cure and Adhesive C has a 3-minute recommended cure, both at 150°C. The DSC results indicate that Adhesive C should have a longer cure time or higher cure temperature than Adhesive B.

(c) Cure calculations

From the DSC measurement data (Table 5.3), and assuming the resin cure reactions to be based on the nth-order kinetics, the calculated E, A and k at different temperatures for Adhesives A, B and C are listed in Table 5.5. The degree of conversion α at different cure times can be solved from the resulting k at specific temperatures and from the rate of conversion in Equation (5.1) for the nth-order reactions.

Table 5.5

Calculated Kinetics Parameters for the Adhesive Curing

Materials	E (kJ/mole)	A (s^{-1})	$k_{120°C}$ (s^{-1})	$k_{130°C}$ (s^{-1})	$k_{150°C}$ (s^{-1})
Adhesive A	67.45	6.6 x 10^6	0.00709	0.0118	0.0306
Adhesive B	78.41	82.2 x 10^6	0.00308	0.00558	0.0168
Adhesive C	67.75	2.73 x 10^6	0.00264	0.00442	0.0115

Employing the first-order equation, $d\alpha/dt = k(1 - \alpha)$, at constant temperature, the degree of conversion: $\alpha(t) = 1 - e^{-kt}$, by applying the boundary condition $t = 0$, $\alpha = 0$. When the second-order reaction is assumed, $\alpha(t) = 1 - 1/(kt + 1)$. The rate constants k at different temperatures were calculated based on the modelling results of E and A values in Table 5.5 for different adhesives. Figure 5.3 shows the conversion degrees versus cure time at specific cure temperatures for Adhesives A, B and C for both first- and second-order reaction assumptions. The first-order model gives a higher degree of conversion than the second-order model does. For example, the first-order curve shows a 99% conversion for Adhesive A cured at 120°C for 11 minutes, while the second-order model shows a 82% conversion at the same cure condition. For the first-order reaction, Adhesive B has a 99% conversion at 150°C for 5 minutes, and Adhesive C has a 99% conversion at 150°C for 7 minutes. Examining the manufacturers' suggested cure schedules (Table 5.2), 120°C, 10 minutes for Adhesive A, 150°C, 5 minutes for Adhesive B, and 150°C, 3 minutes for Adhesive C, result in conversion degrees of 98%, 99% and 87% respectively from the first-order cure model. (Of course, the corresponding degrees of cure would be worse for the second-order case, so these figures can be regarded as the maximum possible degrees of cure.) Adhesive C has a suggested schedule which results in an under-cure; a

higher cure temperature or longer cure time at 150°C is recommended. A
higher cure temperature is the better choice for Adhesive C, because 150°C

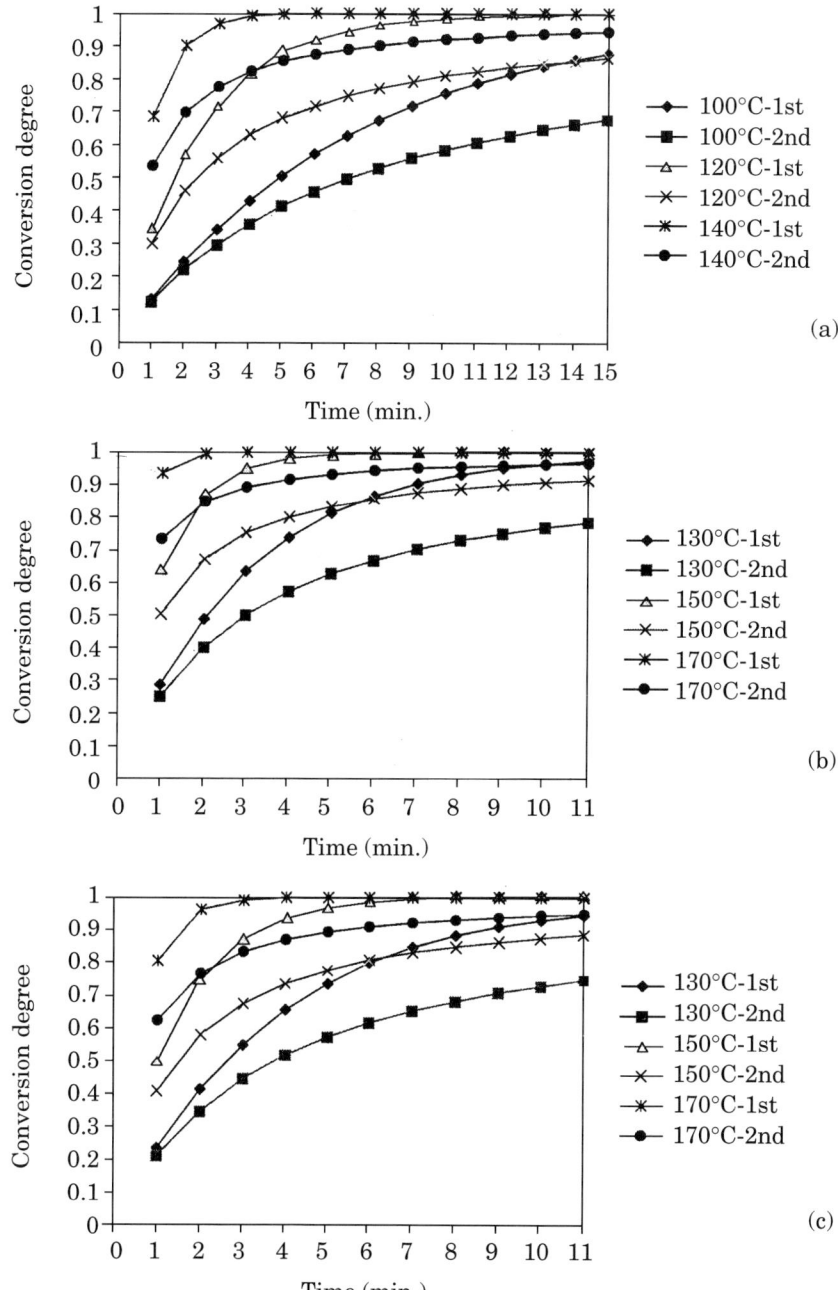

Fig. 5.3 Calculated degree of cure conversion *vs* cure time at different cure temperature for the 1st- and 2nd-order reactions. (a) Adhesive A; (b) Adhesive B; (c) Adhesive C.

is suspected to be lower than $T_{g\infty}$ in the TTT diagram discussed earlier. If the adhesive cures below $T_{g\infty}$, vitrification will occur after gelation. The vitrification process is not controlled by the chemical reaction, but by a diffusion process, resulting in a much slower reaction rate, and Equation (5.1) will not apply. Figure 5.4 shows the degrees of conversion for Adhesive A at 120°C cure, and Adhesives B and C at 150°C cure. Although the short cure cycles are desirable from the manufacturing point of view, the high residual stresses built in the materials curing near the maximum rate need to be considered also.

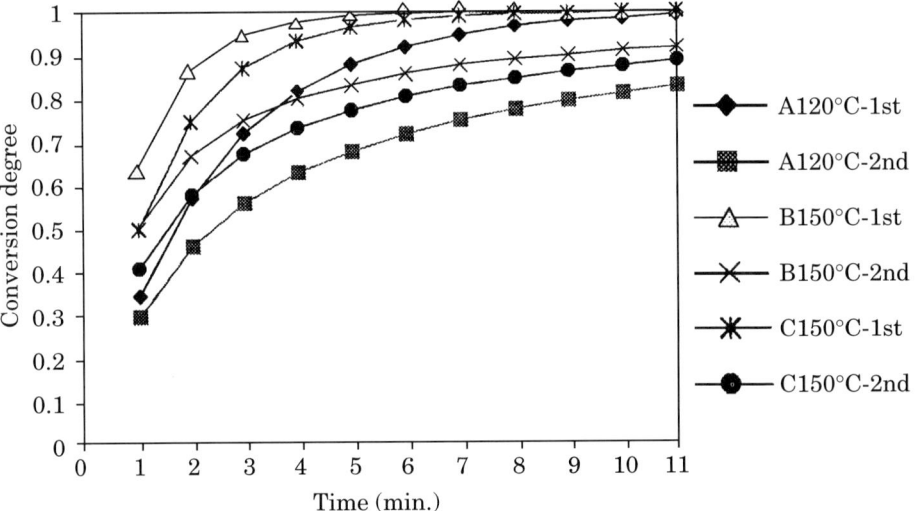

Fig. 5.4 Conversion degree *vs* cure time for Adhesive A at 120°C, Adhesives B and C at 150°C.

A similar result has been obtained[12] by employing a modified auto-catalysis model: $d\alpha/dt = (k_1+k_2\alpha_n^m)(1 - \alpha_n)^n$ (which is actually a linear combination of the auto-catalysis and nth-order models) where $\alpha = H/H_{ult}$ and $\alpha_n = \alpha/\alpha_{iso}(T)$, with H as the heat of reaction measured by dynamic DSC. With this approach, and determining the frequency factor A for Adhesive B from isothermal DSC data (Figure 5.5), an excellent match between the modelled

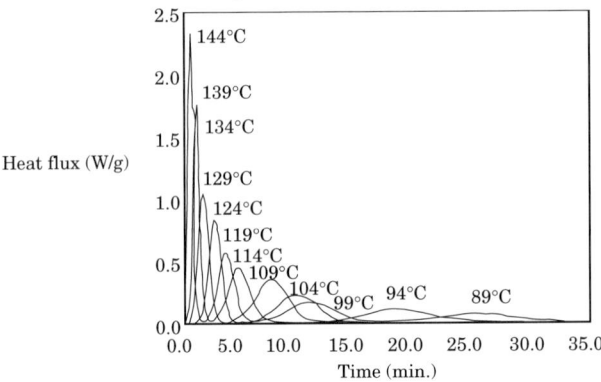

Fig. 5.5 DSC isothermal scan data for Adhesive B.

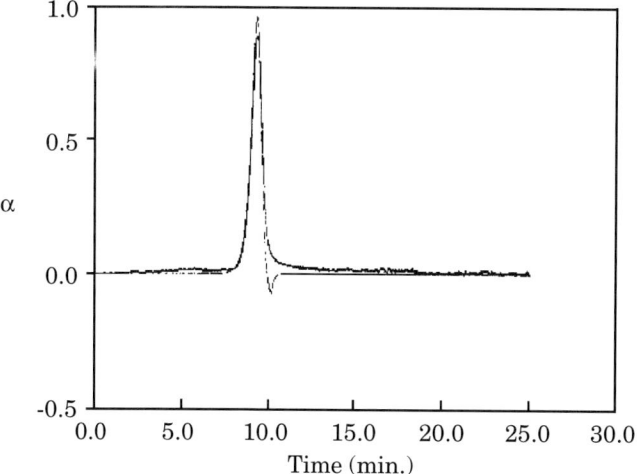

Fig. 5.6 Curve fit of the modified auto-catalysis model with isothermal DSC test data to experimental Adhesive B cure rates (DSC heat of reaction).

and experimental cure rates can be obtained (Figure 5.6), validating the parameters determined experimentally. Plotting degree-of-cure with time (Figure 5.7) produces even more severe estimates of under-cure, but furthermore suggests that a full cure is not possible with an isothermal schedule.

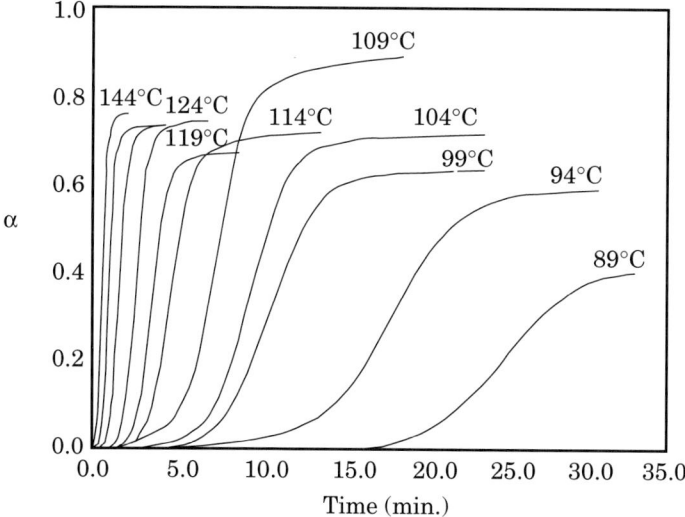

Fig. 5.7 Degree of cure *vs* cure time at different isothermal cure temperatures (auto-catalysis model, Adhesive B).

The cure kinetics models estimate the cure degree for different materials from the DSC experimental results obtained under the same experimental conditions. They give accurate and qualitative information to evaluate and compare the cure conditions of the three materials. It is especially important to establish an optimum cure schedule to match the particular process requirement and to assure complete cure of the material.

(d) Resistance measurements

Electrical measurements were made in a 4-point configuration, using an HP3458A multimeter; the board temperature was monitored with an Omega H82 digital thermometer and a thermocouple wire taped to the test boards with polyimide tape.

The resistivities of these materials were monitored during cure and related to the cure kinetics of the epoxy matrices. The resistivities decreased dramatically (>kΩ-cm to mΩ-cm) around a specific temperature with ramp cure and over a narrow time range (<10 seconds) with isothermal cure. Successive heating (25°C to 150°C) and cooling cycles yielded different degrees of consecutive resistivity decreases for these materials which were originally cured according to the manufacturers' recommended schedules (Table 5.2). Example plots of resistance decreases during the initial cure cycle are shown in Figure 5.8.

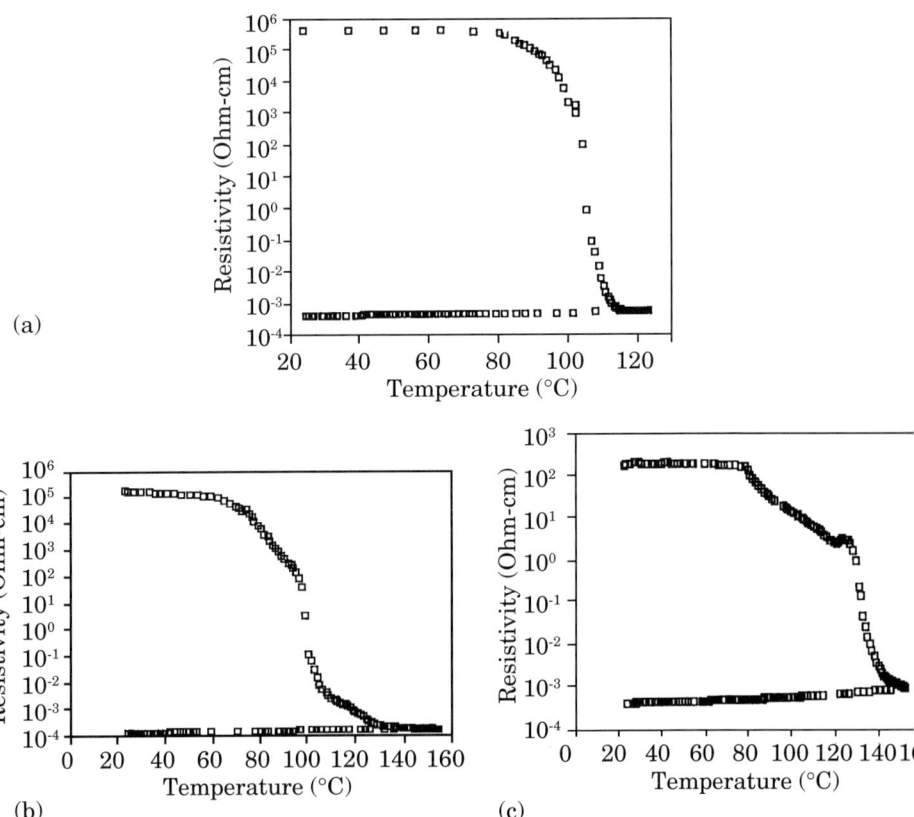

Fig. 5.8 Resistivity *vs* temperature during cure: (a) Adhesive A; (b) Adhesive B; (c) Adhesive C.

Samples were placed in the oven with the uncured adhesive strips and heated with a temperature ramp of 7°C/minute (dynamic cure) to the vendor-suggested cure temperature. The samples were then held at the cure temperature for the suggested times, cooled in the oven to 100°C, and removed. The electrical resistance was monitored continuously throughout these cycles. Other experiments were performed where the samples were inserted into a preheated oven (isothermal cure) at the recommended cure temperatures (120°C for Adhesive A, and 150°C for Adhesives B and C).

The resistivity of Adhesive B is 1×10^5 Ω-cm before cure. It starts to decrease around 80°C, then decreases dramatically around 100°C to 1×10^{-2} Ω-cm. It continues to decrease with additional cure and during cooling. The resistivity ultimately decreases to 1×10^{-4} Ω-cm. It is hypothesised that the drop-off in resistance is associated initially with silver packing as the viscosity decreases. The large transition is associated with gelation. After that the resistance continues to drop upon vitrification and with further cure development. Decreases in resistance upon cooling are relatively small in comparison. A similar decrease in resistivity is observed in Adhesive A during cure. In this case the transition occurs at 105°C. The resistivity goes from 4×10^5 to 4×10^{-4} Ω-cm. For Adhesive C, the resistivity of the material before cure is 200 Ω-cm and starts to decrease at 82°C. It then increases slightly at 124°C. The resistivity decreases dramatically at 134°C to 1×10^{-2} Ω-cm. Resistivity then continues to decrease with additional cure and during cooling. It ultimately decreases to 4×10^{-4} Ω-cm.

With isothermal curing, a test board is inserted into a preheated oven, whereupon the temperature requires a finite time to recover to the original set point, the nominal cure temperature. For a 3-minute isothermal cure at 150°C (Adhesive C in Figure 5.9), the resistivity decreases dramatically at

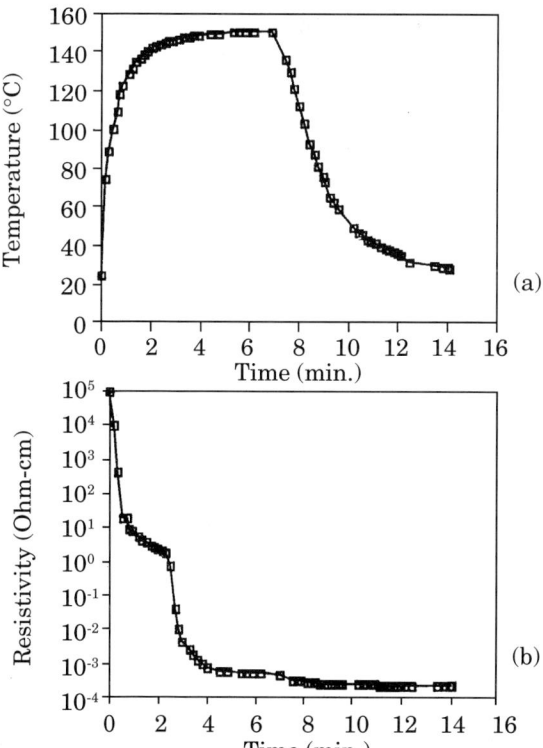

Fig. 5.9 Three-minute isothermal cure of Adhesive C at 150°C: (a) temperature profile; (b) resistivity change.

about 2.5 minutes at a temperature of 145°C, and finally reaches 2×10^{-4} Ω-cm. Longer isothermal cure times of 5 and 10 minutes change the resistivity only slightly.

Resistivity reaches lower ultimate values at higher cure temperatures for the same adhesive. Partial cure at low temperatures, followed by increased heating, gives a less conductive material than that obtained by a one-step cure at the higher temperature.

Although the volume loading of silver in these commercial conductive epoxies is adequate to produce measurable electrical conduction before cure, conduction does not develop until the materials are subjected to the thermal cure process. The initiation of cure occurs at the conduction development temperature and results in substantial shrinkage of the matrix, which then forces the particles into mutual contact.[13] The decrease in resistance may also be attributed to an increase in pressure on the inter-particulate silver contacts, which break the soft tarnish layer on the silver surface. The cure temperature will also contribute to the decarboxylation of any residual insulating stearic acid layer on the silver surfaces, followed by vaporisation of the parent hydrocarbons. These acid layers normally vaporise at 200°C, but the decomposition temperature is reduced by the incorporation of solubilising agents such as long chain organic compounds containing numerous ether linkages in the epoxy resin.[14] In summary, the conduction development is caused by both mechanical and chemical effects associated with the thermal cure process. Mechanical enlargement of the contact area and breakage of the insulating films by shrinkage force between the silver flakes during cure will decrease the contact resistance between the flakes. Chemical decomposition of the organic acid layer on the silver surface will also reduce a contact resistance dominated by electron tunnelling. After cure, metallic contacts between silver flakes are expected, and the contact resistance is controlled by the constriction resistance between the flakes.[15,16]

(e) Electrical properties and degree of cure

Five different cure schedules were selected for each material based on the vendor recommended cure schedules and the DSC experimental results. Table 5.6 shows the detailed cure schedules used and the degree of conversion calculated from the cure kinetics models developed above. Three test boards were used for each cure schedule (two with bare copper finishes and one with a gold finish). The boards were cured by placing them in a preheated oven for the isothermal cure times indicated. Additional times are required for the samples to heat up to their isothermal cure temperatures. The actual cure schedules are longer because the components or samples must come up to temperature. This can add 2 to 4 minutes to the cure schedule depending on the cure temperature required.

Three volume resistivity measurements were made on each test board, and the average resistivities and their standard deviations were obtained from the nine resistance measurements taken from the three boards in each group. The resistivities of the samples were calculated from the adhesive strip geometries measured by a Tencor profilometer. Volume resistivities of the samples were observed to be dependent on the degree of cure. The resistivities of Adhesives A, B and C versus different cure schedules in terms

Table 5.6

Cure Schedules used for the Reliability Study

Materials	Symbols	Soak Temp. & Time	Conversion Degree (%)	
Adhesive A	A5	120°C, 5 min.	1st-order, 88%	2nd-order, 68%
Adhesive A	A10	120°C, 10 min.	98%	81%
Adhesive A	A15	120°C, 15 min.	99.8%	86%
Adhesive A	A100	100°C, 10 min.	75%	58%
Adhesive A	A140	140°C, 10 min.	100%	92%
Adhesive B	B3	150°C, 3 min.	95%	75%
Adhesive B	B6	150°C, 6 min.	99.8%	86%
Adhesive B	B10	150°C, 10 min.	100%	91%
Adhesive B	B130	130°C, 6 min.	87%	67%
Adhesive B	B170	170°C, 6 min.	100%	94%
Adhesive C	C3	150°C, 3 min.	87%	67%
Adhesive C	C6	150°C, 6 min.	98%	81%
Adhesive C	C10	150°C, 10 min.	99.9%	88%
Adhesive C	C130	130°C, 6 min.	80%	61%
Adhesive C	C170	170°C, 6 min.	100%	91%

of conversion degrees (from the first-order reaction model) are shown in Figure 5.10. Resistivities of all adhesives decrease with increased degrees of conversion. For a fully cured material, Adhesive B has the lowest resistivity

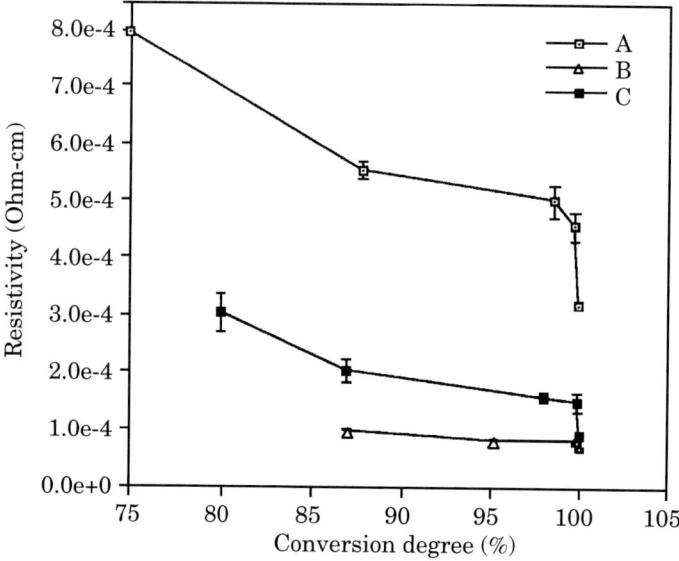

Fig. 5.10 Resistivity *vs* cure conversion degree for Adhesives A, B and C.

at around 7×10^{-5} Ω-cm; Adhesive C has a resistivity of 1×10^{-4} Ω-cm; and Adhesive A has the resistivity 4×10^{-4} Ω-cm, all less than the manufacturer's specifications (Table 5.2). The cure temperature is the most important factor for curing because of the exponential dependence of the reaction rate on temperature, and the minimum cure temperature requirement, $T_{c\infty}$, for complete curing. It is therefore more effective to increase the cure temperature slightly than to extend the cure time more significantly.

(f) Humidity effects

The volume resistivity of each ECA was measured initially and after every 100 hours of exposure to 85°C/85%RH until 900 hours. The under-cured material's resistivity drops initially and then stabilises. The lower the degree of cure, the higher the resistivity drop upon exposure to 85°C and 85% relative humidity. The first measurements after exposure were made at 100 hours. The resistivity could, therefore, have dropped off in less than 100 hours.

Figure 5.11(a) shows the resistivity change of Adhesive A with different cure schedules. These data again indicate that the cure temperature has a

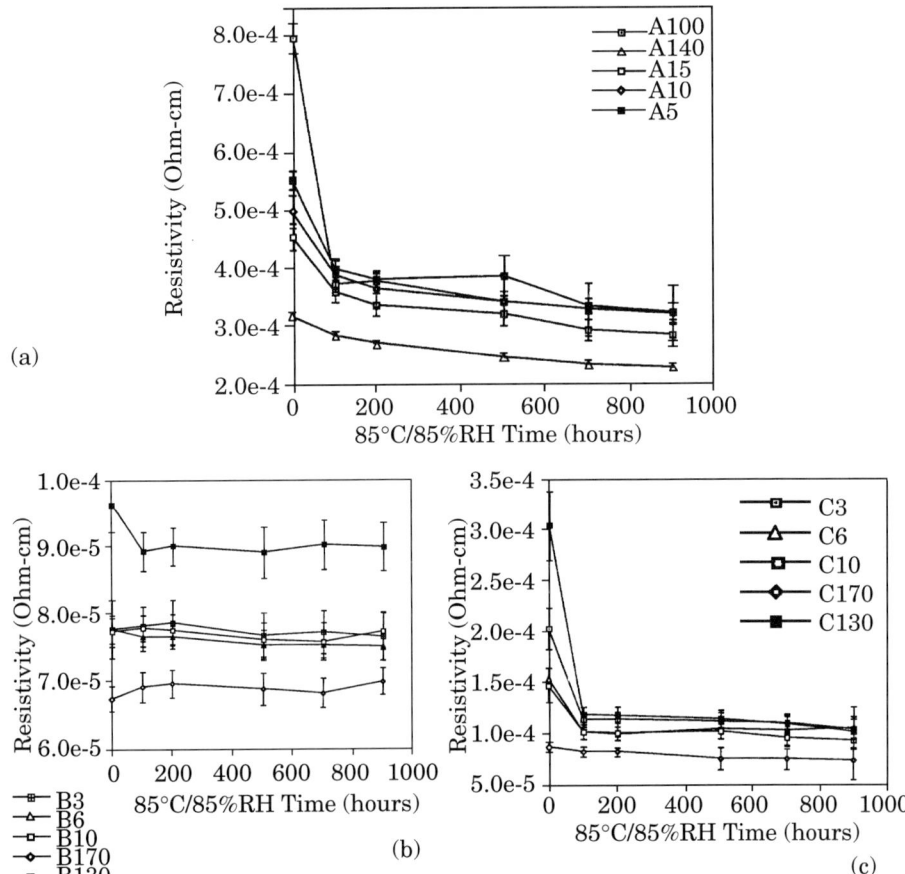

Fig. 5.11 Volume resistivity *vs* 85°C/85%RH exposure time with different cure schedules. (a) Adhesive A; (b) Adhesive B; (c) Adhesive C.

significant influence on resistivity and its stability. Cure time has an effect, but it is secondary in relation to temperature. This is closely related to the cure degree dependence of cure temperature and time. Figure 5.11(b) shows the Adhesive B resistivity change during wet storage. In this case the scale was narrower than in the Adhesive A case. None of the samples show much variation in resistivity upon exposure. The resistivities of the samples cured at 130°C were observed to decrease slightly after 100 hours. The samples cured at 150°C were observed to have very stable resistivities. This suggests that this cure temperature is high enough to produce a stable electrical interconnect structure. Figure 5.11(c) shows resistivity versus humidity for Adhesive C. The larger resistivity variations and decreases during the 85°C/85%RH test are expected as an effect of the under-cure of Adhesive C, which therefore experiences continuing cure while exposed to humidity. Adhesive C cured at 170°C yielded the most stable performance.

5.4   CONCLUSIONS

The cure kinetics of three silver-filled epoxies were studied. The degrees of cure conversion of the materials versus cure time at isothermal cure temperatures were obtained by the simple first- and second-order cure kinetics models developed based on DSC measurement results. Adhesive C has an under-cure schedule suggested by the vendor. The cure kinetics models are useful to provide guidance of the cure schedule selections of the materials to ensure complete cure. The first-order model has proved to be very effective in this particular case. Minimum cure temperature, $T_{c\infty}$, is required to cure the material fully.

A parallel study of a different material, based on the composite auto-catalysed cure model, concluded that complete isothermal cure is not possible, and proposes a dynamic cure sequence instead.[12,17,18] Curve-fitting data provide an interesting 'snapshot' of the temperature dependencies of k_1 and k_2, and of the scatter in m and n (both around one in Reference 17.) Note that, although the simple first-order model gives a good fit to experimental data in the primary work described in this chapter, the auto-catalysis model is required for other materials,[18] and the composite model for others.[17]

Resistivity of the conductive adhesive decreases with increased degrees of cure conversion. Resistivity was found to decrease with higher temperature cures and to a lesser extent with additional cure time. The cure time does not have as great an effect as temperature on the development of electrical properties and their stability. The volume resistivities of the adhesives do not increase during humidity exposure. The resistivity of under-cured samples exposed to 85°C/85%RH decreased with exposure and then stabilised. The mating metallised layer contribution to the total joint resistance is stable under 85°C/85%RH exposure for gold and increases for copper — except in the case of Adhesive B where it is stable for both.

Obviously, the curing issues discussed above also apply to other polymer applications, such as die attach adhesives, where other concerns such as the relationship between stress and cure schedule can be addressed a little more conveniently.[19] Temperature-time cure schedule 'windows' need to be established for conductive adhesives (or supplied by the manufacturers) in a parallel effort to that being undertaken at present for die attach.[20]

REFERENCES

1 Li, L., Lizzul, C., Kim, H., Sacolick, I. and Morris, J. E., 'Electrical, Structural and Processing Properties of Electrically Conductive Adhesives', *IEEE Transactions on Components, Hybrids, and Manufacturing Technology*, **Vol. 16**, No. 8, pp. 843-851, December (1993).

2 Li, L., 'Basic and Applied Studies of Electrically Conductive Adhesives', PhD dissertation, State University of New York at Binghamton (1995).

3 Klosterman, D. and Li, L., 'Conduction and Microstructure Development in Ag Filled Epoxies', Proceedings International Seminar on Conductive Adhesives in Electronics Packaging, Eindhoven, The Netherlands, pp. 5-15, September (1995); *Journal of Electronics Manufacturing*, **Vol. 5**, No. 4, pp. 277-287, January (1996).

4 Wendlandt, W. W., Gallaghet, P. K. and Prime, R. B., in 'Thermal Characterization of Polymeric Materials', Turi, E. A. (editor), Academic Press, New York (1981).

5 Sahimi, M., 'Applications of Percolation Theory', Taylor & Francis, Inc., PA (1994).

6 Enns, J. B. and Gillham, J. K., in 'Polymer Characterization: Spectroscopic, Chromatographic, and Physical Instrumental Methods', Craver, C. D. (editor), American Chemical Society, pp. 27-63 (1983).

7 Ozawa, T., 'Kinetic Analysis of Derivative Curves in Thermal Analysis', *Journal of Thermal Analyses*, **Vol. 2**, pp. 301-324 (1970).

8 Doyle, C. D., 'Estimating Thermal Analysis Stability of Experimental Polymers by Empirical Thermogravimetric Analysis', *Analytical Chemistry*, **Vol. 33**, pp. 77-79 (1961).

9 Kissinger, H. E., 'Reaction Kinetics in Differential Thermal Analysis', *Analytical Chemistry*, **Vol. 29**, pp.1702-1706 (1957).

10 Rorgen, R. and Liu, J., 'Reliability Assessment of Isotropically Conductive Adhesive Joints in Surface Mount Applications', *IEEE Transactions on Components, Packaging, and Manufacturing Technology*, Part B, **Vol. 18**, No. 2, pp. 305-312, May (1995).

11 Du Pont 9000 and 9900 Thermal Analysis Systems, Du Pont Instruments, Thermal Analyzers (1988).

12 Klosterman, D., Li, L. and Morris, J. E., 'Materials Characterization, Conduction Development, and Curing Effects on Reliability of Isotropically Conductive Adhesives', Proceedings 46th Electronic Components & Technology Conference, Orlando, pp. 571-577, May (1996).

13 Miller, B., 'Polymerization Behavior of Silver-filled Epoxy Resins by Resistivity Measurements', *Journal of Applied Polymer Science*, **Vol. 10**, pp. 217-228 (1966).

14 Lovinger, A. J., 'Development of Electrical Conduction in Silver-filled Epoxy Adhesives', *Journal of Adhesion*, **Vol. 10**, pp. 1-15 (1979).

15 Li, L. and Morris, J. E., 'Electrical Conduction Models for Isotropically Conductive Adhesives', Proceedings International Seminar on Conductive Adhesive in Electronics Packaging, Eindhoven, The Netherlands, pp. 35-44, September (1995); *Journal of Electronics Manufacturing*, **Vol. 5**, No. 4, pp. 289-298, January (1996).

16 Li, L., Morris, J. E., Liu, J., Lai, Z., Ljungkrona, L. and Li, C., 'Reliability and Failure Mechanism of Isotropically Conductive Adhesive Joints', Proceedings 45th IEEE Electronic Components & Technology Conference, Las Vegas, pp. 114-120, May (1995).

17 Mei, Y., Wu, S. and Yeh, C., 'Cure Kinetics for Conductive Adhesives', in *EEP*,**Vol. 17**, 'Sensing, Modeling and Simulation in Emerging Electronic Packaging', ASME, pp. 23-27 (1996).

18 Wu, S. X., Zhang, C., Yeh, C., Wille, S. and Wyatt, K., 'Cure Kinetics and Mechanical Properties of Conductive Adhesives', Proceedings 47th IEEE Electronic Components & Technology Conference, San Jose, pp. 550-553, May (1997).

19 Pearson, R. A., Lloyd, T. B., Azimi, H. R., Hsiung, J.-C., Early, M. S. and Brandenburger, P. D., 'Adhesion Issues in Epoxy-based Chip Attach Adhesives', *IEEE Transactions on Components, Packaging, and Manufacturing Technology*, Part A, **Vol. 20**, No. 1, pp. 31-37, March (1997).

20 Hsiung, J.-C. and Pearson, R. A., 'Processing Diagrams for Polymeric Die Attach Adhesives', Proceedings 47th IEEE Electronic Components & Technology Conference, San Jose, pp. 536-543, May (1997).

Chapter 6

CONTACT RELIABILITY MODELLING AND MATERIAL BEHAVIOUR OF CONDUCTIVE ADHESIVES UNDER THERMOMECHANICAL LOADS

SEAN X. WU, KAI X. HU and
CHAO-PIN YEH
Motorola Software Technology Center, Motorola Inc., Illinois, USA

6.1 INTRODUCTION

Polymer-based conductive adhesive materials have become widely used in many electronic packaging interconnect applications, such as tape automated bonding (TAB), chip on glass (COG), chip on ceramic (COC), flip chip on board (FCOB), etc. Using conductive adhesives as interconnect materials offers many distinct advantages over solder alloys, including reduced package size and thickness (finer pitch), improved environmental compatibility, and lowered assembly temperature.[1]

A conductive adhesive (CA) material is typically a composite consisting of a matrix material (normally thermosetting epoxy) and a conducting medium (in the form of particles or flakes) that is dispersed in the matrix material. During component assembly, the epoxy resin is cured to provide mechanical (and sometimes thermal) connection and the conducting medium is utilised for electrical connectivity. The variations from one CA system to another include material compositions and medium treatments (coated or un-coated), curing agents and curing characteristics. These broad variations of a conductive adhesive system, along with variations of substrate, module and perspective metallisations, offer a versatile selection of interconnection configurations.[2] CA materials can be classified into two categories: anisotropic (Z-axis) conductive adhesives (ACA) and isotropic conductive adhesives (ICA). The ACAs provide electrical conductivity in a specific direction, normally in the thickness direction (Z-axis) for conductive films. The ICAs are electrically conductive in all directions and are normally applied in the form of joints as opposed to the anisotropic materials in the form of films.

In Section 6.1, we present a micromechanics approach for conductive adhesive materials. A contact mechanics model is first proposed that addresses pressure-induced conducting mechanisms both for rigid and deformable particle systems. The non-linear thermo-mechanical responses of conductive adhesive materials are then investigated in terms of polymer and particle properties.

One very critical issue for CA materials, that is, the curing physics and characteristics, is addressed in Section 6.3. During the curing process under an elevated temperature and/or UV light, the polymeric molecular crosslink tends to cause a chemical volumetric shrinkage in the CA materials. This shrinkage combined with the thermal expansion mismatch between the CA joints and conducting metal pads can produce considerable post-curing residual stresses in the joints. These residual stresses will continue to evolve during the entire electronic packaging manufacturing processes, such as handling, reliability qualification testing (thermal shock, thermal cycling, humidity, drop, etc.), printed wiring board depanelisation, etc. The distribution and magnitude of such residual stresses can significantly affect the overall thermomechanical, electrical, and further reliability performance of the interconnects. As a result, it is of great interest from a CA manufacturing standpoint, to understand, predict, and optimise the process induced residual stresses in the CA joints. Due to the polymeric characteristics of CAs, they typically possess temperature- and stress-dependent viscoelastic material properties. These non-linear material properties make residual stress and reliability prediction a formidable task. To date, little work has been done in this area. In Section 6.3, a physics-based modelling methodology is proposed to predict the residual stress evolution of the CA joints during the manufacturing process. A realistic, meaningful single component case study is used to demonstrate this methodology. Experiments were first conducted to investigate dimensional and mechanical property changes during the curing process as well as after conductive adhesives have been fully cured. A finite element based model was then developed to incorporate the viscoelastic material properties and curing physics of the CA. Finally, the model was used to demonstrate how the residual stresses could be minimised by optimising manufacturing process parameters.

As CAs become commonly used in component assembly, extensive studies abound in the areas of DC characteristics,[3,4] joint strength/reliability testing,[5] residual stress development,[6] and microstructure based electrical conduction model development.[4] However, little work has been published related to the high frequency, AC impedance characteristics (inductance, resistance, capacitance, etc.) of CA joints when subjected to thermomechanical and/or mechanical loads.[7] From an electrical performance standpoint, it is desirable to ensure impedance stability of electrical signals in the high frequency electronics applications (i.e., crystal oscillators, resonators, etc.). Impedance instability can often cause field failure associated with excessive frequency fluctuations and signal degradation.

In Section 6.4, mechanical strengths and impedance characteristics of CA joints were measured through a systematic test scheme, encompassing three types of tests (bending, shear, and tensile) at different temperatures. It has been found that the joint impedance can change significantly in an indeterministic, probabilistic fashion. The results were sometimes not repeatable even when the same conditions were applied. A hypothesis is proposed to explain this observation.

6.2 ELECTRO-THERMO-MECHANICAL RESPONSES OF ANISOTROPIC CONDUCTIVE ADHESIVE MATERIALS

An extensive body of literature on CAs exists.[8-16] For ACAs, the focus has been on the electrical performance in terms of DC and AC resistance and conductance.

The electrical connectivity in an ACA system is achieved by creating adequate contact surfaces between the metal pads and conducting particles under a predetermined thermomechanical compressive load. It is also observed that two types of conducting mechanisms exist in ACA systems. For a rigid particle system, particles cause conducting pads to indent, thus forming contact adequate surfaces, while for a deformable particle system, the contact surfaces are formed mostly by particle deformation. The definition of rigid and deformable particles will be given later in the deformation analysis.

The electrical contact resistance is a function of the compressive pressure applied during assembly (the force is later removed after epoxy cure).[8,17,18] The force-resistance relationships were studied. Lambert, *et al.*[17] outlined a conceptual design curve that relates the electrical contact and particle deformation. The experimental data for elastomeric polymer-based materials by Fulton *et al.*[8] with conducting columns and by Maalej *et al.*[18] with carbon particles showed an inverse (reciprocal) relationship between contact resistance and applied pressure. Maalej *et al.*[18] further suggested that the resistance decreases with increasing pressure in a logarithmic manner. Such a logarithmic relationship, however, has not been explained on a rigorous analytical basis.

The ACA conductive mechanism can be viewed as an electrical circuit system with many parallel resistive switches (particles), which turn on at a small but different pressure. As the pressure increases, more and more bumps are switched on (make electrical contact), thus decreasing system electrical resistance. A semi-empirical equation exists that relates the resistance to material hardness.[19] This semi-empirical relationship neither provides any contact physics (particle deformation, applied force, etc.) nor details the different contact mechanisms between the rigid and the deformable particle systems.

Another important aspect of a CA system is the thermomechanical performance under reliability qualification testing and field use conditions. The distinction between ACA and ICA becomes vague purely from a thermomechanical response standpoint. An ICA material becomes anisotropic (Z-axis properties different from those in X/Y axes) when the conducting flakes are settled during cure, while an ACA material is essentially in-plane isotropic. The non-linear thermomechanical responses due to particle non-linear deformation are critical for an understanding of the thermomechanical and reliability performance of CA interconnects.

Section 6.2 describes a physics-based micromechanics approach for conductive adhesive materials. A contact mechanics model was first developed to address pressure-induced conducting mechanisms for both rigid and deformable particle systems. The non-linear thermomechanical responses of ACA materials were then investigated using proper polymer and particle material properties. In Section 6.2.2, a deformation analysis that incorporates both the rigid and the deformable particle conducting mechanisms was conducted. Based on this analysis, a physics-based, theoretical force-resistance relationship is established in Section 6.2.2. For linear elastic deformation, a closed-form solution was derived to reveal a logarithmic pressure-resistance relationship. For non-linear plastic deformation, a detailed finite element analysis was conducted. These results provide an analytical foundation for the experimental data obtained by Futon, *et al.*[8] and Maalej, *et al.*[18] Section 6.2.3 further extends this work to develop a uniaxial stress-strain relationship. Section 6.2.4 illustrates the theoretical derivations of an effective coefficient of thermal expansion and thermal stress in an ACA joint. Finally, a brief summary is given in Section 6.2.5.

6.2.1   Deformation Analysis

The deformation-resistance relationship of an ACA joint is derived in this section. The electrical contacts in most CA systems are achieved by simultaneously applying a compressive and a temperature load. The purpose of the compressive load is to make mechanical engagement between conductive particles and metal pads. After the CA joints are cured at an elevated temperature (typically between 120 and 160°C), a permanent, irreversible deformation created by the compressive force will remain in the system to secure electrical contacts. Two types of contact mechanisms are reported: (1) Rigid particle systems, in which the contacts are created through indentation of particles into metal pads; and (2) deformable particle systems, in which particles are squashed to form flat surfaces through which electrical connectivity is made. In the deformable particle mechanism, the metal pads receive little plastic deformation relative to the particles. The rigid particle and rigid metal pad are two extreme, ideal cases. In reality, the contact mechanisms of any ACA material system should be bounded in between these two extreme cases. An examination of such systems will provide enough insight into conducting mechanisms.

As the first step, a single particle system is studied. The schematics of contact mechanisms of a single particle system are shown in Figure 6.1(a) (rigid particle) and 6.1(b) (deformable particle). The multi-particle scenario will be discussed in Sections 6.2.3 and 6.2.4. It should be noted that a conductive joint is typically formed by applying pressure at the curing temperature. During this process, the polymer matrix is in a gelatinous form with virtually no load-carrying capacity. Therefore, in determining the particle deformation, only the metal pads and distributed particles are considered, ignoring the contribution from the epoxy.

In what follows, the two types of conducting mechanisms are treated in a similar fashion. First, the rigid particle system is considered (shown in Figure 6.1(a)). It is assumed that the particle indentation does not change the resistance of the pad metallisation. Given the indentation depths of Δ_1 and Δ_2 in the upper and lower metal pads, respectively, the resistance of the interconnect with the particle radius of r is:

$$R = \int_{-(r-\Delta_1)}^{r-\Delta_2} \rho \frac{dl}{A} = \int_{-(r-\Delta_1)}^{r-\Delta_2} \rho \frac{dl}{\pi(r^2 - 1^2)} = \frac{\rho}{2\pi r} \ln\left[\left(\frac{2}{\varepsilon_1} - 1\right)\left(\frac{2}{\varepsilon_2} - 1\right)\right] \quad (6.1)$$

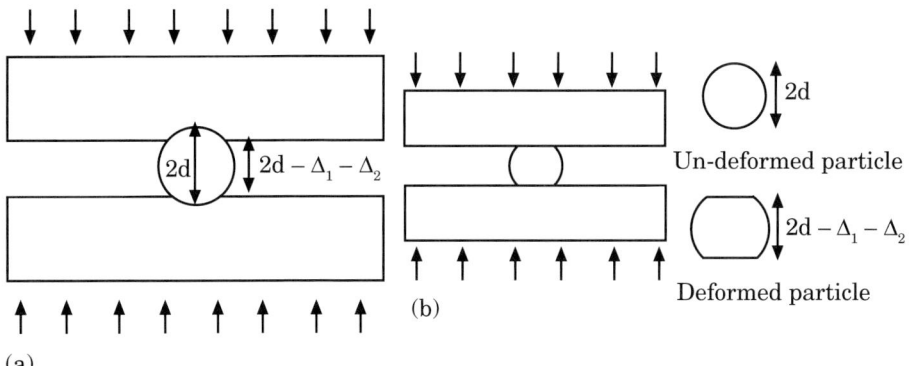

Fig. 6.1 (a) Schematics of a rigid particle system; (b) Schematics of a deformable
particle system.

where ρ is the particle resistivity, $\varepsilon_1 = \Delta_1/r$ and $\varepsilon_2 = \Delta_2/r$. ε_1 and ε_2 measure the
magnitude of particle deformation, and can be interpreted as an overall
particle strain. For small strain, or $\varepsilon_1 \ll 1$ and $\varepsilon_2 \ll 1$, we have:

$$R = \frac{\rho}{2\pi r} \ln\left(\frac{4}{\varepsilon_1 \varepsilon_2}\right) \qquad (6.2)$$

For the case where lower and upper pads have the same amount of deformation
(symmetrical about horizontal plane), $\varepsilon_1 = \varepsilon_2 = \varepsilon$,

$$R = \frac{\rho}{\pi r} \ln\left(\frac{2}{\varepsilon} - 1\right) \qquad (6.3)$$

For the symmetrical and small deformation case:

$$R = \frac{\rho}{\pi r} \ln\left(\frac{2}{\varepsilon}\right) \qquad (6.4)$$

In the case of deformable particles, Equations (6.1) to (6.4) will still be valid
if Δ_1 and Δ_2 now represent the particle deformation in the lower and upper
interfaces, respectively. It should be noted that the cross-sectional area of the
particles is enlarged due to the Poisson's ratio effect in the compressed
conducting particles. The extent of this area enlargement depends on the
cross-sectional location (or x-coordinate). For the purpose of bulky resistance
calculation, it is assumed that area enlargement follows an average Poisson's
law. The deformed area at the location x becomes:

$$A = \pi(r^2 - l^2)\left[1 + \frac{\upsilon(\varepsilon_1 + \varepsilon_2)}{2}\right]^2 \qquad (6.5)$$

where υ is the Poisson's ratio of the particle. Accordingly, Equation (6.1) is modified to account for the effect of Poisson's ratio on the resistance, giving:

$$R = \frac{\rho}{2\pi r \left[1 + \frac{\upsilon(\varepsilon_1 + \varepsilon_2)}{2} \right]^2} \ln\left[\left(\frac{2}{\varepsilon_1} - 1 \right)\left(\frac{2}{\varepsilon_2} - 1 \right) \right] \qquad (6.6)$$

For the symmetrical case, where lower and upper particles are compressed by the same amount:

$$R = \frac{\rho}{\pi r (1 + \upsilon\varepsilon)^2} \ln\left(\frac{2}{\varepsilon} - 1 \right) \qquad (6.7)$$

Equations (6.1) and (6.6) depict the closed-form resistance-deformation relationships for the rigid and the deformable particle systems. Under a deformation-controlled loading scheme, these equations can be used to estimate how much deformation is required to attain a desirable level of contact resistance. In real life assembly practices, however, the deformation-controlled scheme can hardly be the case due to the fact that: (1) the particle deformation can not be easily estimated from applied deformation; and (2) precise deformation control is very difficult to achieve. One would always prefer to know the amount of compressive force necessary to achieve a desirable contact. In the next section, these equations will be used as an intermediate step to obtain the force-resistance relationship.

6.2.2   Force-Resistance Relationship

A force-resistance relationship is derived based on the deformation analysis presented in Section 6.2.2. This is done by solving the contact mechanics problem to obtain the force-deformation relationship. The force-deformation relationship can then be substituted into appropriate resistance equations to derive the desired force-resistance relationship. In the following, a standard elastic contact solution is utilised to give closed-form solutions for both the rigid and deformable particle cases. More generic elastic-plastic contact solutions are given using the finite element method.

Consider an elastic spherical particle with Young's modulus of E_0, and Poisson's ratio of υ_0, in contact with the upper and the lower metal pads with Young's moduli of E_1 and E_2, and Poisson's ratio of υ_1 and v_2. The metal pads are assumed to be infinitely extended. The contact load, P, is applied to the upper pad and the particle. The solution under a small, linear, elastic deformation with a sliding contact boundary condition was given by Hertz[20] and Juvinall:[21]

$$\Delta_1 = \sqrt[3]{\frac{9}{16r}\left(\frac{1 - v_0^2}{E_0} + \frac{1 - v_1^2}{E_1} \right)P^2} \qquad (6.8a)$$

and

$$\Delta_2 = \sqrt[3]{\frac{9}{16r}\left(\frac{1-v_2^2}{E_2} + \frac{1-v_0^2}{E_0}\right)P^2} \qquad (6.8b)$$

Substituting Equation (6.8) into Equation (6.6) gives:

$$R = \frac{2\rho}{3\pi r}\ln\left[\frac{P_0}{P}\right] \qquad (6.9)$$

where P_0 bears a force unit, and depends on particle size and material properties,

$$P_0 = \frac{8\sqrt{2r^2}}{3\sqrt{\left(\frac{1-v_0^2}{E_0} + \frac{1-v_1^2}{E_1}\right)\left(\frac{1-v_2^2}{E_2} + \frac{1-v_0^2}{E_0}\right)}} \qquad (6.10)$$

Two special cases are considered below.

Case (1) Elastic solutions — rigid particle case
In the case of rigid particles, the Young's modulus, E_0, becomes infinite and Equations (6.8) and (6.10) can be simplified into Equations (6.11) and (6.12).

$$\Delta_1 = 3\sqrt{\frac{9}{16r}\left(\frac{(1-v_1^2)P}{E_1}\right)^2} \quad \text{and} \quad \Delta_2 = 3\sqrt{\frac{9}{16r}\left(\frac{(1-v_2^2)P}{E_2}\right)^2} \qquad (6.11)$$

$$P_0 = \frac{8\sqrt{2r^2}}{3}\sqrt{\left(\frac{E_1}{1-v_1^2}\right)\left(\frac{E_2}{1-v_2^2}\right)} \qquad (6.12)$$

Case (2) Elastic solutions — rigid pad metal case
For the rigid pad metal case, the particle is compressed and the amount of deformation in the upper part of the particle equals that in the lower part of the particle. The deformation can be determined by the following equations:

$$\Delta_1 = \Delta_2 = 3\sqrt{\frac{9}{16r}\left(\frac{(1-v_0^2)P}{E_0}\right)^2} \qquad (6.13)$$

where P_0 is given as:

$$P_0 = \frac{8\sqrt{2r^2}}{3}\left(\frac{E_0}{1-v_0^2}\right) \qquad (6.14)$$

Other combinations of material properties, e.g., rigid metal pad on the top or on the bottom only, etc., can also be derived in a similar fashion.

Next, the effects of pressure on the electrical resistance are re-examined in the context of contact mechanics. It should be noted that, from the published experimental investigations,[8,17,18] the resistance is directly related to applied pressure. While this correlation has a direct physical interpretation, it does not provide insight in terms of vital design/fabrication parameters, such as particle volume/weight ratios, material selections, etc. These parameters are very important to the overall manufacturablity, yield and reliability of an ACA interconnect system. For example, one would expect a less compressive force to achieve a desirable contact resistance level with a low particle volume ratio rather than a high particle volume ratio. To put the volume ratio of particles into perspective, it is recalled that Equation (6.9) provides only the force per particle. Assuming that the adhesive thickness is equal to the particle diameter, one can relate the total pressure to the force per particle:

$$p = \frac{3c_p P}{2\pi r^2} \tag{6.15}$$

where C_p is the particle volume ratio. The pressure-resistance relationship becomes:

$$R = \frac{2\rho}{3\pi r} \ln\left[\frac{3c_p P_0}{2\pi r^2 p}\right] \tag{6.16}$$

It is observed that, for the same applied pressure, the less loaded particle system gives better resistance performance per particle. This conclusion appears to be markedly different from the common belief. In fact, the total resistance of a CA film is obtained through parallel connections of all the individual particles. That is:

$$\frac{1}{R_{tot}} = \sum \frac{1}{R} = \frac{N_{tot}}{R} = \frac{3c_p A}{2\pi r^2 R} \tag{6.17}$$

where A is the area of the film.

$$R_{tot} = \frac{4r\rho}{9c_p A} \ln\left(\frac{p_0}{p}\right) \tag{6.18}$$

where p_0 bears a pressure unit and is related to the force exerted by a single particle.

$$p_0 = \frac{3c_p P_0}{2\pi r^2} \tag{6.19}$$

Equations (6.16) and (6.18) reveal that, while increasing the particle volume will generally reduce the overall resistance, the resistance per particle base will also increase for a given pressure.

6.2.2.1   ELASTO-PLASTIC SOLUTIONS

It is known that both the particles and/or the pads will experience plastic deformation during the assembly process. It is crucial that this plastic deformation will sustain permanently so as to provide electrical contact after cure. Also, the distinction between the rigid particle and the deformable particle systems is most appropriately defined in terms of plastic deformation. In a rigid particle system, the particle deformation is limited to elastic and a large part of deformation is due to plasticity in metallisation. In a deformable particle system, however, the deformation of pad metallisation is limited to the elastic regime and a large part of deformation is due to plasticity in particles. In both cases, it is the plastic portion of the total deformation which makes the greatest contribution to the permanent electrical contacts because the elastic deformation, in principle, should recover after cure.

To simplify the analysis, a single particle system (the same system shown in Figure 6.1(a) or 6.1(b)) is considered as an axisymmetric problem. The elastic properties are as follows:

- The upper and lower pads are aluminium and copper with Young's moduli of 70 GPa and 132 GPa, and Poisson's ratio of 0.35 and 0.34, respectively.
- The silver particles with Young's moduli 77 GPa, Poisson's ratio 0.30 with particle diameter of 15 μm.
- For the rigid particle case, the bilinear plasticity of metallisations is considered with yield stress of 36 MPa for aluminium, 56 MPa for copper, secondary slope of 6 GPa for aluminium and 10 GPa for copper.
- For the deformable particles, the bilinear plasticity of particles is considered with a particle yield stress at 172 MPa for aluminium and a secondary slope at 7 GPa.

The system is subjected to a uniform displacement of 6 μm at the upper pad. The deformation fields of the rigid particle case and the deformable particle case are shown in Figures 6.2(a) and 6.2(b), respectively. Also considered are the real conductive adhesive systems with all the associated materials under an assumption of plastic deformation. The deformation and stress fields for the real material system are shown in Figure 6.2(c).

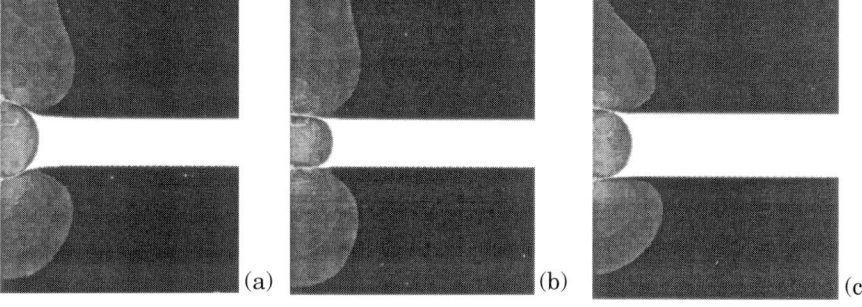

(a)   (b)   (c)

Fig. 6.2 Deformation distribution of different particle systems: (a) rigid particle system; (b) deformable particle system and (c) fully deformable system.

To obtain the force-resistance relationship, the prescribed displacement is gradually applied in several load steps. The resultant force at each load step is calculated. The deformation for the deformable particle case can be extracted from the finite element analysis, as can the pad metallisation for the rigid particle case. The force-deformation relationship can be derived directly and the force-resistance relationship can be obtained through Equations (6.6) and (6.9). The force-resistance and force-deformation relationships for a single particle system are shown in Figure 6.3 for the rigid particle case and in Figure 6.4 for the deformable particle case. For design considerations the level of applied force should be chosen from these curves in such a way that the particle deformation should be confined to ensure the mechanical integrity of the interconnect, but should be large enough to achieve a good electrical contact.

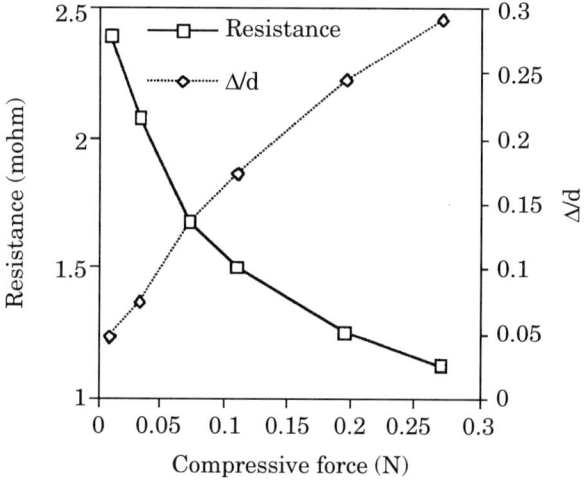

Fig. 6.3 Force-resistance-deformation relationship for a rigid particle system.

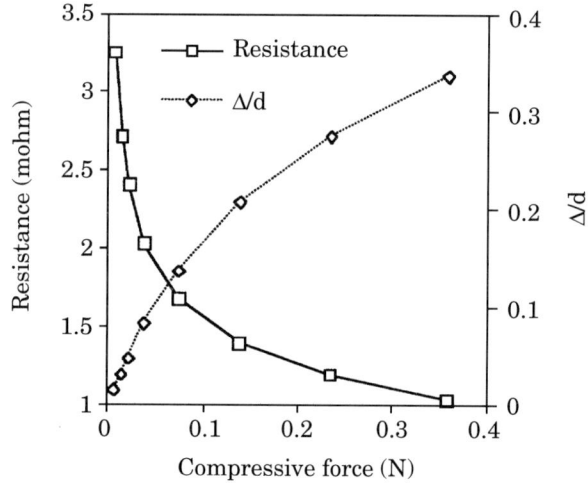

Fig. 6.4 Force-resistance-deformation relationship for a deformable particle system.

This chapter has so far considered the force-resistance relationship only for a single particle under compression. In fact, Equation (6.8) applies to a general system with the restriction that all the particles in the system are assumed to sustain the same amount of forces and the effects due to particle interactions on the deformation behaviour are negligible. To examine the effects of particle interactions, a system with two closely spaced double particles is considered. The distribution of system deformation is shown in Figure 6.5. As the external pressure continues to increase, the particle surfaces will eventually make contact with each other. Following the same procedure as in the single particle case, it was found that the force-resistance relationship per particle base scarcely changes with more than 94% concurrence of contacts with the single particle results.

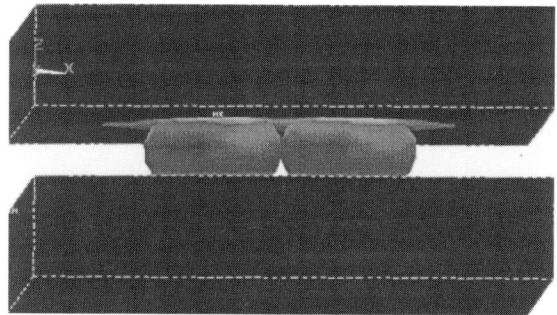

Fig. 6.5 Deformation distribution of multiple particle systems.

6.2.3   Non-linear Stress-strain Relationship

The mechanical response, or stress-strain relationship for post-cure ACAs is considered in this section. The system is a dual-phase composite material, with conductive particles dispensed in the matrix material. Non-linear stress-strain behaviour for composite materials and similarly for polycrystal materials has been studied by several researchers.[22-24,29] In the following text, a micromechanics approach, the Mori-Tanaka method[23,25-27] will be used to investigate the non-linear behaviour of CA materials. The approach presented here follows an approach similar to that proposed by Weng[23] but in a much simpler manner with the interpretation of the micromechanics model. In addition, this approach can accommodate material behaviour where non-linearity can appear instantaneously with no preceding linear elastic deformation. In pursuit of non-linear composite behaviour, the Mori-Tanaka solution is utilised for an auxiliary problem, in which an inclusion embedded in the matrix material is subjected to yet-to-be-determined average matrix stress fields in the real composite arising from a designated load. The uniaxial stress-strain is taken as the case study here. Assume that the stress-strain behaviour of conductive particles can be presented as:

$$\sigma_p = f_p(\varepsilon_p) \tag{6.20}$$

and that the stress-strain behaviour of matrix material is:

$$\sigma_m = f_m(\varepsilon_m) \tag{6.21}$$

Let a representative volume of composite material with a particle volume fraction of c_p be subjected to a remote stress, σ. This gives rise to the (volumetric) average stress and strain of $\bar{\sigma}_m$ and $\bar{\varepsilon}_m$ in the matrix material and $\bar{\sigma}_p$ and $\bar{\varepsilon}_p$ in the conductive particles. The average strain in the composite is given as:

$$\bar{\varepsilon}_c = (1-c_p)\bar{\varepsilon}_m + c_p\bar{\varepsilon}_p \tag{6.22}$$

It can be shown that the average stress in the composite material is precisely the remote stress, σ, regardless of the stress-strain behaviour of the matrix and particle materials. That is,

$$(1-c_p)\bar{\sigma}_m + c_p\sum(\bar{\sigma}_m) = \sigma \tag{6.23}$$

where $\sum(\bar{\sigma}_m)$ is the average particle stress, expressed as a function of the average matrix stress. Therefore, to determine the composite stress-strain relationship, one can simply obtain the values of $\bar{\varepsilon}_c$ for a given remote stress, σ. It is observed that, through Equations (6.20), (6.21) and (6.22):

$$\bar{\varepsilon}_c = (1-c_p)f_m^{-1}(\bar{\sigma}_m) + c_p f_p^{-1}(\bar{\sigma}_p) \tag{6.24}$$

If the average particle stress ($\bar{\sigma}_p$) and the average matrix stress ($\bar{\sigma}_m$) can be related to the remote stress, σ, Equation (6.24) provides the stress-strain solution. It is first noted that, if one can relate the average stress in matrix material ($\bar{\sigma}_m$) to the average particle stress ($\bar{\sigma}_p$) through a function Σ,

$$\bar{\sigma}_p = \sum(\bar{\sigma}_m) \tag{6.25}$$

via Equation (6.23), we can have:

$$(1-c_p)\bar{\sigma}_m + c_p\sum(\bar{\sigma}_m) = \sigma \tag{6.26}$$

Inversely, if a remote stress, σ, is given, Equations (6.24), (6.25) and (6.26) can be used to calculate the average composite strain ($\bar{\varepsilon}_c$), the average particle stress ($\bar{\sigma}_p$), and the average matrix stress ($\bar{\sigma}_m$). These equations should provide the complete stress-strain relationship for the composite except for the correlation between the average matrix stress and the average particle stress.

In general, all the particles in the composite are surrounded by the matrix material, and the particle stress varies from particle to particle due to the particle-particle and the particle-matrix interactions. The Mori-Tanaka method[27] recognised that, for a composite material under a remote stress, the average particle stress can be approximated by enclosing a single particle in an infinitely extended matrix material, subject to the average matrix stress.

This treatment allows one to simplify a complex problem involving particle-particle and particle-matrix interactions into a single particle problem. Equation (6.25) can now be obtained with a little computational effort. For linear elastic problems, Equation (6.25) is given in a closed form. Since the present focus is on the non-linear response, a simple finite element analysis suffices for the task.

As a numerical example, an epoxy-based silver particle system is considered. It is assumed that the post-cure epoxy follows a linear elastic stress-strain relationship and silver particles can be either elastic, or, more likely, plastic, depending on the assembly processes, testing, and/or service conditions. For instance, under a typical -55°C to 125°C air-to-air thermal cycling test, particles can experience significant plastic deformation. The non-linear stress-strain curves are shown in Figure 6.6. When the particle volume ratio increases, the rigidity of the systems increases accordingly. The assumption that the epoxy material behaves elastically explains why the cross-over point of these curves occurs at an unrealistically high strain (6%). In reality, the epoxy matrix should have reached its yield strength long before the strain approaches 6%.

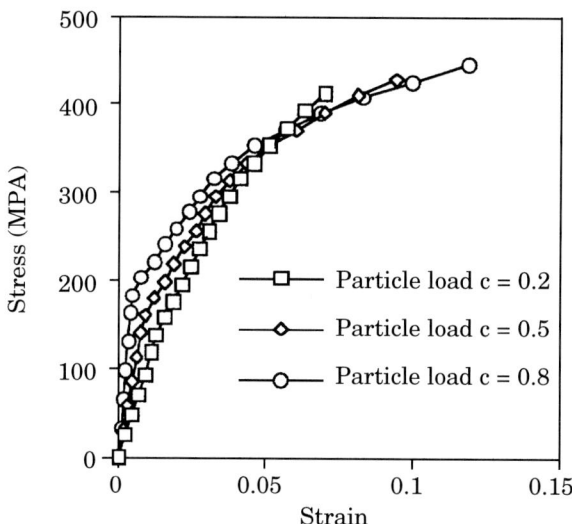

Fig. 6.6 Uniaxial non-linear stress-strain curves for a silver-filled epoxy system.

It is also noted that the Mori-Tanaka method utilised here has certain limitations. Although the method offers adequate accuracy for most CA systems, in which the particle volume ratio is less than 90% and the shear modulus ratio of particle to matrix falls between 0.5 and 100[25-28], accuracy starts to decrease significantly as particles become almost rigid (very high ratio of particle to matrix shear modulus) or become a void.[30-32]

6.2.4 In-plane Effective Coefficient of Thermal Expansion and Thermal Stress

The effective thermal coefficient of expansion (CTE) and the thermal stress for ACA systems under a temperature excursion are considered in this section. When an ACA system is subjected to a net temperature change, ΔT, relative to the reference state, the volumetric change is, at the composite level:

$$\varepsilon_{ij}^c = 3\bar{\alpha}\Delta T \delta_{ij} \tag{6.27}$$

The average strain, viewed from two individual phases, the particles and the matrix, is given as:

$$\varepsilon_{ij}^c = c\varepsilon_{ij}^i + (1-c)\varepsilon_{ij}^m \tag{6.28}$$

Assume that the matrix material behaviour obeys the linear elastic law and the non-linearity of the ACA system stems solely from the plasticity of conducting particles. The stress-strain relationship for the matrix is:

$$\varepsilon_{ij}^M = \frac{1+v_M}{E_M}\sigma_{ij}^M - \frac{v_M}{E_M}\sigma_{kk}^M\delta_{ij} \tag{6.29}$$

and the total stress-strain form for particles can be given as:

$$\varepsilon_{ij} = \frac{1}{2G}\sigma_{ij} - (\frac{v_1}{E_1}\sigma_{kk} - \alpha_1\Delta T)\delta_{ij} + \varepsilon_{ij}^p \tag{6.30}$$

The plastic strain, ε_{ij}^p, is related to deviatoric stresses, S_{ij}. The effective stress, σ_e, and the effective plastic strain, ε_p, (the notation is slightly different from Section 6.2.3 with ε_{ij}^p reserved for plastic strain) are determined by Hencky's Law:[33]

$$\varepsilon_{ij}^p = \frac{3S_{ij}}{2\sigma_e}\varepsilon_p \tag{6.31}$$

Following the same reasoning as in Equation (6.23), the average stress in the composite due to the temperature change is zero. Hence,

$$c\sigma_{ij}^I + (1-c)\sigma_{ij}^M = 0 \tag{6.32}$$

It is important to note that the plasticity does not contribute to the volumetric strain. After substituting Equations (6.29) and (6.30) into Equation (6.28), representing all the stresses through Equation (6.32), and comparing Equation (6.27) with (6.28), one has:

$$\bar{\alpha} = c\alpha^I + (1-c)\alpha^M + \frac{c}{3}\left(\frac{1}{K^M} - \frac{1}{K^I}\right)\frac{\sigma^I}{\Delta T} \tag{6.33}$$

Similar to the procedures described in Section 6.2.4, the key to obtaining the effective CTE of the CA systems then relies on the solution of the average stress in the particle phase, providing a proper mechanism to account for inclusion interactions. This, again, can be accomplished through the Mori-Tanaka method.

6.2.5   Discussion and Summary

Pressure-induced conducting mechanisms were investigated first. The deformation analysis reveals a logarithmic pressure-resistance relationship and is capable of addressing the conducting phenomena for both rigid and deformable particle systems within a contact mechanics framework. It is observed that electrical contacts are made by squashing conducting particles for a deformable particle system while the particle penetration creates a crater in metallisation to make contacts for a rigid particle system. The current analysis provides simple closed-form solutions for the elastic deformation of single-particle contacts and, based on the assumption that the contact forces are evenly distributed in a conductive film, the pressure-resistance responses are correlated to the particle volume fraction. The high volume fraction, while ensuring that there is a sufficient number of particles to make contacts, may limit the particle deformation due to overall increased stiffness, resulting in increased resistance on a per particle basis. The current analysis also offers insight into design considerations whereby a limited amount of deformation (low processing temperature) and sufficiently low electrical resistance are to be simultaneously satisfied. For mechanical performance, a uniaxial non-linear stress-strain relationship is obtained for conductive adhesive systems in terms of polymer and particle material properties. The Mori-Tanaka method is utilised to account for particle-particle and particle-matrix interactions. The thermal expansion behaviour within the elasto-plastic deformation range is also obtained in a similar fashion. In all these calculations, only a very simplified finite element analysis of the problem of a particle embedded in an infinitely extended matrix material needs to be carried out.

6.3   PROCESS INDUCED RESIDUAL STRESSES IN ISOTROPIC CONDUCTIVE ADHESIVE (ICA) JOINTS

CA is a complex composite material system. Like many polymeric materials, CA demonstrates highly non-linear viscoelastic behaviour (stress relaxation and creep) under thermal and thermomechanical loadings. This behaviour can cause serious reliability problems over time. Although many reliability assessment studies of various CA systems have been conducted,[3-5,14] few have addressed the issues concerning the evolution of process induced residual stresses. These issues, which can be critical to the long-term reliability of CA interconnects, include: (1) the underlying mechanisms that cause process induced residual stresses to develop; (2) how to develop a physics-based predictive model, allowing calculation of the process-induced residual stresses; and (3) how to minimise residual stresses through proper selection of design and process parameters such as curing temperature profile. Due to the polymeric characteristics of conductive adhesives, such a prediction model must take into account the viscoelastic material properties.

This section describes experiments conducted to investigate dimensional and mechanical property changes during the curing process as well as after conductive adhesives have been fully cured. A thermomechanical analyser (TMA) and a dynamic mechanical analyser (DMA) were used to measure dimensional changes and to study the viscoelastic properties of fully cured adhesives, respectively. Mechanical measurements were conducted at different temperatures with different frequencies to characterise the viscoelastic characteristics. The results were converted from the frequency domain into the time domain (temperature dependent) to obtain relaxation moduli, which were incorporated into a finite element analysis code. Finally, a finite element analysis was then conducted for a ceramics component structure that is attached to a printed wiring board (PWB) using CA as a case study. The analysis took into account not only the CTE mismatches between different materials, but also elastic, viscoelastic, curing properties to investigate the residual stress development and stress relaxation in the CA joints.

6.3.1 Thermomechanical Material Properties Characterisation for Conductive Adhesives

A thermomechanical analyser (TMA) was used to investigate the dimensional change of the conductive adhesive during and after curing. A rheometrics dynamic spectrometer (RDS II) was used to obtain the viscoelastic material properties of the conductive adhesive.

Specimens and Procedure

The conductive adhesive specimens were cured with a dynamic temperature scan. The dimensional change during the curing process was monitored with the TMA. The temperature range was from 25°C to 250°C with a rate of 10°C/min. The dimensions of specimens were about 4.0 mm by 4.0 mm by 1.0 mm. These specimens were subjected to two separate heating cycles. The first heating cycle was to cure the specimens. The second heating cycle was to obtain the thermal expansion of the fully cured specimens. This two-cycle heating approach has been proven to be valid from previous tests which showed that the specimens became fully cured after the first heating cycle.

For mechanical characterisation tests, the CA specimens were placed in two parallel metal plates and subjected to a cyclic torsional loading. A temperature sweep test was conducted to characterise and obtain the mechanical properties during the cure, followed by a temperature/frequency sweep test to obtain the post-cure mechanical properties. The temperature range for all these tests was from 25°C to 250°C with a rate of 10°C/min with the sweep frequency ranging from 0.1 Hz to 63 Hz. The dimension of the specimens was about 4 mm in radius by 1.5 mm in thickness.

Results

Figure 6.7 shows the dimensional change in CA specimens. During the first heating cycle, the dimensional change was due to thermal expansion and chemical shrinkage. It can be seen that the thermal expansion dominates the dimensional change in the early stage of the first heating cycle. When the temperature reaches a certain level, the cure reaction starts and chemical shrinkage becomes more dominant. The maximum shrinkage occurs at around 150°C, after which the thermal expansion again dominates the dimensional change. Since the slopes of the curves for both the first and the second heating cycles are almost the same at temperatures exceeding 160°C, it can be assumed that the chemical shrinkage plays an insignificant rôle in this temperature range. With the tests conducted, it is very difficult, if not impossible, to differentiate accurately the contributions in dimensional change due to chemical shrinkage from those due to thermal expansion as thermal expansion for uncured and cured material is likely to be different. However, for the purpose of calculating the residual stresses developed during the cure, there is no need to separate these two contributions. It is the absolute dimensional change, or the strain, that contributes to the overall stress distributions.

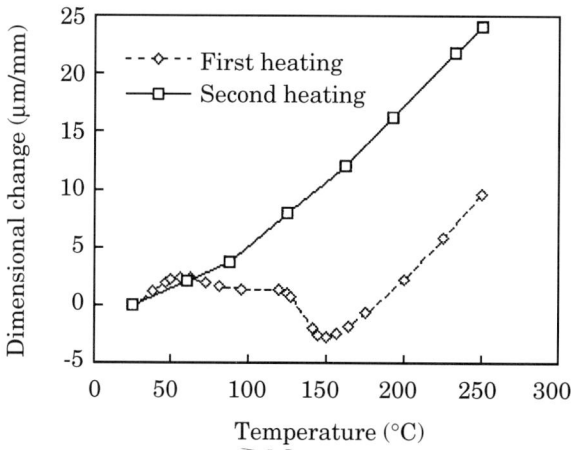

Fig. 6.7 Dimensional change of conductive adhesive.

Figure 6.8 shows the dynamic shear modulus change with temperature during the curing process. In the early stage of the cure, the Young's modulus

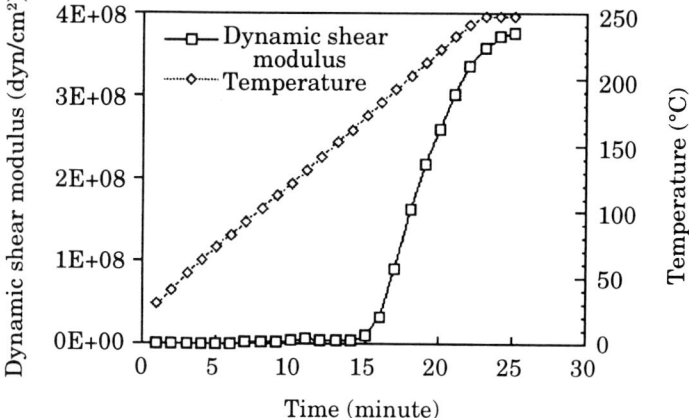

Fig. 6.8 Dynamic shear modulus of conductive adhesive during cure.

of the CA stays at a very low level (in the order of MPa). As the temperature reaches about 100°C, the modulus starts to increase significantly. Contrasting with the dimensional change, the modulus increases continuously with a temperature rise. Figures 6.9 and 6.10 show the modulus as a function of temperature and frequency for fully cured adhesive. The frequency sweep data were used to obtain the relaxation modulus as described in the next section.

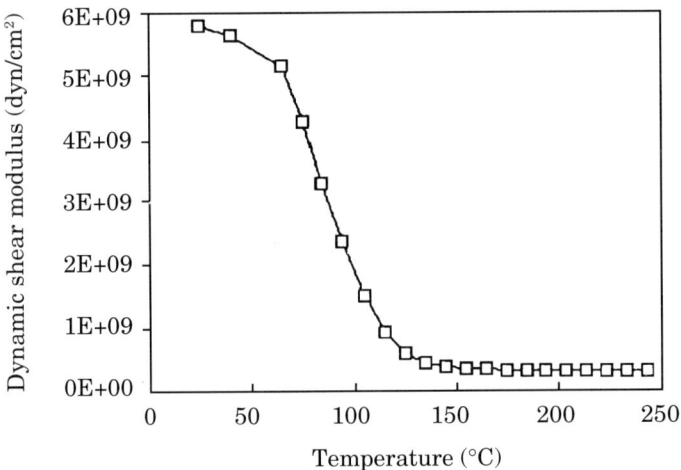

Fig. 6.9 Dynamic shear modulus as a function of temperature and frequency for fully cured conductive adhesive.

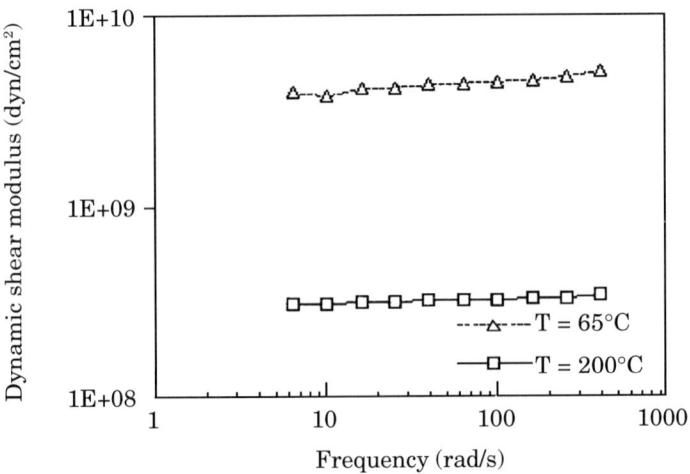

Fig. 6.10 Frequency sweep data of conductive adhesive.

6.3.2   Viscoelastic Behaviour of Conductive Adhesives

For polymeric materials, the constitutive relation can be expressed as:[34]

$$\sigma_{ij} = \int_0^t G_{ijkl}(t-\tau) \frac{d\varepsilon_{kl}(\tau)}{d\tau} d\tau \tag{6.34}$$

where s_{ij} and e_{ij} are stress and strain tensors, respectively; G_{ijkl} is modulus; t is real time; and τ is material time. For isotropic linear materials, the modulus can be expressed in the following discrete form:

$$G(t) = G_e + \sum_{i=1}^{n} g_i \exp\left(-\frac{t}{\lambda_i}\right) \tag{6.35}$$

where G_e is the equilibrium modulus; λ_i is the ith relaxation time; and g_i indicates the relaxation strength of the ith relaxation mode. The storage modulus, G', and loss modulus, G'', from the dynamic tests can be formatted into a similar format:

$$G' = G_e + \sum_{i=1}^{n} g_i \frac{(\omega\lambda_i)^2}{1+(\omega\lambda_i)^2} \tag{6.36}$$

$$G'' = \sum_{i=1}^{n} g_i \frac{(\omega\lambda_i)^2}{1+(\omega\lambda_i)^2} \tag{6.37}$$

where ω is the frequency.

With the experimental data from the dynamic tests, the relaxation spectrum can be determined. Figures 6.11 and 6.12 show the relaxation

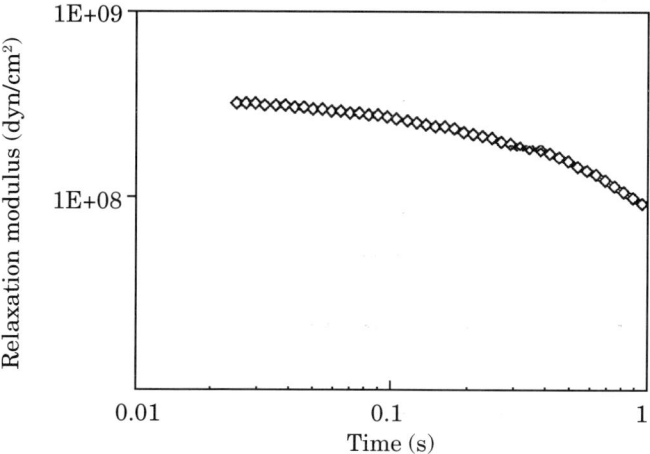

Fig. 6.11 Relaxation modulus at a temperature of 250°C.

modulus at 25°C and 250°C. It can be seen that the stresses relax very rapidly at a high temperature while the stress relaxation at room temperature is moderate.

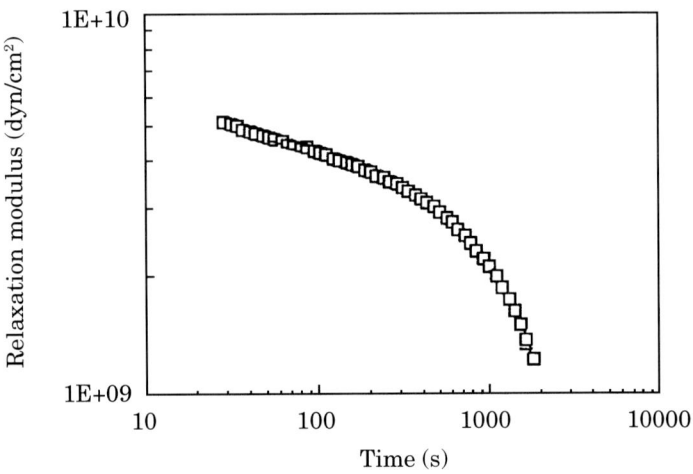

Fig. 6.12 Relaxation modulus at a temperature of 25°C.

6.3.3   Finite Element Model

Geometric Model and Boundary Conditions
   To determine the residual stress evolution during the cure, the finite element method was adopted. As a simple, yet meaningful example, a finite element model was constructed for a ceramic component package mounted on a PWB with CA joints. Due to the geometrical symmetry, only half of the structure was modelled. The geometry was discretised using the 2D plane strain isoparametric elements. The left edge of the finite element model is a symmetry plane and is constrained in the X direction (refer to Figure 6.13).

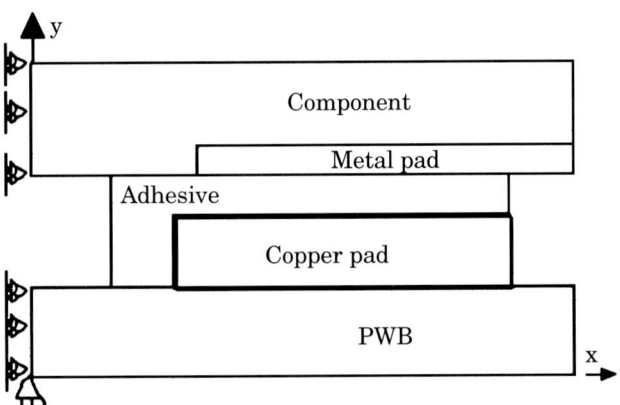

Fig. 6.13 Schematic drawing of geometric model.

A single node at the mid plane on the bottom surface was constrained in the Y direction to prevent rigid body movements. The structure was then subjected to isothermal temperature loads at different process steps. Figure 6.14 shows a partial mesh of the CA joint. Figure 6.15 shows the temperature profile.

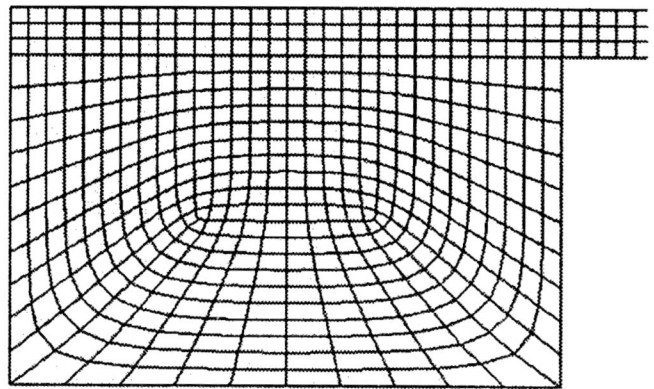

Fig. 6.14 Partial mesh of the adhesive joint.

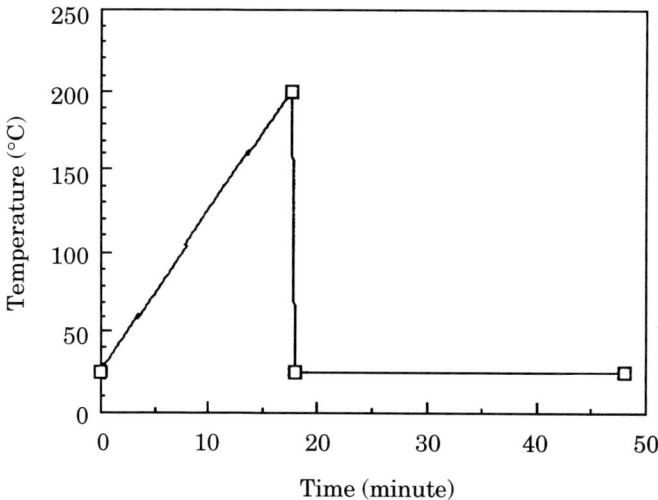

Fig. 6.15 Temperature profile.

Material Properties

Materials used in the structure include ceramics, metallisation (pads on ceramics), CA, copper (pads on the PWB), and PWB. All the materials were assumed to be linear, elastic, and isotropic except the CA, which was treated as a viscoelastic material. Table 6.1 lists the material properties used in the analysis.

Table 6.1

Material Properties used in the Finite Element Analysis

Material	Properties
Ceramics	Elastic modulus = 370 GPa
	Poisson's ratio = 0.25
	CTE = 6 ppm/°C
Conductive adhesive	Modulus — see Figures 6.8 to 6.14
	Poisson's ratio = 0.35
	CTE — see Figure 6.7
Copper	Modulus = 105 GPa
	Poisson's ratio = 0.34
	CTE = 17 ppm/°C
PWB	Modulus = 14 GPa
	Poisson's ratio = 0.25
	CTE = 23 ppm/°C

Finite Element Analysis Results

Figure 6.16 shows the Von Mises stress distribution in the CA joint. The high stresses are located in the areas close to the free edges of the CA joint and the interfaces between adhesive/ceramics (Location A), adhesive/board (Location B), and adhesive/ceramics (Location C).

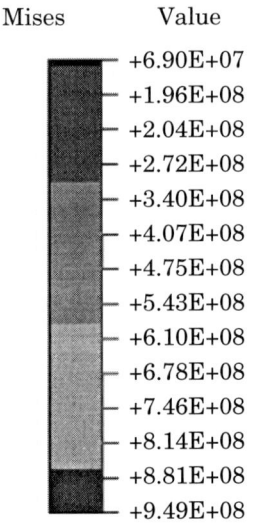

Mises	Value
	+6.90E+07
	+1.96E+08
	+2.04E+08
	+2.72E+08
	+3.40E+08
	+4.07E+08
	+4.75E+08
	+5.43E+08
	+6.10E+08
	+6.78E+08
	+7.46E+08
	+8.14E+08
	+8.81E+08
	+9.49E+08

Fig. 6.16 Von Mises stress distribution in the adhesive joint.

Because the CA changes phases from a gelatinous (liquid) to a solid state during curing, one of the critical tasks in computing the stress/strain in the CA joints was to determine the reference state, i.e., up to what temperature and time can the CA joints still be treated as a stress/strain free state? One obvious choice is the beginning of the heating cycle at room temperature (see Figure 6.15). With this choice, the entire strain and stress fields during the evolution of curing can be computed. However, this is not necessarily a correct selection because there is virtually no stress build-up in the early curing stage when the Young's modulus of the CA is very small. In the early stage of the first heating when the curing process takes place (from room temperature to about 125°C), it is observed that the overall dimensional change is small (see Figure 6.7). Note that, even though the epoxy has a much higher CTE than the copper (approximately 17 ppm°C), the thermal expansion mismatch induced stress is small due to the fact that the increase in overall dimensional change (thermal expansion plus chemical shrinkage) is comparable to that of the copper pad. In addition, in the early curing process, the high viscoelastic properties of the CA will most likely cause most of the stresses/strains to relax, similar to a metal alloy annealing process.

For these reasons, it would not be appropriate to take the starting point of the heating cycle as the reference state. Instead, two other cases were considered. In the first case (referred to as Case 1 hereafter), it is assumed that, before the contribution from the chemical shrinkage starts to outweigh that of the thermal expansion and the elastic modulus of the CA starts to build up, the CA is in the stress-free state. In the second case (referred to as Case 2 hereafter), it is assumed that, before the temperature reaches 240°C, the structure is in the stress-free state and the first heating cycle has no effects on the residual stress development. The reasoning for the latter assumption is that, at a high temperature, the CA exhibits strong viscoelastic behaviour. Any stress built up in the curing process will be relaxed quickly.

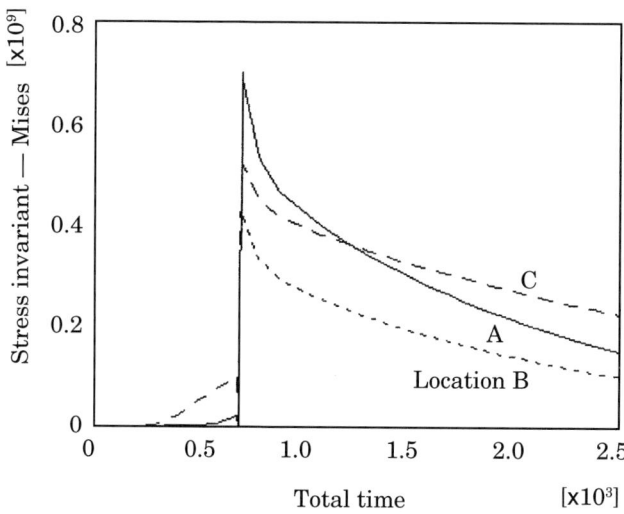

Fig. 6.17 Stress development of Case 1.

While this assumption may be valid, it, however, neglects the effects of the initial strain in the final stress state. Nevertheless, this assumption was used for one of the following case studies. Figures 6.17 and 6.18 show the

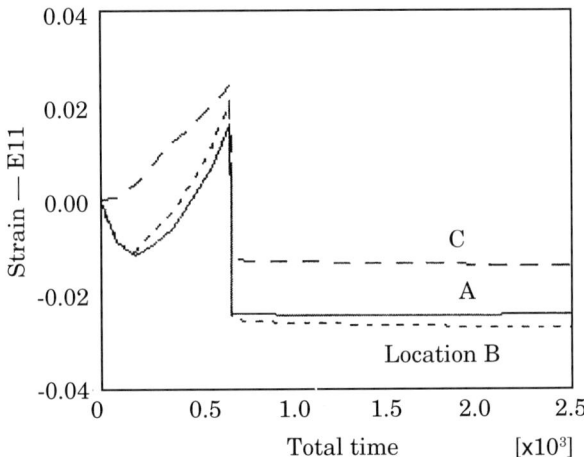

Fig. 6.18 Strain development of Case 1.

development of stresses and strains in the CA for Case 1. Figures 6.19 and 6.20 show the development of stresses and strains for Case 2. In both cases, the stress relaxation occurs very quickly. Within 30 minutes, the maximum stress decays by 50%. It can also be seen that the maximum stress values in Cases 1 and 2 are different. The differences are due to different reference temperatures. In Case 2, the stresses are over-estimated owing to the assumption that the structure is stress-free at 240°C.

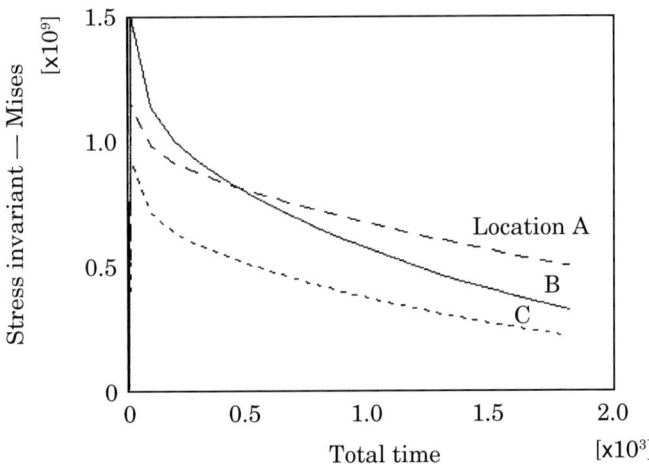

Fig. 6.19 Stress development of Case 2.

Apparently, the residual stresses can be reduced if the cure temperature can be lowered. In fact, this approach has been used in some CA applications. However, simply reducing the cure temperatures alone does not provide a sufficient solution because, even though most chemical reactions have been completed and dimensional change has been stabilised, the mechanical

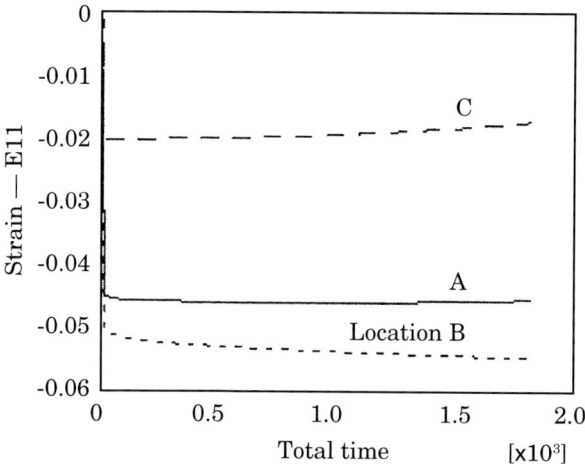

Fig. 6.20 Strain development of Case 2.

properties may still be far from their final values (see Figure 6.8). A better cure schedule will be to promote chemical reaction at a low temperature, then to ramp temperature up to a certain level in which the chemical reaction for the development of mechanical properties will be completed. Since minimum, if any, chemical shrinkage is expected during the temperature ramp, it will not contribute much to the residual stresses in the CA joints. To determine the ramp rate and the final temperature, studies are required for various applications because they depend not only on the adhesive itself, but also on the size and the thermal properties of the materials.

It is interesting to learn that, for both cases, the locations of the maximum stresses continue to evolve with time even when temperature is held constant. The evolution in locations is due to the change in the stiffness ratio between the CA joint and adjacent materials. The ratio change causes stress/strain redistribution in the structure. For the same reason, it is not surprising to see that the stresses in the metal pads (in the area close to the adhesive) increase slightly when held at room temperature (see Figure 6.21). It should

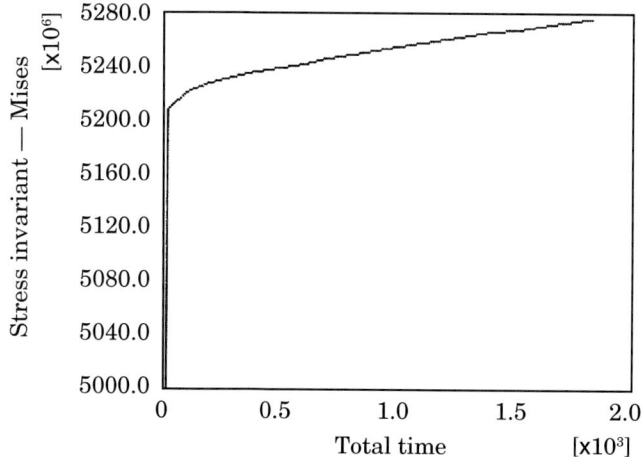

Fig. 6.21 Stress change in the metal pad.

be pointed out that the changes in strain at room temperature are not from creep strains but from the stress/strain redistribution.

In this study, only linear viscoelastic properties were considered. If non-linear viscoelastic properties were to be considered, the results may be slightly different because the relaxation rate will depend not only on time and temperature but also on stress.

6.3.4   Discussion and Summary

Experiments have been conducted to investigate the dimensional change and mechanical properties change during and after the curing process of conductive adhesive. The viscoelastic properties of the conductive adhesive were converted from frequency domain into time domain and were incorporated into the FEA code for analysis. The results indicate that the conductive adhesive has strong viscoelastic characteristics which have to be taken into account when analysing residual stresses in adhesive joints.

The finite element analysis results also indicate that the determination of the stress-free state of a structure with conductive adhesive joints is very important. Incorrect selection of this stress-free state can lead to erroneous stress and strain estimation in the structure. Based on the experimental and numerical analysis data, it is recommended that the chemical reaction be triggered at a lower temperature, then temperature be ramped up to a higher level in order to obtain the desired material properties and reduce process-induced residual stresses.

6.4   HIGH FREQUENCY CHARACTERISATION OF CONDUCTIVE ADHESIVE JOINTS UNDER MECHANICAL AND THERMOMECHANICAL LOADING

The high frequency characterisation described in this section includes a systematic experimental approach, coupled with finite element analyses.

6.4.1   Experimental Procedures

Experimental Set-up
The experimental set-up is shown in Figure 6.22. A component (crystal oscillator) is attached to a PWB with two CA joints. An impedance analyser

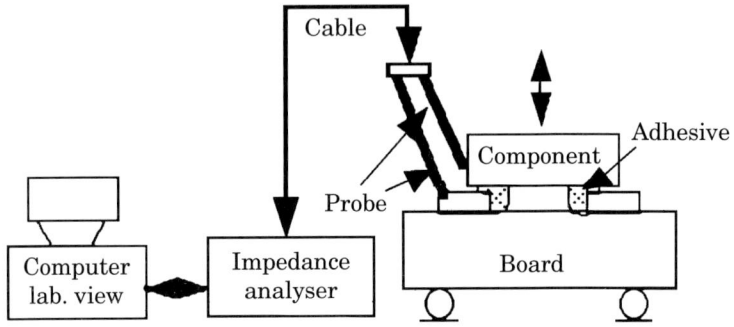

Fig. 6.22 Schematic experimental set-up.

is used to measure the impedance of a conductive adhesive joint across two probe pads, one on the component side and one on the PWB side. An automatic test program is created to control the impedance analyser and to collect experimental data via a GPIB interface card in a PC. Data are taken at intervals of one second.

Two test vehicles were developed and tested in this study. In Test Vehicle I, a component was mounted on a board with CA joints. The test vehicle was then placed in an MTS uniaxial tester and subjected to a simple mechanical load (bending or shear) at room temperature. Two types of mechanical loads were applied to the specimens: monotonic and cyclic. A typical loading profile is shown in Figure 6.23. As the mechanical load is being applied, impedance in the CA joint can be monitored simultaneously. The frequency for the impedance measurement was 10 MHz.

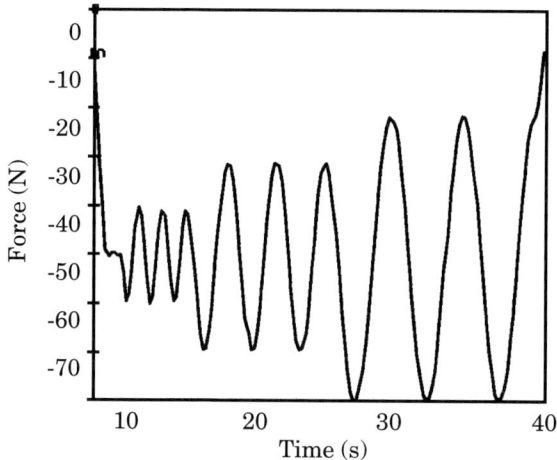

Fig. 6.23 Typical mechanical loading profile.

In Test Vehicle II, two circular copper rods with identical diameter were joined at the ends with a CA joint (see Figure 6.24). To isolate the test vehicle electrically from the MTS machine, a ceramic nut was used to hold one end of the copper rod. A systematic test scheme was developed and carried out

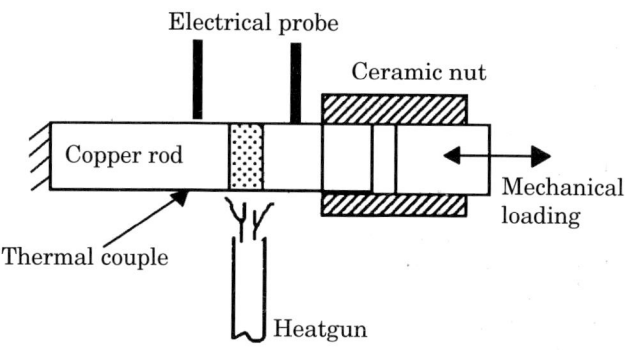

Fig. 6.24 Test vehicle II.

with three types of loading: (1) mechanical (i.e., tensile, shear, bending); (2) thermal (temperature); and (3) combined mechanical and thermal, or thermomechanical loading. The specimen temperature was monitored with a thermal couple. When only the thermomechanical loading was applied, the temperature increased from room temperature to 220°C. When mechanical loading was applied, the highest temperature was limited to the glass transition temperature (T_g) of the CA. For both test vehicles, a preliminary test was conducted to determine the maximum loading that the CA joint can sustain without a failure. The purpose is to determine the appropriate loading in the cyclic loading.

Sample Preparation
In Test Vehicle I, a component with two metal pads on the bottom was attached to a PWB with the CA joints. The joints were cured at 150°C for one hour. The wire length between the probe pad and the joint is approximately 2 mm.

In Test Vehicle II, two circular rods were spliced co-linearly together with a CA joint. The thickness of the adhesive was measured and controlled to a fixed value with a caliper. Any overflowed CA was carefully removed so that it was flush with the rod edges. The prepared vehicle was then placed in an oven to cure the adhesive. Proper co-linear alignment of the two copper rods is crucial during mechanical testing because a slight misalignment can either cause significant errors in the test results or result in premature specimen breakage during specimen mounting.

Three parameters which may affect the impedance of adhesive joints were studied with Test Vehicle II. These parameters are: adhesive thickness (12.5, 50.8, and 101.6 μm); rod diameter (3 and 5 mm); and cure schedule. Three schedules were used to cure the adhesive: 1 hour at 150°C (normal cure), 10 minutes at 150°C (under cure), and 2 hours at 250°C (over cure). After the cure, samples were cooled to room temperature.

6.4.2　Experimental Results

Test Vehicle I Test Results
Figures 6.25 and 6.26 show typical impedance responses under cyclic bending and shear loads, respectively. It can be seen that both resistance and conductance are relatively stable throughout the bending tests. On the other hand, in the shear test, the resistance changes by a small amount whereas the conductance virtually remains the same. Overall, no strong correlation between the stresses and the impedance was observed in both the bending and the shear tests at room temperature with the experimental set-up as shown in Figure 6.22.

Finite Element Analysis for Test Vehicle I
A separate finite element analysis was conducted. The results show that the strain distributions in the CA joint under the bending loads are quite complicated and non-uniform (see Figure 6.27). The strain distributions in the Y direction (perpendicular to the PWB) are in a tensile state in the middle portion of the CA joint but are in a compressive state at both ends of the joint.

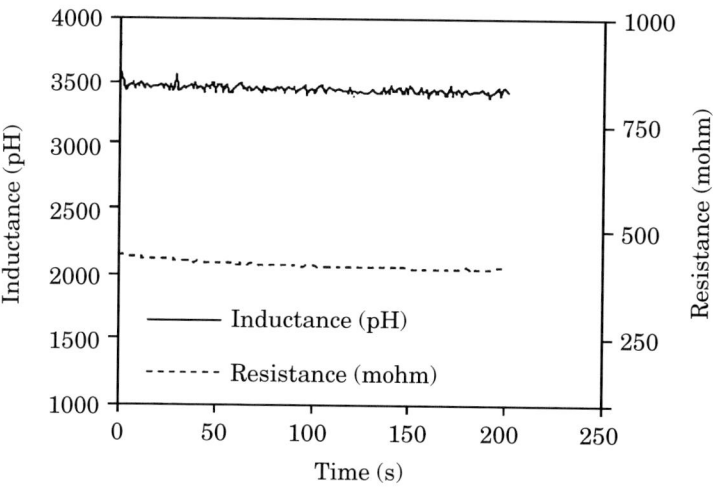

Fig. 6.25 Impedance change during bending test.

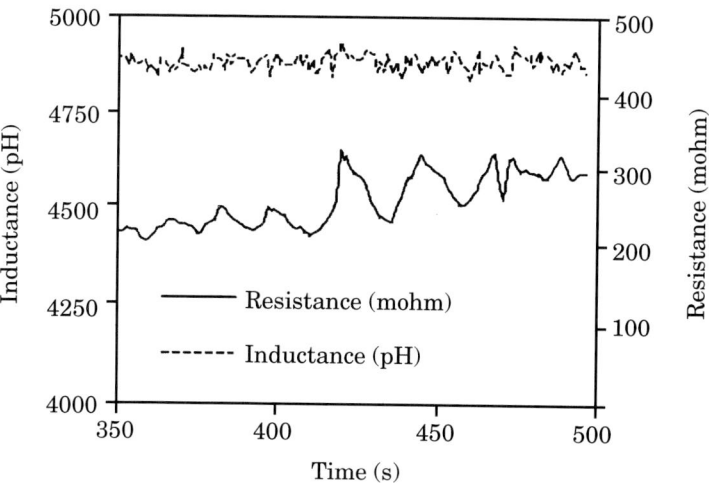

Fig. 6.26 Impedance change during shear test.

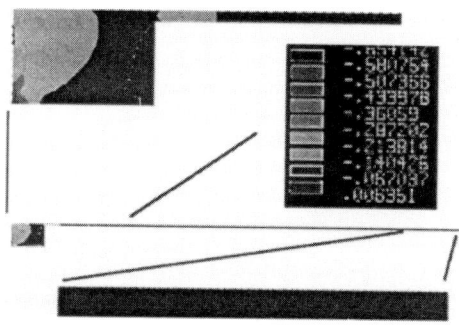

Fig. 6.27 Strain distribution in the CA joint under bending tests.

As discussed in the next section, the CA strain, especially when in the tensile state, is a more influential parameter than the CA stress from the electrical performance standpoint. These experimental results should not lead to the conclusion that the impedance fluctuation of conductive adhesive joints does not depend on mechanical loading.

Test Vehicle II Test Results

Figure 6.28 shows the tensile test (cyclic loading) results at room temperature. Again, neither resistance nor inductance shows a strong correlation between the impedance fluctuation and the mechanical loading.

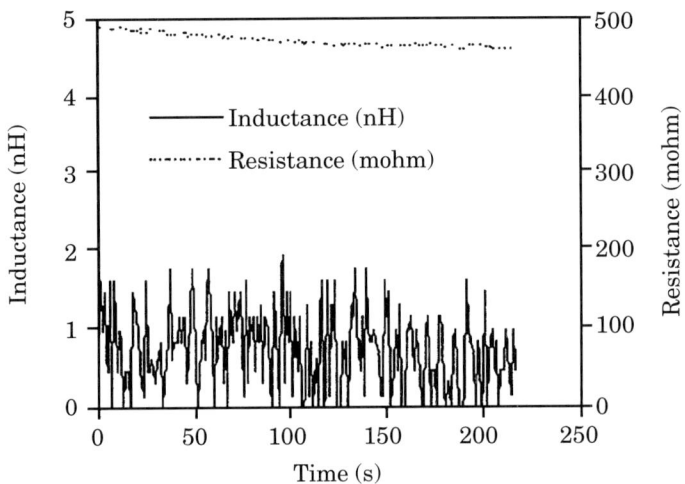

Fig. 6.28 Impedance change during tensile test at room temperature.

Figures 6.29 and 6.30 show the inductance changes for under-cured and over-cured specimens (2 mil thick), respectively. The specimens were subjected

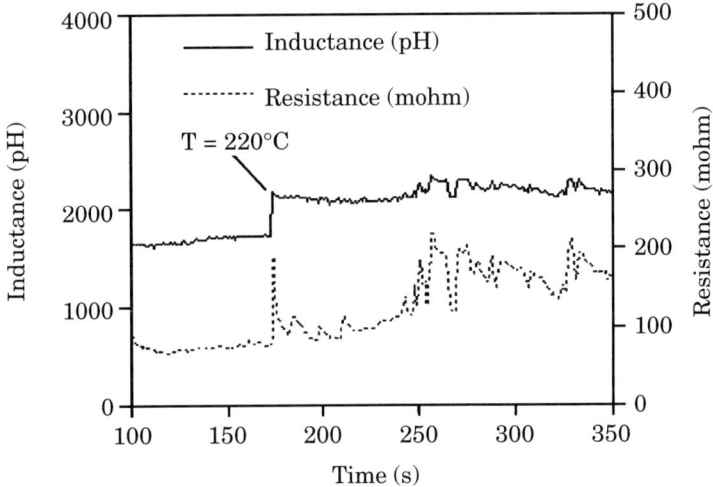

Fig. 6.29 Temperature effects on the impedance of the over-cured CA joint.

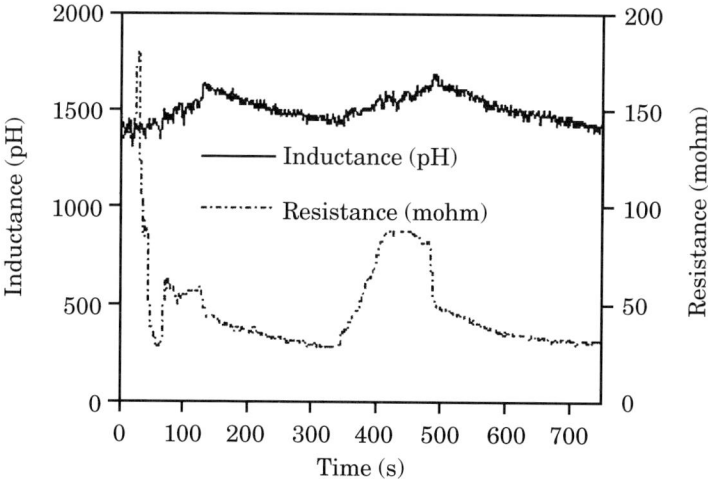

Fig. 6.30 Temperature effects on the impedance of the under-cured CA joint.

to only thermal loading (see Figure 6.31 for the temperature profile). The under-cured specimens were subjected to two heating cycles (the CA is fully cured after the first cycle) and the over-cured specimens were subjected to only one heating cycle. For the under-cured specimens, an instability zone of inductance and resistance exists at the beginning of the first heating cycle. Beyond this zone, both parameters increase with temperature. For the over-cured specimens, on the other hand, no such instability zone exists at the beginning of the heating cycle. Both the inductance and the resistance are relatively stable and do not change until the temperature reaches 220°C. When the temperature is kept at 220°C, there is a jump in inductance (~0.5 nH). This may be due to the degradation of the adhesive since it is over-cured. Although the jump is not huge, it does raise electrical and reliability performance concerns in real product applications where the surface mounted reflow temperature typically reaches as high as 230°C.

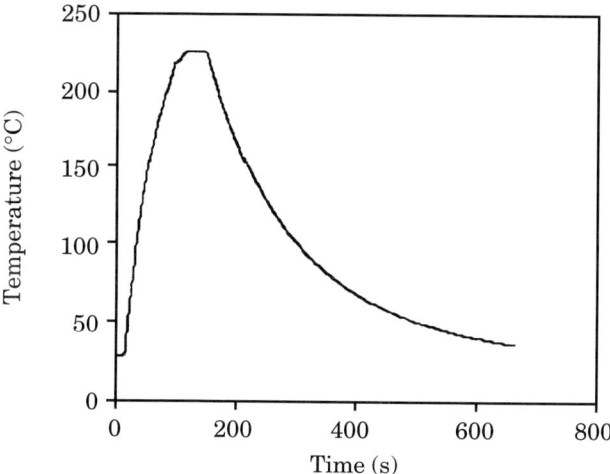

Fig. 6.31 Typical temperature profile.

Another test was also conducted for the under-cured specimens. A specimen was first heated to 220°C, then dipped into liquid nitrogen (LN$_2$) at -170°C for about 30 to 60 seconds. No abnormal impedance change was observed even though the CA joint experienced a dramatic thermal stress. It should be noted that the CA tends to shrink when dipped into the LN$_2$.

Of the twenty normally cured specimens, the inductance changes in the majority of the specimens were similar when subjected to a thermal loading (see Figure 6.32). The inductance increased approximately 0.3 nH when the

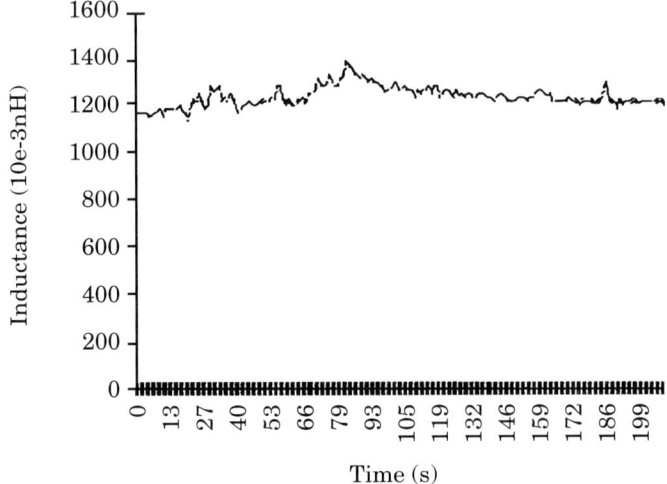

Fig. 6.32 Temperature effect on the inductance of the CA.

temperature increased from room temperature to 220°C. The same trend was observed for all three different CA joint thicknesses and two different joint diameters, indicating that either the thickness or diameter alone has a minimum impact on the electrical performance. There are two exceptions, however. For these cases, the impedance became unstable when temperature reached the high end. Furthermore, the CA joint changed from inductive to capacitive at about 130°C during the cooling down stage. The capacitance oscillated for a certain period of time, then asymptotically approached 1.4 pF. Instead of decreasing with temperature, the resistance started to increase at the transition point from inductive to capacitive. At room temperature, the resistance reached 1.5 ohm.

Postulation

It is postulated that this phenomenon is due to the change in the interface between the copper and the CA. The capacitance, C, between two parallel plates obeys[35] the following equation:

$$C = e \; A/d \tag{6.38}$$

where e is the permissivity constant. The permissivity of the polymer materials is about 26.655 x 10^{-12} Fm^{-1}. A is the area of the plate. With 5 mm diameter specimens, A = 1.963 x 10^{-5} μm^2. d is the distance between plates.

It has been observed that, in the area close to the metal pad, silver flakes tend to align in parallel with the pad. A detailed examination under a microscope indicates that the real contact area between the pad and the flakes accounts for only a tiny portion of the total pad surface area. Assume that only 1% of the copper surface is in contact with the flakes (A is approximately 1.963×10^{-7} μm^2). In order to obtain a 4 pF capacitance, the distance needs to be 1.3 mm. When the temperature rises far above the glass transition temperature of the epoxy resin, the mismatch in thermal expansion between the flakes and epoxy within the adhesive becomes much more prominent. At an elevated temperature, the epoxy resin expands much more than the silver flakes because the epoxy has a higher CTE and a lower modulus than those of the silver flakes. Especially in the area close to the interface, the stress/strain induced by the CTE mismatch can reach a maximum. It is possible to cause the flakes to separate from the copper. However, to observe a capacitive CA joint, all the flakes need to be completely separated from the copper pads. The probability of this occurring is low. This explains the sporadic occurrence of the capacitive CA joints when subjected to a temperature increase.

At low temperature, however, the epoxy, which becomes stiffer, tends to contract, which bring flakes close to each other and to the metal pads, thus enhancing the flake-to-flake and the flake-to-pad contact conditions. It is understandable that no capacitive CA joint is found because the contact between the flakes and the metal can be preserved better when the CA joint is dipped into LN_2. For the same reason, a capacitive CA joint is unlikely to occur in the bending test because some portion of the joint is always in a compressive state.

In brief, when the normal strain in the CA joint at the interfaces is in a tensile state, the possibility of disconnections between flakes and flakes as well as between flakes and pads will be enhanced. This may explain why electrical performance degrades in the CA joints under such loading conditions.

In the case of thermal and mechanical loading, both the thermal and the mechanical loads were applied in a sequential manner. In one test, a tensile force (100 Newton) was first applied, followed by a temperature increase. The specimen broke at the T_g of the CA material. In another test, the specimen was first heated to around the T_g, and a force was subsequently applied with a rate of 5 Newton/second. In this case, the specimen also broke. The purpose of these tests was to investigate the effect of loading sequence on the electrical characteristics of CA joints. In total, three specimens were tested. Figure 6.33 shows the impedance time history during a test where a mechanical load was applied first. When the specimen began to experience an elevated temperature, there was a disturbance in resistance. Furthermore, heating did not change either the resistance or the inductance until the specimen was about to break. When the specimen broke, the inductance increased suddenly, and then dropped to zero.

6.4.3   Discussion and Summary

In this section, the AC electrical performance (impedance) of an isotropic conductive adhesive joint was characterised at high frequency under various mechanical and thermal loading combinations. A stress/strain finite element

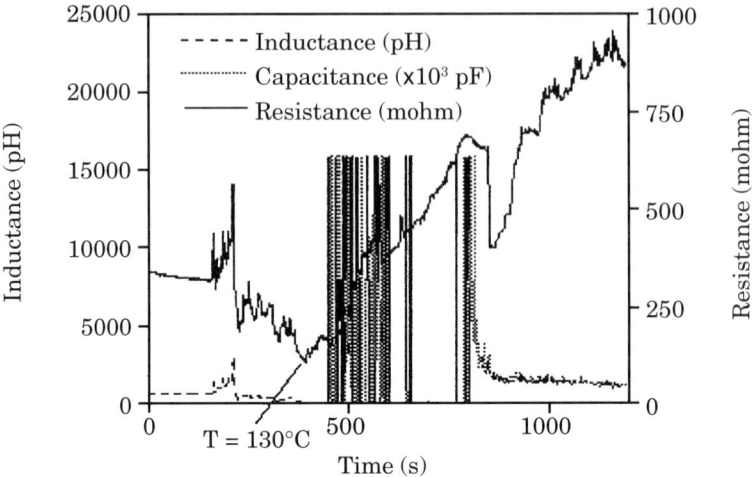

Fig. 6.33 Impedance of a CA joint.

analysis was conducted as an attempt to correlate the stress/strain field with the impedance fluctuation observed in the tests. The thickness and the diameter of the CA joints alone do not affect the electrical performance. However, either over-cure or under-cure of the CA joints may give rise to unstable electrical characteristics. At a high temperature, due to the large, non-uniform deformation of the adhesive between epoxy resin and flakes near the adhesive/pad interfaces, the flakes may disengage from the copper pads with a small distance, resulting in undesirable impedance changes and frequency shifts.

6.5   ACKNOWLEDGEMENTS

The authors gratefully acknowledge the co-operation of Steve Wille, Ted Lind, Xinyu Dou, Gary Mui, and Karl Wyatt of Motorola, Inc., for their helpful discussions and suggestions.

REFERENCES

1   Ogunjimi, A. O. *et al.*, 'A Review of The Impact of Conductive Adhesive Technology on the Interconnection', *Journal of Electronics Manufacturing*, **Vol. 2**, No. 3, p. 109 (1992).

2   Whalley, D. C. *et al.*, 'A Comparison of the Behavior of Isotropic and Anisotropic Conducting Adhesives', *Manufacturing Aspects in Electronic Packaging*, **PED-Vol. 65** (1993).

3   Keusseyan, R. L. *et al.*, 'Electric Contact Phenomena in Conductive Adhesive Interconnects', *International Journal of Microcircuits and Electronic Packaging*, **Vol. 17**, No. 3, p. 236 (1994).

4   Li, L. *et al.*, 'Electric, Structure and Processing Properties of Electrically Conductive Adhesives', *IEEE Transactions on Components, Hybrids, and Manufacturing Technology*, **Vol. 16**, No. 8, p. 843 (1993).

5   Liu, J., 'Reliability of Surface-Mounted Anisotropically Conductive Adhesive Joints', *Circuit World*, **Vol. 19**, No. 4, p. 4 (1993).

6   Wu, S. X. *et al.*, 'Process Induced Residual Stresses in Conductive Adhesive Joints', Proceedings Second International Conference on Adhesive Joining and Coating Technology in Electronics Manufacturing, Stockholm, Sweden, p. 133 (1996).

7   Otsuka, K., 'High Frequency Characterization of Conductive Adhesive and Its Interconnection Technology Trend in Japan', Proceedings Second International Conference on Adhesive Joining and Coating Technology in Electronics Manufacturing, Stockholm, Sweden, p. 114 (1996)

8   Futon, J. A. *et al.*, 'Electrical and Mechanical Properties of a Metal-Filled Polymer Composite for Interconnection and Testing Applications', Electronic Component Technology Conference (ECTC), pp. 71-77 (1989).

9   Chung K., Dreier, G., Fitzgerald, P., Boyle, A., Lin, M. and Sager J., 'Z-axis Conductive Adhesive for TAB and Fine Pitch Interconnects', ECTC, pp. 345-354 (1991).

10 Basavanhally, N. R., Chang, D. D., Cranston, B. H. and Segar, S. G., Jr., 'Direct Chip Interconnect with Adhesive Conductor Films', *IEEE Transactions on CHMT.*, **Vol. 15**, pp. 972-976 (1992).

11 Buratynski, E. K., 'Thermomechanical Modeling of Direct Chip Interconnection Assembly', ASME, **Vol. 115** pp. 382-391 (1993).

12 Chang, D. D. *et al.*, 'An Overview and Evaluation of Anisotropically Conductive Adhesive Films for Fine Pitch Electronic Assembly', *IEEE Transactions on Components, Hybrids, and Manufacturing Technology*, **Vol. 16**, No. 8, pp. 828-835 (1993).

13 Rak, S., Oaken, A., Ostrem, F., Petrites, M., Polak, T. and Schieleit, D., 'Electrically Conductive Adhesives — Effects of Different Platings on Electrical and Mechanical Strength Properties', Proceedings Summer Motorola AMT Symposium, pp. 545-552 (1994).

14 Klosterman, D. *et al.*, 'An Investigation of the Conductive Metal Interfaces in Ag Filled Adhesives', Proceedings of the First International Conference on Adhesive Joining Technology in Electronics Manufacturing, Berlin (1994).

15 Klosterman, D. and Li, L., 'Conduction and Microstructure Development in Ag Filled Epoxies', Proceedings International Seminar on Conductive Adhesives in Electronics Packaging, Eindhoven, Netherlands, pp. 5-15 (1995).

16 Huang, Y. and O'Malley, G., 'Electrical Characterization of Anisotropic Conductive Adhesive', Proceedings Winter Motorola AMT Symposium, pp. 257-263 (1995).

17 Lambert, W. R., Mitchell, J. P., Suchin, and Futon, J. A., 'Use of Anisotropically Conductive Elastomers in High Density Separable Connectors', ECTC, pp. 99-106 (1989).

18 Maalej, N. *et al.*, 'A Conductive Polymer Pressure Sensors', Proceedings IEEE Engineering in Medicine & Biology Society 10th Annual International Conference, pp. 770-771 (1988).

19 Holm, R., 'Electrical Contacts', 4th Edition, Springer Verlag, New York (1967).

20 Hertz, H. R., *J. Reine Angew. Math. (Crelle's J.)*, **Vol. 92**, pp. 156-171 (1881).

21 Juvinall, R. C., 'Engineering Considerations of Stress, Strain and Strength', McGraw-Hill, New York (1967).

22 Hutchinson, J. W., 'Bounds and Self-Consistent Estimates for Creep of Polycrystalline Materials', Proceedings of the Royal Society, A 348, pp. 101-123 (1977).

23 Weng, G. J., 'The Theoretical Connection between Mori-Tanaka's Theory and the Hashin-Shtrikman-Walpole Bounds', *International Journal of Engineering Science*, **Vol. 28**, pp. 1111-1120 (1990).

24 Bao, G., Hutchinson, J. W. and McMeeking, R. M., 'The Flow Stress of Dual-phase, Non-hardening Solids', *Mechanical Materials*, **Vol. 12**, pp. 85-94 (1991).

25 Taya, M. and Chou, T.-W., 'On Two Kinds of Ellipsoidal Inhomogeneities in an Infinite Elastic Body: An Application to a Hybrid Composite', *International Journal of Solids Structures*, **Vol. 17**, pp. 553-563 (1981).

26 Weng, G. J., 'Some Elastic Properties of Reinforced Solids with Special Reference to Isotropic Containing Spherical Inclusions', *International Journal of Engineering Science*, **Vol. 22**, pp. 845-856 (1984).

27 Mori, T. and Tanaka, K., 'Average Stress in Matrix and Average Elastic Energy of Materials with Misfitting Inclusions', *Acta Metallurgica*, **Vol. 21**, pp. 571-583 (1973).

28 Benveniste, Y., 'A New Approach to the Application of Mori-Tanaka's Theory in Composite Materials', *Mechanical Materials*, **Vol. 6**, pp. 147-157 (1987).

29 Huang, Y., Hu, K. X., Wei, X. and Chandra, A., 'A Generalized Self-Consistent Mechanics Method for Composite Materials with Multiphase Inclusions', *Journal of Mechanical and Physical Solids*, **Vol. 42**, pp. 491-504 (1994).

30   Christensen, R. M. , 'A Critical Evaluation for a Class of Micro-Mechanics Models', *Journal of Mechanical and Physical Solids*, **Vol. 38**, pp. 379-404 (1990).

31   Hu, K. X., Chandra, A. and Huang, Y., 'Multiple Void-crack Interaction', *International Journal of Solids Structures*, No. 30, pp. 1473-1489 (1993).

32   Huang, Y., Hu, K. X., and Chandra, A., 'A Generalized Self-Consistent Mechanics Method for Microcracked Solids', *Journal of Mechanical and Physical Solids*, **Vol. 42**, pp. 1273-1291 (1994).

33   Mendelson, A., 'Plasticity: Theory and Applications', Robert E. Krieger Publishing, Malabar, Florida (1983).

34   Christensen, R. M., 'Theory of Viscoelastics: An Introduction', 2nd edition, New York: Academic Press (1982).

35   Kraus, J., 'Electromagnetics', New York, McGraw-Hill (1973).

Chapter 7

DESIGN AND MODELLING OF SOLDER-FILLED ACAs FOR FLIP-CHIP AND FLEXIBLE CIRCUIT APPLICATIONS

J. K. KIVILAHTI
Helsinki University of Technology, Espoo, Finland

P. SAVOLAINEN
Nokia Research Center, Helsinki, Finland

7.1 INTRODUCTION

The interest in using new packaging materials and chip mounting processes for fine-pitch assembly of electronic components has been markedly increasing during the past few years.[1-3] Due to the continuous pursuit of higher interconnection density, area array bare chip mounting, both at module and board levels, will be considered over other packaging technologies. This is the case in portable communication devices and in smart cards — provided the improved performance and higher reliability of the devices (Figure 7.1) can be achieved cost-effectively and in an environmentally compatible manner. It is generally agreed that flip chip is a well qualified direct chip level interconnection technology to meet the above-mentioned challenges.[4] However, it seems likely that more universal implementation of flip chip will grow only gradually until such issues as the availability of known good die (KGD), reliable under bump metallurgy (UBM) with high Sn content, and inexpensive reworking capability and testing are satisfactorily resolved.

Even though metallurgical bonding is the predominant interconnection method used for electronics assembly, much attention has been paid recently to new interconnection materials such as anisotropically conductive or z-adhesives (ACA). Z-adhesives provide electrical conductivity through the adhesive layer being an insulator in the xy-plane of flip-chip or flexible substrate joints. Conductive particles in the adhesive are compressed between the bumps and the corresponding pads on the substrate when hot press bonding is performed. If conductive fillers are solder particles, they can react with conductors and form microscopic solder joints inside the polymer.

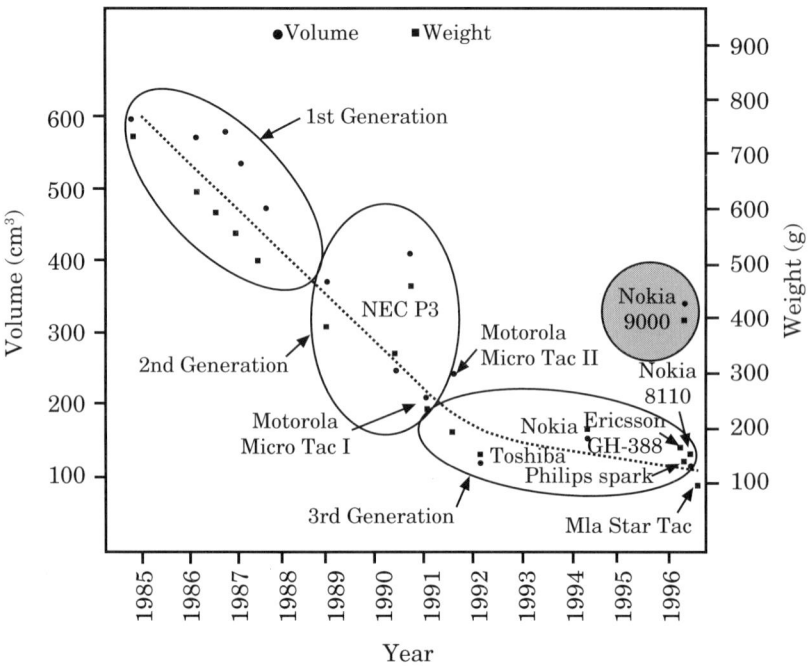

Fig. 7.1 Weight and volume reduction of cellular telephones.

Z-adhesives offer several advantages for high density electronics assembly. These include very high density interconnects and low process temperatures as well as lead-free, fluxless bonding which eliminates the need for post-assembly cleaning. In addition, the polymer matrix provides an underfill for flip chip and, thereby, eliminates further process steps.

Z-adhesives may also provide potential solutions to future soldering problems which are likely to be encountered in ultra-fine pitch assembly. Concurrently with the development of higher density packaging technologies, increasing joint densities are unavoidably associated with decreasing solder joint volumes, which will make the larger part of the solder mass partake in the intermetallic reactions between solder, bump and substrate metallisation.[5] As illustrated in Figure 7.2, the solder volumes per interconnection in conventional through-hole technology are in the range of 0.1-1 mm^3, and the intermetallic layers occupy only a small fraction of the total volume of the joint. Considering direct chip attachment, the solder volumes are significantly smaller. For example, if the bumps are 0.1 mm per side, the final solder volume is 0.510^{-4} mm^3 when the solder joint thickness is 50 μm after reflow. Hence, the relative amount of intermetallics is considerably larger than in through-hole or even in surface mount soldering. In such cases, the total mass of the original solder may transform into the matrix of various intermetallics, which, owing to their inherent brittleness, make microjoints mechanically too weak to support cyclic thermal loads. This 'small volume effect' can be avoided, for example, by using z-adhesives filled with inert particles or with the solder particles being thermodynamically or kinetically compatible with conductor pads, and thereby the benefits of both soldering and adhesive joining being successfully combined.[6,7] Likewise, solder-filled z-adhesives can provide a useful solution to paste printing in fine and especially ultra-fine pitch electronics assemblies, where adequate printing accuracy is very difficult to achieve.

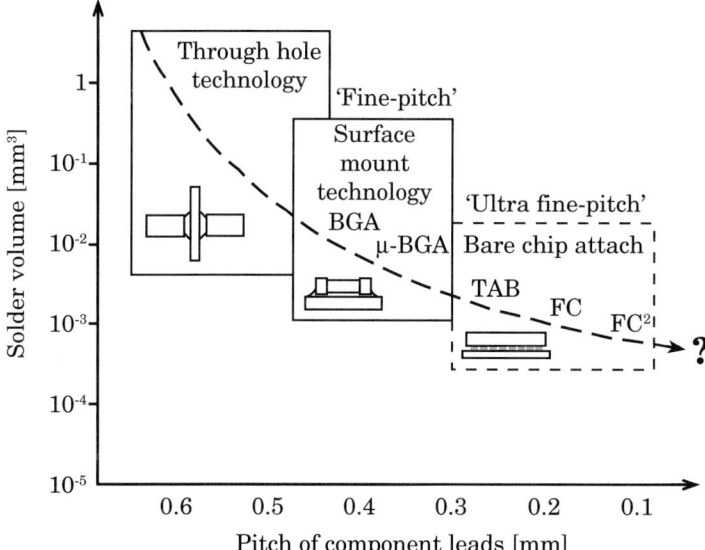

Fig. 7.2 Trend in solder volumes in conventional and fine-pitch assembly.

However, even though the fundamental problem related to the usage of small solder particle-filled z-adhesives has been solved by employing metallurgically compatible materials, there are still issues to be resolved before the z-adhesive joining process will be fully utilised in volume flip-chip production. For example, thermosetting polymers require a relatively long time to cure and most of the z-adhesives must be bonded under relatively high pressure. Compared with soldering, adhesive flip chip needs a very accurate component alignment and placing system, as no self-alignment occurs. A humid environment may cause problems, especially with certain noble metallisations, because polymers take up water, resulting in unstable electrical contacts.[8,9] This is likely to arise from local electrochemical corrosion. Swelling of the polymer matrix can also separate the filler particles from the pads physically. These and other issues are considered in some detail in the following sections by placing the emphasis on solder materials and bonding processes used with solder-filled z-adhesives.

7.2 CONDUCTIVE ADHESIVES

Basically, there are two different types of adhesives used in electronics: conductive adhesives and non-conductive or structural adhesives. The conductive adhesives can be either intrinsically conductive or composite materials of polymer matrix filled with conductive material. Intrinsically conductive polymers display a wide range of conductivities, but they are relatively sensitive to moisture and oxidation. There are also limitations in producing conductive layers or joints with these polymers, since they can be brittle and insoluble. At present they are not used commercially as conductive adhesives. Isotropically conductive adhesives (ICAs) typically contain conductive filler, generally silver flakes, between 20 and 35 vol.%. The matrices are mostly one- or two-component epoxies or epoxy-based resins, such as epoxy-silicones or epoxy-urethanes. ICAs are heat and/or IR-radiation curable and the curing cycle varies from 10 minutes to 2 hours. ICAs are utilised, for example, as solder replacement for surface mount technology (SMT) components and die-attach adhesives.[10-12]

Z-adhesives (or anisotropic conductive adhesives, ACAs) are also composite materials consisting of polymer matrix and conductive filler. The volume fractions of conductive fillers in the polymer matrix are considerably smaller than in the case of ICAs: typically between 0.5 and 10 vol.%, which enables ACAs to be used in fine and ultra-fine pitch applications. The interconnection density achievable depends on the average size, amount and distribution of conductive particles. Some currently available adhesives are already used in volume production of 0.1 mm pitch interconnections but the latest adhesives are capable of bonding even 0.070 mm pitch electrodes without the risk of short circuiting.[13,14] It can be seen from Figure 7.3 that a good contact percentage can be achieved with a wide range of particle loading. On the other hand, the amount of short circuiting increases noticeably when more than 12% of the filler particles is used.[15] Hence, one must find the optimum loading in terms of conductivity and risk of short circuiting.

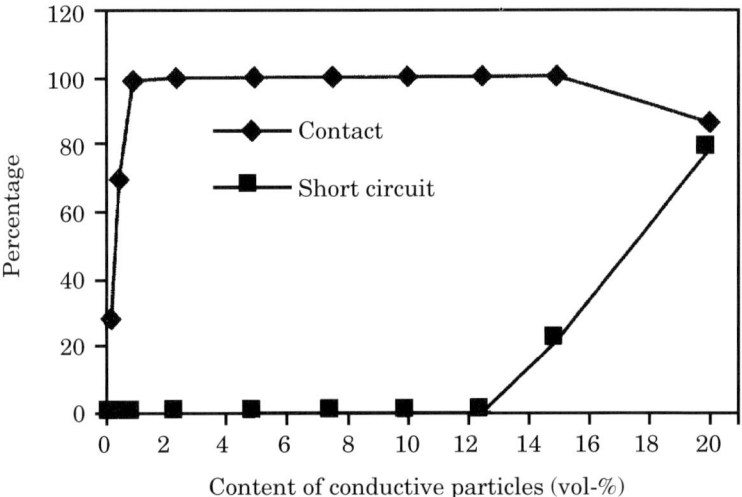

Fig. 7.3 Dependence of conductive particle content on percentage of contact and short circuits.[15]

The matrix materials for z-adhesives are mainly epoxy-based resins because of their high strength and high reliability, and also because the adhesion of epoxies to most materials used in electronics assembly is good. The drawback of using epoxy-based materials is that rework is difficult since the cross-linked matrix is resistant to most solvents. Because of easy processing and the possibility to rework, the interest in thermoplastic adhesives is growing and new polymers with enhanced properties are under development.[16-18]

Fillers for z-adhesives are particles of electrically conductive substances, e.g., graphite, nickel, metal-coated polymer balls or solder particles, mixed with the matrix. Hard, solid metal particles do not deform during the bonding process. Often they are irregular in shape and the particle size distribution is quite large, which leads to a situation whereby the contacts between the particles and pads are point contacts.[19] It has been shown that lower resistivity and higher reliability can be achieved with adhesives filled with metal coated polymer particles. These adhesives have been studied extensively during recent years.[20-22] The particles deform during the bonding process, increasing the electrical contact area.[23,24] In addition, the reliability is increased during thermal cycling, as it is possible to match the coefficients of thermal expansion of the particle core and the matrix, which ensures that both the particle and the matrix expand or shrink at the same rate during temperature changes. The production of the polymer particle cores enables strict control of the particle size distribution and it is also possible to produce very small particles.

In the above cases, the contact between the particles and the pads is of a mechanical nature. The best possible conductivity and reliability can be expected when the contact is truly metallurgical, i.e., the particles react with the pads, forming soldered microcontacts within the adhesive. Thus, there has been a growing interest in solder-filled z-adhesives.[25-29] Tin-lead-based as well as lead-free solder particles have been used as filler materials, but tin-bismuth- or tin-indium-based alloys are better suited to the purpose because of their considerably lower melting temperature. A lower melting temperature allows more variation of the process parameters without compromising the properties of the interconnections. This is because the solder particles are overheated significantly above their melting temperature, which enhances the reaction between particles and contact pads.

7.3   METALLURGY OF MICROSOLDERING

Adhesive joining technology, when based on metallurgical microjoints, offers additional advantages compared with the technologies commonly used for adhesive joining. A major advantage of the metallurgical interconnects is better electrical performance. Soldered micro-joints also sustain mechanical and thermal stresses. Since this technology relies considerably on the factors controlling the microsolderability of conductive areas, adhesion and wetting are briefly considered in the following sections before thermodynamics and kinetics of microsoldering.

7.3.1   Non-reactive and Reactive Wetting

Successful joining requires strong adhesion, which implies immediate wetting of the substrates. In adhesive bonding, wetting proceeds without chemical reactions between adhesive and substrates, while in soldering intermetallic reactions affect the rate and extent of the wetting.

By definition, 'adhesive is a substance which holds components together and resists separation when applied to the surfaces'.[30] Because the strength of the joint depends on the physical forces between the adhesive molecules and atoms or molecules of the substrates, the adhesive and the substrates must maintain very close contact, and the adhesive should spread easily on the surfaces of the substrates during the bonding process. The adhesive must fulfil three requirements to be able to make proper contact: (1) the adhesive's viscosity needs to be very low at some phase of the bonding process; (2) the liquid adhesive must wet the substrates well and (3) it must displace air and any other contaminants that may be present on the surface.[31]

In order to assess the ability of an adhesive/substrate combination to meet these criteria, one must consider the wetting equilibria, the surface-free energies of the adhesive and the substrates, and the free energy (or surface tensions) of the adhesive/substrate interface as well as studying the kinetics of the wetting process. Wetting equilibria and surface and interfacial free energies determine the thermodynamic conditions for the formation of intimate contact and, thus, the creation of strong bonds (Figure 7.4). The adhesive wets the substrate spontaneously when the contact angle θ is zero. The surface tensions at the three-phase contact are: γ_{LV} (liquid/vapour), γ_{SL} (solid/liquid) and γ_{SV} (solid/vapour) and are related to the contact angle by the well known Young's equation: $\gamma_{SV} = \gamma_{SL} + \gamma_{LV} \cos\theta$ The contact angle θ for a given system results from the balance of two competing forces: a driving force arising from the reduction of γ_{SV} by the liquid ($\gamma_{SV}-\gamma_{LV}$) acting on the periphery of the liquid drop, and a resisting force due to the increase of total liquid surface energy. Spontaneous wetting occurs when $\gamma_{SV} \gtrless \gamma_{SL} + \gamma_{LV}$. The energy required to separate a unit area of interface into two original surfaces is the thermodynamic work of adhesion. It can be expressed with the Young-Dupré equation:[32]

$$W = \gamma_{LV} (1+ \cos\theta) \qquad\qquad (7.1)$$

Accordingly, by measuring the contact angle, one can determine the work of adhesion when the surface energy of the liquid in equilibrium with its vapour is known.

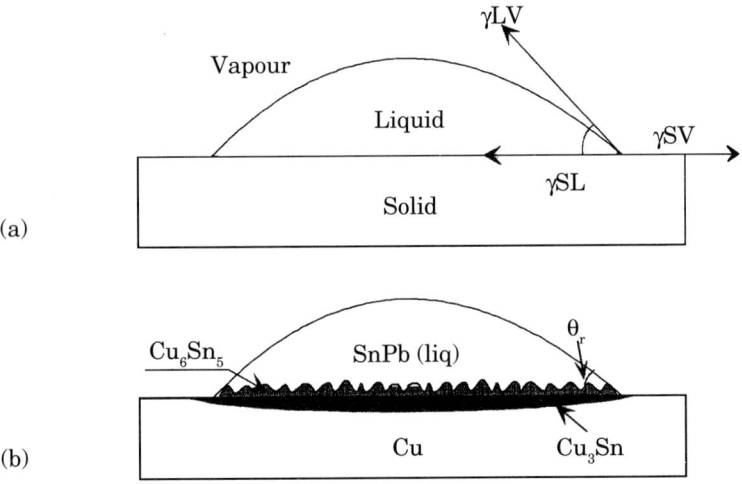

Fig. 7.4 A liquid drop at equilibrium on a solid surface (a) and reactive wetting of Cu conductor by liquid Sn-based solder alloy resulting in two intermetallic compounds (b).

It is essential that the adhesive has low viscosity during the bonding process, since the kinetics of wetting may be the determining factor in formation of intimate contact. On the other hand, the roughness of the substrate surface may influence the kinetics of wetting, because in some cases the rate and extent of interfacial contact are increased with roughening of the surface. The bonding operation should be conducted in an environment free of atmospheric contamination and with low relative humidity. This guarantees that adsorption of atmospheric water, hydrocarbons, dust or other impurities on the surface is minimised. An essential step is to clean the substrates carefully to remove any contaminants from previous process steps.

Generally, the Young-Dupré equation can also be applied to soldering, but is then based on the surface energies of an essentially inert system only. However, in conventional soldering or joining with solder-filled adhesives, intermetallic compounds are formed and substrates always dissolve to some extent into the liquid solder, altering its composition — as illustrated in Figure 7.4(b). These processes may change the situation considerably.[33,34] It is evident that the rate and extent of intermetallic reactions affect the wetting between the liquid solder and the substrate.

It has been suggested that the chemical reaction and/or diffusion of component atoms across an interface from one phase to another will decrease the corresponding interfacial energy by an amount equal to the free energy of the effective chemical reaction per unit area at the interface.[34,35] This will change mainly the interfacial energy at the solid-liquid interface, increasing the driving force for wetting at the early stage of the spreading process. Furthermore, the driving force for wetting has been shown to be considerably larger when the Gibbs free energy of formation of the number of compounds at the solid/liquid interface is included, compared only with the surface energy imbalance.[34]

However, these predictions have not yet been confirmed experimentally and the rôle of intermetallic formation with regard to the wetting kinetics is still unclear. The solid-liquid surface energy term, γ_{SL}, is affected by the intermetallic formation, dissolution and mixing, oxidation, surface contamination and so on. Even though this term is generally the smallest of the three surface tensions, it can still be very important for the wetting and spreading kinetics, as has been pointed out by Aksay *et al.*[36]

It is evident that both the interfacial energy and the Gibbs (free) energy affect the driving force of wetting in reactive wetting. Before any intermetallic reaction takes place, significant dissolution of solid may occur and, hence, there are two separate Gibbs energy contributions to the free energy of the wetting. Because the two Gibbs energies can have significant effects, it is worth discussing this in more detail. Moreover, these considerations are important for understanding the energetics and kinetics of microstructural (phase) evolution during soldering processes — in particular when small solder volumes are involved as in joining with solder-filled adhesives.

7.3.2 Energetics and Kinetics of Microsoldering

Thermodynamics of materials provides fundamental information on the stability of phases (microstructures), as well as on the driving forces for intermixing by dissolution, chemical reactions and diffusion processes and, therefore, is very useful for studying solder/conductor or coating/substrate interactions, in particular in systems where materials are used in diminutive amounts. Likewise, thermodynamics provides phase diagrams that contain information on metastable equilibria — usually not available in experimentally determined equilibrium diagrams. Even though complete phase equilibrium is not encountered in joining or interconnection applications, because the contact regions are under continuous microstructural evolution, local equilibrium is, however, generally attained at interfaces. Thus, the tie-lines of binary or ternary phase diagrams as well as stability diagrams can be used for determining the phases (or microstructures) that can be in *local* stable or metastable equilibrium with each other in conventional, reactive soldering or non-reactive (intermixing) solder/conductor systems shown in Figure 7.5.

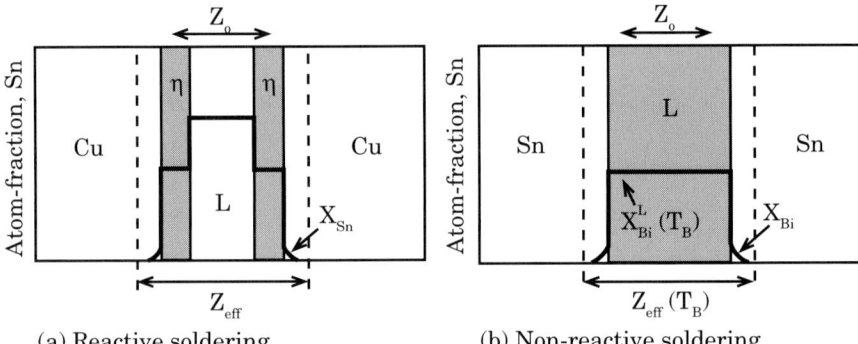

(a) Reactive soldering   (b) Non-reactive soldering

Fig. 7.5 Schematic representation of the effective joint region (a) in 'reactive' soldering and (b) in non-reactive soldering.

In a multicomponent system containing n_1 moles of component 1, n_2 moles of component 2 and v_i moles of component i, the chemical reaction can be represented by:

$$v_1 A_1 + v_2 A_2 + \dots = v_I A_I + v_{II} A_{II} + \dots$$

where A_1, A_2,... are the reactant components, A_I, A_{II},... are the reaction products, v_1, v_2,... are the number of moles of the reactant component and v_I, v_{II},... are the number of moles of the reaction products. The Gibbs energy change for the above reaction is:

$$\Delta G = \Delta G^0 + RT \ln \left(\frac{a_I^{v_I} a_{II}^{v_{II}} \dots}{a_1^{v_1} a_2^{v_2} \dots} \right) \tag{7.2}$$

The quantity in the bracket is related to the activities of components in phases of arbitrarily chosen non-equilibrium concentrations. On the other hand, the activities of the components are related to their chemical potentials by the equation:

$$a_i(T, x_i, p = 1) = \exp \left[\frac{1}{RT} \left(\mu_i - \mu_i^0 \right) \right] \tag{7.3}$$

where $\mu_i^0(T)$ is the standard chemical potential of component i, R is the gas constant, T is temperature and a_i is the activity of component i with reference to the standard used in the calculation. The term ΔG^0 represents the change in the standard Gibbs energy of the components A_1, A_2,... in their standard states reacting at constant temperature producing A_I, A_{II},... in their standard states. For example, in the case of the Cu-Sn-Bi system shown in Figure 7.6, it is natural to define the standard states for Cu, Sn and Bi their stable solid phases: Cu(fcc), Sn(bct) and Bi(rhombo-hedral), respectively. Accordingly, the driving forces for the formation of the η and ε intermetallics — with respect to either the binary or ternary liquid — as well as the driving forces for diffusion of the component atoms can be read directly from Figure 7.6. More detailed presentation of the Gibbs energy diagrams can be found elsewhere.[38]

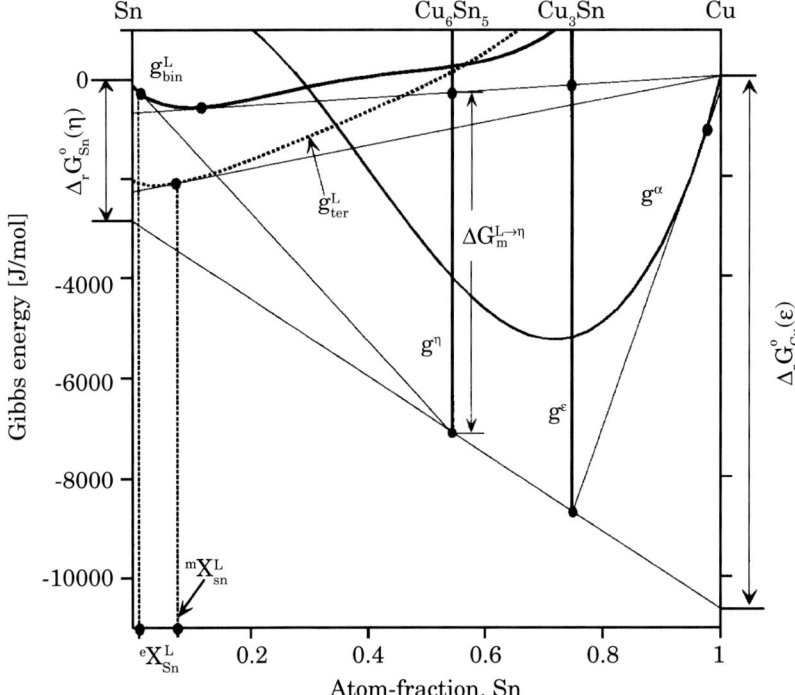

Fig. 7.6 The Gibbs energy diagram for the Cu-Sn system at 235°C showing the Gibbs energy of reaction for the ε and η intermetallics.[37]

On the other hand, it is noted that any intermetallic reaction is preceded by the dissolution of a solid substrate into liquid solder. For the dissolution reaction, there is a separate driving force ΔG and only after the molten solder is saturated (i.e., $x_{Cu}^L > {}^e x_{Cu}^L$) by the substrate metal, does the chemical reaction begin, as described above. It is important to notice that both ΔGs are dependent on the activities of the components taking part in the reactions. Naturally, the condition $\Delta G < 0$ must be fulfilled before any reaction can proceed.

In the case of the system composed of solution phases — like L and α in Figure 7.6 — the molar Gibbs energy of formation and chemical potentials of individual components are related as follows:

$$\frac{\Delta G}{\sum\limits_{\phi} n^{\phi}} = \Delta g = \sum_{\phi=1}^{m} y^{\phi} \sum_{i=1}^{n} \mu_i x_i = f(T, a_i), \qquad (7.4)$$

where y^{ϕ} is the volume fraction of phase ϕ in the system and x_i is the mole fraction of component i. A phase diagram giving valuable information on expected microstructures in a soldered joint can be constructed by minimising the total Gibbs energy of the individual phases of the system at various temperatures under constant pressure. This implies, of course, that the activities of the components are known as a function of temperature and composition.

The dissolution of the base metal into the molten solder always precedes the nucleation of the intermetallics. It is a particularly significant process also in non-reactive wetting as in the case of Sn or Sn-based solder coatings.[39] The dissolution rates of some important conductive or coating metals into eutectic SnPb solder are presented in Figure 7.7.[40] These dissolution rates are strongly dependent on the thermodynamics of the base metal/solder system exemplified by the copper-tin-bismuth system in Figure 7.6. The driving force for dissolution is extremely high for the very first copper atoms (the tangent of the Gibbs energy curve of liquid phase goes to minus infinity), but disappears when the (metastable) equilibrium is attained.

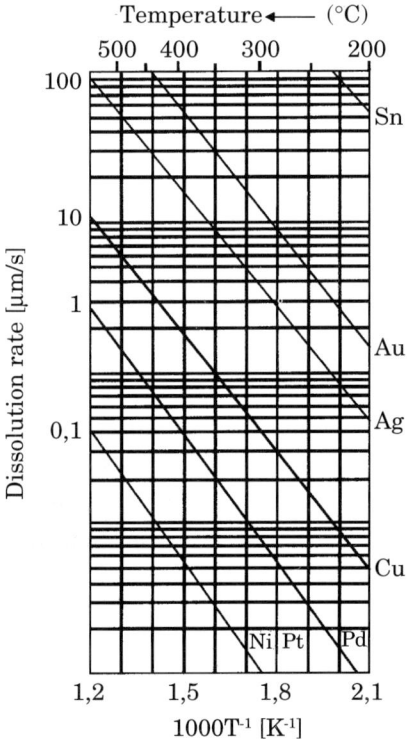

Fig. 7.7 Dissolution rate of various metals into eutectic Sn37Pb solder as a function of temperature.[40]

In reactive systems the stability of the intermetallic compound in equilibrium with the solder also affects the stable solubility limit. When intermetallic compounds at the substrate metal/liquid interface are 'precipitated', further dissolution of the base metal can even be totally prevented because of the elimination of the driving force and, especially, if the base metal does not diffuse through the reaction layer.

It can be shown that the dissolution rate increases with increasing solubility but decreases with the increasing stability of the intermetallic compound.[39] Since tin does not react chemically with tin-lead or tin-bismuth solders, its dissolution depends only on the solubility limit which is high compared with reactive metal-solder systems, which explains the fast dissolution rate of tin. The above consideration implies, of course, that the diffusion of metals is about the same in liquid SnPb or SnBi solders.

As stated above, dissolution of the base metal into molten solder is essential for nucleation of the intermetallic compounds formed between the base metal and the reactive component in the solder. Due to the dissolution the composition of the base metal reaches the *metastable solubility* limit at the solid/liquid interface (see Figure 7.6). This maximum metastable solubility is larger than the stable one and limits the amount of base metal that can be dissolved before nucleation of the intermetallic compound. Due to this supersaturation the melting point of the liquid, enriched by the base metal, rises, leading to heterogeneous nucleation and subsequent growth of the intermetallic compound *by solidification*. This explains the experimental observations in several base metal/solder systems where thick intermetallic layers are formed even during a very short bonding time — a fact that can not be predicted by a normal diffusion-driven layer growth (linear or parabolic).

To predict the actual diffusion path in a ternary or multicomponent system, i.e., whose phases are in local equilibrium with each other in a joint region, kinetic data are also needed. The fact that the phase diagrams, when combined with kinetic information, provide an efficient method for designing reliable microjoining and interconnection materials and process, becomes even more important when smaller solder joint volumes or thinner metallisations will be encountered in very high density electronic assemblies in the future.

It is important to realise that the connection between the thermodynamics and kinetics of interfacial reactions is also based on the activities of the components of the system in question, because the intrinsic diffusion fluxes of component atoms in solder/substrate systems are related to the thermodynamic activities of the components.[41] Thus, the phase sequence in a binary diffusion couple, for example, when joining two dissimilar metals, can be predicted directly from the phase diagrams, if mass transport is known as a function of time. In soldering, however, most solder-based metal systems — in addition to being in a liquid state — contain more than two elements, which complicates the quantitative analysis of reaction layers considerably. For example, in ternary diffusion couples such as SnPb solder in contact with a Cu conductor, two-phase regions can exist and theoretically many phase sequences and, hence, diffusion paths are possible. The most important constraint for the diffusion path to fulfil is the conservation of mass. While no material is lost or created, the diffusion path must cross in the ternary phase diagram the connection line (C.L.) between the end members at least once.[42] A quantitative modelling of this type of diffusion couples is given elsewhere.[43]

On the other hand, when solder volumes are small — as they are, indeed, in solder-filled z-adhesives — thermodynamic and kinetic considerations can also be carried out with the help of a special concept of 'local nominal composition' (LNC) of the effective joint region.[44] Since in joining applications the equilibria are attained only at the interfaces, the LNC can be defined only locally in an effective joint/contact region, where the concentrations (and other properties) of the components differ from those of the original contact materials. Basically, the LNC approach combines the thermodynamic and diffusion kinetic approaches and can be used for modelling the microstructural evolution occurring in microjoints and in thin material layers as a function of time, as will be illustrated in the next section in the case of the Cu-SnBi system.

7.4   SOLDER FILLERS FOR Z-ADHESIVES

Quite extensive research and development work is being carried out on solder-filled adhesives. Most of the filler alloys used are based on the Sn matrix, and at present more emphasis is also being placed on Pb-free solder alloys. This is understandable considering the benefits that the use of alternative alloys to lead-bearing solders can provide. First, lower processing temperatures fit better with the lower curing behaviour of most thermosetting adhesives, thus producing less thermal damage to components and reduced thermal stresses. Secondly, alloys with different melting temperatures allow multiple processing steps of complex assemblies requiring surface mounting of previously soldered sub-assemblies.[45,46] Thirdly, advanced solder alloys are needed to improve the resistance of soldered assemblies to thermal damage by increased thermal fatigue resistance.[47,48] Fourthly, health and environmental concerns arising from the use of Pb are abolished.

Most of the lead-free solder alloys are based on tin with additional elements such as Bi, In, Ag, Cu and Sb, which are used as major or minor alloying elements in various combinations.[49,50] For designing new filler particles, an extensive thermodynamic study of various solder metal combinations was carried out. The results of this study are presented schematically in Figure 7.8 showing that the available possibilities/choices can be categorised in three sub-systems, when Cu is taken as a conductor metal and Sn is the solder solvent. System 1 represents those ternary alloy systems which do not contain any additional intermetallics: the Cu-M binaries, where M = Pb, Bi, Zn, Tl, Cd,... show very wide miscibility gaps with practically no mutual solubilities of the component atoms. Sn-M systems show simple eutectic equilibria which also include the most commonly known solder SnPb system. In addition to Bi, there are only a very few metals which are expected to have any technological interest or environmental acceptance as a solder component in this system. In system 2 the Sn-M binaries, where M = Zn, Al, Si, are of the eutectic type, and therefore are unable to form intermetallics. However, they react strongly with copper, producing numerous intermetallics and ordered phases, which will restrict their use as major elements in solders. System 3 contains only binaries with complex intermetallic reaction products, and therefore are used — indium being an exception — only as minor alloying elements.

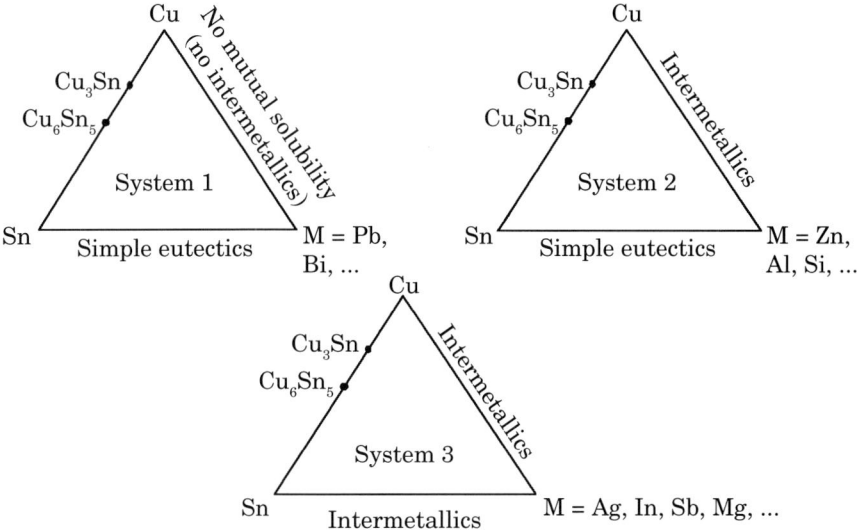

Fig. 7.8 Different types of ternary Cu-Sn-M systems.

Consequently, it is evident that there are only a few major alloying elements in the periodic system which are feasible as solder metals, and thus there are in practice very few binary alloys which have melting temperatures matching that of eutectic Sn-Pb solder. The most obvious choices for solder fillers to be used for microsoldering Cu conductors are the following Pb-, Cd- and Tl-free binaries: SnBi, SnIn, SnZn and the ternaries: SnBiZn, SnInZn, SnAlZn. The eutectic SnBi (139°C) and SnIn (120°C) binaries have a melting point below 183°C, while that of the SnZn system is 199°C. Generally, the melting temperature ranges of the ternary alloys vary strongly with composition, and therefore the factual liquidus and solidus temperatures must be determined for each specific alloy. At present, they can be calculated, however, quite accurately by using the latest assessed thermodynamic data on the system.[37] This minimises effectively the work needed for specifying a proper alloy for a particular application.

On the other hand, when developing solder-filled adhesives providing adequate conductivity and reliability of microsoldered (adhesive) joints, the following objectives — in addition to the above-mentioned melting temperatures — are met: liquid particles should wet and bond to metal conductors so that the area of electrical contact will be as large as possible; they are expected to avoid excessive oxidation and to solidify without marked disintegration of microstructure. The microstructure of a solder alloy, in contact with conductors, should remain stable and metallic in order to withstand stresses of either mechanical or thermal origin. Hence, the use of solder-filled z-adhesives implies careful consideration of several materials and processing requirements. When selecting alternative solders to tin-lead alloys, aspects other than technical ones must also be considered. For example, components used in Pb-free alloys should be available in sufficient quantities (e.g., Bi and In) and compatible with existing and future materials.

Considering the above requirements for solder-fillers, it is evident that SnBi particles (or Bi particles) are among the best candidates for use in z-adhesives. Even though eutectic SnBi solder may need somewhat more aggressive fluxes than Pb-Sn alloys to obtain good wettability with bare Cu, many of the mechanical properties are superior to those of conventional SnPb solders. Moreover, eutectic SnBi solder has a low melting point of 139°C, and its constituents are relatively abundant as well as economically feasible. There are also other Pb-free alloys available that can make Bi production independent of Pb refining.[51] Bi is relatively noble, which raises the electrode potential of Sn-based alloys with increasing Bi content. As a pure element, it is only weakly oxidising in air and humid environments, which also facilitates wettability. However, Bi itself has a relatively high melting point (271°C) and is mechanically weak due to its inherent brittleness. As the United Nations Environmental Programme does not consider Sn and Bi to be harmful elements — contrary to Pb and Sb as well as their compounds — SnBi alloys can be regarded as a safe choice for solder alloys as well as for coating material in the future.[52] Other possible feasible filler alloys can be produced by alloying SnBi with small amounts of minor elements from system 2 and/or 3. One attractive system is SnBiIn, which needs to be studied more carefully before specifying the most viable alloy compositions. This system shows several ternary eutectics, the melting points of which range from about 56°C close to the binary SnIn eutectic (120°C). Their usefulness should be studied and assessed critically on the basis of their compatibility with the conductor metals or (protective) coatings used.

There is, however, a fundamental problem that may hamper the use of most Sn-based fillers — including SnBi and SnBiIn particles — when used together with conductor metals or coatings that dissolve too fast in liquid Sn-based particles. The reaction between a solder alloy (such as Sn58Bi or Sn37Pb) and conductor metals produces intermetallic layers (e.g., $AuSn_4$ or Cu_6Sn_5). The problem can be even greater if the fast dissolving metal is a thin noble coating like Au or Pd, since the dissolution will expose locally the underlying, generally less noble metal.[7]

7.4.1   Reactive Bonding of Cu Conductors with SnBi-filled Adhesive

With solder particle-filled z-adhesives, the volumes of solder particles are already in the range of 10^{-5}-10^{-6} mm^3 or even lower. Because the volume of the solder particles is very small, like the filler particles in Figure 7.9, it is generally difficult to avoid fast dissolution and supersaturation of liquid filler particles. This will lead to rapid decomposition of the original microstructure of the solder during bonding as the volumes of the solder particles are so small. As shown in Figure 7.10, the thicknesses of the intermetallic layers (Cu_3Sn and $AuSn_4/Ni_3Sn_4$) are limited by the amount of the reactive element in the solder. Since Bi does not dissolve or react with most of the conductor or coating metals, it will remain as elemental bismuth between the intermetallics and, therefore, the microjoints are mechanically weak due to the inherent brittleness of bismuth and intermetallics. Moreover, the resistivity of bismuth is almost a decade higher than that of tin. Thus, due to the small volumes of the solder particles, it is very difficult to prevent the generation of this type of microstructure.

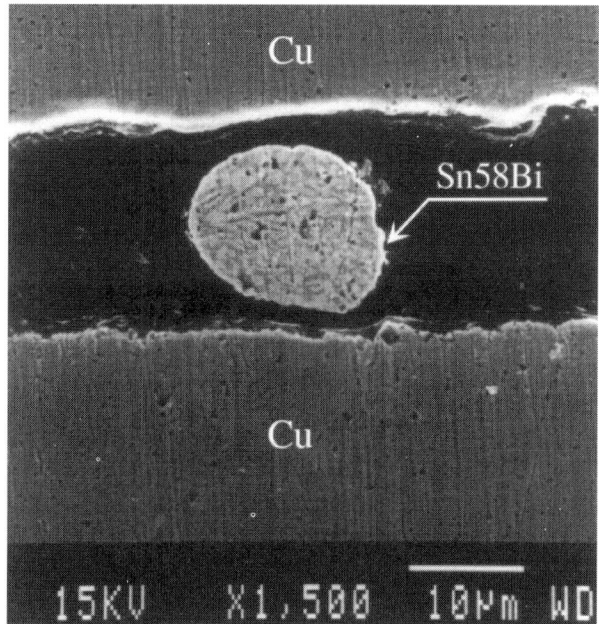

Fig. 7.9 Eutectic SnBi particle with a volume of about 2 x 10⁻⁶ mm³ is located in an epoxy adhesive between the Cu conductors.

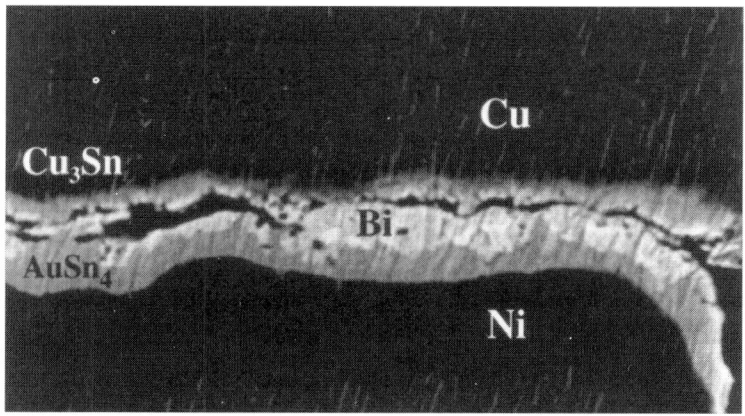

Fig. 7.10 SEM micrograph showing a microjoint adhesively bonded at 180°C for 1 min. between Ni/Au and Cu metallisations.

As stated before, the concept of local nominal composition can be used together with the relevant phase diagrams of the bonding system to explain the observations related to the 'solder volume effect'. When joining Cu conductors with the eutectic SnBi particle-filled adhesive, the ternary phase

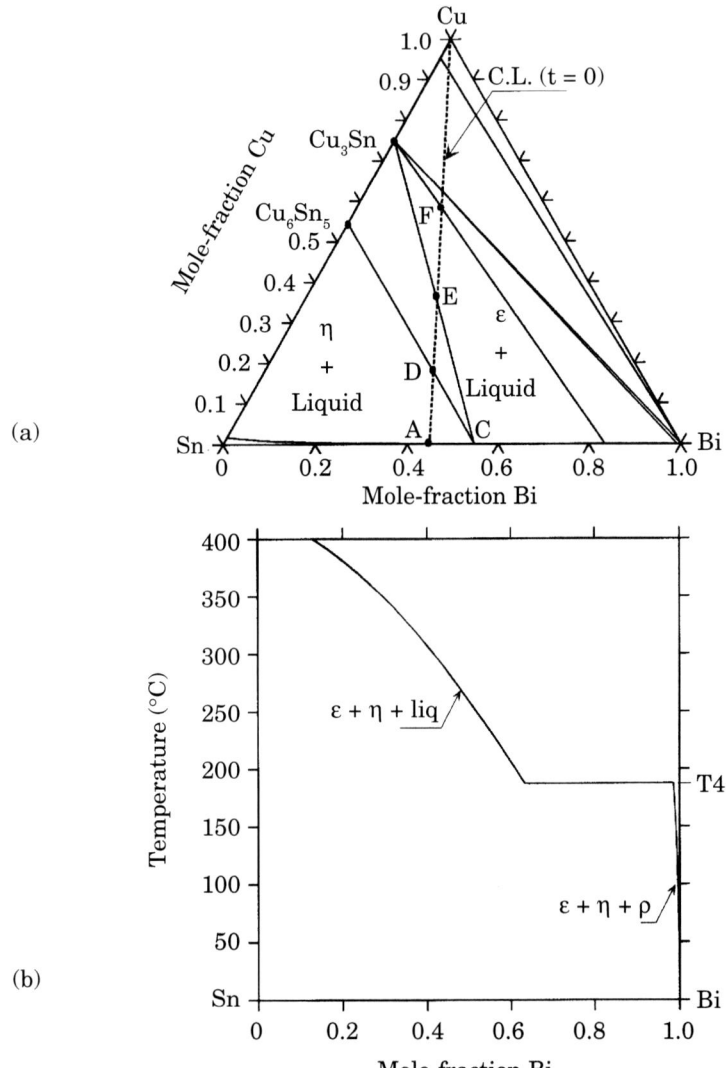

Fig. 7.11 (a) The isothermal section of the Cu-Sn-Bi system at 235°C.[7] Note the connection line (C.L.). (b) Location of apex C of the three-phase triangle at different temperatures in the CuSnBi system.

diagrams of the system are needed. One such diagram assessed at 235°C is shown in Figure 7.11(a).

At the beginning of microsoldering processes, the effective joint region corresponds to the original volume of the filler material (solder), and enlarges when the conductor metal enters by dissolution and/or by chemical reactions. It is essential to notice that the amount of filler material, i.e., the number of moles of all components in the filler as well as their ratios, will not change with time in the effective joint region. Therefore, the local nominal composition of the effective joint region, LNC, locates on the connection line (C.L.) between the original solder composition and that of the conductor metal. Immediately after the first contact, Cu dissolves rapidly into the molten solder until it has reached the metastable solubility limit (which is higher than point A) at the liquid/copper interface. This maximum attainable supersaturation of copper in the liquid is essential for the formation of the Cu_6Sn_5 intermetallic, which attains a local stable equilibrium with the liquid of the metastable composition at the phase boundary. Since the volumes of the SnBi particles are small, the maximum supersaturation of Cu is reached very rapidly throughout the entire solder volume and, therefore, the solder composition will change from point A to B, while the local nominal composition point moves from A to point B'. The formation of intermetallics such as η-Cu_6Sn_5 or ε–Cu_3Sn directly from the Sn-based liquid alloy is so fast that mechanisms other than those in the solid state must operate.[5]

Therefore, it is suggested that a thin layer of Cu_6Sn_5 (or Cu_3Sn) is formed rapidly by heterogeneous nucleation from the supersaturated melt at the Cu/liquid interface. Because of the dissolved copper the melting points of the particles are increased above the bonding temperature — either locally (large particle) or overall (small particle) in the liquid particles. As the Sn is consumed from the solder by the growth of the Cu_6Sn_5 phase, the solder composition moves towards point C along the liquidus while the local nominal composition moves along the contact line towards point D. It should be noted, however, that the (ε-η-liq) three-phase equilibrium point C moves towards the Bi-rich corner in the Cu-Sn-Bi phase diagram when the bonding temperature is lowered, as has been illustrated in Figure 7.12.

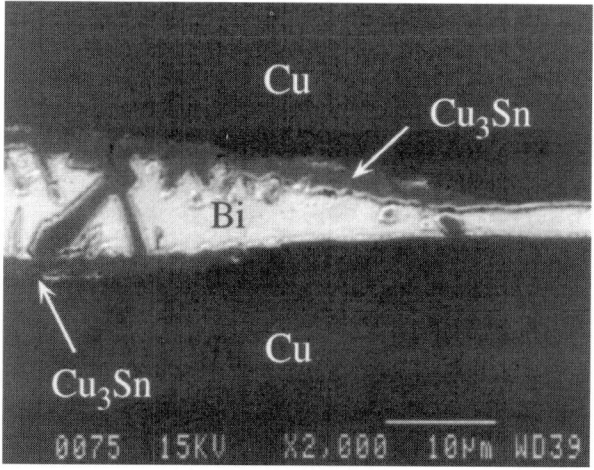

Fig. 7.12 Cross-section of a microjoint bonded at 180°C with a thin layer of the eutectic SnBi alloy.

Figure 7.12 shows in more detail that the once formed η-layer will transform into the ε-phase and a pure Bi layer is formed during the bonding operation. When the η-phase continues to grow, the composition of the solder passes point C following the metastable η/liquid solubility line. After point C the η-phase becomes too metastable compared with the ε-phase, and this initiates a rapid transformation of the η-phase into the ε-phase with the help of the liquid. During the transformation the local nominal composition moves from point D to E. After consumption of the h-phase, the ε-phase continues to grow, while the LNC moves along the connection line in the $(\varepsilon + \text{Liq})$ phase region, where the corresponding tie-lines fix the liquid composition. Eventually, the $(\varepsilon - \text{Liq} - \text{Bi})$ triangle is reached and pure solid bismuth becomes stable following the disappearance of the liquid phase.

7.4.2   Non-reactive Bonding of Sn-coated Cu Conductors with SnBi-filled Adhesive

To avoid the formation of brittle microcontacts during adhesive joining, resulting from excessive chemical interaction between Sn-based alloy particles and conductor metals or their coatings, a new technique for bonding fine-pitch electronic components with ACAs containing fusible metal particles has been developed.[6] According to this technique the contact areas to be joined are coated chemically or electrochemically with a thin layer of metal, which is metallurgically compatible with the solder particles in the sense that no intermetallic formation can occur between liquid solder particles and solid electrodes. This is provided, of course, the coating is thick enough so that the SnBi or Bi particles cannot melt the coating locally down/up to the Cu substrate. Generally, coating thicknesses of about 10 μm are used successfully.

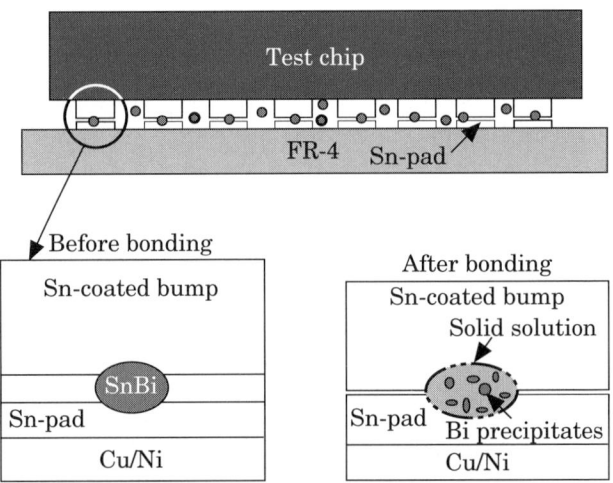

Fig. 7.13 Schematic representation of test chip bonded on Sn-coated Cu contact pads with Sn58Bi-filled epoxy adhesive.

The basic concept of non-reactive bonding is illustrated in Figure 7.13. The eutectic SnBi particles are compressed between Sn-coated Cu layers, so that they will break the oxide layers of the coatings locally before melting. As the particles melt during heating (above 139°C), the bismuth dissolves rapidly into the tin coatings and simultaneously melts some more tin. The extent of the liquid phase in the microjoint region will depend on the volume of a molten particle and the temperature of bonding, T_B, in Figure 7.5(b). While Bi atoms diffuse into solid Sn-rich solution, the liquid will gradually solidify, mostly isothermally, and, depending on the temperature, time and relative volume of the filler particles, the solidification can go to completion at the bonding temperature.

On the other hand, if one has a pure Bi particle between Sn-coated conductors at the bonding temperature, diffusion of component atoms in the opposite direction to the original joint interface gives rise to a thin layer of solid solution. As soon as Bi has saturated the Sn-rich solution phase and Sn has saturated the Bi-rich solution phase, rapid irreversible melting will occur provided the temperature is above 139°C. Since the diffusion of bismuth along the grain boundaries of the Sn-rich phase is relatively fast, the Bi is consumed from the liquid phase which also reduces the amount of liquid. In the case of small Bi particles, isothermal solidification will occur producing relatively fine precipitates of Bi in an Sn-rich matrix. Figure 7.14 shows two such joints where the precipitated Bi particles occupy the areas where the original particles were melted. Since there is the activity gradient of Bi in the joint, the Bi atoms tend to diffuse away from the region of the contact area, while Sn atoms diffuse in the opposite direction. The rate of levelling out of the Bi can be accelerated by annealing the joint at elevated temperatures, which also increases the solubility of Bi in solid tin. This will decrease both the Bi content and the mechanical strength of the joint region continuously, but what is more important: the ductility increases with time. Since the Sn coating next to the Cu is in the solid state, the intermetallic reactions between Cu and Sn proceed very slowly during the bonding operation. Thus, with the help of the SnBi or Bi particles, the Sn-coated conductors are fused together sporadically. It should be noticed that the melting is transient; the remelting of the bonding zone will occur at higher temperatures than the first melting (139°C).

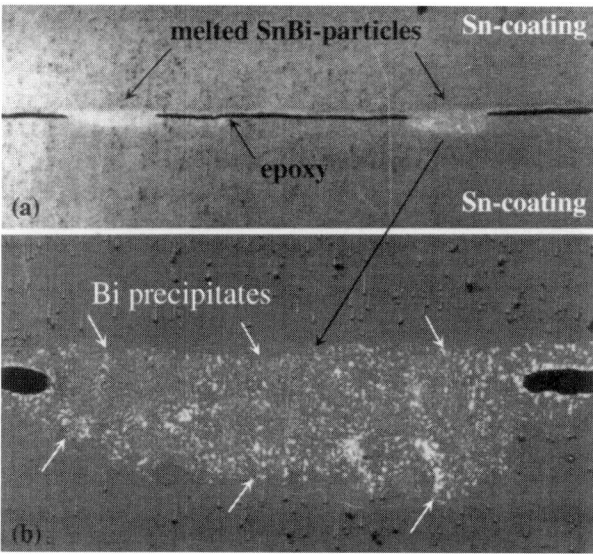

Fig. 7.14 SEM micrograph showing a microjoint between adhesively bonded Sn layers with Sn58Bi particles at 180°C for 1 min. (Note white Bi precipitates in Sn-matrix.)

7.4.3   SnPb-bumped Flip Chips Bonded on FR-4 with Bi Particle-filled Adhesive

What has been stated above on non-reactive bonding applies also to the SnPb solder bump/Bi-particle system. The metallurgical reactions occurring in this flip-chip system can be inferred from Figure 7.15 showing the vertical section from the eutectic Sn26Pb alloy into the Bi corner of the ternary phase diagram as well as the Gibbs (free) energy diagram related to it at 160°C.[54] At the typical bonding temperatures used in this study, SnBi- or Bi-particles dissolve rapidly into thin liquid formed on top of the SnPb bumps. The difference in activity of the component atoms is the driving force for their dissolution as well as for their intrinsic diffusion fluxes, J_{Bi}, J_{Sn} and J_{Pb}, are

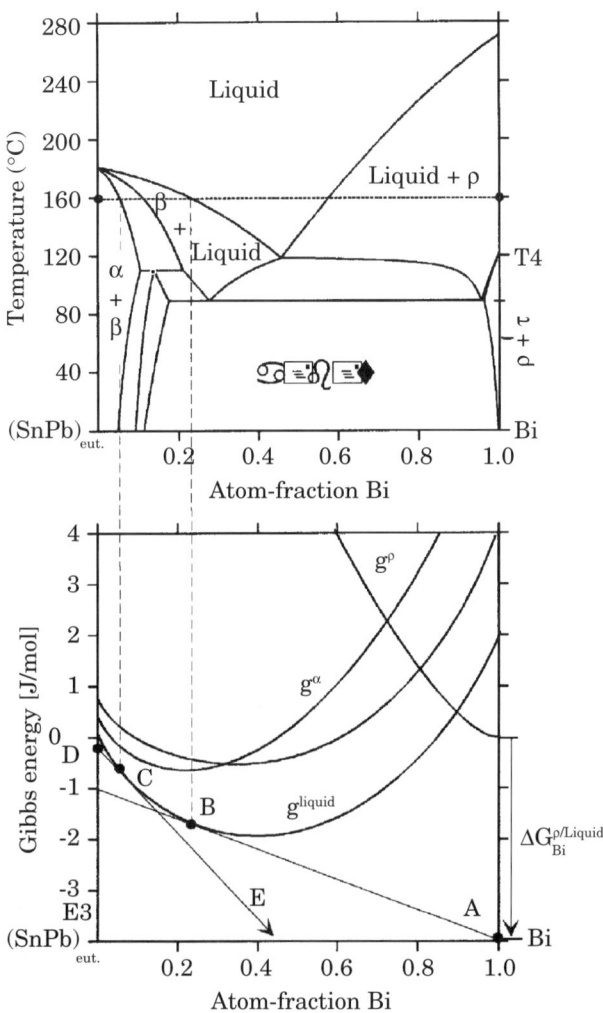

Fig. 7.15 Temperature-composition graph for tin-bismuth with presentation of Gibbs energies of phases at 180°C.

proportional to their activity gradients.[41] The chemical potentials — and thus the activit͏ of the components — can be read directly from the intersection poınts of the tangent to the g^{liq}-curve at point B and the vertical axes. The activity of Bi in the liquid layer with a eutectic ratio of Sn to Pb is 0.33 (with respect to solid pure Bi) while it is about 0.1 in the saturated SnPb solid solution at the composition point C. Hence, the activity difference driving the dissolution of Bi into the liquid alloy at B is 0.67 and the corresponding driving force is about 4000 J/mol.

Thus, with the help of the Bi (or SnBi) particles the Sn- or SnPb-coated conductors and Sn37Pb bumps are fused together locally. After solidification, practically pure Bi particles precipitate out of the saturated solid solution — either during the cooling or later at room temperature. Accordingly, there are activity gradients of Bi in the joint region driving Bi atoms to diffuse away from the original bonding zone. The rate of levelling out of the Bi can be accelerated by annealing the joint at elevated temperature, which also increases the solubility of Bi both in the Pb-rich (α) and Sn-rich (β) solid solutions. Depending on the amount of Bi in the eutectic or near eutectic structure of the joint region, the microjoints start to remelt above about 90°C. It should be noted that, in principle, the melting is transient; therefore, the remelting of the joint regions can be controlled to some extent by the amount of Bi present as well as by the time and temperature used for bonding.

To study the interaction of pure Bi particles with eutectic PbSn alloy experimentally, solder-bumped test chips were bonded on SnPb-coated copper conductors on FR-4 with conductive z-adhesive. The thickness of the SnPb coating varied from 5 to 15 µm. The bonding was carried out with the parameters and the device described earlier. Figure 7.16 shows the microstructure of the flip-chip joints observed with the SEM/EPMA technique. Due to the absence of intermetallics, there are only precipitated Bi particles

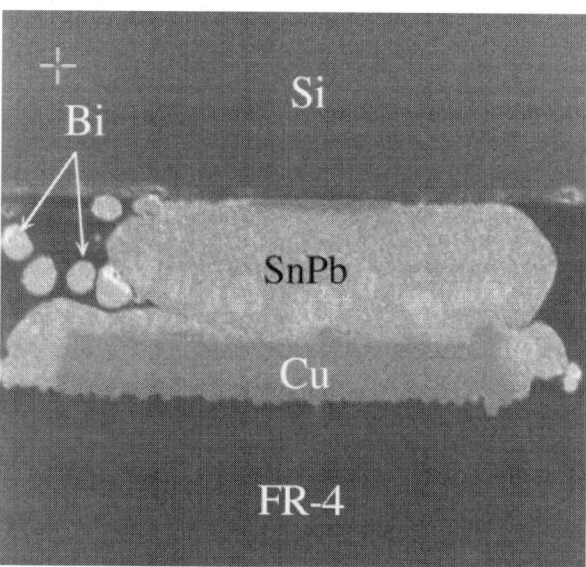

Fig. 7.16 SEM micrograph showing an SnPb-bump bonded into an SnPb-coated Cu contact pad with the Bi-filled adhesive.

which now occupy a volume which is larger than the volume of the original particles located between the mating surfaces. Therefore, good electrical and mechanical properties were measured. Moreover, it was observed that the polymer matrix protects solid Bi particles against further oxidation during storage as well as isolating the liquid particles effectively from the atmosphere during the bonding process. The matrix also has a mildly fluxing effect when the curing agent is activated by heat. Hence, the Bi particles are able to mix fast with the base metal as described above.

7.5   RELIABILITY RESULTS

The contact resistance values of the joints were measured during a heat and humidity test (60°C/95% RH). The results are shown in Figures 7.17(a) and (b). The z-adhesive containing Sn-58Bi-filler particles performed well

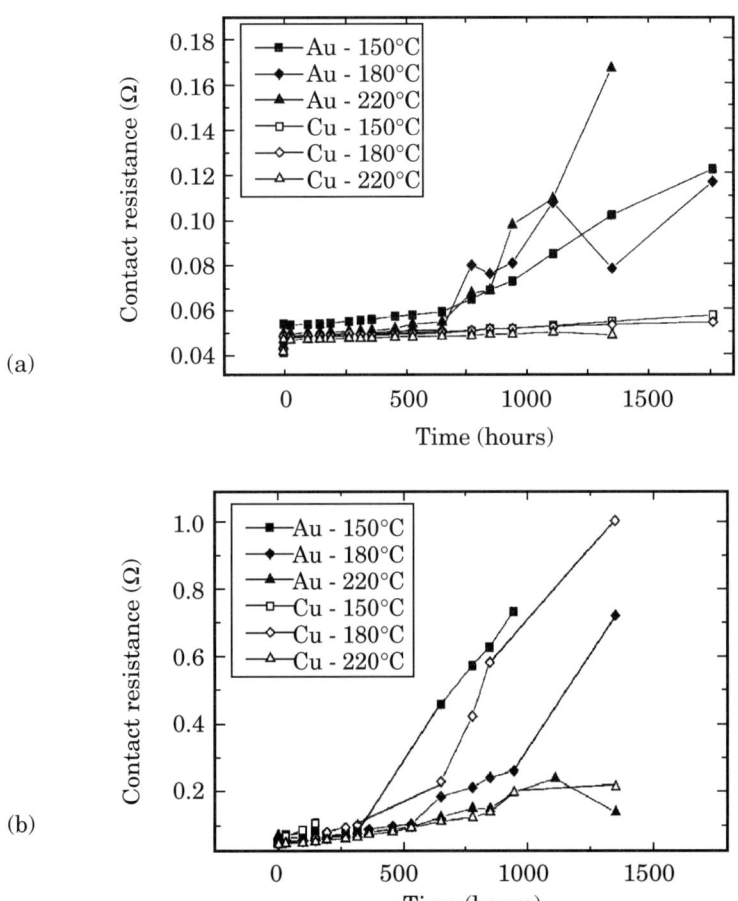

(a)

(b)

Fig. 7.17 (a) Contact resistance values of joints produced with Sn-58Bi-filled adhesive during the 60°C/95%RH-test. (b) Contact resistance values of joints produced with Sn-7.8Zn-0.7Al-filled adhesive during the 60°C/95%RH-test.

during the test with bare copper conductors. The contact resistance values increased less than 10% from the initial value, regardless of the bonding temperature. With Au/Ni metallisation the contact resistance values start to increase after 600-700 hours. Furthermore, the scatter of the results with the Ni/Au metallisation is considerable. The Sn-7.8Zn-0.7Al-filled adhesive failed the test because all the joints opened before 1500 hours. This results from the high melting temperature of the alloy as well as from the lack of metallurgical bonding between the filler particles and the conductor metallisations. On the basis of the results obtained from the high humidity, high temperature tests, it can be concluded that the epoxy matrix withstands this test well.[8]

The behaviour of different substrate metallisations during the 60°C/95%RH test can be explained with the help of potential-pH equilibrium diagrams and the electrochemical series of the metals. Because the substrate/solder system consists of different metals, galvanic corrosion can occur during the test. Gold as a noble metal is a cathode and the solder alloys and in particular the exposed substrate metallisation are anodes. Because the area of the gold surfaces is very large compared with that of the solder joints (ratio is about 0.03-0.04),[8] the anodic dissolution reaction can be fast. On the basis of the pH-potential diagrams of the different metals (that of Ni is in Figure 7.18), it is obvious that all the metals can oxidise in a humid environment. Tin, zinc and nickel can also form hydroxides when they react

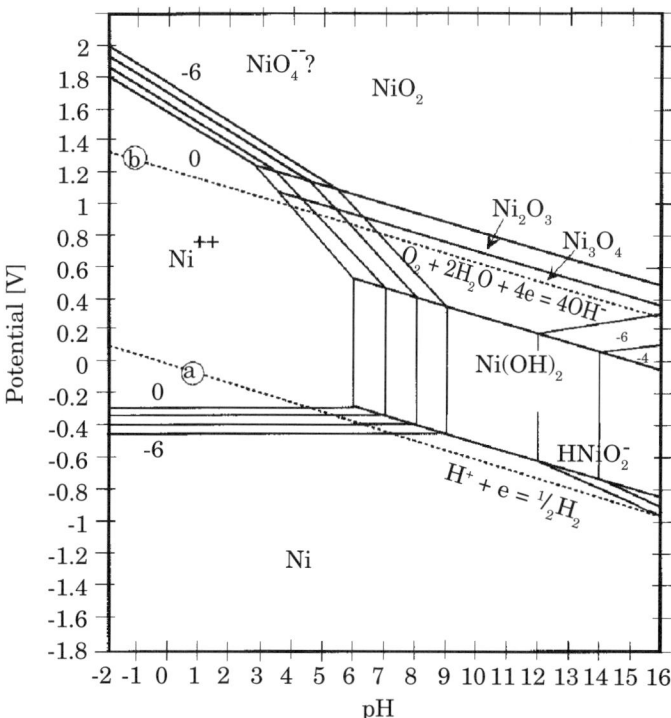

Fig. 7.18 pH-potential equilibrium diagram of nickel in water at 25°C.[55]

with water and oxygen. The Sn-58Bi alloy forms a solution with an electrochemical potential close to the potential of copper. Therefore the rate of the dissolution reaction is very low with the Au/Ni metallisation and almost zero with bare copper. Due to the higher Zn content and very active Al, the Sn-7.8Zn-0.7Al alloy is relatively unstable compared with gold and copper. Therefore, when enough water and oxygen have diffused to the polymer matrix, the solder alloy starts to dissolve, decreasing the electrical conductivity of the joint. Considering the results of the 60°C/95%RH tests, the incubation time of water is about 500 hours.

   Potential corrosion problems can be eliminated by choosing conductor and bump metallurgies such that they are compatible with the solder filler, as described earlier. This was tested by electroplating Cu conductors on flexible circuits with 5 to 15 μm tin. As shown in Figure 7.19, the Sn58Bi-filled adhesive exhibited good interconnection reliability in a hot and humid environment with the Sn-coated Cu metallisation on flex circuits.

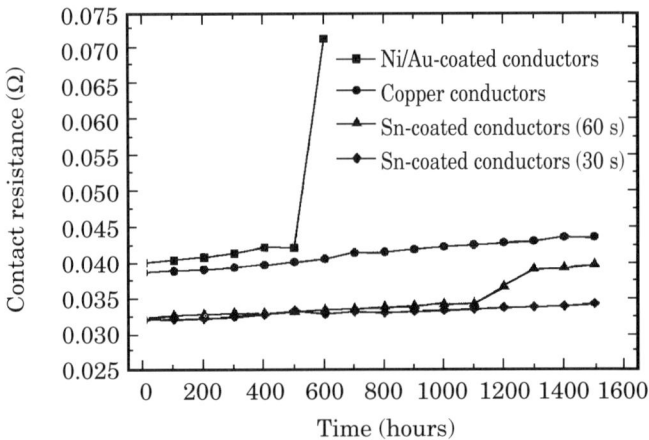

Fig. 7.19 Daisy chain resistance values of flexible test circuits with various conductor metallisations bonded with Sn58Bi-filled ACA.[54]

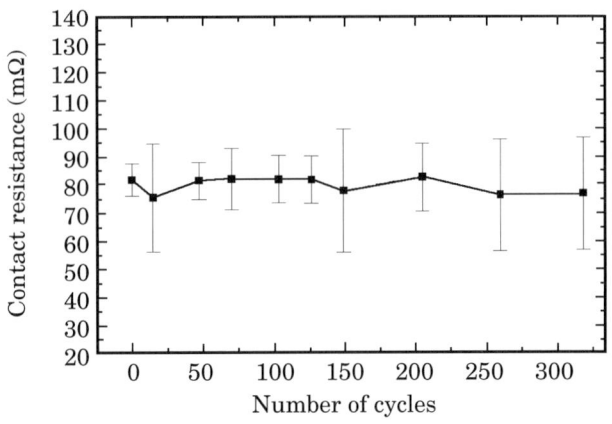

Fig. 7.20 Resistance values of flex-to-flex interconnections bonded with Sn-58Bi-filled ACA (-40°...+100°C, three-hour cycle).

It is also evident that the Sn coating improves the conductivity of the interconnection by almost 25%.[53] This most likely results from the increased contact area that is achieved in two ways. First, the tin layers are soft and may be deformed by pressure during the bonding operation. Secondly, the reaction between the molten SnBi particle and tin is a dissolution reaction, which does not cause the segregation of tin and bismuth. This in turn leads to a situation where the molten metal occupies and bonds together a larger area of the conductors. Lower resistance values are achieved due to the larger contact area.

The epoxy matrix withstands the high humidity, high temperature test relatively well. The glass transition temperature of the epoxy is about 105°C, therefore the adhesive can be used up to 100°C without problems. Maximum water uptake of the epoxy in the humid environment is 10%, which is a relatively high value. However, the results obtained from two long-term exposures to a hot and humid environment show that high water diffusion does not create problems in terms of swelling of the matrix which could physically separate the substrates.[8]

The tests with flexible circuits showed that solder-filled ACAs have good reliability in the temperature cycling test (Figure 7.21).[54] The interconnection resistance values remain stable through 300 cycles between temperatures of -40°C and +100°C (three-hour cycle). The high reliability results from the flexibility of both substrates, which allows the CTE mismatch to be relieved without high stresses. In addition, the CTE mismatch in this case is much smaller than with rigid substrates. The situation, however, is different with flip chip, when a relatively rigid substrate, such as FR-4, is used with an Si chip. Both substrate material and chip have markedly different coefficients of thermal expansion (CTE) and, furthermore, the CTE of the adhesive differs considerably from those values. When temperature excursions occur, high stresses are introduced into the joint and, if the materials are not capable of deforming, failure is expected to occur. For example, flip chips bonded with the SnBi-filled ACA have a high failure risk during temperature cycling because the joint microstructure consists of brittle Bi and similarly

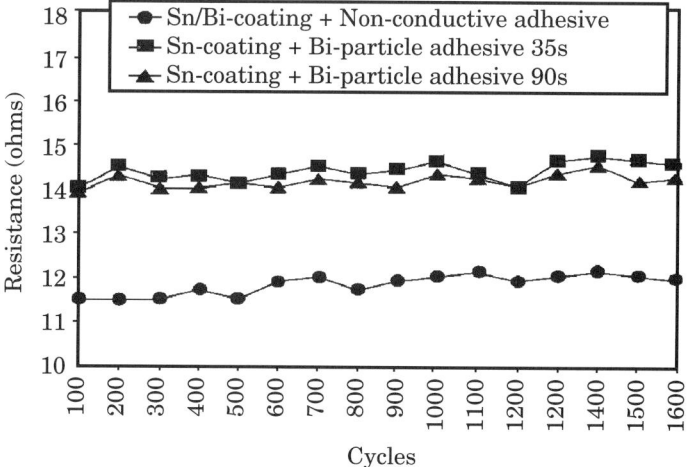

Fig. 7.21 Results of thermal cycling test with flexible test structures.

brittle Sn/Cu or Sn/Ni intermetallics. If solder-filled ACAs are used for flip-chip bonding, one must select metallurgically compatible substrate metallisations, which provide ductile, homogeneous microstructures, as discussed earlier. Reliability evaluations of solder-ACA flip chips are under way.

Throughout the above discussion the filler particles have melted locally inside the adhesives and produced sporadic soldered microjoints which act as electrical contacts between the electrodes. To increase the total area of the electrical contacts, the solder particles can be replaced by metallurgically compatible solder coatings which are fused together with non-conductive adhesive. Since the preliminary results with the Sn/In system indicated that fusible solder coatings together with non-conductive adhesives can provide a viable interconnection method,[53] this is developed further in another study.[54] Thus, to compare the interconnection methods, flexible test structures were bonded both with Bi-filled z-adhesives and with non-conductive solder coatings utilising Sn and Bi. Figure 7.21 shows clearly that the flexible circuits passed the thermal cycling tests well. On the other hand, the joints bonded with non-conductive adhesive and the Sn/Bi coatings are about 15% better than those obtained with the Sn coating and the Bi-filled adhesive. This is most probably due to the larger contact areas of the joints made with the non-conductive adhesive and fusible Sn/Bi coatings.

Overall, the results showed that reliable, intermetallic-free joints can also be produced with non-conductive adhesives when used together with metallurgically compatible solder coatings. Detailed scanning electron microscopy and microanalysis confirmed that true metallurgical bonding can be achieved with the help of fusible solder coatings.

7.6   SOLDER-FILLED ADHESIVES IN FLIP-CHIP APPLICATIONS

Factors affecting the manufacturability of interconnections with ACAs are storage, application, bonding (assembly) process, testing and rework. In addition, the total system cost versus system performance must be evaluated in order to establish the feasibility of ACAs compared with other options.

Because of their relatively high reactivity, the adhesives are stored at low temperatures, which prevents curing prior to assembly. Hence, the user must have storage capability near the assembly line in order to keep the adhesives in optimum conditions. In addition, to avoid contamination of the adhesive from humidity, it must be brought to room temperature well in advance. Thus, some extra cost and care are inevitable when using ACAs.

The application of the adhesive depends on its form. Film adhesives are usually provided on a reel, and automatic application is possible. If the adhesive is a paste, stencil or screen printing or syringe dispensing are used to apply it. This gives some flexibility compared with film adhesives, but, on the other hand, pastes usually require longer cure cycles. In some cases, it is advantageous to pre-dry the paste between printing or dispensing and the actual bonding process.

There is a variety of bonding equipment for anisotropic conductive adhesives ranging from manual laboratory bonders to fully automatic machines that can be integrated into the production line. The bonders usually consist of a heating tool connected to a pressurising unit and component alignment system. Unlike solders, the adhesives are not self-aligning and, therefore, very accurate component alignment and placement methods must be used. The alignment accuracy needed depends on the pad size of the parts to be assembled.

At present, the greatest challenge in using ACAs in volume production of flip-chip devices lies in the relatively time-consuming involved process. The bonding cycle per chip is relatively long (5 to 60 seconds) and, when several chips are bonded to the same substrate, the throughput is low. Hence, one must decrease the process time of the adhesive or look for solutions for bonding all chips simultaneously. The ideal solution would be to develop such a process that all active as well as passive components can be bonded in one process step. This process would be equivalent to reflow soldering.

An additional limitation due to the pressure requirement is that the process flow is complicated when using double-sided boards. As bonding pressure is applied, the substrate must be supported from below, which means that any component on that side would be damaged. Thus, assembly must be sequenced in such a way that components bonded with ACAs are attached first and all other components in the subsequent process steps.

Devices assembled with ACAs can be tested electrically like soldered devices. The reworkability of the adhesive joint depends on the adhesive type. Thermoplastic adhesives are easily softened by applying heat and the component can be easily removed. The adhesive residue is then cleaned by suitable solvents or left in place. Thermosetting adhesives are more difficult to rework. The matrix can be softened by heating above its glass transition temperature and the component is then removed. However, the adhesive residue is very difficult to clean with solvents, and mechanical cleaning may damage the substrate. Consequently, the best approach is to optimise the process in such a way that rework is minimised.

The minimum pitch achieved with an ACA depends on the particle size and distribution within the adhesive. Generally, the commercially available ACAs exhibit homogeneous particle distribution and, therefore, the particle size is a limiting factor. In order to avoid the risk of short circuiting, the space between adjacent conductors/bumps should be about five times the particle size. For example, if the adhesive is filled with 5 µm particles, the feasible distance between conductors is 25 µm. The adhesives on the market today are suitable for applications with pitches down to 75 µm.

Small particle sizes require very strict control of the planarity of the bumps and contact pads. Let us consider 5 µm particles, for example metal coated, deformable polymer particles. The particles should be deformed during the process by 40 to 60% of their original size. This means that the heights of the deformed particles after bonding vary between 2 and 3 µm. This can be achieved if the height differences of the bumps and contact pads are within one micrometre. If both bumps and pads are 20 µm high, the maximum allowed variation of the height is 0.25 µm. Consequently, the highest bumps/pads are 20.25 µm and the distance from the surface of the substrate to the bottom of the chip is 40.5 µm. However, there may be bumps/pads with a height of 19.75 µm, and the substrate/chip distance is 39.5 µm. As a result, the particles deformed to 2 µm are between the 20.25 µm bumps and pads, and the particles between 19.75 µm bumps and pads are deformed to 3 µm from the original size of 5 µm. In general, the smaller the particles, the stricter is the co-planarity requirement.

The best test vehicle for defining the performance of ACAs in terms of processing as well as interconnection properties is an area array flip-chip device. It is beneficial to design the test chip in such a manner that as many individual interconnections can be measured as possible. This allows the monitoring of performance variations in different parts of the device. Combining electrical measurement with proper non-destructive testing methods should allow an evaluation of the effects of the assembly process on the performance of the device. In addition, the electrical properties and the reliability of the adhesive interconnection can be measured and proper data can be assessed for manufacturing.

7.7   CONCLUSIONS

Joining with solder-filled z-adhesives provides a technically feasible interconnection method for bare chips and flexible circuits, especially when bump materials and coatings on substrate conductors are compatible with solder particles of the adhesive. If adhesives filled with Sn-based alloy particles are used for bonding, so much conductor metal may dissolve into the liquid particles that the original eutectic microstructure of the particles will decompose in the microjoints into mechanically weak phase constituents. A local nominal composition approach based on combined thermodynamic and diffusion-kinetic theories can be used to explain the microstructural transformations occurring, especially, in small volumes as well as for modelling new solutions to this type of problem. One solution is to use metals which are unable to react chemically and thereby to produce brittle intermetallic compounds. Another solution is to influence the dissolution kinetics of the metals to be bonded. As an example of the previous solution, an adhesive filled with either the eutectic SnBi or pure Bi particles was used to bond successfully Sn-coated conductors or SnPb-bumped chips on Sn-coated contact pads on FR-4. Solutions of the latter type are currently under investigation.

REFERENCES

1   Gross, D., 'Portable Communications: Trends in Systems and Component Technology', *Journal of Electronics Manufacturing*, No. 4, pp. 203-209 (1994).

2   Dolan, T., Tierney, T. and Browne, J., 'Analysing the Strategic Implications of Interconnect Technologies', *Journal of Electronics Manufacturing*, No. 4, pp. 113-124 (1994).

3   Ogunjimi, A. O., Boyle, O., Whalley, D. J. and Williams, D. J., 'A Review of the Impact of Conductive Adhesive Technology on Interconnection', *Journal of Electronics Manufacturing*, No. 2, pp. 109-118 (1992).

4   'Chip on Board Technologies for Multichip Modules', edited by J.H. Lau, van Nostrand Reinhold, New York (1994).

5   Kivilahti, J. K. and Kulojärvi, K., 'A New Reliability Aspect of High Density Interconnections, Design and Reliability of Solders and Solder Interconnections', Proceedings TMS Annual Meeting, Orlando (1997).

6   Kivilahti, J. and Savolainen, P., 'Anisotropic Adhesives for Flip-Chip Bonding', *Journal of Electronics Manufacturing*, No. 5, pp. 245-252 (1995).

7   Kivilahti, J. K., 'Modeling Joining Materials for Microelectronics Packaging', *IEEE CPMT — Part B*, Vol. 18, pp. 326-333 (1995).

8   Savolainen, P. and Kivilahti, J., 'Electrical Properties of Solder Filled Anisotropically

Conductive Adhesives', *Journal of Electronics Manufacturing*, No. 5, pp. 19-26 (1995).

9   Chang, D. D., Fulton, J. A., Ling, H. C., Schmidt, M. B., Sinitski, R. E. and Wong, C. P., 'Accelerated Life Test of Z-axis Conductive Adhesives', *Transactions IEEE CHMT*, **Vol. 16**, pp. 836-842 (1993).

10   Liu, J., 'Reliability of Surface Mounted Anisotropically Conductive Adhesive Joints', *Circuit World*, **Vol. 19**, pp. 4-12 (1993).

11   Burkhart, A., 'Conductive Polymeric Adhesives Solve SMD Assembly Problems', *Adhesives Age*, pp. 36-39, October (1990).

12   Lyons, A. M. and Dahringer, D. W., 'Handbook of Adhesives Technology', Pizzi, A. and Mittal, K., Eds., Marcel Dekker, New York, pp. 565-584 (1994).

13   Adachi, K., 'Packaging Technology for Liquid Crystal Displays', *Solid State Technology*, **Vol. 36**, pp. 63-71 (1993).

14   Matsuoka, H. and Tsukagoshi, I., 'A New Type of Anisotropic Conductive Film with High Connection Reliability and Finer Pitch Densities', Proceedings International Seminar on Recent Achievements in Conductive Adhesive Joining Technology in Electronics Manufacturing, Gothenburg (1993).

15   Takashi, W., Murakoshi, K., Kanazawa, J., Ikehata, M., Iguchi, Y. and Kanamori, T., 'Solderless COG Technology using Anisotropic Conductive Adhesive', Proceedings IMC Yokohama, pp. 93-98 (1992).

16   Dietz, R., Peck, D. and Firmstone, M., 'Reworkable Thermoplastic Adhesive for High Definition Printing', Proceedings Adhesives in Electronics, Berlin (1994).

17   Estes, R., 'Polymer Flip Chip P_FC: A Technology Assessment of Solderless Bump Process and Reliability', Proceedings of Adhesives in Electronics, Berlin (1994).

18   Gilleo, K., Cinque, T., Corbett, S. and Lee, C., 'Thermoplastic Adhesive — The Attachment Solution for Multichip Modules', Proceedings IEPS, San Diego, pp. 232-242 (1993).

19   Savolainen, P. and Kivilahti, J., 'Characterisation of Polyimide-glass-metal Joints Bonded with Anisotropic Electrically Conductive Adhesives', *Microelectronics International*, pp. 13-16, May (1996).

20   Yamaguchi, Y., Tsukagoshi, L. and Nakajima, A., 'Anisotropic Conductive Film', *Circuit Technology*, No. 4, pp. 362-370 (1989).

21   Hogerton, P. B., Carlson, K. E., Hall, J. B., Krause, L. J. and Tingerthal, J. M., 'An Evaluation of a Heat-Bondable, Anisotropically-Conductive Adhesive as an Interconnection Medium for Flexible Printed Circuitry', Proceedings IEPS, pp. 1026-1033 (1990).

22   Chung, K., Dreier, G., Fitzgerald, P., Boyle, A., Lin, M. and Sager, J., 'Z-Axis Conductive Adhesive for TAB and Fine Pitch Interconnections', Proceedings 41st ECTC, pp. 345-354 (1991).

23   Shiozawa, N., Isaka, K. and Ohta, T., 'Electric Properties of Connections by Anisotropic Conductive Film', *Journal of Electronics Manufacturing*, No. 5, pp. 33-37 (1994).

24   Morishita, H., Kokogawa, T., Adachi, K., Ishizu, A. and Takasago, H., 'Optimum Condition of Fine Pitch Bonding using ACF', Proceedings IMC, Yokohama, pp. 88-92 (1992).

25   Ando, H., Kobayashi, N., Numao, H., Matsubara, Y. and Suzuki K., 'Electrically Conductive Adhesive Sheet, Circuit Board and Electrical Connection Structure Using the Same', European Patent 0 147 856 (1985).

26   Gilleo, K., 'An Anisotropic Adhesive for Bonding Electrical Components', European Patent 0 265 077 (1987).

27   Pennisi, R., Papageorge, M. and Urbisch, G., 'Anisotropic Conductive Adhesive and Encapsulant Material', US Patent 5 136 365 (1992).

28   Savolainen, P. and Kivilahti, J., 'A Solder Alloy Filled Z-axis Conductive Epoxy Adhesive', *Journal of Adhesion*, **Vol. 49**, pp. 187-196 (1995).

29   Kang, S. K., Rai, R. and Purushothaman, S., 'Development of High Conductivity Lead (Pb)-Free Conducting Adhesives', Proceedings 1996 ECTC, Orlando, pp. 565-570 (1996).

30   Kinloch, A. J., 'Durability of Structural Adhesives', A. J. Kinloch, ed., Applied Science Publishers, London, pp. 1-43 (1983).

31   Kinloch, A. J., 'Adhesion and Adhesives: Science and Technology', Chapman and Hall, London (1987).

32   Adamson, A. W., 'Physical Chemistry of Surfaces' (Fifth edition), Wiley-Interscience Publication, John Wiley & Sons, Inc., NY (1990).

33   Lea, C., 'A Scientific Guide to Surface Mount Technology', Electrochemical Publications Ltd, Ayr, pp. 308-377 (1988).

34   Yost, F. G. and Romig, A. D., 'Thermodynamics of Wetting by Liquid Metals', in 'Electronics Packaging Materials Science', R. Jaccodine, K. A. Jackson and R. C. Sundahl, Eds., Materials Research Symposium Proceedings, Pittsburgh, No. 108, pp. 385-390 (1988).

35   Kim, H. K., Liou, H. K. and Tu, K. N., 'Morphology of Instability of the Wetting Tips of Eutectic SnBi, Eutectic SnPb, and Pure Sn on Cu', *Journal of Materials Research*, No. 10, pp. 497-504 (1995).

36   Aksay, I. A., Hoge, C. E., and Pask, J. A., in 'Surfaces and Interfaces of Glass and Ceramics', V. D. Frechette, W. C. LaCrouse, and V. L. Burdick, Eds., Materials Science Research, Plenum Press, New York, **Vol. 7**, pp. 299-321 (1973).

37   IPMA — the Thermodynamic Databank for Interconnection and Packaging Materials (org. J. Kivilahti), Helsinki University of Technology (1996).

38   Gaskell, D. R., 'Metallurgical Thermodynamics', in 'Physical Metallurgy', R. W. Cahn and P. Haasen, Eds., 3rd Edition, Elsevier Publishers BV, pp. 271-326 (1983).

39   Rönkä, K. J., Vuorinen, V. and Kivilahti, J. K., 'Wetting of Copper, Nickel and Tin by SnPb and SnBi Solders', January (1999).

40   Klein Wassink, R.J., 'Soldering in Electronics' (2nd Edition), Electrochemical Publications Ltd, Port Erin, Isle of Man (1989).

41   van Loo, F. J. J., 'Multiphase Diffusion in Binary and Ternary Solid State Systems', *Prog. Solid State Chemistry*, No. 20, pp. 47-99 (1990).

42   Kirkaldy, J. S. and Young, D. J., 'Diffusion in the Condensed State', The Institute of Metals, London, pp. 172-272 (1987).

43   Rönkä, K. J., van Loo, F. J. J. and Kivilahti, J. K., 'A Diffusion-Kinetic Model for Predicting Solder/Conductor Interactions in High Density Interconnections', *Journal of Metallurgical & Materials Transactions*, **Vol. 29A**, pp. 2951, December (1998).

44   Rönkä, K. J., van Loo, F. J. J., and Kivilahti, J. K., 'The Local Nominal Composition — A Useful Concept for Microjoining and Interconnection Applications', (submitted 1996).

45   Allenby, B. R., Ciccarelli, J. P., Artaki, I., Fischer, J. R., Schoenthaler, D., Carroll, T. A., Dahringer, D. W., Degani, Y., Freund, R. S., Graedel, T. E., Lyons, A. M., Plewes, J. T., Gherman, C., Solomon, H., Melton, C., Munie, G. C. and Socolowski, N., 'An Assessment of the Use of Lead in Electronics Assembly: Part 1', *Circuit World*, **Vol. 19**, pp. 18-24 (1993).

46   Vianco, P. T. and Frear, D. R., 'Issues in the Replacement of Lead-bearing Solders', *Journal of Materials*, pp. 14-19, July (1993).

47   Nicholson, A. and Bloomfield, D., 'The Use of Bismuth Alloy Systems for Reflow and Wave Soldering', *Soldering & Surface Mount Technology*, No. 10, pp. 23-26, February (1992).

48   Frear, D. R., Grivas, D. and Morris, J. W., 'Thermal Fatigue on Solder Joints', *Journal of Materials*, pp. 18-22, June (1988).

49   McCormack, M. and Jin, S., 'Progress in the Design of New Lead-free Solder Alloys', *Journal of Materials*, pp. 36-40, July (1993).

50   Morris, J. W., Freer Goldstein, J. L. and Mei, Z., 'Microstructure and Mechanical Properties of Sn-In and Sn-Bi Solders', *Journal of Materials*, pp. 25-27, July (1993).

51   Mojebuoboh, F., 'Bismuth — Production, Properties and Applications', *Journal of Metals*, pp. 46-49, April (1992).

52   *Metal Bulletin*, p. 29, August (1996).

53   Kulojärvi, K., Savolainen, P. and Kivilahti, J. K., 'Bonding Flexible Circuits and Bare Chips with Anisotropic Electrically Conductive and Non-conductive Adhesives', Proceedings 10th European Microelectronics Conference, Copenhagen, pp. 28-34, May (1995).

54   Puhakka, K., Kulojärvi, K, Savolainen, P. and Kivilahti, J. K., 'Bonding Flexible Circuits and Flip Chips with Solder-Filled Z-adhesives, Non-Conductive Adhesives and Fusible Coatings', *International Journal of Microelectronics Packaging* (in print).

55   Pourbaix, M., 'Atlas of Electrochemical Equilibria in Aqueous Solutions', Pergamon Press, London (1966).

Chapter 8

RECENT ADVANCES AND EVALUATION OF ANISOTROPICALLY CONDUCTIVE ADHESIVES FOR MICROELECTRONICS ASSEMBLY

A. M. LYONS
Bell Laboratories - Lucent Technologies, New Jersey, USA

C. P. WONG
Georgia Institute of Technology, Atlanta, USA

8.1   INTRODUCTION

Isotropically conductive adhesives (ICAs) have been used for a number of years to attach chips to package lead frames in the semiconductor industry and for general interconnection of components to flexible circuits in various consumer product applications. These materials conduct equally in all directions. To obtain isolation between adjacent pads, ICAs are screen or stencil printed only on the circuit contact pads. For fine pitch applications, this process becomes problematic for two reasons. First, printing paste at fine pitches is difficult without applying so much adhesive that shorts between adjacent traces occur during assembly. Secondly, the small amount of adhesive deposited on the contact pads, coupled with the very high conductive filler content, lowers adhesive bond strength. Loss of bond integrity is especially apparent from mechanical shock and drop tests.

In the last few years a new class of adhesives that are conductive in one direction only have been developed. These are referred to as anisotropically conductive adhesives (ACAs) and can be obtained either as films (ACAFs) or as pastes (ACAPs). These anisotropically conductive adhesives provide electrical as well as mechanical interconnections between conductive pads on parts to be permanently assembled. The conductivity of these materials is restricted to the Z-direction (perpendicular to the plane of the board) with electrical isolation provided in the X -Y plane. Because of the anisotropy, ACAs may be deposited over the entire contact region, greatly facilitating material application. Larger volumes of adhesive may be deposited, covering a larger bond area and ensuring mechanically robust interconnections. The lower conductive filler loadings also improve adhesive bond strength. Thus, ACA materials offer an adhesive method for achieving robust, fine pitch interconnections.

The most commercially significant ACAs are based on the single particle bridging concept. Interconnections with pitches below 50 μm have been demonstrated with these materials. ACAs are the subject of many recent studies[1-8] and numerous companies offer ACA products (see Appendix 8.1). Examples of typical interconnections using ACAs are shown in Figure 8.1. Figure 8.1(a) shows the interconnection of a flexible circuit to a liquid crystal display (LCD) using a narrow strip of ACAF, and Figure 8.1(b) shows the attachment of a tape automated bonded (TAB) circuit connected to a second flexible circuit using a picture frame of ACAF. In general, the adhesive material is applied to one interconnection surface, such as a display with a pad array. A part, such as the flexible circuit, is aligned to the display with standard placement equipment and then bonded by the simultaneous application of heat and pressure. A wide variety of assembly options are possible using ACA materials.

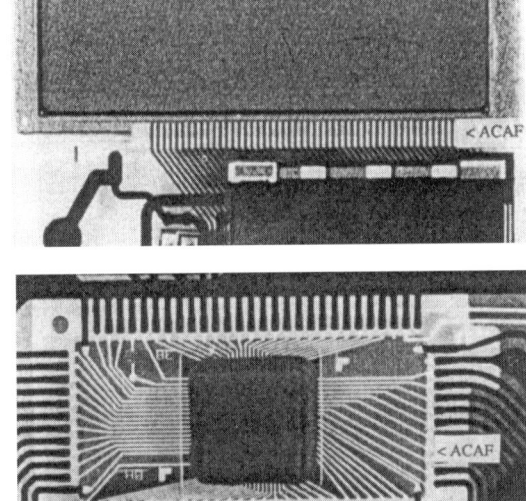

(a)

(b)

Fig. 8.1 Examples of typical interconnections using ACAs. (a) shows the interconnection of a flexible circuit to a liquid crystal display (LCD) using a narrow strip of ACAF, and (b) shows the attachment of a tape automated bonded (TAB) circuit connected to a second flexible circuit using a picture frame of ACAF.

8.2 MATERIALS AND CONDUCTION MECHANISMS

A The Anistropically Conductive Adhesive: General Considerations

In general, ACA materials are prepared by dispersing electrically conductive particles in an adhesive matrix at a concentration far below the percolation threshold. The concentration of particles is controlled such that enough particles are present to assure reliable electrical conductivity between the assembled parts in the Z-direction while too few particles are present to achieve percolation conduction in the X-Y plane. When designing materials to achieve fine pitch interconnections, several important variables must be considered and are application dependent. These variables include adhesive characteristics as well as particle type.

Two basic types of adhesives are available: thermoplastic and thermosetting. Thermoplastic adhesives are rigid materials at temperatures below the glass transition temperature (Tg) of the polymer. Above this temperature, polymer flow occurs. When using this type of material, assembly temperatures must exceed the Tg_g to achieve good adhesion. Thus the Tg_g must be sufficiently high to avoid polymer flow during use conditions, but the Tg_g must be low enough to prevent thermal damage to the electronic circuits during assembly. The principal advantage of thermoplastic adhesives is the relative ease with which the interconnection can be disassembled for repair operations.

Thermosetting adhesives, such as epoxies and silicones, form a three-dimensional cross-linked structure when cured under specific conditions. Curing techniques include: heat, UV light, and added catalysts. As a result of this irreversible cure reaction, the initial uncross-linked material is transformed into a rigid solid. The curing reaction is not reversible. This fact may hinder disassembly and interconnection repair. The ability to maintain strength at high temperature and the formation of robust adhesive bonds are the principal advantages of these materials. The effect of polymer matrix on electrical performance is discussed in more detail in the following section.

The principal criterion used for selecting the adhesive is that robust bonds are formed to all surfaces involved in the interconnection. Numerous materials surfaces can be found in the interconnection region including: SiO_2, Si_3N_4, polyester, polyimide, FR-4, glass, gold, copper, and aluminium. Adhesion to these surfaces must be preserved after standard tests such as temperature-humidity-bias ageing and temperature cycling. Some surfaces may require chemical treatments to achieve good adhesion. In addition, the adhesive must not contain ionic impurities that would degrade electrical performance of the interconnections.

ACA adhesives come in two distinct forms: pastes and films. The most significant difference between these forms is the method employed to apply the material to the substrate. Paste materials are either printed (screen, stencil or dip techniques) or dispensed with a syringe. Film materials are supplied by the adhesives manufacturer in a reel and the end-user must have dedicated equipment to cut, align and tack the adhesive into position on the substrate. Screen or stencil printing offer significant advantages over films for applying ACAPs rapidly over large areas with a minimum of capital equipment needs. In addition, the thickness of the adhesive deposit can be readily adjusted by the end-user to accommodate substrate metallisation thickness or IC chip bump height variations. Film bonding is advantageous when the substrate is non-planar, as in the case of assembled liquid crystal displays (LCDs).

Little information is available concerning the chemical composition of the adhesives used for ACAs. Most journal publications refer to the composition as simply an "epoxy-type" adhesive for proprietary reasons. One recent article[9] breaks with this trend and describes in detail the factors influencing the optimisation of an ACAF formulation. Items discussed include the types of epoxy resins, curing agents, coupling agents and conductive particles evaluated. In all cases, manufacturers and trade-names were included. Information that is especially useful to end-user and formulator alike is the discussion of how resin ratio (i.e., the ratio of solid bis-A to liquid bis-F resin) affects the stress-strain, 90° peel strength and loop tack strength values of the films. These properties are important for evaluating the process of tacking a film to a substrate, as well as how the adhesive can flow into contact with the device during cure. This paper also describes the formulation of four other commercially available ACAFs, including a thermoplastic system based on a styrene-b-ethylene-butylene-b-styrene block copolymer. The stress strain behaviour of the films is compared with their electrical interconnection performance during ageing at 85°C/85% relative humidity.

The materials used as conductive particles must also be carefully selected. Silver offers moderate cost, high electrical conductivity, high current carrying ability, and low chemical reactivity, but problems with electromigration may occur. Nickel is a lower cost alternative, but corrosion of nickel surfaces has been found during accelerated ageing tests. The material that offers the best properties is gold; however, costs may be prohibitive for large-volume applications. Plated particles may offer the best combination of properties at moderate cost. Some ACA materials use solder particles to ensure electrical contacts with high reliability by creating a metallurgical bond.

B Conduction Mechanisms:

Conduction mechanisms are highly dependent upon the type of conductive particle that is formulated into the adhesive matrix. In all cases discussed in this review, pressure is required during assembly to displace excess adhesive such that single particles span the gap between component and substrate metallisation surfaces. The particle type determines the nature of the electrical contact at the particle-surface interface. Three types of contact mechanisms will be discussed based on: rigid, compliant and solder based particles. Conduction has also been observed when components are assembled to substrates under pressure with adhesives containing no conductive particles. This type of conduction mechanism will be discussed for comparison with the particle-filled adhesive systems.

Contact theory (see Holm[10]) provides a good basis for understanding these different conduction mechanisms. We will not present a complete description of how contact theory can be applied to ACA interconnections; however, several important factors that influence ACA conduction mechanisms will be illustrated. The contact resistance (R) of an interconnection can be described by $R = R_c + R_f$ where the constriction resistance (R_c) arises from current flow being constricted through small conducting spots, and the film resistance (R_f) results from insulating films at the conductor surface. In the case of ACAs, the conductive particles can be viewed as the "asperities" or conducting spots described by Holm. The apparent contact surface area (A_a), or bond pad, is significantly larger than the load bearing contact area (A_b). Assuming that all particles touching both substrate and component surfaces make electrical contact, then A_b is equivalent to the area of the electrically conducting spots such that $A_b = \pi n a^2$ where a is the average radius of the conductive spot (i.e., the radius of the spot formed at the substrate/particle interface) and n is the number of spots. If the particle concentration is sufficiently low, then each particle contributes to R_c independently and $R_c = 2(\rho/4na)$ where ρ is the resistivity of the particles.

The radii of the conductive spots are dependent upon the relative hardness of the contact materials (H) and the applied load (P) such that $P = \xi H A_b$ where ξ is a factor, ranging from 0 to 1, that depends upon the elasticity of the system. Assuming that the particles are either rigid (and significantly harder than the metallisations) or compliant, then $\xi = 1$. By combining the above equations it is seen that $R_c = 0.886\rho(H/nP)^{1/2}$. In both cases, the initial load (P) is applied externally during assembly. After assembly, however, the load is maintained by curing the adhesive. The case for particles that are harder or softer than the substrate/component metallisations will be discussed in more detail in the following sections.

1 Rigid Particles

For particles that are hard relative to the substrate and component metallisations, the ACA conduction mechanism is based upon applying sufficient pressure during assembly such that the particles penetrate into, and plastically deform, the metallisations. With these rigid particle systems, the particle size distributions are broad. Thus the initial load is supported by the few largest particles and $A_b \ll A_a$. As these largest particles penetrate and deform the underlying metal, more particles will form electrically conductive bridges. Eventually an equilibrium will be achieved where the final contact pressure will depend not only upon H and P, but also the particle size distribution and metallisation thicknesses.

Figure 8.2 illustrates the plastic deformation of both chip and substrate metallisations resulting from the high contact pressure exerted by a silver plated glass particle. The aluminium chip metallisation exhibits plastic yielding, similar to that produced by a spherical indenter during a Brinell hardness test. Plastic deformation of the relatively harder Au-Ni-Cu substrate metallisation is less pronounced. The reliability observed for this type of interconnection could be explained by cold welds formed at the particle-metallisation interfaces.[10]

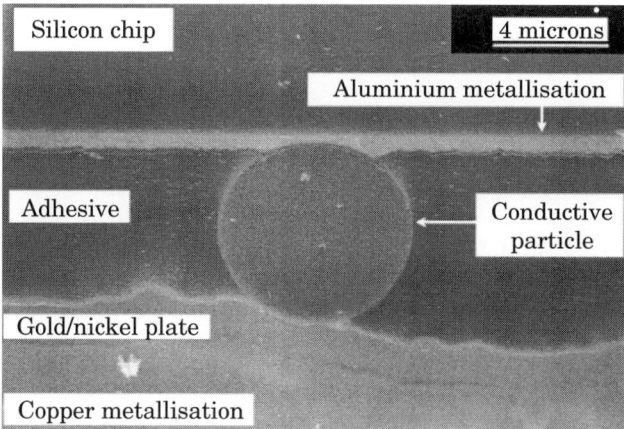

Fig. 8.2 SEM micrograph of an ACA interconnetion between a flex circuit and an unbumped aluminium metallised silicon chip. The hard silver plated glass particle penetrates and plastically deforms the relatively soft aluminium chip metallisation and plated copper metallisation on the flex circuit.

Film resistance values for this type of interconnection are limited to the conductive particle surfaces; any films present on the chip/substrate metallisations will be broken during assembly for all but the smallest particles making contact. For rigid particles with a noble metal coating, film resistance values will be negligible.

The intimate particle-substrate contacts formed during assembly are maintained in the final interconnection by curing the adhesive. The elastically deformed portion of the indentations will exert a continuous contact pressure on the interconnections. In the case of heat cured systems, the higher coefficient of thermal expansion (CTE) of the adhesive matrix, compared with that of the particles, exerts an additional load on the contacts after cooling the assembly to ambient temperature.[11] Creep of the matrix would relax these loads. This explains, in part, why thermosetting matrices, which are less susceptible to creep, outperform thermoplastic based ACAs. Shrinkage of UV curable adhesives serves a comparable function of exerting applied loads. Increasing the Tg of either heat or UV cured systems will also improve reliability.

2 Compliant Particles

Compliant particles are the most widely used conductive fillers for ACAs and are typically composed of gold and nickel plated polymer spheres. The ACA conduction mechanism is based upon applying sufficient pressure during assembly such that the particles themselves plastically deform and make contact over an area greater than their initial diameter. An example of a deformed plated particle is shown in Figure 8.3. As the size distribution of these particles is typically very narrow, with a range of sizes <5%, most particles trapped between chip and substrate participate in the electrical interconnection. A minimum pressure is required to guarantee that the particles are able to overcome local surface asperities. The calculation of $R_c = 2(\rho/4\Sigma a)$ and $P = HA_b$ would be relatively straightforward compared with the rigid particle case if the particles were isotropically conductive.

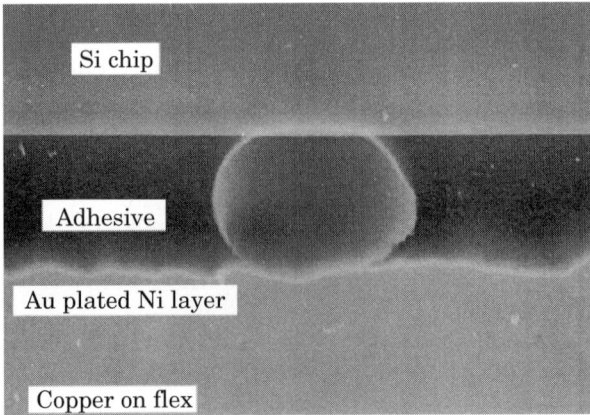

Fig. 8.3 SEM micrograph of an ACA interconnection between a silicon chip and a PWB substrate. The compliant plated polymer particle is significantly compressed and conforms to the metallisation surfaces.

With plated polymer spheres other conditions apply. At higher loads, the contact area increases rapidly, but the conduction path becomes limited by the plating thickness. Higher pressures decrease the contact resistance because the limiting conduction path length decreases; the increase in contact area is relatively less significant. The effect of controlled particle compression on contact resistance values has been recently reported.[12] Dielectric spacer particles of different sizes (4-10 μm diameter) were formulated into an ACAF containing 10 μm diameter plated polymer spheres. Larger particle deformations resulted in lower initial contact resistance values. The most stable values, for interconnections tested at 85°C and 85% RH, were reported for 40% particle compression levels. Presumably higher compression levels can lead to reliability problems.

Film resistance values for compliant particle interconnections can occur on either the chip or substrate metallisation surfaces as no plastic deformation of these surfaces occurs. The particles, which do plastically deform, are usually plated with a thin exterior gold layer.

As with rigid particle systems, curing the polymer matrix under applied pressure maintains particle-substrate contacts. Continuous contact pressure can act on the interconnections resulting from spring-like deformation of the plated polymer particles. Polymer particles with high crosslink densities minimise deleterious relaxation and creep effects. No additional loads are expected from CTE mismatch effects during cooling as the CTE difference between the polymer particle cores and the polymer matrix is relatively small.

3 Solder Particles

In these systems, solder particles form metallurgical bonds to both the substrate and component metallisations. This mechanism eliminates the need of the polymer adhesive to maintain the particles under a compressive load. The quality of the bond depends strongly upon the interaction between the filler particles and the component and substrate metallurgies.

Much of the work on flip-chip interconnections with solder filled ACAs has been reported by Savolainen and Kivilahti.[13-15] They found that SnPb as well as Pb-free Sn alloys form intermetallics with copper and nickel based metallisations. Intermetallic formation consumes all the tin from the relatively small solder particles, leaving a layer of relatively pure bismuth or lead, the two most commonly used alloying elements. The resulting bond is shown schematically in Figure 8.4(a). Bismuth is brittle and the layer can easily crack. This results in a purely mechanical contact, not a metallurgical bond. The low mechanical strength of Pb can also cause problems as the layer can be deformed by very small mechanical stresses. In addition, both Bi and Pb are relatively poor conductors of electrical current. Thin gold layers, used to protect the base metals from oxidation, readily dissolve into the solder alloys and do not prevent intermetallic formation.

To avoid the formation of intermetallics, a transient melting technique was developed[13] as shown schematically in Figure 8.4(b). Sn or SnPb was plated on to the PWB traces and chip bumps. During bonding, as the SnBi particles begin to melt, Bi diffuses into the Sn surfaces, causing further localised melting. As the Bi is depleted from the particles, the melting temperature of the progressively Sn-rich particles increases and the particles solidify at the bonding temperature. Cross-sections of these bonds show no indication of intermetallic layer formation.

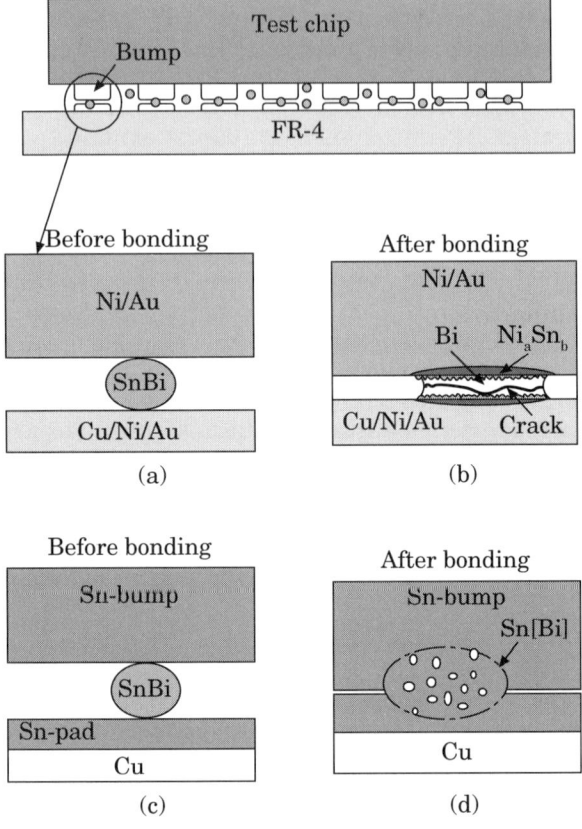

Fig. 8.4 Schematic illustrations of ACA interconnections formed with solder particles. (Figure courtesy of Jorma Kivilahti)

Constriction resistance values are negligible in systems with true solder joints due to the very large particle diameters that result from applying pressure to the soft solder particles. Film resistance values are also negligible in these systems, again assuming metallurgical bonding. Oxides on the solder particle, chip or substrate metallisations could prevent solder wetting and thus significantly increase resistance values. Savolainen and Kivilahti[14] found, however, that no added flux was necessary to achieve good solder particle-surface wetting. They speculated that the adhesive matrix acted as a fluxing agent. Other studies have found the addition of flux to be advantageous.[16]

The adhesive does not need to maintain a compressive load on the interconnection as described for rigid and compliant particles in the previous sections, due to the formation of metallurgical bonds. The adhesive is required for two reasons: to enhance the mechanical integrity of the interconnection and provide environmental protection. These are the essential functions of underfill materials used in conventional flip-chip solder interconnections.

Solder filled ACAs have been used to fabricate multilayer PWBs.[17]

4 No Particles

Systems where no particles are used in the adhesive will be described in section IV E, "Technologies for Extremely Fine Pitch Applications". These interconnections most closely resemble those described by Holm.[10] Asperities on the mating metallisation surfaces displace the adhesive and make electrical contact. Very reliable interconnections can be formed, especially when both surfaces are plated with a noble metal. Assembly yields, however, are extremely sensitive to coplanarity of the contacts.[12]

C Electrical Properties

1 Frequency Response:

Because of the composite structure of ACAs, the possibility of signal frequency dependent phenomena is a concern. The fundamental principle in achieving high frequency performance in any interconnection system is to minimise inductance and capacitance, or have uniform controlled impedance. The shortest interconnection length gives the lowest inductance. The interconnection length of an ACA material is determined by the diameter of conductive particles, which can range from 0.5 to 30 µm, significantly shorter than pins or wirebonds. Therefore, the inductance of an adhesive interconnection should be negligible. The capacitance resulting from the adhesive dielectric matrix is mainly dependent upon the physical layout of the interconnection. Only the dielectric located between the signal and ground lines will show stray capacitance. Recent experiments have demonstrated excellent performance of ACAs at high frequencies.[18]

2 Current Carrying Capability:

Since the amount of conductive metal is small and varies in ACAs, one must evaluate the current carrying capability of each material. Even for a given material, the electrical properties will be determined by the geometries of the component and substrate for each application.

AC current carrying capability has been demonstrated using an active bipolar IC bonded with an ACAF to a flexible circuit.[19] These results show that an ACAF filled with plated metal particles can carry at least 20 mA root mean square (RMS) current at 2 MHz. For carrying high radio frequency current, it appears that the surface of the conductive particles should be smooth.

DC electrical contact resistance values are highly dependent on particle type, particle concentration and assembly parameters (especially applied pressure). Measurements on ACAFs filled with three types of conductive particles exhibited current-carrying capabilities dependent upon the particle metal concentration.[19] Silver plated nickel, silver plated glass and gold plated polymer spheres could carry 200, 20 and 5 mA respectively. Electrical properties of ACAs filled with either solid silver particles (coated with a thin epoxy resin) or gold plated polymer spheres were compared by Date *et al*.[29] Resistance values of 6 and 150 mW with current carrying capabilities of 4000 and 500 mA were reported, again reflecting the higher conductivity of solid *vs* plated particles. Watanabe *et al*.[20] measured the current voltage characteristics of ACAF films filled with both Au plated polymer spheres and Ni particles, and measured resistance values ranging from 3-10 mΩ by a four-point probe technique on 70 x 100 μm bumps. Interconnections formed with both materials could carry 2000 mA at 8 mV DC.

D Component and Substrate Geometry Effects

Design consideration for the substrate include the height, width and spacing of conductors. The width and spacing are determined by pad size and pitch of the components. For a specific conductor pitch, as the conductor width increases, the conductor spacing decreases. As a result, it becomes more difficult to maintain electrical x-y isolation with a specific ACA material. The primary benefits of enlarging conductor widths is to accommodate any lateral misregistration between pad and conductor during the bonding operation and increase the number of particles in the interconnection. The ACA material selected for a specific application should contain particles that are significantly smaller than the minimum space between adjacent conductors.

ACA thickness depends upon the substrate conductor height, the conductive particle diameter and the component conductor height. By using an ACA that is slightly thicker than the sum of these values, adhesive flow during assembly will minimise void formation. As shown in Figure 8.5, voids between the adhesive and the component can form if insufficient adhesive was available during bonding. Voids will lower the strength of the bond and provide sites for moisture accumulation. Both of these phenomena will degrade the performance and reliability of the interconnection. In contrast, if the ACA is too thick or if the bonding pressure and temperature are too low,

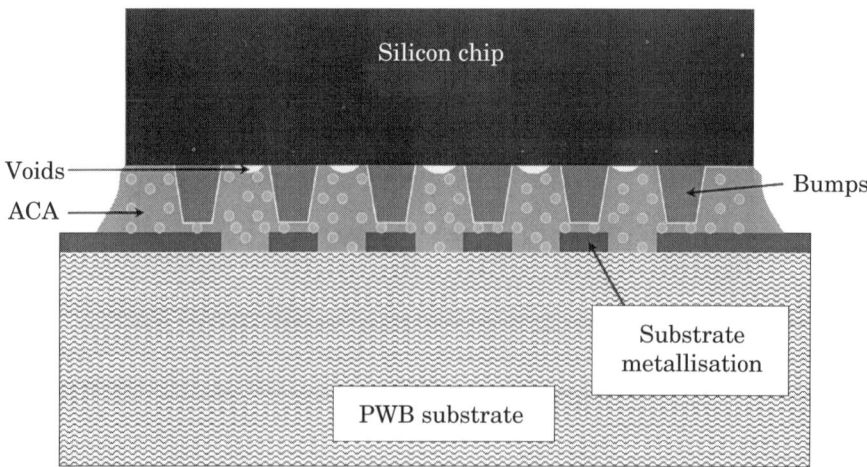

Fig. 8.5 The effect of insufficient adhesive thickness on final bond line properties is illustrated. Void formation will reduce bond strength and create sites for moisture accumulation.

then sufficient adhesive flow may not occur, resulting in open circuits, as shown in Figure 8.6.

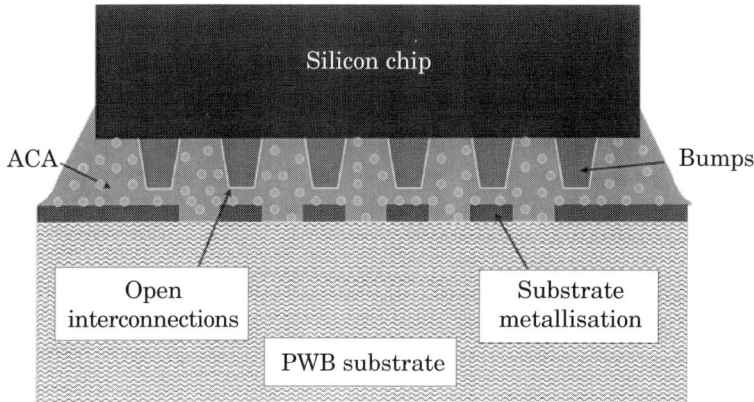

Fig. 8.6 The effect of excess adhesive thickness on final bond line thickness is illustrated. If the assembly conditions are not optimised, then excess adhesive may increase bond resistance or prevent electrical interconnection formation.

The type of substrate selected for ACA interconnections will influence the assembly process. Flex circuits offer numerous advantages for flip-chip assembly over other substrates such as glass or rigid printed wiring boards (PWBs). Unlike glass, flex is compliant. This is especially true at elevated assembly temperatures and when an adhesive is used to laminate copper foil to a polyimide substrate. This compliance allows the copper metallisation to conform about irregularities, such as unusually large partilces in the adhesive or plating asperities, as shown in Figure 8.7. Unlike rigid PWBs,

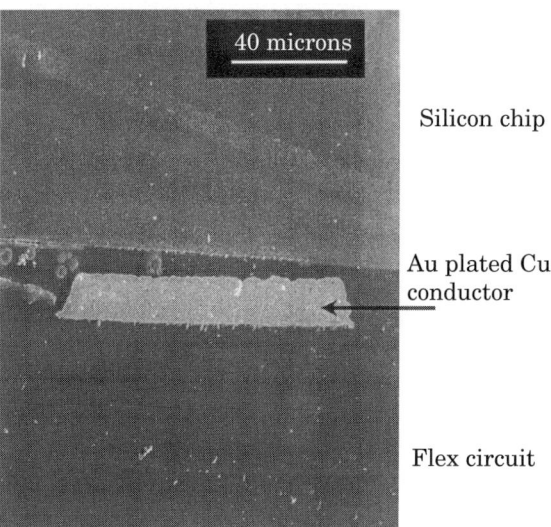

Fig. 8.7 SEM micrograph of an ACA interconnection between a silicon chip and a flex circuit demonstrating the deformation of the flex about an unusually large particle.

flex has a smooth flat surface. Thus the distance between a chip and the substrate is uniform over the entire perimeter. And, unlike silicon and glass, the height of the copper traces may reduce the need to bump the IC chips[22,23] as pressure applied to the chip is focused on the contact pads.

The ideal substrate conductor surface finish is a noble metal plating such as gold flash over a nickel plated copper layer or Pd over copper. Bare copper without any surface treatment typically results in poor interconnection reliability due to the formation of oxides.[21] In general, the key is to minimise surface oxides before the bonding operation and prevent oxidation during testing and use.

For components, the contacts should provide a large flat surface to maximise the number of particles that can contribute to the interconnection. When attaching SMT packaged components, gull-wing devices offer the best geometry for interconnection. Not only do the ends of the pads present a flat surface for bonding, but the shape of the leads provides compliance to the interconnection that can accommodate some degree of non-planarity. Through-hole components present a cross-sectional area that is too small to achieve high interconnection yields.

When bare die are to be interconnected with ACAs, bumps are generally required. The required bump height is dependent upon the ACA adhesive thickness available, as well as the CTE mismatch between chip and substrate. Bumps with flat surfaces will provide the lowest resistance values as more particles will be trapped in the interconnection. The most critical parameter for chip interconnections with ACAs is coplanarity of the bumps. As shown in Figure 8.8, a bump that is significantly shorter than its neighbours may not be electrically interconnected. Higher assembly pressures, compliant metal plated polymer particles and the use of compliant substrates can help alleviate bump coplanarity tolerances. The development of an ACA assembly process that does not require chip bumping ensures contact coplanarity on the chip;[22,23] mating substrate contacts must be either compliant or coplanar. Significant cost savings will result from the elimination of bumps due to the reduction of process steps and the increased availability of singulated chips.

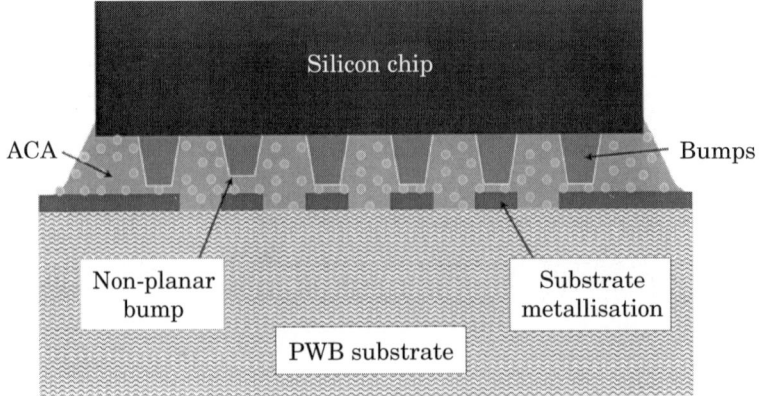

Fig. 8.8 Schematic illustration of the effect of bump non-planarity on ACA interconnection formation.

8.3   ACA ASSEMBLY

All ACA assembly processes require the application of pressure during adhesive cure. Curing the adhesive is straightforward as standard methods can be employed to supply the energy required to initiate the chemical reaction. Typically heat, and less frequently ultra-violet (UV) radiation are used; these energy sources are easily incorporated into the process. Applying pressure during cure, however, requires special equipment. Most ACA processes affect adhesive cure in a specially designed alignment machine. Heat is supplied from the thermode used for component pick-up, whereas UV is usually brought through the substrate by optical fibre bundles.

A Bare Die and SMT Assembly Processes

During the assembly of bare die with ACAs, the alignment machine must serve three functions: align the chip to the substrate, apply pressure uniformly to the entire chip, and supply sufficient energy to cure the adhesive. Because of the multiple requirements and tight tolerances, machines are expensive to own and maintain. Cure time reduces throughput and significantly increases machine operating costs. Using an ACAF further increases costs as additional equipment is required to cut, align and tack the adhesive on to the substrate. In addition, adhesive films must be tailored to individual chip dimensions, bump heights and bond line thicknesses.

The severe demands placed on the alignment machine by standard ACA assembly processes have significantly limited the implementation of ACA materials. Alternative assembly processes are required to expand the use of ACA materials to applications beyond interconnections to glass substrates.

A new approach to using ACAs has recently been described.[22,23] In this process, the cure step is shifted from the alignment machine to a batch curing fixture (BCF) where a conformal silicone bladder applies pressure uniformly to all assemblies. Many types of components, ranging from bare die to SMT packages, can be assembled with ACAs using this approach. An overview of the BCF assembly process is shown in Figure 8.9 and a cross-sectional view is shown in Figure 8.10.

(a)   (b)   (c)

Fig. 8.9 A photographic overview of the Batch Curing Fixture. Populated circuits placed on to the 8 in. x 8 in. vacuum chuck (a), stretched silicone rubber bladder placed above the circuits to create a sample chamber (b), and bladder drawn into conformal contact with the circuits by evacuating the underlying chamber (c).

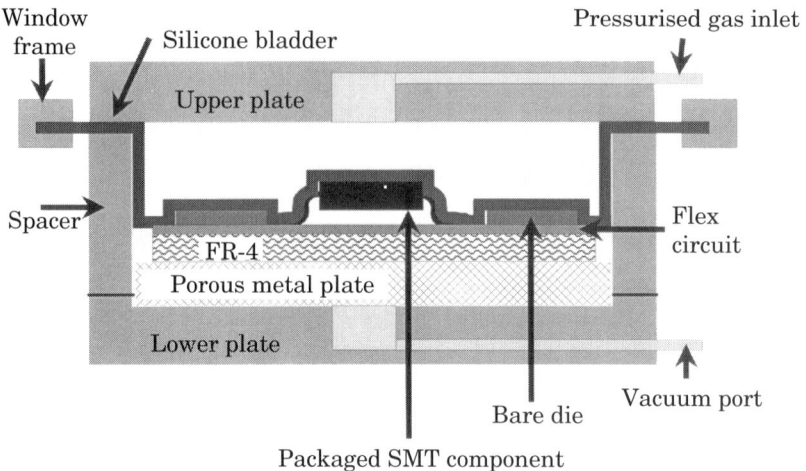

Fig. 8.10 Schematic cross-section of the BCF illustrating the sample and pressure chambers, as well as the bladder in conformal contact with the components.

When implementing the BCF process, the first step is to apply the ACA to the substrate. An ACAP adhesive will maximise the throughput of the BCF process for two reasons. Paste adhesives can be formulated with specific rheological properties[22,23] such that components placed into an ACA paste are held securely due to their "tacky" nature. This eliminates the need to supply heat and pressure to the component in the alignment machine. The second reason is that stencil printing paste is an inherently less expensive process than cutting, aligning, and tacking film based adhesives. Film materials can be used, but film tacking, as well as component tacking in the alignment machine, would be required.

After printing, the components are aligned and placed into the paste. The populated circuits are then transported from the placement machine to the BCF for cure. The BCF sample chamber can be designed to accommodate single or multiple circuits, depending upon sample size and process flow.

In the BCF, the populated circuits are placed on a heated porous metal plate, as shown in Figure 8.9(a). A stretched silicone rubber bladder is placed above the circuits to create a sample chamber (Figure 8.9(b)). Pressure is initially applied to the interconnections by first evacuating the sample chamber (Figure 8.9(c)). Ambient pressure above the bladder forces it into conformal contact with the populated circuits. Immediately after evacuating the chamber, the BCF is clamped shut. Compressed gas (100-500 p.s.i.) is introduced above the bladder during the cure cycle. A cross-sectional cartoon of the BCF under pressure is shown in Figure 8.10. Pressure can be maintained during cooling of the samples and is vented before opening the BCF and removing the completed circuits.

The chip to flex alignment achieved during the initial placement step is maintained to within ± 5 μm after final cure, as demonstrated with glass

chips as shown in Figure 8.11.[22] This ability to closely reproduce initial
alignment accuracy is achieved, despite transporting the populated circuits
from the alignment machine to the BCF, due to the tacky nature of the ACA
paste as well as the compliance of the silicone bladder. The bladder ensures
that pressure is uniformly transmitted to the silicon chips regardless of
substrate-bladder coplanarity.

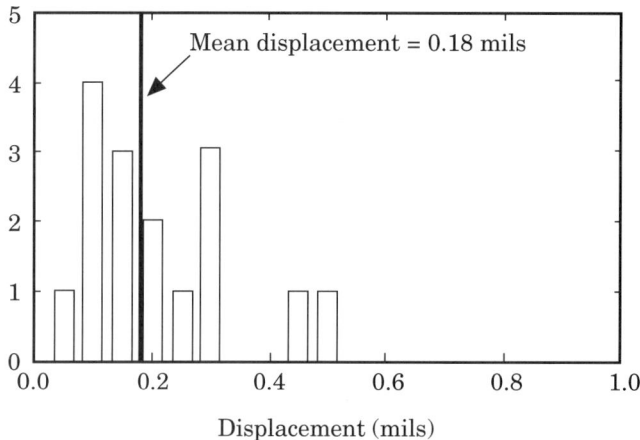

Fig. 8.11 Displacement of glass chips after cure in the BCF plotted as a function of
frequency. Average displacement distance is 5 μm.

The principal advantage of the BCF process is that it frees the alignment
machine to *only* place die. Thus throughput in the machine is significantly
improved, approaching the rates achievable for flip-chip solder
interconnections (only the increased alignment accuracy slows the machine).
Equipment costs are reduced as the machine need not be constructed with
the ability to apply pressure or heat, and coplanarity requirements are
relaxed.

Assembly considerations for SMT components are similar to those described
for flip-chip processes. Throughput is an even greater concern as placement
times for SMT components are even shorter than those for bare die. The need
to shift the cure process away from the alignment/placement machine
becomes greater. A BCF process for SMT components has been developed to
address these concerns.[24] ICA processing has an advantage over ACA
systems as pressure is not required during cure. Alignment and cure
equipment used for solder reflow can also be used for ICAs. Problems with
interconnection reliability and mechanical bond strength limit ICA
applications.[25]

B Registration and Coplanarity Concerns
Placement accuracy is a critical element in using ACAs. Unlike the reflow
solder bump interconnect processes, conductive adhesives do not have the
self-alignment capability that corrects minor misregistration between pad
and substrate conductors. Thus, the placement accuracy required depends
upon the pad size and pitch of the parts to be assembled. Alignment
tolerances exceed ± 25 μm for 100 μm contact pads on 200 μm pitch.

Coplanarity between chip and substrate also imposes severe constraints on the assembly equipment. Requirements exceed ± 1 μm over a 2 cm long IC. This tight tolerance is required to maintain uniform compression of the conductive particles and prevents stresses from adversely affecting interconnection reliability. For SMT component assembly, alignment tolerances are relaxed; however, greater accuracy is still required than for solder assembly processes.

C Assembly Parameters

Important process parameters for ACA assembly are temperature, load, tacking time (the time needed for the adhesive to soften and flow), and bonding time (final cure time). For typical ACAF processes, one of the interconnecting parts is preheated to a temperature below the ACAF bonding temperature, but high enough to partially soften the film so that it has the ability to flow and fill void areas. The bonding load should be high enough to allow the conductive spheres to make good physical contact between conductors but not high enough to damage any of the parts. Finally, the tacking time should be sufficient to give adequate time for the film to flow before cure begins so that it seals the contact area during the final bonding process.

BCF process details have been discussed in section 8.3A, process details for extremely fine pitch flip-chip processes are discussed in the next section (8.4). A step-by-step process description for very fine pitch flex to PWB substrates has been published;[26] other descriptions of flex to rigid ACA interconnection processes have also been published.[27,28]

8.4 TECHNIQUES FOR EXTREMELY FINE PITCH APPLICATIONS

ACA materials prepared with conductive particles randomly distributed in the adhesive matrix form reliable interconnections to components with pad pitches of 200 μm or finer. For extremely fine pitch applications, such as LCD driver chips with pitches ≤100 μm, additional material and processing techniques have been developed. These techniques are designed to reduce or eliminate the possibility of particles forming conductive chains in the X-Y plane that would create shorts between adjacent conductors. The following sections describe the numerous approaches that have been reported to extend the pitch capabilities of ACAs.

A Epoxy Coated Conductive Particles:

One technique uses conductive particles coated with a thin dielectric layer.[29] The particles remain insulating unless sufficient pressure is applied during bonding to break through the thin dielectric. Thus only particles trapped between substrate and chip metallisation can conduct whereas particles between contacts cannot. The thin dielectric layers are applied by an emulsion polymerisation technique whereby silver particles dispersed in an epoxy resin were added to an aqueous emulsion of amine. Upon heating, a thin cured epoxy coating was formed. These coated particles were isolated, then dispersed in an adhesive matrix; both ACAPs and ACAFs were formulated.

B Magnetic Field Enhanced Particle Dispersions:

Uniform dispersions of conductive particles can be created magnetically in ACAFs.[30] In a vertical magnetic field, ferromagnetic spheres (e.g., plated nickel) dispersed in a viscous adhesive matrix repel one another to produce a uniform two-dimensional particle distribution. This structure is preserved by either cooling or curing the matrix within the field. The magnetically processed ACAF gives fewer pad-to-pad variations in contact resistance values and reduces undesirable shorting or voltage breakdown locations. A complementary process has recently been reported[31] where the adhesive matrix, rather than the particles, is magnetically aligned. The applied magnetic field acts upon a ferromagnetic adhesive fluid in which conductive, non-magnetic particles are dispersed. The alignment of the adhesive causes the conductive particles to be uniformly distributed. Once ordered, the arrays of conductive particles can be maintained for several days in the liquid state without external magnetic fields. A variety of ferrocolloids based on polymerisable resins can be employed. The advantage of this technique is that a broad array of conductive particles, including solder and gold plated polymer spheres, can be incorporated into the ACA.

C Adhesive Flow Control:

Even when particles are uniformly distributed in an ACA, the flow of an adhesive during chip assembly can force conductive particles away from the contact area. This decreases the concentration of particles in the contact area while increasing the concentration (and the probability of a short circuit) in the areas between contacts. The viscosity of the adhesive influences this flow phenomenon. Particle motion is limited in high viscosity adhesives. However, these materials require higher bonding temperatures and pressures and longer bonding times to ensure sufficient polymer flow and good adhesion. Low viscosity adhesives typically exhibit higher adhesive strengths as the materials can more rapidly flow and wet the surfaces to be bonded; however, excessive particle flow can occur. To address this problem, Hitachi has developed a double-layer ACAF[32,33] which consists of non-filled and conductive particle filled adhesive layers. The rheological behaviour of the two adhesive layers was adjusted to minimise particle flow and maximise adhesion. Experiments demonstrated that the number of conducting particles trapped between a bump and the substrate was greater with a double layer film than with a conventional single layer material. This resulted in lower contact resistance values and the ability to achieve interconnections at 10 µm spacings without short circuits.

Samsung and Zymet have developed a different approach to restricting particle flow away from contact pads.[34,41] Insulating, peak shaped polymeric 'dams' are created around contact pads which limit particle flow. The dams are created by coating a negative acting photoimageable dielectric on to a glass substrate with opaque electrode pads. UV light is exposed through the backside of the glass substrate, curing the dielectric in the exposed areas. The unexposed dielectric is removed from the contact pads before applying the ACA. Bumps are fabricated on the chip such that the bump diameter is smaller than the contact pad area. When the chip is aligned and bonded to the glass substrate, the bumps fit within the dams. Care must be taken to create dams of the appropriate height, and opaque metallisation on the glass is required. Any adhesive system, including ACAPs, can be used with this system.

D Particle Localisation:

Localisation or placement of conductive particles only on the contact pads of an IC chip has been achieved by several novel processes.[35,36] In one process,[35] a UV-curable adhesive is applied to an LSI wafer and exposed through a mask such that only the material above the metallic contact pads on the IC remains tacky. The surface is then coated with metallised polymer spheres, 10 μm in diameter; the spheres adhere only to the tacky regions above the contact pads. The chips are diced and assembled to LCD substrates which have also been coated with a UV-curable adhesive. Pressure is applied to the assembly, and the UV-curable adhesives (both on the substrate and on the uncured adhesive holding the conductive spheres to the chip) flow so as to fill the bond line as well as to allow the conductive particles to make electrical contact to both chip and substrate metallisations. The final assembly is cured by UV light before pressure is released. This process can be used for 50 μm pitch interconnections without risk of short circuits. Disadvantages include the need to process whole wafers. The ability of the conductive particles to remain on the contact pads during wafer dicing and chip removal from tape may be problematic.

A similar approach has been reported[36] where gold plated polymer conductive particles are mixed with an adhesive and printed on to the LCD glass substrate. A non-conductive epoxy adhesive is coated around the conductive particles. An unbumped, aluminium metallised IC is aligned and bonded to the substrate under the simultaneous application of heat and pressure. Finally, a ceramic cap is bonded to encapsulate the chip and retard corrosion of the aluminium contact metallisation. This approach has many merits as bare isolated die, without bumps, can be used. The need for a ceramic cap, however, increases costs and increases the substrate area required for chip interconnections.

E Unfilled Adhesive Systems:

Chip on glass interconnections have been reported where bumped chips are interconnected to glass substrates by non-conductive adhesives. One approach[37] uses gold bumps and a UV curable adhesive that exhibits significant shrinkage during cure. Chips with extremely uniform bump heights are required. Other approaches deposit compliant solder alloys either on the LCD substrate,[38] or on the gold bumped IC;[39] interconnection is achieved by curing a non-conductive adhesive. These techniques minimise bump planarity issues as the solder layer imparts compliance, but require special deposition techniques to deposit the alloys. Unbumped chips have been interconnected to flex circuits using an unfilled adhesive.[23] Contacts on the chip are inherently coplanar and the flex circuit contacts are highly compliant. Interconnections are reliable but assembly yields are low as the metallisation on the flex could not deform sufficiently to contact the recessed chip metallisation consistently.

F Fixed Conductor Arrays:

Other methods have been reported to create rigidly defined arrays of conductive bumps fixed within a polymer film. Two general approaches will be described, based either on plating metallic bumps or printing arrays of isotropically conductive adhesives. The first plating approach was introduced by Sumitomo and Canon,[40,41] and called vertical interconnecting sheet (VIS). It was prepared by coating a metal foil with a photodefinable polyimide. An array of 5 μm holes was defined in the polyimide and transferred into the underlying metal foil. Gold was plated through the holes, into the cavities below the polyimide; plating was continued such that the gold plated through the holes and formed a bump above the polyimide surface. The underlying metal foil was etched away to create a free-standing film. The film could be used to form interconnections by thermocompression bonding. The usefulness of this material is limited due to its cost, handling problems, and the lack of protection offered to the bare die.

Another approach has been recently reported by AMP[42] where metal bumps (e.g., nickel) are plated through a resist coated metal substrate. The resist is removed and an adhesive is coated over the bump array. The adhesive-bump composite is peeled off the metal substrate to form a free-standing film. Bump pitches down to 20 μm were reported. This approach addresses some of the cost, handling and chip protection issues reported for VIS. Fewer steps are required to manufacture the material and the adhesive matrix should improve handling and provide protection for the bare chip.

Screen and stencil printing techniques have been developed to create ordered arrays of isotropically conductive adhesive bumps in a dielectric polymer matrix. One technique called Polymer Flip Chip (PFC)[43] has been reported where isotropically conductive adhesive and dielectric polymer layers are printed directly on to the silicon wafer before dicing. The aluminium contact pads on the wafer are first metallised to prevent aluminium corrosion. Additional isotropically conductive adhesive bumps are printed on to the substrate. After assembly, an underfill adhesive is required to ensure good adhesion and reliability. Fine pitch interconnections (75 μm bumps on 130 μm pitch) have been reported. The disadvantages of this approach include the numerous high yield, fine-pitch printing processes required on full wafers.

An alternative approach is known as Area Bond Conductive (ABC) adhesives.[44,45] These materials are formed by stencil printing an array of isotropically conductive adhesive dots on a release film and then screening a high strength dielectric epoxy adhesive around the conductive dots. The pattern is dried to form a tack-free, B-staged, two component adhesive film. During assembly, the chip is aligned and thermally tacked to the adhesive; the adhesively coated chip is removed from the carrier film and aligned and bonded to the substrate. This approach requires that high precision printing steps be performed by the adhesive vendor, as opposed to the end-user for the PFC process. Full wafer processing is not required.

8.5 CHARACTERISATION OF ACAs

After an extensive review and some initial experimentation of various characterisation techniques, it was determined that the procedures listed in

Table 8.1 would give the best information for comparison of ACAs. The table also contains the information provided by the techniques. Below the individual techniques are described in more detail and the types of information that can be obtained with their use discussed. To demonstrate the techniques, four ACAFs were chosen and subjected to the characterisation and evaluation process.

Table 8.1

Characterisation Methods

Technique	Information
Optical Microscopy	Morphology
Scanning Electron Microscopy (SEM)	Detailed morphology
Energy Dispersive X-ray (EDX)	Material identification
Differential Scanning Calorimetry (DSC)	Cure properties and glass transition temperature
Thermogravimetric Analysis (TGA)	Stability and decomposition
Dielectrometry	Cure kinetics
Fourier Transform Infrared Spectroscopy (FTIR)	Cure time and polymer type
Mechanical Push-off	Adhesion
Assembly test (at ambient and 85°C/85%RH)	Electrical properties and reliability

A Microscopy

Various types of microscopy can be used to examine ACAF materials and the type is chosen based on the type of information being sought. Overall surface detail, particle shape, particle type, and a rough measure of the loading of particles in the ACAF require low magnification and are best done with optical microscopy or low magnification SEM. Figure 8.12(a) shows this type of microscopy. For higher magnification of a film, SEM is ideal and gives more detailed information on the conductive particles and other possible fillers. Figure 8.12(b) shows a typical photomicrograph of an ACAF particle. These data were obtained by SEM.

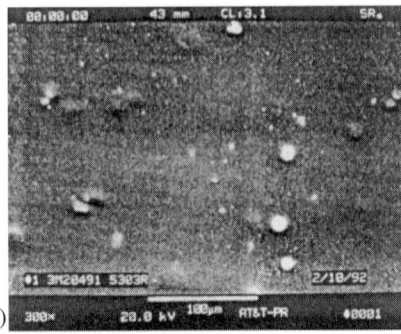
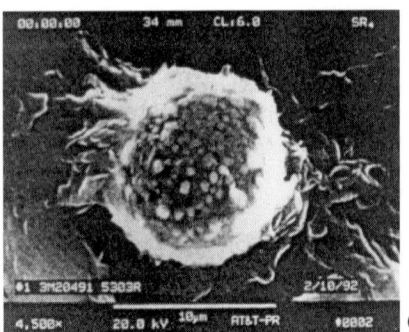

(a)   (b)

Fig. 8.12 Examples of microscopy. Optical (a) and SEM (b).

B Energy Dispersive X-Ray (EDX)

EDX systems are often coupled with SEMs, because they can use the electron imaging beam of the SEM to excite X-ray emissions from elements in the sample. The identity of the elements and a semiquantitative measurement of the amounts of those elements can be determined from the energy and flux of the emitted X-rays. This technique can be used to analyse the surface composition of the conductive particles or other fillers.

Table 8.2 shows the types of data that can be obtained from the commercial ACAFs examined. This information gives a general view of the types of particles, coatings, and particle sizes that occur in a range of the adhesive films.

Table 8.2

Particle Characterisation

Material	Particle Size (microns)	Particle Type
A	5-7	Au/Ni
B	8-12	Ag/Glass
C	12	Ni/Polymer
D	20	Au/Ni

C Fourier Transform Infra-red Spectroscopy (FTIR)

Absorption of infra-red radiation is widely used to analyse polymeric materials. FTIR is a very sensitive tool for measuring the vibrational energy of the reactive functional groups of polymer films such as heat curable epoxies and silicones. Further, the presence of various polymer types and their modification can be identified with FTIR. In addition, FTIR can be used to measure completeness of cure in some polymer systems by measuring the change in an absorption band. For example, the strong absorption of Si-H at 2100 cm^{-1} shows the presence of an uncured silicone in a sample. During a hydrosilation cure of the sample, the decrease of Si-H absorption is an indication of curing and could be easily measured by its peak height or peak area. Stabilisation of the Si-H absorption is a good indication of the final cure state of the materials.

Figure 8.13 shows the IR spectra of the four polymer films and demonstrates the wide variety of polymer variations found in the films. One can, however, pick out chemical moieties that are common to all these materials and compare those moieties to standard materials or spectral tables to determine the polymer variations present.

D Differential Scanning Calorimetry (DSC)

Differential scanning calorimetry (DSC) measures the heat change in a material during a physical or chemical transition. It measures both the heat capacity of endothermic and exothermic transitions of a sample and provides quantitative information regarding the enthalptic changes. A DSC scan plots energy supplied against average programmed temperature. The peak areas can be quantitatively related to the enthalptic changes. Tg (glass transition temperature) can be readily obtained and kinetic cure information can also be calculated. For the commercial ACAF materials, DSC scans from ambient to 250°C were taken at a prescribed rate. Figure 8.14 shows the DSC scan of a typical uncured ACAF material. A general exothermic peak, such as peak I in the figure, provides qualitative information regarding each ACAF material's cure temperature. When the materials are fully cured, there should be no heat loss or gain in the region of the cure temperature during subsequent DSC scans. The four ACAFs being evaluated showed cure temperatures to be in the range from 140° to 160°C. Peak II shows the point at which polymer degradation begins. These data provide additional

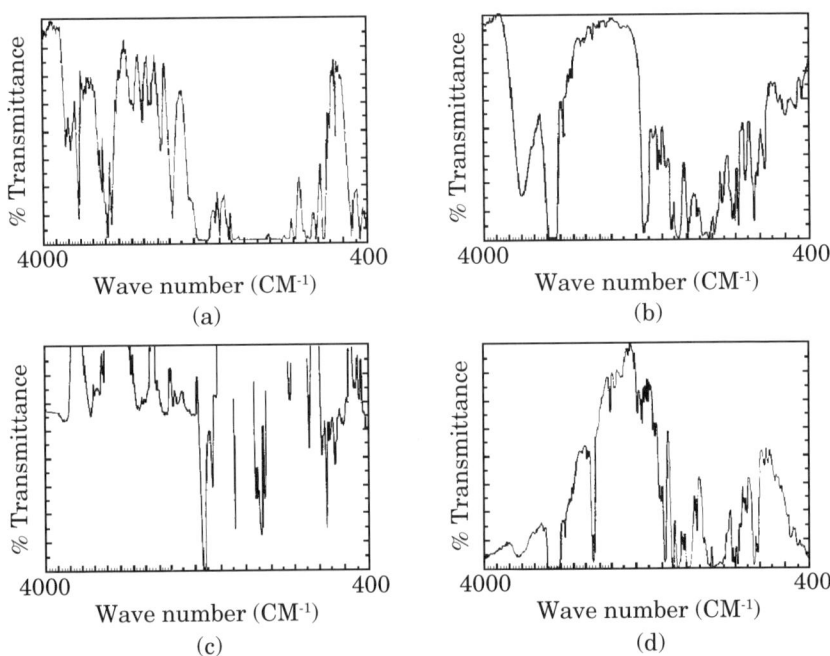

Fig. 8.13 IR spectra from four ACAFs.

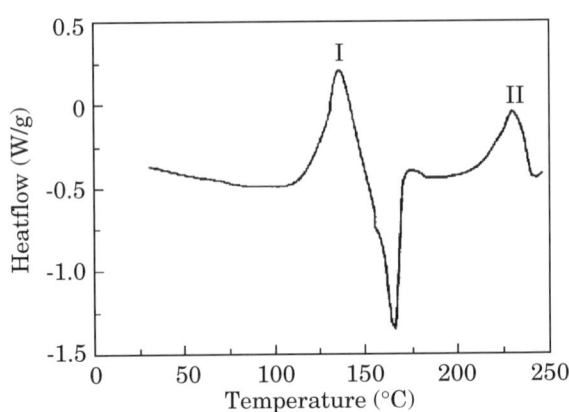

Fig. 8.14 DSC scan from a typical uncured ACAF.

information regarding the thermal stability of the ACAF. More detailed thermal stability information can be obtained by thermogravimetric analysis (see Section F).

E Microdielectrometry

Dielectrometry is the measurement of dielectric change in a sample at a particular frequency during a physical or chemical change in that sample. The recent development of high sensitivity microdielectrometry, capable or making measurements in the frequency range of 0.05 Hz to 10 kHz, allows one to study dielectric changes in polymeric films.[4] A Micromet Instruments Eumetric System II microdielectrometer with a miniature IC sensor capable of using a wide range of frequencies (from 0.05 Hz to 10 kHz) was used to monitor the loss factor (E) in the ACAF films. To make the measurement, a layer of the film was placed on a miniature IC sensor and put inside a programmable oven. The temperature of the oven was set to a temperature (i.e., 130°, 140° or 150°C) and the loss factor (E) at various frequencies (0.05, 1, 100, 1000, 10000 Hz) was monitored periodically during the curing time. Results of the microdielectric loss factor (E) measurements are shown in Figure 8.15. During an isothermal cure of the ACAF film using low frequency sweep experiments, it was possible to use this sensitive tool for measuring a material's complete cure and thus determine its exact cure time at a given temperature. As an example, Figure 8.15(a) shows an ACAF's E measurement

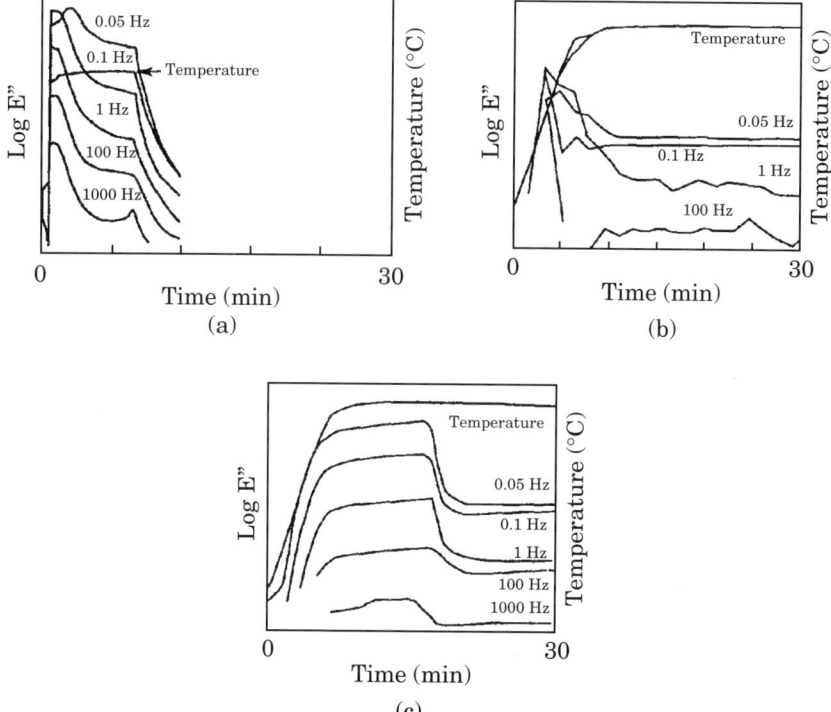

Fig. 8.15 Microdielectric loss factor plotted as a function of time (a) and temperature (b) and (c).

versus curing time at 140°C. The initial Es increase with various frequency scans (0.05, 0.1, 1, 100 Hz) and these increases are due to the thermal randomisation of dipoles within the ACAF resin during the heating period from ambient to 140°C. When the material temperature reaches 140°C, all Es begin to decrease rapidly. This indicates rapid cure at this temperature. When E reaches its equilibrium state, i.e., no further change in E with time, the material is completely cured. The low frequency sweep experiments (0.05, 0.1, 1 Hz) provide a sensitive method of determining a polymer's cure time.[46] Figures 8.15(b) and (c) show results obtained for the ACAF films A and D, respectively. With curing times of ~35 minutes for the A material and ~15 minutes for the D material at 140°C, the length of the cure time is inversely proportional to the cure temperature. In later experiments the cure temperature was increased to 160°C to decrease the cure time needed.

F Thermal Gravimetric Analysis (TGA)

The stability of a polymer film can be evaluated by heating it through a range of temperatures and measuring its weight loss. The temperature at which weight loss begins is the temperature at which change (loss of water, degradation, etc.) of the polymer starts. Thermal gravimetric analysis (TGA) is a thermal analytical technique that automates this procedure. A TGA output is displayed in Figure 8.16. As can be seen, this ACAF begins to lose

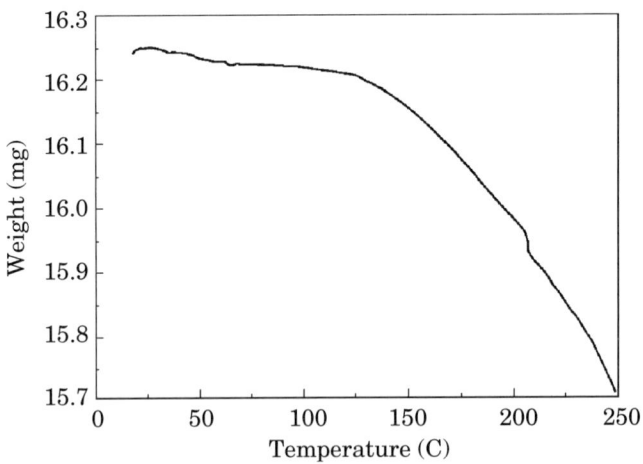

Fig. 8.16 TGA trace for a typical ACA where weight is plotted as a function of temperature.

weight at 140°C and shows a large loss above 150°C. This is an example of a partially cured resin to demonstrate the effect of low stability. Evolution of volatiles during cure would be problematic as voids would form at the adhesive interface. When completely cured, the four materials analysed all showed the start of degradation between 190° and 220°C and no material resisted major degradation above 240°C, in air.

G Mechanical Adhesion

Adhesion of parts connected with ACAFs was measured using a push-off type tester. A set of parts is assembled with an ACAF and one part is securely held in the tester while a measured force is applied to the edge of the other part. When separation of the parts occurs, the force is recorded. The ACAFs in the set of four under examination were tested using a silicon chip with circuitry connected to an FR-4 printed wiring board. In all cases, the push-off force was greater than 8 lbs and in some cases greater than 16 lbs. For comparison, bond strength requirements for die attach adhesives are 900 p.s.i. (6 MN/m²) as per MIL-A-87172.

8.6 RELIABILITY OF ACA INTERCONNECTIONS

The reliability of ACA interconnections depends on the specific formulation, process, substrate and component combination. No *a priori* assumptions can be made as each system must be evaluated separately. Certainly ACA interconnections can be reliable as the use of these materials in LCD assemblies demonstrates. Optimisation of materials, processes and surfaces will result in robust interconnections for a particular application.

A Test Vehicle Design:

When developing a new ACA application, the design of an appropriate test vehicle can significantly improve results. The test vehicle must mimic the materials and geometries of the final assembly. In addition, the test vehicle should be designed to facilitate failure mode analysis. An example of a flip-chip test vehicle[22] is shown in Figure 8.17. This vehicle is composed of two independent daisy chains that allow for measuring electrical interconnection yield as well as electrical isolation between adjacent conductors. There are 32 interconnections per daisy chain (64 I/O per chip); each contact pad measures 100 x 100 µm with a separation distance between daisy chains of 100 µm. Test points are included to allow for evaluation of isolated groups of interconnections. The chip and substrate can be built of different materials, depending upon the final application.

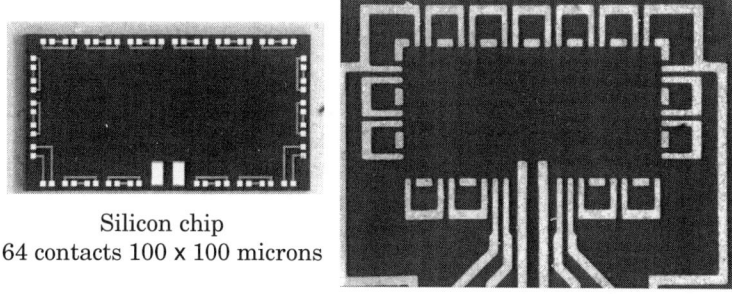

Silicon chip
64 contacts 100 x 100 microns

Kapton flex circuit
Electroless Au over 1/2 oz Cu

Fig. 8.17 Photographs of an ACA flip-chip test vehicle with mating chip (a) and flex circuit substrate (b).

Figure 8.18 shows a test vehicle for flex to rigid PWB interconnections. When the circuits are successfully interconnected, they form a group of six daisy chains in three pairs. Probe points for testing the through resistance are located on the FR-4. This design provides 14 contact points per daisy chain and the pairs of daisy chains are interdigitated to allow for measurements of isolation resistance. Contact pads measure 150 µm x 150 µm and are on 300 µm pitch.

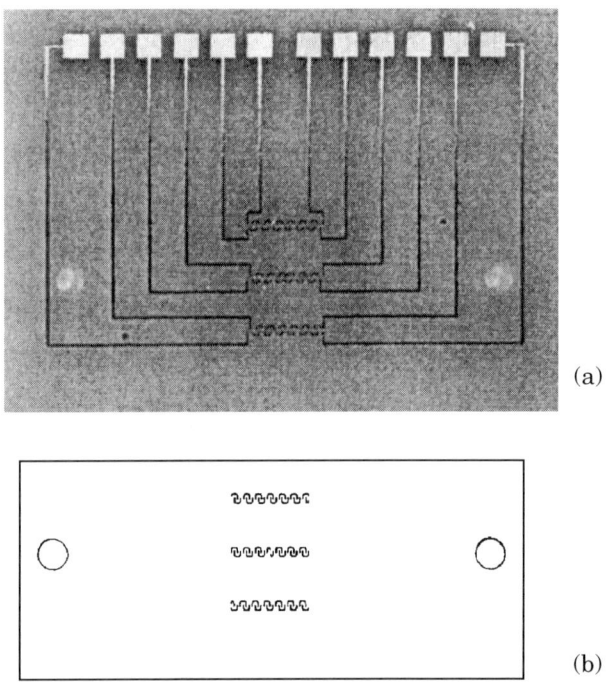

(a)

(b)

Fig. 8.18 Photographs of an ACA flex to rigid PWB test vehicle.

B Accelerated Life Testing

The long-term performance of ACA interconnections can be evaluated using accelerated environmental tests. Elevated temperature and relative humidity (RH) environments accelerate many ACA failure mechanisms. Typical tests conducted at 85°C/85% RH can cause chemical changes in the adhesive matrix, or at important interfaces. This is especially true with interconnections made to unprotected aluminium metallisation.[36,23] Temperature cycling and temperature shock tests effectively accelerate failures due to mechanical stresses, such as those that result from materials with mismatched CTEs.

8.7   CONCLUSIONS

An overview has been given of current ACA materials and assembly processes that have been discussed in the literature. Both anisotropically conductive adhesive films (ACAFs) and anisotropically conductive adhesive pastes (ACAPs) were discussed. ACAs were emphasised for flip-chip interconnections as this technology is not yet mature but offers great potential for low-cost, very fine pitch, electronic assemblies. Details concerning numerous ACA materials and assembly processes for pitches less than or equal to 200 μm were reviewed. The electrical properties and conduction mechanisms of ACA interconnections were discussed with attention focused on the effect of conductive particle chemistry.

A fundamental obstacle to implementing ACA processes is the need to apply pressure during adhesive cure while maintaining tight alignment and coplanarity tolerances between chip and substrate. Currently, most ACA processes rely on the alignment machine to cure the adhesive, resulting in low throughput and high assembly costs. The recently developed Batch Curing Fixture process, which transfers the cure step from the alignment machine to an inexpensive pressure frame, may provide a route to a generic low-cost ACA assembly process.

Various analytical techniques have been outlined that are useful in the characterisation of ACAs for use in fine pitch assembly, including: microscopy for evaluating the ACA materials and component surfaces prior to and after bonding; EDX and FTIR for determining material composition; DSC and microdielectrometry for optimisation of the cure reaction; and TGA and mechanical strength measurements for evaluation of adhesive and interface stability. Robust interconnections can only be achieved if both materials and processes are optimised for a particular application and bond geometry.

It is hoped that this review will enable current and future users of ACAs to gain better insight into the design factors that affect interconnection yields and reliability.

REFERENCES

1 Basavanhally, N. R., Chang, D. D. and Cranston, B. H., 'Direct Chip Inter-connect with Adhesive-connector Films', in *Proceedings Electronic Components Technology Conference*, pp. 487-491, May (1992).

2 Chang, D. D., Crawford, P., Fulton, J. A., McBride, R., Schmidt, M., Sinitski, R. and Wong, C. P., 'An Overview and Evaluation of Anisotropic Conductive Adhesive Film for Fine Pitch Electronic Assembly', *IEEE Transactions on Components, Packaging, and Manufacturing Technology*, **Vol. 16**, No. 8, p. 828 (1993).

3 Tsukagoshi, I., Nakajima, A., Goto, Y. and Muto, K., Hitachi Technical Report, No. 16, pp. 23 (1991).

4 Chang, D., Fulton, J., Ling, H., Schmidt, M., Sinitski, R. and Wong, C. P., 'Accelerated Life Test of Z-axis Conductive Adhesives', *IEEE Transactions on Components, Packaging, and Manufacturing Technology*, **Vol. 18**, No. 8, p. 836 (1993).

5 Liu, J., Boustedt, K. and Lai, Z. H., 'Development of Flip-chip Joining Technology on Flexible Circuitry using Anisotropically Conductive Adhesives and Eutectic Solder', Proceedings Surface Mount International, San Jose, p. 102 (1995).

6 Ogunjimi, Y., Mannan, S., Whalley, D. and Williams, D., 'The Assembly Process for Anisotropic Conduction Joints', Proceedings International Seminar in Conductive Adhesive Joining in Electronics Packaging, Philips, Eindhoven, The Netherlands, ISBN No. 91-630-3729-7, p. 127 (1995).

7 Wong, C. P., Lu, D., Meyers, L., Vona, S. and Tong, Q., 'Fundamental Study of Electrically Conductive Adhesives', Proceedings of the First IEEE International Seminar on Polymeric Electronic Packaging, p. 80 (1997).

8   Liu, J., Ljungkrona, L. and Lai, Z. H., 'Development of Conductive Adhesives Joining for Surface-mounting Electronics Manufacturing', *IEEE Transactions on Components, Packaging and Manufacturing Technology-Part B*, **Vol. 18**, No. 2, p. 313 (1995).

9   Asai, S., Saruta, U., Tobita, M., Takano, M. and Miyashita, Y., *Journal of Applied Polymer Science*, **Vol. 56**, pp. 769-777 (1995).

10 Holm, R., ' Electrical Contacts; Theory and Application', 4th edition, Springer-Verlag, New York (1967).

11 Lai, Z. and Liu, J., 'Anisotropically Conductive Adhesive Flip-Chip Bonding on Rigid and Flexible Printed Circuit Substrates', *IEEE Transactions CPMT, Part B*, **Vol. 19**, No. 3, pp. 644-660 (1966).

12 Shiozawa, N., Isaka, K. and Ohta, T., 'Electric Properties of Connections by Anisotropic Conductive Film', *Journal of Electronics Manufacturing*, **Vol. 5**, No. 1, pp. 33-37 (1995).

13 Kivilahti, J. and Savolainen, P., 'Anisotropic Adhesives for Flip-Chip Bonding', *Journal of Electronics Manufacturing*, Vol. 5, No. 4, pp. 245-252 (1995).

14 Savolainen, P. and Kivilahti, J., 'Electrical Properties of Solder Filled Anisotropically Conductive Adhesives', *Journal of Electronics Manufacturing*, **Vol. 5**, No. 1, pp. 19-26 (1995).

15 Savolainen, P. and Kivilahti, J., 'A Solder Alloy Filled Z-Axis Conductive Epoxy Adhesive', *Journal of Adhesion*, Vol. 49, pp. 187-196 (1995).

16 Pennisi, R. W., Papageorge, M. V. and Urbish, G. F., US Patent No. 5,136,365, issued 8/4/92.

17 Casson, K. L., Myers, C., Gilleo, K. B., Suilmann, K. B., Mahagnoul, E. and Tibesar, M., US Patent No. 5,502889, issued 4/2/96. See also Sheldahl's Z-Link Brochure.

18 Otsuka, K., Watanabe, I. and Takemura, K., 'High Frequency Characterization of Conductive Adhesive and Its Interconnection Technology Trend in Japan', Proceedings Adhesives in Electronics '96 Conference, Stockholm, Sweden, pp. 114-125, June (1996).

19 Chang, D. D., Fulton, J. A., Lyons, A. M. and Nis, J. R., 'Design Considerations for the Implementation of Anisotropically Conductive Adhesive Interconnections', Proceedings Nepcon West, p. 1381 (1992).

20 Watanabe, I., Takemura, K., Shiozawa, N., Watanabe, O., Kojima, K. and Ohta, T., 'Flip Chip Interconnection to Various Substrates Using Anisotropic Conductive Adhesive Films', *Journal of Electronics Manufacturing*, **Vol. 5**, No. 4, pp. 273-276 (1995).

21 Liu, J., 'On the Failure Mechanism of Anisotropically Conductive Adhesive Joints on Copper Metallization', *International Journal of Adhesion and Adhesives*, **Vol. 16**, No. 4, pp. 285-287 (1996).

22 Lyons, A. M., Hall, E., Wong, Y.-H. and Adams, G., 'A New Approach to Using Anisotropically Conductive Adhesives for Flip-Chip Assembly', *IEEE Transactions on CPMT, Part A*, **Vol. 19**, No. 1, pp. 5-11 (1996).

23 Lyons, A. M., Kammlott, G. W., Wong, Y.-H. and Adams, G., 'A Batch Curing Process for the Assembly of Flip Chip Interconnections with Anisotropically Conductive Adhesive Pastes', Proceedings Adhesives in Electronics '96 Conference, Stockholm, Sweden, pp. 68-75, June (1996).

24 Lyons, A. M., Seger, S. G. Jr. and Dahringer, D. W., Bell Laboratories Technical Memorandum 11518-900920-15.

25 Zwolinski, M., Hickman, J., Rubin, H., Zaks, Y., McCarthy, S., Hanlon, T., Arrowsmith, P., Chaudhuri, A., Hermansen, R., Lau, S. and Napp, D., 'Electrically Conductive Adhesives for Surface Mount Solder Replacement', Proceedings Adhesives in Electronics '96 Conference, Stockholm, Sweden, pp. 333-340, June (1996).

26 Bruner, D. M., 'Z-Axis Adhesive Film Interconnect Using 150 Micron and 75 Micron Pitch Flex Circuits', *International Journal of Microcircuits and Electronic Packaging*, **Vol. 18**, No. 3, pp. 311-318 (1995).

27 Reinke, R. R., Proceedings 41st Electronic Components Technical Conference (ECTC), p. 355 (1991).

28 Kreutter, N. P., Grove, B. K., Hogerton, P. B. and Jensen, C. R., 'Effective Polymer Adhesives for Interconnect', Proceedings 7th Electronic Materials and Processing Congress, Cambridge, MA, pp. 249-256, August (1992).

29 Date, H., Hozumi, Y., Tokuhira, H., Usui, M., Horikoshi, E. and Sato, T., 'Anisotropic Conductive Adhesive for Fine Pitch Interconnections', Proceedings ISHM, pp. 570-575 (1994).

30 Jin, S., Tiefel, T. H., Chen, L.-H. and Dahringer, D. W., 'Anisotropically Conductive Polymer Films with a Uniform Dispersion of Particles', *IEEE Transactions on CHMT*, **Vol. 16**, No. 8 (1993).

31 McArdle, C. and Burke, J., 'Novel Uniaxial Conductive Adhesives Comprising Polymerisable Ferrofluids and Conductive Magnetic Holes', Proceedings Adhesives in Electronics '96 Conference, Stockholm, Sweden, pp. 154-159 (1996).

32 Watanabe, I., Takemura, K., Shiozawa, N., Watanabe, O., Kojima, K. and Hirosawa, Y., 'Development of Double-layer Anisotropic Conductive Adhesive Films, Anisolm', Hitachi Chemical Technical Report, No. 26, pp.13-16 (1996).

33 Watanabe, I., Shiozawa, N., Takemura, K. and Ohta, T., 'Flip Chip Interconnection Technology Using Anisotropic Conductive Adhesive Films', in 'Flip Chip Technologies', J. H. Lau, ed., McGraw-Hill, New York, pp. 301-315 (1996).

34 Lee, C. H. and Loh, K. I., 'Fine Pitch COG Interconnections Using Anisotropically Conductive Adhesives', Proceedings 45th Electronic Components Technical Conference (ECTC), Las Vegas, NV, pp. 121-125, May (1995).

35 Nukii, T., Kakimoto, N., Atarashi, H., Matsubara, H., Yamamura, K. and Matsui, H., 'LSI Chip Mounting Technology for Liquid Crystal Displays', Proceedings ISHM, Chicago, IL, pp. 257-262 (1990).

36 Sakuma, K., Nozawa, K., Sato, E., Yamasaki, Y., Hanyuda, K., Miyasaka, H. and Takeuchi, J., 'Chip On Glass Technology with Standard Aluminized IC Chip', Proceedings ISHM, Chicago, IL, pp. 250-256 (1990).

37 Hatada, K. and Fujimoto, H., Proceedings 39th Electronic Components Technical Conference (ECTC), pp. 45 (1989).

38 Kondoh, Y. and Saito, M., 'A New CCD Module Using the Chip On Glass (COG) Technique', Proceedings ISHM, Chicago IL, pp. 487-494 (1990).

39 Saito, M., Mori, M., Hongu, A. and Niitsuma, A., 'COG (Chip On Glass) Technique for LCD Using a Low Melting Point Metal', Proceedings ISHM, Chicago, IL, pp. 263-268 (1990).

40 'Pad Grid Arrays Attached by Gold Bumps', H. Markstein, ed., *Electronic Packaging & Production*, p. 28, December (1993).

41 Lee, C. H., 'Anisotropic Conductive Flip Chip-on-Glass Technology', in 'Flip Chip Technologies', J. H. Lau, ed., McGraw-Hill, New York, pp. 317-339 (1996).

42 Ishibashi, K. and Kimura, J., 'A New Anisotropic Conductive Film with Arrayed Conductive Particles', *IEEE Transactions on CPMT, Part B*, **Vol. 19**, No. 4, pp. 752-757 (1996).

43 Estes, R. H. and Kulesza, F. W., 'Conductive Adhesive Polymer Materials in Flip Chip Applications', in 'Flip Chip Technologies', J. H. Lau, ed., McGraw-Hill, New York, pp. 223-267 (1996).

44 Bolger, J. C. and Gilleo, K., 'Area Bonding Conductive Epoxy Adhesive Preforms for Grid Array and MCM Substrate Attach', MCM Conference, Santa Cruz, CA, March (1994).

45 Czarnowski, J. M., Reynolds, M. E. S., Hayes, M. T., Ellis, C. D., Johnson, R. W. and Palmer, M. J., 'Evaluation of Area Bonding Conductive Adhesives for Flip-Chip Attach of Area Bonded Die', Proceedings International Electronics Manufacturing Technology Symposium, Austin, TX, October (1996).

46 Wong, C. P., 'Effect of RTV Silicone Cure in Device Packaging', American Chemical Society Symposium series, **Vol. 346**, p.511 (1987).

APPENDIX 8.1

Anisotropically Conductive Adhesive Suppliers

3M, AI Technology, Hitachi Chemical, Hysol, Loctite, Sheldahl, Sony Chemical, Three Bond, Zymet.

Chapter 9

MANUFACTURABILITY, RELIABILITY AND FAILURE MECHANISMS IN CONDUCTIVE ADHESIVE JOINING FOR FLIP-CHIP AND SURFACE MOUNT APPLICATIONS

JOHAN LIU
IVF, Mölndal, Sweden

PONTUS LUNDSTRÖM
Ericsson Components, Stockholm, Sweden

9.1 INTRODUCTION

During recent years, many novel electronics packaging methods and techniques have been developed. The driving forces are mainly miniaturisation of electronic components, lower cost, higher reliability and environmental compatibility. Surface mount technology, as one of the major packaging methods, is facing smaller pitch than 0.4 mm. Difficulties have been observed in working with lead-containing solder pastes in terms of printability for this type of pitch. Therefore BGA and CSP technology are taking the market share. Anisotropically conductive adhesives (ACAs) can be stencil printed over the entire pad line without individual apertures. Therefore, they are very suitable for extremely fine pitch technology. Since lead is one of the most toxic elements and there is a growing concern over tin-lead based solder joint reliability in harsh electronics environments, there is an increasing interest in looking into the alternatives for replacement of lead-containing solders in volume production. Isotropically conductive adhesives (ICAs) are considered to be one of the major candidates for this.

In fact, conductive adhesive joining technology has been used for many years in the area of hybrid technology, LCD interconnect and chip-on-glass technology. It is only recently that efforts have been made to develop new conductive adhesives for surface mount and low-cost flip-chip electronics volume manufacturing. Such efforts include the new formulation of ICAs without solvent and modified curing schedules. Today it is possible to buy, off-the-shelf, conductive adhesives that are tailored for a specific electronic packaging process. New high strength and high-reliability thermosetting-type anisotropic conductive adhesives have also been developed for flip-chip application on rigid and flexible circuitry. New thermoplastic conductive adhesives for flip-chip and die-attach applications offer a unique advantage for repair of the die. High strength ACAs are used for flip-chip assembly with 70 μm pitch on glass substrate.[1] Parallel to this, a great deal of research work is currently under way in an effort to understand and develop processes and technologies for conductive adhesive joining.[2]

9.2 CONCERNS WITH SOLDER JOINTS

One of the reasons conductive adhesives have been considered interesting is the concern about solder joint reliability especially in harsh environments. Let us consider the following. The melting point of tin-lead based eutectic solder is:

$$T_m = 183°C \ (456K) \tag{9.1}$$

The operating temperature range of all electronics is roughly:

$$T_i = \text{-20 to } 120°C \ (253 \text{ to } 393K) \tag{9.2}$$

The ratio of operating temperature to melting point is then:

$$T_i/T_m = 0.55 \text{ to } 0.86 \tag{9.3}$$

The approximate recrystallisation temperature of Sn and Pb occurs at $T_i/T_m = 0.47$ (for Pb) and 0.53 (for Sn).[3] Therefore, it is probable that tin-lead solder will show grain growth and coalescence phenomena at its upper operating temperature range. Hence, for high temperature and harsh environment applications, the reliability of the solder joint can be questioned.

9.3 NECESSARY CONDITIONS FOR A GOOD CONDUCTIVE ADHESIVE JOINT

In order to obtain a good adhesive joint, the adhesive must wet the bonding surface. A necessary condition for this is that the surface tension of the adhesive is lower than the surface tension of the bonding surface. Epoxy, polyimides, polyester and polyurethanes are major polymers used as base matrix for conductive adhesives. These materials have lower surface tension values than Sn, Pb, Cu, Au and Pd etc., as can be seen in Figure 9.1. Therefore, a good adhesive joint is expected when bonding on SnPb, Cu and Au systems. As will be discussed in Sections 9.9.1.1 and 9.9.1.2, water molecules can easily penetrate through the adhesive and oxidise/hydrate the surface, thus reducing the electrical and mechanical performance of the joint.

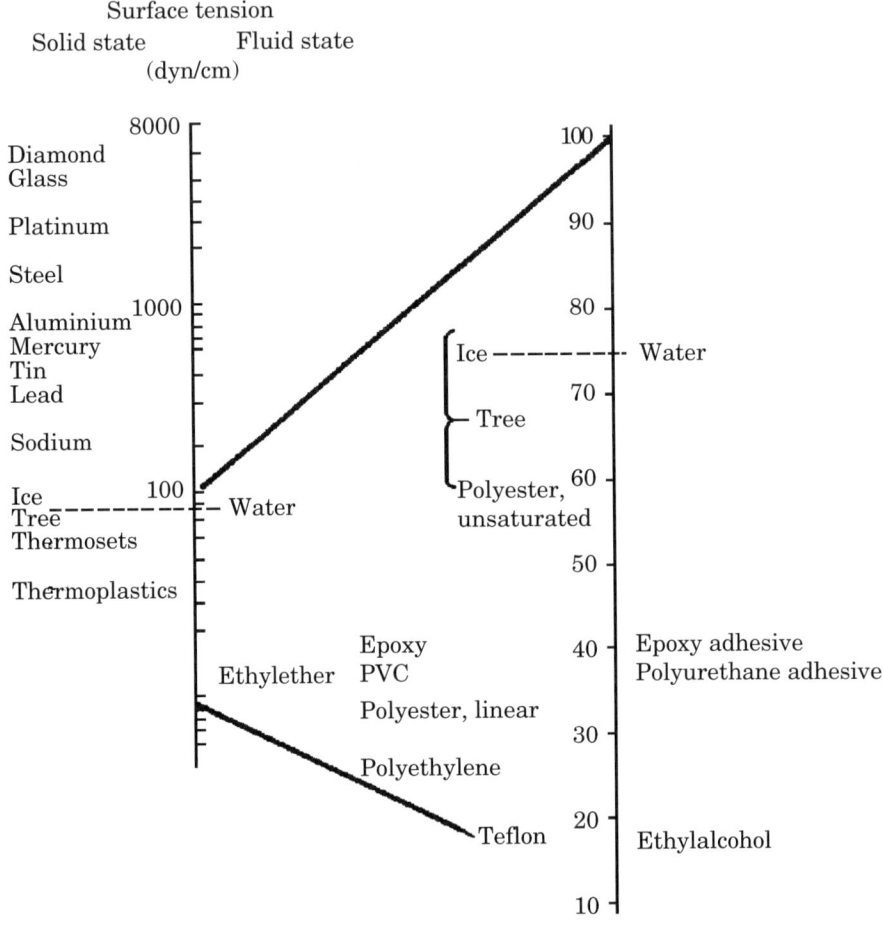

Fig. 9.1 Surface tension of various metals and polymer materials.[4]

9.4   MICROSTRUCTURES OF VARIOUS CONDUCTIVE ADHESIVES

Figure 9.2 shows the microstructure of an isotropically conductive adhesive joint for a surface mount chip component on FR-4 substrate. The metallic filler content is high enough (between 25-30 volume percent) to cause direct metallic contact. To see the electrical conduction mechanism, it is necessary to use high resolution electron microscopy as shown in Figure 9.3. This shows clearly that the electrical conduction in an ICA joint takes place through direct metallic contact.

In an ACA joint, the filler particle is normally between 5 and 10 volume percent. Therefore, it does not cause any direct metallic contact, as is illustrated in Figure 9.4. It is only after pressurisation during curing that

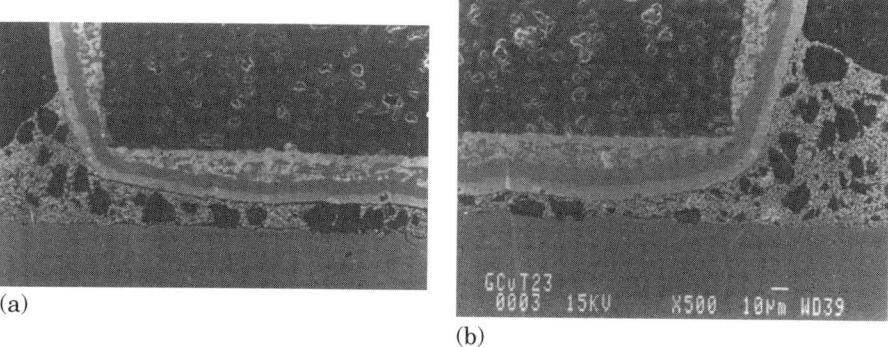

(a)

(b)

Fig. 9.2 ICA joining for a surface mount chip component on FR-4 substrate. (a) and (b) show the two joints for the chip component.

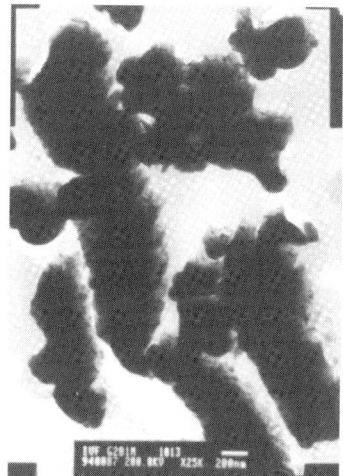

Fig. 9.3 TEM microstructure showing the electrical conduction mechanism of an ICA using Ag paste.

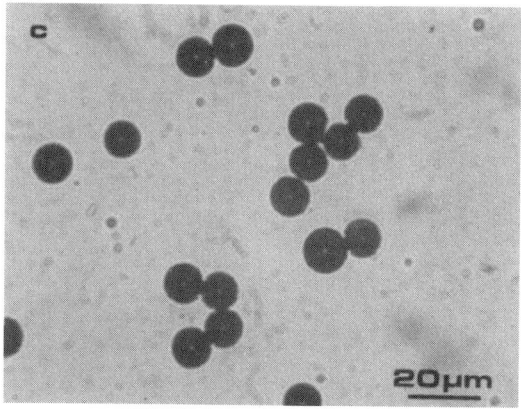

Fig. 9.4 A normal ACA conductive adhesive paste with filler of 5 vol% using Ni/Au coated plastic cores.

electrical conduction becomes possible in the pressurisation direction, as shown in Figure 9.5.

Fig. 9.5 ACA joint for a flip-chip component on FR-4 substrate using nickel filler.

9.5   THE EFFECT OF CURING DEGREE ON THE JOINT RELIABILITY

There is no doubt that proper curing is very important for joint reliability. Several groups have studied the effect of curing degree on joint reliability.[5,6] Attempts have been made to deal with the curing phenomenon as predicted by Arrhenius Law.[7] It seems that the electrical resistance of the joint is related to the curing degree especially for non-noble metal surfaces, as can be seen in Figure 9.6. Figure 9.6 shows the electrical resistance *vs* curing time for an epoxy conductive adhesive cured at 150°C and at various curing times after damp heat treatment at 85°C, 85%RH, for 1000 hours on the Sn37Pb bonding surface.[6] The corresponding curing degree varies between 65 and 90%. The curing degree was determined by the DCS measurement.

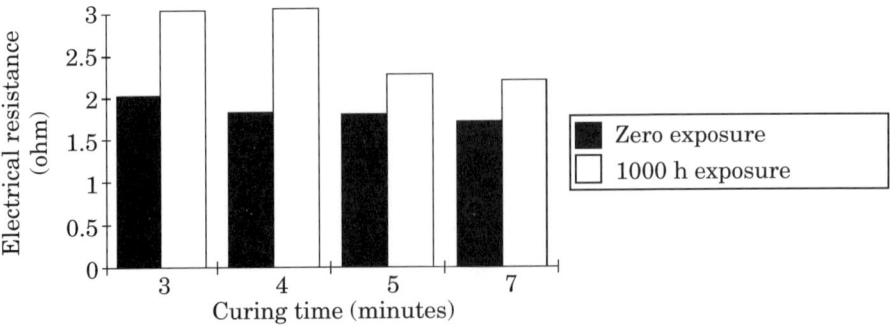

Fig. 9.6 Contact resistance of 10 Sn37Pb plated chip components in series before and after exposure to humidity up to 1000 hours, at 85°C and 85% RH, using an epoxy based conductive adhesive on Sn37Pb-plated boards.

Below a critical curing degree (for this adhesive, the critical curing degree is 77%), the electrical resistance of the joint increases significantly. The reason is that a not fully cured epoxy can absorb a significant amount of moisture which in turn causes oxidation/hydration of the Sn37Pb bonding surface. If a noble metal, for instance Au or Pd, is used as the bonding surface, no electrical resistance change occurs despite the fact that the curing degree can be very low, as shown in Figure 9.7.

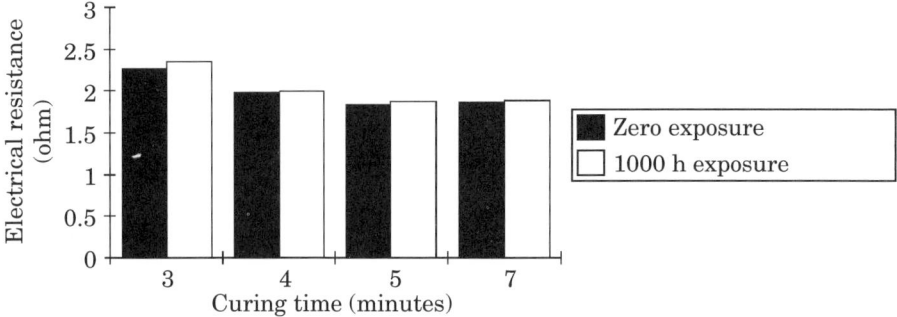

Fig. 9.7 Contact resistance of 10 Ag/Pd plated chip components in series before and after exposure to humidity up to 1000 hours, at 85°C and 85% RH, using the same epoxy based conductive adhesive as that used to obtain the data in Fig. 9.6 on Au-plated boards.

Once a critical curing degree has been reached (72%), it seems that the shear strength of the joint on the Sn37Pb bonding surface can be maintained at a constant level, as shown in Figure 9.8.

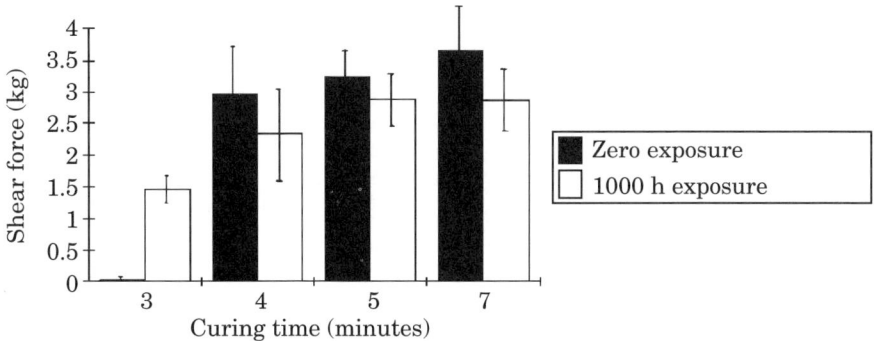

Fig. 9.8 Average shear strength of 10 Sn37Pb plated chip components as a function of curing time, before and after exposure for 1000 hours at 85°C and 85% RH, using the same epoxy conductive adhesive as that used to obtain the data in Fig. 9.6 and Sn37Pb-plated boards.

However, on the noble metal bonding surface, the shear strength of the joint is almost independent of the curing degree in the range between 67 and 92%, as can be seen in Figure 9.9.

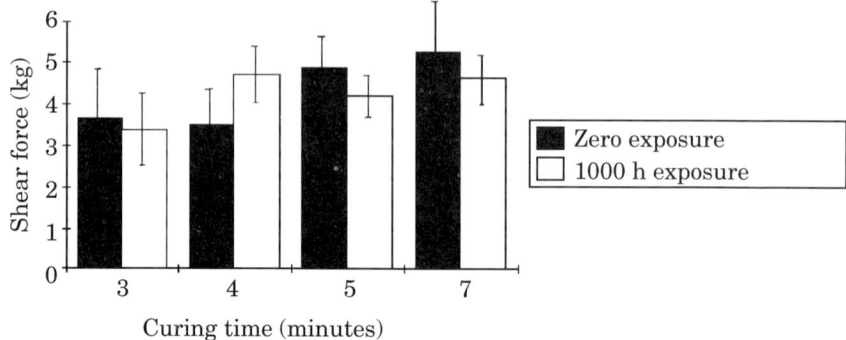

Fig. 9.9 Average shear strength of 10 Ag/Pd plated chip components as a function of curing time, before and after exposure for 1000 hours at 85°C and 85% RH, using the same epoxy conductive adhesive as that used to obtain the data in Figure 9.6 and Au-plated boards.

Recent results also show that full cure can lead to good joint quality.[8]

In summary, it can be said that a minimum curing degree appears to be required to provide a certain level of mechanical and electrical performance in the adhesive system. Once this is achieved, increasing curing times does not result in significant improvement.

The above results also indicate that, for conductive adhesive joining, a noble metal surface is preferable to a non-noble metal surface.

9.6   MANUFACTURABILITY AND PROCESS FLOW FOR CONDUCTIVE ADHESIVE JOINING

In order to use ACAs for fine pitch surface mount or flip-chip components, a thermal bonding machine needs to be incorporated in the manufacturing line. With the bonding machine, pressure and heat can be applied simultaneously to form the ACA joints. Therefore, the procedures shown in Figures 9.10 or 9.11 can be used for high volume electronics manufacturing

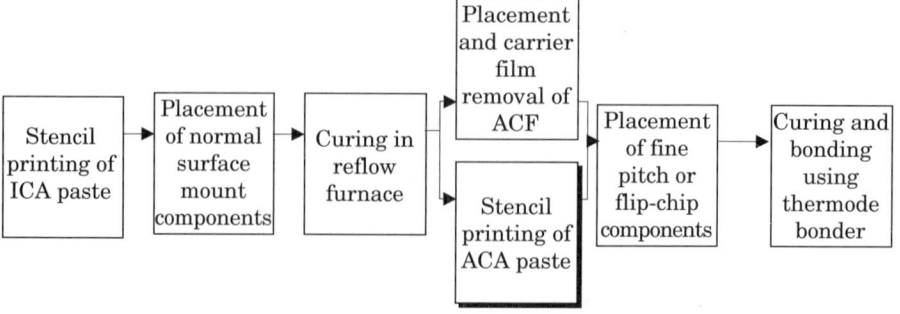

Fig. 9.10 Volume manufacturing process using stencil printing of ICAs followed by dispensing of ACA paste or using anisotropic conductive film (ACF).

processes based on conductive adhesive joining technology. Down to a 0.5 mm pitch surface mount process, a normal stencil printing or dispensing process can be used as it is viable to dispense the conductive paste in this way. It is in the range of 0.3-0.4 mm for surface mount while for smaller pitch (70-150 μm) flip-chip, ACA joining technology is interesting.

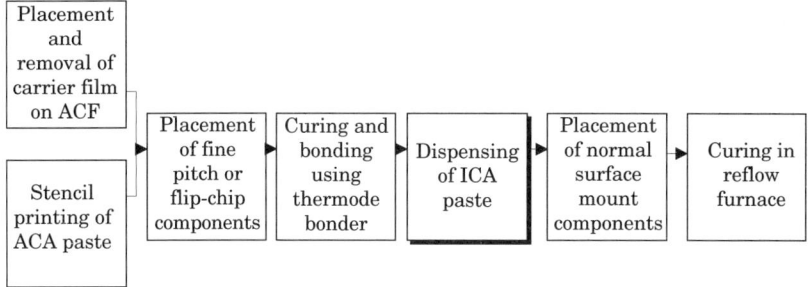

Fig. 9.11 Volume manufacturing process using stencil printing of ACA paste or using anisotropically conductive film (ACF) followed by dispensing of ICA paste.

ACA technology can in principle be mixed with soldering technology if the ICA technology is replaced by soldering. In fact, Casio's transistor radio is produced in this way where ACF flip-chip technology is mixed with soldering on FR-4 substrate using SBU-technology.[9]

For anisotropically conductive paste, stencil printing technology can be used. This is a benefit from the manufacturing viewpoint as existing equipment can be used. A disadvantage of ACA pastes is that the filler distribution is affected by the printing process. This may lead to improper filler distribution causing bridging and shorting between pads. The ACA adhesive is printed over the entire pad area, as shown in Figures 9.12 and 9.13 for surface mount and flip-chip applications.

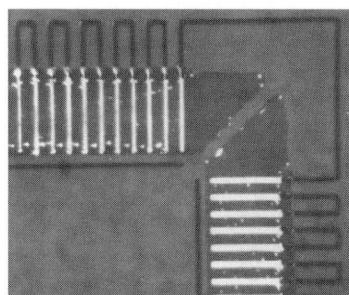

Fig. 9.12 Printing of ACA paste for surface mount application.

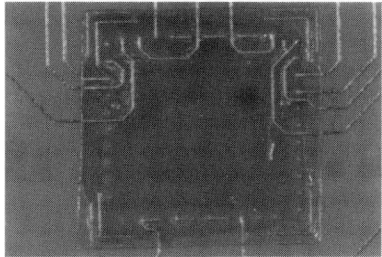

Fig. 9.13 Printing of ACA paste for flip-chip application.

When working with ACA films, the filler distribution is only affected during the bonding process. However, the carrier film must be removed by prebonding using a thermode bonder using light pressure and at the same time applying heat. The film is supplied in an appropriate width to cover the bonding area. The adhesive is then prebonded to the board. After prebonding the carrier film is removed and the adhesive is ready for the final bonding. Figure 9.14 shows the mechanism for carrier film removal in an automatic bonding line. The carrier film on the ACF film is cut to the correct size and placed on the board.[10] Lighter pressure is then exerted to tack the film on the substrate. After this, the top layer carrier film is removed in the same way. Finally, the chip component is placed before final bonding. Figure 9.15 shows such a bonding machine and process flow when flip-chip bonding ACF film on FR-4 substrate.[11] Figure 9.16 shows a photograph of an ACF on the bonding area after prebonding and after the carrier film has been removed for the flip-chip application.

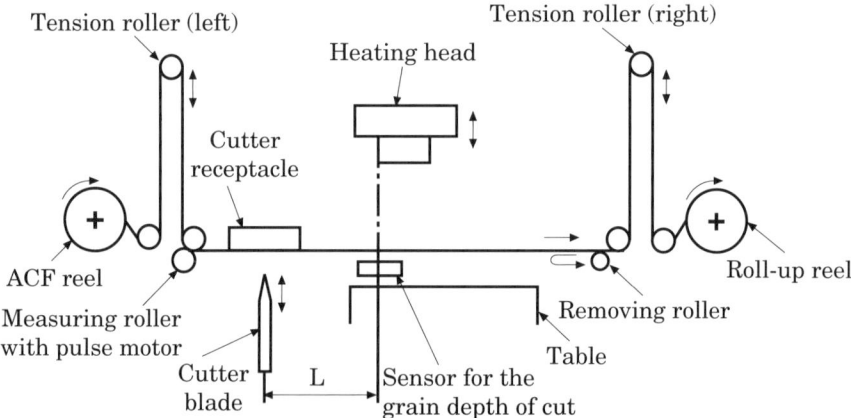

Fig. 9.14 Carrier film removal mechanism in an automatic bonding line.

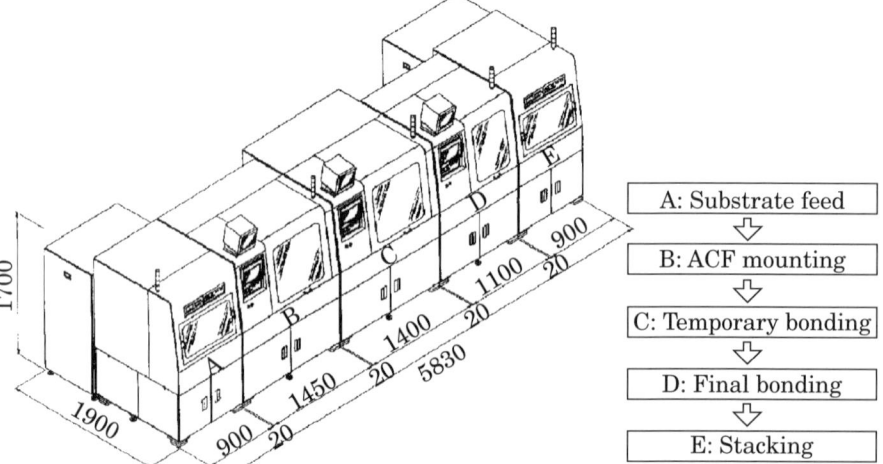

Fig. 9.15 Automatic process flow for flip-chip bonding using ACF film on FR-4 substrate.

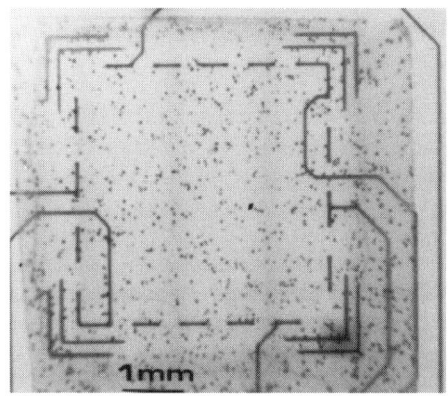

Fig. 9.16 ACF film placed on a bonding area for the flip-chip application.

As ACF requires an automatic handling system to remove the carrier film and attach the adhesive on to the board, it brings additional cost to the manufacturing process. Therefore, ACA paste technology based on stencil printing in combination with an in-line ACA bonder may be the most appropriate technology from the cost viewpoint. However, as yet, ACA pastes have not been developed and used to the same extent as ACA film technology. Future developments in paste technology may alter this situation.

Curing and bonding of ACAs are carried out using a thermode. The fine pitch bonder consists of a head with thermode blades (hot bars). The head is also used for picking components from trays using vacuum. A camera is also placed on the head for vision. The vision system reads the fiducial marks on the board for proper positioning.

A typical bonding profile that can be achieved in the bonder is shown in Figure 9.17. As can be seen, there are a number of parameters, i.e., pressure and heating ramp rate, bonding time, bonding temperature, release temperature and idling temperature, that affect the bonding quality.

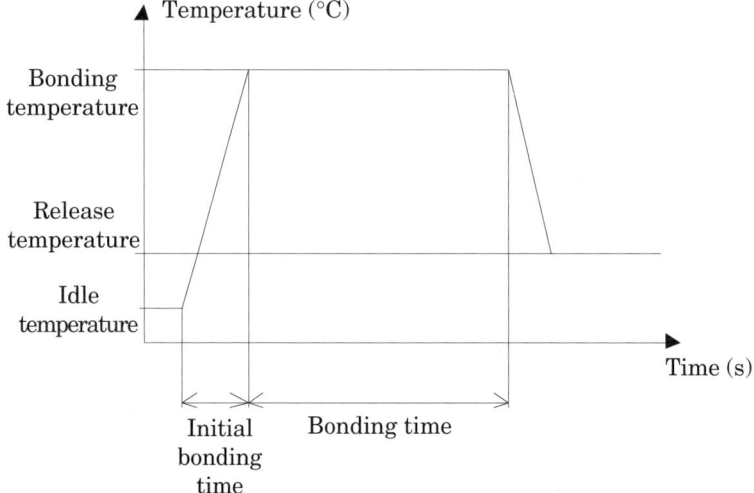

Fig. 9.17 Temperature profile of the thermode during bonding.

9.7 INSPECTION

One of the problems with conductive adhesives seems to be related to inspection. Since conductive adhesives do not wet the bonding surface in the same way as do solders, it is impossible to inspect the conductive adhesive joint manually. Non-destructive testing methods such as X-ray do not work very well either since the Ag particles overlap each other and the contrast is too small. Ultrasonic microscopy can detect pores and fairly large cracks in conductive adhesives. However, conductive adhesive joints have to be considered from both electrical and mechanical properties standpoints as it seems that there is no automatic relationship between the mechanical and electrical properties of the joint. This is shown in Figure 9.18. This conclusion is drawn from electrical and mechanical performance data analysis.

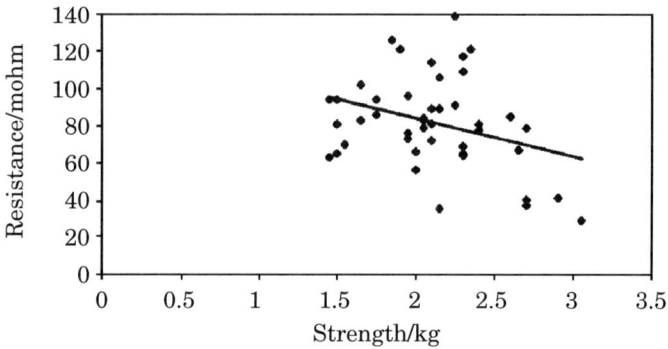

Fig. 9.18 Electrical contact resistance *vs* mechanical shear strength for 45 mounted chip capacitors (type 0805) after dispensing a thermosetting conductive adhesive on an FR-4 substrate.

9.8 REPAIR

Repair is one of the areas that requires further investigation. Various repair methods have been reported including liquid nitrogen low temperature repair. However, the majority of repairs to conductive adhesive joints is believed to be carried out in a similar way to that of solder joints, i.e., by heating the component to a certain temperature. Thus thermoplastic conductive adhesives are melted and removed and the thermosetting type conductive adhesive joints are softened. After this, the components can be removed. Figure 9.19 shows repair of an adhesively joined surface mount QFP component. The repair work is done by heating the adhesive joints to a temperature between 250 and 285°C for over 35 seconds. The time to reach the desired temperature was 20 seconds. Details of the repair conditions are given in Table 9.1.

The first repair test of the adhesive joints is carried out under the same conditions as for solder joints. Under these conditions, i.e., 250°C for 35 seconds of reflow time, the adhesively joined QFP components can not be removed. A further temperature increase to 285°C is necessary to soften the adhesive joints completely for both types of adhesives. 35 seconds of reflow time was then sufficient to remove QFP packages. After removal of the components, some adhesive residues are normally left on the boards. These residues can be removed by dissolving in chemical solvents such as acetone, or mechanically polished away using sand paper. However, these methods may damage the circuit board. Also chemical solvents should not be used from the environmental point of view. Therefore a better method is to dispense new adhesive directly on the old pattern without removing the adhesive residues. In this way, repair work can be carried out. However, this process requires the component to be placed in exactly the same position as the old component, as the old joint always leaves a footprint there.

Table 9.1

Repair of a Thermosetting Type ACA Joint of a QFP Component
Preheating and Cooling Time are 20 seconds[12]

Trial No.	Reflow Temp. (°C)	Reflow Time (s)	Possible to Remove Component
1	250	35	No*
2	285	72	Yes
3	285	53	Yes
4	285	35	No*

*These repair process parameters are used for repair of the same soldered QFP components.

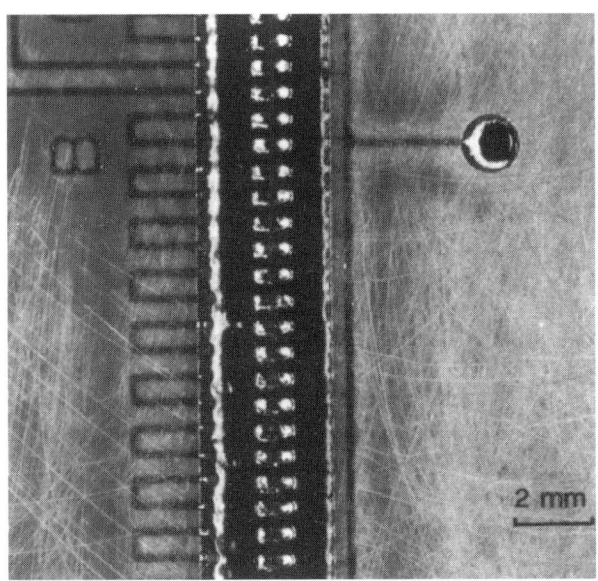

Fig. 9.19 Repair of an adhesively joined surface mount QFP component after component removal.

The higher temperature required to repair the joint leads to concern about the joint reliability of components near the repaired ones.

Another strategy for dealing with repair is simply to throw away the assembled module if this can be tolerated from the cost point of view.

9.9   FAILURE MECHANISMS

One of the most important features that makes conductive adhesives different from solders is that a conductive adhesive consists of a metal filler part to conduct electricity and a polymer part to act as an adhesive matrix to establish the mechanical strength of the joint. Therefore, failures can be due to the degradation of the polymer matrix as well as the degradation of the metal part.

9.9.1   Oxidation/Hydration

9.9.1.1   Sn37Pb SURFACE

Figure 9.20 shows an ESCA analysis spectrum recorded on an Sn37Pb surface before treatment which has been stored in room temperature for 1.5 years. The analysis indicates the presence of both Sn and Pb oxide. By examining the surface with different take-off angles, as is shown in Figure 9.21, the oxide thickness can be determined. The thickness of the Sn oxide is calculated as 74 Å.[13] The Pb oxide present is only 26 Å, which is much thinner than the tin oxide.

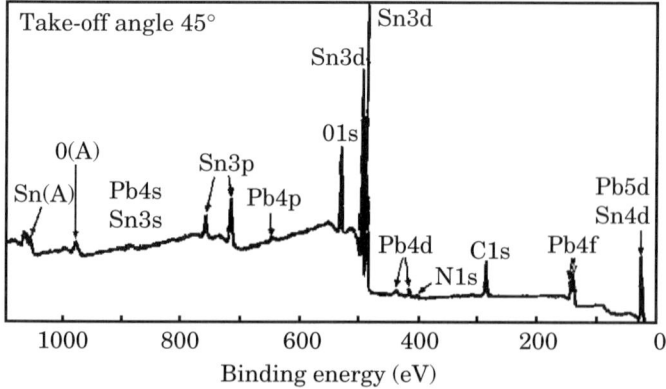

Fig. 9.20 ESCA analysis spectrum recorded on an Sn37Pb surface before treatment.

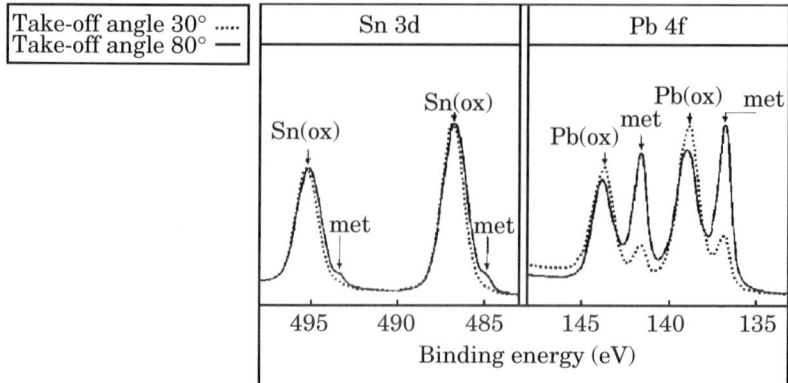

Fig. 9.21 Angle resolved ESCA spectra from Sn37Pb surface.

Transmission electron microscopy (TEM) analysis shows that the Sn and Pb grains exist independently instead of as an Sn37Pb eutectic structure in the Sn37Pb matrix, probably as a result of coalescence of the Sn37Pb eutectic at room temperature. Thus, it can be suggested that the Sn-rich phase is covered by Sn oxide and the Pb-rich phase is covered by Pb oxide. After 68 hours in an 85°C/85%RH environment, both tin and lead are present as pure metal grains, as can be seen from Figure 9.22. However, after 1000 hours

(a)

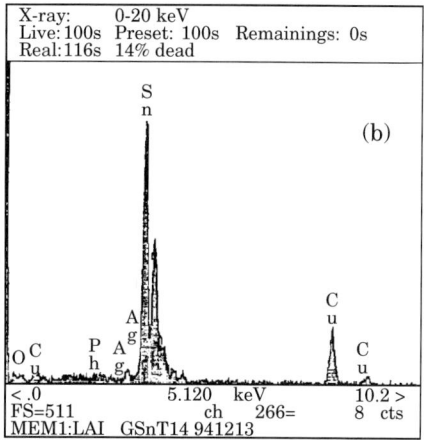 (b)

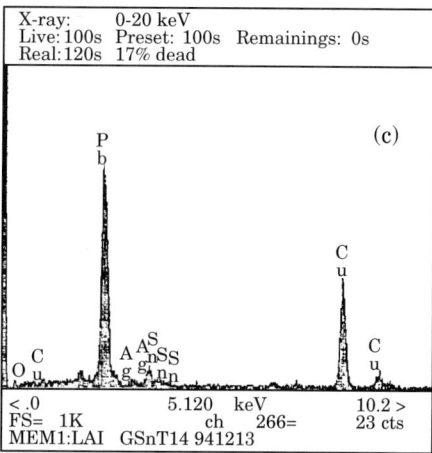 (c)

Fig. 9.22 (a) TEM photograph of the microstructure of the Sn37Pb after 68 hours in the 85°C/85% RH environment; (b) EDX spectrum of the Sn phase; (c) EDX spectrum of the Pb phase.

in such an environment, water has penetrated through the Sn37Pb layer. As a result of this, Pb was converted to an amorphous structure as observed by TEM. But using EDS analysis in TEM, only Pb and oxygen signals can be detected. Figure 9.23 shows the analysis of an epoxy based conductive adhesive joint on the Sn37Pb joint after humidity testing for 1000 hours. The diffuse diffraction ring in Figure 9.23 indicates that the structure formed is amorphous, which indicates that it is $Pb(OH)^2$ that is formed and not PbO, as PbO has a crystalline structure.[14] The ESCA analysis of the pure Sn37Pb

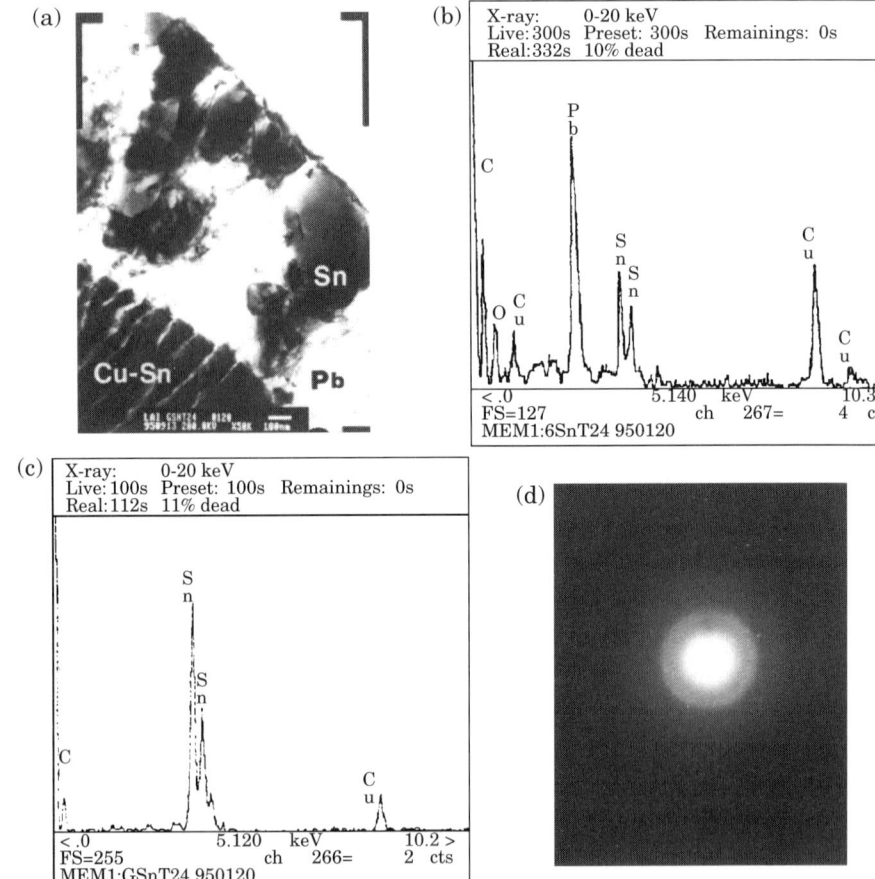

Fig. 9.23 (a) TEM photograph of an epoxy based conductive adhesive joint on an Sn37Pb surface after the 85°C/85% RH test for 1000 hours; (b) EDX spectrum of Pb in its oxidised state; (c) Sn phase without oxygen; (d) diffuse diffraction ring indicating that the Pb oxide has an amorphous structure.

surface shows that the chemical shift of the oxygen signals indicates that the structure formed is from the OH group and not from Pb_2O_3 or Pb_2O which also have an amorphous structure.[15] Pb hydration in the joint has taken place after humidity testing for 158 hours, as can be seen from Figure 9.24. Two Pb grains (indicated by arrows in Figure 9.24) have been attacked by water to form hydroxide. This did not occur with the Pb grains near the Sn37Pb – Cu interface. However, after testing for 500 hours the Pb grain close to the Cu – Sn37Pb interface is also hydrated.

From Figure 9.25, it can be seen that the relative resistance was not altered very much for the joints with Sn37Pb finished copper pads. This could be attributed to Sn, which did not oxidise further during the test, However, the formation of amorphous Pb-hydroxide can lead to degradation of mechanical properties of the joints as Pb-hydroxide often has a powdery structure and to an increase of the electrical resistance as lead hydroxide is an inorganic and insulating material.

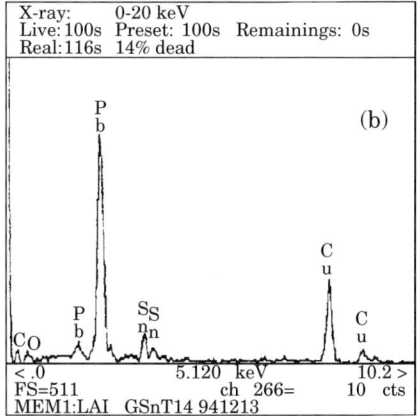

Fig. 9.24 Pb oxidation in an epoxy based conductive adhesive joint on an Sn37Pb surface has taken place after testing for 158 hours. (a) TEM photograph; (b) EDX spectrum.

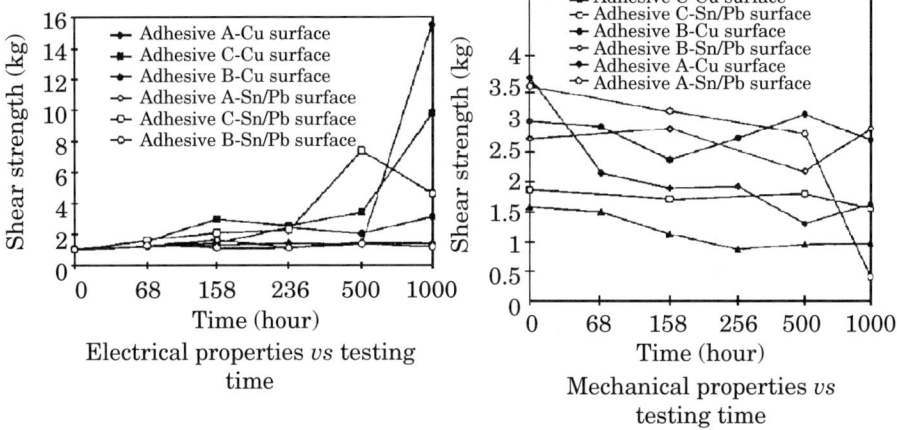

Electrical properties *vs* testing time

Mechanical properties *vs* testing time

Fig. 9.25 Electrical and mechanical properties of the conductive adhesive joints *vs* testing time in 85°C, 85%RH constant humidity test.

9.9.1.2 Cu SURFACE

Figure 9.26 shows the conductive adhesive/copper interface. As can be seen from Figure 9.26, no oxide is observed. However, after a humidity test for 1000 hours in an 85°C/85%RH environment, a distinct layer, approximately 100 nm thick, is formed on the Cu pads.[13] Figure 9.27(a) (bright field image) and Figure 9.27(b) (dark field image from the first diffraction ring in Figure 9.27(d)) show the morphology of the oxide structure. Its composition containing copper and oxygen is shown in Figure 9.27(c). The diffraction rings in the diffraction pattern obtained from the oxide layer indicate that the layer consists of crystalline grains with a fine grain size. The radii of the rings in the diffraction pattern correspond to the spacing of the crystallographic planes of Cu_2O. It is therefore concluded that the oxide formed is Cu_2O, which is a poor conductor.[16] Thus, the electrical resistance on the copper joint will increase during the humidity treatment.

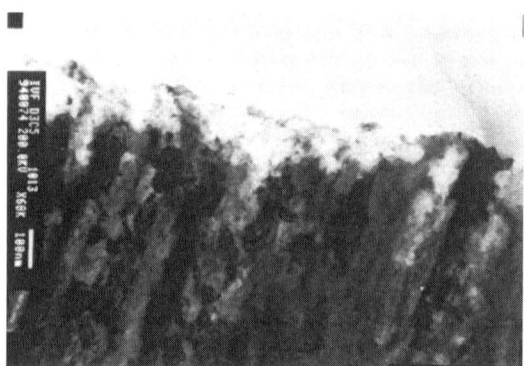

Fig. 9.26 TEM photograph of the conductive adhesive and copper joint interface before humidity test.

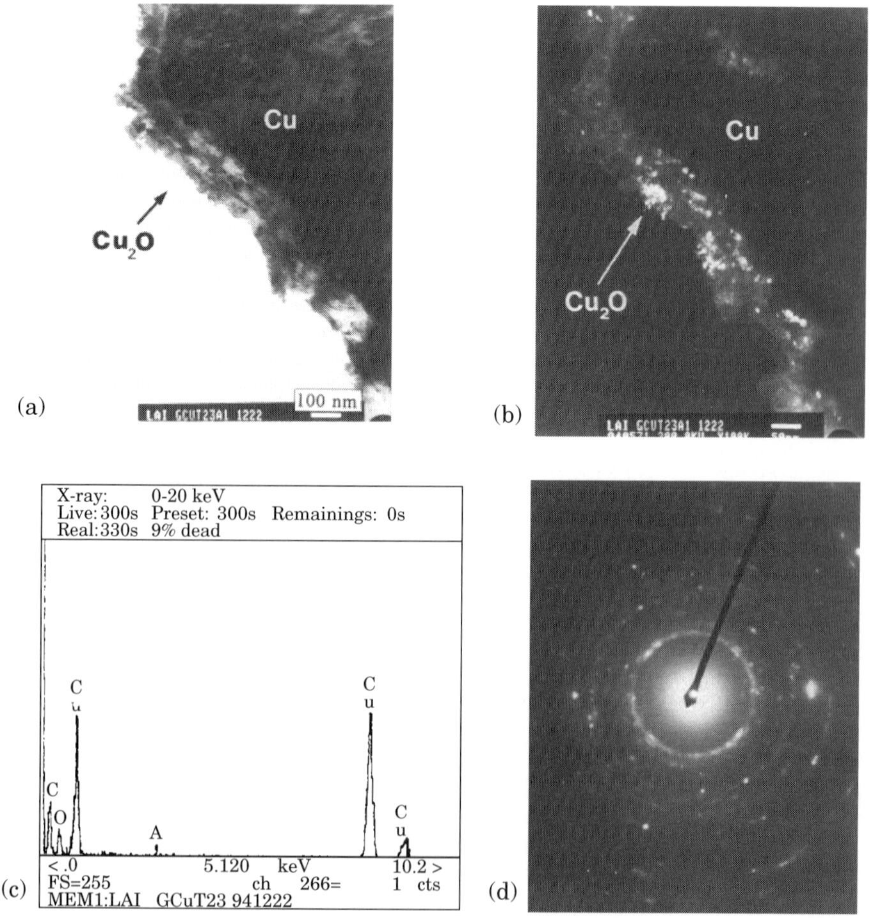

(a)

(b)

(c)

(d)

Fig. 9.27 (a) Bright field image and (b) dark field image from the first diffraction ring in (d) show the morphology of the oxide structure. Its composition containing copper and oxygen is shown in (c).

Figure 9.28 shows the electrical resistance change of a gold plated QFP80 component joined using three epoxy based conductive adhesives on an electroless Au plated FR-4 board as a function of testing time in the 85°C/85% RH environment up to 2000 hours. No electrical resistance change can be observed. It can be concluded that a noble-metal surface such as Au or Ag/Pd is preferable.

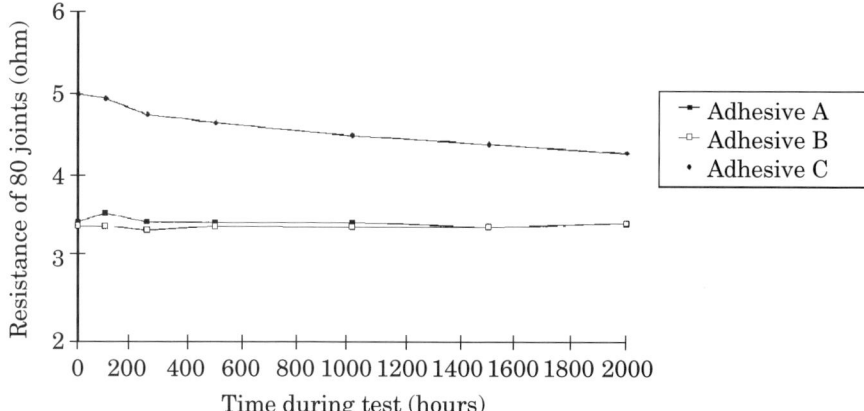

Fig. 9.28 Electrical resistance change of a gold plated QFP80 component joined using three epoxy based conductive adhesives on an electroless Au plated FR-4 board as a function of testing time in the 85°C/85% RH environment up to 2000 hours.

9.9.1.3 THEORETICAL TREATMENT OF OXIDATION AND CRACK GROWTH

Assuming ohmic behaviour of the conductive adhesive joint, the electrical conducting path can be schematically shown as in Figure 9.29.

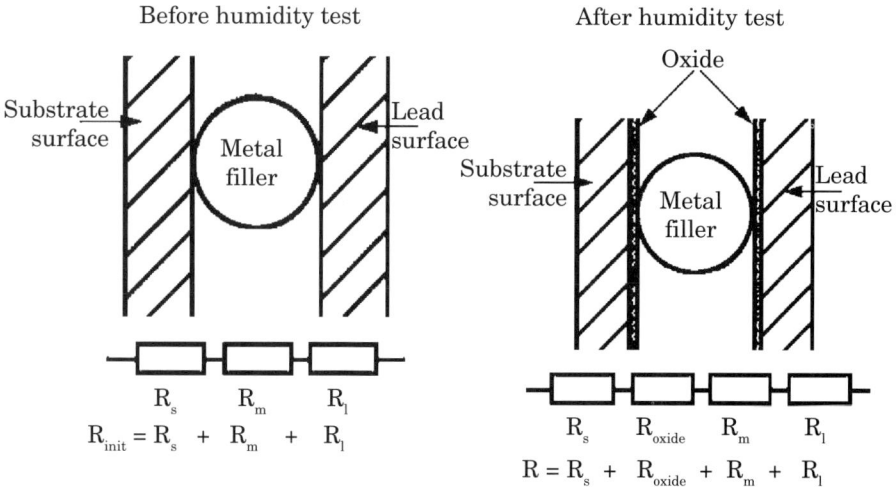

$$R_{init} = R_s + R_m + R_l$$

$$R = R_s + R_{oxide} + R_m + R_l$$

Fig. 9.29 Electrical conduction path through an anisotropically conductive adhesive joint before and after humidity testing.

Before exposure to the humid environment, the total resistance in a joint is:[17]

$$R_{before} = R_s + R_m + R_l = R_{init} \qquad (9.4)$$

where R_{before} is the total resistance in a conductive adhesive joint between a substrate and a component lead. R_s is the resistance through the substrate and R_m is the resistance through the metal filler. R_l is the resistance through the component lead, and R_{init} the total resistance before oxidation. For an 0805 chip component bonded using a typical conductive adhesive, R_{init} is approximately equal to 0.1-0.2 Ω.

After oxidation, the total resistance is:

$$R = R_s + R_{oxide} + R_m + R_l = R_{init} + R_{oxide} \qquad (9.5)$$

Where R_{oxide} is the resistance through the oxide layer which can be expressed as:

$$R_{oxide} = \rho_{oxide} \frac{l_{oxide}}{A} \qquad (9.6)$$

where ρ_{oxide} is the volume resistivity in the oxide layer, l_{oxide} the oxide layer thickness and A is the contact area.

Since polymer structures normally contain a large amount of free volume and metal oxides are often in a crystalline or in a meta-crystalline state, it is reasonable to propose that the diffusion rate of oxygen is much faster in polymers than in metal oxides. In other words, the oxygen diffusion rate through the oxide layer will control the oxide growth rate and consequently the increase of the resistance in the oxide layer.

Assuming the following Einstein equation holds:

$$l_{oxide} = \sqrt{2 D_{oxide} t} \qquad (9.7)$$

where D_{oxide} is the diffusion parameter of oxygen through the oxide layer and t is the available time for the oxygen diffusion. Combining the above-mentioned equations, one obtains a relationship between the time and the resistance change as expressed by:

$$\frac{R}{R_{init}} = 1 + \frac{l_{oxide} \, \rho_{oxide}}{A_0 \, R_{init}} \sqrt{\left(\frac{t}{t_0} \right)} \qquad (9.8)$$

where A_0 is the original contact area. A_0 is approximately equal to half of the pad size. For an 0805 chip component, A_0 is equal to 1.1 x 10^{-6} μm^2. t is the elapsed time and t_0 is the total testing time. Equation (9.5) can be used to calculate the relative electrical resistance change after humidity testing if the oxide layer thickness and the other parameters are known.

Due to moisture penetration, the polymer-based conductive adhesive joint will expand and the total metal contact area will decrease. The crack normally starts at the interface between the adhesive and the adherent. It has also been previously suggested that the electrical conducting mechanism in a conductive adhesive joint should be treated from a contact theory point of view. Thus, the contact area A can be expressed as:

$$A = A_0 \left(1 - \frac{t}{t_0} \right)$$

(9.9)

Then, the electrical resistance change can be expressed as:

$$\frac{R}{R_{init}} = 1 + \frac{l_{oxide} \, \rho_{oxide}}{A_0 \left(1 - \frac{t}{t_0} \right) R_{init}} \sqrt{\frac{t}{t_0}}$$

(9.10)

Equation (9.7) takes into account both crack growth and oxide growth during testing.

Figure 9.30 shows the results calculated using Equations (9.8) and (9.10) and the parameters given in Table 9.2. The calculations show that, if no crack

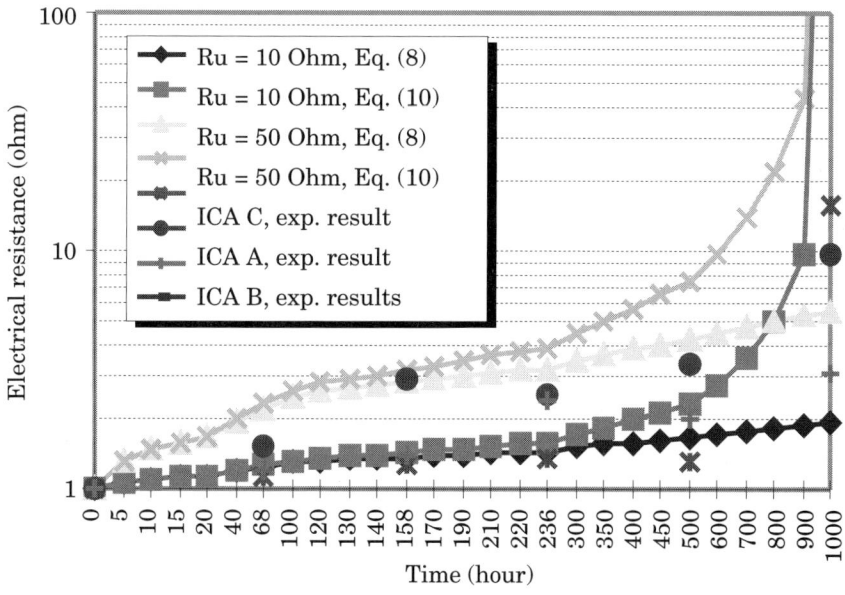

Fig. 9.30 Calculated and experimentally observed results of electrical resistance change as a function of humidity testing time for copper surface.

Table 9.2

Parameters used to Calculate the Electrical Resistance Change *vs* Elapsed Time during 85°C, 85%RH up to 1000 hours for Conductive Adhesive Joining of an 0805 Chip Component on Copper Bonding Surface

Bonding Surface	Oxide	Volume Resistivity ρ_{oxide} (Ωm)	Original Contact Area A_0 (μm^2)	Oxide Layer Thickness (nm)	Diffusion Constant D (m^2/s)	Original Electrical Resistance R_0 (Ω)
Copper	Cu_2O	10-50	1.1×10^{-6}	20	5×10^{-20}	0.2

is formed, the electrical resistance will increase, but no catastrophic failure will be expected. If a complete crack is formed by the end of the testing, the electrical resistance will go to infinity. It should also be noted that, if a crack is formed, the increase in the electrical resistance is smaller at the beginning and becomes significant by the end of testing.

In the same figure, the experimental results obtained earlier are also given. The theoretically calculated results can explain the experimental observations quite well. However, after 500 hours, the theoretical calculations are much higher than the experimentally observed values. If only the oxidation of the copper metal surface is considered, the experimental results after 500 test hours can not be explained. This means that fracture must have taken place during humidity testing. In fact, cracks have already been observed after 158 hours of exposure time.[18]

The present model only takes into account oxide and crack growth. It also assumes that there is always a total disaster failure when the testing is complete. This may not always be the case. The model also shows that oxidation alone can not contribute to the electrical resistance increase during testing. Crack formation can contribute to the large electrical resistance increase observed.

9.9.2   Polymer Degradation due to Moisture Attack

Moisture sorption effects may be reversible or irreversible, and are usually small enough to make detection of the molecular changes during absorption/adsorption very difficult.

Figure 9.31 shows the FTIR spectra of an anisotropic conductive adhesive: (a) after curing and 41 hours' conditioning at 85°C and 85% RH, (b) after curing, and (c) the difference spectrum (a)-(b). (c) thus represents the changes occurring due solely to exposure to moisture conditions at 85°C and 85% RH.[19]

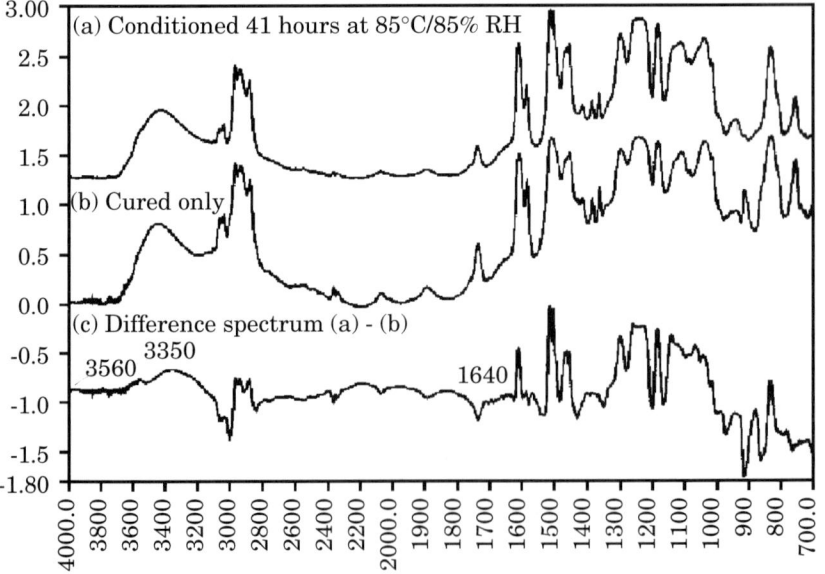

Fig. 9.31 FTIR spectra of an anisotropic conductive adhesive: (a) after curing and 41 hours' conditioning at 85°C and 85% RH, (b) after curing, and (c) the difference spectrum (a)-(b).

The most obvious real changes are the negative bands at 868, 916, 1345, 3005 and 3058 cm⁻¹, implying decreasing epoxy functionalities and thus further progress of the cure reaction. The new bands at 3560 and 3350 cm⁻¹ may both be attributed to hydroxyl groups, of which the former are free groups, which could be formed on further curing, or as an oxidation product resulting from thermo-oxidative/degradative processes. The latter are attributed to hydrogen-bonded hydroxyl groups, indicating the type of bonding of the adsorbed water to the epoxy resin. The slight rise at about 1640 cm⁻¹ indicates the presence of absorbed water in the epoxy resin. Finally, new ester linkages, again indicative of further curing, are indicated by the presence of a broad absorption region between 1000 and 1300 cm⁻¹.

Figure 9.32 compares the molecular events occurring on further exposure to these same conditions. The figure shows the difference spectra (a) after 41 hours' conditioning, (b) after 162 hours' conditioning, (c) after 821 hours' conditioning, all at 85°C and 85% RH. It is observed first that the subtracted spectra all show the same profile, indicating that the subtraction procedure has been consistent and that the subtraction spectra are valid.

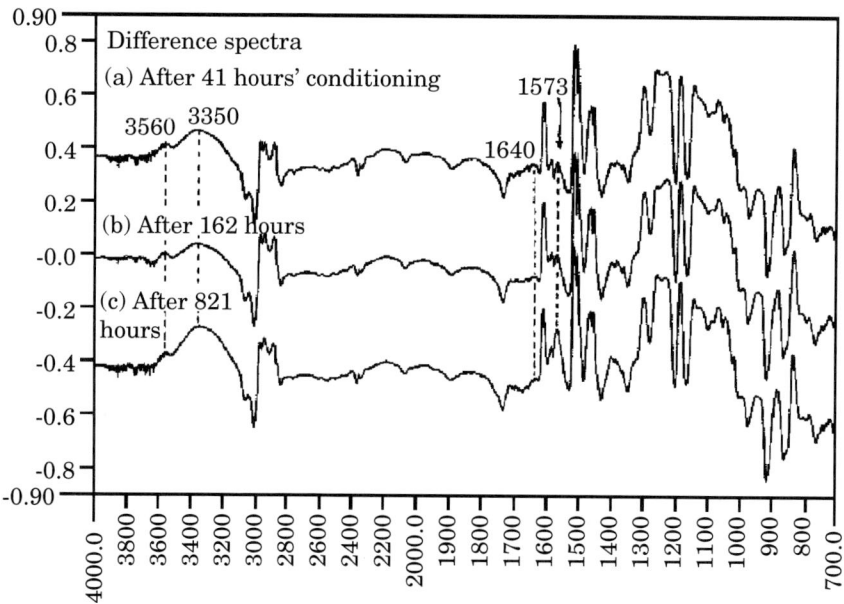

Fig. 9.32 FTIR difference spectra (a) after 41 hours' conditioning, (b) after 162 hours' conditioning, (c) after 821 hours' conditioning, all at 85°C and 85% RH.

Closer scrutiny of this figure also shows that the bands at 3560, 3350, 1640 and 1573 cm⁻¹ are increasing in intensity with increasing conditioning time. Both the increases at 3350 and 1640 cm⁻¹ follow the increasing adsorption of water in the epoxy. The steadily growing absorption at 1573 cm⁻¹ is tentatively attributed to unsaturated vinyl structures ('C=C') which are formed as a result of degradative reactions. Moisture degradation is believed to occur by hydrolysis of the ester linkages ('R-(C=O)-OR'). Such hydrolytic attack breaks the polymer chain creating two new end groups, a hydroxyl and a carbonyl. Although it is difficult to see a new emerging carbonyl group in this figure, the presence of the band at 3560 cm^{-1}, which indicates free hydroxyls, supports the suggestion of degradative reactions occurring with increasing exposure to heat and humidity at 85°C and 85% RH.

In conclusion, it can be said that, on exposure of the cured adhesive to 85°C and 85% RH, both moisture adsorption and further curing can be observed. After a certain time, however, further curing will not be observed; instead, degradation effects may be seen.

9.10   RELIABILITY AND QUALITY OF THE ACA FLIP-CHIP JOINT

ACA flip-chip joining technology on FR-4 and flexible circuitry represents a novel and interesting technology as a low-cost alternative to soldering technology. The benefits of ACA technology compared with soldering are:[20]

— Possibility to obtain a materials and environmentally compatible system. For instance, gold can be used as the interconnecting material across the interfaces. This will prevent galvanic corrosion across the interconnect.
— Bumping is not an absolute requirement. In some cases, only a barrier layer or under bump metallisation is needed.
— Simplicity for array and small pitch chip assembly. Below 100 μm pitch is possible.
— Few process steps and simple processing techniques. Conventional stencil printing machines can be used for application of ACA pastes.
— Low thermal shock during assembly due to curing.
— Underfilling is not necessary when using anisotropically conductive adhesives.

The drawbacks of this technology compared with soldering are:

— Lack of reliability data.
— Pressure is required during bonding. This makes the in-line process different from the conventional flip-chip process.
— The adhesive bonding process does not have the same self-alignment capability as solder.

9.10.1   The Effect of Bonding Pressure, Particle Size and Bump Geometry

There are many variables which affect bonding quality. They include the following:

— Board coplanarity.
— Bump height and uniformity.
— Pressure distribution and pressure application rate.
— Particle distribution.
— Cure temperature and cure time.
— Temperature ramp rate.
— Alignment accuracy.

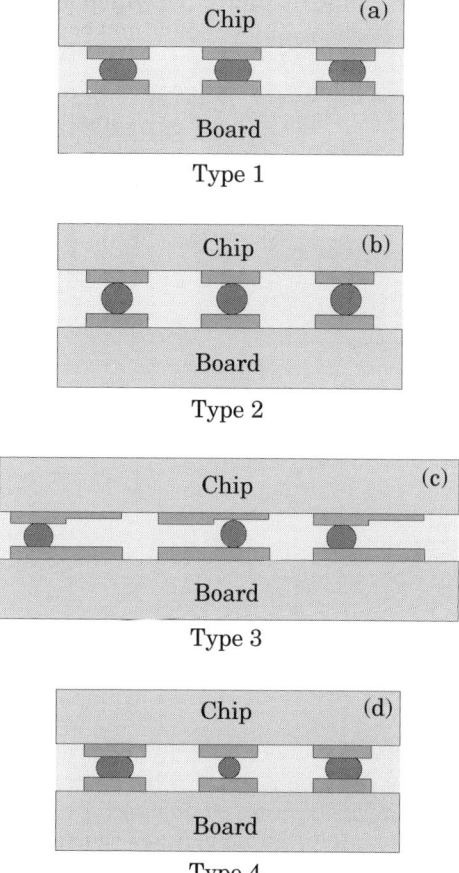

Fig. 9.33 Schematic diagrams of four types of ACA joints caused by different bump geometry, variation in filler size and difference in bonding pressure.

Figure 9.34 summarises schematically the different types of joint structures that may occur during ACA flip-chip bonding.[21] The Type 1 joint shows uniform particle size and is the most reliable with respect to withstanding various environmental tests owing to the strong and uniform atomic interaction between the heavily deformed particles and the contacts from the chip and from the board.

Type 2 and Type 3 joints consist of conducting particles with a uniform size but different bump/pad shape. Type 4 has different particle sizes. Type 2 joints consist of undeformed or slightly deformed conducting particles, due to too low a load on the bonded joints. This is caused by either low applied bonding pressure or inhomogeneous pressure distribution on the chips during flip-chip bonding. The conductive character of this type of joint is very unstable, especially at elevated temperature. An additional threat to these joints is the large difference in thermal expansion of conductive particles in the anisotropically conductive adhesive and the adhesive matrix. In this kind of joint, no resistive force exists to oppose the formation of conductive gaps.

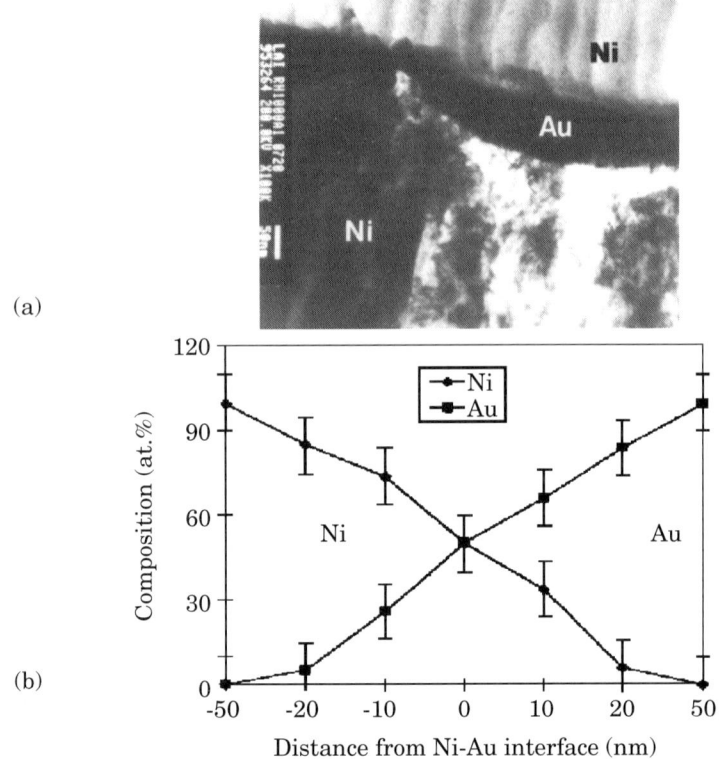

(a)

(b)

Fig. 9.34 Atomic bonding between a nickel filler in an ACA material and the Au bonding surface. (a) TEM microstructure photo showing the atomic bonding between particles and pads; (b) interdiffusion between the nickel and gold surface.

Conductive failure of Type 2 joints can therefore occur easily in the high temperature region. However, during cooling, conductivity could be recovered due to contraction of the adhesive. This type of joint occurs more frequently in bumped die. Therefore, during the temperature cycling test, the conductivity may drop in the high temperature region, as can be seen in Figure 9.35.

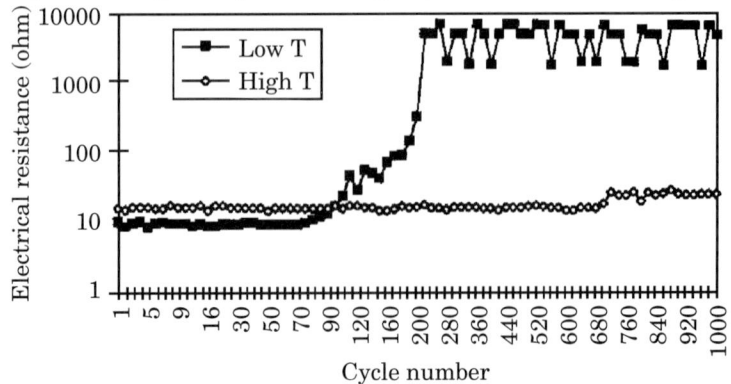

Fig. 9.35 In the Type 2 joint, failure occurs in the higher temperature region during the temperature cycling test (-40 to +125°C).

Type 3 joints can result from shape or height variations of the contact areas such as in bumpless die. Electrical degradation can also occur in the high temperature region if the inter-atomic force between deformed particles and conducting areas on the chip and the board is not strong enough. However, provided that, at elevated temperature, the strong inter-atomic force of deformed joints is sufficient to maintain electrical contact, the distance between the bonded chip and board will be maintained. Therefore, the influence of thermal expansion of the adhesive on the undeformed particles or the thermal stress caused by the mismatch of the CTEs between the chip and the substrate can be eliminated. The electrical performance of the whole chip can therefore withstand thermal attack. When the temperature decreases, on the other hand, the contraction of the adhesive will be greater than that of the conducting particles. The spacing between chip bumps and board pads cannot reduce as much as the adhesive contraction on account of the restriction from the pressed particles. In this case, the conductivity performance will depend on the status of the undeformed particles at low temperature. In other words, failure occurs more easily in lower temperature regions. This is illustrated in Figure 9.36.

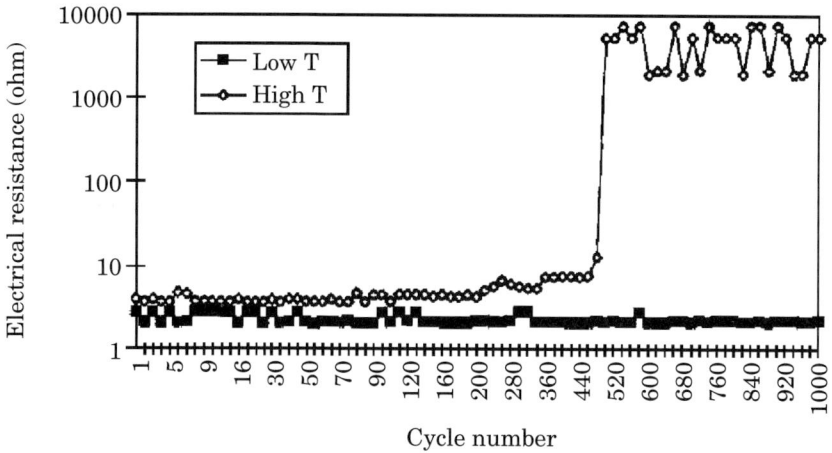

Fig. 9.36 In the Type 3 joint, failure occurs in the lower temperature region during the temperature cycling test (-40 to +125°C).

The concave barriers in the bumpless die readily produce uneven deformation of the conductive particles as shown in Figure 9.37. A particle in the projecting part of the barrier has been heavily deformed, while that in the hollow has been only slightly deformed.

Finally, the conductivity of Type 4 joints is also unstable due to the weak atomic bonding between the smaller particles and the contact area. Failure can easily occur both at low and high temperatures, as illustrated in Figure 9.38.

Given the fact that bumpless die have an intrinsically concave shape, it will be difficult to obtain good reliability especially on rigid FR-4. This is because there is a greater chance that fillers are not deformed inside, thus causing failure in lower temperature regions. Therefore, high reliability is obtained when using bumped die under proper pressure and filler size control. This is demonstrated by a number of experimental results, i.e., on FR-4, bumped die are reliable and unbumped die lead to unreliable joints.

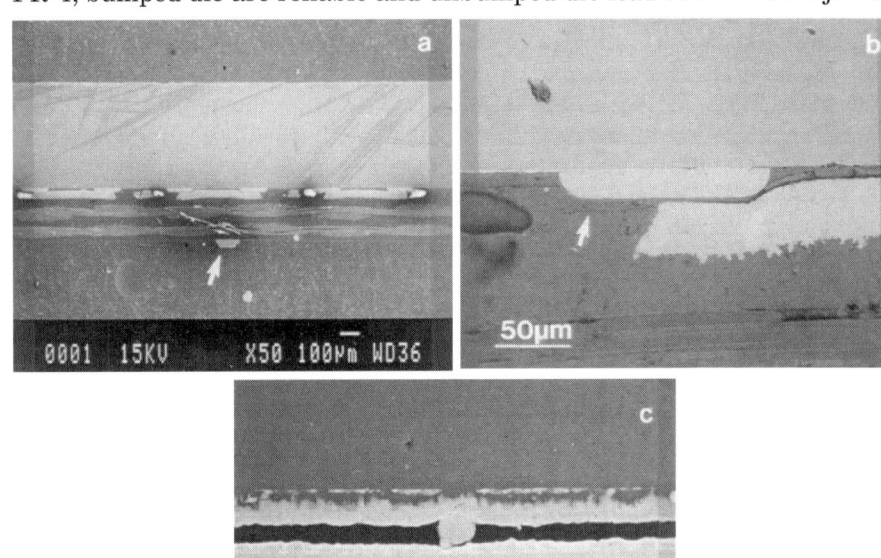

Fig. 9.37 Inhomogeneous deformation of particles in an ACA joint with a bumpless die. (a) shows the general configuration: the arrows indicate a deformed and an undeformed particle; (b) shows the severely deformed particle in (a); (c) shows the slightly deformed particle in (a).

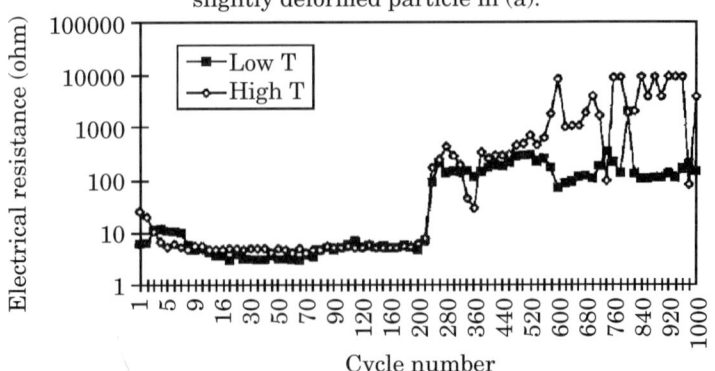

Fig. 9.38 Example of Type 4 joint. Failure occurs in both high and low temperature regions after temperature cycling from -40 to +125°C.

9.10.1.1 QUALITATIVE ANALYSIS OF THE CRITERIA FOR A GOOD ACA JOINT

Figure 9.39 presents schematic diagrams illustrating two different situations which have been observed on conducting tracks separated by a metal particle and surrounding adhesive. In Figure 9.39(a) the particle has been highly deformed so that the original spherical particle becomes an oblate spheroid, while in Figure 9.39(b) the particle is only slightly deformed so that it remains virtually spherical. Consequently, the adhesive in the regions just beyond the contact area (for example, ABC in Figure 9.39(a) and A'B'C' in Figure 9.39(b)) will act as a wedge which could induce decohesion at A or A' if the wedge is thermally expanded.

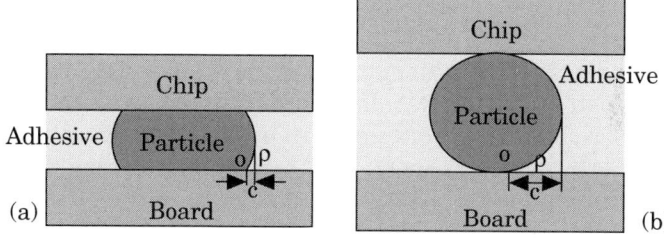

Fig. 9.39 Schematic diagram of deformed and undeformed particles in an ACA joint. (a) shows the deformed particle while (b) shows the undeformed particle.

The distribution of the stress caused by adhesive thermal expansion is uneven due to the discontinuities in the structure and the material of the ACA joint. High stress will be localised on the tips of the wedge. An exact mathematical analysis of stress concentration is very difficult or impracticable. Therefore, Figure 9.39 is further simplified by Figure 9.40 in two dimensions without loss of the general concept.

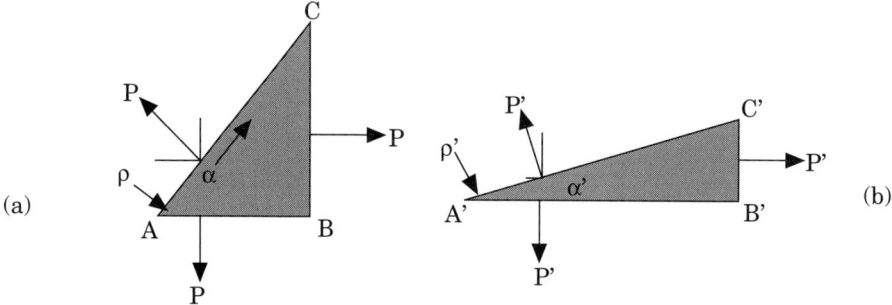

Fig. 9.40 Simplified model showing the deformed particle (a) and undeformed (b) situation.

Because the adhesive has a much higher coefficient of thermal expansion than the conducting particle, the thermal stresses developed at the sides AB, BC and AC are hydrostatic pressure P. The same situation occurs in Figure 9.40(b), except that the pressure is denoted by P'. The wedge opening angles are α' and α' respectively (α' is probably smaller than α). Probably due to the thermal expansion of the adhesive in the region ABC (Figure 9.40(a)), there will be a frictional force F per unit area on the surface AC. However, neither this force nor the horizontal component of P, i.e. Psinα, produces a wedging effect, therefore the effect of F will not be considered further. In fact, it is the force combination Pcosα acting on AC and AB per unit area which contributes to tearing at tip A. Assuming that the radius of curvature at the tip is ρ, then an approximate estimation of the stress concentration at A may be expressed by:

$$P \cos\alpha \sqrt{\frac{AB}{\rho}} \tag{9.11}$$

When this stress is high enough to pull the atomic planes apart, normally at A, decohesion will occur at A. If the atomic force between two atoms at A is denoted by N, and the atomic distance in a direction perpendicular to the atomic force is b, then the atomic bond breaking stress will be simply N/b^2. Thus, the criterion for the decohesion at A is:

$$P \cos\alpha \sqrt{\frac{AB}{\rho}} = \frac{N}{b^2} \tag{9.12}$$

In other words, the thermal stress Pi required to initiate decohesion at A is determined by:

$$P_i = N\left(\frac{1}{b^2}\right)\sqrt{\frac{\rho}{AB}}\,\frac{1}{\cos\alpha} \tag{9.13}$$

Similarly, in Figure 9.40(b), the necessary thermal stress P'i for decohesion initiation at A' is determined by:

$$P'_i = N'\left(\frac{1}{b^2}\right)\sqrt{\frac{\rho'}{A'B'}}\,\frac{1}{\cos\alpha'} \tag{9.14}$$

Because in Figure 9.39(a) the particle has been highly deformed, the atoms at A are more closely related, making N > N', although the atomic distance b is almost the same. Since ρ ≥ ρ', AB < A'B' and α > α', obviously P_i > P'_i. This means that, in a case like Figure 9.39(b), a lower thermal expansion stress will be sufficient to induce electrical failure at the contact region while the same thermal stress is still unable to do so in a situation such as that shown in Figure 9.39(a).

9.10.1.2 EFFECT OF THE TEMPERATURE RAMP RATE

Figure 9.41 shows the temperature ramp rate used during flip-chip bonding. For the bumped die, a good flip-chip joint quality is obtained with both a low and a high ramp rate. For the unbumped die, a good quality joint is obtained only with a low ramp rate if the pressurisation speed is very low.[22] Figures 9.42 to 9.49 show the assembled joints on glass substrate through the glass substrate and in cross-sections.

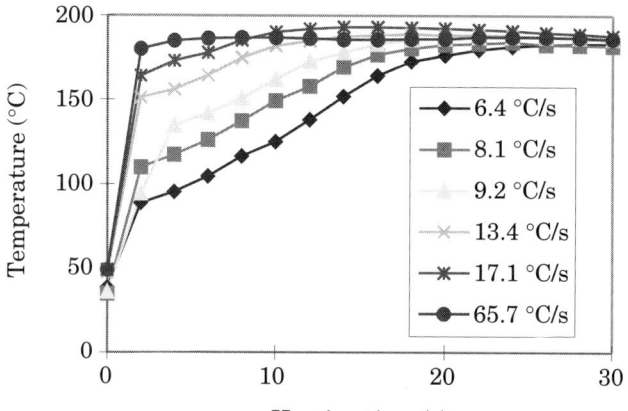

Heating time (s)

Fig. 9.41 Temperature ramp rate used to bond the ACA flip-chip joint.

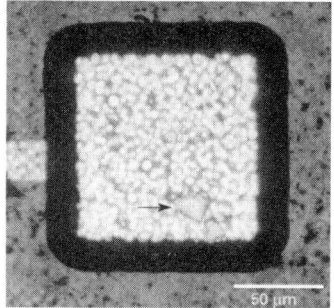

Fig. 9.42 Bumped die assembled on glass substrate with a temperature ramp rate of 8.1°C/s and an applied force of 15 N/chip. A deformed particle is indicated by an arrow.

Fig. 9.43 Bumped die assembled on glass substrate with a ramp rate of 65.7°C/s and an applied force of 15 N/chip. A deformed particle is indicated by an arrow.

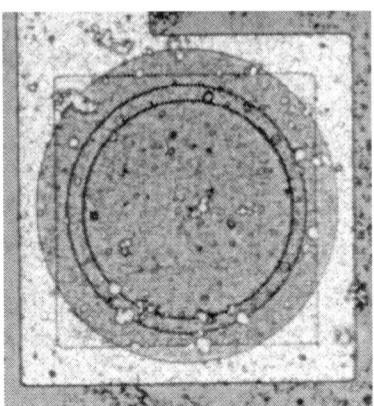

Fig. 9.44 Unbumped die assembled on glass substrate with a ramp rate of 8.1°C/s and an applied force of 15 N/chip.

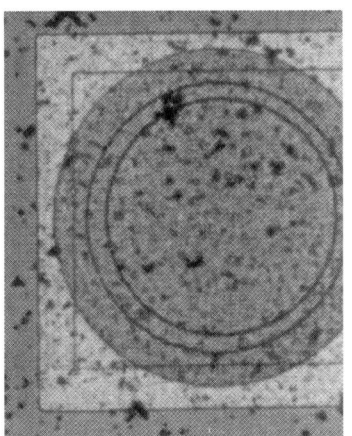

Fig. 9.45 Unbumped die assembled on glass substrate with a ramp rate of 65.7°C/s and an applied force of 15 N/chip.

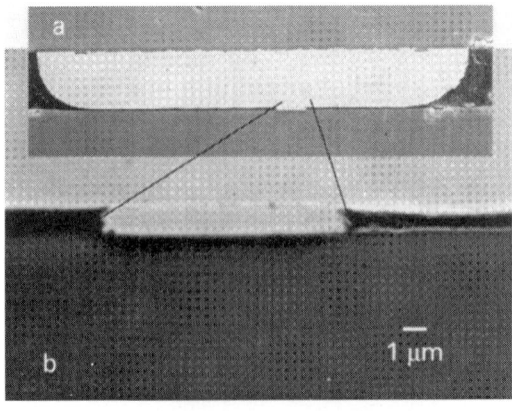

Fig. 9.46 (a) Cross-section of bumped die assembled with a ramp rate of 8.1°C/s and (b) a deformed particle at a higher magnification.

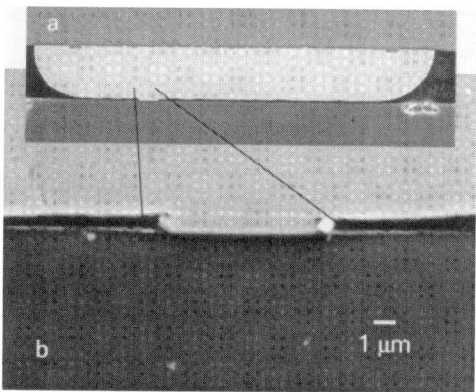

Fig. 9.47 (a) Cross-section of bumped die assembled with a ramp rate of 65.7°C/s and (b) a deformed particle at a higher magnification.

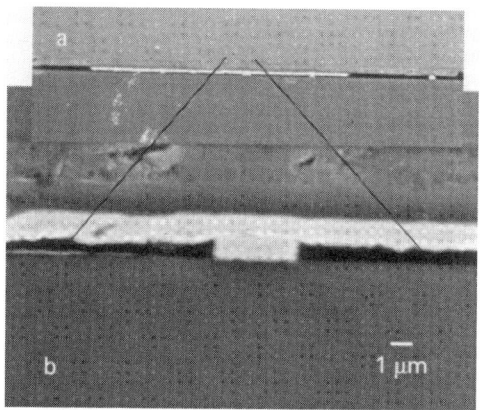

Fig. 9.48 (a) Cross-section of unbumped die assembled with a ramp rate of 8.1°C/s and (b) a deformed particle at a higher magnification.

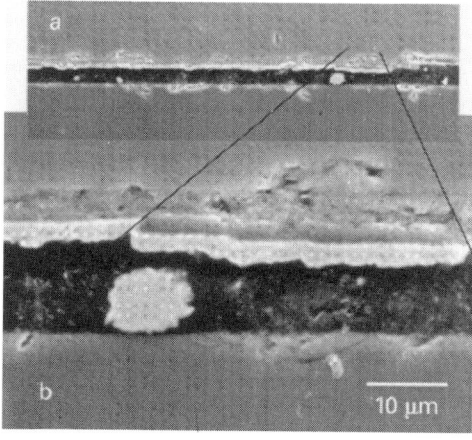

Fig. 9.49 (a) Cross-section of unbumped die assembled with a ramp rate of 65.7°C/s and (b) non-deformed particles at higher magnification.

The white-looking particles indicated by the pillow in Figures 9.42 and 9.43 have been deformed during assembly and the dark particles have not been deformed. From the above figures, it can be seen that, for the bumped die, the temperature ramp is not an important parameter, i.e., good deformable joints can always be obtained. However, for the unbumped die, it is important to have a low ramp rate of the temperature. If too high a temperature ramp rate and too low a pressure application rate are used, the adhesive is already cured before full particle compression has been reached, as is shown in Figure 9.49. As a result, no good ACA joints can be obtained.

9.10.1.3   EFFECT OF BONDING PRESSURE DISTRIBUTION

Bonding pressure distribution is important because uneven pressure on the chip can cause localised high pressure, resulting in elastic stress and uneven deformation of conducting particles. Table 9.3 shows the results of the test before and after calibration of pressure distribution in an ageing test at 125°C.

Table 9.3

Measured Electrical Resistance of Epoxy Based ACA Joints with Bumpless Die during Ageing Test (125°C) on FR-4 and Polyimide Flexible Substrates up to 1000 hours

Pressure Distribution	Board Type	Test Number	Electrical Resistance (ohm)				
			0 h	100 h	250 h	500 h	1000 h
Before	rigid	1	14.3	23.0	23.3	23.5	23.9
	rigid	2	22.1	66 K	66 K	112 K	310 K
	rigid	3	13.2	13.3	13.8	15.1	21.5
	flexible	4	53.3	35.4	133.7	297	320
	flexible	5	12.7	open	open	open	open
	flexible	6	open	open	open	open	open
After	rigid	1	12.5	12.5	12.4	12.2	12.3
	rigid	2	12.7	12.7	12.5	12.4	12.5
	rigid	3	12.4	12.4	12.2	12.2	12.3
	flexible	4	12.3	12.6	12.4	12.3	12.4
	flexible	5	12.6	12.5	12.4	12.3	12.5
	flexible	6	13.6	15.0	16.9	16.5	17.1

9.10.1.3.1   Factors Affecting Pressure Distribution During Bonding

A uniform bonding pressure distribution means that the pressure on every particle between the conducting areas of the chip and the board is about the same for producing uniform deformation of these particles. The pressure distribution is influenced by the following factors:

— position of the chip holder in the bonding machine;
— homogeneity of particle size;
— configuration, height variation of the bump within and across the whole chip.

An example of the difference in pressure distribution is given in Figure 9.50.

⬜ (a)   ⬜ (b)

Fig. 9.50 Uniform (a) and non-uniform (b) pressure tracks of bumpless die on rigid
FR-4 board.

It is clear that uneven particle size can also produce uneven distribution
of the bonding pressure. The question is which size is the most suitable. A
large particle size will be unfavourable for particle settlement on the
conducting areas, while fine particles can scarcely achieve a strong enough
inter-atomic effect due to the height variation of the contact surface. The
majority of ACAs seem to use a filler size in the range of 3-5 μm with
minimum variation in size.

9.10.1.4   EFFECT OF ELECTRICAL DESIGN

The electrical conductor track design can have a strong influence on joint
reliability.

Table 9.4 shows such an example. It can be seen that failure occurs mainly
in the area between measurement points 2 and 3 instead of between 1 and
2 although they contain the same number of joints (8 joints). The electrical

Table 9.4

Electrical Resistance (Ω) of ACA Joints with Bumpless Die on Rigid FR-4 and on
Flexible Substrates during Ageing Test at 125°C for 1000 hours

Board	Test Number	Measured Points	Electrical Resistance (ohm)				
			0 h	100 h	250 h	500 h	1000 h
FR-4 Rigid	1	1/2	1.7	1.6	1.6	1.7	1.7
		2/3	1.9	2.0	2.0	2.1	2.2
	2	1/2	1.5	1.6	1.5	1.6	1.6
		2/3	1.9	2.0	2.0	2.1	2.1
	3	1/2	1.5	1.5	1.6	1.5	1.6
		2/3	1.9	2.0	2.0	2.1	2.1
Polyimide Flexible	1	1/2	1.7	1.9	2.3	2.6	8.2
		2/3	1.9	2.0	2.3	2.2	71.8
	2	1/2	1.7	2.3	5.3	6.6	68.4
		2/3	1.9	2.3	open	open	open
	3	1/2	1.5	1.5	1.6	1.5	2.1
		2/3	1.5	open	open	open	open

conductor routes for the chip are shown in Figure 9.51. By comparing the
pressure tracks of the rigid and the flexible (Figure 9.52(a) and b)), it can be
seen that the bonding pressure with the flexible board is always uneven. The
excess pressure, indicated by an arrow, in the upper part of the pressure
tracks on the flexible board indicates a high pressure localised somewhere in

the region between measured points 2 and 3. Figure 9.53(a) shows the corresponding structure with the bumpless die. The uneven pressure distribution leads to a non-uniform deformation of the contacting pads on the flexible board. From Figures 9.51 to 9.53, it can be seen that the most severe deformation takes place in the highly pressed area where a conducting line on the reverse side of the board passes (indicated by an arrow in Figure 9.51). After ageing at 125°C for 100 hours, a conducting gap was formed due to the spring-back of the heavily pressed chip or the board from their original bonded positions (indicated in Figure 9.53(b)), with the result that the electrical resistance of the part (i.e., between measurement points 2 and 3) increased from 1.9 ohm to infinity (open circuit). Proper design of the flexible circuitry is therefore very important for good ACA flip-chip bonding.

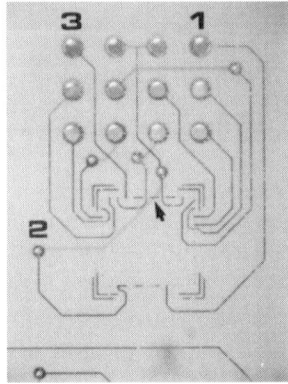

Fig. 9.51 Conductor configuration for bumpless die on a flexible polyimide board.

Fig. 9.52 Pressure tracks (1.4 x) on bumpless die on rigid FR-4 board and on a flexible polyimide board. (a) shows the pressure distribution on the rigid board (the bonding force was 17 N); (b) shows the pressure on the flexible board (from left, the bonding force was 90, 60, 35, 17 N).

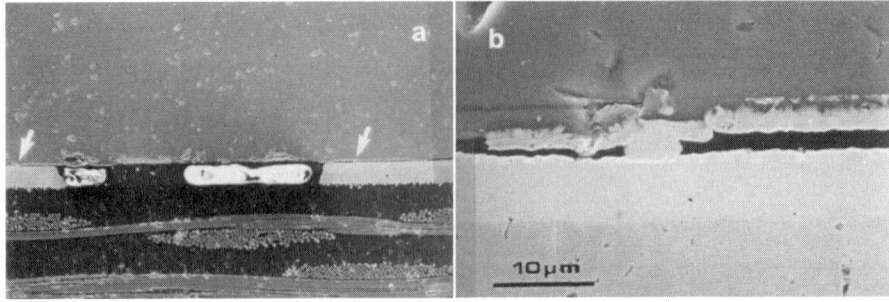

Fig. 9.53 The joining structure with the bumpless die after ageing at 125°C for 100 hours, which corresponds to the upper part of pressure tracks in (b); (a) shows the uneven deformation of the bonding areas, the most severe deformation occurring where a conductor on the reverse side of the flexible board passes below; (b) shows the conductive gap formation in the severely deformed bonding area.

9.10.1.5   EFFECT OF BUMP UNIFORMITY

If there is a large variation of the bump height across the chip, it will be difficult to exert a uniform pressure over the entire chip. This is illustrated in Figure 9.54. In this chip, about 9 μm height variation has been observed in a total of 40 bumps. (The required bump height was set as 20 μm.) This will lead to poor bonding quality.

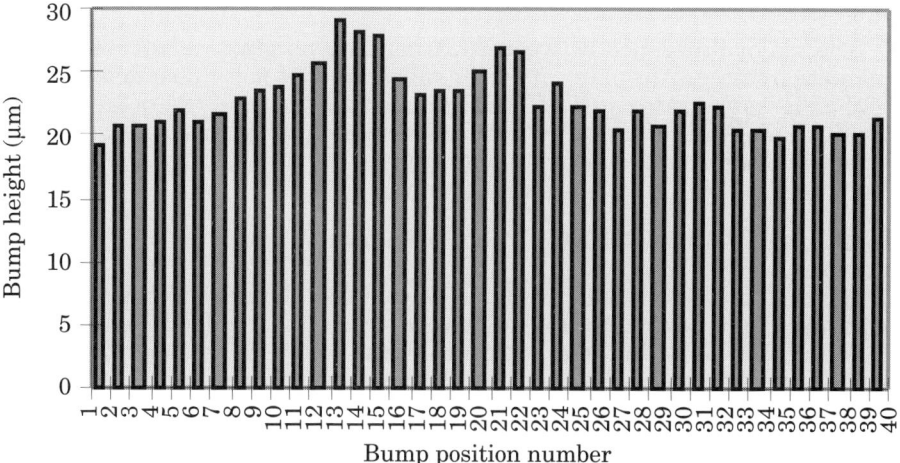

Fig. 9.54 Bump height variation within one chip with 40 bumps. The designated value was 20 μm.

If the height variation is within 1μm, as illustrated in Figure 9.55, good bonding is possible.

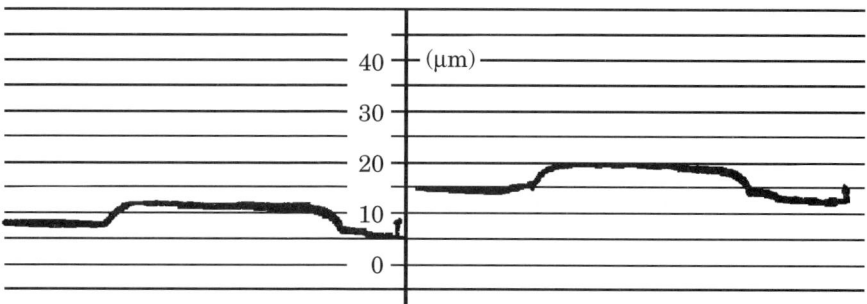

Fig. 9.55 Bump height variation less than 1 μm leading to a good possibility of obtaining a good ACA flip-chip joint.

Therefore the bumping process and quality control flow diagram described in Figure 9.56 can be used to guarantee bumping quality.

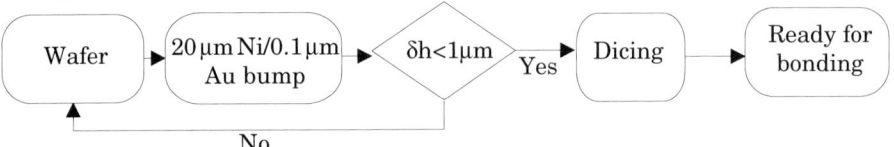

Fig. 9.56 Process and quality control flow diagram for low-cost electroless Ni/Au bumping for ACA flip-chip assembly.

9.10.1.6   EFFECT OF BOARD PLANARITY

The major difference between ACA bonding on glass substrate and on printed circuitry is the planarity of the substrate. The non-linear deformation of the FR-4 substrate causes deformation of approximately 2 μm area under the dynamic bonding pressure as discussed on Chapter 4. Therefore, substrate with a higher glass transition temperature or greater stability than FR-4 is necessary for high reliability applications.

9.11   HIGH FREQUENCY PROPERTIES

As conductive adhesives are made of composite material, it is naturally envisaged that these materials will have inferior high-frequency performance to metallic solders. Limited literature exists today on the high-frequency behaviour of conductive adhesives.[23-25] However, this inferior performance has not proven to be the case for ACAs.

9.11.1   FR-4

On the FR-4 substrate, up to 2 GHz, the ACA flip chip does not seem to perform any worse than the solder joint, as shown in Figure 9.57. The large transmission loss is from the silicon itself. Beyond 2 GHz, it is probably not appropriate to use FR-4 substrate.[25]

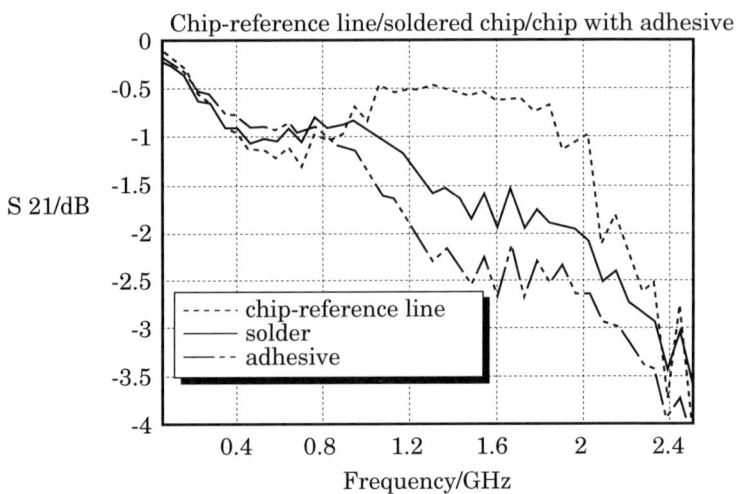

Fig. 9.57 ACA and soldered flip-chip joint up to 2 GHz.

9.11.2   High-frequency Duroid Substrate

Figure 9.58 shows the signal transmission S21 on a high-frequency Duroid substrate up to 20 GHz.[24] Again, it can be seen that there is no difference between soldered and ACA joints. The major loss is from the silicon chip itself.

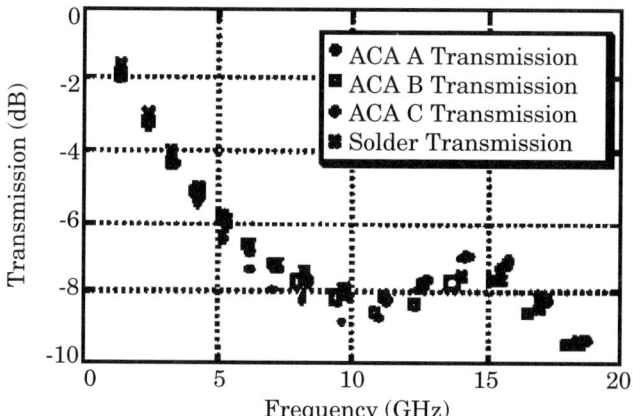

Fig. 9.58 Transmission properties S21 on a high-frequency Duroid substrate for an ACA and a soldered flip-chip joint.

9.12   THERMAL RESISTANCE OF CONDUCTIVE ADHESIVE JOINT IN FLIP-CHIP APPLICATION

The thermal performance of an adhesively assembled chip is of vital interest as power dissipation in the chip increases. The steady state temperature profile of a mounted chip may be described roughly with the thermal resistance R_{jp}. The temperature rise from the board to the chip is given by the following equation:[26]

$$T_{chip} - T_{board} = P \times R_{jp} \qquad (9.15)$$

where P = power dissipated in the chip.

For ACA simulation, the following conditions are used:

- Chip size 4.5 x 4.5 mm
- Chip thickness 0.6 mm
- Power in the chip is only dissipated in a thin area close to the flip-chip side
- Power dissipated 4 W
- Active area on the chip is uniformly out to the pad row
- Flip-chip pad size 0.1 x 0.1 mm
- 10 particles in contact in each joint as an average
- Pitch 0.2 mm

- 76 pads close to the chip periphery
- Bump thickness 5 µm
- Bump material gold
- Footprint pad height 35 µm
- Board used FR-4 board
- ACA material height 3 µm

The mounted anisotropic flip chip has a very short thermal passage over the joint but only a very low percentage of metal contact in the joint. Assuming an average of 10 fillers in each contact in an ACA joint and that only 20% of the metal ball is in contact with the chip bump, the result from the simulations gives:

$$R_{jp} = 7 \text{ K/W} \tag{9.16}$$

$$\tau_{chip} = 200 \text{ ms} \tag{9.17}$$

and τ defines the chip thermal time constant. This may be compared with the ideal case where 100% of the deformed filler is in ideal contact with the bump:

$$R_{jp} = 2.6 \text{ K/W} \tag{9.18}$$

and the time constant is:

$$\tau_{chip} = 100 \text{ ms} \tag{9.19}$$

The results indicate very clearly how thermal performance (R_{jp}) is affected by the contact area. A chip power dissipation of 5 W gives a temperature difference from board to chip of 35 K or 13 K.

For ICA simulation, the following conditions are used:

— Chip size 4.5 x 4.5 mm
— Chip thickness 0.6 mm
— Power in the chip is only dissipated in a thin area close to flip-chip side
— Active area on the chip is uniformly out to the pad row
— Flip-chip pad size 0.1 x 0.1 mm
— Pitch 0.2 mm
— 76 pads close to the chip periphery
— Underfill material epoxy
— Bump thickness 5 µm
— Bump material gold
— Footprint pad height 35 µm
— FR-4 board used
— ICA height 30 µm
— ICA material thermal conductivity 2 W/mK
— Epoxy underfill between the joints

The mounted isotropic flip chip has a medium length thermal passage over the joint and a low percentage of metal in the joint. The spaces between the joints are filled with epoxy underfill material. The results from the simulations give the thermal resistance between chip and board:

$$R_{jp} = 8.8 \text{ K/W} \tag{9.20}$$

A chip power dissipation of 5 W gives a temperature difference from board to chip of 44 K, and τ defines the chip thermal time constant.

$$\tau_{chip} = 280 \text{ ms} \tag{9.21}$$

The time constant defines an easy means of describing the unsteady state behaviour of the chip temperature. After a power step into the chip, the chip temperature is given by the following equation as a function of time t:

$$T = T_0 x (1 - e^{-\frac{t}{\tau}}) \tag{9.22}$$

where T_0 is the steady state temperature.

From the above analysis, it is seen that the ACA joint has better thermal performance than the ICA joint.

9.13   ISSUES AND CONCERNS

Conductive adhesives for surface mount applications have been tested and examined during the past seven years. It can be concluded that no single conductive adhesive has such good electrical and mechanical performance that it can work as a 'drop-in' replacement. Instead, modification of production process steps, component geometry and component metallisation or of the conductive adhesive itself are necessary to replace solder.[32]

9.13.1   Prediction Methodology for Estimation of Real Service Life after Accelerated Testing

One of the major questions that needs to be addressed is the estimation and prediction of the real service life of a conductive adhesive joint. As conductive adhesives consist of a metal part and an epoxy part, they are composite materials. Therefore, it is unlikely that the acceleration laws used for prediction of the real service life of pure metals and the pure polymers can be used directly for conductive adhesives.

It is apparent that mechanical fatigue and creep are an important factor causing failure of the adhesive joint and also the moisture can attack a conductive adhesive joint through both bulk and interfacial diffusion. Therefore, it will be interesting to study the low-cycle mechanical fatigue behaviour of the conductive adhesive joint in a humid environment.

Figure 9.59 shows such testing equipment. This equipment is able to qualify low-cycle mechanical fatigue in a humid and in a dry atmosphere. Thus, the effect of moisture on the low-cycle fatigue life of the joint can be studied.

Another issue is that, when bonding on printed circuitry with ACA technology, it is important to understand the non-linear deformation behaviour of the substrate during bonding. This appears to be critical in obtaining a high quality ACA joint. Further investigation is necessary to clarify this matter.

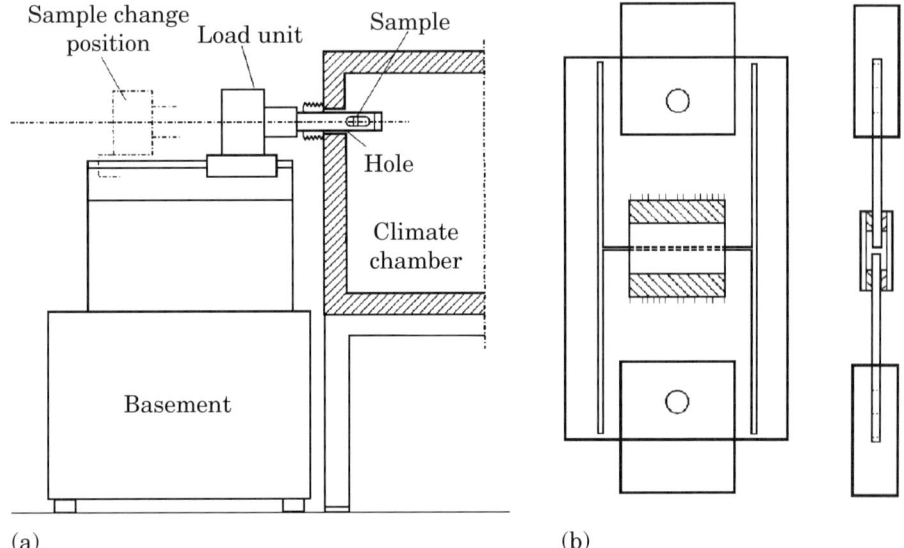

(a)   (b)

Fig. 9.59 (a) Schematic drawing of a low-cycle fatigue tester that can be operated in a climatic chamber. Thus the moisture effect on the fatigue life can be taken into account; (b) the test board designed for testing.

9.13.2   Bending Performance

As ICAs are so heavily loaded with metal particles to guarantee electrical performance, the mechanical properties of the joint are affected. For instance, on an ICA joined surface mount board 250 x 300 cm^2, cracks were observed in the surface mount QFP joints at the centre of the board when bending the board on the 10 mm cylindrical rod placed in the centre of the board. Therefore, better adhesive/metal particle ratio optimisation is necessary to enhance the bending performance.

9.14   DEVELOPMENT TRENDS IN ACA CONDUCTIVE ADHESIVE JOINING

ACA conductive adhesives are developing with the following approaches and characteristics:

— Double layer
— Arrayed ACF
— Insulation layer on top of the conducting layer
— Fast UV-curable.

The double layer type of ACF is described in Chapter 10 of this book. The purpose of the double layer ACF is apparently to increase the number of particles settling on the bumps/pads. The arrayed ACF is described in a number of papers.[27-30] By using the arrayed ACF, it is expected that a high number of pin counts can be coped with. The insulation layer on top of the conducting layer represents another interesting development trend.[29] The purpose of this is to increase the packaging density without causing shorting. By using the insulation layer, the particles physically contact each other in the horizontal layer, but in the vertical conduction layer the insulation is broken during pressurisation and bonding. The UV-curable systems are described in Chapter 4. Using UV-curable ACAs, it is possible to increase the processing and in-line assembly speed. Today, the following principles for achieving UV-curable ACA systems exist:

— Usage of photoinitiators to initiate in-line cure before IC placement and post-cure off-line using heat.
— Dark cure in-line after IC placement using the principle of in-depth cure.

9.15   CONCLUSIONS

Conductive adhesives for low-cost flip-chip and surface mount applications on printed circuitry are an emerging technology. It has been shown that conductive adhesives play a significant rôle in electronics packaging applications and are expected to do so for years to come. It is clear that the wider use of adhesives has been recognised in recent years. An increasing amount of performance data has been generated by a large number of research projects world-wide. More products based on adhesive joining technology are appearing, especially in the field of low-cost flip-chip assembly. However, further reliability data and real service life prediction tools are necessary for this environmentally friendly and low-cost technology to be fully accepted.

9.16   ACKNOWLEDGEMENTS

Johan Liu wishes to thank his colleagues: Zonghe Lai, Katrin Gustafsson, Rolf Sihlbom, Roger Rörgren, Cynthia Khoo, Lennart Cider and Anders Sihlbom who have been engaged in conductive adhesive research at IVF and who have generated a tremendous quantity of research results during the last seven years. The authors would also like to acknowledge the collaboration of Markus Denervik and Piotr Starski, Chalmers University of Technology, Sweden, in the study of high-frequency behaviour of conductive adhesives. Finally, they wish to acknowledge the financial support from The National Swedish Board for Industrial and Technical Development (NUTEK) and Nordisk Industrifond (NI) in the research programme 'Techniques for better adhesive joints'.

REFERENCES

1 Kubota, T., Kimura, T. and Ushiki, S., 'COG (Chip-on-glass) Mounting of Si and GaAs Devices', Proceedings Japan International Electronic Manufacturing Technology Symposium, Tokyo, Japan, pp. 188-191, June (1991).

2 Liu, J., 'An Overview of Advances of Conductive Adhesive Joining Technology in Electronics Applications', *Materials Technology*, **Vol. 10**, Nos. 11/12, pp. 247-252 (1995).

3 Guy, A., 'Physical Metallurgy for Engineers', Addison-Wesley Publishing Company, Inc., p. 258 (1962).

4 'Adhesive Bonding on Aluminium, *Aluminiumteknik*, **Vol. 2**, October (1989) (in Swedish).

5 Li, L., 'Basic and Applied Studies of Electrically Conductive Adhesives', PhD dissertation, State University of New York at Binghamton (1995).

6 Khoo, C., Liu, J., Ågren, M. and Hjertberg, T., 'Influence of Curing on the Electrical and Mechanical Reliability of Conductive Adhesive Joints', Proceedings International Electronics Packaging Society Conference, Austin, Texas, USA, pp. 483-501, September/October (1996).

7 Boyle, O., Whalley, D. and Williams, D., 'A Study of the Process Parameters involved in the Manufacture of Conductive Adhesive Joints', 1993 Interim report, Grant GR/H/21241 (1994).

8 Liu, J., Lundström, P., Gustafsson, K. and Lai, Z. H., 'Conductive Adhesive Joint Reliability under Full-cure Conditions', presented at Interpack '97 Pacific Rim/ASME International, Intersociety Electronic and Photonic Packaging Conference, Hawaii, USA, June (1997), also published in *EEP*, **Vol. 19**, No. 1, pp. 192-196 (1997).

9 Electronics in Casio RF transistor radio, model MR80, available in Japan, July (1997).

10 Private communication with Shintori Hori, Hitachi Chemicals, Japan (1994).

11 Technical brochure from Misuzu FA, Japan, December (1996).

12 Liu, J., 'Reliability of Surface-mounted Anisotropically Conductive Adhesive Joints', *Circuit World*, **Vol. 19**, No. 4, pp. 4-11 (1993).

13 Liu, J., Gustafsson, K., Lai, Z. and Li, C., 'Surface Characteristics, Reliability and Failure Mechanisms of Tin, Copper and Gold Metallizations', *IEEE Transactions on CPMT, Part A*, **Vol. 20**, No. 1, March (1997).

14 Weast, R., 'CRC Handbook of Chemistry and Physics', CRC Press, pp. B-89-90 (1980).

15 Gustafsson, K., Nylund, A., Liu, A. and Olefjord, I., 'Surface Characteristics of Sn37Pb Metallization for Electronics Packaging Applications', Proceedings ECASIA'97, Göteborg, Sweden, June (1997).

16 Samsonov, G. V., 'The Oxidation Handbook', second edition, IFI/Plenum Data Company, p. 204 (1982).

17 Liu, J., 'On the Failure Mechanism of Anisotropically Conductive Adhesive Joints on Copper Metallisation', *International Journal of Adhesion and Adhesives*, **Vol. 16**, No. 4, pp. 285-287 (1996).

18 Li, L., Morris, J., Liu, J., Lai, Z., Ljungkrona, L. and Li, C., 'Reliability and Failure Mechanism of Isotropically Conductive Adhesives', Proceedings 45th Electronics Components Technology Conference, Las Vegas, USA, pp. 114-120, May (1995).

19 Khoo, C. and Liu, J., 'Moisture Sorption in Some Popular Conductive Adhesives: What Really Happens?', *Circuit World*, **Vol. 22**, No. 4, pp. 9-15 (1996).

20 Liu, J., Boustedt, K. and Lai, Z., 'Development of Flip-chip Joining Technology on Flexible Circuitry using Anisotropically Conductive Adhesives and Eutectic Solder', *Circuit World*, **Vol. 22**, No. 2 (1996).

21 Lai, Z. and Liu, J., 'Anisotropically Conductive Adhesive Flip-chip Bonding on Rigid and Flexible Printed Circuit Substrates', *IEEE Transactions on CPMT, Part B: Advanced Packaging*, **Vol. 19**, No. 3, pp. 644-660, August (1996).

22 Gustafsson, K., Mannan, S., Liu, J., Lai, Z., Whalley, D. and Williams, D., 'The Effect of Ramping Rate on the Flip-chip Joint Quality and Reliability Using Anisotropically Conductive Adhesive Film on FR-4 Substrate', ECTC'97, San Jose, California, USA, May (1997).

23 Dillaman, B. L., Wentworth, S. M. and Johnson, R. W., 'Attenuation and Reliability of Conductive Adhesive Interconnects', Proceedings Electronics Packaging Conference, Austin, Texas, September/October (1996).

24 Denervik, M., Sihlbom, R., Lai, Z, Starski, P. and Liu, J., 'High-frequency Measurements and Modelling of Electrically Conductive Adhesive Flip-chip Joint', Interpack '97, Hawaii, USA, pp. 177-184, June (1997).

25 Sihlbom, R., and Liu, J., 'High Frequency Signal Simulation of Electrically Conductive Adhesives', Proceedings International Seminar in Conductive Adhesive Joining in Electronics Packaging, Eindhoven, Philips, The Netherlands, pp. 199-220, September (1995).

26 Sihlbom, A., 'Thermal Simulations of the Unsteady State Thermal Response in Flip-chips, Comparing Anisotropic and Isotropic Adhesive Thermal Performance', Document No. ASM6043, Status report No. 1 of the Solderless Flip-Chip Program 'Flip-chip joining using conductive adhesives, phase II, SFC-II', IVF, May (1996).

27 Ishibashi, K. and Kimura, J., 'A New Anisotropic Conductive Film with Arrayed Conductive Particles', *IEEE Transactions, Part B: Advanced Packaging*, **Vol. 19**, No. 4, pp. 752-757, November (1996).

28 McArdle, C. and Burke, J., 'Novel Uniaxial Conductive Adhesives Comprising Polymerisable Ferrofluids and Conductive Magnetic Holes', Second International Conference on Adhesive Joining and Coating in Electronics Manufacturing, pp. 154-159, June (1996).

29 Bolger, J. and Gilleo, K., 'Area Bonding Conductive Epoxy Adhesive Preforms for Grid Array and MCM Substrate Attach', Proceedings IEEE Multi-Chip Module Conference, pp. 77-82 (1994).

30 Gotoh, Y. and Watanabe, I., 'Novel Anisotropic Conductive Films with Area-arrayed Conducting Particles', Hawaii, USA, June (1997).

31 Casio, US patent 5,180,888, January 19 (1993).

32 Liu, J., Ljungkrona, L. and Lai, Z., 'Development of Conductive Adhesive Joining for Surface-mounting Electronics Manufacturing', *IEEE Transactions on Components, Packaging, and Manufacturing Technology — Part B*, **Vol. 18**, No. 2, pp. 313-319, May (1995).

33 Liu, J., 'Conductive Adhesive Joining for Electronics Packaging Applications', document given as intensive course in the Second International Conference on Adhesive Joining and Coating Technology for Electronics Manufacturing, Stockholm, Sweden, June (1996).

Chapter 10

ANISOTROPIC CONDUCTIVE ADHESIVE FILMS FOR FLIP-CHIP INTERCONNECTION

ITSUO WATANABE and KENZO TAKEMURA
Hitachi Chemical Co. Ltd, Tsukuba, Japan

10.1 INTRODUCTION

Anisotropic conductive adhesive films (ACFs) consisting of conducting particles and adhesives provide both attachment and electrical interconnection between electrodes. They are widely used for high density interconnections between LCD (liquid crystal display) panels and TAB (tape automated bonding) as a replacement for traditional soldering or rubber connectors. High connection reliability and very fine pitch interconnections of ACFs have seen rapid development as LCD technologies have progressed since the early 1980s.

In LCD packaging, the TAB technique is the most popular procedure for interconnecting LCD panels and driver ICs. However, TAB technology has limitations in achieving interconnections smaller than 70 µm pitch. To realise very fine pitch interconnections, chip-on-glass (COG) technology has received considerable attention in LCD packaging.[1-3] Recently, LCD panels assembled by the chip-on-glass (COG) technique using ACF have been commercialised in Japan.

ACFs have many advantages over soldering in flip-chip packaging[5-10] such as low temperature assembly, high density interconnects, fluxless bonding and low fabrication cost. Therefore, their use is also expected to increase as new interconnect materials in semiconductor packaging which requires smaller and thinner dimensions, and very high density interconnects.

So far the author's company has developed a variety of ACFs (trade name: Anisolm) for output and input lead connections in LCD packaging. Recently, ACFs have been developed for flip-chip interconnection to various substrates such as ITO-coated glass substrates, FR-4 printed circuit boards (PCBs) and flexible printed circuits (FPCs). In this chapter, ACFs for flip-chip interconnection are described through discussions of the interconnection principle, materials, approaches for very fine pitch interconnections and the connection reliability of ACF joints.

10.2 PRINCIPLES OF ACF INTERCONNECTION

ACFs are adhesive films with anisotropic conductive properties induced by dispersing 0.5~5 vol% of conducting particles into polymer matrices such as thermoplastic and thermosetting resins. The volume fractions of the conducting particles in polymer matrices are much lower than those of isotropic conductive adhesives such as Ag pastes to prevent conducting particles from contacting each other in the X-Y plane of the films. Figure 10.1 illustrates the dependence of the volume fractions of conducting particles on the conductivity of ACF filled with Ni particles. The dependence of the volume fractions of conducting particles on the conductivity is strongly related to the direction of the film. That is, a film filled with low volume fractions of conductive particles (0.5~5 vol%) gives a transverse resistance of less than 1 Ω while providing high resistance in the X-Y plane. By controlling the volume fractions of conducting particles, anisotropic conductivity can be imparted to the adhesive film. Of course, the dependence of the volume fractions of conducting particles on anisotropic conductivity is closely related to the size and shape of the conducting particles.

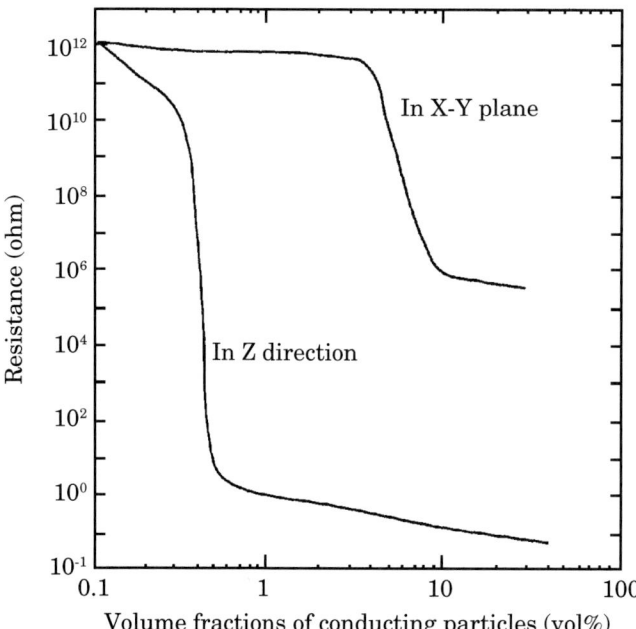

Fig. 10.1 Dependence of the volume fractions of conducting particles on the conductivity of ACF filled with Ni particles.

Figure 10.2 illustrates the principle of ACF interconnection. The adhesive resin melts with the application of heat and pressure, and conducting particles dispersed in the matrix are trapped between conductor surfaces. As a result of this, the film has high transverse conductivity, while also having high insulation resistance because all the conducting particles in the X-Y plane of the films exist independently. These mechanical contacts between conducting particles and bonding electrodes are retained by the strong adhesion strength of the polymer matrix. Therefore the thermal and mechanical properties of the polymer matrix have a significant influence on the interconnection reliability of ACFs, as mentioned in the next section.

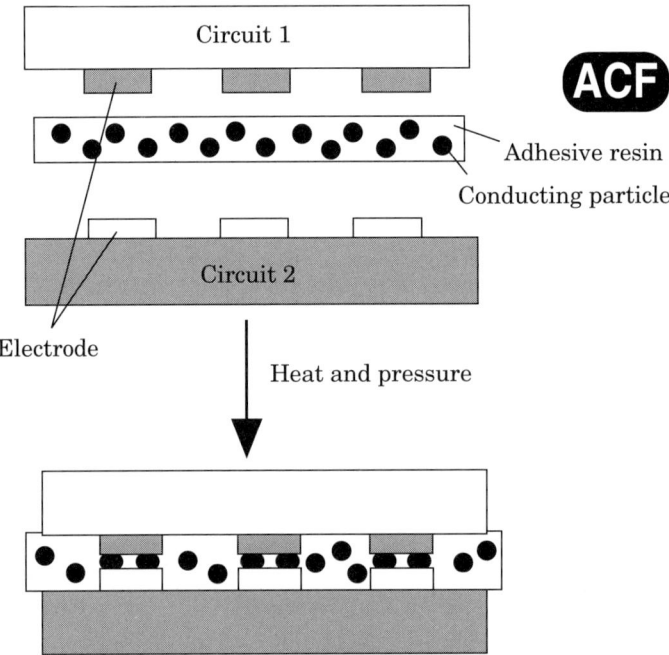

Fig. 10.2 The principle of ACF interconnection.

10.3   MATERIALS

10.3.1   Adhesives

In the early stages of the development of ACFs, thermoplastic adhesives such as poly(styrene-butadiene-styrene) and poly(styrene-ethylene-styrene) were used as a polymer matrix. Thermoplastic adhesives have good reworkability because they are thermally reversible and can be dissolved in common organic solvents, although they also have shortcomings such as low heat resistance and high contact resistance due to their high melt viscosity. In order to overcome these problems, therefore, thermosetting adhesives such as epoxy resins are used as polymer matrices from the viewpoint of improving the interconnection reliability. Epoxy resins, in particular, are commonly used as adhesive resins because of their strong adhesion to a variety of substrates and their high glass transition temperature. In addition, they have a low melt viscosity because their starting materials consist of oligomers and can easily be squeezed between bonding electrodes and conducting particles. Consequently, they have a high transverse conductivity, as mentioned later.

The transverse electrical properties of ACFs are represented by contact resistance between bonding electrodes. The contact resistance between bonding electrodes is the total of the resistance of the bonding electrode, the contact resistance between conducting particles and bonding electrodes, and the resistance of conducting particles. In ACF interconnections, the exclusion of adhesive resins between bonding electrodes and conducting particles has a significant influence on the contact resistance. When adhesive resins with high melt viscosity are used, adhesive resins between contact areas become insulation barriers and provide high resistance in the Z-direction. On the other hand, when adhesive resin with low melt viscosity is used, it is easy to exclude from between contact interfaces and provides good electrical contacts. Epoxy-based ACFs for flip-chip interconnection have a melt viscosity of less than 20 Pa·S at bonding temperature. These values are almost comparable with those of typical underfill encapsulant materials at room temperature. In this case, a contact resistance lower than 10 mΩ is obtained in flip-chip interconnections, as mentioned later.

10.3.2   Conducting Particles

Metal (Ni/Au) coated polymer spheres (diameter: 5~10 μm) are commonly used in fine pitch interconnection because the distribution of the diameter of polymer spheres is fairly uniform, hence they can easily be dispersed uniformly into adhesive resins. These metal-coated polymer spheres provide high connection reliability, since the contact area increases by the elastic deformation of the spheres in ACF interconnects, as shown in Figure 10.3.

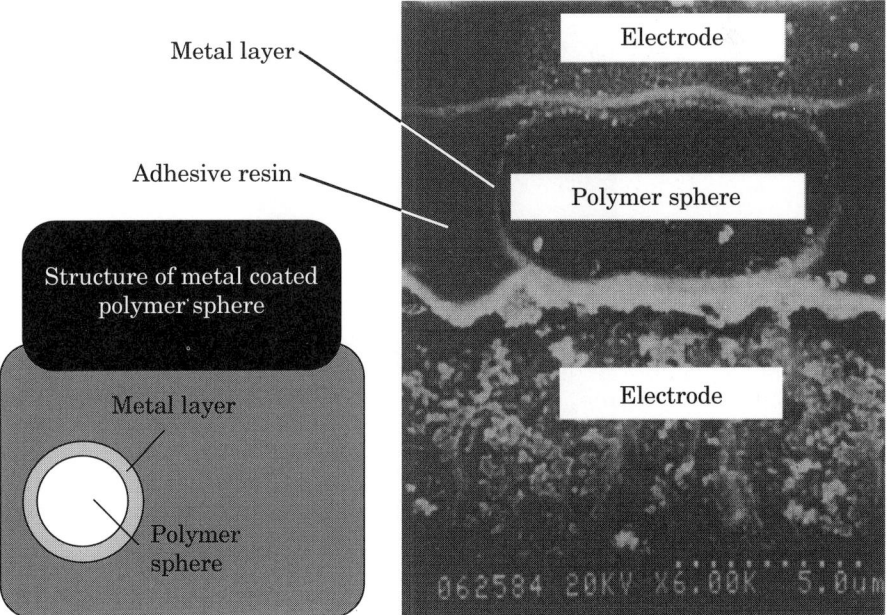

Fig. 10.3 Cross-section of interconnection using ACF filled with Ni/Au coated polymer spheres.

The contact resistance and the current-carrying capacity in ACF interconnects decrease as the deformation ratio of conducting particles increases.[2,11] Today ACFs filled with Ni/Au coated polymer spheres are mainly used for interconnecting LCD panels and TAB, as shown in Figure 10.4.

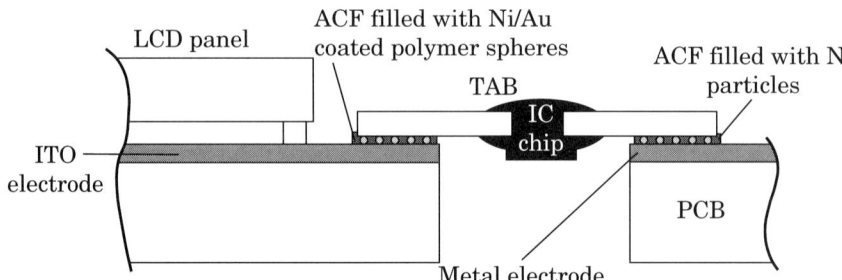

Fig. 10.4 Practical example of ACF interconnection using ACFs in LCD packaging.

Ni particles are also used as conducting particles for interconnecting metal electrodes which can easily be oxidised, although they are difficult to deform, unlike metal-coated polymer spheres. Ni particles are suitable for breaking the oxide layer on the metal electrodes of the interconnects. In particular, Ni particles with many spines (see Figure 10.5) are used for this purpose. ACF filled with Ni particles has been used as an interconnecting material between TAB and PCBs (see Figure 10.4) for LCD modules in mass production.[12] Similar ideas for ACFs filled with Ni particles can be applicable for flip-chip interconnection, as described later.

Fig. 10.5 SEM micrograph of Ni particles.

10.4   APPROACHES FOR VERY FINE PITCH INTERCONNECTIONS

Today TAB interconnection technology for flat panel displays using ACFs is capable of 70 μm pitch. However, finer pitch interconnections are required for ACFs to accomplish higher resolution and smaller displays in flat panel displays and flip-chip packaging technologies. ACFs basically have three functions, namely high electrical conduction in the Z-direction, high electrical insulation in the X-Y plane, and encapsulant. Flip-chip interconnection using ACFs is accomplished by applying heat and pressure to the back side of the chip, as shown in Figure 10.6. The adhesive resin is squeezed out of the clearance between bonding electrodes with an accompanying flow of conducting particles facing the chip into the conductor spaces during the bonding process. Therefore, it becomes more and more difficult to maintain in-plane electrical insulation with single-layer ACFs, as the conductor spacings of interconnections are decreasing. In addition, it is necessary to get more conducting particles into an adhesive matrix in order to trap enough conducting particles to make electrical contact with both small conductor surfaces, since the electrodes for flip-chip interconnection are smaller than those for TAB interconnection. Consequently, it should be considered that a higher volume fraction of conducting particles in ACFs may cause a short circuit problem in these applications.

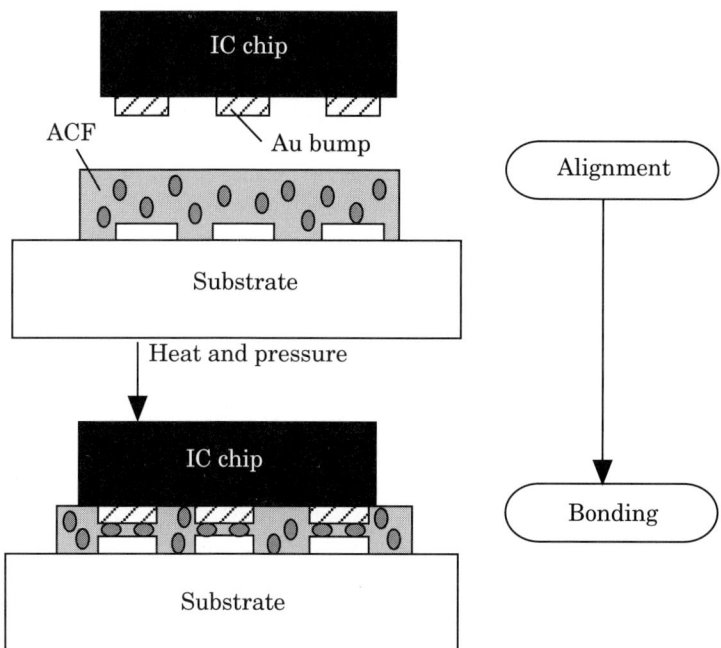

Fig. 10.6 Flip-chip interconnection using ACF.

In order to trap sufficient conducting particles to make electrical contact with both conductor surfaces but prevent electrical contact between the different conductive particles even in fine pitch applications of less than 50 μm pitch, double-layer ACFs whose functions include high electrical conduction in the Z-direction, high electrical insulation in the X-Y plane and encapsulant have been proposed.[3,11] Figure 10.7 shows the structure of double-layer ACFs. Double-layer ACFs consist of non-filled and conducting

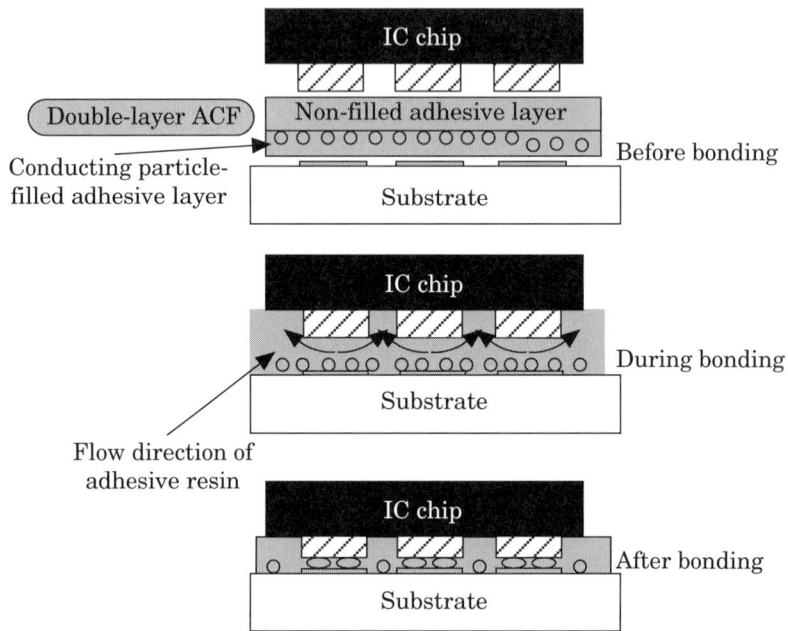

Fig. 10.7 Structure of double-layer ACF.

particles filled adhesive layers. In this case, a non-filled adhesive layer interfaces with the bumps of the chip, as shown in Figure 10.6. Conductor spaces are mostly filled with an adhesive resin of a non-filled adhesive layer during the bonding process. As a result of this, the number of conducting particles in conductor spaces is less than that of a single-layer ACF. It has been demonstrated that the number of conducting particles trapped on a bump in a double-layer ACF is much higher than those in a single-layer ACF. This indicates that, even though the particle density in double-layer ACFs is low, conducting particles for making electrical contact with both conductor surfaces are trapped more effectively between conductor surfaces in double-layer ACFs. Consequently, the risk of short circuits occurring in double-layer ACFs is expected to be lower than that in single-layer ACFs.

Figure 10.8 shows the influence of layer structure on the probability of short circuits in conductor spaces. In the case of a single-layer ACF, electrical insulation resistance of more than 10^{12} Ω is maintained down to 20 μm conductor spacing, but short circuits occur with conductor spacing of less than 10 μm. On the other hand, in the case of double-layer ACFs, electrical insulation resistance higher than 10^{12} Ω is maintained even in 10 μm conductor spacings. It has been demonstrated that double-layer ACFs give high in-plane insulation resistance of more than 10^{12} Ω even with 15 μm spacings and low interconnection resistance of less than 100 mΩ with a COG assembly.[11] (The chip is 1.7 mm x 17 mm and has 362 gold bumps. The bump size is 50 μm x 90 μm and bump height 10 μm.)

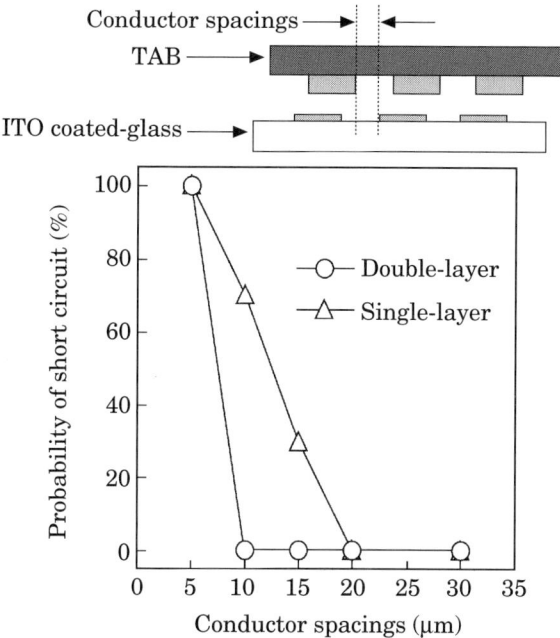

Fig. 10.8 Influence of layer structure on probability of short circuits in conductor spaces.

10.5 FLIP-CHIP INTERCONNECTION TO ORGANIC SUBSTRATES[13-14]

10.5.1 Flip-chip Interconnection with Bumped Chips

ACFs are expected to perform as promising interconnect materials for flip-chip interconnection technology owing to several advantages such as low temperature assembly, high density interconnection, low cost and fluxless bonding which eliminates the need for cleaning. Figure 10.9 illustrates the process flow for flip-chip interconnection using ACFs. ACFs provide a simpler flip-chip interconnection process because there is no need for an underfill encapsulant process, compared with soldering and isotropic conductive adhesive joining. However, thermal and mechanical stresses and strains induced by CTE (coefficient of thermal expansion) mismatches between the chip and the organic substrates need to be considered in flip-chip interconnections to organic substrates such as FR-4 PCB and FPCs. In order to apply ACF to flip-chip interconnection to PCBs, the reliability of adhesive resins of ACF has been enhanced by formulating with epoxy resins, modifiers and flexibilising agents.

It is also of concern that contact resistance may not be low since interconnection using ACF relies on mechanical contact as described earlier, unlike the metal bonding of soldering. Bonding process parameters such as temperature, pressure and curing time have a significant influence on the interconnection resistance between both electrodes. When the bonding temperature is lower than 160°C where an epoxy resin used as an adhesive can be cured, the mechanical contact between bonding electrodes is not maintained. Also, if the bonding pressure is too low, conducting particles dispersed in adhesive films can not make good electrical contacts with bonding electrodes. Figure 10.9 shows the influence of bonding pressure on the contact resistance between the bumps of a chip (10 mm x 10 mm with 288

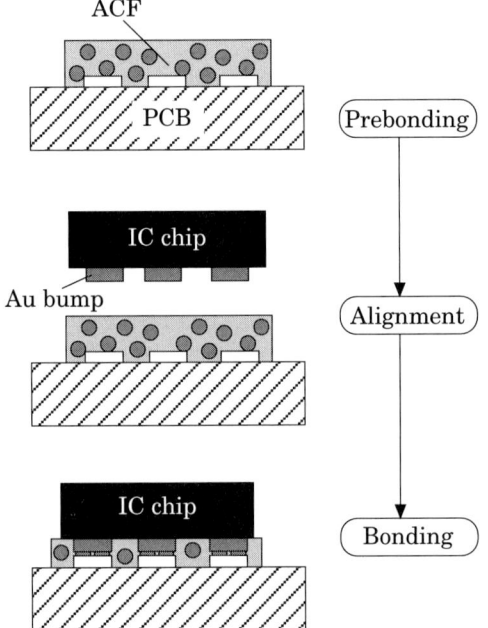

Fig. 10.9 Process flow for flip-chip interconnection using ACFs.

gold bumps; bump size 80 μm x 80 μm and bump height 15 μm) and Ni/Au electrodes on an FR-4 substrate (PCBs fabricated of FR-4 and plated with a layer of Ni/Au that has been deposited on 10 μm copper). As shown in Figure 10.10, contact resistance decreases with increasing bonding pressure. When

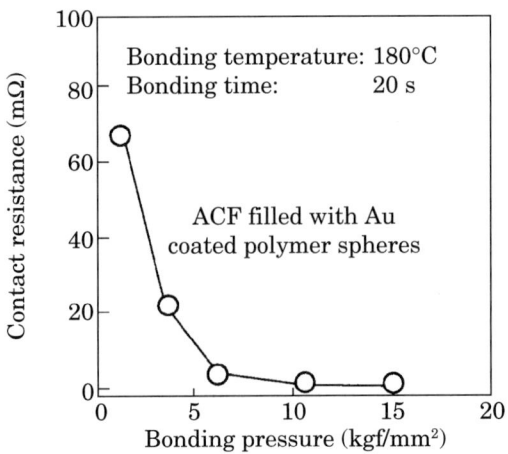

Fig. 10.10 Influence of bonding pressure on the contact resistance of ACF joints in flip-chip interconnection to a PCB.

the chips and substrates are bonded for 20 s at 180°C under a pressure of more than 6 kgf/mm² (based on the bump area), a contact resistance of less than 10 mΩ is obtained.

Despite interconnection due to mechanical contact, the contact resistance in flip-chip attach using ACFs is as low as 3 mΩ. In addition, as seen in Figure 10.11, the current-voltage characteristics of ACF joints measured by

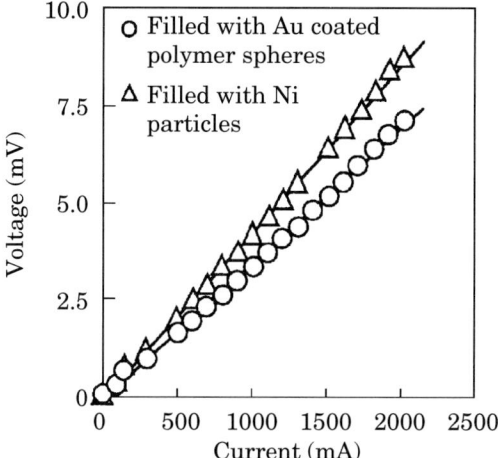

Fig. 10.11 Current-Voltage characteristics of ACF joints in flip-chip interconnection to a PCB.

a four-point probe method show that the current-carrying capacity is 2000 mA, which is sufficient for flip-chip interconnection. The fact that the contact resistance is low suggests that not only mechanical contacts between conducting particles and conductor surfaces but also direct metallic contacts may be established between conductor surfaces.

Figure 10.12 shows the contact resistance between the bumps of the chip and Ni/Au electrodes on an FR-4 substrate bonded with ACF after being

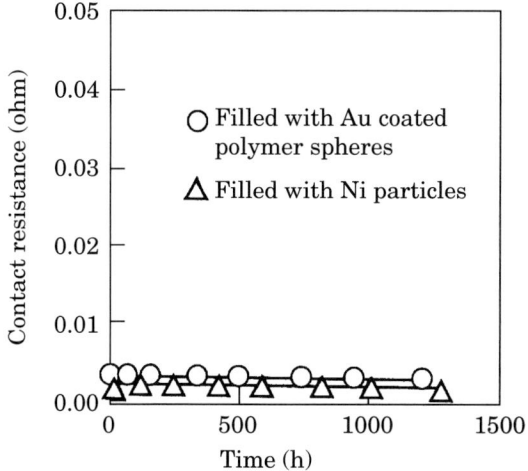

Fig. 10.12 Contact resistance of ACF joints in flip-chip interconnection to a PCB after exposure to high temperature humidity test (85°C/85%RH).

subjected to a high temperature humidity test (85°C/85%RH). Initial low contact resistance of less than 10 mΩ was maintained even after high temperature humidity testing for more than 1000 h. Likewise, the reliability of the ACF joints was confirmed by a thermal cycling test (-40°C/+125°C) of 1000 cycles, as shown in Figure 10.13. Although there is concern that, in flip-chip interconnection to FR-4 PCBs, thermal and mechanical stresses and strains induced by CTE mismatches between the chip and the substrate lead to an increase in resistance or electrical failure in flip-chip joints, the thermal cycling testing indicates that the ACF reduces the strain on the flip-chip joint and enhances the connection reliability like an underfill encapsulant in

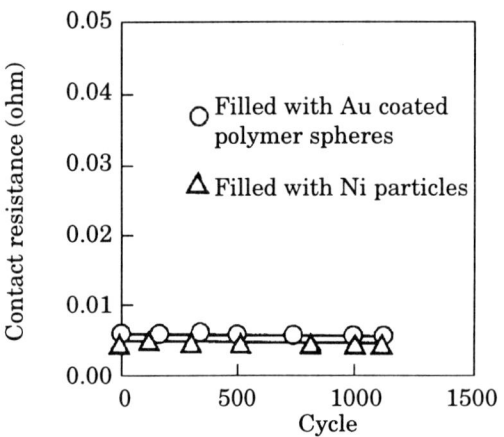

Fig. 10.13 Contact resistance of ACF joints in flip-chip interconnection to a PCB after exposure thermal cycling test from -40°C to 125°C.

flip-chip solder bump technology.[15] When the ACF interconnects are exposed to a high temperature environment, the adhesive resin expands more than the bonding electrodes due to CTE mismatches between the adhesive resin and bonding electrodes. Therefore, the behaviour of contact resistance as a function of heating temperature was investigated. Figure 10.14 shows the

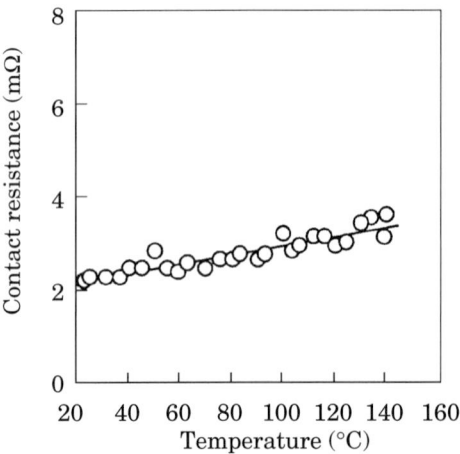

Fig. 10.14 Temperature dependence of contact resistance in flip-chip interconnects on FR-4 PCB using ACF.

temperature dependence of contact resistance in flip-chip interconnects on FR-4 PCBs using ACF. The contact resistance is stable even at 140°C. The slight increase of the contact resistance in the high temperature region is due to the temperature dependence of resistivity of conducting particles and bonding electrodes.

It was also confirmed that an insulation resistance higher than $10^8\Omega$ was obtained in flip-chip attach using ACF (bump spacings: 30 μm) even after being exposed to a high temperature/humidity bias test (85°C/85%RH, 5 V) for 1000 h.

10.5.2 Flip-chip Interconnection with Bumpless Chips to Various Organic Substrates

ACF can be applicable for unbumped flip-chip interconnection to FR-4 PCBs, when bumps are produced on substrate electrodes.[13] The use of unbumped chips allows a reduction in the costs of the flip-chip bonding process, since Au bumping on to the chip is not required.

Figure 10.15 shows the contact resistance of bumpless interconnections on various organic substrates. Contact resistance strongly depends on the types

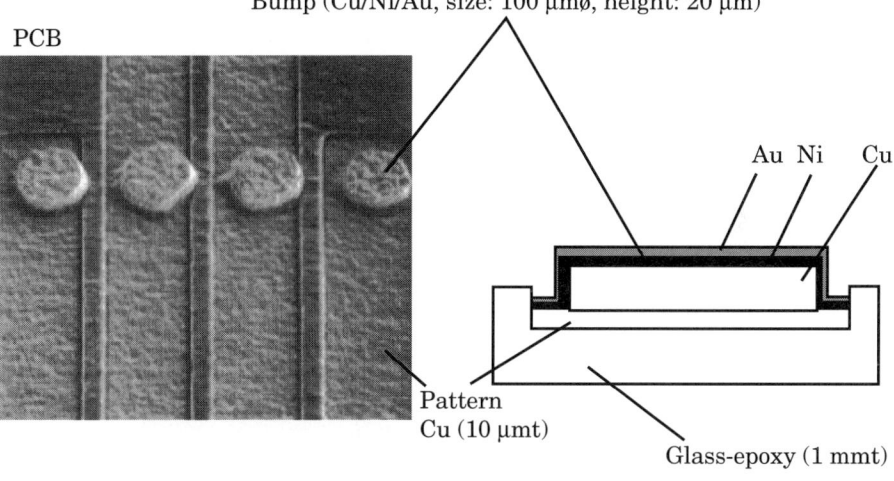

Bump (Cu/Ni/Au, size: 100 μmø, height: 20 μm)

PCB

Au Ni Cu

Pattern
Cu (10 μmt)

Glass-epoxy (1 mmt)

Bump pitch: 150 μm

Fig. 10.15 Contact resistance of bumpless interconnection on various substrates.

of substrates and conducting particles. When PCBs with Ni/Au bumped pads (see Figure 10.16) are used in bonding, low and stable contact resistance is obtained. This result suggests that the bump formation on the board is very effective in making a good electrical contact in bumpless interconnection as well as on the chip. Also it seems that FPCs are more suitable for bumpless interconnection than rigid FR-4 boards, although the contact resistance with FPCs is still higher than with FR-4 boards with Ni/Au bumped pads. It is thought that FPCs are flexible enough to deform along the edge of the SiN insulation layer around the Al pads of the chip, as shown in Figure 10.17. Hence, FPCs seem to be favoured for interconnecting bumpless chips using ACF.

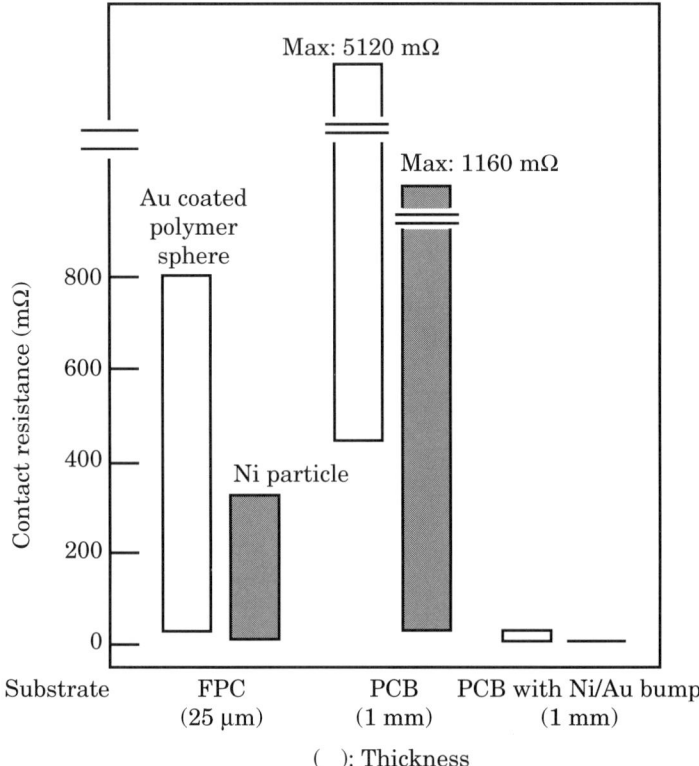

Fig. 10.16 SEM micrograph of a PCB with Ni/Au bumped pads.

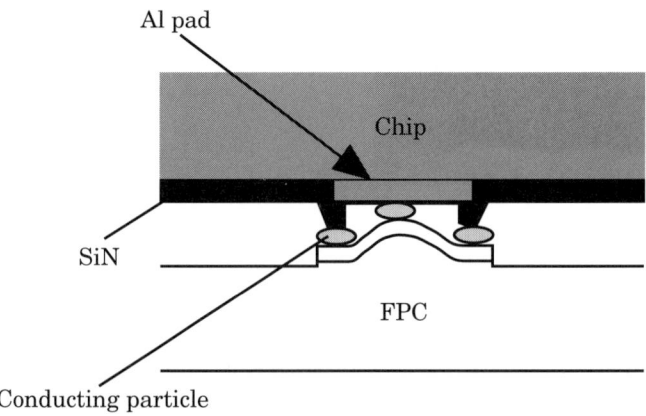

Fig. 10.17 Schematic of exaggerated interconnects in bumpless flip-chip interconnection to FPC using ACF.

The initial resistance is also dependent on the conductive particles. The Ni particle filled adhesive films have lower resistance than Au coated polymer sphere filled adhesive in all substrates. Ni particles break the oxide layer of the Al pads on the chip and make good electrical contacts between the Al pads of the chip and the substrate electrodes. The thickness of the oxide layer of the Al pads was about 40 Å (estimated from XPS measurement). In particular, when FR-4 substrates with Ni/Au bumped pads are used in bonding, Ni particle filled ACF gives an interconnection resistance of less than 10 mΩ as well as with the bumped chips. These results indicate that the bump location does not matter in flip-chip attach using ACF, and Ni particles in an adhesive film are very effective in making good electrical contacts between Al pads and substrate electrodes.

Figure 10.18 shows the contact resistance of unbumped flip-chip interconnects using ACF after exposure to high temperature humidity testing (85°C/85%RH, 1300 h). The initial contact resistance and fatigue life strongly depend on the types of conducting particles. The Ni particle filled adhesive films have lower resistance and longer fatigue life than Au coated polymer sphere filled adhesive films in unbumped flip-chip attach on to FR-4 boards with bumped pads. These results also suggest that Ni particles prevent further oxidation of Al even after exposure to the high temperature humidity test. However, further investigations are necessary to clarify the mechanism of long fatigue life in ACF interconnects between Al and Au electrodes.

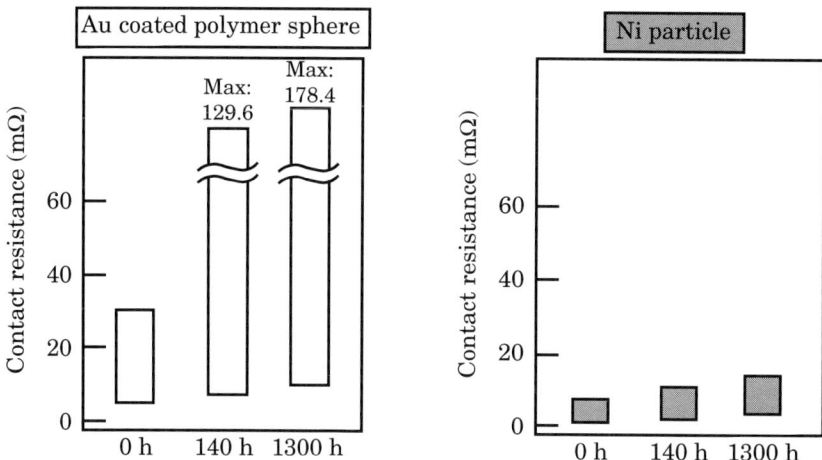

Fig. 10.18 Contact resistance of unbumped flip-chip interconnects using ACF after exposure to high temperature humidity test (85°C/85%RH).

10.6   CONCLUSION

This chapter described the principle of ACF interconnection, some approaches for very fine pitch interconnection and the electrical characteristics of ACFs for flip-chip interconnection. It has been shown that double-layer ACFs consisting of non-filled and conducting particles filled adhesive layers are suitable for very fine pitch interconnections. ACFs developed for flip-chip interconnection have shown stable contact resistance of less than 10 mΩ even after exposure to a high temperature humidity test (85°C/85%RH for 1000 h) and a thermal shock test (from -40°C to 125°C, for 1000 cycles). It has also been found that a low and stable contact resistance is obtained with flip-chip attach of unbumped chips using ACF filled with Ni particles, when

FR-4 PCBs with Ni/Au bumped pads are used in bonding. In this case, it has been confirmed that the low contact resistance between the Al pads of the unbumped chip and Ni/Au substrate electrodes is maintained after high temperature humidity testing (85°C/85%RH, 1300 h). This unbumped flip-chip interconnection technology using ACF has the potential to provide a low-cost flip-chip packaging process. Thus, ACF is expected to play an important rôle as a new interconnect material for solder replacement in flip-chip packaging technology.

10.7   ACKNOWLEDGEMENT

The authors are very grateful to their co-workers in the Tsukuba Research Laboratory of Hitachi Chemical Co. Ltd, A. Nagai, O. Watanabe and K. Kojima.

REFERENCES

1   van Noort, H. M., Kloos, M. J. H. and Schafer, H. E. A., 'Anisotropic Conductive Adhesives for Chip on Glass and Other Flip Chip Applications', Adhesives in Electronics '94 (1994).

2   Shiozawa, N., Isaka, K. and Ohta, T., 'Electric Properties of Anisotropic Conductive Adhesive Films', Adhesives in Electronics '94 (1994).

3   Hirosawa, H., Tsukagoshi, I., Matsuoka, H., Watanabe, I., Takemura, K., Shiozawa, N. and Ohta, T., 'Double-layer Anisotropic Conductive Adhesive Films', Display Manufacturing Technology Conference, Digest of Technical Papers, **Vol. 2**, pp. 17-18 (1995).

4   Takakahashi, W., Murakoshi, K., Kanazawa, J., Ikehata, M., Iguchi, Y. and Kanamori, T., 'Solderless COG Technology Using Anisotropic Conductive Adhesives', Proceedings IMC 1992, Yokohama, pp. 93-98 (1992).

5   Liu, J., 'Reliability of Surface-mounted Anisotropically Conductive Adhesive Joints', *Circuit World*, **Vol. 19**, No. 4, pp. 4-11 (1993).

6   Basavanhally, N. R., Chang, D. D., Cranston, B. H. and Seger, S. G., 'Direct Chip Interconnect with Adhesive-Connector Films', Proceedings 42nd IEEE Electronic Components & Technology Conference, pp. 487-491 (1992).

7   Yamaguchi, Y., Tsukagoshi, I. and Ohta, T., 'Anisotropic Conductive Adhesive Films', Technical Report of IEICE, EMD92-69, pp. 29-36 (1992).

8   Chang, D. D., Fulton, J. A., Lyons, A. M. and Nis, J. R., 'Design Consideration for the Implementation of Anisotropic Conductive Adhesive Interconnection', Proceedings Nepcon West, pp. 1381 (1992).

9   Chung, K., Devereaux, T., Monti, C., Yan, M. and Mescia, N., 'Z-axis Conductive Adhesives as Solder Replacement', Proceedings 1993 Surface Mount Technology International, pp. 554-560 (1993).

10 Chang, D. D., Crawford, P. A., Fulton, J. A., McBride, R., Schmidt, M. B., Simtski, R. E. and Wong, C. P., 'An Overview and Evaluation of Anisotropically Conductive Adhesive Films for Fine Pitch Electronic Assembly', *IEEE Transactions on Components, Hybrids, and Manufacturing Technology*, **Vol. CHMT-16**, No. 8, pp. 828-835 (1993).

11 Watanabe, I., Takemura, K., Shiozawa, N. and Ohta, T., 'Flip Chip Interconnection Technology Using Anisotropic Conductive Adhesive Films', in 'Flip Chip Technology', ed. J. H. Lau, McGraw Hill, Chapter 9, pp. 301-315 (1996).

12 Kawaguchi, H., Aota, K. and Ohga, M., 'Fine Pitch Solderless Interconnection Technology for LCD Module of Notebook PC', Proceedings ISHM'95, pp. 266-271 (1995).

13 Watanabe, I., Takemura, K., Shiozawa, N., Watanabe, O., Kojima, K. and Ohta, T., 'Flip-chip Interconnection to Various Substrates Using Anisotropic Conductive Adhesive Films', *Journal of Electronics Manufacturing*, **Vol. 5**, No. 4, pp. 273-276 (1995).

14   Watanabe, I., Takemura, K., Shiozawa, N., Watanabe, O., Kojima, K., Nagai, A. and Tanaka, T., 'Anisotropic Conductive Adhesive Films for Flip-chip Interconnection', Proceedings IMC 1996, Omiya, pp. 328-332 (1996).

15   Suranarayana, D., *et al.*, 'Flip-chip Solder Bump Fatigue Life Enhanced by Polymer Encapsulation', Proceedings 40th Electronic Components Technology Conference, **Vol. 1**, pp. 338-344 (1990).

Chapter 11

RELIABILITY OF ELECTRICALLY CONDUCTIVE ADHESIVE JOINTS IN SURFACE MOUNT APPLICATIONS

JANNES C. JAGT
Philips Centre for Manufacturing Technology, Eindhoven,
The Netherlands

11.1   INTRODUCTION

Isotropic electrically conductive adhesives have already been in use for many years, but until recently were used merely as die-attach adhesives[1-4] to bond chips to lead frames in order to establish a thermal contact and/or make an electrical (ground) connection. The main advantage of conductive adhesives over Au-Si eutectic bonding is their lower thermal stress, due to the lower bonding temperature and higher flexibility. The higher flexibility is also favourable, of course, during subsequent large temperature variations.

In low power applications, and for plastic packaged components, conductive adhesives are by far the most frequently used bonding system. Also, in the field of hybrid circuit technology, electrically conductive adhesives have been used for quite a long time, and appear to offer higher reliability than soldering.[5,6,7] Use in hybrid microwave integrated circuits (60 GHz) has been reported recently.[6]

Other applications are, for example, in making electrode contacts in components,[8] quartz oscillators,[9] interconnection of flexible circuits ('flex') to LCDs or flex to rigid circuit boards with anisotropic conductive adhesive film (ACAF),[10] flip chip on glass,[11] LSI mounted membrane switches (PET film),[7] SMD components to polyester flex,[86] bonding of ceramic chip capacitors,[13] capacitors on FR-4 in registration and identification systems[14] and ignition systems.[15]

The use of conductive adhesives for bonding surface mount components, in spite of several potential advantages, is by no means an established practice today. Possible benefits of conductive adhesives in this application area are:

(i)   They are more environmentally friendly than solders, as they are lead-free and do not require fluxes and flux cleaning, as is still done for certain applications.

(ii) They have higher resolution capability than present solder pastes due to smaller particle size (especially anisotropically conductive adhesives).

(iii) They can be cured at much lower temperatures than used for soldering (thermally sensitive components and substrates).

(iv) Non-solderable (cheap) substrates can be used (e.g., glass, polyester flex).

(v)   They are less sensitive to fatigue than solder.

(vi) Fewer process steps are needed than for (wave) soldering (no temporary SMD adhesive, no flux, no flux cleaning).

Concerns do, however, exist with respect to:

(i)   the lower conductivity (Table 11.1);

(ii) sensitivity to environmental factors (reliability);

(iii) the different wetting behaviour compared with solder (no fillet formation like solder); higher accuracy needed for stencil printing;

(iv) the absence of self-alignment for small components;

(v)   silver migration, which could occur under certain conditions, but does not seem to be a problem under normal practical test conditions,[83] see also Section 11.4.6.

In recent years, several industrial and independent research institutes and universities have been investigating and evaluating the application possibilities and reliability aspects of conductive adhesives in surface mount applications. The electrical demands here are much higher than for most of the previously mentioned applications. The present status of these reliability investigations is reviewed below.

Table 11.1

Volume Resistivity (Bulk) and Thermal Conductivity of Various Materials

Material	Volume Resistivity (Ωcm)	Thermal Conductivity (W/m.K)
Gold	2.2×10^{-6}	295
Silver	1.6×10^{-6}	408
Nickel	6.8×10^{-6}	69
Copper	1.7×10^{-6}	394
Graphite	8.0×10^{-4}	155
Sn/Pb solder	1.0×10^{-5}	50
Epoxy resin	1.0×10^{14}	0.2
Epoxide/silver adhesive	1.0×10^{-4}	4
Silver/glass	1.0×10^{-5}	90
Epoxide/Al_2O_3	1.0×10^{13}	1
Epoxide/diamond	1.0×10^{14}	12

11.2   ISOTROPIC CONDUCTIVE ADHESIVE SYSTEMS

Conductive adhesives used in die attach, hybrid technology, or, e.g., for making contacts in components, generally consist of thermohardening resins such as (i) epoxies, (ii) polyimides, (iii) silicones, and (iv) acrylic adhesives, or alternatively thermoplastic adhesives (v). To achieve electrical conductance,

Fig. 11.1 SEM micrographs showing differences in size of Ag flakes of conductive adhesives CA-2 and CA-5 from Ref. 68.

carbon particles may be used for low conductivity applications such as keyboards or shielding. For the more demanding applications, Ni, Au, or Ag (or AgPd) particles are used. The less noble metals are more readily oxidised during environmental exposure. Because the price of silver is lower than that of gold, and because it has less tendency to form agglomerates, silver is the most frequently used filler material; it is generally used in amounts of 70-80% (w/w). Silver may become oxidised to some extent under environmental conditions, but the oxide formed is also conductive.

In general, silver flakes are used, varying in size from a few microns to approximately 25 microns. Broad size distributions are reported to offer improved conductance over narrow ones. Bimodal distributions also appear to give improved conductivity.[33-35]

Gold is sometimes used for highly demanding military and space applications,[31] to eliminate the risk of silver migration. The mechanism of conduction has been studied by several groups.[32]

11.2.1   Epoxies

Both one- and two-pot versions are available on the market. Mostly the resins are of the DGEBA type (diglycidyl ether of bisphenol-A). Sometimes DGBF (diglycidylether of bisphenol-F) is used instead, or epoxy-novolac type resins.[16-18] Most systems use amine type hardeners: e.g., di- or polyamines, polyaminoamides, imidazoles or dicyandiamide (Dicy).[17] Anhydride hardeners are also used (moisture sensitive during processing). Catalytic curing with tertiary amines or borohalogenamino complexes is a third possibility.[17]

In one-component versions, the hardeners can be present as dispersed particles that will melt (or decompose) at the curing temperature, thereby starting the curing reaction.

In general, the one-component versions should be cured at temperatures above 100°C. The curing speed of the various systems available on the market varies considerably. The fastest curing speed of one-component systems, as determined by DSC studies (e.g., Reference 68) is approximately 5 min. at 150°C. This is still longer than used for the non-conductive SMD adhesives (3-5 min. at 125°C). In most of the investigations reported in the literature, however, considerably longer curing times are used, mostly in the order of 15-30 min. at 150° or 125°C in a convection type oven. Detailed studies of the influence of curing time on electrical and mechanical properties using in line curing equipment, such as IR, hot air or combi ovens, are still lacking in the literature. A few studies, however, give some indication. Gustafson[19] mentions that, for die attach, hot plate curing is twice as fast as convection curing and infra-red curing even faster, and Guy[20] briefly describes IR oven curing for 4 min. at 150°C.

Examples have been described in the literature, showing that insufficient curing[21-26] may decrease durability in harsh environments. Orthmann[63] reports that, for a 120 µm layer of a well-known die attach adhesive (Epotek H20E), a 15 min. cure at 120°C gives optimum results, and longer curing does not improve results. Liu[21-26] indicates that overcure of some adhesives may lower durability, although in other cases no such effect is seen.

Undercured adhesives will have a lower cross-link density, and therefore be more susceptible to moisture. Overcured adhesives may tend to have a higher Tg, and can become too brittle and more easily form cracks.

Very high curing temperatures and fast ramp-up rates increase the risk of outgassing and void formation.[27] Generally, epoxy systems are claimed to be solvent-free by suppliers. Investigation with TGA measurements (thermo gravimetric analysis) for several adhesives[68] showed some solvent or reactive diluent to be present, probably in order to adjust rheology. A problem mentioned in the older die attach literature[28] is bleeding of the adhesive, i.e., separation of liquid adhesive and filler. This behaviour is very dependent on the topography (capillary action) and wetting characterisics of the substrate surface.

Some of the classical die attach adhesives are also used for bonding surface mount components, but several suppliers have recently developed improved systems, e.g., in References 29 and 30 the addition of penetrating particles is mentioned, which should increase oxide tolerance. Also, the addition of reducing agents has been mentioned.[29,30] Both should improve the durability of joints on PbSn surfaces. A flexibilised and fast curing adhesive has been developed which cures in 3 min. at 150°C and is claimed to give very good electrical performance on PbSn surfaces after damp heat (85°C/85% RH).[37-42] The results reported, however, were achieved on alumina using a test pattern without actual components. Other specially designed flexibilised adhesives are also reported.[43,44]

The majority of conductive adhesives suitable for SMD bonding are one-pot ('one-component') systems, but two-pot systems are also available, and are in principle curable at lower temperatures. They require careful mixing before application and degassing to avoid void formation and dot size variations or even dot placement failures during dispensing.

11.2.2   Polyimides[45]

These systems have been used to a certain extent for die bonding.

They have high thermal stability, low ion content, offer high strength, but are somewhat brittle and need difficult processing, i.e., high curing temperature and rather long curing times. Moreover, they contain considerable amounts of solvent. Their usefulness for surface mount applications seems rather low.

11.2.3   Silicones[47,48]

One- and two-pot silicones with metal fillers are also available on the market. They are very compliant but have rather high resistance values and low strength, and need long curing times or high temperatures. Adell *et al.*[49] mention poor electrical conductivity for silicone adhesives after environmental tests, while mechanical properties in moist environment remained relatively good. Hvims mentions poor adhesion strength for both one- and two-component silicone adhesives, but reasonably good electrical performance for a one-component silicone adhesive filled with silver plated copper particles.[50,51] One-component systems (moisture curing) cure rather slowly, two-component systems faster (mainly addition type).

11.2.4   Electroconductive Ag-filled Acrylates

Conductive acrylate systems are also available, but not much has been reported about their durability in environmental tests. Bauer and Tränkner report[57] that QFP100 joints made with a one-component acrylate adhesive (curing 15 min. at 120°C) showed similar resistance increase on PbSn surfaces to an epoxy adhesive during temperature cycling. Adell *et al.*[49] reported poor high-temperature stability for an acrylic adhesive compared with epoxy and silicones. UV- or visible light curing is also mentioned.[59,60]

In addition, electroconductive cyanoacrylates with, e.g., Ag, Ni, or Mo fillers,[61] have been described in the literature, but no durability data are known, and no products seem to be available on the market.

11.2.5   Thermoplastic Adhesives

Thermoplastic adhesives have been proposed in the past[52] for die attach. Potential advantages mentioned are resilience, faster bonding and easy rework possibility. Disadvantages are: (i) the use of solvent to obtain pastes of suitable rheology, causing a risk of void formation with high ramp-up rates and (ii) lower strength. Systems based on conductive PEEK (polyether ether ketone) film[53] are claimed to be more suitable for hermetic sealing of metal enclosures on hybrid circuits than epoxies, because of higher thermal stability, resistance to temperature cycling (-65 to +150°C), and easier rework. Processing temperature, however, is very high (approximately 400°C). More recently, thermoplastic paste adhesives based on high-melting plastics (PES, polyether sulphone)[54] have become commercially available, as well as lower-melting, low Tg adhesives[55] for die attach applications. Excellent thermal cycling stability (-65°C to +150°C), resistance to damp heat (85°C/85%RH), and compatibility with thermosonic Au bonding are claimed. The optimum processing temperature in the latter case is 175-200°C, overall processing time 30 min. Workers at IBM[56] recently described a new Pb-free conductive adhesive of thermoplastic nature and filled with metal particles coated with a low melting metal. The adhesive is capable of metallurgical bonding. It has a resistivity comparable to that of solder; the joints with Cu substrates are claimed to have a better durability in T/H (85°C/85%RH) than Ag-filled epoxies.

11.3   RELIABILITY INVESTIGATIONS

11.3.1   Test Conditions

The requirements placed on adhesive bonds depend greatly on the application area, the highest requirements applying to outdoor applications, and especially automotive applications. The assembly has to withstand relatively high temperatures and large temperature variations. To simulate these environmental ('climate') demands, special climatic tests should be passed. The most demanding tests are temperature shock or thermal cycling, e.g., -55° to + 125° for 1000 cycles, or even from -65° to +150°C, damp heat at

85°C and 85%RH for 1000 h, and hot storage at 125° or 150° for 1000 h. Some frequently used environmental tests are indicated in Table 11.2.

Table 11.2

Reliability Tests for Various Applications[21]

	Automotive (under bonnet)	Telecom	Military	Industrial	Purpose (Failure Mech.)
Temperature cycling	-55° to +125°, 30 s, 600 cy, IEC-68-2-14	-10° to +100°C (<300C/min. until 50% failure)	-65° to 150°C, 1000 cy, Mil-Std-883D Method 1010.7 test cond.D	-55° to 85°C, 25 cy, IEC-68-2-14 (test Na)	Resistance to cyclic T-loads (Brittle fracture and fatigue)
Humidity test	85°C, 85% RH, 2000 h, IEC-68-2-3 (test Ca)	85°C, 85% RH, 15-50 V, 1000 h	85°C, 85% RH, 1320 h	85°C, 95% RH, 5 V DC, 1000 h, IPC-S-815A, class 3 or IEC-68-2-2 (test Ca) 56 d and 5 V	Resistance to moisture (Migration)
Humidity cycling	-10° to 65°C, 96% RH, 10 cy, 240 h, IEC-68-2-38 (test Z/AD)	25° to 55°C, 95% RH, 144 h, IEC-68-2-30	-	25° to 55°C, 95% RH, 144 h, IEC-68-2-30 (test Db)	Simulation of failure during transport; condense
Mechanical shock and vibration test	Shock: 100 g, 6 ms l/direction, IEC-68-2-27 (test Ea), IEC-68-2-6 (test Fc), IEC-68-2-35 (test Fda)	Sine vibration IEC-68-2-6 (test Fc), Random vibration IEC-68-2-35 (test Fda)	500 g, 1 s, Mil-Std-883D, method 2002.3, test cond.A	-	Mechanical force
Ageing test	-	-	-	IEC-68-2-2 (test Ba), 125°C, 1000 h	Behaviour during product life
Free fall	1000 mm, IEC-68-2-32 (test Ed)	-	-	-	Drop (brittle fracture)

d = day

Environmental test results have been reported by several groups of investigators. Because the various investigations differ considerably in terms of adhesives used (usually coded), and in component and board metallisations and test conditions, a direct comparison is difficult, therefore some of the most elaborate ones are described separately below.

11.3.2 Results at Munich University (Orthmann, Habenicht)

Ag paste conductor lines

One of the earlier more elaborate investigations of the use of electrically conductive adhesives for SMD assembly to printed wiring boards, and comparison with soldering, was reported by Wipfelder and Orthmann in 1989,[62] and later by Orthmann in a dissertation study at Munich University, and following papers.[63-66] The earlier literature on conductive adhesives for chip bonding and use in hybrid technology is also reviewed in these references. Orthmann's papers describe the electrical and mechanical behaviour before and after environmental testing for conductive adhesive joints with Epotek H20E of various SMD components to FR-4 printed wiring board with conductor lines also made of the Ag-filled adhesive. The components were generally finished with a AgPd layer.

The optimum curing conditions for the H20E adhesive (15 min. at 120°C) were established using a lap-shear geometry. Insufficient curing of conductive adhesive joints gave inferior strength and electrical conductance after environmental testing. Also, an optimum thickness of adhesive (125 µm) was established with the lap shear geometry.

It was observed that, especially for larger resistors (2412), SOT-23, IC-6 and IC-24, the failure level (R increase more than 3x) after temperature cycling (-40° to 150°C) was much higher than for soldered components (Figure 11.2).

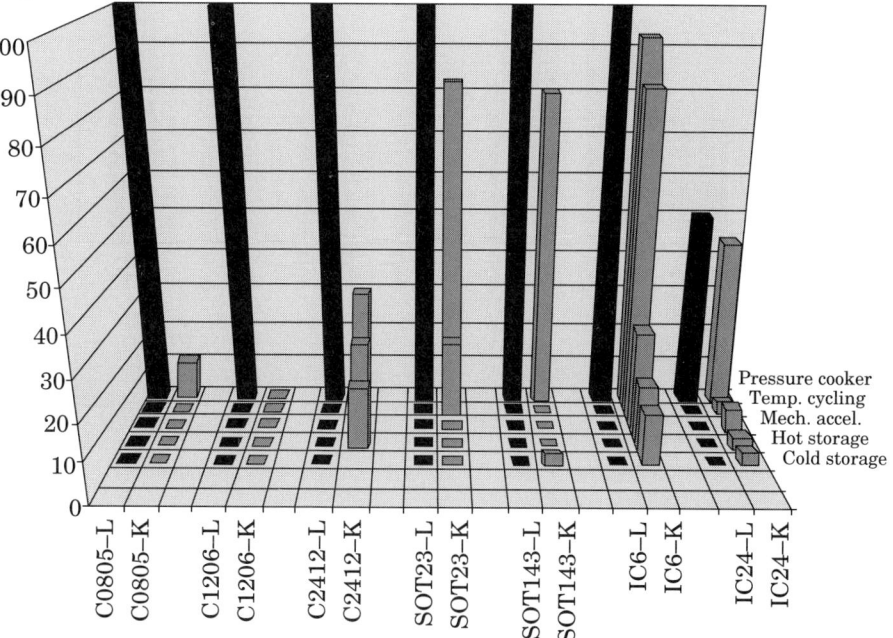

Fig. 11.2 Failure rates (%) of soldered surface-mount components and components bonded with conductive adhesive in cold storage, hot storage, mechanical shock test, thermal cycling and pressure-cooker tests, reported by Habenicht *et al.*, see Ref. 64 (K = adhesive, L = solder).

Hot storage testing at 150°, cold storage at -40°C, and mechanical acceleration at 20,000 g for 1 min. generally had less effect on joint resistance. For C 2412, however, considerable failures were also found in hot storage, and for IC-6 all tests led to some failures. A pressure-cooker test at 120°C had a devastating effect on both solder joints (on copper boards) and conductive adhesive joints, and was set aside as being too severe. Also, the mechanical shear strength of the adhesive joints was reduced after temperature cycling and hot storage especially for SOT-23, SOT-143 and IC-6. The mechanical strength of adhesive joints was generally slightly lower than for soldered joints, but for the SOT-23, SOT-143 and IC-6 it was considerably lower (Figure 11.3).

For the smaller R components, the resistance remains more or less constant in the various climatic tests. The high failure rate of C 2412 and IC-6 components (Figure 11.2) can be ascribed to large expansion differences between component and board, and the relatively small adhesive surface.

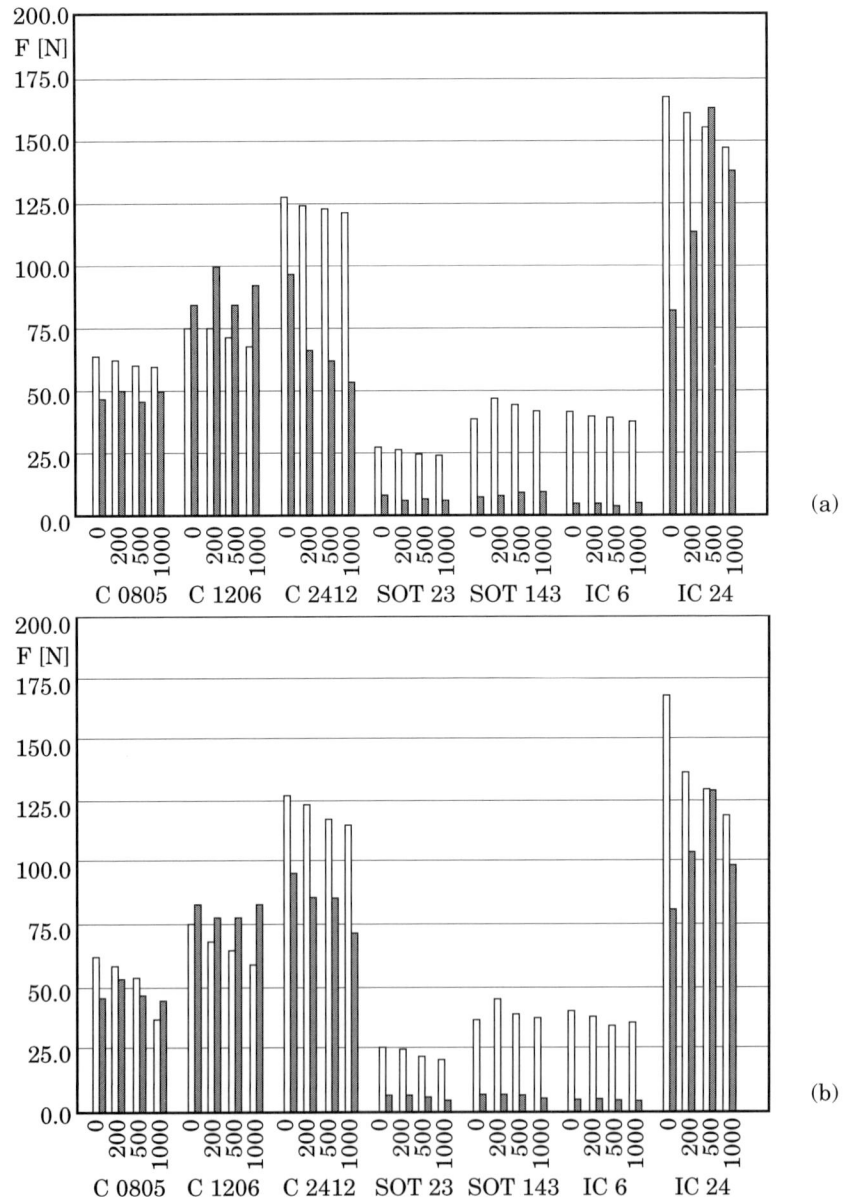

Fig. 11.3 Lap-shear strength of soldered and conductive adhesively bonded surface-mount components (a) after thermal cycling (-40°C to +150°C) and (b) after hot storage (150°C), according to Ref. 64 (□ = solder, ■ = adhesive).

It was also found (for lap-shear joints on pretinned Cu substrates) that Sn-containing leads showed larger resistance increases than AgPd. This behaviour was ascribed to the formation of a less conductive intermetallic layer consisting of Ag_3Sn. As will be further discussed in the section on failure mechanisms, this observation has not been confirmed by other investigators to date. Formation of Ag_3Sn between metallic Ag and Sn/Pb layers at increased temperature is, however, well known in the literature.[67]

Noble metallised copper conductor lines

In a more recent study of bonding capacitors on to a small FR-4 board[14] of an identification module, Orthmann reported that the conductive adhesive joints (different adhesive, as mentioned above) withstood 5000 cycles from -65°C to 150°C, while solder joints failed at 700 cycles, due to thermomechanical stresses. Noble metallisations were used on component and board (Ag, Pd, Au). The initial bond strength of the conductive adhesive joints (measured on lap shear joints, ASTM 1002) was lower by a factor of approximately 3 than for solder joints, but the strength of solder joints diminished considerably during temperature cycling to 1-5 N/mm^2 (cracking observed), while the adhesive bond strength remained fairly constant.

11.3.3   Reliability Investigations at IVF

Rörgren and Liu[21,22] investigated six conductive adhesives (Table 11.3) to attach 160 leaded (0.65 mm pitch) QFPs (quad flat packs) and 0805 chip components to a special test PCB with either flash gold (0.1 μm on 4-5 μm Ni), passivated copper, or tin/lead metallisation (hot air solder levelled, HASL; 10 μm).

Table 11.3

Adhesives used in Reliability Investigations at IVF[22]

Adhesive & Type	Viscosity (Pa.s)	Potlife	Glass Transition	Volume Resistivity (Ωcm)	Shear Strength (MPa)	Curing Time (min.)	Curing Temp. (°C)
ICA 1 (1 comp.)	65	3 days	80	2.10^{-4}	11	10-15	130-150
ICA 2 (2 comp.)	25-35	3-4 days	85	$1-4.10^{-4}$	10	30	130-140
ICA 3 (2 comp.)	50	2 days	50	$2-4.10^{-5}$	8	90	130-140
ICA 4 (1 comp.)	160-200	4 days	80	5.10^{-3}	5	20-30	120-130
ICA 5 (1 comp.)	310-350	4 days	80	1.10^{-3}	4	20-30	120-130
ICA 6 (2 comp.)	150-200	8-12 hr	75	$2-5.10^{-4}$	14	10-15	170-180

The reliability of the joints after constant humidity at 60°and 95%RH was tested as well as after temperature cycling from -40° to 85°C. Electrical performance and mechanical shear strength were evaluated. The components were standard pretinned, gold-plated, or with AgPd terminal finish (0805).

Migration tests

Surface insulation resistance (SIR) was tested with the QFP components under a bias of 5 V. The surface insulation resistance values were found to vary depending on the type of board metallisation, but no dendrite formation whatsoever was visible after the completed humidity test. SIR values varied from 100 MΩ for pretinned boards to 3 GΩ for Au PCBs and 10 GΩ for copper PCBs, which is quite good. Scarcely any difference was observed for the various adhesives. The low values for pretinned boards are ascribed to flux residues.

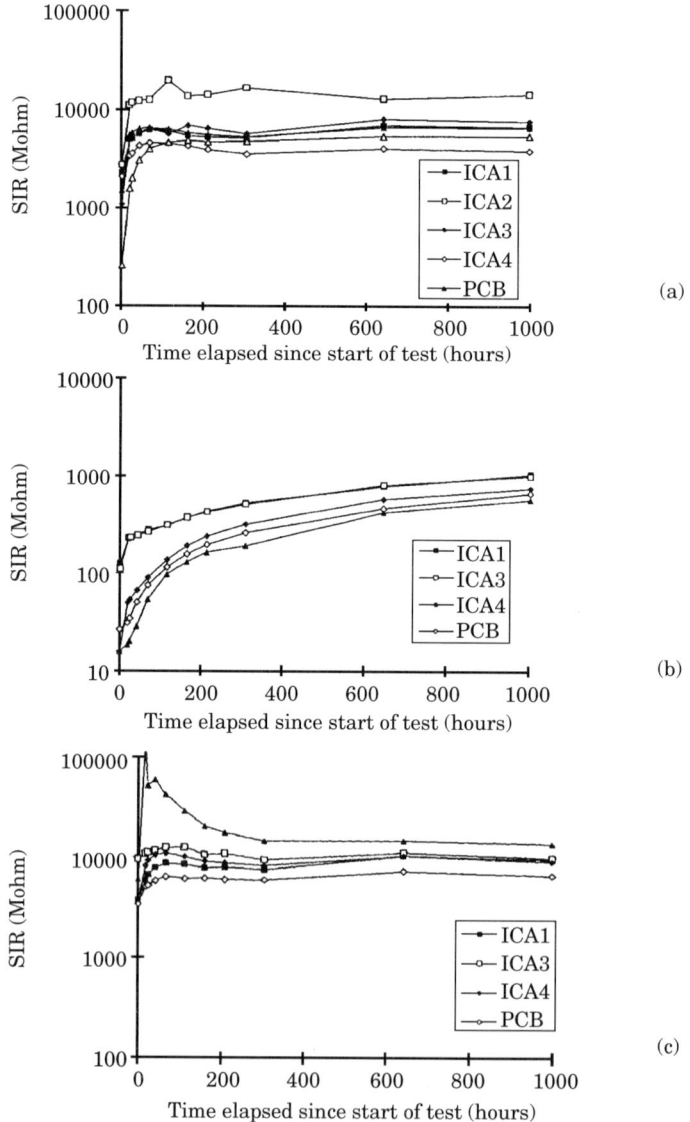

Fig. 11.4 Surface insulation resistance (SIR) values for Au-plated QFP160 components during constant humidity testing (60°C, 90% RH), 5 V bias with isotropic adhesives (see Table 11.3) on gold PCBs (a), pretinned PCBs (b), and copper PCBs (c) according to Ref. 22.

According to the investigators, the Ag-filled epoxies are less sensitive to migration than silver inks used in hybrid applications. The absence of migration phenomena is explained by the encapsulation of silver particles with an epoxy resin.

Joint resistance

The change in resistance values observed after humidity exposure of pretinned 0805 jumpers was found to be very dependent on the adhesive

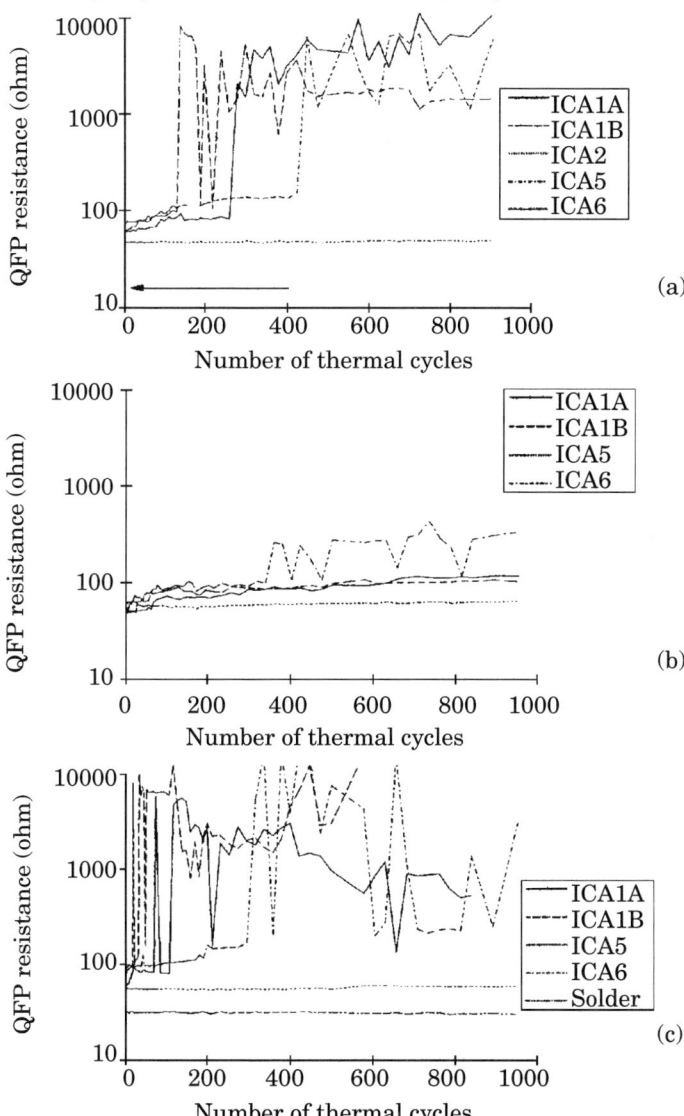

Fig. 11.5 Total joint resistance of QFP 160 (SnPb) on gold finished (a), bare copper (b), and pretinned PCBs (c), after 1000 hours of temperature cycling, -40°C to 85°C, according to Ref. 22.

type. Some adhesives showed a resistance increase by a factor of 3. Only one of the adhesives (ICA 1, Table 11.3) showed less than 20% increase in joint resistance on all metallisations. Remarkably, values on tin-plated boards were not significantly different from those on Au-plated boards.

The electrical performance of SnPb-metallised QFPs after temperature cycling tests (-40°C to 85°C) was also quite dependent on the adhesives used. On gold-plated PCBs only one of the adhesives (ICA 5, Tables 11.3 and 11.5) showed a stable resistance value. All other adhesives exhibited large increases up to a factor of ten or hundred, even after 100 cycles. With the solder-plated boards, the same adhesive, ICA 5, gave stable resistance values, while the others showed very rapid deterioration of resistance values. Adhesive ICA 1, performing best on 0805, did not do so in temperature cycling of the QFPs, which was ascribed to its lower flexibility.

More recently Liu *et al.*[23] also performed RCT testing from -40°C to +125°C (1000 cycles) for gold-plated QFPs on Au finished PCBs. All the adhesives investigated failed under these conditions. With a coating on the leads, however, one of the adhesives passed the test (Figure 11.8(a)).

Mechanical performance

The shear strength of C 0805 (AgPd) joints was also tested before and after humidity testing at 60°C (90%RH). The electrically best performing adhesive (ICA 1) also showed the highest shear-strength values before and after the test (30-44 N for various metallisations). For the other adhesives, values below 24 N were found, which generally decreased in humidity testing. After temperature cycling from -40° to 85°C, again the adhesive ICA 1 showed the highest shear strength. The other adhesives all gave more or less decreased (10-50%) shear-strength values.

The high shear strength of adhesive ICA 1 was ascribed to the lower viscosity and the related easy flow, resulting in better wetting of the substrate and less void formation. One of the other adhesives unexpectedly showed a very low shear strength after thermal cycling, probably due to a very thin bondline.

Failure samples

SEM photographs of failure samples after temperature cycling show either delamination of component lead from adhesive, or crack formation at

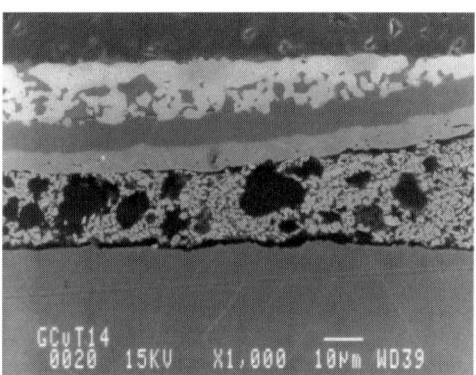

Fig. 11.6 SEM micrograph of good performing adhesive joint (ICA V) of pretinned QFP on Cu PCB, after 1000 hours of temperature cycling (-40°C to +85°C), according to Ref. 22.

the adhesive/PCB interface. The best-performing adhesive on QFPs (ICA 5) had very small silver flakes and a large number of black spots ascribed to voids and flexibilising agent.

Before environmental exposure, shear fractures generally occurred between bond pad and adhesive; after temperature cycling, fracture was observed between component lead and adhesive.

One particular mechanism that could explain the strong increase in joint resistance during temperature cycling is related to the compliance of the polymer, i.e., during cycling the metal particles would move apart, and not entirely regain their original contact. Although resistance values at high temperature are higher than at lower temperature (see Figure 11.7), no evidence was observed for this mechanism, as no gradual increase in resistance was found (Figure 11.5). The quite sudden increases sometimes observed tend to support the occurrence of delaminations. At times such delaminations may close more or less at the low temperature extreme. Therefore misleading results may be obtained if R is only measured at the low temperature extreme. It was expected that in such cases the resistivity amplitude would also increase during cycling. This was not observed at all (Figure 11.7, pretinned QFPs). It can be seen, however, that completely failing joints (delamination) may seem to be good conductors when looking only at the low temperature extreme, e.g., in Figure 11.7 the bad sample of ICA 6a seems to conduct well if measured only at low temperature.

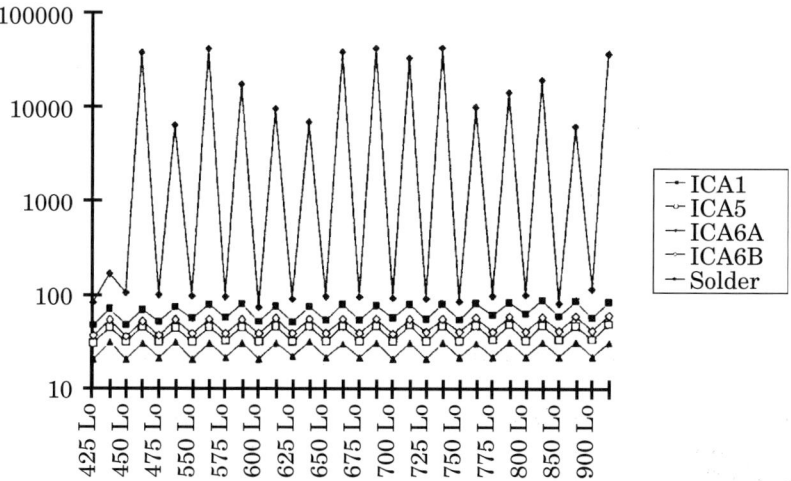

Fig. 11.7 Resistance of adhesive joints of pretinned QFPs during 500 cycles from -40°C to +85°C, according to Ref. 22.

Drop tests

A serious problem with the reliability of conductive adhesive joints on FR-4 boards, even in the case of noble metallised QFPs (80 or 160, 0.5 or 0.3 mm pitch) and gold flash on the boards, is the poor resistance to drop and bending tests. None of three selected adhesives survived 6x drop testing from 1.5 m height in a special test jig, with a specially designed split board pattern. In combination with an extra coating on the leads, or a conformal coating, however, the test was passed (less than 2% increase in resistance).[23]

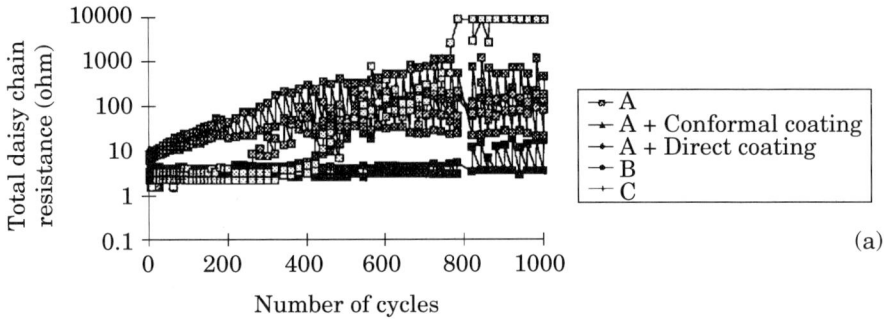

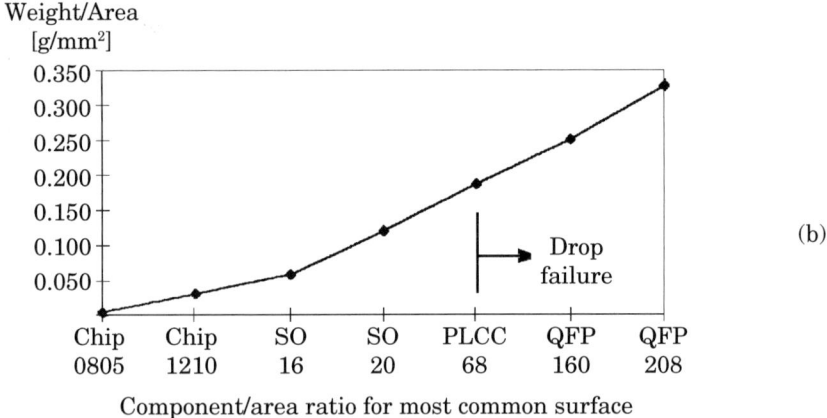

Fig. 11.8 (a) Resistance of adhesive joints of gold-plated QFP 80s to gold finished PCBs during thermal cycling from -40° to +125°C. Measurements during cold and hot cycle. Adhesive A with direct coating on the leads shows best performance.[23] (b) Drop failure risk is more severe for SMDs with higher weight/area.[23]

11.3.4   Reliability Investigations at Philips and TNO

Jagt *et al.* at Philips[68] made a comparison of the electrical and mechanical behaviour of eight different adhesives (Table 11.4) using R1206 components with SnPb 90/10, or AgPd terminations on FR-4 boards with passivated copper, SnPb 60/40, and Au.

Some of the adhesives selected have a rather low Tg, around or below room temperature, others around 80°C. The adhesive joints were tested in Hot Storage at 150°C for 1000 h, in Damp Heat at 85° and 85%RH for 1000 h and Rapid Change of Temperature from -40° to +125°C for 1000 cycles. In none of the tests did the volume resistance of the adhesives change significantly. The joint resistance for SnPb-leaded components was found to increase sharply during Damp Heat and RCT testing for all adhesives, but most for the more flexible low Tg adhesives. After Hot Storage also resistance increase was found, but less severe than in the other tests. With AgPd-terminated components, results were much better than for SnPb, the best performing adhesives (CA-1,2) showing practically no increase in resistance values on boards with gold or protected copper. On SnPb-finished boards, small to significant resistance increases were found, depending on the adhesive used. Again the flexible low Tg adhesives gave results inferior to those of the higher Tg adhesives (see Figure 11.9).

It can be concluded that the resistance increasing influence of SnPb on the component side appears to be much larger than on the board side.

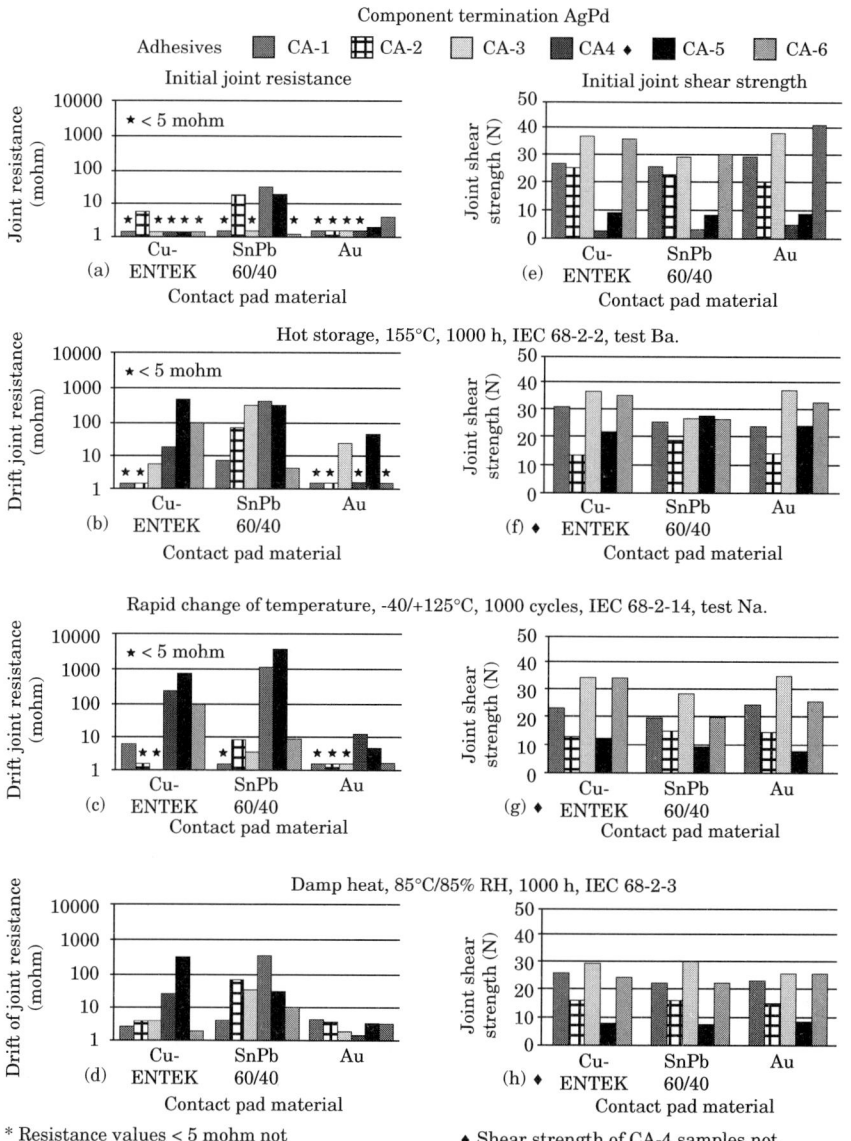

* Resistance values < 5 mohm not accurately measurable

♦ Shear strength of CA-4 samples not measurable after environmental tests

Fig. 11.9 Electrical resistance and shear strength values for R1206 jumpers with AgPd terminations after various climate tests, according to Ref. 68.

Two types of adhesives (CA 7 and 8, Table 11.4), which were claimed by the supplier to give better results on SnPb, indeed showed no, or almost no, increase in the 85°C/85%RH test. However, results on the most critical RCT (-40° to +125°, 1000 h) test were not reported for these adhesives.

Table 11.4

Adhesives used in Reliability Investigations at Philips[68] ((a) Type of adhesive, rheological properties and weight loss measured with TGA; (b) Curing characteristics measured with DSC and thermomechanical analysis (TMA))

(a)

Adhesive No.	Type of Adhesive	η (100 s^{-1})[(1)] [Pa.s]	τ_0[(2)] [Pa]	Δ weight (200°C, 120 min) [%]
CA-1	Epoxy	79	0	6.1
CA-2	Epoxy	46	255	1.4
CA-3	Epoxy	39	~0	9
CA-4	Epoxy-Urethane	37	43	16
CA-5	Epoxy-Silicone	75	0	1.7
CA-6	Epoxy	4	80	8
CA-7	Epoxy	31	150	2.5
CA-8	Epoxy	75	23	~0.5

(1) Viscosity at shear rate 100 s^{-1} and 23°C (cone-plate).
(2) Apparent (calculated) yield value at 23°C.

(b)

Adhesive	DSC [(1)] Dynamic Scan (5°C/min.) T_{max} (°C)	H_{dyn}[(4)] (J/g)	Isothermal Scan [(2)] T_{iso} (°C)	H_{iso}[(5)] (J/g)	$t_{90\%}$ (min.)	TMA (1) Dyn. Scan [(3)] T_g (°C)	TCE x 10^{-5}/°C
CA-1	160	92	150	93	12.5	74	10/37
CA-2	113/124	106	150	115	4.5	79	10/42
CA-3	111	114	125	111	6	26	10/46
CA-4	n.d.	n.d.	n.d.	n.d.	n.d.	n.d.	n.d.
CA-5	143	23	150	31	7	n.d.	n.d.
CA-6	131	129	125	152	9	51	7/33
CA-7	135	89	150	93	4	n.d.	n.d.
CA-8	135	98	150	96	4	n.d.	n.d.

(1) Mettler DSC 30, — TMA 40.
(2) DSC isothermal scan: heating 100°C/min., $t_{(90\%)}$ = time for 90% conversion, incl. heating up.
(3) The 2 TCE values are for temp. <Tg and temp. >Tg respectively.
(4) H = reaction enthalpy.
(5) H_{iso} = measured enthalpy for isothermal scan.

Two remarks should be made concerning the poor results with most adhesives in the case of pretinned component terminations. First, the composition of SnPb at the board and at the component termination is not the same; components generally had an SnPb 90/10 composition, while SnPb 60/40 was present on the board side. Secondly, the bonding area at the component is smaller than at the board side. Furthermore, the deteriorating effect of SnPb on joint resistance seems to be more pronounced if more Sn is present in the solder composition.[69,70]

No correlation was found in these investigations between changes in mechanical shear strength and changes in resistance after climate testing, although the stronger increase of resistance in RCT than in Hot Storage points to an influence of thermomechanical effects. After hot storage, in some cases an increase in shear strength was found, probably due to further curing, but the resistance value in most cases increased. With RCT and Damp Heat exposure, generally a decrease in shear strength was found for both solder-plated and AgPd-terminated components.

For some adhesives, moisture uptake at room temperature and 100% RH was determined in order to detect a possible correlation with the resistance increases observed in damp heat testing. Indeed, the order of water uptake roughly correlated with the resistance deterioration in this test (Figure 11.10).

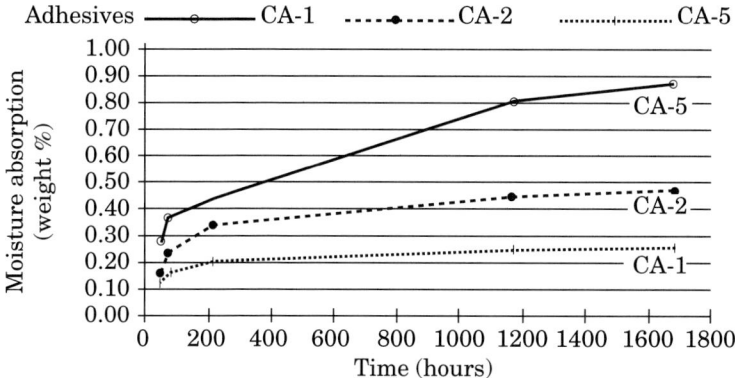

Fig. 11.10 Moisture absorption of cured conductive adhesive samples (2 x 5 x 40 mm) at room temperature and 100% RH.[68]

Attempts to measure the reaction shrinkage of the adhesives, and a possible correlation thereof with resistance variations of adhesive joints, were unsuccessful. Accurate determination of shrinkage in TMA appeared to be difficult, possibly due to evaporation of volatile components. Similar observations were made by Li Li.[71]

Evidence that oxidation of SnPb may occur during Damp-Heat testing was obtained by XPS, but delamination effects were also observed, and some evidence for an Ag-depleted layer at the component side after Damp Heat (see section on failure mechanisms) was found.

Botter (TNO)[70] reported that the resistance increase during cyclic humidity testing at 25° and 80° and 98% RH for approximately 300 to 400 h appeared to be worse for combinations of gold-plated boards and tin-metallised components than in the case where both components and board were solder-coated. He ascribed this to the formation of a micro-electrochemical cell, which will corrode especially Sn, and to a much lesser extent also Cu and Pb (which show oxide passivation contrary to Sn). The adhesive is considered to play an important rôle in this process by taking up water. It is assumed that the ionic content of the adhesive (Cl⁻) is also of influence in this process. Furthermore, Botter indicates that a larger contact area (R1206) is less sensitive to resistance increase than a smaller one (R0603), and that pure Sn-metallised components (or boards) give much worse results than, e.g., SnPb

60/40. With AgPd-finished components and board metallisations of Au, pure Pb, and Cu, little or no increase of electrical contact resistance was found in cyclic humidity testing. For SO-8 components with NiPd metallisation good results were also obtained. With SEM/EDAX it could be shown that, with Sn metallisation, extensive oxidation occurs under the test conditions indicated. Oxidation was only observed in the vicinity of or underneath the adhesive material. Also the presence of Cl at the fractured surface was detected.

With R0603 and R1206 — contrary to SOT-23 and SO-8 components — abrupt changes in resistance sometimes occurred during humidity cycling. During heat-up from 25 to 80°C the resistance may increase by more than 200 mohm. This is believed to be due to crack formation. Upon cooling, the cracks may close, more or less, leading to a decrease in resistance. It was also reported that R1206 components are less sensitive to resistance increase than R0603, probably due to the larger contact area.

11.3.5   Biased Temperature/Humidity Testing

Investigators at Epoxy Technology[72] described 85°C/85% RH exposure results after 500 hours with and without bias of 5 V dc for 20, 100, and 500 ohm resistors (size 2512 and 3614), and zero ohm jumpers, for five different adhesives (A-E).

Results on bare Cu boards without bias were considerably better than with pretinned boards. With pretinned boards, with some adhesives (B,D,E) SnPb-terminated resistors gave better results than AgPt-terminated, which sometimes (D,E) showed high resistance increases of up to several ohms. With Au terminated resistors, resistance values remained more or less constant.

With bias, resistance values increased dramatically both on Cu and SnPb board metallisation, except for one adhesive (E) which showed lower values after 85°C/85% RH exposure with SnPb 500 ohm resistors in both cases. With SnPb finished 100 ohm resistors, however, some increase was found with adhesive E, and another adhesive, B, gave better results.

During temperature cycling (-55° to +125°C), adhesive B again showed stable resistance values for SnPb-terminated components and pretinned boards. With Au- and AgPt-finished components on pretinned boards, large resistance increases were found. With bare Cu boards, results were generally considerably better, but in some cases with SnPb- (C and D) and in others with AgPt- (A,C and E) plated components, large resistance increases occurred. No good explanation is available at present for these results. For some catastrophic failures (unfortunately also with the good performing adhesive E), however, poor adhesion was supposed to be the cause.

11.3.6   Investigations at Binghampton

In a dissertation study[71] and related reports,[73-75] Li Li and Morris described the effect of 1000 hours of 85°C/85% RH exposure on the joint resistance of pretinned 0805 jumper resistors (SnPb 95/5), adhesively bonded (Table 11.5) to HASL pretinned boards or bare copper boards. The resistance increased quite dramatically for two adhesives A and C, but with a third adhesive, B, an increase of only 27% was obtained for the pretinned boards and a 127%

increase for the bare copper boards. Joints with adhesive C, showing a very large R increase, also had very low shear strength. No increase of the bulk resistivities of A, B and C was found after 85°C/85% RH testing.

Table 11.5

Adhesives used in Reliability Experiments at State University of New York at Binghampton[71] (Properties measured with TMA (cured block samples))

Adhesive	T_g (°C)	CTE (<T_g) ppm/°K	CTE (>T_g) ppm/°K
A	90	56	155
B	90	61	168
C	90	78	218

The large increase of resistance for adhesive C was ascribed at least partly to low stencil printing quality, which could also cause the large variations in initial resistance values. SEM investigation of cross-sections of joints made with adhesive C showed that in several cases no fillet to the component had formed at all. A joint with fillet showed an increase of only 5% in resistance value after 500 h in the test.

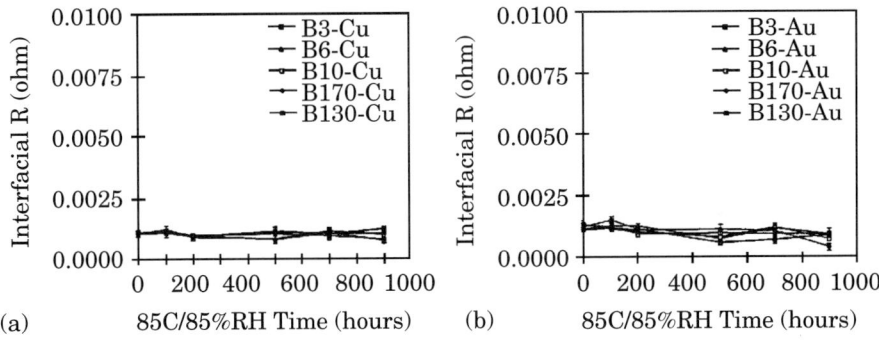

(a)   85C/85%RH Time (hours)   (b)   85C/85%RH Time (hours)

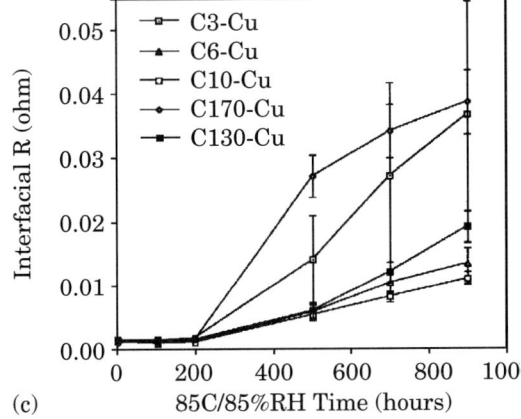

(c)   85C/85%RH Time (hours)

Fig. 11.11 Interfacial resistance during 85°C/85% RH for adhesive B on Cu substrate, after different cure schedules (a), *ibid* for adhesive B on Au (b), *ibid* for adhesive C on Cu (c), according to Ref. 71.

Also, the cure parameters for adhesive A appear to be critical: A was cured for only 87%, while the better performing adhesive B was almost 100% cured. Separate investigations showed a large dependence of the interfacial resistance for adhesives A and C bonded to Cu (passivated) boards on curing conditions. On Au the effect was less pronounced. Interfacial resistance of B on Cu was fairly independent of the curing conditions (Figure 11.11).

Cracks were sometimes observed after 85°C/85% RH testing at the adhesive-PCB interface (for adhesive A and B) or at the terminal lead (for A). For adhesive B, voids were also observed in the adhesive layer, apparently without much effect (see above).

In some cases the adhesive layer was very thin (adhesive C), producing failure at the component side. Again, the stencil-printing thickness and/or the bonding force applied during component placement appear to be critical factors.

TEM studies of some samples showed that a 60 nm thick oxide layer formed on Cu in the case of adhesive A after 1000 h of 85°/85% RH, which was not present after 68 h. On pretinned boards no significant oxide layer was detected after 1000 h.

11.3.7   Reliability Results with Epoxies and Silicone Adhesives from a Nordic Project

Hvims[50,51] reported an evaluation study of 15 different adhesives (Table 11.6) on two different metal surfaces for 0603, 0805, 1206, SO-28,

Table 11.6

Adhesives used in Nordic Project[50]

Adhesive	Filler	T_g (°C)	Vol. Resistivity (Ωcm)	Cure Schedule (time)	Cure Schedule (°C)
A (1-c epoxy)	Ag flakes	90	6×10^{-5}	1 h	130
B (1-c epoxy)	Ag-plated Cu flakes	n.d.	4.5×10^{-3}	30 min	125
C (1-c epoxy)	Ag flakes	130	2.5×10^{-4}	1 h	150
D (2-c epoxy)	Ag flakes	90	2×10^{-4}	5 min	120
E (1-c epoxy)	Ag flakes	>200	7×10^{-5}	30 min	150
F (1-c epoxy)	Ag flakes	80	1×10^{-3}	6 min	150
G (2-c epoxy)	Ni	n.d.	1	2 h	65
H (1-c epoxy)	Ag flakes	n.d.	1×10^{-3}	1.5 h	120
I (1-c polyimide)	Ag flakes	249	5×10^{-4}	1 h	140
J (2-c epoxy)	Ag flakes	85	5×10^{-4}	30 min	150
K (1-c epoxy)	Ag flakes	91	2×10^{-4}	15 min	140
L (1-c silicone)	Ag-plated Cu flakes/balls	-55	1×10^{-2}	168 h	25
M (2-c epoxy)	Ag flakes	160	5×10^{-3}	30 min	99
N (2-c epoxy)	Ag flakes	150	5×10^{-4}	1 h	150
O (2-c silicone)	Ag flakes	n.d.	6×10^{-4}	1 h	150

n.d. = not determined

SQFP-48, QFP-100 and PLCC-68 components. Results were not described in detail, but in general electrical stability of 1206 resistors, after temperature cycling from -20° to 90°C for 48 cycles (30 min/30 min) and 85°C/85% RH for 168 h, was much better with Ag/Pd terminations and Au-plated boards than with Sn/Pb metallisations and Sn/Pb-plated boards. Some Ag-filled one-component epoxy adhesives showed reasonable results with Pb/Sn, but it should be kept in mind that the test conditions here are milder than in the investigations mentioned previously. Results with the two-component epoxies used were worse than for the one-component, and silicone adhesive (one-component) was inferior to epoxies both electrically and mechanically. Resistance increases generally were highest in the temperature-humidity test. Migration tests with parallel conductor lines at spacings varying from 0.8-0.1 mm did not show signs of silver migration after temperature-humidity testing (5 V-12 V) for any of the adhesives.

11.3.8   Reliability Investigations by a US Consortium — Drop Tests

In an investigation recently reported by a US consortium,[77,78] 25 commercially available adhesives were evaluated with respect to stability of joint resistance of various pretinned IC components on boards with bare copper, or tin/lead. Test conditions were 500 hours at 85°C/85% RH. A set of requirements was formulated for a surface mount conductive adhesive, i.e., (i) a volume resistivity of 1 mohm.cm, (ii) less than 20% shift in resistance after ageing, and (iii) the ability of an adhesively bonded PLCC-44 to withstand six drops from a height of 60 inches. None of the adhesives investigated passed all the requirements. All of the adhesives failed after six drops at 36 inches. For a drop height of 18 inches, only two adhesives passed. For the drop tests, PLCC-44 components were bonded to (half) lap-shear substrates provided with a square patch of adhesive.

Also, lap-shear tests were performed with standard ASTM samples and an adhesive bondline of 5 mil. After 85°/85% RH testing, lap-shear strength decreased by 10-80%. No direct correlation was found, however, between lap shear strength and drop testing.

A first electrical analysis of the adhesives was performed by using a cross bridge structure (Figure 11.12) consisting of two copper rods bonded together

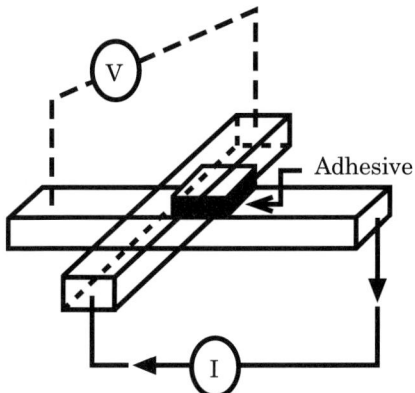

Fig. 11.12 Cross bridge structure according to Ref. 77.

with adhesive in a cross configuration. Samples with bare copper, OSP copper, Ni/Pd and Ni/Au bonded with the best performing adhesive showed a small decrease in resistance upon ageing. Sn/Pb samples showed a considerable increase and wide variation in resistance values.

Drop testing with boards

Printed circuit boards with a variety of components (QFP, PLCC, SOIC and BGA) were drop tested also. Unaged boards were subjected to three drops from a height of 36 inches on to a vinyl-covered concrete floor. Surface mounted discrete components and axial through-hole resistors survived the drops without any significant increase in joint resistance. The IC components all showed open joints, or separated completely from the board after three drops. PLCCs and LCC packages were usually lost after as few as one or two drops. Drop-testing with a conformal coating and non-conductive staking adhesive under the component body prevented component loss, but did not improve electrical properties. This is contrary to results from IVF, discussed earlier,[23] where electrical benefit was reported from a coating on component leads.

Temperature / Humidity testing

Temperature/Humidity (T/H) tests were performed at 65°C/85%RH, as well as 85°C/85% RH, for 1000 hours. A change of 50 mohms in individual

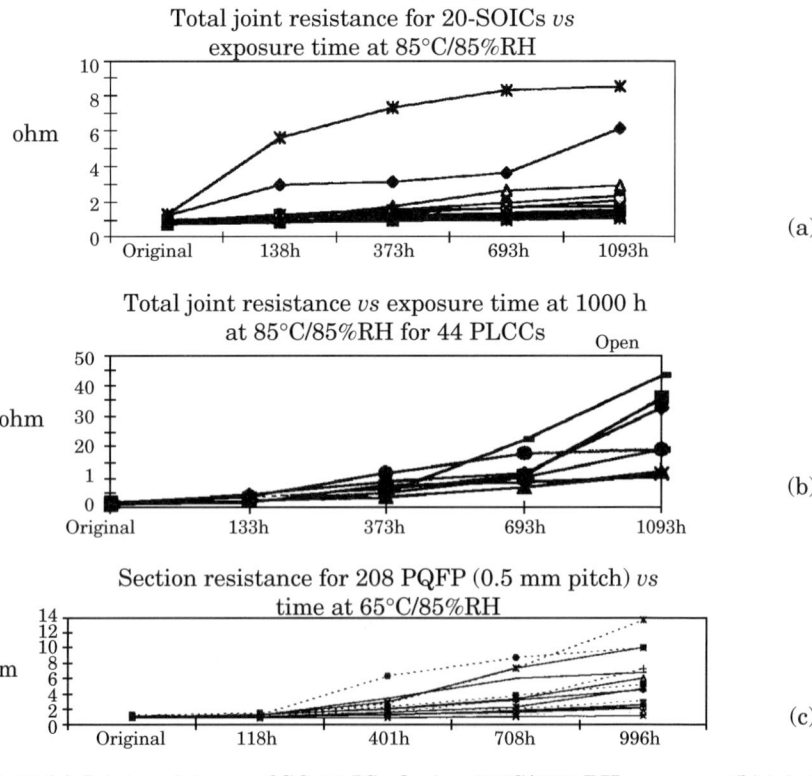

Fig. 11.13 (a) Joint resistance of SO-20 ICs during 85°C/85% RH exposure, (b) joint resistance of PLCC-44s during 85°C/85% RH exposure, (c) section resistance of PQFP-208s (0.5 mm pitch) during 65°C/85% RH exposure, see Ref. 77.

joint resistance was still considered to be acceptable. The deterioration of resistance in T/H tests was dependent on lead geometry and the dimensions of the SMDs. The trends in the resistance increase were:

PTH< 1206 < LCC< SOIC20 < Fine pitch < PLCC 84 < PLCC 44.

While the resistance increase for PTH (axial through-hole resistors) and 1206 components in 85°C/85%RH was < 20 mohms, SOICs did pass the 65°C/85% RH T/H test, but in the 85°C/85% RH exposure 30% of the joints showed an unacceptable increase in resistance, up to 7 ohms (Figure 11.13(a)). QFP components showed a lot of variation. An unacceptable resistance drift already occurred in 65°C/85% RH T/H (Figure 11.13(c)). PLCCs showed gradual resistance increases in 65°C/85% RH exposure, and very large resistance jumps for some individual joints in 85°C/85% RH, other joints being well within the limit (Figure 11.13(b)). This is probably due to the non-compliance of the J-lead configurations, which in combination with the small contact area leads to high stresses in the joints. Cross-sectioning and SEM investigations, however, did not clearly reveal this. Sometimes good joints showed considerable crack formation and bad joints did not.

11.3.9   Miscellaneous Other Investigations

Gaynes *et al.*[76] tested three thermohardening and one thermoplastic silver-filled adhesive by making lap shear joints with a comb pattern made of copper (40 fingers, 0.25 mm wide, 0.25 mm thick) and exposing them to 85°C/85% RH for 1000 h, 0-100° Temperature Cycling for 2000 h and 120° Hot Storage for 2000 h. The copper was finished with a Pd alloy, gold (both on Ni), Ni or Sn. One of the thermohardening adhesives (A) showed very good contact resistance on the Pd alloy (see Figures 11.14 and 11.15), even after environmental testing only 4.4 mohm being measured, against 4.0 mohm

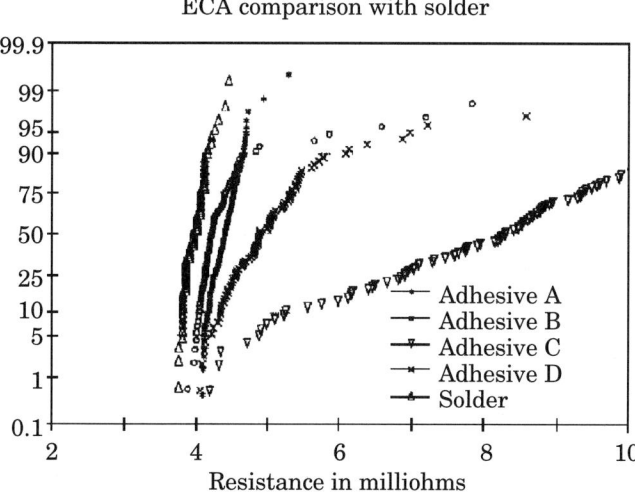

Fig. 11.14 Comparison of various selected conductive adhesives (A-D) and solder on Pd alloy surfaces, with respect to cumulative percentage increase in contact resistance, according to Ref. 76. Distribution of resistance values of adhesive A is very close to that of solder.

for solder. Results on Au were less good, on Sn inferior and on Ni worst (Figure 11.15). Also, the thermal ageing test gave poor results in the case of gold, which was ascribed to the Ni hardening layer.

Mechanically, adhesive joints were found to be less robust than solder. Encapsulation was suggested for mechanical protection.

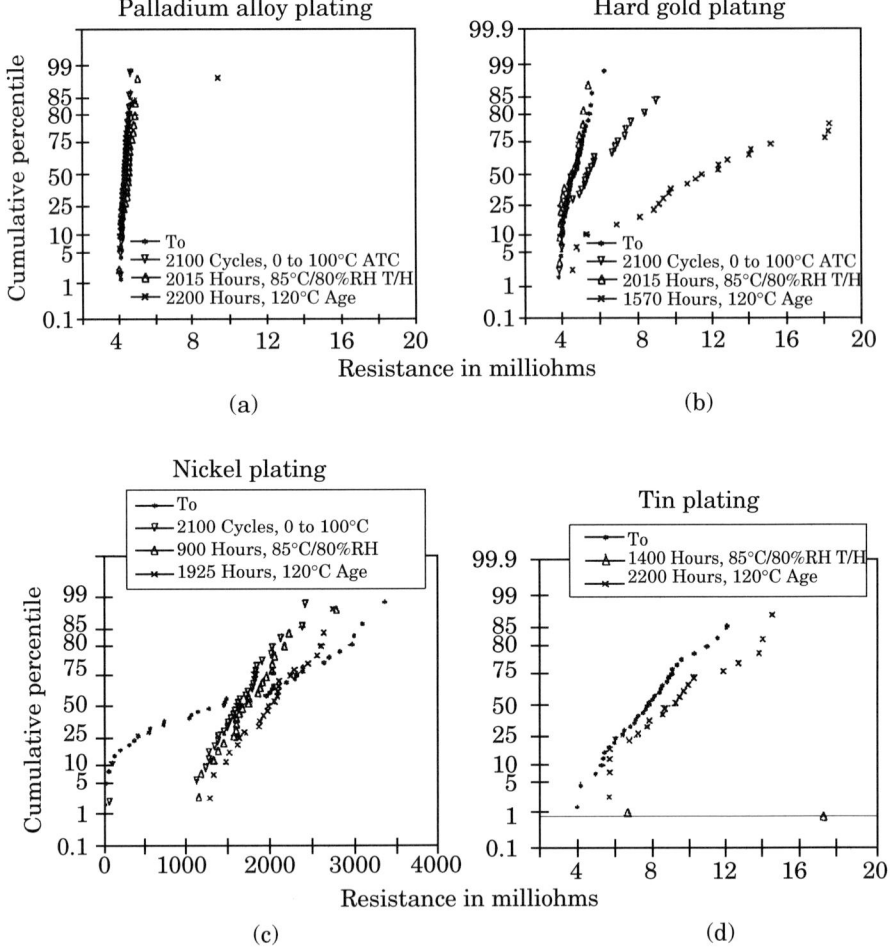

Fig. 11.15 Cumulative increases in contact resistance of adhesive A on Pd alloy plated substrate (a), hard gold plated (b), nickel plated (c), and tin plated (d) substrates after various climate tests, see Ref. 76.

Nguyen *et al.*[37] at Ablestik Laboratories investigated mechanical and electrical properties of adhesive joints made of Ag-filled epoxies (flakes <10 μm) specially designed for component attach on fine-pitch circuits. Joints with relatively coarse patterns of AgPd thick film on alumina were used (two substrates glued together with approximately 100 μm 8175 adhesive). After 1000 hours of 85°C/85%RH with 100 mA bias, only small increases in contact resistance (approximately 14%) were observed. Substrates covered with Sn/Pb/Ag (62/36/2) showed a larger increase, i.e., some 31%

increase after 85°C/85% RH exposure. With the more flexible and faster curing 8175A (3 min. at 150° *vs* 30 min. for 8175), however, the resistance increase after 85°C/85% RH was almost nil.

Shear-strength values for 8175 joints made by glueing Kovar tabs plated with Cu, Ag, Ni or SnPb 60/40 on alumina substrates with Ag/Pd, Ag, Cu and Au conductors[38-41] generally did not deteriorate significantly after hot storage at 150°C, exposure to 85°C/85% RH, and thermal cycling from -65°C to +150°C for 1000 h. Resistance values of Cu tabs bonded to Ag and Ag/Pd conductors generally increased less than 3% after 85°C/85% RH, and thermal cycling (-40 to + 125°C). Electromigration testing according to IPC-TM-650 with uncoated substrates at 85°C and 90% RH and 10 V dc bias did not reveal signs of migration after seven days. More recently,[42] also studies with Au-plated tantalum capacitors bonded to thick film gold-alumina substrates were reported. Ta capacitors are critical components, showing visual failures due to cracks at the interface of adhesive and component after environmental testing from -65°C to 150°C. Several factors were assumed to be of importance, such as a relatively low CTE of adhesive, high Tg, low E modulus, and high adhesion (giving highest percentage cohesive failure). Adhesion showed the closest correlation to the visual performance. Oxygen/argon plasma-treatment was reported to improve visual performance, although no significant increase in shear strength was observed. No electrical results were shown, however.

Contrary to the results above, investigators at IVF[23] observed a significantly higher increase of resistance with Au-plated QFPs on Au-metallised FR-4 after thermal cycling from -40°C to +125°C for all adhesives tested.

Gilleo of Alpha Metals reported[29,30] some reliability results on a new type of Ag-filled conductive adhesive that is claimed to be able to break the oxide layers on substrates. This adhesive was reported to exhibit a decrease in resistance after climate tests (60°C/90%RH 1000 cycles; -55°/85°C, 25 cycles) for solder-plated R1206 and PLCCs on Ag-PTF polyester flex. On FR-4 with bare copper, a small increase (<10%) was found after 85°/85%RH.

11.4   FAILURE MECHANISMS

Several mechanisms reported in the papers cited previously are compared and discussed in this section, namely (i) oxidation and corrosion of SnPb, (ii) crack formation, (iii) thin layer showing depletion of silver, (iv) creep in the adhesive layer, and (v) formation of an intermetallic compound.

11.4.1   Oxidation and Corrosion

The observation that SnPb-finished component terminations and pretinned Cu patterns on the board show relatively large R increases during damp heat testing and thermal cycling is ascribed by most of the authors to oxidation of SnPb. Pores in SnPb on Cu may also lead to hole corrosion of SnPb near Cu. This type of corrosion is accelerated by Cl⁻ ions. In the older DGEBA-type adhesives a fair amount (e.g., 170 ppm for H20E) of Cl⁻ has been detected,[21-26] but newer versions appear to be much better. In some cases,[24,71] formation of a Cu_2O layer is considered as the cause of resistance increase after damp heat (85°C/85% RH).

The thickness of the oxide layer formed on PbSn after damp-heat exposure, according to Reference 68, is in the order of 100 nm or more as measured by XPS (Table 11.7).

Table 11.7

XPS Analysis and Depth Profiling with Ar Ion Sputtering for Damp Heat (85°C/85% RH) Exposed Sample, and Reference Sample of R1206 (PbSn), after Cleavage from Board[68]

Sputter Time (min.)	CA-6 Damp Heat Sample at % O	CA-6 Control Sample at % O
0	(23) [1]	47
0.5	35	30
1	21	2
2	15	0
5	15	0

Kratos Axis HS with MgKα-radiation under 90°

Depth profiling by Ar sputtering: approx. 13 nm/min. for SiO_2

Spot size: 70 μm

(1) Value too low due to strong C signal at surface.

11.4.2   Crack Formation

Several investigators also found cracks in electrically poorly performing adhesive joints.[71] Crack formation has been observed after humidity exposure at the Cu/adhesive interface, or at the adhesive/PbSn interface.[21-26,68,69,71,73] In some cases, a relation between mechanical strength and crack formation is suggested. Li Li reported[71] that minimum shear-force samples showed a high percentage resistance increase after humidity exposure, but other investigators did not see a clear correlation between strength and electrical properties. One group of investigators[77,78] mentions the occurrence of cracks even in 'good' samples. Work described in Reference 69 revealed crack formation in many of the pretinned R 1206 samples, which showed a large increase in resistance values after damp heat (85°C/85% RH), or rapid change of temperature (-40°C to 125°C). As can be seen in SEM BSE micrographs (Figure 11.16)[69] with oxygen and Pb mapping, some local oxidative deterioration of PbSn can also occur at very distinct places. At these places some Cl⁻ concentration is observed. In addition, coarsening of Pb grains can be observed after damp heat, but neither of these two observations was considered to be the main reason for the R increase. However, under the more severe cyclic humidity conditions used by Botter (TNO),[70] stronger local oxidation of PbSn was observed.

Figure 11.17 shows similar crack formation to that described above at the PbSn/Ag interface after RCT tests. Remarkably, despite the resistance increase from 33 mohm to 810 mohm, the shear strength of 38 N before the test was still 25 N after testing. This may mean either that the crack does not extend over the entire surface, or alternatively the R1206 components had also become bonded to the component body, outside the metallisation.

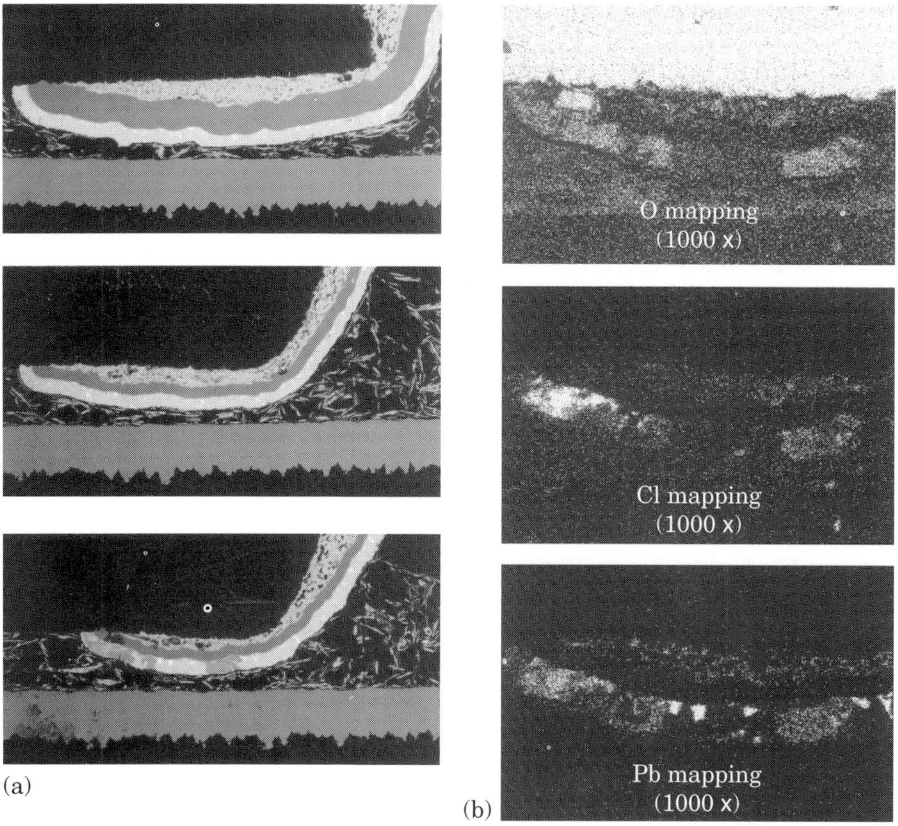

(a)

(b)

O mapping
(1000 x)

Cl mapping
(1000 x)

Pb mapping
(1000 x)

Fig. 11.16 (a) SEM BSE micrographs (400 X) of three R1206 (SnPb 90/10) components bonded with CA-3 to Cu (passivated) pad on FR-4 board after 1000 hours at 85°C/85% RH exposure.[69] In all three cases, delamination at the component adhesive interface is observed. In one case (lower photomicrograph) significant deterioration of SnPb is also observed (see also Fig. 11.16(b)). (b) One deteriorated R1206 with O, Cl and Pb mapping.[69]

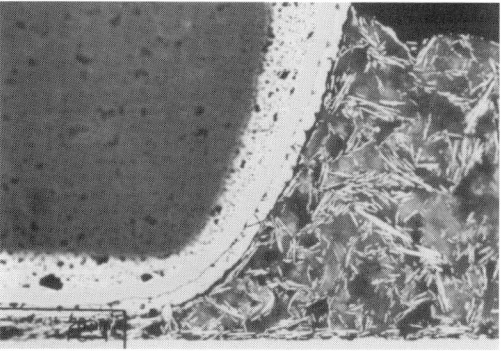

Fig. 11.17 SEM micrograph of R1206 (Sn/Pb 90/10) joint with CA-3 to passivated Cu board.[69] Although cracks are formed along SnPb/adhesive surface and electrical resistance increased dramatically, joint strength is still considerable.

With AgPd terminated resistors on pretinned Cu pads, which did not show any significant resistance increase, no large cracks were observed (Figure 11.18); only occasionally small interruptions between the Ag/Pd layer on the component and the adhesive layer were observed.

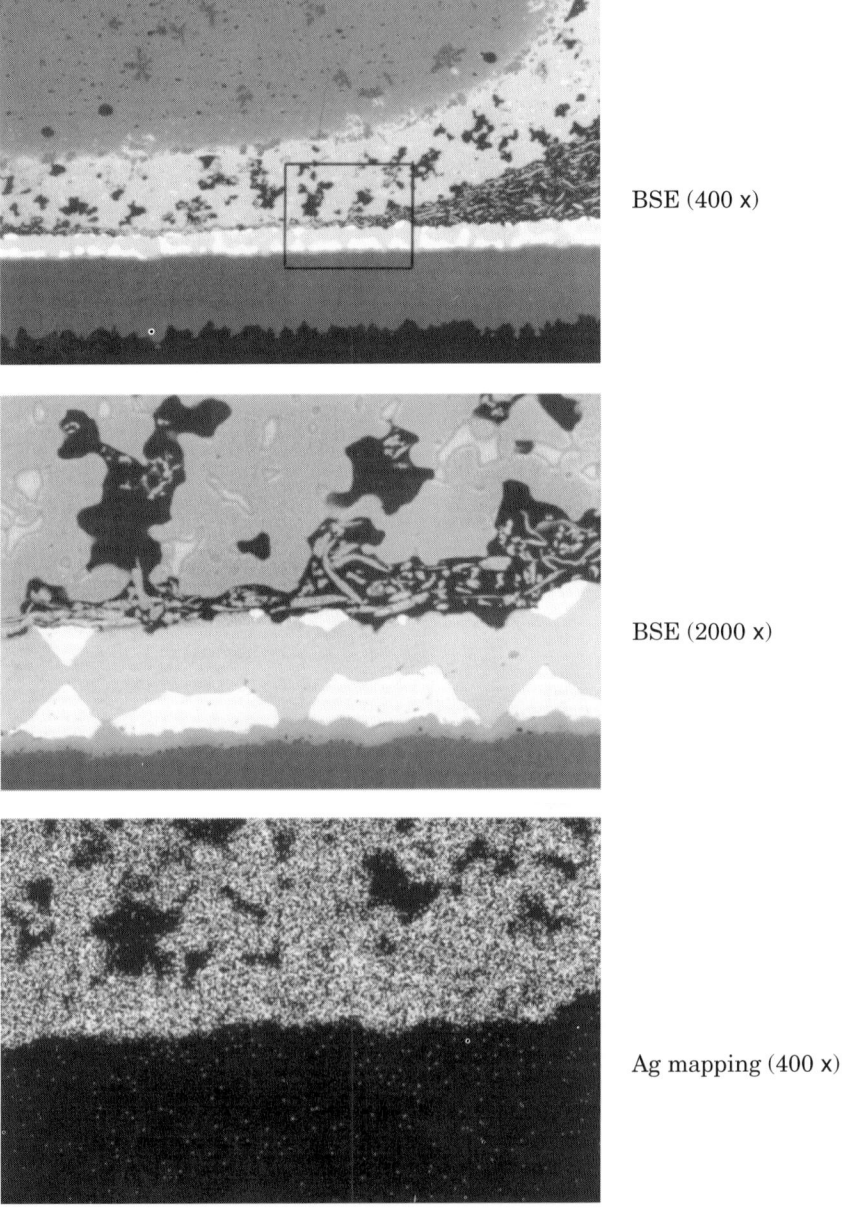

BSE (400 x)

BSE (2000 x)

Ag mapping (400 x)

Fig. 11.18 SEM BSE micrographs of R1206 with AgPd termination joint (CA-6) to pretinned FR-4 board (SnPb 60/40) after 1000 hours of 85°C/85% RH exposure. No large cracks are observed.[69]

11.4.3 Depletion of Silver in Surface Layer of Adhesive

Jagt *et al.*[69] reported evidence of a thin silver-depleted layer between PbSn metallisation and adhesive layer. Auger spectra in combination with Ar-ion sputtering at the adhesive surface after cleavage of the component (adhesion failure at component interface in both cases) indicated a difference before and after damp heat testing. After damp heat testing, a thin layer was present at the adhesive surface (more than 50 nm) without silver. See Figure 11.19 and Table 11.8. Since the observations were made after cleavage at the component side, it cannot be ruled out that crack formation had also occurred. Possibly creep effects at a crack could also lead to a silver-depleted layer at the adhesive surface. It was reported earlier that epoxy resins tend to form electrically insulative layers around metal wires.[80]

An alternative explanation could be the diffusion of Ag into the PbSn layer. Attempts to detect Ag in the PbSn layer, however, failed. At present it is unclear whether or not this is a generally occurring mechanism.

Table 11.8

Auger Analysis and Depth Profiling of Cleaved R1206 (Sn/Pb 90/10) Bonded with CA-6 (Table 11.4) to FR-4 (Cu passivation), see also Figure 11.19 [69]

Pos. Comp. / PWB		Sputter Time (min.)	at % Ag
PWB	□ 1		9.1
	□ 2		-
	○ 1		3.3
	○ 2		0.9
	○ 3		-
Comp.	□ 1		0.3
	□ 2		-
	□ 3		8.3
Comp.	□ 1	3	1.0
	□ 2	3	-
	□ 3	3	26
Comp.	□ 1	10	1.1
	□ 2	10	-
	□ 3	10	39
Comp.	□ 1	20	1.3
	□ 2	20	1.1
	□ 3	20	47
Comp.	□ 1	30	1.1
	□ 2	30	1.2
	□ 3	30	51

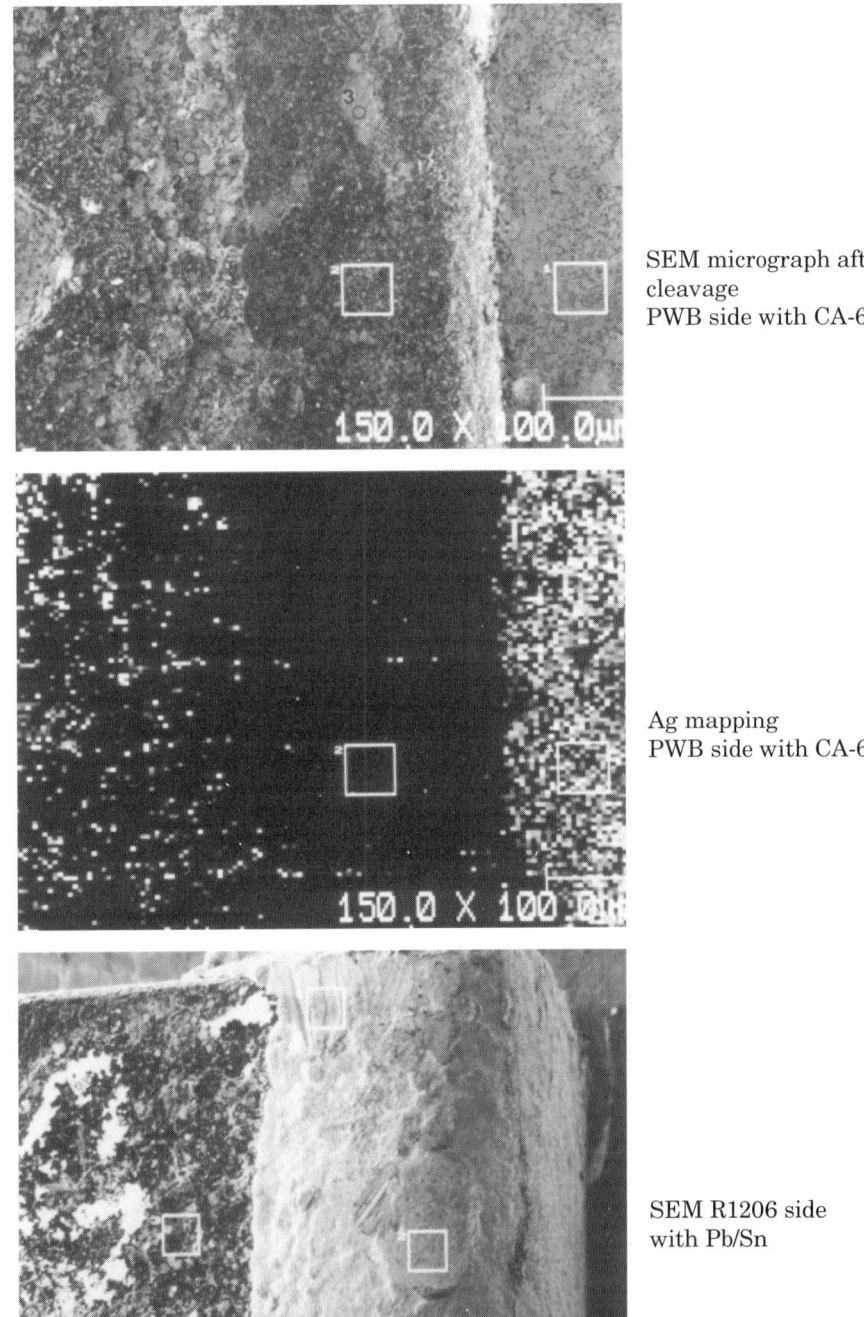

SEM micrograph after
cleavage
PWB side with CA-6

Ag mapping
PWB side with CA-6

SEM R1206 side
with Pb/Sn

Fig. 11.19 SAM microprobe analysis of R1206 with Sn/Pb 90/10 metallisation, bonded with CA-6 to Cu (passivated) FR-4 board.[69] See also Table 11.8.[68]

11.4.4   Creep Effects in the Adhesive Layer

Several authors have suggested an influence of creep effects in the adhesive layer on durability. It has been observed by Keusseyan *et al.*[79] that adhesive showing relatively large compliance mechanically survived more than 3000 cycles of RCT without losing much adhesive strength, but underwent large resistance increases. This phenomenon is thought to be due to the cyclic shear motion of the component lead relative to the substrate, and subsequent visco-plastic deformation of the adhesive. During movements of the metal particles, the adhesive will flow in between, leading to loss of contact points. The fact that the bulk resistance of conductive adhesives does not increase significantly in climate tests, as found by several investigators,[68,71] may seem not to support this explanation, but these measurements are generally performed using a comb geometry and under those conditions the adhesive is not subjected to similar strain movements to those in the adhesive joints.

11.4.5   Formation of an Intermetallic Layer

Increase of resistance after environmental testing by formation of an intermetallic layer of Ag_3Sn was suggested by Habenicht, Orthmann and Wipfelder.[64] The occurrence of such a layer was detected by optical microscopy, and with a scanning electron microscope provided with EDAX, after storage of pretinned lap-shear samples at 150°C. The conductance of this layer is reduced, but mechanical strength is not deteriorated. The use of a solder finish in combination with Ag-filled adhesives was rejected for this reason, and also because of the generally higher contact resistance between Pb/Sn and Ag. During formation of an intermetallic layer, Sn moves into the Ag layer and forms the intermetallic phase at the surface of the Ag flakes. At the same time, Ag atoms diffusing towards the Pb/Sn layer form an intermetallic phase at the Pb/Sn surface (see Figure 11.20). According to Orthmann, the main diffusion direction is from Sn to silver, however. In addition, diffusion of silver due to the Kirkendall effect (hole formation in particles) may decrease the contact area between silver flakes.

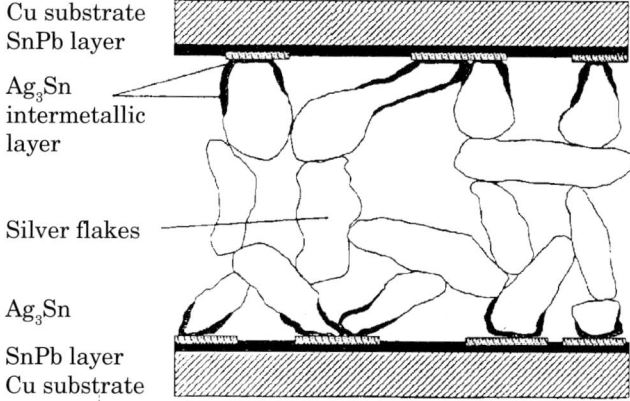

Fig. 11.20 Schematic representation of intermetallic Ag_3Sn formation, according to Ref. 63.

Table 11.9

Overview of Reliability Investigations with Isotropic Conductive Adhesives

Company / Inst. / Univ.	Adhesive	Component	Comp. Metall.	Board Metall.	Test Conditions	Remarks / Conclusions
Univ. Münich/ Siemens (Orthmann)	Epotek H20E	R2412, SOT23, SOT143, IC-6, IC-24	AgPd (SnPb)	FR-4 + Ag-paste metall.	-40°/+150°C; +150°C; -40°C; shock	R(AgPd) ≈ const., but for 2412 and IC-6 in TC (-40/+150°): $R\uparrow$, $\tau\downarrow$ due to $\Delta\alpha$ with board. With SnPb laps: $R\uparrow$, $\tau\downarrow$
IVF (Liu *et al.*)	6 coded adh.	R0805 QFPs	AgPd, SnPb	FR-4; passiv. Cu SnPb	-40°/+85°C; -40°/+125°C; 60°C/90%RH (DH)	R0805: only ICA1<20% $R\uparrow$ on all metallisations in DH. QFP (SnPb), -40/85°C: only ICA5→ $R\approx$c on Au and SnPb. DH: oxid. Cu. -40/125°: for QFP(Au) on Au all ICAs fail. Drop test → delam. +$R\uparrow$. Glob top beneficial. SIR good. No Ag migration.
Philips CFT (Jagt *et al.*)	8 coded adh.	R1206	SnPb, AgPd	FR-4; Au, passiv. Cu, SnPb	85°C/85%RH (DH); +150°C; -40°/125°C	SnPb on Rs→$R\uparrow$, but CA-7,8 →$R \approx$ c in DH. R_{vol}=c. With AgPd $R\approx$c for some CAs after tests. No correl. electr. with mech. results. Evidence for oxid. of Sn/Pb and delamin.
TNO (Botter)	2 coded adh.	R1206, R0603, SO8, SOT23	SnPb, SnAgPd, AgNiPd, Au	FR-4; Cu, SnPb, Sn, Pb, Au, Pd	25° to 80°C/98%RH	Sn causes $R\uparrow$. Cu and Pb → little $R\uparrow$. Evidence for el. chem. corrosion.
Epoxy Technology (Pernice *et al.*)	4 coded adh.	R2512, R3614	SnPb, AgPt, Au	Cu, SnPb	85°C/85%RH (DH) with bias; -55/+125°C	Boards: Cu better than SnPb. Rs: SnPb better than AgPt on SnPb board. Au→$R\approx$c. Bias: with SnPb Rs on Cu or SnPb, CA-E,B → $R\approx$c after DH. -55°/125°C: SnPb Rs on SnPb: only CA-B→$R\approx$c, Au or AgPt→$R\uparrow$.
Univ. Binghampton (Li Li, Morris)	3 coded adh.	R0805	SnPb95/5	FR-4; Au, Cu, SnPb	85°C/85%RH	R0805 (SnPb 95/5) on SnPb or Cu board, only adh.C → low $R\uparrow$. $R_{vol}\approx$c. Influence thickness+fillet adh. + cure degree. TEM: ox. Cu after DH, no SnPb ox. layer (board).

Source	Adhesives	Components	Component metal.	Substrate/finish	Test conditions	Comments
Nordic Project (Hvims et al.)	15 coded adh.	R1206, R0805, R0603, SO28, SQFP48, QFP10, PLCC68	AgPd	FR-4; Au, SnPb	-20/+90°C, 48 cy; 85°C/85%RH 168 h	AgPd termin. + Au board better than SnPb termin. + SnPb board. 1-comp. epoxy better than 2-comp. Silicones inferior. No Ag migration.
US consortium (Zwolinski et al.)	25 coded adh.	QFPs, PLCC44, SOIC, BGA	SnPb	FR-4; Cu passiv., SnPb, NiPd, NiAu	85°C/85%RH (DH), 500 h; 65°C/85%RH	All adhesives fail in drop tests (6 × 60 in. height with PLCC 44). R 1206 (SnPb) passed DH, but SOICs, QFPs, PLCCs did not (R↑>50 mΩ). Also in 65°/85%RH QFPs + PLCCs → large R↑.
IBM (Gaynes et al.)	4 coded adh.	Comb pattern of Cu + finish	-	Pd alloy, Au, Ni, Sn	85°C/85%RH 0°/100°C (2000 h); 120°C (2000 h)	One adh. → low R_c on Pd after tests. Au less good than Pd, Sn bad, Ni worst.
Ablestik (Nguyen et al.)	Ablebond 8175, 8175A	Alumina substrate and Kovar tabs	Cu, Ag, Ni, SnPb	Alox+ AgPd, Sn/Pb/Ag (62/36/2), AgPd, Ag, Cu, Au	85°C/85%RH 150°C; -65°/150°C	For 8175 on AgPd/alumina, 85°C/85% RH → R_s↑ = 14%; Sn/Pb/Ag (62/36/2) → R↑ = 31%; with 8175A R_c = c after 85°C/85%RH.
Alpha Metals (K. Gilleo)	Polysolder	R1206, PLCC-44, 68	SnPb, Au	Polyester-PTF flex, FR-4, Cu	60°/90%RH; vibr., shock; 85°C/85%RH; 60°C/90%RH; -55°C/+85°C, 25 cy; 85°, 500 h	On flex (AgPTF), SnPb SMDs → R↓. On FR-4 (Cu), 85°/85% RH, SnPb SMDs → <20% R↑.

τ = shear strength, R↑ = resistance increase, R ≈ c = resistance constant, R_c = contact resistance, R_v = volume resistance, TC = thermal cycling, DH = damp heat, SIR = surface insulation resistance, ICA = CA = (isotropic) conductive adhesive

Schäfer *et al.*[81,82] performed a transmission electron microscopy (TEM) study after pressure-cooker testing (30 h, 121°C, 100 % RH, 2 bar) of adhesive joints of pretinned R chips on Ag conductor lines on an alumina substrate. They reported the existence of an amorphous intermediate layer of Sn-Pb between the solder and the silver flakes, and diffusion of nano Sn-Pb-O particles (10-20 nm) into the Ag layer. Agglomeration of these particles on Ag flakes near the Sn/Pb layer gives an Sn-Pb-O layer of higher resistance. No evidence was found by these investigators, however, for Ag_3Sn formation.

11.4.6   Ag Migration

In the presence of water (electrolyte) and an electric field (DC voltage), silver can undergo migration phenomena with the formation of dendritic trees, eventually leading to electrical shorts between adjacent conductor patterns. The phenomenon is well known with silver-containing solders, Ag-filled polymer pastes, and Ag-filled lacquers.[83] Ag migration for conductive adhesives has not been observed under test conditions relevant in practice, e.g., 85°C/85% RH or 60°C and 90% RH under 5 V or 12 V bias and conductor pattern spacings ranging from 0.8 mm down to 0.1 mm.[83] It has been claimed that silver migration is less likely to occur in conductive adhesives than in silver inks used in the hybrid industry, because the silver particles are encapsulated with an epoxy polymer layer.[21-26]

However, under more severe conditions, e.g., if conductor patterns are connected by a liquid water film or water drop, migration does occur.[84,85] The risk of Ag migration under severe climatic conditions can be totally eliminated by covering the Ag layer with a suitable organic coating, thus preventing direct contact between the silver layer and water.[23]

11.5   CONCLUSIONS

From the large variety of investigations with conductive adhesives reported so far (see Table 11.9 for overview), it is quite obvious that the type of metallisation of the component leads, and to a lesser extent also the board metallisation, have a very dominant influence on electrical reliability. Au, NiPd and AgPd component metallisations form rather stable and durable joints in combination with Ag-filled epoxy adhesives, although generally not as good as solder joints. In situations where large stresses are built up in solder joints, and fatigue failures are observed, conductive adhesives may give better results (see, e.g., Reference 14).

PbSn metallisations are generally not favourable for conductive adhesives; although some adhesives show better reliability with PbSn metallisations than others, the overall results after harsh environmental testing (e.g., 85°C/85% RH and -40°C to +125°C TC) are not good enough. Some reports about inferior results with noble metals on one (e.g., component) side and the less noble metals on the other (e.g., board, or *vice versa*), due to electrochemical cell formation, need further confirmation and clarification.[70]

At present, the influence of the various process parameters on the electrical properties of the joint is known only globally and needs a more systematic study, for instance of the risk of undercure, fillet size, and bond line thickness, the effect of fast IR cure, cure temperature and time, Tg and moisture level.

With respect to the choice of adhesive, most of the epoxy adhesives show much better electrical durability than acrylate, silicone, or thermoplastic alternatives. Very flexible and low Tg adhesives have inferior electrical properties compared with higher Tg ones. This may be due to increased water uptake and creep of the adhesive at temperatures above Tg.

The validity of the climatic tests for real life durability, however, is questionable in those cases where the test temperatures exceed Tg. If the Tg is situated within the temperature range of the tests, large variations in permeability, water uptake and flexibility can occur. Under normal life conditions, depending on the adhesive, the Tg will not be exceeded in a lot of applications. High Tg values might be favourable in this respect, but they may also lead to higher stresses during thermal cycling (TC). Further improvement of adhesives with respect to both T/H sensitivity and TC resistance is desired.

There is also a large influence of component geometry on test results. The larger components like IC-8, QFPs, but also certain smaller ones like SOT-23 have a relatively small adhesive surface area, and the dimensioning of leads is not very favourable, causing unwanted peel forces on the joints. Some improvement can be achieved by applying non-conductive adhesive underneath the component body or on the leads, at the cost of an extra process step. Clearly, the present components are not designed optimally for conductive adhesive bonding.

The poor behaviour of most adhesives in drop tests is somewhat surprising, given their advantage of higher flexibility than solder. The cohesive strength of the adhesive joints is lower than that of solder and, moreover, in many cases the adhesion strength to the surface is the limiting factor. Again the situation can be much improved by using an extra coating or glob top on the leads or underneath the component body, but direct improvement of adhesive strength would be preferable.

The various possible failure mechanisms (crack formation, delamination, oxidation of PbSn or Cu, and creep) have been identified, but to what extent each of the mechanisms actually contributes to the deterioration of joint resistance in durability tests for different adhesives, components, and metallisations still needs to be resolved.

As an overall conclusion, it can be stated that reliable connection of surface mount components to printed circuit boards is definitely possible with the right selection of adhesive and metallisation. Because the present lead geometries are not at optimum and most common (PbSn) metallisations are not suitable for conductive adhesives in demanding applications, a 'drop-in' replacement for solder is not likely in most cases. In the near future, conductive adhesives will probably be used primarily in those niche applications where the use of solder is problematic. A ban on lead for environmental reasons, however, could quickly initiate much wider use.

11.6   ACKNOWLEDGEMENT

The author gratefully acknowledges the help of his colleagues at Philips CFT: Piet Beris, Gerard Lijten and Harry van Noort in collecting the literature, discussions on the various topics, and for their critical review of the manuscript.

REFERENCES

1   Opila, R. L. and Sinclair, J. D., 'Electrical Reliability of Silver Filled Epoxies for Die Attach', Proceedings IEEE/IRPS, pp. 164-172 (1985).

2   Chung, K. *et al.*, 'MCM Die Attachment Using Low Stress, Thermally Conductive Epoxies', *Surface Mount Technology*, pp. 42-45, May (1991).

3   Shukla, R. K. and Mencinger, N. P., 'A Critical Review of VLSI Die-Attach in High Reliability Applications', *Solid State Technology*, pp. 67-74, July (1985).

4   Brunner, H., 'Leitungsmechanismus und Funktionsverhalten elektrisch leitender Klebungen am Beispiel eines Leistungstransistors', dissertation University of Munich (Institut für Werkstoffen und Verarbeitungswissenschaften), February (1987).

5   Horntvedt, J. E., 'Experience of using Conductive Adhesives in Hybrid Circuitry', Proceedings International Seminar on Recent Achievements in Conductive Adhesive Joining Technology in Electronics Manufacture, IVF, Gothenburg, Sweden, September (1993).

6   Fernandez, L., 'Epoxy Techniques for Hybrid Microwave Integrated Circuits', Proceedings ISHM (1974).

7   Yoshinuma, K., *et al.*, 'An LSI-mounted Membrane Switch using Conductive Adhesive', *Fujikura Technical Review*, pp. 101-105 (1995).

8   Private communication with Messrs Souffriau and Luycks (Emerson and Cuming, Inc., Westerlo, Belgium).

9   Teuscher, J. H. and Garell, R. L., 'Stabilization of Quartz Crystal Oscillators by a Conductive Adhesive', *Analytical Chemistry*, No. 67, pp. 3372-3375 (1995).

10 Lijten, G. F. C. M., van Noort, H. M. and Beris, P. J. M., 'Durability of Anisotropically Conductive Adhesive Joints in Surface Mount Applications and in Flexible to Rigid Board Interconnection', *Journal of Electronics Manufacturing*, **Vol. 5**, No. 4, pp. 253-261 (1995); see also Proceedings International Seminar: Latest Achievements in Conductive Adhesive Joining in Electronic Packaging, Eindhoven, pp. 117-126, September (1995).

11 van Noort, H. M., Kloos, M. J. H. and Schäfer, H. E. A., 'Anisotropic Conductive Adhesives for Chip on Glass Bonding and other Flip Chip Applications', *Journal of Electronics Manufacturing*, **Vol. 5**, No. 1, pp. 27-31, March (1995); see also Proceedings First International Conference on Adhesive Joining Technology in Electronics Manufacture, Berlin, November (1994); Schäfer, H.E.A. and van Noort, H. M., 'Conductive Adhesive Processing for Chip-on-Glass', *ibid.*

12 Schubert, A. *et al.*, 'Mechanisch-thermische Zuverlässigkeit von Chipkarten', *VTE*, **Vol. 8**, No. 5, p. 247 (1996).

13 Moshammer, A., 'Chip-Condensatoren: Kleben statt Löten', *Elektronik*, No. 13, pp. 104-107 (1991).

14 Orthmann, K., 'Leitklebstoffe — mehr als ein Lötersatz (Teil 1)', *Adhäsion*, **Vol. 39**, No. 7, pp. 32-35 (1995); *ibid.*, Teil 2, *Adhäsion*, **Vol. 39**, No. 9, pp. 26-29 (1995).

15 Barbieri, R., Copari, G. and Rudland, D., 'The Use of Adhesive Technology in the Replacement of Solder for the Manufacture of the New FIAT 500 Ignition System', Proceedings ISHM-Nordic, Gothenburg, Sweden, pp. 97-103, September (1993).

16 Hennemann, O.-D., Mieskes, H. and Dorbath, B., 'Entwicklung von neuen Klebtechnologien in der Elektronik, Teilvorhaben: Materialentwicklung für die Anwendung von Leitklebstoffe', Adhäsion Büchreihe, H. Vogel Verlag München (1991).

17 Bolger, J. C. and Mooney, C. T., 'Failure Mechanisms for Epoxy Die Attach Adhesives in Plastic Encapsulated ICs', 33rd Electronic Components Conference, Orlando, FL, May (1983).

18 Bolger, J. C. and Mooney, C. T., 'Die Attach in Hi-Rel P-Dips: Polyimides or Low Chloride Epoxies?', *IEEE Transactions on Components, Hybrids, and Manufacturing Technology*, **Vol. CHMT-7**. No. 4, pp. 394-398, December (1984).

19 Gustafsson, P., 'Adhesives for Die Attach to Lead Frame and Substrates', Proceedings IVF Seminar, Gothenburg, p. 16, October (1991).

20 Guy, J., 'Manufacturing of 25 mil Pitch Surface Mount Assemblies using Conductive Adhesives', Proceedings Printed Circuits and Electronics Assemblies (Nepcon East),

Boston, pp, 374-380 (1994).

21 Rörgren, R. and Liu, J., 'Reliability of Isotropically Conductive Adhesive Joints in Surface Mount Application', First International Conference on Adhesive Joining Technology in Electronics Manufacturing, Berlin, November (1994).

22 Rörgren, R. S. and Liu, J., 'Reliability Assessment of Isotropically Conductive Adhesive Joints in Surface Mount Applications', *IEEE Transactions on Components, Packaging, and Manufacturing Technology, Part B: Advanced Packaging*, **Vol. 18**, No. 2, pp. 305-312, May (1995).

23 Liu, J. and Weman, B., ' Modification of Process and Design Rules to Achieve High Reliable Conductive Adhesive Joints for Surface Mount Technology', Second International Symposium on Electronics Packaging, Shanghai, China, December (1996).

24 Liu, J., Ljungkrona, L. and Lai, Z., 'Development of Conductive Adhesive Joining for Surface-Mounting Electronics Manufacturing', *IEEE Transactions on Components, Packaging, and Manufacturing Technology — Part B*, **Vol. 18**, No. 2, pp. 313-319, May (1995).

25 Liu, J., Rörgren, R. and Ljungkrona, L., 'Avoiding Environmental Regulation by using Conductive Adhesives', European Surface Mount Conference, Brighton, UK, November (1994).

26 Liu, J., Rörgren, R. and Ljungkrona, L., 'High Volume Electronics Manufacturing using Conductive Adhesives for Surface Mounting', Proceedings Surface Mount International, San José, pp. 291-302, August/September (1994).

27 Ogunjimi, A.O. *et al.*, 'A Review of the Impact of Conductive Adhesive Technology on Interconnection', *Journal of Electronics Manufacturing*, **Vol. 2**, pp. 109-118 (1992).

28 Ireland, J. E., 'Epoxy Bleedout in Ceramic Chip Carriers', *International Journal for Hybrid Microelectronics*, **Vol. 5**, No. 1 (1982).

29 (a) Gilleo, K., 'Poly-Solder-C: A Breakthrough in Junction Stability under Humidity Aging and Thermal Cycle Stress', Adhesives in Electronics, First International Conference on Adhesive Joining Technology in Electronics Manufacturing, Berlin, November (1994); (b) Gilleo, K., 'SMT+Flex = Maximum Versatility and Reliability', *Electronic Packaging & Production*, pp. 56-59, July (1992).

30 Gilleo, K., 'Assembly with Conductive Adhesives', *Soldering & Surface Mount Technology*, No. 19, pp. 12-17, February (1995).

31 Kooring, C. W. L. and Riphagen, D., 'Application of Conductive Adhesives in Microcircuits for "Long-Life" Equipment', *Electrocomponent Science & Technology*, **Vol. 7**, pp. 69-75 (1980).

32 See Chapter 3 of this book.

33 Lyons, A. M., 'Electrically Conductive Adhesives: Effect of Particle Composition and Size Distribution', ANTEC '90, pp. 843-845 (1990).

34 *ibid*, *Polymer Engineering and Science*, **Vol. 31**, No. 6, March (1991).

35 Pandiri, S. M., 'The Behavior of Silver Flakes in Conductive Epoxy Adhesives', *Adhesive Age*, pp. 31-35, October (1987).

36 See Reference 60: Appendix, p. 24.

37 Nguyen, G. P., Williams, J. R., Gibson, F. W. and Winster, T., 'Electrical Reliability of Conductive Adhesive for Surface-Mount Applications', Proceedings ISHM '93, pp. 50-55 (1993).

38 Nguyen, G. P. *et al.*, 'Conductive Adhesives: Reliable and Economical Alternatives to Solder Paste for Electrical Applications', DVS Berichte, Proceedings EuPac '94, Essen, pp. 218-223 (1994).

39 Nguyen, G. P. *et al.*, 'Conductive Adhesives: Reliable and Economical Alternatives to Solder Paste for Electrical Applications', Proceedings Surface Mount International Conference, pp. 310-318 (1992).

40 Nguyen, G. P. *et al.*, 'Conductive Adhesives', *Circuits Assembly*, pp. 36-39, January (1993).

41 Nguyen, G. P. *et al.*, 'Electrical Reliability of Conductive Adhesives for Surface-Mount Applications', International Seminar on Recent Achievements in Conductive Adhesive Joining Technology in Electronics Manufacturing, Gothenburg, Sweden, September (1993).

42   Youn, A., 'Adhesive Attachment of Tantalum Capacitors: Solutions to Persistent Problems', Adhesives in Electronics '94, First International Conference on Adhesive Joining Technology in Electronics Manufacturing, Berlin, November (1994).

43   Van Den Bosch, A. and Luyckx, G., 'Conductive Adhesives, A Feasible Challenge?', Adhesive in Electronics '96: Second International Conference on Adhesive Joining and Coating Technology in Electronics Manufacturing, Stockholm, Sweden, pp. 160-166, June (1996).

44   Hennemannn, O.-D., Mieskes, H. and Dorbath, B., 'Entwicklung von neuen Klebtechnologien in der Elektronik', Adhäsion Buchreihe, Heinrich Vogel GmbH, Munich (1991).

45   Pujol, J. M. *et al.*, 'Electroconductive Adhesives: Comparison of Three Different Polymer Matrices, Epoxy, Polyimide and Silicone', *Journal of Adhesion*, **Vol. 27**, No. 4, pp. 213-229 (1989).

46   See also Ref. 16, p. 22.

47   Lutz, M. A. and Cole, R. L., 'High Performance Electrically Conductive Silicone Adhesives', *Hybrid Circuits*, No. 23, pp. 27-30, September (1990).

48   See also Ref. 16, p. 19 and Ref. 45.

49   Adell, J. A. *et al.*, 'Adhesives for Electronic Applications', *Hybrid Circuits*, No. 31, May (1993).

50   Hvims, H. L., 'Conductive Adhesives for SMT and Potential Applications', *IEEE Transactions on Components, Packaging, and Manufacturing Technology, Part B: Advanced Packaging*, **Vol. 18**, No. 2, pp. 284-291, May (1995).

51   Hvims, H. L., 'Solder Replacement', *Soldering & Surface Mount Technology*, No.17, pp. 12-19, May (1994).

52   Ying, L., 'A Novel Approach, Thermoplastic Die Attach Adhesive'; King, H. A., 'Organic Solder, A New Type of Adhesive Conductor for Electronics', SAMPE Electronic Materials & Process Conference, Santa Clara, California, June (1987).

53   Shores, A. A., 'Adhesive Bonding Hybrid Microcircuit Substrates with a Thermoplastic Film', *SAMPE Quarterly*, pp. 49-53, April (1988).

54   Ongley, P. E. *et al.*, 'New Innovations in Thermoplastic Die Attach Adhesives for Microelectronic Packaging', Proceedings International Seminar: Latest Achievements in Conductive Adhesive Joining in Electronics Packaging, Philips, Eindhoven, pp. 91-111, September (1995).

55   Firmstone, M. G. *et al.*, 'Benefit of Thermoplastic Conductive Adhesives in Advanced Electronics Packaging Applications', Proceedings International Seminar: Latest Achievements in Conductive Adhesive Joining in Electronics Packaging, Philips, Eindhoven, pp. 69-85, September (1995).

56   Kang, S. K. *et al.*, 'New High Conductivity Lead (Pb)-Free Conducting Adhesives', Proceedings IEEE International Symposium on Electronics and the Environment ISEE, Orlando, FL, pp. 177-181, May (1995).

57   Bauer, A. and Tränkner, M., 'Reliability of Conductive Adhesive Joints on Solder Covered Surfaces', DVS Berichte, No. 158 , Proceedings EuPac '94, Essen, pp. 209-212 (1994).

58   Adell, J. A. *et al.*, 'Adhesives for Electronic Applications', *Hybrid Circuits*, No. 31, May (1993); K. F. Schoch and A. I. Bennett, 'Electrical Evaluation of Conductive Adhesives', *Transactions IEEE*, pp. 291-293 (1985).

59   Bayer, H. and Hekele, W., 'UV Cure Options for Conductive Resin Systems', Adhesives in Electronics '96, Second International Conference on Adhesive Joining and Coating Technology in Electronics Manufacturing', Stockholm, Sweden, pp. 38-42, June (1996).

60   Hvims, H. L., Preliminary Report Conductive Adhesives in SMT, Elektronik Centralen, Hoersholm, Denmark, Appendix, p. 46 (1993).

61   Chorbadjiev, K. G. and Kotzev, D. L., 'The Effect of Fillers upon the Properties of Electroconductive Cyanoacrylate Adhesives', *International Journal of Adhesion and Adhesives*, **Vol. 18**, No. 3, pp. 143-146 (1988).

62   Wipfelder, E. and Orthmann, K., 'Elektrisch leitfähige Klebstoffe für elektronische Bauteile', *Adhäsion*, No. 11, pp. 26-31 (1989).

63   Orthmann, K., 'Elektrische und mechanische Eigenschaften von Leitklebungen im Vergleich

zu Lötungen bei der Leiterplattentechnik', Heinrich Vogel GmbH, München (1991).

64 Habenicht, G. *et al.*, 'Elektrische und mechanische Eigenschaften von SMD-Leitklebungen und Lötungen', *Adhäsion*, No. 11, pp. 10-15 (1991).

65 Orthmann, K., 'Leitklebstoffe — mehr als ein Lötersatz (Teil 1)', *Adhäsion*, **Vol. 39**, No. 7, pp. 32-34 (1995).

66 *ibid* (Teil 2), *Adhäsion*, **Vol. 39**, No. 9, pp. 26-29 (1995).

67 Kay, P. J. and Mackay, C. A., 'The Growth of Intermetallic Compounds on Common Basis Materials Coated with Tin and Tin-Lead Alloys', *Transactions of the Institute of Metal Finishing*, **Vol. 54**, pp. 68-74 (1976).

68 Jagt, J. C., Beris, P. J. M. and Lijten, G. F. C. M., 'Electrically Conductive Adhesives: A Prospective Alternative for SMD Soldering?', *IEEE Transactions on Components, Packaging, and Manufacturing Technology, Part B*, **Vol. 18**, No. 2, pp. 293-297 (1995).

69 Jagt, J. C., 'Isotropic Conductive Adhesives: Durability Aspects and Failure Causes', Seminar on Electrically Conductive Adhesives at Delco Electronics, February (1996).

70 Botter, E., 'Factors that Influence the Electrical Contact Resistance of Isotropic Adhesive Joints during Climate Chamber Testing', Adhesives in Electronics '96, Second International Conference on Adhesive Joining and Coating Technology in Electronics Manufacturing, Stockholm, Sweden, pp. 30-37, June (1996).

71 Li, L., 'Basic and Applied Studies of Electrically Conductive Adhesives', Dissertation, State University of New York at Binghamton (1995).

72 Pernice, R. F., Hannafin, J. J. and Estes, R. H., 'Evaluation of Isotropic Conductive Adhesives for Solder Replacement', Proceedings 27th International Symposium on Microelectronics (1994).

73 Li, L. *et al.*, 'Electrical, Structural and Processing Properties of Electrically Conductive Adhesives', *IEEE Transactions on Components, Hybrids, and Manufacturing Technology*, **Vol. 16**, No.8, pp. 843-851, December (1993).

74 Kim, H. *et al.*, 'Processing, Structural and Electrical Properties of Electrically Conductive Adhesives', *Transactions IEEE*, pp. 311-319 (1993).

75 Li, L. and Morris, J. E., 'Structure and Selection Models for Anisotropic Conductive Adhesive Films', *Journal of Electronics Manufacturing*, **Vol. 5**, No. 1, pp. 9-17, March (1995).

76 Gaynes, M. A., Lewis, R. H., Saraf , R. F. and Roldan, J. M., 'Evaluation of Contact Resistance for Isotropic Electrically Conductive Adhesives', *IEEE Transactions on Components, Packaging, and Manufacturing Technology, Part B: Advanced Packaging*, **Vol. 18**, No. 2, pp. 299-304, May (1995).

77 Zwolinski, M. *et al.*, 'Electrically Conductive Adhesives for Surface Mount Solder Replacement', Adhesives in Electronics '96, Second International Conference on Adhesive Joining and Coating Technology in Electronics Manufacturing, Stockholm, Sweden, pp. 333-340, June (1996).

78 *ibid*, Proceedings Surface Mount International, San José, pp. 391-401, September (1996).

79 Keusseyan, R. L. and Dilday, J. L., 'Electric Contact Phenomena in Conductive Adhesive Interconnections', Proceedings International Symposium on Microelectronics, ISHM '93, pp. 44-49 (1993).

80 See Ref. 60, Appendix, p. 41.

81 Schäfer, H. *et al.*, 'AEM Investigations of Interfaces of Electrically Conductive Adhesive Joints', DVS Berichte, **Vol. 141**, *Verbindungstechnik in der Elektronik*, pp. 134-141, February (1992).

82 Schäfer, H. *et al.*, 'Beständigkeit elektrisch leitfähiger Klebverbindungen', *Adhäsion*, **Vol. 38**, pp. 30-33 (1994).

83 For silver migration, see Ref. 50, Ref. 71, pp. 26-28, and D.D. Chang *et al.*, *IEEE Transactions on Components, Hybrids, and Manufacturing Technology*, **Vol. 16**, No. 8, pp. 836-842 (1993).

84 (a) Hennemann, O.-D., Mieskes, H. and Dorbath, B., 'Entwicklung von neuen Klebtechnologien in der Elektronik', Adhäsion Buchreihe, Heinrich Vogel GmbH, München, p. 30 (1991). (b) see Ref. 70.

85 Wong, W., 'Electronically Conductive Adhesives: Conduction Mechanisms, Mechanical Behavior and Durability', University Microfilms International, Ann Arbor, USA, Dissertation Clarkson University, Potsdam, NY, USA (1995); UMI order No. DA9527571.

86 Private communication with Mr S. Corbett of Polyflex Circuits.

Chapter 12

ELECTRICALLY CONDUCTIVE JOINTS USING NON-CONDUCTIVE ADHESIVES (NCAs) IN SURFACE MOUNT APPLICATIONS

ANDREAS BAUER

CEM — Centrum für Mikroverbindungstechnik in der Elektronik,
Neumünster/Itzehoe, Germany

THOMAS GESANG

Fraunhofer Institut für Fertigungstechnik únd Angewandte
Materialforschung (IFAM), Bremen, Germany

12.1 INTRODUCTION AND LITERATURE REVIEW

Electrically conductive adhesive joints can be formed using non-filled organic adhesives, i.e., without any conductive filler particles. The bulk material of these adhesives or polymers insulates well and shows high electrical break-down voltages. Hence, the technique is called 'Joining with Non-conductive Adhesives (NCAs)', although it must be taken into account that very thin layers (below 1 µm) of polymers or other organic substances can contribute to electrical conductivity by different conduction mechanisms like tunnelling, hopping and charge carrier injection (see 12.5 and Reference1). Intrinsically conductive organic materials, e.g., synthetic metals[2,4] have not been utilised to date in adhesive formulation and are not dealt with in this chapter.

The electrical connection is achieved by sealing the two contact partners under pressure and heat. Thus, a small gap contact is created, approaching the two surfaces to the distance of the surface asperities. The formation of contact spots depends on the surface roughness of the contact partners. Approaching the two surfaces first a small number of small contact spots are formed which allow the electric current to flow. When the parts are pressed together during the sealing process, the number and area of the single contact spots are increased according to the macroscopic elasticity or flexibility of the parts and the microhardness and plasticity of their surfaces, respectively (see Figure 12.1). The joining pressure applied effects a mechanical contact load at all these spots. When the joining pressure is maintained during cooling, the adhesive filling the gap around the contact spots partly 'freezes' this contact load as well as providing the mechanical strength of the bond. The curing shrinkage of the adhesive and a thermal contraction of the adhesive which is larger than that of the contact metal causes an additional contact load. Figure 12.2 summarises the influential parameters for the formation of an NCA joint.

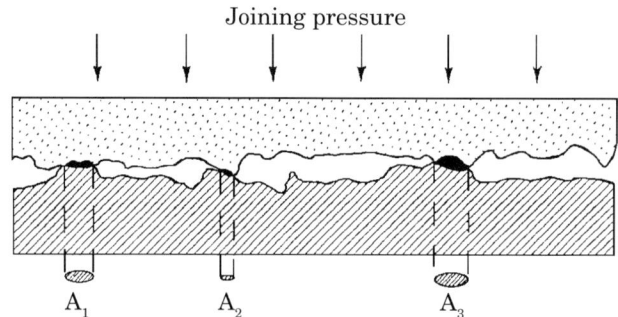

Fig. 12.1 Schematic of the contact formation for electrically conductive adhesive joints using non-conductive adhesives. The overlap at the contact points corresponds to a microdeformation of asperities which causes an enlargement of contact areas A1 to A3.[36]

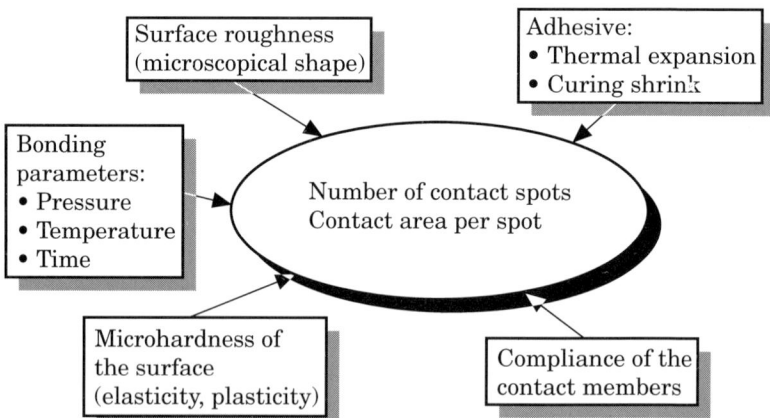

Fig. 12.2 Parameters influencing the formation of a conductive adhesive joint with non-conductive adhesive (NCA).

Conductive joining with non-conductive adhesives provides a number of advantages compared with other adhesive bonding techniques using isotropically or anisotropically conductive adhesives. NCA joints avoid short-circuiting and are not limited, in terms of particle size or percolation phenomena, to a reduction of connector pitches. Further advantages are cost-effectiveness of the adhesives, ease of processing regarding the possibility of non-structured adhesive application, good compatibility with a wide range of contact materials, low temperature cure and environmental friendliness by avoiding flux media or washing.

12.1.1   Literature Review

The formation of stationary electrical contacts by joining with non-filled adhesive is a fairly new technique in microelectronics packaging. The joining method was first reported in 1983 in a patent application by Cognard and Ganguillet[5], who performed tests with several material combinations. The function principle, however, was not accurately interpreted. Other patents and publications followed until 1987.[6,7]

A first industrial application using galvanically formed Au-bumped chips for a flip-chip on glass technology (COG) at Matsushita Corporation was reported by Hatada in 1988.[8,9] In this case a light-setting insulating adhesive was used which was hardened by UV irradiation through the glass substrate with pressure from the chip side. The advantage of the reported material combination is the excellent coplanarity of the glass substrate as well as the bumped chip.

Pape[10,11] pointed out the feasibility of NCA joints with epoxy and cyanacralate adhesives using test samples of polyester foil with a Ni surface and SMT components with a solder-covered surface, passing reliability testing up to 200 h. A contact resistance smaller than 100 mΩ and a joint strength of more than 10 N/mm^2 was achieved.

Kristiansen *et al.*[12] investigated the reliability of NCA joints using flexible circuits (Kapton with Cu metallisation) on liquid crystal display panels (ITO surface) as well as on FR-4 PCB. A stable contact resistance over 1000 h humidity testing (80%/85°C) and 1000 temperature cycles (-30°C to 90°C) was observed. Further experiments by Kristiansen *et al.* employing fine-pitch SMT components on FR-4 boards both with solder-covered surfaces showed the feasibility of NCA joining, whereas an evaluation of reliability features was not possible.[13]

Schäfer *et al.*[14,15] investigated NCA joints of flexible circuits with Cu connectors and indium-tin-oxide structures (ITO) on liquid crystal displays. This work proved the feasibility of this technology and showed that even copper surfaces are sufficiently stable in humid climate (40°C/95% RH, 480 h) with an appropriate surface pretreatment prior to bonding.

NCA joints have recently been applied to flip-chip bonding on rigid or flexible printed circuit boards in surface mount technology. Electrical contacts and the underfilling are created in one sealing step.

Aschenbrenner *et al.*[16-20] used mechanically formed Au stud bumps on the chip side, printed circuit boards (FR-4) or flexible substrates (Espanex) with Cu/Ni/Au metallisation and a thermosetting/thermoplastic adhesive film. The use of these relatively large (65-80 μm height), highly deformable gold stud bumps reduces the coplanarity requirements of the process. The connections showed low contact resistances (< 7 mΩ) and a good reliability performance in thermal cycling (-55 to 125°C, 1000 cycles) and constant humidity exposure (85°C/85%, 1000 h). NCA joining in flip-chip technology with mechanically created Au bumps is a promising option for low-cost, low volume production because no additional mask processing steps at wafer level are required.

Kivilahti *et al.*[21,22] studied NCA joints of Au-bumped flip chips on FR-4 or flexible substrates with fusible SnIn coatings. Metallurgical contacts are achieved which show good reliability performance. In this case the metallurgical compatibility of the solder coating and the contact partner is questioned.

Nagle *et al.*[23] evaluated flip-chip technology with NCA joints using bumped chips (electroless NiAu) and FR-4 substrate with copper tracks coated by solder or electroless NiAu. A copper track plated with fusible solder forming a metallurgical contact and a NiAu plated structure forming a pressure contact are shown in Figures 12.3 to 12.5. NCA flip-chip assembly is found

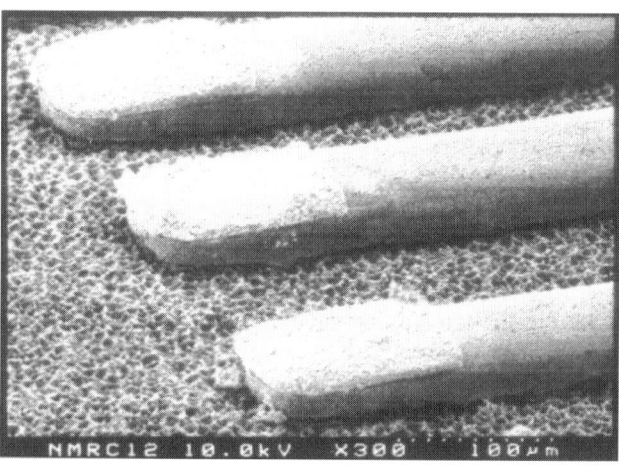

Fig. 12.3 Solder coatings (5 μm layer of electroplated Sn60Pb40 solder) on the ends of copper tracks on an FR-4 substrate prior to NCA flip-chip assembly. (Courtesy of R. Nagle, NMRC, Cork, Ireland)

Fig. 12.4 Microsection of an NCA flip-chip joint with fusible solder coating. FR-4 substrate with 5 μm solder layer on the copper tracks; flip chip with 10 μm electroless NiAu bumps. The area between the connectors is filled with non-conductive adhesive. (Courtesy of R. Nagle, NMRC, Cork, Ireland)

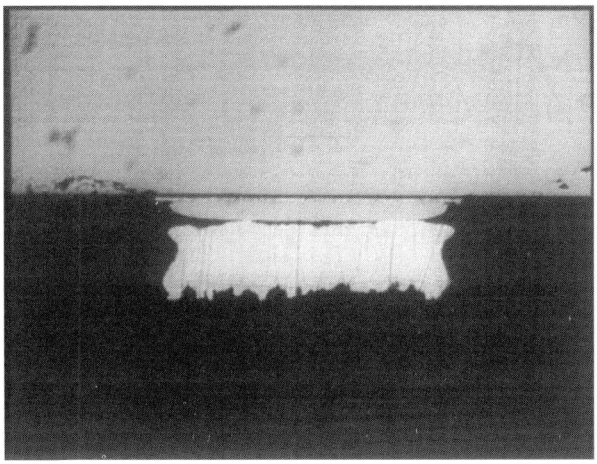

Fig. 12.5 Microsection of an NCA flip-chip joint with NiAu coated surfaces. FR-4 substrate with copper tracks (23 μm x 100 μm) and 10 μm electroless NiAu bumps on the flip-chip side. The surrounding area is filled with non-conductive adhesive. (Courtesy of R. Nagle, NMRC, Cork, Ireland)

to ensure good electrical connection, with contact resistances of about 30 mΩ, when sufficient coplanarity of the joining partners is guaranteed. Solder coatings appear to improve the long-term reliability of the contacts in humidity testing (85°C/85%) even when compared with flip-chip joints using anisotropic conductive adhesives.

The investigations reported in References 24-30 are based on work carried out at the Centrum für Mikroverbindungstechnik (CEM), Neumünster, and at the Fraunhofer Institut für Angewandte Materialforschung (IFAM), Bremen between 1993 and 1996, and are summarised in the following sections. Experiments on NCA joining of fine-pitch SMT components, high current performance and the conduction mechanism will be discussed.

12.2 NCA JOINING AND THEORY OF CONTACT FORMATION

In principle, the situation in a conductive NCA joint is similar to that of releasable electrical contacts, which have been investigated for several decades. In this well-known field of material research and technology, a complete theory of electrical contacts was developed. An excellent introduction to this theory is given in the book of R. Holm.[31] Other publications describe the formation of contact resistances[32,33] or develop models for the size of the contact area.[34-36] The Hertzian theory predicts the dependence between the size of contact spots and the pressure distribution across the contact area, applying a purely elastic model for a sphere on a plane as the idealised contact spot geometry:[35]

$$r = (3F_n \bullet R/4E')^{1/3} \text{ and} \tag{12.1}$$

$$P_{max} = 3F_n/2 \pi r^2 \tag{12.2}$$

where

r = radius of the area of a contact spot
R = radius of the sphere
F_n = normal force
E^n = effective modulus of the materials
P_{max} = maximum value of the Hertzian stress

According to Holm,[31] the contact resistance observed can be explained by a constriction resistance and a film resistance. The constriction resistance is related to the confinement of the current flow on to the small area of conducting spots (see Figure 12.6). The film resistance is caused by insulating

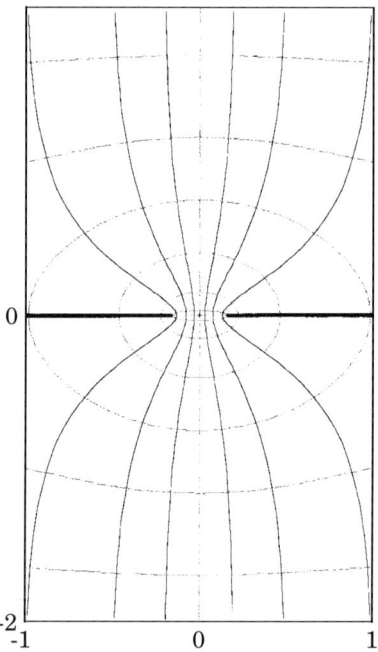

Fig. 12.6 Current flow and the equipotential lines of an idealised circular contact spot geometry between two long rods.

or poorly conducting films (tarnish films or, in the case of NCA joints, thin adhesive layers) which reduce the fraction of metallic contact of the contact areas or contribute with a film resistivity or tunnel resistivity to the contact resistance. The constriction resistance, R_c, of a circular contact area with radius a can be calculated as:

$$R_c = \rho/2a \tag{12.2}$$

where ρ is the bulk resistivity of the symmetrical contact partners. Taking into account that the temperature in the contact rises due to the heat dissipation of the current, an additional factor has to be introduced:

$$R_c = (1 + \frac{2}{3} \cdot \alpha \, \Theta) \cdot \rho/2a \tag{12.3}$$

where α is the temperature coefficient of the metal resistivity and Θ is the so-called maximum supertemperature of the contact spot (i.e., the difference between the maximum contact spot temperature T_c and the bulk temperature T_0: $\Theta = T_c - T_0$). Assuming that the generated heat and the electrical current take the same flow paths in a symmetrical contact, the maximum supertemperature can be calculated from the thermal conductivity, λ, the electric resistivity, ρ, and the contact voltage, U:[31]

$$\int_{T_0}^{T_0 + \Theta} \rho\lambda dT = U^2/8 \qquad (12.4a)$$

$$\text{or } \{\rho\lambda\}\Theta = U^2/8 \qquad (12.4b)$$

where a mean value $\{\rho\lambda\}$ in the temperature range can be calculated.

As an example, Table 12.1 shows the calculated values for copper, whereby the results are valid for all metals above room temperature according to Widemann-Franz's law: $\rho\lambda = \text{const}$.[37] The supertemperature in the contact spots can reach considerable values and it is even possible to reach the melting temperature of the contact metal. It is obvious that such high temperatures cause a change in the elastic and plastic properties of the metal at the contact spots (i.e., softening or melting), and therefore usually enlarge the contact area so that the contact voltage is reduced. These effects are known as the softening drop or melting drop of the contact resistance. However, in the case of NCA joints the influence of the thin adhesive layer in the intermediate joining gap around the contact spots has to be added. This will be discussed in 12.5.

Table 12.1

Calculated Values of the Supertemperature Θ for Copper at Different Contact Voltages (* softening temperature of Cu, ** melting temperature of Cu; all data taken from Ref. 31

U	[V]	0.03	0.12	0.3	0.41
Θ	[°C]	16	190*	700	1063**
$(1 + 2/3 \cdot \alpha\,\Theta)$		1.04	1.5	2.8	3.8

A contact is called metallic when a direct metal-to-metal contact is formed, and quasimetallic when a very thin film (< 1 nm) allows a good penetration of electrons by means of the tunnel effect. According to Reference 32, only gold or high percentage gold alloys as contact members allow the formation of almost pure metallic contacts with little or no surface films. In most other cases thin tarnish films or other organic films are present on the contact surface, creating a film resistance R_f which contributes to the contact resistance. In a real contact, both areas with metallic and areas with quasimetallic contact behaviour will be found within the load bearing contact spot. In NCA joints, additionally thin adhesive films must be regarded which were not squeezed out during the joining process (for further discussion refer to 12.4). The film resistance then becomes:

$$R_f = \eta/\pi a^2 \qquad (12.5)$$

where η is the (specific) film resistivity and a is the radius of a circular contact spot area. The total contact resistance becomes:

$$R_{contact} = R_c + R_f \qquad (12.6)$$

For a complete treatment of the theory of contacts, the reader is referred to Reference 31. Regarding NCA joints, the theory of electrical contacts has to be modified slightly with respect to the presence of adhesive in the intermediate gap between the contact partners.

In summary, the contact performance and reliability of the joint are seen to be highly dependent on the type of contact partners. Not only do the chemical state and mechanical properties of the surface material influence the quality of the joint but also the geometrical form and mechanical properties of the bulk material (e.g., compliance of a foil or workpiece).

12.3 APPLICATIONS IN FINE-PITCH SURFACE MOUNT TECHNOLOGY

Various applications in surface mount technology have already been investigated, as outlined earlier. The studies presented here deal specifically with the adhesive interconnection of fine-pitch surface mount components (QFP-160) to rigid printed circuit boards (see Figure 12.7).

Fig. 12.7 Fine-pitch surface mount component QFP-160 bonded on an FR-4 PCB substrate. (Length of marker: 10 mm)

12.3.1 Materials and Manufacturing Process

The investigations focus on a solder-covered surface complemented by Cu and Pd surfaces. The QFP-160 connector leads with a pitch of 0.65 mm in gull-wing form (Figure 12.8) consist of Cu97Fe3-leadframe material electroplated with PbSn solder. The Cu surfaces were made by stripping the PbSn solder and coating with a corrosion inhibitor. The substrates used were Cu-plated FR-4 printed circuit boards used either bare, with hot air levelled Pb-Sn solder or with chemical Pd plating. The adhesives used were a thermosetting two-component epoxy resin and a reactive thermoplastic film adhesive.

The joining process was performed with a commercially available heat seal press (HSC) with pneumatic pressure application, as used for heatsealing of anisotropic adhesives. Special pressing tools moulded to the shape of the component had to be constructed to seal two or four sides of the element

Fig. 12.8 Connector lead of the QFP-160 component showing the gull-wing geometry.

simultaneously. The joints were formed at a pressure of ca. 1 N/mm² (0.3 N per lead for a nominal contact area of 0.29 mm² per lead). The cure conditions were 10 min. at 120°C for the epoxy and 30 s at 180°C for the thermoplast (for temperature profiles, see Figure 12.9). There is still potential for optimisation of the cure.

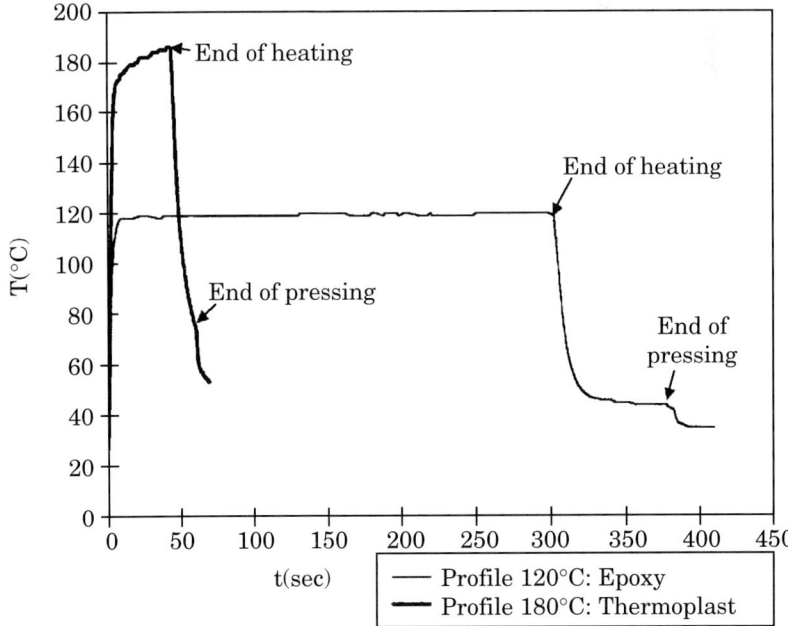

Fig. 12.9 Temperature *vs* time profiles of the joining process for epoxy and thermoplastic adhesives.

In order to achieve homogeneous pressure and temperature profiles, one of the main features of this pressing tool is the coplanarity of the heating electrodes. The temperature profile depends on the heat conduction within the tool and the thermal contact to the leads, which is also dependent on the local pressure at each lead. At the corners of the element a temperature decrease of less than 5°C was observed when a suitable heating electrode design was employed (see Figure 12.10). The pressure profile depends on the elasticity and coplanarity of the sample and the tool.

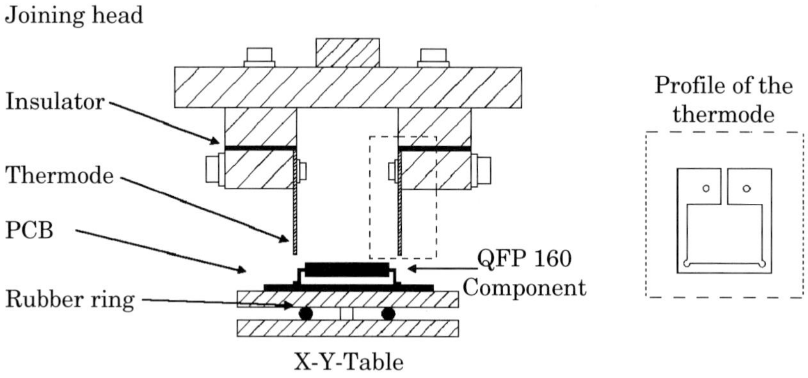

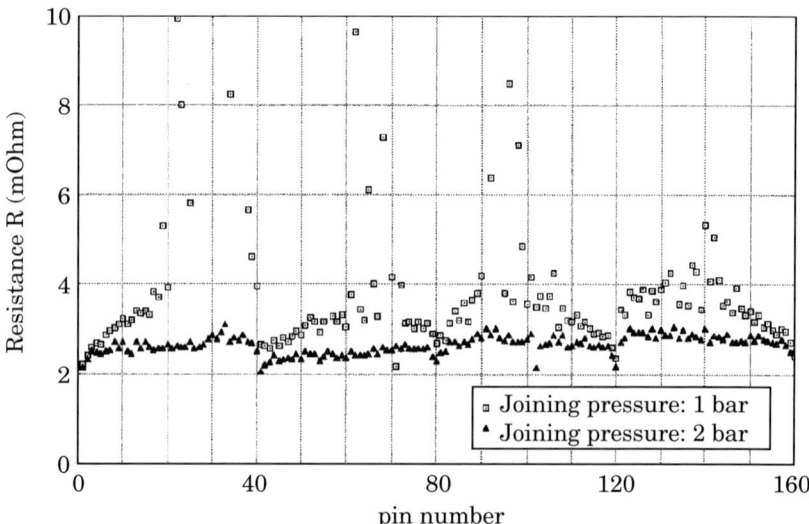

Fig. 12.10 Sketch of one of the heating electrodes used.

A minimum joining pressure, here ca. 0.3 N/lead, is required to allow a reliable connection of each of the 160 leads. Figure 12.11 shows the influence of the joining pressure on the distribution of contact resistances over the 160 leads and its dependence on the joining pressure in the case of solder-plated surfaces. A joining pressure of 0.4 N/lead (triangles in Figure 12.11) makes it possible to connect all 160 leads of a component with a contact resistance of about 3 mΩ and a statistical scattering of below 1 mΩ.

Fig. 12.11 Distribution of contact resistance over 160 connector leads for joining pressures of 0.2 N/lead (circles) and 0.4 N/lead (triangles).

In order to achieve a reliable joining process, an important parameter is the geometrical form of the leads, especially the angle of their contact faces to the substrate plane. Lead forms and geometric tolerances of SMD leads are commonly adapted to the soldering process. However, for NCA joining the requirements are different. The two different lead forms shown in Figure 12.12 (a) and (b) are both within the specified tolerance of the chosen QFP component which is optimised for the soldering process. During the adhesive sealing process the specimen in Figure 12.12 (a) suffers elastic deformation, frozen by the adhesive, which can damage the joint at a later stage. A suitable lead form for NCA joining is shown in Figure 12.12 (b).

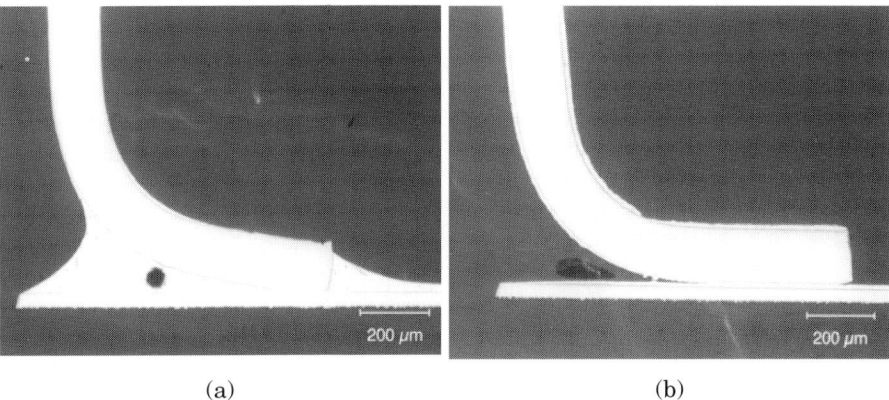

(a)   (b)

Fig. 12.12 Comparison of two different gull-wing lead forms: (a) soldered joint; (b) NCA joint on a copper-clad printed circuit board. The form of the gull-wing lead in (a) is optimised for the soldering process but less suitable for NCA adhesive joining whereas the gull-wing lead in (b) shows an optimal geometry for NCA joining.

12.3.2 Morphology and Electrical Properties of the Joints

The contact areas are found to be much smaller than the nominal lead contact area. Due to this difficulty in the definition of the contact area, all measurement values are given in resistances, not in specific area resistivities. The actual contact area per gull wing lead strongly depends on the surface material and its capability to deform plastically. The solder-plated surfaces are widely deformed and tend to create extended areas where the adhesive is almost completely displaced from the joining gap (see Figure 12.25 later). Also, the formation of a reliable contact on all 160 leads depends on the plastic deformability of the surfaces. The cross-sections in Figures 12.13 and 12.14 show the morphology of a typical NCA joint of solder-coated surfaces with an epoxy adhesive. The fine adhesive gap shown in Figure 12.14 was further investigated by TEM. Relatively extended regions with metallic contact surrounded by an adhesive gap of less than 1 μm were observed (Figure 12.15). Using thermoplastic adhesive to join the solder-coated surfaces, such areas with extended metallic contact were not observed.

Different morphologies of the contact region are observed when non-deformable surfaces, such as Cu or Pd, or flexible joining partners like foil materials are used. In contrast to solder-coated contact members, NCA joints

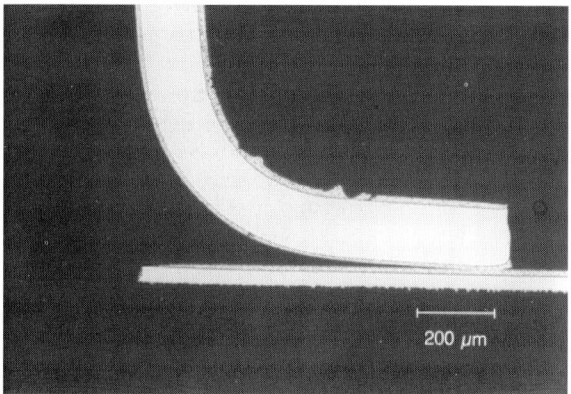

Fig. 12.13 Cross-section of a conductive adhesive joint with non-conductive epoxy adhesive (overview). Gull-wing lead and copper track on the printed circuit board are solder plated.

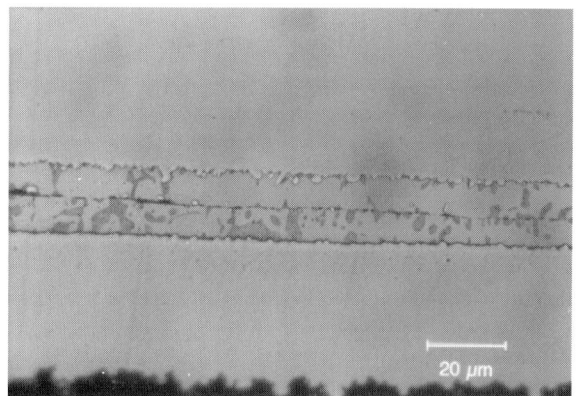

Fig. 12.14 Detail of the contact area of the NCA joint with solder-plated contact partners shown in Fig. 12.13. A very fine adhesive gap filled with epoxy adhesive and a number of contact spots can be seen.

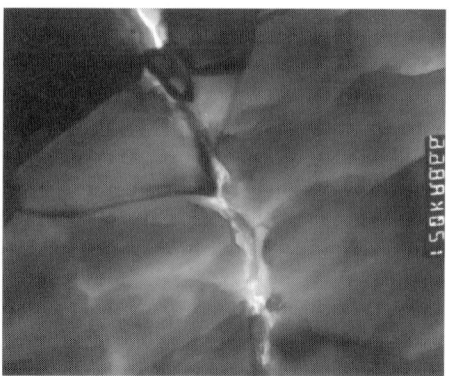

Fig. 12.15 TEM image of a conductive adhesive joint with non-conductive epoxy adhesive between two solder-plated contact members showing local metallic contacts. (Magnification: 120,000X, 200 kV)

between copper surfaces show considerably fewer contact regions at the tip of the lead (see Figures 12.16 and 12.17). Extremely small contact spots in one of these regions shown in Figure 12.18 were observed by TEM

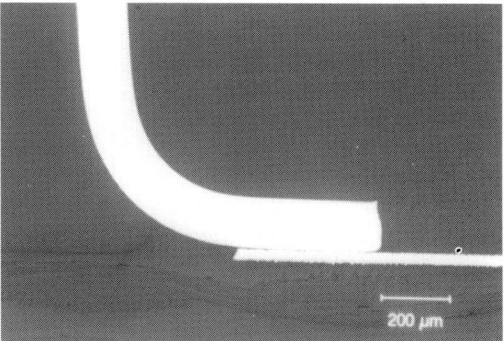

Fig. 12.16 Cross-section of a conductive adhesive joint with non-conductive thermoplastic adhesive. Both contact members, the gull-wing lead and the connection line on the printed circuit board, provide bare copper surfaces.

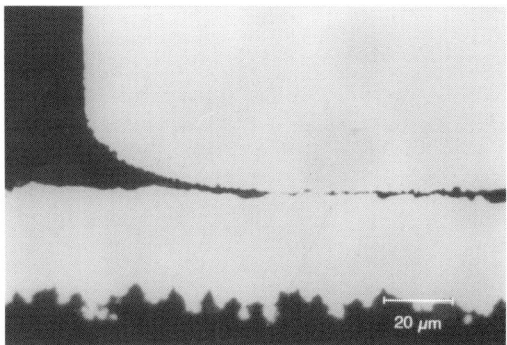

Fig. 12.17 Detail of the contact area of the NCA joint with copper surfaces shown in Fig. 12.16. The poorly deformable surface material allows only small contact areas with very few contact spots.

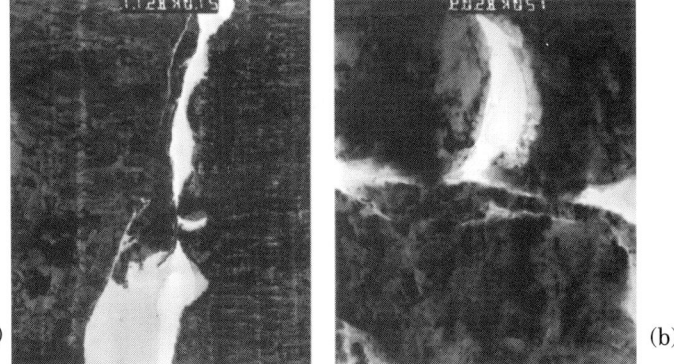

(a)   (b)

Fig. 12.18 TEM image of one of the few contact spots in a conductive adhesive joint with non-conductive epoxy adhesive between a copper gull-wing lead (right in Fig. 12.18 (a) and a copper connector on the printed circuit board (left in Fig. 12.18 (a); (b) detail of the same specimen. (Magnifications: (a) 21,000X, (b) 120,000X, 200 kV)

investigations. A model calculation of the constriction resistance for circular contact spots based on the diameter taken from Figure 12.18 (b) amounts to $R_c = 60$ mΩ per contact spot ($\varnothing$ 300 nm, $\rho_{Cu} = 1.8 \bullet 10^{-3}$ mΩ x cm). To obtain the observed contact resistance of 3 mΩ, parallel circuiting of 20 such contact spots is required, which is a fairly reasonable value.

In summary, the process described enables one to connect simultaneously all 160 leads of a component with contact resistances below 3 mΩ and a small statistical scattering of about 1 mΩ for solder-covered surfaces. The contact resistances achieved for the different systems can be seen in Figure 12.20. Typical contact patterns of solder-plated QFP-160 elements joined with epoxy and thermoplastic adhesive in comparison with a soldered element are shown in Figure 12.19.

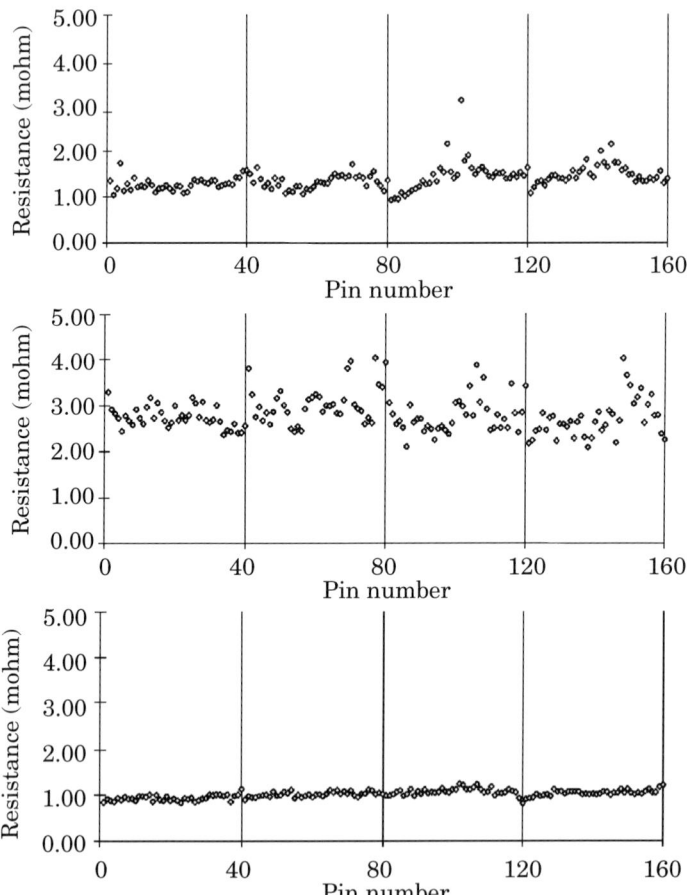

Fig. 12.19 Typical patterns of contact resistances along the 160 leads of a QFP component with solder-covered surfaces: (a) joined with non-conductive thermoplastic adhesive with: R = 1.39 mΩ ± 0.25 mΩ, (b) joined with non-conductive epoxy adhesive with: R = 1.46 mΩ ± 0.24 mΩ, (c) soldered joints with: R = 1.00 mΩ ± 0.08 mΩ as reference values. Due to the 4-point measurement set-up, the given resistances contain a constant contribution of the bulk resistances of the lead and the connector line and have to be regarded as an upper limit for the desired contact resistance.

12.3.3 Reliability

The reliability of the joints in terms of contact resistance and mechanical strength was examined after climatic cycling (-55°C to 125°C/1000 cycles) and constant humidity exposure (85°C/85% RH for 1000 h). Figures 12.20 and 12.21 show the results of the various reliability tests with solder-plated and bare copper surfaces of the contact members tested with both epoxy and reactive thermoplastic adhesive. Comparing the contact resistance results of the two surface systems (see Figure 12.20), the problems of bare copper contact members in moisture are obvious. The results of shear

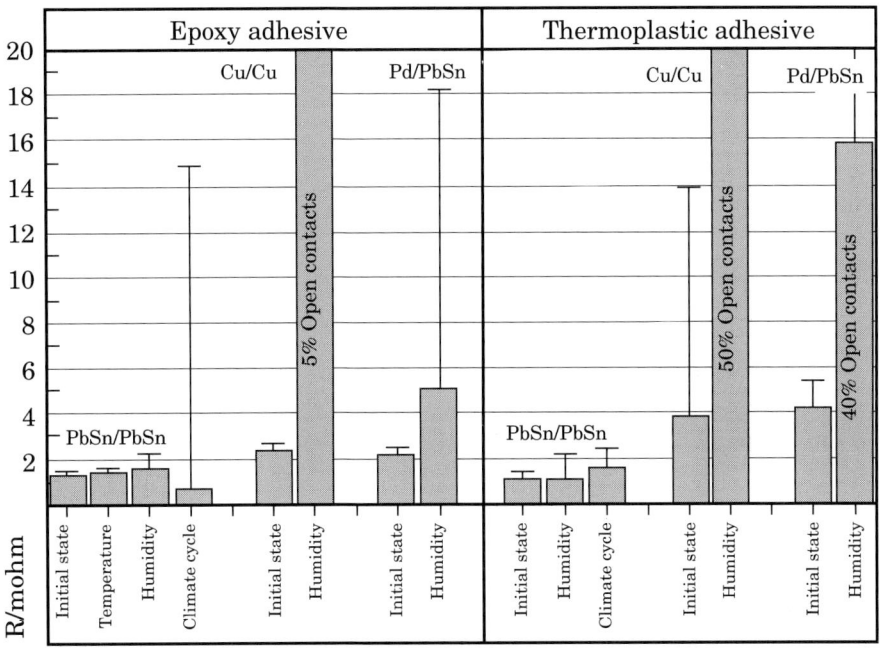

Fig. 12.20 Contact resistance for various material systems (surface combination/ adhesives) after different ageing treatments: climatic cycling (-55/125°C, 1000 cycles), constant humidity exposure (85°C/85% RH, 1000 h) and constant temperature exposure (125°C, 1000 h).

tests (Figure 12.21) also indicated a better reliability of solder-plated surfaces. A strict correlation between high contact resistances and low shear strength for single leads is not observed. The reactive thermoplastic adhesive in combination with solder-plated contact partners showed the best results in reliability testing and seems to be a suitable combination for surface

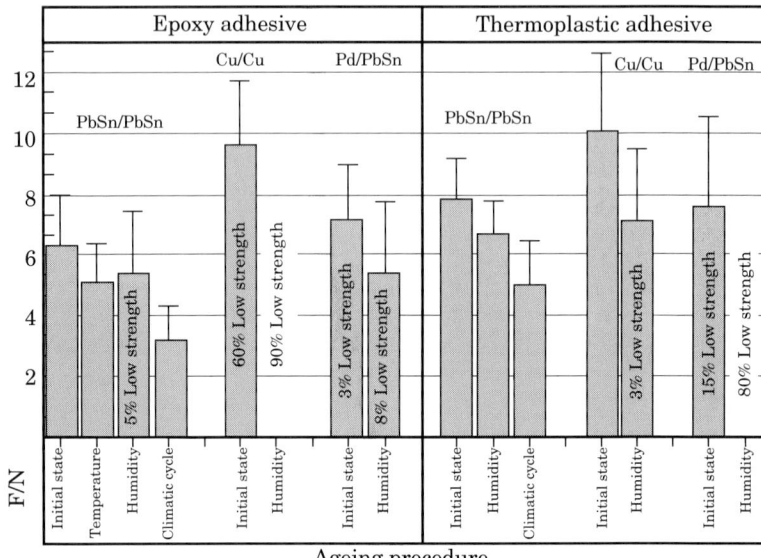

Fig. 12.21 Mechanical strength for various material systems (surface combination/adhesives) after different ageing treatments: climatic cycling (-55/125°C, 1000 cycles), constant humidity exposure (85°C/85% RH, 1000 h and constant temperature exposure (125°C, 1000 h).

mount applications. The epoxy adhesive leads to a certain rise in contact resistance in some instances.

In-line contact resistance measurements at single contact leads were performed in constant humidity (see Figure 12.22) and in temperature

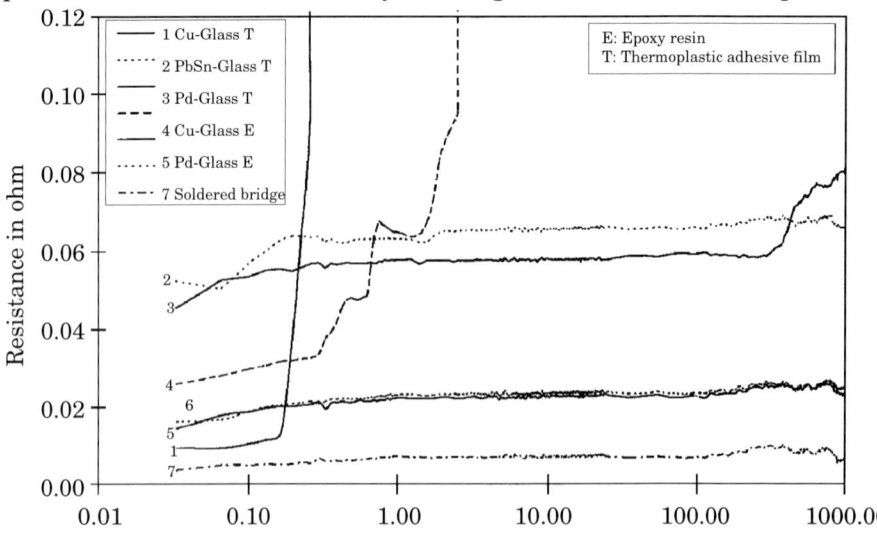

Time in h

Fig. 12.22 In-line contact resistance measurements for single-contact pins in 85°C/85% RH for 1000 h. (1 to 5: PbSn/PbSn, Cu/Cu and Pd/PbSn - surfaces; all glass reinforced FR-4 substrates)

cycling tests (Figure 12.23) with a larger number of different contact members. Copper/copper contacts show a fairly rapid degradation of contact resistance in constant humidity (see Figure 12.22), while contact systems containing deformable solder plating (Pd/solder and solder/solder) behave in a relatively stable manner over 1000 hours.

In the thermal cycling test the influence of different thermal expansion of component and substrate in the case of the aramide reinforced PCB can be observed (for thermoplastic adhesive, refer to Figure 12.23).

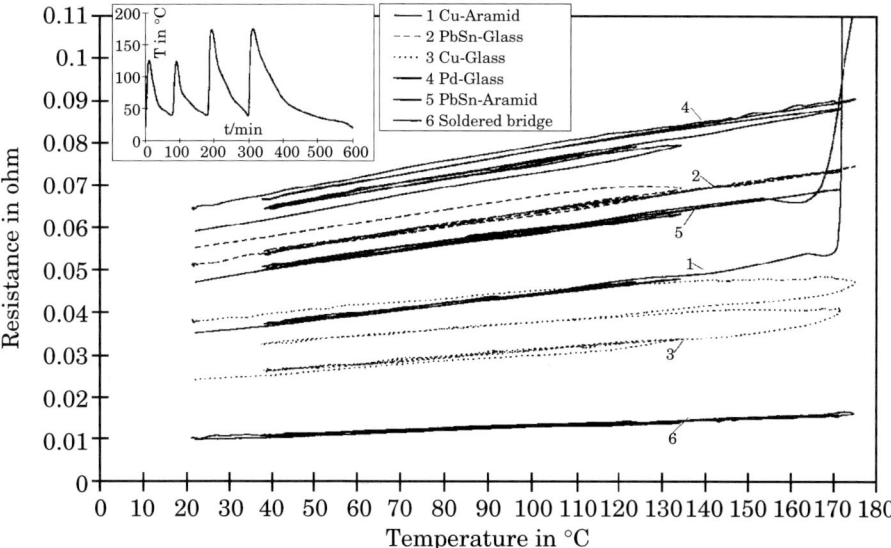

Fig. 12.23 Temperature characteristic of the contact resistance of NCA joints with thermoplastic adhesive for different material systems. The temperature profile shown in the inset runs two fast temperature ramps to 150°C and 180°C each. The figure shows a linear thermal coefficient of the resistances. The systems with aramide reinforced FR-4 substrates (CTE: 10 x 10^{-6}/K for the substrate *vs* 16 x 10^{-6}/K for the leadframe) fail at the 180°C ramps.

12.3.4 Summary

Electrically conductive adhesive connections with non-conductive adhesive provide low contact resistances of less than 10 mΩ per gull-wing lead in SMD applications. With suitable process parameters and an optimised pressing tool, a low variation of contact resistances of high pin count SMD components can be achieved. Critical features in the process are the homogeneity of the temperature profile and the planarity of the pressing tool.

As outlined above, the requirements for reliable NCA fine-pitch joints are plastic deformable surfaces which do not tend to corrode in a moist environment and adjusted coefficients of thermal expansion of the component (leadframe material) and the substrate. Solder-plated contact members have relatively large contact areas due to the plastic deformation of surface layers. The mechanical strength of the joints decreases in humidity but is sufficient to hold the components in place.

12.4   INVESTIGATIONS OF THE CONDUCTION MECHANISM

Several investigations of the electrical properties of the contacts and the conduction mechanism of NCA fine-pitch joints have been carried out. Some of the observations are discussed below. The technological contact resistance of individual pins (leads) amounts to 1-10 mΩ. This low value — which comes close to that of a soldered joint — indicates a metallic conduction mechanism.

Upon joining, the parts (pin and track) are pressed together and the adhesive is forced out of the gap. The resulting contact resistance of the cured joint depends on the viscosity of the adhesive (which increases towards the end of its pot life). With increasing viscosity the mean contact resistance of 160 pins increases from 2.6 over 3.3 up to 4.4 mΩ. This can be explained by one of the following mechanisms:

— For purely metallic conduction through the contact area between pin and track (which, according to fracture analysis, is much smaller than the nominal area of the pin), a high viscosity of the adhesive hampers the growth of the contact area during the time when pressure and heat are applied. Thus, the contact resistance is larger.
— When there is combined conduction via regions with metallic as well as quasimetallic contact (where ultra-thin adhesive layers prohibit direct metallic contact), the area and thickness of this ultra-thin adhesive layer influence the resulting resistance. Again, a high adhesive viscosity will lead to a thick layer and a high resistance.

12.4.1   Voltage and Temperature Characteristics

The current *vs* voltage characteristics were investigated. The current varied from -200 mA up to +200 mA; the voltages were < 1 mV. For both adhesives, the resulting diagrams go through zero and are fully linear (not shown). This points to metallic conduction.

Finally, the temperature characteristics of the contacts were observed in the temperature range from 10 K to 330 K and compared with theoretical curves of various conduction mechanisms. Figure 12.24 shows a typical

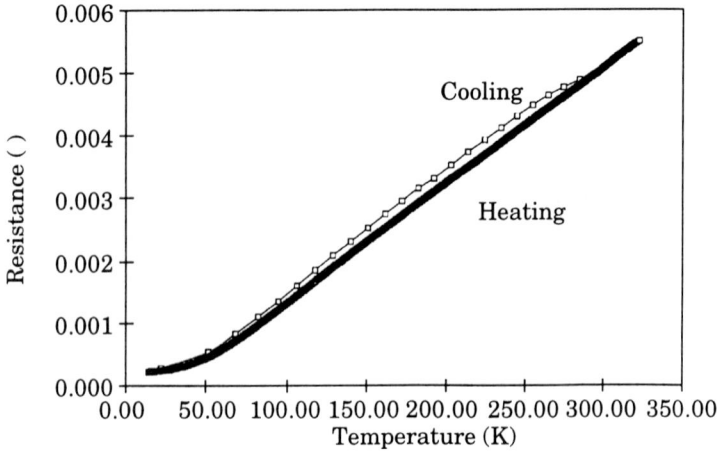

Fig. 12.24 Temperature characteristics of the contact resistance. Surfaces: solder, epoxy adhesive: Structalit X-941-052-051.

experimental characteristic. The upper curve was obtained while cooling down from room temperature, the lower curve (having a very high density of measured points = squares) while heating. The hysteresis is related to the thermal capacity of the system. A comparison of the temperature characteristics shown in Figure 12.24 with the conduction mechanisms known — among others conduction via ultra-thin or thicker organic films — concurs only with purely metallic conduction. A very good fit to the Ziman equation[37] of metallic conduction is possible (not shown).

12.4.2 Analysis of Fracture Surfaces

The following methods were applied for the analysis of fracture surfaces:

— Light microscopy (BF, DF, polarisation, differential interference contrast) — LM;
— Infra-red spectroscopy (grazing incidence or microscopy with chemical imaging) — IRS;
— Auger electron spectroscopy (AES: chemical imaging, depth profiling) with scanning electron microscopy (SEM: with X-ray micro-analysis);
— Transmission electron microscopy (TEM: with X-ray micro-analysis);
— X-ray photoelectron spectroscopy (XPS: with small spot chemical imaging, depth profiling, and angle resolved XPS).

The representative fracture surfaces investigated stem from a joint with solder-covered surfaces (Sn60Pb40) and epoxy adhesive. LM and SEM show the residual adhesive clearly. However, somewhere in the middle, there is a rough region with no visible adhesive. Figures 12.25 (a) and (b) show the fracture surfaces with:

— Pin (arrow A);
— Residual adhesive (arrow B);
— The rough region with no visible adhesive (arrow C) for pin and track, respectively.

 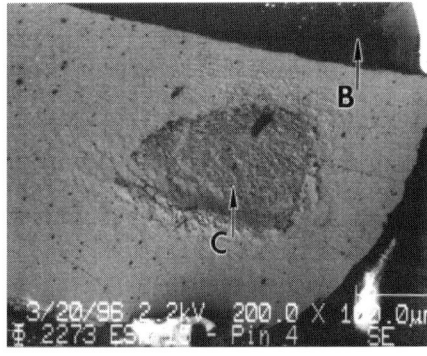

(a)   (b)

Fig. 12.25 SEM image of the fracture surfaces: (a) of the pin and (b) of the track. On the right in (a) the pin is heading towards the housing of the component. (Marker length: 100 μm, (a); AES: Phi 2340, (b) AES: Phi 2273)

Further investigations provided more information on those regions with 'no visible adhesive'. In summary, the following results were obtained:

— The fracture surfaces of the pins comprise a continuous, isolating layer with ≈2 nm thickness. This is probably adhesive (not an inorganic isolating material). Holes in this layer — which can form a metallic contact — can not be excluded, but the diameter then has to be < 1 μm.
— The fracture surfaces of the tracks comprise a continuous, carbon-rich layer with ≈10 nm thickness (possible holes % : « 1 μm). This layer presumably consists of a phase with good electrical conductivity such as graphitised organic compounds.
— The metal which for both fracture surfaces lies beneath the layers has a composition that is significantly different from the composition in the bulk. For both fracture surfaces there is an enrichment of Sn.

12.4.3   Model for the Conduction Mechanism

All the results mentioned above (and further findings not detailed here) can be explained by the following model for the conduction mechanism [in brackets the most important indications]:

— The electrical conductivity is primarily induced by metallic contacts [temperature characteristics of the conductivity, viscosity dependence of the contact resistance, current *vs* voltage diagrams].
— The area ratio of the metallic contacts to the total interface can vary considerably depending on the materials of the surfaces, adhesive, and joining conditions. For identical parameters, materials with a higher ductility feature a larger area of the metallic contacts [TEM: SnPb *vs* Cu].
— Parts of the interface with no metallic contacts can also contribute to conduction. These parts can form large areas and have a thickness of a few nanometres [AES, IRS, TEM, viscosity dependence of the contact resistance].
— A graphitisation of parts of the adhesive — increasing the conductivity by several orders of magnitude — can not be excluded [AES].
— Reliable conduction via metallic contacts is only possible when the cured adhesive maintains those contacts which have formed at high pressure and temperature ['joints' formed as usual but without adhesive showed poor conductivity of most pins and fell apart quickly].
— For SnPb surfaces, conduction is created neither by metallic diffusion of the two parts nor by soldering ['joints' without adhesive; conditions not allowing diffusion or soldering; conductivity also for Cu surfaces].

12.5   HIGH CURRENT AND THERMAL PROPERTIES

Electrically conductive adhesive joints with non-filled adhesive showed very low contact resistances in the range of some 10 mΩ to 100 mΩ and evidence of a high current load capability.[24] This led to the idea to use NCA joints for power carrying contacts in power electronics. Dealing with the problems of heavy wire bonding on solder die bonded devices, it can be an approach to replace wire bonding in connecting clips with the described technique. The process would be much simpler than clip soldering.

In the following section some basic experiments are discussed, pointing out the potential and also the problems associated with power applications of NCA joints. In the example reported, the investigations focus on test structures using flexible or semi-flexible foils, mainly copper, which could be used as clip material.

12.5.1 Experimental Set-up

To measure small contact resistances of some $\mu\Omega$, a sample geometry in the form of a Kelvin contact of a 100 μm copper foil and a polished DCB substrate structure (Direct Copper Bond, 300 μm Cu) was chosen (see Figure 12.26). The surface roughness of both contact members, the Cu foil and the substrate, was determined by profilometer measurements to about 1 μm. The adhesive bonding process was performed using a commercially available heat seal press. The adhesive used was a standard two-component epoxy resin, which was cured for 5 min. at 120°C at a pressure of 0.5 N/mm². The pressure was maintained for an additional 2 min. while cooling down.

The nominal contact area of this geometry is a square of 2 mm edge length. A four-point measurement of current and contact voltage was carried out as shown in Figure 12.26. In this way, only a nominal contact resistance can be

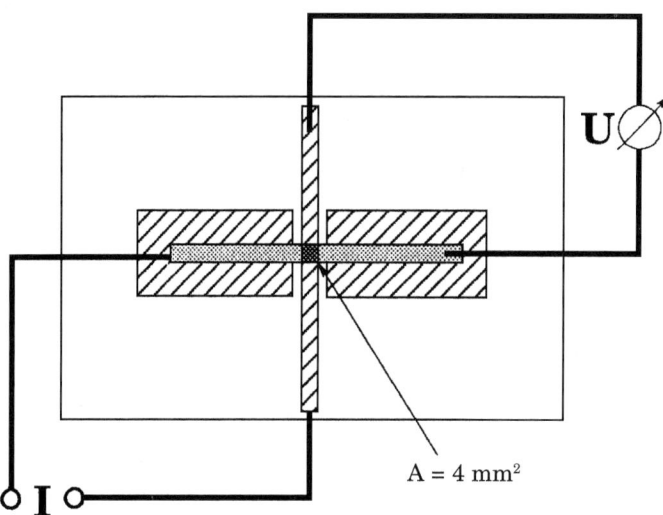

Fig. 12.26 Sketch of the sample geometry and contact resistance measurement set-up using the 4-point method. The DCB structure is insulated against the ground plate.

calculated. The real values of contact resistance can be considerably larger since the lateral resistance across the contact area (occurring inside the contact partners) is of the same order of magnitude as the contact resistance itself. The cross-section shown in Figures 12.27 and 12.28 gives an impression of the geometrical shape and the microstructure of the samples. The section was cut along the stripe of copper foil and shows the different parts of the DCB substrate.

Fig. 12.27 Cross-section of the test structure in the direction of the copper foil, overview. The DCB substrate shows the layer sequence Cu/ceramic/Cu.

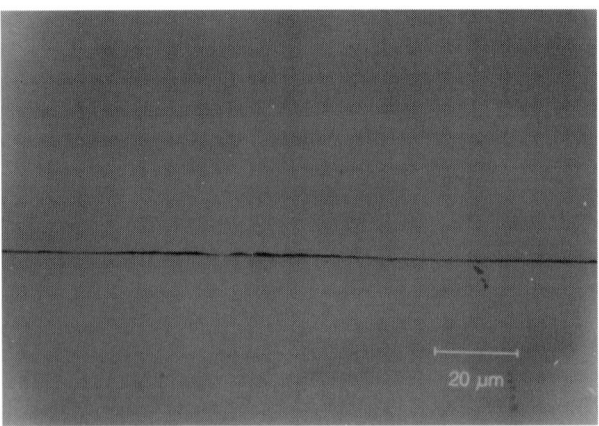

Fig. 12.28 Detail of the contact region. The joining gap shows a width of about 1 μm. A contact point near the surface asperity can be suspected. Since the probability of finding such a contact point with the section line at the contact interface is very low, such contact points were not observed directly.

The measurements were performed by applying constant currents to one sample for about 1 hour with successively increasing values. Additionally, the contact resistance was observed after a break of some minutes (with zero current). During current application, the average temperature of contact was measured at the topside of the copper foil with a thermoelement. This temperature can not be quoted as the real temperature at the contact interface, but it gives an indication of the heat generated in the bond. The whole set-up was mounted on to a heat sink (cold plate at 25°C) and was set into a vacuum chamber to provide stable thermal boundary conditions.

Supplementary measurements of the temperature dependence of the contact resistance were performed up to 160°C within an oven by applying a temperature gradient of 10 K per hour. A test current of 100 mA was used.

12.5.2 Effects of High Current Load

The development of the contact voltage of a typical sample is shown in Figure 12.29. The corresponding temperature curves are given in Figure 12.30.

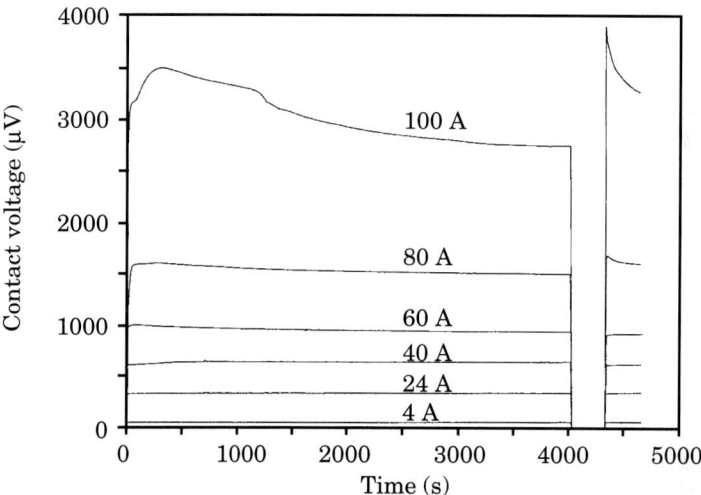

Fig. 12.29 Development of the contact voltage of a typical sample while loading with different currents.

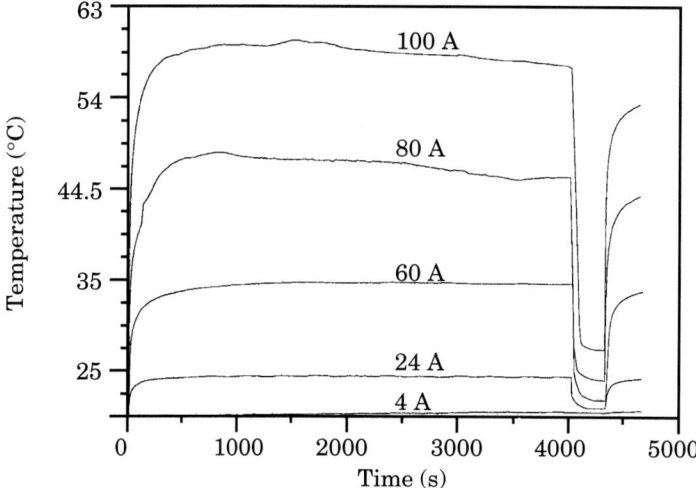

Fig. 12.30 Mean temperature of the contact region for the current load experiments shown in Fig. 12.5, measured on the upper surface of the copper foil.

The sample shows a relatively time stable contact resistance below a current of 60 A. Above a current of 80 A, a drop of the contact voltage to a stationary value is observed in the first minutes of a load cycle. The effect becomes larger with higher currents. The following load cycles feature different peak forms with a similar decrease of the contact voltage. This can be explained as a softening drop of the copper contact spots at a local temperature of 190°C (softening temperature of copper) in accordance with Table 12.1, section 12.2. Using a corresponding contact voltage of 0.12 V, the calculation of the contact resistance gives 1.5 mΩ which gives an estimation of the real value of the contact resistance.

The current-voltage plot for this sample (see Figure 12.31) shows a constant resistance (nominal 15 μΩ) up to 60 A. Above this current, larger contact resistances are observed. This can be explained as the effect of local heat generation at the contact spots which produces a greater constriction resistance (due to the positive temperature coefficient of resistivity of copper) and to the expansion of the surrounding adhesive layer with subsequent loss of pressure at the contact spot. In this case, an irreversible degradation of the contact occurs since the contact resistance does not recover completely even if the sample is cooled down to room temperature. As shown in Figure 12.31, another sample with a smaller contact resistance (nominal 7.7 μΩ) can be charged with up to 100 A (25 A/mm²) without any increase in contact resistance.

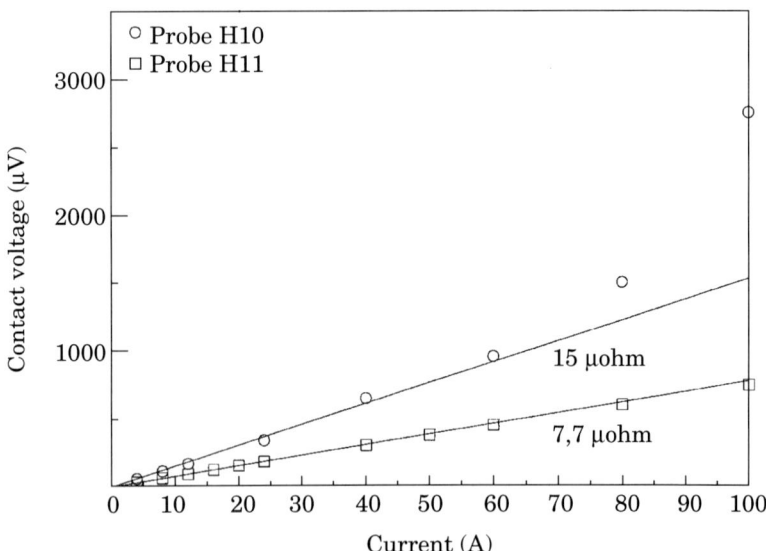

Fig. 12.31 Voltage-current characteristics of two samples with different contact resistance. The values of the sample H10 are taken from Fig. 12.5 at 4000 s.

12.5.3 Temperature Dependence of Contact Resistance

To prove the assumption that local heat generation at the contact points causes an increase of contact resistance, the temperature dependence of the contact resistance was examined. The sample was exposed to an external temperature treatment from room temperature to 180°C (see Figure 12.32). In the range from 50°C to 150°C, an almost constant temperature coefficient of 22 x 10^{-3} 1/K was observed. Compared with the temperature coefficient of copper, which is about 4 x 10^{-3} 1/K, it is evident that effects other than metallic conduction give rise to the high value of temperature coefficient observed. A possible interpretation is the above-mentioned expansion of the adhesive gap, which reduces the compressive forces on the contact points and subsequently reduces the elastically enlarged contact areas. This is also in accordance with the excessive increase of resistance at temperatures above 150°C, which is probably due to the enlarged thermal expansion coefficient of the adhesive above its glass transition temperature. The 'switch-off' effect observed at 175°C causes an irreversible degradation in the contact which leads to an increase of the contact resistance of some orders of magnitude. However, operating in the linear range of temperature coefficient the contact resistance is almost reversible.

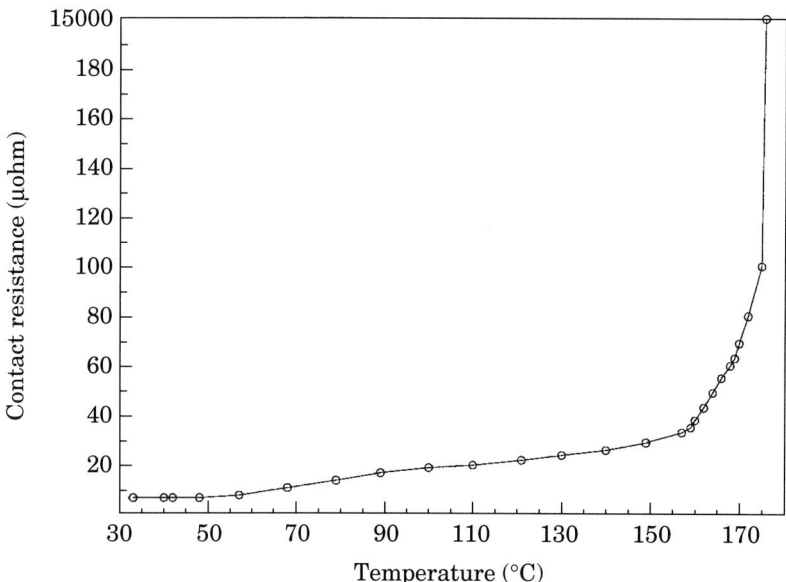

Fig. 12.32 Temperature dependence of the contact resistance. In the temperature range from 60°C to 150°C a temperature coefficient of ca. 22 x 10^{-3} 1/K can be calculated.

12.5.4   Visualisation of Hot Spots

A visualisation of contact spots by temperature measurement with an infra-red camera was not possible in the case of copper foils due to the high thermal conductivity of copper and the subsequently large heat spreading even in a thin foil. On the other hand, with two 25 μm thick Ni-foils (λ_{Ni} = 70 W/m°K, λ_{Cu} = 380 W/m°K), in some cases it was possible to observe a hot spot.

For example, Figure 12.33 shows a hot spot at a current of 12 A. With a larger current, the hot spot burned out to a 200 μm wide hole and another appeared in a different place.

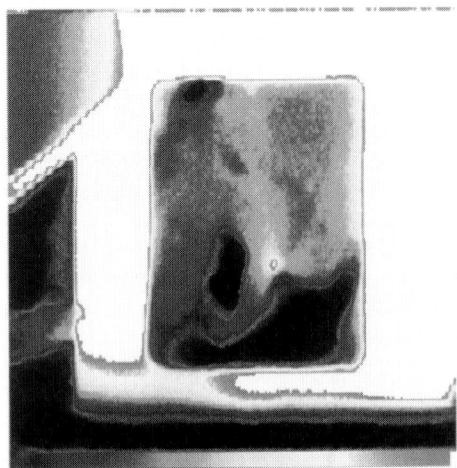

Fig. 12.33 Visualisation of a single hot spot in an NCA joint of two 25 μm Ni foils loaded with a current by an infra-red imaging camera. The emissivity of the surfaces has not been calibrated.

12.5.5   Summary

Electrically conductive contacts with non-conductive adhesives are able to carry high current loads up to 25 A/mm². The contact resistances were found to be of the same order of magnitude as the copper foils considered. The stability of the joints at high current loads is limited by the thermal expansion and degradation of the adhesive in the vicinity of the contact spots. Thus, the technique is not suitable for high power applications.

The recent investigations were carried out with unconditioned surface roughness and a standard adhesive as a first approach. Further developments can employ surface treatments, surface plating and optimised adhesives to extend the stable range of current load and to reach industry relevant process conditions. These optimisations should enable NCA joints to be produced for electronic applications with moderate power requirements.

12.6   CONCLUDING REMARKS

The authors have tried to give an overview and examples of recent applications of electrically conductive adhesive joining with non-conductive adhesive. Although the technique is not used in large-scale industrial production at present, it has potential for a number of special joining applications.

Possible future application fields of electrically conductive joints using non-conductive adhesives in surface mount and chip-on-board technology are flip-chip joining, surface mount joining of fine-pitch components or the connection of flexible circuits. Recent developments involve a combination of NCA joining and soldering by means of solder-coated surfaces.

Process investigations on a laboratory scale showed that electrically conductive joints can be achieved with low contact resistances (< 10 mW) and other interesting properties in terms of current load capability and thermal conductivity. Regarding the process, the following advantages can be stated:

— cost-effective joining technique due to cheap adhesives;
— ease of processing with unstructured adhesive application;
— good compatibility with a wide range of contact materials;
— no limitation as regards further reduction of connector pitches.

As outlined above, there are a number of requirements to be fulfilled in order to obtain reliable NCA joints:

— First-rate coplanarity of the joining partners is required to obtain reproducible process conditions.
— In order to overcome coplanarity problems, the surfaces or contact partners should be plastically deformable on a scale related to the unevenness of the joining partners. Such contacts allow more extended contact areas.
— The joining partners should have comparable coefficients of thermal expansion to minimise the mechanical stress as the thickness of the adhesive layer is only in the order of 1 μm. Another advantage would be the use of at least one flexible joining partner which does not introduce stress into the adhesive joint.
— The surfaces of the contact partners should not have any tendency to corrode in moisture. In the case of solder-plated contact partners with relatively large contact areas, corrosion effects might be reduced due to the very small joining gap or suppressed in the case of metallurgical contacts.

The reliability data on conductive NCA joints available today relate only to special material systems and a few joining partners. Further investigations on the electrical behaviour and long-term reliability will be needed in order to give a more definitive answer on the applicability to large-scale industrial processes and to point out the potential of this technique.

REFERENCES

1 Pope, M. and Swenberg, C. E., 'Electronic Processes in Organic Crystals', Oxford University Press, New York, pp. 273-336 (1982).
2 Skotheim, T., 'Handbook of Conducting Polymers', Marcel Dekker Inc. (1986).
3 Wnek, G. E., 'Electrically Conductive Polymers', *MRS Bulletin*, November-December (1987).
4 Kaner, R. B. and MacDiarmid, A. G., 'Elektrisch leitende Kunststoffe', *Spektrum der Wissenschaft*, pp. 54-59, April (1988).
5 Cognard, J., Gangguillet, C. and Asulab S.A., 'Process for Connecting Two Conductors', Patent Application No. 83 10015, France, 15.06.1983.
6 'Elastomeric Module-to-Board Connector System', *IBM Technical Disclosure Bulletin*, **Vol. 28**, No. 3, August (1985).
7 Hieber, H. and Thews, W., 'Process for making an electrically conductive adhesive connection', European patent: EP 237114/B1 920708/Application: A2 870916 (1987).

8   Iinuma, Y., Hirohara, T. and Inoue, K., 'TV couleur: Techniques des écrans et cristaux liquides', *TLE*, No. 534, pp. 18-23, May (1988).

9   Hatada, K., Fujimoto, H. and Kawakita, T., A New LSI Bonding Technology — Micron Bump Bonding Assembly Technology', Proceedings IEEE CHMT International Electronic Manufacturing Technology Symposium, pp. 23-27 (1988).

10   Pape, K., 'Leitende Klebverbindungen mit nichtleitenden Klebstoffen,' *DVS-Berichte*, **Vol. 110**, pp. 159-162 (1988).

11   Pape, K., 'Elektrische Kontakte, hergestellt mit nichtgefüllten Klebstoffen', *Elektronische Produktion & Prüftechnik*, pp. 40-44, May (1989).

12   Kristiansen, H. and Bjorneklett, A., 'Fine-pitch Connection to Rigid Substrate using Non-conductive Epoxy Adhesive', *Journal of Electronic Manufacturing*, No. 2, pp. 7-12 (1992).

13   Kristiansen, H., Liu, J. and Bjorneklett, A., 'A Comparison of Non-Conductive and Anisotropic Conductive Adhesive for Surface Mount Application', Proceedings 10th Microelectronics Conference, ISHM-Nordic, pp. 35-43, May (1995).

14   Schäfer, H., Wiegmann, G. and Hennemann, O.-D., 'Electrically Conductive Adhesive Joints with Non-filled Adhesives', EuPac'96, *DVS-Berichte*, **Vol. 173**, pp. 30-32 (1996).

15   Schäfer, H., 'Zuverlässige Kontaktdruck-Klebtechnik als Verbindung der Anschluß-metallisierungen von LCD-Zellen mit flexiblen Leiterplatten', Series: 'Innovationen in der Mikrosystemtechnik', **Vol. 33**, Mikroverbindungstechniken für Flüssigkristallanzeigen, VDI/VDE-IT, Teltow, pp. 107-127 (1995).

16   Aschenbrenner, R., Gwiasda, J., Eldring, J., Zakel, E. and Reichl, H., 'Flip Chip Attachment using Non-Conductive Adhesives and Gold Ball Bumps', Proceedings IEPS Conference, Atlanta (1994).

17   Aschenbrenner, R., Gwiasda, J., Eldring, J., Zakel, E., and Reichl, H., 'Gold Ball Bumps for Adhesive Flip Chip Assembly', 1st International Conference on Adhesives in Electronics, Berlin, November (1994).

18   Aschenbrenner, R., Gwiasda, J., Eldring, J., Zakel, E. and Reichl, H., 'Flip-Chip Montage mit nichtleitenden Klebstofffolien und Gold Ball Bumps', *VTE*, No. 2, pp. 98-103 (1995).

19   Jung, E., Aschenbrenner, R., Zakel, E. and Reichl, H., 'Flip Chip Interconnection to Organic Substrates: A Comparison between Adhesive Bonding and Soldering', 10th Microelectronics Conference, Copenhagen, Denmark, ISHM-Nordic, pp. 44-53, May (1995).

20   Zakel, E. and Reichl, H., 'Flip Chip Assembly using Gold, Gold-Tin, and Nickel Metallurgy', in Lau, J. H., 'Flip Chip Technologies', McGraw-Hill, pp. 415-490 (1995).

21   Kulojärvi, K., Savolainen, P. and Kivilahti, J., 'Bonding Flexible Circuits and Bare Chips with Anisotropic Electrically Conductive and Non-conductive Adhesives', Proceedings 10th Microelectronics Conference, ISHM-Nordic, Copenhagen, Denmark, pp. 28-34, May (1995).

22   Puhakka, K., Kulojärvi, K., Savolainen, P. and Kivilahti, J., 'Bonding Flexible Circuits and Flip Chips with Solder-Filled Z-Adhesives, Non-Conductive Adhesives and Fusible Coatings', 2nd International Conference on Adhesive Joining and Coating Technology in Electronics Manufacturing, Stockholm, Sweden, pp. 351-364, June (1996).

23   Nagle, R., Stam, F. and Barett, J., 'Evaluation of Adhesive Based Flip-Chip Interconnect Techniques', 2nd International Conference on Adhesive Joining and Coating Technology in Electronics Manufacturing, Stockholm, Sweden, pp. 351-364, June (1996).

24   Bauer, A. and Schmid, H., 'Electrical Properties of Conductive Adhesive Connections with Non-Conductive Adhesive', 1st International Conference on Adhesives in Electronics, Berlin, November (1994).

25   Bauer, A. and Oeverdiek, H., 'High Current Performance of Electrical Conductive Contacts with Non-Filled Adhesives', Proceedings International Seminar on Latest Achievements in Conductive Adhesive Joining in Electronics Packaging', Eindhoven, pp. 155-160 (1995).

26   Bauer, A., Oeverdiek, H., Gesang, T. and Schäfer, H., 'Conductive Adhesive Joints with Non-Conductive Adhesives for Fine-Pitch SMT-Applications', EuPac'96, *DVS-Berichte*, **Vol. 173**, pp. 27-29 (1996).

27   Gesang, T., Bauer, A., Schäfer, H. and Oeverdiek, H., 'Conductive Adhesive Joints with Non-Filled Adhesives for Surface Mount Technology', 2nd International Conference on Adhesive Joining and Coating Technology in Electronics Manufacturing, Stockholm,

pp. 365-368, June (1996).

28   Gesang, T., Bauer, A. and Bornholdt, O., Abschlußbericht zum AIF-Forschungsvorhaben No. 9627: 'Elektrisch leitfähiges Kontaktieren von Fine-Pitch-Baulementen mit nichtgefüllten Klebstoffen', Forschungsvereinigung Schweißen und Schneiden e.V., Deutscher Verband für Schweißtechnik (DVS), Düsseldorf.

29   Oeverdiek, H., 'Funktion und Zuverlässigkeit leitfähiger Engspaltklebverbindungen', Diploma Thesis at Fachhochschule Lübeck, Fachbereich Physikalische Technik, Lübeck, August (1995).

30   Pick, M., 'Zuverlässigkeit leitfähiger Engspaltklebverbindungen', Diploma Thesis at Fachhochschule Lübeck, Fachbereich Elektrotechnik, Lübeck, August (1996).

31   Holm, R., 'Electric Contacts', Springer Verlag, Berlin (1967).

32   Morzkowski, R., 'Connector Contacts: Critical Surfaces', *Advanced Materials & Processes inc. Metal Progress*', No. 12, pp. 49-54 (1988).

33   Malucci, R. D., 'Multispot Model of Contacts Based on Surface Features', Proceedings 36th IEEE Holm Conference on Electrical Contacts, pp. 625-634 (1990).

34   Greenwood, J. A., 'The Area of Contact Between Rough Surfaces and Flats', *Journal of Lubrication Technology*, pp. 81-91, January (1967).

35   Fluss, H. S., 'Hertzian Stress as a Predictor of Contact Reliability', *Connection Technology*, No. 12, pp. 12-21 (1990).

36   Malucci, R. D., 'Dynamic Model of Stationary Contacts Based on Random Variations of Surface Features', *IEEE Transactions on CHMT*, **Vol. 15**, No. 3, pp. 339-347 (1992).

37   Kittel, C., 'Introduction to Solid State Physics', J. Wiley & Sons, New York (1976).

38   Ziman, J. M., 'Electrons and Phonons', Clarendon Press, Oxford (1960).

Chapter 13

USE OF CONDUCTIVE ADHESIVES AS DIE-ATTACH FOR POWER ELECTRONICS APPLICATIONS

ARE BJORNEKLETT

Ericsson Components AB, Stockholm, Sweden

13.1   INTRODUCTION

Over the last two or three decades, the use of electrically conductive, silver-filled, epoxy adhesives has been increasing steadily in the microelectronics industry. The primary application areas are interconnection of electrical conductors, attachment of passive electronic components such as resistors and capacitors, and attachment of encapsulated active electronic components or bare silicon chips to substrates or packages. The primary physical property of these adhesives is high and stable electrical conductivity. Typically, they offer a specific electrical resistivity of 10^{-4} Ωcm or about two orders of magnitude higher than the best metallic conductors. This conductivity is appropriate for many interconnect applications in electronic components. This section of the book is concerned with conductive adhesives for attachment of power semiconductor die characterised by medium to high power dissipation.

Attachment of semiconductor chips to substrates and packages is an important step in the fabrication of microelectronics devices. A typical microelectronics assembly is shown in Figure 13.1. The semiconductor chip

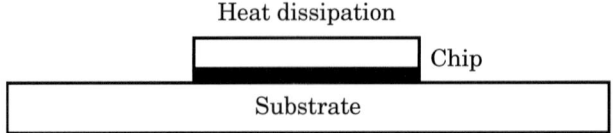

Fig. 13.1 A typical microelectronics assembly. A conductive adhesive joint attaches the semiconductor die to a substrate. Both high electrical and thermal conductivities are needed.

is usually silicon. The chip is attached to a chip carrier or substrate. The chip carrier may in its simplest form be a piece of metal or ceramic acting as a heat spreader or a heat sink. The chip carrier can also be a complex multilayer structure of ceramic and metal or polymer and metal. In this case, the metal layers are patterned and the layers are interconnected with so-called vias so that a large number of electrical signals can be routed through the structure. The most important materials for chip attachment are:

- Silicon-gold eutectic (hard solder);
- Lead/tin/indium/silver based alloys (soft solder);
- Glass filled with precious metals (often silver);
- Polymer based adhesives filled with precious metals (often silver).

Silver-filled adhesives, often epoxies or polyimides, are probably among the most extensively used chip attachment materials due to a simple process and relatively inexpensive equipment. Typical curing temperatures are well below the melting point of common solder alloys and far below the melting point of silicon-gold, eutectic solders and glass. The low cure temperature allows the use of a number of materials in the assembly – for instance, polymer materials that are not compatible with the higher temperatures encountered in the other processes used in the assembly.

The requirements imposed on the chip attachment are increasing as a consequence of the trends in the electronics industry. The average size of semiconductor chips is increasing. This leads to growing difficulties of managing the thermomechanical stresses induced in the chip by differences in the coefficients of thermal expansion. While the chip size becomes larger, the number of electronic circuit elements on the chip increases even faster due to the decreasing dimensions of the elements processed into the chip. The operating speed of the circuits is also increasing. These factors lead to a greater power dissipation and more stringent requirements on the thermal conductivity of the assembly in order to maintain a reasonable operating temperature in the semiconductor chip.

Reliability is an increasingly important issue as complex electronic control systems are utilised in automotive and aircraft applications. The chip attach plays a major rôle with respect to failure modes such as hot spots and fractures of the semiconductor chip. Hot spots are associated with voids in the chip attachment material that cause local heating due to the large thermal resistance in the void. The hot spots may eventually lead to burn-out of the chip because of non-linear, thermo-electrical phenomena. The voids are created during manufacturing by the outgassing of solvents or by fatigue during temperature cycling. Fracture of semiconductor chips is caused by either thermomechanical stress generated during the assembly process or from the cyclic stress loading imposed on the assembly during temperature cycling. Voids or chip fractures caused by thermal fatigue during temperature cycling are the most serious modes of failure because they occur during the operational lifetime of the electronic system. Failures occurring at the assembly stage should be discovered at the final testing of the system before it becomes operational.

A most demanding die attach adhesive application is power electronics devices that are used to control heavy electrical machinery. High thermal conductivity, as well as electrical conductivity, is of ultimate importance in this application. The heat dissipation is in excess of $100 \, \text{W/cm}^2$ in many power electronics applications. In fact, some applications are in excess of $1000 \, \text{W/cm}^2$. Die attach adhesives are still not suitable for the most extreme devices. However, there are still a large number of power electronics applications that utilise die attach adhesives.

13.2 THERMAL CONDUCTIVITY OF ADHESIVES

A parameter of primary importance for die attach adhesives in power electronics is thermal conductivity. The performance of a power electronics device or module is, to a large extent, limited by the heat conduction capability of the package. Adhesives filled with particles of silver or another thermally conductive material are two-phase materials. The adhesive represents the matrix and the particles represent the filler phase. The calculation of thermal conductivity for such materials is generally difficult.

The conductivity of a two-phase material depends on the conductivities of the matrix and filler and the volume fraction of filling material and its geometry. In some cases, the resistance in the interface between matrix and filler may be of significant influence. However, such a material may be considered as a 3-phase material with the interface as the third phase. The following review of theories will not include interface phenomena. A particularly simple case is when the filler phase is comprised of fibres or rods arranged in the direction of conduction. The conductivity of such materials is described by a parallel coupling of the resistance in the matrix and the filler. This can be seen in Figure 13.2.

Direction of heat flow ⟶

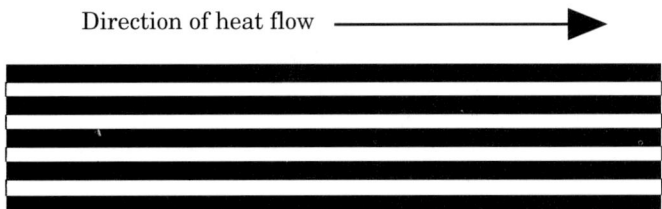

Fig. 13.2 A parallel coupled thermal conductor.

$$\frac{1}{\rho_C} = \frac{1 - \phi_F}{\rho_M} + \frac{\phi_F}{\rho_F} \tag{13.1}$$

or because conductivity is the reciprocal of resistivity:

$$\lambda_C = (1 - \phi_F)\lambda_M + \phi_F\lambda_F \tag{13.2}$$

In these equations, ρ is resistivity and λ is conductivity. The subscripts C, M and F refer to composite, matrix and filler respectively. The volume fraction of filler material is ϕ_F. Slabs or plates arranged so that the direction of conduction is normal to their face is another equally simple case described by a series coupling of resistances, see Figure 13.3.

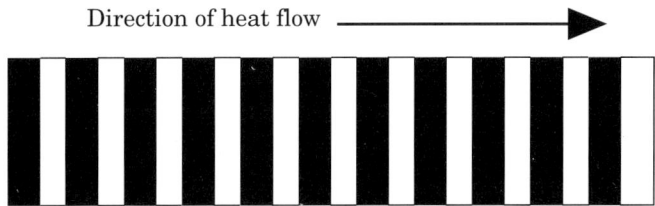

Fig. 13.3 A series coupled thermal conductor.

$$\frac{1}{\lambda_C} = \frac{1 - \phi_F}{\lambda_M} + \frac{\phi_F}{\lambda_F} \tag{13.3}$$

The general case of a particulate filler of arbitrary size and shape is far more complex and no general theory has been developed as yet. However, in the general case, Equations (13.2) and (13.3) represent the upper and lower limits of the conductivity.

Theories have been developed for special cases with particulate fillers of regular geometry such as spheres, ellipsoids or cubes arranged in a regular lattice.[1,2] A major shortcoming of these theories is the fact that the particles in most filled adhesives are irregular in shape and of different sizes. They are also randomly distributed in the adhesive. Calculations with regular geometry may be of limited value in these cases. Please see Figure 13.4.

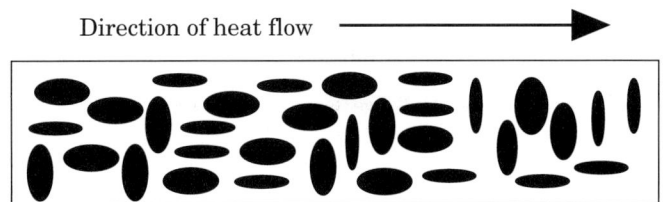

Fig 13.4 A disordered thermal conductor.

A semi-empirical theory due to Lewis and Nielsen[3] has eliminated some of these difficulties. In their theory, the thermal conductivity of the two-phase material λ_C is given by:

$$\lambda_C = \lambda_M \frac{1 + AB\phi_F}{1 - B\psi\lambda_M} \tag{13.4}$$

where:

$$B = \lambda_M \frac{\lambda_F/\lambda_M - 1_F}{\lambda_F/\lambda_M + A}$$

and:

$$\psi = 1 + \left[\frac{1 - \phi_m}{\phi_m^2} \right] \phi_F$$

In this equation, A is a geometrical parameter reflecting the shape of the filler particles, see Table 13.1, and λ is the thermal conductivity. The subscripts C, M and F refer to composite, matrix and filler respectively. The volume fraction of the dispersed material is ϕ_F. The maximum packing fraction of the filler material is ϕ_m.

Table 13.1

The Shape Parameter A and the Maximum Packing Fraction ϕ_m in the Lewis and Nielsen Theory of Thermal Conduction in Two-phase Materials for Various Particle Geometries

Particle Shape	A	ϕ_m
Cubes	1.5	1.000
Spheres	2.0	0.601
Randomly oriented rods:		
length/diameter = 10	4.9	0.520
length/diameter = 35	30	0.520

A major achievement of the Lewis and Nielsen theory is the introduction of the geometry dependent parameter, A. This parameter takes care of the fact that elongated particles yield a higher conductivity than spherical particles if the volume ratio ϕ_F is equal. There is a relationship between the aspect ratio of the particles and A. The Lewis and Nielsen theory also includes the concept of maximum packing fraction of filler particles. The maximum packing fraction, ϕ_m, reflects that it is impossible to load more filler material into the matrix than ϕ_m. Table 13.1 gives some values of A and ϕ_m for particles of different shape. The theory has been successfully employed to interpret experimental data on thermal conduction of two-phase materials.

An interesting observation to be made from Equation 13.4 is that B is close to 1 for high contrast composites. A metal-filled epoxy is a high contrast composite. The thermal conductivity of the filler is typically 2 to 3 orders of magnitude larger than the thermal conductivity of the matrix. In the case of silver-filled epoxy, the thermal conductivity of the matrix phase is 0.2 W/mK. The thermal conductivity of the filler is 417 W/mK. This implies that the conductivity of the filler has a negligible influence on the composite conductivity. The thermal conductivity of such composites is essentially determined by the volume fraction ϕ_F and the geometrical properties A and ϕ_m.

Table 13.2 shows calculations based on the Lewis and Nielsen theory. They demonstrate some of the interesting features of this theory. The thermal conductivity of an epoxy adhesive filled with various amounts of different materials is calculated. The filler materials are silica, alumina,

silver or diamond particles with thermal conductivities 1.7, 25, 417 and
1200 W/mK respectively. Three different particle geometries are used in the
calculations: spheres with A = 1.5, randomly oriented rods or fibres with a
length/diameter ratio of 10 (A = 4.9) and length/diameter ratio of 35 (A = 30).
It is evident from the calculations that the parameters of significant importance
are the volume fraction and the geometry of the filler material. The thermal
conductivity of the filler material is less important except for the silica filler
with low thermal conductivity.

Table 13.2

Calculated Thermal Conductivities for Epoxy filled with Silica, Alumina, Silver
and Diamond Powder

| Geometry | Volume Fraction of Filler | | | |
Parameter A	10%	20%	30%	40%
Silica filler, k = 1.7 W/mK				
1.5	0.24	0.30	0.38	0.51
4.9	0.27	0.37	0.49	0.68
30	0.32	0.46	0.61	0.77
Alumina filler, k = 25 W/mK				
1.5	0.26	0.34	0.47	0.73
4.9	0.33	0.52	0.85	1.64
30	0.75	1.48	2.60	4.69
Silver filler, k = 417 W/mK				
1.5	0.26	0.34	0.48	0.75
4.9	0.34	0.54	0.91	1.86
30	0.90	1.88	3.61	7.88
Diamond filler, k = 1200 W/mK				
1.5	0.26	0.34	0.48	0.76
4.9	0.34	0.54	0.92	1.88
30	0.90	1.91	3.67	8.12

(The thermal conductivity of the epoxy matrix is 0.2 W/mK. The calculations were carried out with
three different particle shape parameters: A corresponding to spheres, A = 1.5, rods or fibres with
a length to diameter ratio of 10, A = 4.9, and 35, A = 30. All thermal conductivities are in units of
W/mK.)

Commercially available silver-filled epoxies have a weight fraction of
silver in the 65-80% range with corresponding volume fractions in the
0.18-0.30 range. The thermal conductivity of these epoxy adhesives is in the
1.5-4 W/mK range. It is clear from Table 13.2 that the silver particles are
elongated.
    The implication of these results with regard to design and development of
high thermal conductivity adhesives is that the shape and arrangement of
the filler particles in the adhesive are of considerable importance. The
volume fraction of filler is also important. According to the theory, the
thermal conductivity of the filler is less significant.

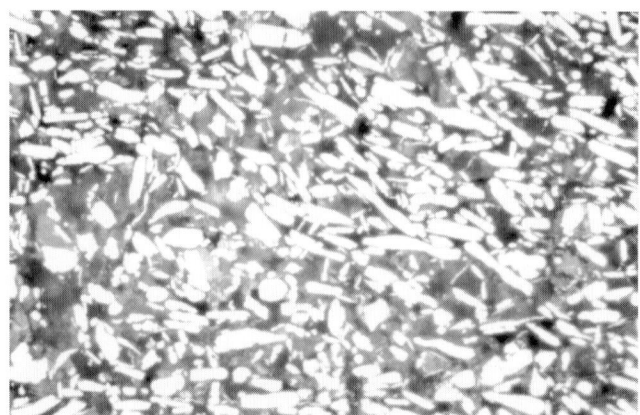

Fig 13.5 Cross-section of a commercially available silver-filled epoxy adhesive. The silver particles have an elongated shape which increases the thermal conductivity.

The temperature dependency of the thermal conductivity may also be of interest as some electronic components and particularly power electronic components may operate at temperatures between 150 and 200°C. Figure 13.6 shows the thermal conductivity as a function of the temperature for two common die attach adhesives.[4] Results show that the thermal conductivity increases up to the glass transition temperature. At temperatures above the glass transition, the thermal conductivity decreases. The thermal conductivity increases with increasing volume fractions of silver.

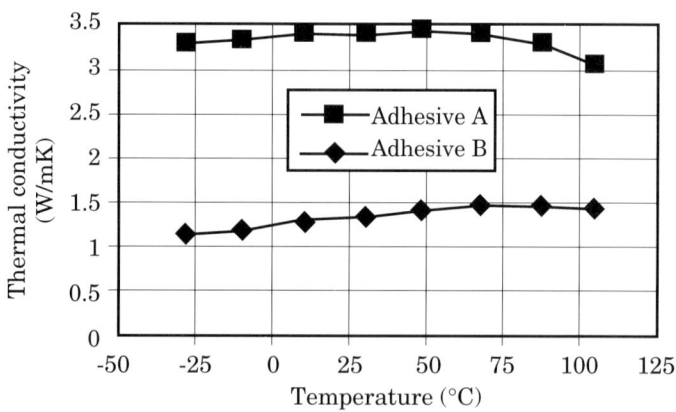

Fig. 13.6 Temperature dependency of thermal conductivity.[4]

13.3　THERMAL RESISTANCE OF ADHESIVE JOINTS

It is a fact that the parameter of practical importance in an electronic package or hybrid is the thermal resistance of the die attachment and not the thermal conductivity of the material itself. The chip temperature at a given power dissipation is determined by the thermal resistance. There are, in principle, two ways of reducing the thermal resistance and thereby the chip temperature: (1) increasing the thermal conductivity, or (2) reducing the thickness of the adhesive.

The thermal resistance in a bond layer of area, A, and thickness, t, consisting of a material with thermal conductivity, λ, is given as:

$$R = \frac{t}{\lambda A} \tag{13.5}$$

where R is the thermal resistance (K/W), t is the thickness of the adhesive joint, A is the area of the adhesive joint and λ is the thermal conductivity of the adhesive (W/mK).

From a thermal management point of view, it is desirable to reduce the thickness of the adhesive as much as possible in order to minimise the thermal resistance in the bond layer. There is, however, a limit to how much the thickness can be reduced. It is shown that a thermal contact resistance is present in the bond layer that will limit the benefit of reducing the thickness.[4]

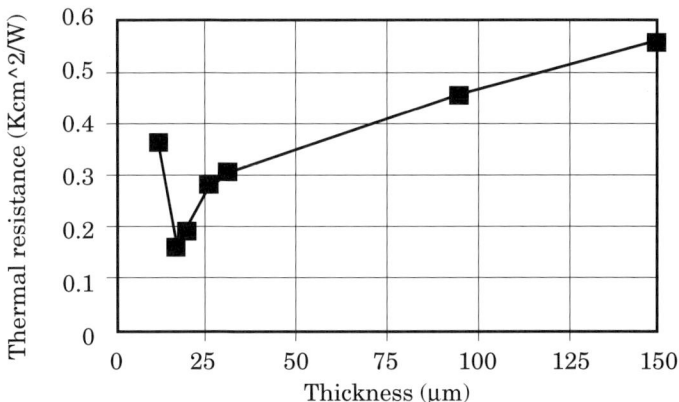

Fig. 13.7 The thermal resistance of a die attach adhesive as a function of the thickness.[4]

When the thermal resistance of the bond layers is compared with the bulk thermal conductivity, there appears to be a residual thermal resistance in the bond layers, more pronounced in thin layers. The residual thermal resistance is higher for chips bonded to substrates with large mismatch in the coefficient of thermal expansion between the chip and the substrate. The mismatch causes mechanical stress in the adhesive that may result in formation of microcracks and local spots of de-bonded areas in the interface between chip and adhesive or substrate and adhesive. This damage induced in the bond layer yields an additional thermal interfacial resistance of approximately 0.1-0.2 Kcm^2/W, in series with the bulk thermal resistance. When the bulk thermal resistance is low, as in the case of a thin bond layer, the thermal interfacial resistance may contribute more to the total thermal resistance than the bulk resistance.

There exists an optimal thickness of the adhesive joint. Too thin a joint gives too much thermal interface resistance and too thick a joint gives too much bulk thermal resistance. The optimal thickness depends on the mismatch in the thermal expansion coefficient between the chip and the substrate/package. The optimal adhesive thickness will also change if the chip size changes. Large area joints should be handled carefully.

The bulk thermal conductivity is an insufficient criterion for die-attach adhesives in applications that are critical with regard to thermal management. Thermal resistance measurements should preferably be carried out in order to obtain accurate values for the thermal performance of the adhesive.

13.4   THERMAL STRESS IN ADHESIVE JOINTS

Thermomechanical stress in adhesive joints is, as shown in the previous section, an important parameter to consider. It is therefore relevant to refer to an analysis of the stress in adhesive joints between materials of dissimilar thermal expansion carried out by Chen and Nelson.[5]

Consider a semiconductor die bonded to a rigid substrate with an adhesive layer of thickness, t. The geometry is shown in Figure 13.8. In a rigid substrate, there is no significant bowing or straining. The diagonal length of the die is 2L and the thickness is h_d. The thermal expansion coefficients are usually not equal in the substrate and the die. This causes a shear stress in the adhesive upon temperature changes. The difference in coefficient of thermal expansion between the die and the substrate is Δa.

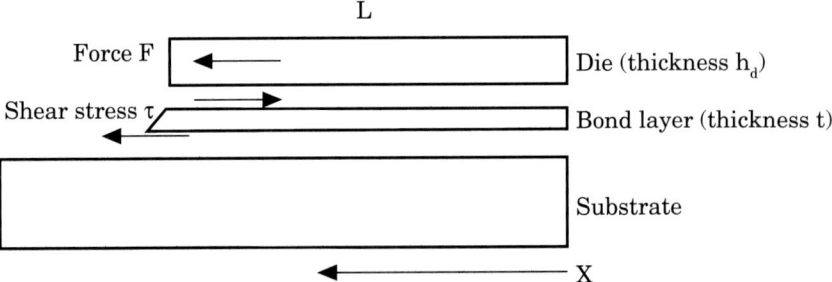

Fig. 13.8 Schematic outline of a die bonded to a substrate. Only half of the die is shown. A shear stress is present in the adhesive as well as a force in the die due to mismatch in the thermal expansion coefficients.

Chen and Nelson[5] have calculated the shear stress by considering the balance of forces in the adhesive layer and the die. If τ is the shear stress in the adhesive, and F is the force caused by thermomechanical stress in the die, then these quantities must obey the equation:

$$\frac{\partial F}{\partial x} = \tau \tag{13.6}$$

With this equation as a starting point, Chen and Nelson arrived at the following expression for the shear stress in the bond layer as a function of the distance x from the centre of the chip:

$$\tau = \frac{\Delta\alpha\Delta TG\sinh \beta x}{\beta t \cosh \beta L} \tag{13.7}$$

where G is the shear modulus of elasticity in the adhesive and ΔT the temperature range. The temperature range may, for instance, be the difference between the cure temperature and the room temperature if the stress developed during the manufacturing process is considered. The parameter β in Equation (13.2) is given as:

$$\beta^2 = \frac{G}{t}\left[\frac{1}{E_d h_d} + \frac{1}{E_{sub} h_{sub}}\right] \qquad (13.8)$$

where E_d and E_{sub} are the tensile modulus of elasticity in the die and the substrate respectively. The thickness of the substrate is h_{sub}. In the case of a rigid substrate (e.g., much thicker than the die), the expression for β simplifies to:

$$\beta^2 = \frac{G}{t}\frac{1}{E_d h_d} \qquad (13.9)$$

The maximum shear stress will occur for x = L or at the corners of the die and is given as:

$$\tau_{max} = \frac{\Delta\alpha\Delta T G \tanh \beta L}{\beta t} \qquad (13.10)$$

In adhesives with a very low shear modulus, βL will be small and, since tanh βL is approximately equal to βL for small βL, Equation (13.5) can be simplified to:

$$\tau_{max} = \frac{\Delta\alpha\Delta T G L}{t} \qquad (13.11)$$

This situation corresponds to a stress-free die which is rarely the case except for silicone adhesives. In adhesives with a high shear modulus, tanh βL will be close to 1 and Equation (13.5) simplifies to:

$$\tau_{max} = \Delta\alpha\Delta T\sqrt{\frac{G}{t}}\sqrt{E_d h_d} \qquad (13.12)$$

In both the soft and hard adhesive limits, there is an inverse relationship between the maximum shear stress t_{max} and the thickness of the bond layer t. A thinner bond layer will result in a larger shear stress.

The mechanical stress in the chip itself should also be considered. Some adhesives may induce very high stresses in the semiconductor chip with risk for cracking. The thermal stress in the chip can be analysed both by Finite Element simulation Methods (FEM) and by measurement.

Measurements are typically performed by utilising a test chip with integrated strain gauges.[6] The strain gauges are electrical resistors in which the resistance depends on the mechanical stress. A large number of strain gauges can be spread across the surface of the chip so that a good picture of the stress distribution can be obtained. Figure 13.9 shows the mechanical stress as measured with a silicon test chip bonded to a copper substrate together with a finite element simulation. There is a reasonably good correspondence between the results.[6]

The two lateral stress components, along a line dividing the chip into two equal rectangular areas, are shown. The measured stress was compressive. The stress component parallel to the line is strongly reduced as one approaches the edge of the chip. The other component is approximately constant.

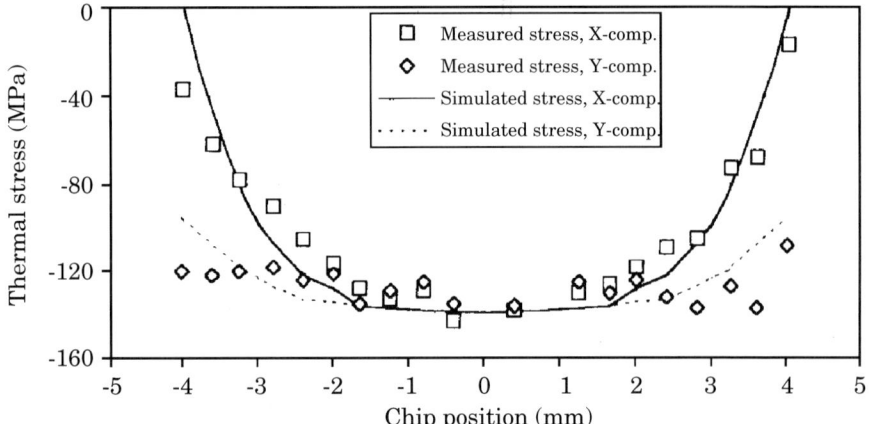

Fig. 13.9 Measured and simulated mechanical stress in a silicon die bonded to copper substrate.

13.5   CRACKING, DELAMINATION AND THERMAL FATIGUE OF ADHESIVE JOINTS

The thermal stress in the die-attach layer can give rise to serious reliability problems. If the thermal stress becomes too large, the die may either simply pop off by a delamination process or by a brittle fracture of the bond layer. Even at moderate levels of thermal stress, problems may arise from thermal fatigue. Cyclic variations in temperature lead to cyclic thermal stresses which in turn induce crack growth in the die-attach layer or a slow delamination process.

Electronic systems are often subjected to a thermal cycling test as a part of quality assurance and qualification. MIL-STD-883C, Method 1010.6, is commonly used. Condition B of this test specifies thermal cycles between -55 and 125°C and the number of cycles is typically between 10 and 1000. The temperature range in this test is more severe than in most real applications. However, the number of cycles in real applications may outnumber those of the test considerably. Automotive electronics components may be cycled between 10 and 80°C once or twice every day for ten or more years. Components in low earth orbit spacecrafts may be cycled 14 times per day or 5000 cycles per year caused by consecutive sunlight and shadow. Numbers may be even higher for power on/off cycles. An electrical vehicle in city traffic may start and stop within periods of a few minutes causing temperature cycling of drive electronics components. Temperature control electronics may switch on/off within a period of a few seconds to minutes depending on the thermal time constant of the thermal mass under control.

The heat transfer characteristics of the die-attach layer are of particular importance in electronic systems with high power dissipation. The fatigue process creates cracks or delaminated areas which then increase the thermal resistance of the bond layer. A deteriorating heat transfer capability of the bond is thus caused by the thermal cycles.

Investigation of silver-filled die bonds has shown that crack growth is initiated at the edges and, in particular, at the corners of the bonded area.[7] This is illustrated in Figure 13.10 where various stages of bond layer fatigue are shown schematically. Figure 13.11 shows a cross-section between two diagonal corners of a bond area. The half diagonal length of the area is L and the length from the centre to the crack tip is l.

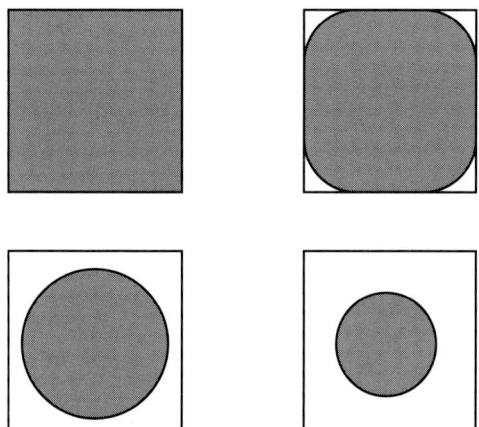

Fig. 13.10 Various stages of thermal fatigue of an adhesive joint. The white area represents the cracked part of the joint.

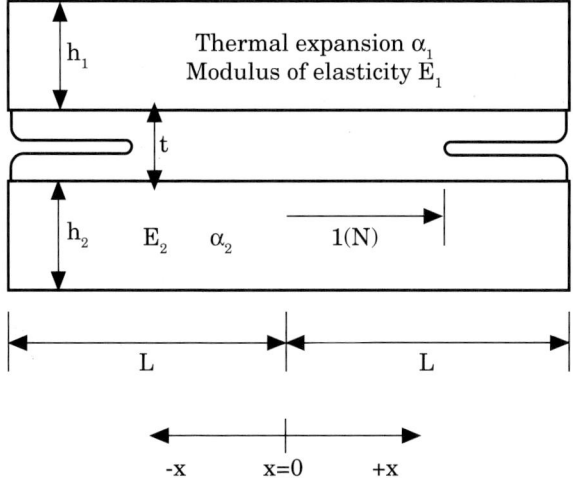

Fig. 13.11 Schematic cross-section of an adhesive joint and the adherends.

A physical model describing thermal fatigue of adhesive bonds has been developed.[8] The model gives the thermal resistance of the bond layer as a function of the number of thermal cycles. The model gave a consistent description of the thermal fatigue characteristics of silver-filled epoxy adhesives in die-attach applications on substrates with different thermal expansions.

The starting point for the thermal fatigue model is an equation describing the propagation rate of the crack tip as a function of geometrical, material and environmental parameters. This equation, known as the Paris-Erdogan Equation,[9] gives the crack growth rate in materials exposed to cyclic stress as:

$$\frac{dl}{dN} = -C(\Delta K)^m \tag{13.13}$$

In this equation, dl is the increase in crack length per cycle dN, C and m are material constants, and ΔK is the difference in stress intensity factor between low and high temperatures. The stress intensity factor describes the stress field close to a crack tip in terms of the far field stress and the crack geometry. Simple expressions for K exist in the case of simple stress fields and crack geometry, but a cracking bond layer does not possess a simple stress field. As a first approximation, K can be taken as proportional to the dominant far field stress in the bond layer which is the shear stress.

Equation (13.11) can be solved in terms of the crack length as a function of the number of temperature cycles l(N).

$$l(N) = L\left[C(1-m)(N+1)\left(\frac{\Delta\alpha\Delta TG}{t}\right)^m\right]^{\frac{1}{1-m}} \quad \text{Low G} \tag{13.14}$$

$$l(N) = L - CN\left[\Delta\alpha\Delta T\sqrt{\frac{G}{t}}\sqrt{\frac{E_1h_1E_2h_2}{E_1h_1+E_2h_2}}\right]^m \quad \text{High G} \tag{13.15}$$

In these equations, Δa is the difference in thermal expansion between the chip and the substrate. ΔT is the temperature difference between the high and the low temperature of the cycle. G is the shear modulus of the adhesive, t is the thickness of the bond layer, and L is the diagonal half length of the bond area. E_1 and E_2 are the moduli of elasticity in the die and the substrate and h_1 and h_2 are the thicknesses of the die and the substrate. C is a constant depending on the adhesive.

From a thermal management point of view, the interesting result is the effect of the crack growth on the thermal resistance of the bond layer. The cracked part of the bond layer will maintain some heat transfer capability, but far less than the uncracked part. If t is the thickness of the bond layer and λ is the thermal conductivity of the adhesive, then the thermal conductivity is given as R(N):

$$R(N) = \frac{t}{4\lambda l(N)^2} \tag{13.16}$$

where l(N) is given by Equation (13.14) for low-G adhesives or (13.15) for high-G adhesives.

The models have been fitted to a set of experimental data obtained by using silicon test chips with dimensions 8 x 8 x 0.38 mm, see Figures 13.12 and 13.13.[8] The test chips were bonded to substrates made of copper and copper-coated aluminium with two different silver-filled epoxy adhesives, Adhesive A and Adhesive B. The substrates were subjected to temperature cycles between +10 and +150°C, and the thermal resistance from the chips to the substrate was recorded after each cycle. The High-G model, Equations (13.15) and (13.16), was selected for Adhesive A. The High-G model was unable to reproduce the shape of the experimental data for Adhesive B. The Low-G model was therefore selected for Adhesive B.

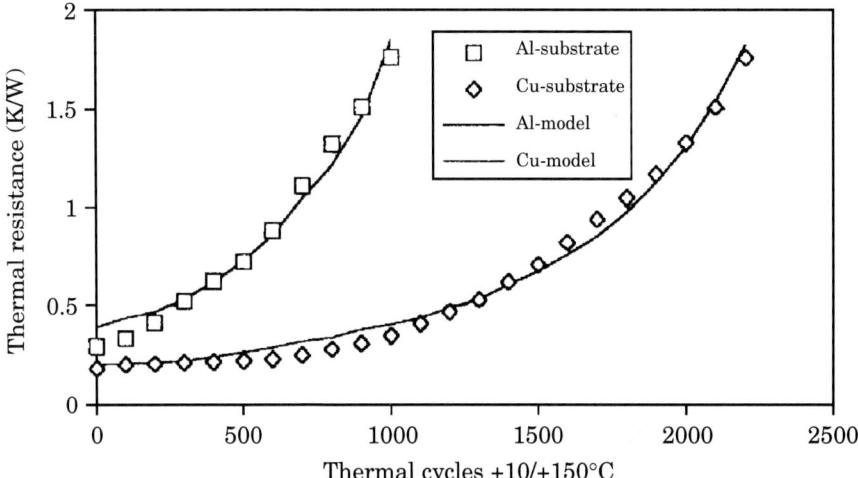

Fig. 13.12 The data points show the thermal resistance of test chips attached to copper-coated aluminium and copper substrates as a function of the number of thermal cycles between +10 and +150°C. The chips were bonded with Adhesive A.

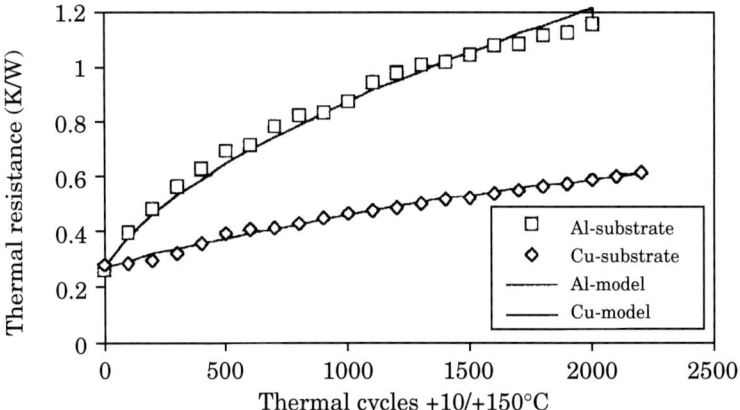

Fig. 13.13 The data points show the thermal resistance of test chips attached to copper-coated aluminium and copper substrates as a function of the number of thermal cycles between +10 and +150°C. The chips were bonded with Adhesive B.

13.6   DESIGN AND OPTIMISATION OF DIE ATTACH

This section is concerned with how to design and verify a practical die attach. The first thing to check out is whether the die attach will conduct the heat away from the die within an acceptable temperature difference between the die and the heat sink. Thermal analysis and design software such as FEM are very helpful at this stage. It is also quite useful to do some thermal measurements with a thermal test chip or some kind of dummy structure to determine the effective thermal conductivity that can be expected in the joint. As mentioned above, the effective thermal conductivity can be considerably below the bulk thermal conductivity referred to in the data sheet.

When a sufficiently good thermal performance is obtained, the next step would be to verify the mechanical properties of the die attach. Die shear strength measurements should be carried out in order to check for delamination or cracking of the bond layer. It is also important to check that the die attach adhesive does not exert such thermal stresses to the die that there is a risk of premature die cracking.

Life testing will be the next step. Samples may, for instance, be subjected to high temperature storage, high temperature in combination with high humidity, mechanical vibrations and temperature cycling. The amount of testing depends on the application. The most critical test is often the temperature cycling.

The samples should be tested after the life testing in order to determine the amount of deterioration. Thermal resistance measurement is a convenient way to determine deterioration of adhesive joints. Cracks and delamination show up as an increase in thermal resistance. The relative increase in thermal resistance can therefore be used as a direct measure for degree of deterioration.

It can be efficient to utilise a Design Of Experiment (DOE) method for the optimal selection of a die-attach adhesive. The Taguchi method is suitable for such purposes.[10] Table 13.3 shows an experimental plan based on the

Table 13.3

Experimental Plan based on the Taguchi Method for Optimisation
of Die-attach Adhesives

Experiment No.	Type of Adhesive	High Temperature Storage	High Humidity Storage	Substrate Metallisation	Adhesive Thickness
1	Adhesive A	Yes	Yes	Nickel	30 µm
2	Adhesive A	No	No	Gold	50 µm
3	Adhesive B	Yes	Yes	Gold	50 µm
4	Adhesive B	No	No	Nickel	30 µm
5	Adhesive C	Yes	No	Nickel	50 µm
6	Adhesive C	No	Yes	Gold	30 µm
7	Adhesive D	Yes	No	Gold	30 µm
8	Adhesive D	No	Yes	Nickel	50 µm

(Eight separate experiments are performed according to the table. The response parameter is a relative increase in thermal resistance after a certain number of temperature cycles.)

Taguchi method for optimisation of adhesive material, substrate metallisation and adhesive thickness. The external environmental parameters are high temperature storage, high humidity storage and temperature cycling.

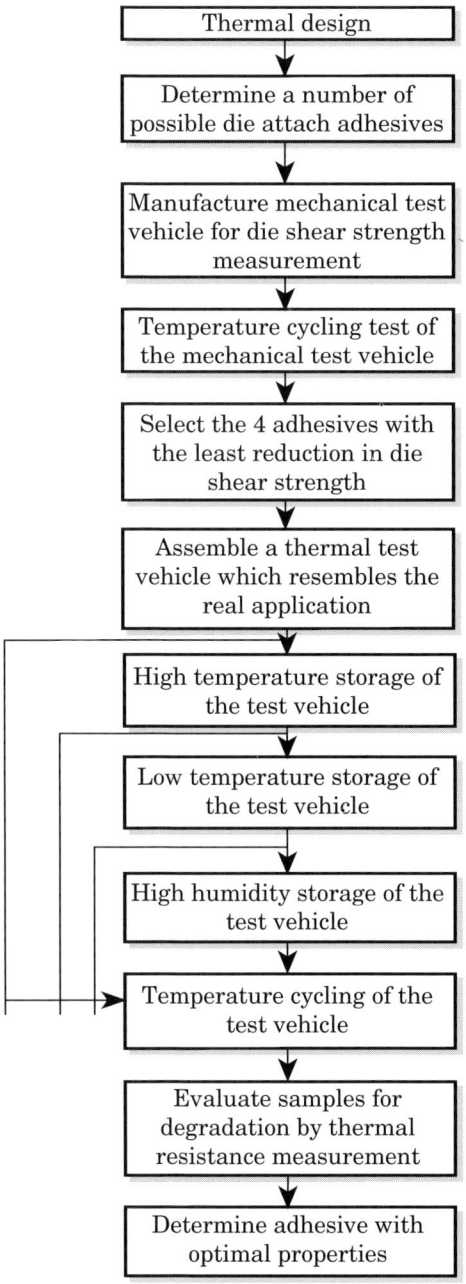

Fig. 13.14 A typical test and verification flow for die-attach adhesives is shown above.

REFERENCES

1 Maxwell, J. C., 'A Treatise on Electricity and Magnetism', 3rd Edition, Dover, New York, Chapter 9 (1954).

2 Bruggeman & Landauer, American Institute of Physics Conference Proceedings, No. 40, edited by J. C. Garland and D. B. Tanner, American Institute of Physics, New York, p. 2 (1978).

3 Nielsen, L. E., 'The Thermal and Electrical Conductivity of Two-Phase Systems', *Industrial Engineering Chemistry Fundamentals*, **Vol. 13**, No. 1 pp. 17-20.

4 Bjorneklett, A., Halbo, L. and Kristiansen, H., 'Investigation of the Thermal and Mechanical Properties of Die Attach Adhesives', Proceedings International Electronic Packaging Conference, pp. 509-522 (1992).

5 Chen, W. T. and Nelson, C. W., 'Thermal Stress in Bonded Joints', *IBM Journal of Research & Development*, **Vol. 23**, No. 2, pp. 179-188, March (1979).

6 Lanchbery, J. F. and Shorthouse, G., 'Measurement of Stress and Temperature Distribution in Large Area Dies', Proceedings 8th International Electronic Manufacturing Technology Symposium, Baveno, Italy, May (1990).

7 Bjorneklett, A., Tuhus, T., Halbo, L. and Kristiansen, H., 'Thermal Resistance, Thermomechanical Stress and Thermal Cycling Endurance of Silicon Chips Bonded with Adhesives, Proceedings IEEE Semiconductor Thermal Measurement and Management Symposium, Austin, TX, USA, pp. 136-143 (1993).

8 Bjorneklett, A., Tuhus, T. and Kristiansen, H., 'A Model for Thermal Fatigue of Large Area Adhesive Joints between Materials with Dissimilar Thermal Expansion', Proceedings IEEE Semiconductor Thermal Measurement and Management Symposium, San Jose, CA, USA, pp. 138-141 (1994).

9 Sobczyk, K. and Spencer, B. F., 'Random Fatigue, from Data to Theory', Academic Press, Inc. (1992).

10 Taguchi, G., 'Introduction to Quality Engineering', American Supplier Institute International, Inc., Dearborn, Michigan, USA (1986).

Chapter 14

REPLACING SOLDER WITH ISOTROPICALLY CONDUCTIVE ADHESIVES IN DIE BONDING OF POWER SEMICONDUCTORS

OUTI RUSANEN
VTT, Oulu, Finland

14.1   ISOTROPICALLY CONDUCTIVE ADHESIVES

Conductive adhesives consist of a polymer matrix filled with conductive particles. The polymer matrix and its characteristics are mostly responsible for the adhesive's ability to bond and withstand mechanical stresses. The electrical conductivity of the adhesive depends in particular on the filler material and its particle size, shape, amount and distribution. Polymer matrices, and especially filler materials, are able to conduct heat. Table 14.1 lists the criteria for selecting the polymer and filler materials.

Table 14.1

Criteria for Selecting Polymer and Filler Materials for
Conductive Adhesives

Criteria for Selecting Polymer Matrix	Criteria for Selecting Filler Material
Sufficient adhesion for different surfaces	Sufficient electrical and thermal conduction
Ability to withstand high amounts of filler materials	Does not form insulating oxides
Low amount of ionic contaminants	Corrosion resistant
Suitable for production and rework	Good adhesion to the polymer matrix
Low shrinkage due to cure	Not an environmentally or occupationally harmful substance
Low outgassing during cure	
Ability to withstand commonly used solvents	
Ability to withstand mechanical stresses	
Not an environmentally or occupationally harmful substance	

The most commonly used filler particles are metals. For cost savings, insulating material particles with metal plating can also be used. In a survey of adhesives, it has been found that 158 out of 201 electrically conductive adhesives have silver as the filler material. In 12 adhesives, gold is used, 8 types use nickel, 5 types use copper, and in 18 adhesives another material is used.[1] The shape, size and distribution of the filler particles also affect the conductivity of the adhesives.

To improve the adhesives' electrical and thermal conductivities, the amount of conducting filler particles may be increased. Experiments have, however, shown two results. One is that the maximum amount of silver particles in an epoxy matrix is approximately 30% by volume, and the second is that the adhesion of the adhesive is severely degraded.[2] The amount of silver in isotropically conductive adhesives is therefore typically between 70 and 80% by weight.

In isotropically conductive adhesives, the use of epoxies has been 'the state-of-the-art' for a long time. This is due to the many beneficial properties of epoxies. They have low shrinkage, good adhesion, and resistance to thermal and mechanical shocks. They also have good resistance to moisture, solvents and chemical attacks. The desirable properties may further be improved with a suitable choice of solvents, fillers, colorants, flame retardants, flexibilisers and cure accelerators.

Recently, conductive adhesives with thermoplastic polymer matrices have emerged on the market. They facilitate rework and may offer a short bonding process. Suitable polymer matrix materials may be polyurethane, polyimides or polysulphones among others. Because the thermoplastic adhesive matrices consist of long polymer chains, their rheological properties must be improved with the substantial use of solvents.

Working with thermoplastic conductive adhesives does not differ much from working with epoxy-based adhesives. The only significant difference is in the processing time or the time span. After applying a thermoset epoxy adhesive, the component mounting time is limited by the adhesive's pot life. After applying a thermoplastic adhesive, the adhesive normally needs to be dried. After this, the components or substrates can be stacked for storage or even transport, and also for later use.

14.2   COMPARING ADHESIVE DIE BONDING WITH SOLDERING

14.2.1   Adhesion and Mechanical Properties

When soldering, the solder alloy is melted and brought into contact with the adherend metallisation. The molten solder alloy wets the adherend surface and, upon solder solidification, forms a metallic contact. Wetting is possible only if the solder is able to come into immediate contact with the metallic surface of the solid metal part; then sufficient attraction is ensured. Any firmly adhering contamination, such as oxides on the surface to be soldered, will act as a barrier to metallic continuity, thus preventing wetting[3]. The strong interaction between solder, especially its tin content, and some base metals may also result in the formation of intermetallic layers.[4]

With adhesive bonding, the liquid state adhesive is applied to the adherend surface and, on adhesive cure, it hardens and mechanically interlocks into adherend surface irregularities. The adhesive and adherend do not need to interact except when the adhesive is in its liquid state. At that time, it must be able to wet the adherend surface. Adhesives are able to wet many kinds of surfaces such as metals, metal oxides, wood and even some polymers. The difference between a solder joint and an adhesive joint is further illustrated in Figure 14.1.

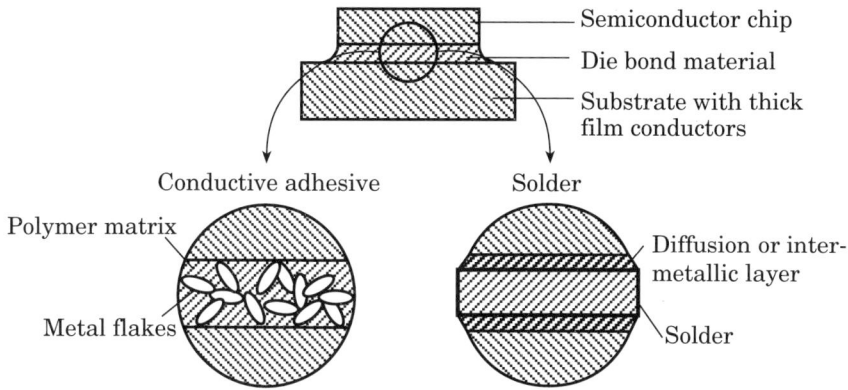

Fig. 14.1 Solder and conductive adhesive as a die bond material.

Once the bond is formed, its reliability, or lifetime, depends upon many die bond material properties such as tensile strength, shear strength and creep. In solder joints, fatigue, as a rule, is caused by cyclic deformation as a result of temperature changes produced by irregular currents in the electronics equipment. The results of such fatigue are cracked joints which may eventually cause a complete interruption of the connection.[4] In low-cycle thermal or mechanical fatigue, the adhesive joints, notably those based on epoxy, are able to exhibit significantly better reliability than equivalent solder joints. This is due to the intrinsic elasticity of the epoxy.[4] Some numerical figures representing the mechanical properties of tin-lead solders and conductive adhesives may be found in Table 14.2. It must be stressed that the figures given for solder in Table 14.2 are only approximations, since

Table 14.2

Mechanical Properties of Die Bond Materials

Property	Tin / Lead Solders	Conductive Adhesives
Modulus of elasticity	32 N/mm^2 for eutectic tin-lead solder at room temperature[4]	From 0.14 to 6 N/mm^2 according to adhesive manufacturers
Tensile strength	37-38 N/mm^2 (Ref. 3)	9-11 N/mm^2 (Ref. 3)
Shear strength	From 12 to 52 N/mm^2 Sn62Pb36Ag2 and from 14 to 55 N/mm^2 for Pb95Sn5, depending on test strain rate and temperature[4]	From 10 to 50 N/mm^2 according to adhesive manufacturers

various aspects such as solder alloy constituents, solder microstructure just after solidification, storage after solidification, and operating temperature of solder joint affect the properties. The figures given for conductive adhesives are also approximations since adhesives perform differently under varying conditions.

14.2.2   Electrical and Thermal Conductivity

Tin-lead solders are superior electrical and thermal conductors compared with isotropically conductive adhesives. The electrical and thermal resistances of the die bond layer are often only a small part of the module's total electrical or thermal resistances. Therefore, conductive adhesives perform satisfactorily as die bond materials for most applications.

The bulk volume resistivity of silver-filled epoxy is, at best, approximately ten times higher than the volume resistivity of eutectic tin-lead solder ($\approx 170 \cdot 10^{-6} \ \Omega \cdot cm$).

The bulk thermal conductivity of silver-filled adhesives ranges from 1 W/m·K to 8 W/m·K. The thermal conductivity of eutectic tin-lead solder is approximately 50 W/m·K. The inferior thermal conductivity of the conductive adhesive may cause an increase of thermal resistance in the die bonded transistor structure. Theoretically, this increase can be negated by using thinner layers of adhesive than of solder. (Typically, the solder layer thickness is around 100 μm.) In practice, however, the thermal resistance in adhesive die bonding layers shows a strong residual part, probably due to interfaces or micro-cracks in the adhesive.[5] This means that uniform bonding of interfaces dictates the thermal resistance rather than the bulk resistivity or layer thickness of the adhesive.

14.2.3   Processing

For adhesive assembly, the components are placed on spots of uncured, isotropically conductive adhesives just as components to be reflow soldered are placed on to spots of solder paste. The substrates are then subjected to thermal treatment in order to cure the adhesive, during which time it sets to form a permanent and conductive layer. Cleaning is not needed after the adhesive has been cured.

Both isotropically conductive adhesives and solder pastes may be applied by either dispensing or screen or stencil printing. To achieve a quality joint, it is necessary to print or otherwise place enough adhesive for a strong bond. On the other hand, the adhesive amount is limited so that bridging is avoided. Unlike solder, adhesives do not have a high surface tension, and will not pull back to the joints where there are wettable surfaces. Adhesives adhere equally well to the substrate and, once a smear or a bridge is created, it cannot be easily removed. For this reason, a clean, distinct, well-defined print is critical. The amount of adhesive that should be placed is less than the amount of solder paste that is traditionally placed. This is because solder paste is typically about 50% flux by volume. In addition, in a soldered joint, some of the solder will wick up the leads due to surface tension and wetting forces. This does not happen in joints manufactured with adhesives, which further reduces the amount of adhesive needed.[6]

Component placing requires more accuracy while working with adhesives than when working with solder paste. If the component is misplaced, it might cause the adhesive to smear across the adjacent pads. At that time, it will probably be necessary to remove the components, clean the substrate with alcohol or acetone and print a new adhesive. Downward placement of the adhesive also needs special care. On some placement machines, the components are dropped into the paste. This is not a problem for solder pastes because the solder will wet the lead during reflow. With adhesive usage, this may be a problem. If the component lead is sitting on top of the adhesive, but not in it, it will not form a strong bond. It will probably not form any bond at all. The adhesive will cure and there will be a component sitting on top of a cured adhesive bonded to pads. It is important that the components are placed in the adhesive.[7]

Many of the adhesives cure at lower temperatures than the typical solder paste reflow process. Curing usually takes place at constant temperatures between 100°C and 150°C. This reduces thermomechanical stresses due to temperature gradients.

14.2.4   Cost Approximation

Silver-filled epoxy adhesives cost more than eutectic tin-lead solder creams. Often, the adhesives must be stored at sub-zero temperatures, which adds to their transport costs. On the other hand, the amount of isotropically conductive adhesives used is less than that of solder paste.

When replacing solder with conductive adhesives, the cost of manufacturing is lessened because the process is simplified. Convection ovens used for adhesive curing are simpler and cheaper than soldering ovens (equipment). Also, there is no need for flux removal, which saves additional work, solvents and equipment.

14.2.5   Environmental Considerations

Tin-lead solder is the most common joining material in electronics. Lately, the toxicity of lead has caused some concern. In the United States, Congress has proposed the Lead Exposure Reduction Act of 1990 which aims to reduce and finally eliminate lead-containing solders and other lead-containing products such as paint. The bill was not passed, but the issue on lead is still under discussion. Regarding lead-free solders, the development focuses on bismuth-tin alloys.[7]

Silver-containing epoxy adhesives are not ideal as regards environmental issues. From the viewpoint of recycling or repair, thermoplastic polymers are preferable. They are commercially available, but up until now have rarely been utilised compared with epoxies. Epoxy products are also irritating to the skin and the eyes, thus may cause allergic reactions through contact by sensitised persons. Once an allergic reaction to these substances has been developed, the worker will be excluded from all work with epoxy and polyurethane for life. Precautions such as wearing gloves and arranging for proper ventilation are necessary in the working environment. Once cured or polymerised, epoxy substances are neither reactive nor allergenic.[8]

Additionally, no harmful substances are permitted in the adhesives or auxiliary substances, e.g., the use of solvents should be avoided as far as possible. As the harm of potential metals distributed in the environment is not usually known, the metal content should be as small as possible. For example, silver works as a disinfectant for micro-organisms, and nickel is known as an allergen. Furthermore, biological effects may not be excluded. Metal content, as small as possible (technologically), is also economically favourable.[8]

The Swedish Research Institute, IVF, has performed a study on the environmental impact of a tin-lead solder and a conductive adhesive. The result varies according to the evaluation method. If waste is emphasised, then conductive adhesives are a better option for the environment. When the environmental load from the extraction and production of silver is emphasised, then tin-lead solder is the better choice.[9]

14.3   POWER SEMICONDUCTOR DIE BONDING WITH ISOTROPICALLY CONDUCTIVE ADHESIVES

Semiconductor components which dissipate more than one watt may be defined as power semiconductors. This is a rather loose definition of the term. Other definitions for a power semiconductor are that a component's current exceeds a few hundred milliamperes or that the maximum voltage over the component exceeds 50 V.[10]

A power module consists of several power semiconductors that are die bonded on to one substrate. The module has all the necessary inner and outer connections as well as module encapsulation (Figure 14.2). Packaging several bare semiconductors on to one module rather than making a module of individually packaged semiconductors offers several advantages such as improved cost-effectiveness and reliability. An important reliability issue is heat transfer from the semiconductor. The dissipated power heats up the component and, eventually, the whole module. If bare semiconductor components are die bonded to a substrate which is attached to a copper cooling plate, heat is able to transfer effectively into a cooling element. The thermal resistance of such a module is around 1 K/W. If individually packaged semiconductors are attached to the substrates, the module's thermal resistance may easily exceed 10 K/W.

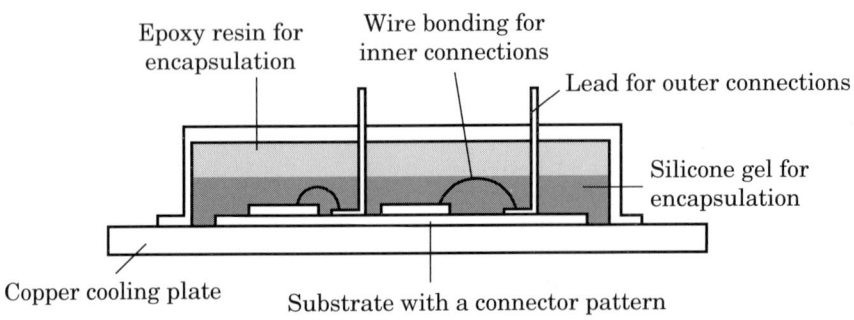

Fig. 14.2 A typical power module construction.

In power modules, die bonding with solder has been 'the state of the art'. Solder offers unique capabilities to make a stable, mechanical connection which also has low electrical and thermal resistivities. The characteristics of a solder joint have fulfilled the user's need, even though the cyclic operation of power modules may cause reliability problems with solder fatigue. On the other hand, module manufacturing with solder has offered a number of challenges. Bare semiconductors are sensitive to any impurities and, therefore, flux residue removal must be performed with the greatest care.

Semiconductor die bonding is often carried out with a high lead content solder such as Pb95Sn5 which has a melting point of approximately 300°C. The high soldering temperature complicates flux removal. If no flux is used, the soldering must take place in a reactive atmosphere such as a gas mixture of hydrogen-nitrogen. This requires expensive equipment and the soldering process is difficult to control. The other problems with manufacturing originate from the module's large thermal mass which further complicates soldering, since the time that the solder is in a liquid state should be a matter of only a few seconds. Reworkability of a module is also complex as local heating of only one semiconductor is almost impossible. Power modules must have good capability for transferring heat.

The manufacturing of power modules is simplified when the solder in die bonding is replaced by isotropically conductive adhesives. The most obvious reason for this is the elimination of the cleaning steps. Rework is also easier since adhesive joints do not need to be heated locally. The whole module may be heated to an appropriate temperature and the faulty component is then removed mechanically. A new component is placed and the adhesive may be cured again with no harm done to the previously cured adhesive joints.

The use of adhesives also promotes the so-called step of manufacturing. Expensive semiconductor chips can be die bonded first with an adhesive and then cured. Once the semiconductor components are tested, module assembly may continue. The curing temperatures of conductive adhesives are typically around 150°C. That is lower than the liquidus temperature of eutectic tin-lead solder. Thus, the stresses originating from the different thermal expansion coefficients of module materials are lessened. An adhesive joint is also more flexible than a solder joint, which further improves its reliability with mechanical stresses.

14.4   EXPERIMENTAL RESULTS FROM REPLACING SOLDER WITH ISOTROPICALLY CONDUCTIVE ADHESIVES

14.4.1   Test Adhesives

The adhesives used in die bonding are chosen for their maximised electrical and thermal conductivities. Their silver content is between 70 and 80% by weight. All adhesives tested had an epoxy polymer matrix and are denoted as adhesives A, B and C. Adhesive A is a stress absorbing adhesive that is designed for hybrid die attach. Adhesive B is a so-called 'low T_g' adhesive. It has a glass transition point of -20°C. The low T_g should result in adhesive flexibility which makes bonding materials with highly mismatched TCEs (coefficient of thermal expansion) possible. Adhesive C is an adhesive designed specifically for chip bonding in microelectronics and optoelectronics applications. Table 14.3 lists some of the adhesive properties.

Table 14.3

Data on Test Adhesives

Property	Adhesive A	Adhesive B	Adhesive C	Sn62Pb36Ag2
Volume resistivity in mΩ-cm	0.2	<0.4	0.1...0.4	0.017
Thermal conductivity in W/mK	3.7	8	1.6	50
Glass transition point in °C	79	-20	160...180	-
Coefficient of thermal expansion in ppm/K	54...167	120	45...75	25
Modulus of elasticity in kN/mm^2	6.9	0.14	-	32
Adhesive shear strength in N/mm^2	42	8.5...10.6	48	-
Adhesive viscosity (cps)	47,000	-	25,000	-
The shape and approximate size of the conducting silver particles in the adhesive	rounded rectangles, 2...10 μm	flakes and rounded rectangles, 1...5 μm	flakes and rounded rectangles, 1...10 μm	-
Cure conditions used for the adhesives in the test modules in °C/h	150/1.5	150/4	180/2	-

14.4.2   Manufacturing Test Module

A power module was designed and manufactured to study the performance and reliability of isotropically conductive adhesives in die bonding. The test module has power transistors, diodes and structures for measuring corrosion, migration and bond resistance. Figure 14.3 shows a photograph of the test module.

Fig. 14.3 The power module used for testing (alumina size 51 x 102 mm²).

The manufacturing of power modules with conductive adhesives causes some problems. The mechanical strength of adhesive bonded to the outer leads (connectors) is not as good as those attached with solder. Once the adhesive in the modules cures, the leads are prone to break during handling. This is not the case with soldered leads. The situation may improve if adhesives with a lesser silver content are used.

14.4.3   Electrical Effects of Replacing Solder with Isotropically Conductive Adhesives

The voltage-current relationships of the transistors are quite insensitive to the die bond material as is shown in Figure 14.4. Earlier work shows that the electrical resistance of a die bond is a few milliohms (thickness and area of the bond are 30 μm and 25 mm² respectively). Based on this earlier work, it is estimated that the electrical resistivity of the transistor's die bond is around 1 m for adhesives A and B, and 2.5 m for adhesive C (same dimensions as above). Thus, the die bond resistance does not have a significant effect on the transistor's electrical characteristics.

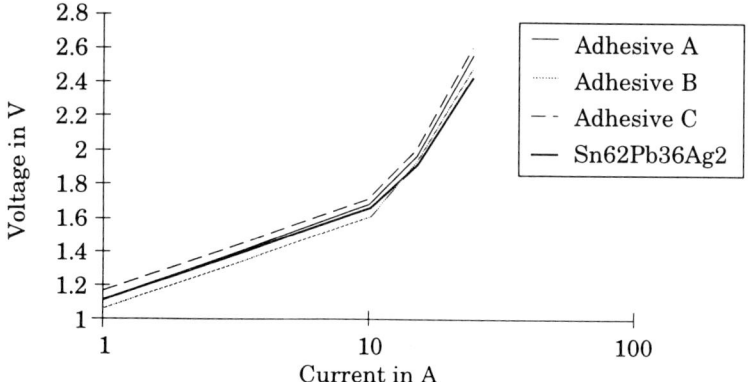

Fig. 14.4 The transistor's voltage-current relationship.

14.4.4   Thermal Effects of Replacing Solder with Isotropically Conductive Adhesives

In this study, the thermal resistance of a power module is simulated and measured. Figure 14.5 shows a thermal model of the case where different materials and the module's capability to transfer heat into ambient are represented by a thermal resistance.

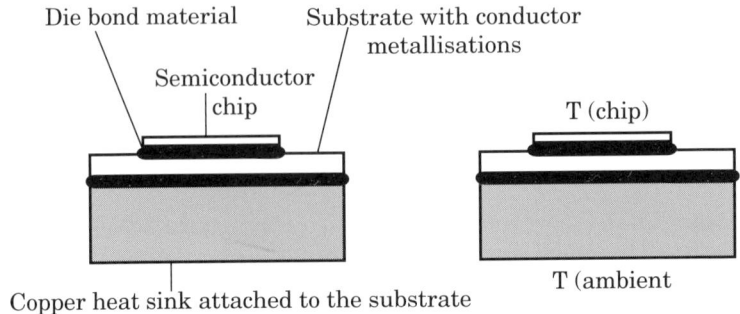

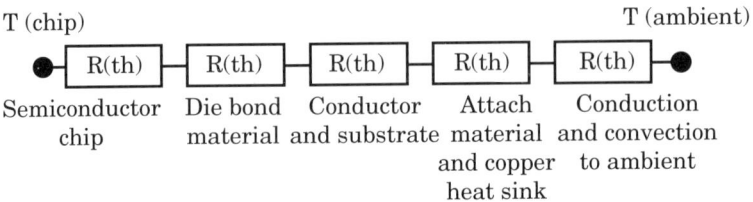

Fig. 14.5 Thermal model of a power module. The different materials and the module's capability to transfer heat into ambient are represented by a thermal resistance.

The measured thermal resistances show that good adhesion between joined surfaces is essential for optimised heat flow. The heat conductivity of an adhesive is only a secondary factor affecting the structure's thermal resistance. Figure 14.6 shows simulated and measured values of the modules with a copper cooling plate.

The agreement between simulated and measured values is only fair. The variation is caused by module manufacturing flaws. The large scattering of thermal resistance is due to improper bonding between the alumina substrate and the copper cooling plate. When looking at the minimum measured values, it can be seen that the solder die bond is superior as a thermal conductor. Nevertheless, the thermal conductivity of the adhesives is adequate for a wide range of applications.

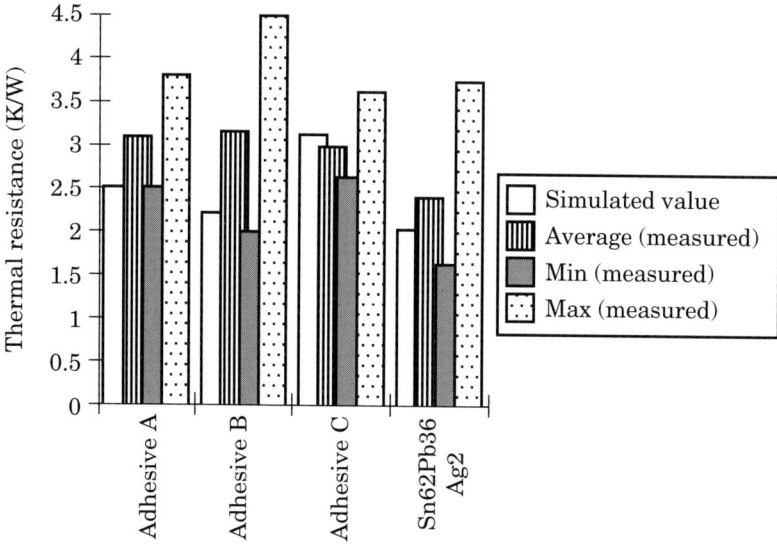

Fig. 14.6 Thermal resistance values for test modules with copper cooling plates. In the simulations, the thickness of the solder die bond is 90 μm, and of the adhesive die bond 50 μm. The diode size is 5.3 x 5.3 mm².

14.5 RELIABILITY ASPECTS OF REPLACING SOLDER WITH ISOTROPICALLY CONDUCTIVE ADHESIVES

The failure mechanisms of adhesive bonds are accelerated by environmental effects such as heat, humidity and mechanical stresses in the bond. Humidity has the greatest effect. On adhesive interfaces, it diminishes adhesion strength which may eventually lead to an adhesion failure. Conductive adhesives generally endure mechanical stresses and relatively high temperatures (~150°C) without a detrimental loss of properties such as electrical conductivity and adhesion strength.

To study the reliability of adhesive joints, the test modules undergo an extensive ageing programme. The test procedures include:

— thermal cycling between -40°C and +125°C for 100 cycles;
— operational cycling between 20°C and 100°C, for 10,000 cycles;
— elevated humidity and temperature at 85%RH/85°C for 1000 hours.

After ageing all modules, they are visually checked. Some undergo destructive shear strength testing and some are analysed with a SEM. The following sections summarise the results of the ageing tests.

14.5.1 Reliability in Thermal and Operational Cycling

The results of the thermal cycling are successful for all test materials even though the temperature range is as wide as -40°C to +125°C (100 cycles). This testing showed that adhesives may endure mechanical stresses without a deterioration in performance (Figure 14.7).

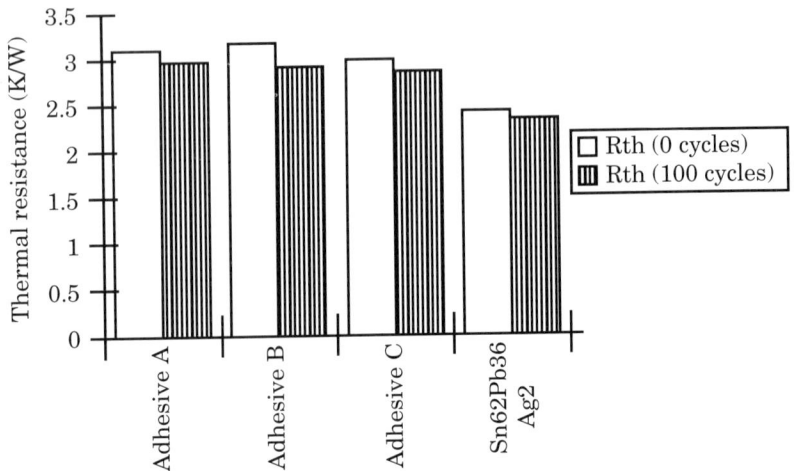

Fig. 14.7 Thermal resistance values for test modules with copper cooling plates before and after thermal cycling (-40°C to 125°C). The diode size is 5.3 x 5.3 mm².

In the operational cycling, a heat generating current (8.5 A) is fed alternately through the diodes and transistors. Each module is heated for 30 s and then allowed to cool for 7 min and 30 s. The heating current is restricted so that the maximum temperatures of the chips are kept below 100°C. The number of operational cycles is 10,000. All adhesives that undergo operational testing perform in a reasonable manner. Figure 14.8 shows the effect of operational cycling on the thermal resistance of diodes. Surprisingly, the solder joints completed the operational test as well as the adhesives. The homogeneity and dimensions of solder joints in the test module have most likely improved their fatigue endurance. Cracking of a solder joint is typical when the solder joint dimensions are small compared with component size, which is not the case with die bonding. Furthermore, the test module soldering took place in a vapour-phase oven, resulting in homogeneous solder joints.

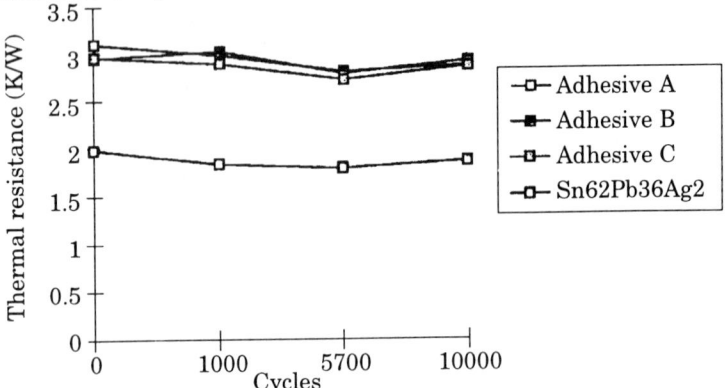

Fig. 14.8 The effect of operational cycling on thermal resistance of diodes. The size of a diode is 5.3 x 5.3 mm².

Another surprising result is the relationship between the adhesive's glass transition point and reliability during testing. It is a common guideline that adhesives should not be used at temperatures above their glass transition temperatures since the mechanical properties of the adhesives show changes in the region of glass transition. This study shows, however, that, in conductive adhesives, transition temperature is not critical for the performance of a die bond (Table 14.4). It may be argued that the mechanical bonding of a semiconductor chip is an undemanding task compared with bonding a large structure such as a car windscreen or an aircraft door.

Table 14.4

Test Adhesives, their Glass Transition Temperatures and Performance in
Thermal and Operational Cycling Tests

Adhesive	Glass Transition Point	Thermal Cycling -40 to +125°C	Operational Cycling ~20 to +100°C
Adhesive A	80°C	good	fair
Adhesive B	-20°C	fair	fair
Adhesive C	180°C	good	fair

14.5.2   Reliability in Elevated Humidity and Temperature Ageing

In this study, elevated humidity and temperature (85%RH/85°C for 1000 hours) ageing deteriorates the test structures and test modules most. At worst, damp heat causes debonding of the adhesive joints to the degree that the die bonds are fractured depending on the adhesive and adherend metallisations. The test module has AgPt thick-film conductors and does not perform well in damp heat ageing.

Earlier work has shown that, in damp heat, the choice of adherend metallisation is critical. The effect of damp heat ageing on different component metallisations may be seen in Figure 14.9. The most reliable adherend metallisation is gold, as can be expected. Gold is a noble metal that does not form stable compounds with oxygen, sulphur etc. When Ni-plated metal plates are die bonded to gold thick-film conductors, the electrical resistance of the structure is no longer stable during elevated humidity and temperature ageing, even if all bonds remain conductive during ageing. When Ni-plated metal plates are die bonded to Cu and AgPt thick-film conductors, the ageing effects become fairly evident with some fractured joints.

The test module includes a corrosion test chip. It has two aluminium conductor chains whose resistance is monitored during damp heat testing. The changes in the measured resistances are negligible, less than 1%. It may be concluded that the low level of impurities in adhesives does not induce corrosion.

The structure used for silver migration testing also gives negative results. There is no migration visible on the test module after 1000 hours in 85%RH/ 85°C. This finding agrees with other studies.[11] It could be that the polymer matrix's ability to wet and surround the conducting silver particles prevents migration under humid conditions.

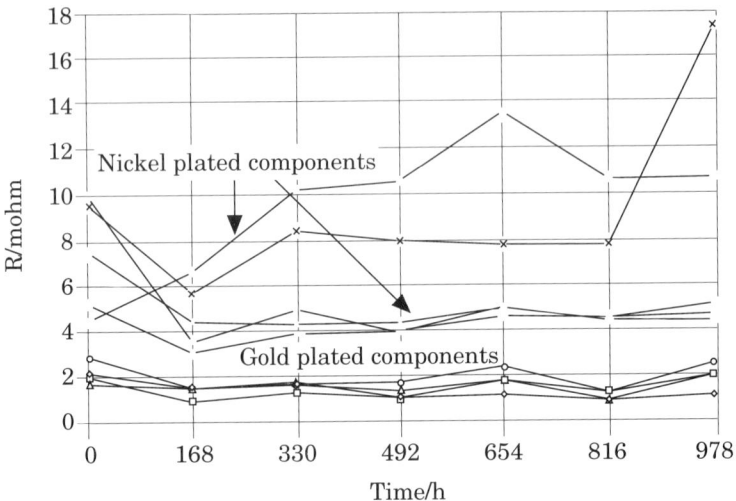

Fig. 14.9 The effects of ageing at 85%RH/85°C on the junction resistance of adhesive joints of Au- and Ni-plated components bonded to thick-film Au metallisation.

14.5.3   Analysing Test Adhesive Reliability

Adhesive A performs best of all the test adhesives. Its ability to bond and stay bonded after the elevated ageing test is unique among the conductive adhesives tested. All metallisations tested (Au, Ni, Cu and AgPt) survive damp heat testing. The superior performance and ability to bond starts with good initial wetting of the adhesive (Figure 14.10). The homogeneous adhesive interfaces are resistant to humidity and mechanical stresses.

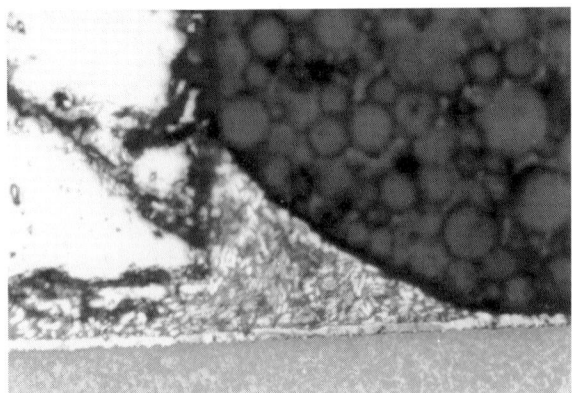

Fig. 14.10 A microscope picture taken from a cross-section sample. In the picture, the die is bonded with adhesive A and the adhesive has wetted the die side.

The test module with adhesive B performs poorly in 150°C ageing and 85%RH/85°C ageing. The high temperature testing takes place at 170°C above its glass transition point, which results in faulty adhesive joints. In 85%RH/85°C ageing, the humidity penetration is probably increased by elevated temperature. It should be remembered that the damp heat performance is a function of adherend metallisation also. In the earlier tests, adhesive B was used to bond gold-plated components on to Au thick-film conductors. These test structures remain stable during 1000 hours of 85%RH/85°C conditions.

Adhesive B contains more silver than the other test adhesives and thus its bonding ability may not be optimal. The poor quality bond most probably accelerates the deterioration of the adhesive joints. It may then be argued that the die bonding process with Adhesive B should be optimised in order to produce better quality bonds. Adhesive B survives operational and thermal cycling fairly well, probably because it has the lowest E-modulus of the test adhesives. Figure 14.11 shows a SEM photograph of test adhesives A, B and C.

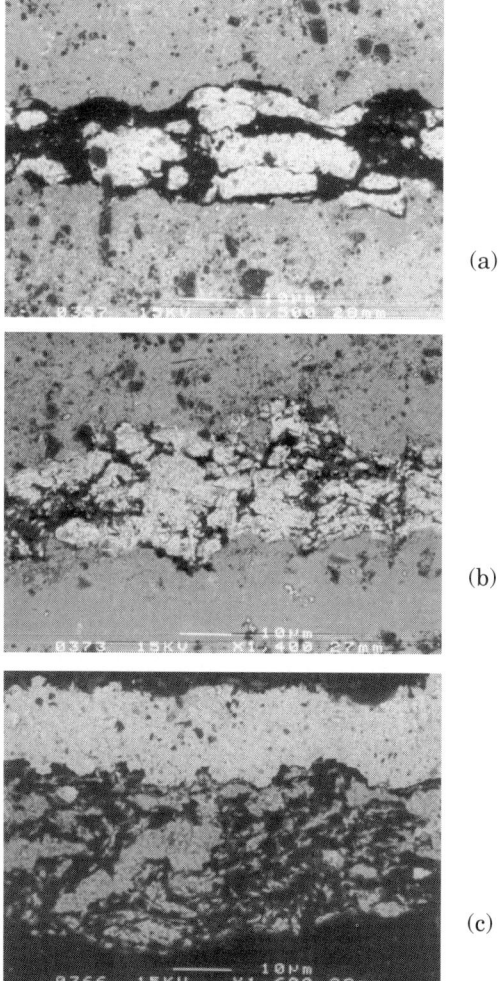

(a)

(b)

(c)

Fig. 14.11 SEM photographs from test adhesives A, B and C. The darker areas show adhesive polymer in which lighter coloured silver particles are embedded. In the pictures of adhesives A and B, some of the adherend surface is also visible at top and bottom of the picture.

The 85%RH/85°C ageing proves unfortunate for test modules with adhesive C. This adhesive has a high glass transition point, which may be the result of polar groups in its main molecular chain. These polar groups in molecular chains may enhance water penetration into the adhesive and make it less resistant to humidity.[12] Again, the damp heat performance is a function of adherend metallisation. In the earlier tests, adhesive C was used to bond gold-plated components on to Au thick-film conductors. These test structures remain stable during 1000 hours of 85%RH/85°C conditions.

Figure 14.12 shows a microscope photograph taken from a cross-section sample. In the photograph, adhesive C does not show any wetting. It may be argued then that the disastrous performance at elevated humidity and temperature ageing is a result of adhesive characteristics and an improper bonding process. The wetting of the adhesive C may have been aided by external pressure during or after component placing. The adhesive survives the other ageing test adequately, which indicates that the bonding process is not a complete failure.

Fig. 14.12 A microscope photograph taken from a cross-section sample. In the picture, the die is bonded with adhesive C and the adhesive has not wetted the die side. The crack between die and adhesive results from sample preparation.

14.6   CONCLUSIONS

The manufacturing of power modules is simplified when solder die bonding is replaced by the use of isotropically conductive adhesives. The most apparent reason for this is the elimination of the cleaning steps.

Isotropically conductive adhesives are inferior electrical conductors compared with tin-lead solders. In spite of this, the voltage current relationships of power transistors are insensitive to the die bond material. The electrical resistance of isotropically conductive adhesive bonds is in the range of a few milliohms.

Isotropically conductive adhesives are also inferior thermal conductors compared with tin-lead solder. Nevertheless, the thermal conductivity of the adhesives tested is adequate for a wide range of applications. The measured thermal resistances show that good adhesion between joint surfaces is essential for optimised heat flow. The heat conductivity of the adhesive material is only a secondary factor affecting the module's thermal resistance. Suitable values of electrical and thermal conductivity do not guarantee reliable performance in adhesive die bonding. Above all, a conductive adhesive must be able to make homogeneous bondlines. Increasing the amount of silver particles beyond a certain limit may also increase the adhesive bond's electrical and thermal resistance.

When gold surfaces are adhesively bonded, the joints are usually reliable. With careful adhesive selection, other metal surfaces may also be bonded. Damp heat presents the most demanding conditions for conductive adhesives and may lead to the debonding of joints. Accelerated testing with elevated temperature or operational cycling, on the other hand, has been well endured by most adhesives tested.

Isotropically conductive adhesives offer a viable option for soldering, even in power module manufacturing.

REFERENCES

1   Wipfelder, E. and Ortmann, K., 'Elektrisch leitfähige Klebstoffe für elektronische Bauelemente', *Adhäsion,* No. 11. pp. 26-30 (1989).

2   Brunner, H., 'Leistungsmechanismus und Funktionsverhalten elektrisch leitender Klebungen am Beispiel eines Leistungstransistors', *Schweißtechnische Forschungsberichte,* Deutscher Verlag für Schweißtechnik (DVS) GmbH, Düsseldorf, Germany, **Vol. 10**, No.177, pp. 51,131.

3   Klein Wassink, R.J., 'Soldering in Electronics', Electrochemical Publications Ltd, Ayr, Scotland, pp. 35, 149, 162, 187, 188 (1989).

4   Lea, C., 'A Scientific Guide to Surface Mount Technology', Electrochemical Publications Ltd, Ayr, Scotland, p.306 (1988).

5   Bjorneklett, A., Halbo, L. and Kristiansen, H., 'Investigation of the Thermal and Mechanical Properties of Die Attach Adhesives', Proceedings International Electronic Packaging Conference, Austin, Texas, pp. 509-522, September (1992).

6   Greaves, J. B. Jr, 'Manufacturing with Conductive Adhesives', Nepcon West conference, Anaheim, California, pp. 587-590, March (1994).

7   Hartwig, A. and Hennemann, O.-D., 'Debonding of Adhesively Joined Electronic Circuits to the Purpose of Recycling', IVF Seminar on 'Recent Achievements in Conductive Adhesive Joining Technology in Electronics Manufacture', Gothenburg, Sweden, September (1993).

8   Westphal, H., 'The Toxicology of Electrically Conductive Adhesives — A Review of Epoxies', First International Conference on Adhesive Joining Technology in Electronics Manufacturing, Berlin, November (1994).

9   Segerberg, T., 'Life Cycle Assessment of Tin-lead Solder and Conductive Adhesive in Surface Mount Technology', IVF Report 95051, The Swedish Institute of Production Engineering Research (1995).

10   VTT, Mikroelektroniikan kehittämisohjelma (1987-1990), Tehokomponentit, Loppuraportti, Helsinki (1990).

11   Hvims, H. L., 'Electrically Conductive Adhesives for SMT', ECR-255, ElektronikCentralen (1993).

12   ASM International, 'Engineered Materials Handbook', **Vol. 3**, 'Adhesives and Sealants', ASM International, p. 623 (1990).

Chapter 15

OVERVIEW OF CONDUCTIVE ADHESIVE INTERCONNECTION TECHNOLOGIES FOR DISPLAY APPLICATIONS

HELGE KRISTIANSEN
SINTEF Electronics and Cybernetics, Oslo, Norway

JOHAN LIU
IVF, Mölndal, Sweden

15.1 INTRODUCTION

The importance of display devices, the most common user-machine interface, has increased as the information society progresses. Liquid crystal displays (LCDs) are now becoming the most important of these devices, because they, compared with traditional CRTs (cathode ray tubes), combine a compact and flat shape with low power consumption. In addition, LCDs are light and are easily compatible with large-scale integrated chips. The image quality of LCDs has improved significantly. However, for them to be more widely applied and to surpass cathode ray tubes (CRTs) in image quality, technical developments are needed such as high resolution and large capacity. Dramatic cost improvements are necessary also, particularly in the large screen segment, before LCDs can compete in price with CRTs.

Japanese companies continue to dominate the large area LCD market, but several Korean and Taiwanese companies have begun mass production. In Europe, Philips is one of the companies that manufactures its own LCD displays. In the USA, Planar International focuses on electroluminescent technology. Manufacturing yields have increased significantly and prices have dropped sharply because of over-capacity and competition.

This means that suppliers are now focusing on lowering material costs and increasing throughput by the use of larger substrates and factory automation. Japanese suppliers have begun to move LCD assembly offshore, for example to the Philippines. Furthermore, most Japanese companies are shifting their focus to the high end of the market, moving from 10.4 in. displays to 11.3 in., 12.1 in. and even 17.7 in. displays with increasing resolution and full colour.

The other end of the high performance display market is the small sized, 1-3 inch-diagonal, with high resolution. These displays are used for camera viewfinders or light valves for liquid crystal projectors. Simple matrix LCDs, used for character displays, are another part of the market.

15.2 LCD CONSTRUCTION

LCDs consist of two glass plates that sandwich aligned liquid crystal polymers. The glass plates are lined with polarising film oriented at right angles. Consequently, light from a backlight (or reflected ambient light) can not shine through the assembly unless it is re-oriented at 90°. The liquid crystals tilt and thus alter the polarisation of the light under electrical excitation, acting as optical shutters. Colour filters add colour to the image.

In order to achieve an image, individual areas — pixels — of the display must be individually addressable. This is achieved by defining a grid of conductor lines that can apply a voltage to any specific pixel and tilt the angle of the liquid crystals. The standard LCD conforms to the VGA display standard with 640 x 480 pixels. SVGA displays with 800 x 600 pixels are also available. XVGA displays with 1024 x 768 pixels are now reaching the market and suppliers are working on a future 1280 x 1024 pixel display. Since each pixel of a colour display consists of typically three colours (red, blue, green), three times as many 'cells' must be individually addressable.

The photolithography processes required to make LCDs are similar to those in integrated circuit manufacturing, even though the resolution is much lower. However, the size and continuous image of the LCD panel require special steppers.

The back panel is a glass substrate on which the TFT drive array is formed. The result is a set of transistors aligned in a complex array that selectively excites individual pixels. The transistor array is formed through a series of metal depositions, photolithography and etching steps. ITO (indium tin oxide) is used as the standard metallisation for electrically conductive signal lines, due to its transparency. If further metallisation steps are required these can be carried out by adding TiW(/Cu)/Au. This metal system has good wire bonding capabilities, low resistivity and is cost effective. Solder can be applied when Cu is the main conductor. A flash with gold is used to prevent oxidation.

15.2.1 Driver IC packaging

In the field of flat panel displays, device technology and packaging technology have significant influences on display performance. The electrical interconnect between the LCD and the LCD driver circuit is an area that needs improvement to achieve finer pitch, easier assembly and greater connection reliability. With increasing pixel count and resolution, driver electronics are becoming more complex and packaging has become a challenge. For LCD driver packaging, the ideal assembly process would have the following characteristics:

— low processing cost;
— reliability suited to the final application;

— high-density, fine-pitch capability;
— low product profile;
— acceptable joint resistance;
— ease of inspection;
— reworkability.

The overall trend in LCD driver IC packaging has been to move the driver IC closer to the LCD itself. Initially, the IC was placed, as a QFP, on a printed circuit board which was in turn connected to the LCD panel via a flexible circuit. In a next step, the driver IC was placed on a board as a bare die, thus saving board real estate and potentially allowing a dedicated board to be moved directly adjacent to the LCD panel. In both cases, the electrical connection between the driver electronics and the glass was effected either by elastomeric connectors or by heat seal.

Elastomeric connectors consist of alternating segments of electrically conducting and isolating silicone rubber. A metal frame with a certain spring action is used to compress the connector between the LCD and the substrate, as the contact needs a uniform pressure. These connectors are often referred to as zebra strips because of their striped appearance. Elastomeric connectors can be used when the contact pitch is 0.4 mm or greater. The electrical conductivity is limited, consequently this 40-year old technology is now typically used only for small LCDs in watches, calculators and office equipment.

The third step in IC packaging was the use of polyester heat seal connectors. These are thin polyester films, patterned with conductive polymer thick film traces. This method is routinely used today for monochrome, lower density pixel displays. One end of the traces is bonded to ITO traces on the glass panel, while the other end is connected to the printed circuit board (PCB) containing the driver electronics. The bonding, in most cases, is obtained by a thermoplastic adhesive. The PCB can then be folded behind the LCD to reduce the total area.

This flexible film concept was extended by using a TAB package directly connected to the LCD panel. Today this is the predominant packaging approach for large area LCDs. In most cases, the TAB is directly connected to the ITO traces on the glass using anisotropic conductive adhesive (ACA) or film (ACF).

In chip on glass (COG) technology, the driver LSI chips have moved all the way on to the LCD glass itself. COG is typically done by flip chip, often using conductive adhesives. ITO traces fan out from the IC to the display area, as well as to the point where a polyimide flexible circuit is connected to the glass substrate, to supply power and picture information. Chip on glass (COG) mounting is currently being used in a number of products, in particular when the pixel density is high.

Both TAB and flip-chip connections with adhesives will be discussed in more detail later in this chapter.

15.3   ADHESIVES FOR LCD DRIVER CONNECTION

Many different types of adhesives are used to connect driver LSI chips to LCDs, including thermoplastic adhesives and thermosetting adhesives.

During the past few years, interest has mainly been in the development of thermosetting adhesives for interconnection of LCD modules to flexible circuitry or rigid boards. The reason is that thermosetting adhesives have been shown to have better long-term stability and reliability properties than thermoplastic adhesives.[1,2]

There are two different mechanisms used for curing the adhesive, heat curing and UV curing. Heat curing appears to be most common. However, the use of the transparent glass substrate in the LCD makes UV curing an interesting alternative since the bonding process can be done quickly by only irradiating with UV light at room temperature. In this way other materials in the assembly are not damaged by the heat. Liquid crystals are particularly heat sensitive and cannot withstand soldering temperatures.[3,4]

Adhesives used can also be classified according to their electrical conductivity. Since the polymer matrix itself is non-conducting, electrical conductivity is obtained by adding conductive particles to the adhesive. According to the amount of added particles, adhesives are classified as non-conductive adhesives (no added particles), anisotropic conductive adhesives (5-10 volume percent with particles) and isotropic conductive adhesives (25-35 volume percent).

15.3.1 Anisotropic Conductive Adhesive

The use of anisotropic conductive adhesives (ACAs) for LCD applications has stimulated significant interest. Conventional ACA is an adhesive consisting of conductive particles dispersed in an adhesive matrix. These particles can be pure metals such as gold, silver or nickel, or metal-coated particles with plastic or glass cores. The volume fraction of particles is well below the percolation threshold, so the particles typically range from 5 to 20 µm in diameter. Due to the low volume fraction, there are no continuous conductive paths among the particles in the x-y plane of the film.

During the connection process, the adhesive is sandwiched between the chip I/O pads or the flexible TAB component electrodes, and the bond pads of the glass (see Figure 15.1). During this operation some of the conductive particles are trapped between the opposite contact pads, making a conductive

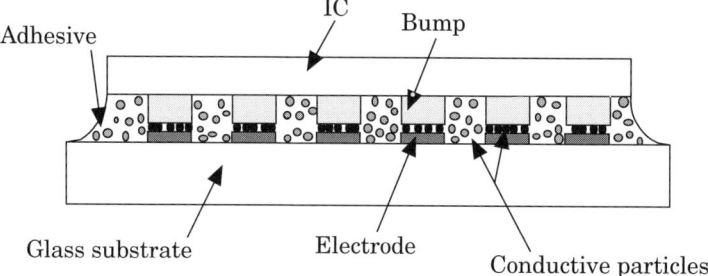

Fig. 15.1 A typical connection using an isotropically conductive adhesive. Some of the conductive particles are trapped between the electrodes on the substrate and the bumps on the chip (or the conductors of a TAB component). These particles contribute to electrical bridging between the connecting areas. The lack of continuous connections between the particles gives a very high insulation resistance in the lateral dimension.

path. Besides acting as a matrix, the purpose of the adhesive is to lock the position of the two parts after alignment and to maintain a compressive force between the conductors and the conductive particles. Because there is no contact between particles, the electrical contact is only achieved perpendicular to the film. Pressure together with heat or UV light is then applied to cure the adhesive and form a permanent bond. These adhesives are available in paste form as anisotropic conductive adhesives (ACAs) and in film form as anisotropic conductive films (ACFs). In film form, the adhesives are typically packaged in tape-on-reel format.

The low processing temperature of anisotropic conductive adhesives is one of the primary reasons for their widespread use for LCD driver attachment. In addition, the technology is fine pitched due to lack of solder bridging or smearing of conductive adhesive. Using an ACA simplifies the mounting process. There is no need for precise placement of the adhesive. These anisotropic conductive materials are continuously improving both in manufacturability and reliability.

Table 15.1

Some Anisotropic Conductive Adhesives for Display Applications from Liu *et al.*[5]

Company	Product Name	Product Form	Cure Mechanism	Filler	Temp. Range (°C)
Hitachi	Anisolm 7000 series	Tape	Thermosetting	Gold-plated plastic balls	-40 to 100
Sony	CP 7131	Tape	Thermosetting	Tin-lead balls	-40 to 100
Sumitomo	Sumizac 1000 series	Tape	Thermosetting	Gold-plated plastic balls	-30 to 100
3M	3M-5303R	Tape	Thermosetting and thermoplastic	Nickel-plated plastic balls	-40 to 100
Hysol	TG-9000R TS-9000R	Paste	Thermosetting	Silver or gold particles	40 to 80
Sheldahl	Shel-zac	Sheet	Thermoplastic	Tin-lead balls	-30 to 80
ECPI	ECPI	Sheet	-	Silver or gold plated rubber	-40 to 120
Zymet	ZXUV101	Paste	UV	Gold	-30 to 100
LCD-mikroelektronik	F 001-008	Tape	Thermosetting or UV	Gold	-40 to 130
Polytel	Uniax ET-201, ET-209	Paste	Thermosetting	Nickel	-55 to 185

15.3.1.1 ACA PARTICLE DISTRIBUTION

A serious technical shortcoming in conventional anistropic conductive adhesives is that particle distribution on the bumps after the bonding process can not be predetermined. Even when the conductive particles supposedly have a uniform distribution within the base resin, the number of particles on the bumps will differ from bump to bump. This particle distribution after bonding has been studied quantitatively by Williams and Whalley.[5]

In practice, the distribution of conductive particles will depend on the dispensing methods. These include pin transfer, screen printing, stencil or syringe dispensing. Different methods have been suggested to reduce this element of randomness. These will be discussed later.

ACA, in paste form, has the additional shortcoming of short-term storability because the particles tend to settle down inside the resin as a result of weight variation between conductive particles and resin. This phenomenon is more pronounced than with pure metal particles.

15.3.1.2   BONDING PARAMETERS

Application of film adhesives is well suited to LCD applications, and requires only cutting the right length and pre-bonding to the glass. Pre-bonding is typically performed at 80-100°C, at a pressure of 50-100 N/cm² for 3 - 5 seconds. A protective liner is then removed from the film and the kapton flex foil or the component is aligned. Typical bonding parameters for anisotropic conductive adhesives[6] are 170-180°C, at a pressure of 200-400 N/cm² for 20-30 seconds. Preferably, the adhesives should be cooled under pressure. Adhesives can be found in different thicknesses, designed for different bump heights and metallisation thicknesses.

15.3.2   Isotropic Conductive Adhesive

In an isotropic conductive adhesive (ICA), the electrical contact is obtained through a network of contact points between individual particles. This network is complex and the total interconnect resistance depends on the contact resistance between the individual particles. Isotropic conductive adhesives are typically filled with silver or silver palladium particles, the latter to reduce the risk of silver migration. These adhesives are used to some extent in LCD applications. A few COG applications will be discussed later in this chapter.

15.3.3   Non-conductive Adhesive

The purpose of a non-conductive adhesive (NCA) is the same as for the ACA, namely to provide conductive paths between the different components to be connected. Instead of introducing new conductive particles to the system, however, the NCA bonding method relies upon direct electrical contact between the two conductor surfaces.[7] When two nominally flat surfaces are forced into contact, they meet only in a limited number of small areas. With mechanical pressure, a 'metal to metal' contact is created between the ITO and the metallisation on the flexible circuit. This contact is therefore characterised by a number of contact spots and a number of cavities. During the connection process an external load is applied to increase the contact pressure, thereby increasing the number and the area of the contact points. Using non-conductive adhesives, the contact points are responsible for the transport of electrical current. The epoxy-filled cavities supply the adhesive forces needed to keep the materials together. After the connections are made, shrinkage in the cured adhesive and the mechanical properties of the materials involved will be responsible for the compressive force needed to maintain the electrical contacts. This technology is called 'electrical connection with non-conductive adhesive'. The number and area of the contact points depend upon the surface finish as well as the hardness (micro-hardness) of the materials involved.

15.3.3.1   CHIP ON FLEX (TAB)

TAB bonding is currently the predominant interconnection technology for LCD driving ICs and will continue to be in the foreseeable future for larger displays. These displays satisfy consumer needs for large-size LCDs such as notebook and sub-notebook computers.

ACAs in film form have achieved wide acceptance for the outer lead bonding (OLB) of the TAB component to glass,[8] from larger notebook computer displays to smaller alphanumeric displays found in pagers (beepers). LCD applications provide by far the largest market for TAB technology worldwide. One advantage of TAB is that drivers may be tested and burned in prior to final assembly. Gang inner lead bonding also provides a short cycle time for high volume throughput.

The current industry limit for ACF bonding is approximately 200 leads per TAB frame at 100 µm pitch. One of the limiting factors is the dimensional stability of the polyimide carrier of the TAB tape or the flex circuit. As the TAB tape is heated during the bond cycle, the polyimide expands in x and y directions. Although this expansion is relatively small, especially with newer polyimides, the accumulated error on fine TAB tape is sufficient to cause misalignment of the tape leads with respect to the ITO traces on the glass, resulting in open and short circuits over a long bond length. The 70 µm pitch will limit OLB TAB packaging technology for quite some time.

Ultra-fine pitch patterns can be produced by reducing the thickness of Cu. However, reducing the thickness of Cu foil decreases the lead strength.

At SINTEF Electronics and Cybernetics, Norway, non-conductive adhesives have been used to connect TAB circuits to glass.[9] The parts were aligned in the bonding equipment and the adhesive (Epotek 353ND from Epoxy Technology) was cured for 1 minute at 150°C under pressure. The reduced temperature, compared with ACF bonding, was an advantage as it reduced the thermal expansion of the flexible circuit. The mechanical alignment was simplified by the use of a non-conductive adhesive, as opposed to anisotropic conductive film.

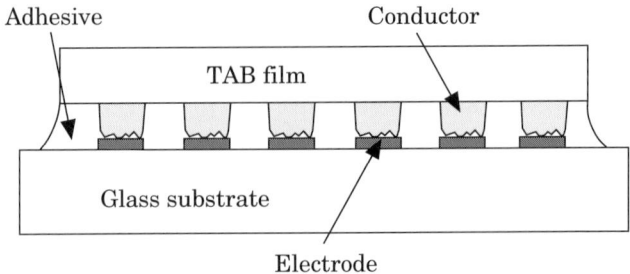

Fig. 15.2 The NCA connection technology for TAB on glass, developed at SINTEF.

The contact resistance obtained was significantly lower than with the use of ACA when employing bare copper tracks or gold-plated tracks. The contact resistance was stable to 1000 thermal cycles within 1%. The sample connected with tin/lead plating gave poor results. Compared with ACA bonding, the variation in contact resistance between the different samples was much smaller, indicating a more stable and reproducible contact.

15.4   CHIP ON GLASS TECHNOLOGY

Due to the limitations of TAB technology, bonding the IC chips directly to the glass substrate of the LCD panel might be a better choice when the pitch is less than 70-100 μm. Small size and high resolution LCDs such as viewfinders, video-game equipment displays, or light valves for liquid-crystal projectors have been using flip-chip on glass technology for their IC-driving packaging.

Since the announcement by Citizen in 1983 of a chip on glass (COG) driver assembly process for their LC pocket TV, many different types of COG assembly processes have been developed. The majority of the work comes from Japanese companies such as Matsushita, Seiko, Citizen etc. Some of the technologies proposed are discussed below. Unlike TAB to glass, which is a mature and fairly standard assembly process, COG has many variations. There are no standard materials or assembly processes. All the major LCD module manufacturers have one or more COG processes in development and/ or in production, but not many COG technologies have been applied in high volume applications.

In principle, COG can satisfy many of the requirements of an ideal assembly process. One advantage of COG is the reduction in packaging cost for the display module compared with TAB. There is no base tape or inner lead bonding required. This means fewer process steps and a potential for higher yield due to the elimination of one interconnect level. Another advantage is that finer pitches can be bonded. For high-definition LCDs, pixel size decreases and pixel count increases. COG allows the driver to be bonded directly to the ITO traces on the glass without increasing the size of the panel. Thus, the use of COG technology reduces the size of the packaged FPD module. Because COG display drivers can have bond pads arrayed across the entire surface of the die, the number of drivers which can be processed on a wafer increases, providing significant cost savings on LSI chips. Chip on glass technology also gives a significant reduction in the size of the LCD system.

Chip on glass technology does, however, cause difficulties, such as coplanarity. Uneven heights can cause bumps to be improperly bonded. In some cases excessive pressure on other bumps can cause glass breakage. The bonding pressure imposed on the backside of the IC must be controlled precisely according to the total number of particles on the IC bumps to achieve a reasonable elastic region of particles when depressed. The bonding pressure influences contact resistance as well as particle deformation. The coplanarity of the collet and the table of the bonding equipment is important in order to achieve a uniformly depressed ratio of particles distributed over the entire area of the chip.

The contact area between the TAB component and the glass substrate has a length in the order of millimetres. The use of COG technology implies that the contact area is reduced by an order of magnitude, due to the small quadratic contact pads. This causes the specific contact resistance (contact resistance per area) to be more important. In addition, the alignment influences the achievement of low contact resistance. To increase the bump size, bumps could be aligned in a staggered manner rather than in a straight line.

Another limitation on COG is that existing inspection and test equipment for the testing of dies is based on probe technology. This is not suitable for contacting very fine-pitch pads of high pin count display drivers. As pitch continues to decrease and pin count continues to increase, the development of test and inspection equipment for FPD drivers will be of prime importance for the future of COG. New test and inspection methods which can provide stable contacts to high density panels and driver chips need to be developed. This limitation applies, to some extent, to the glass panels. However, on the panels there is no absolute need for addressing individual pixels during testing.

15.4.1   General Discussion

The following four types of bonding process using the flip-chip technique have been reported:

— anisotropic conductive film applied to the interconnection layer;
— isotropic conductive adhesive applied to different types of bumps;
— pressure connection with bumps;
— soldering with eutectic solder.

This review will focus on the first three technologies, which use adhesive bonding.

COG technology will in most cases require bumped bond pads on the chip. This is not a standard silicon process. The bumps can be obtained in several different ways. The most frequently used method is to plate gold bumps in a process similar to bump formation for TAB inner lead bonding.

In stud-bump technology, bumps are formed on the LSI chip by using a conventional ball bonder. In this way, the traditional sputtering and plating processes used in 'normal' bump formation can be omitted. Also, other methods for bumping the chips have been used, and will be discussed later.

Underfill is known to increase the mechanical strength and the reliability of a flip-chip assembly.[10] Using NCA and ACA (ACF), the underfill process is a part of the electrical interconnect process. However, in the case of ICA and solder bonding, an additional underfill process is needed after electrical interconnection has been achieved.

15.4.1.1   PROCESS AND RELIABILITY

The temperature differences in the adhesive can cause uneven flow and curing conditions, creating possible reliability problems. Endoh *et al.*[11] have performed transient temperature analysis of the bonding process, which revealed significant temperature differences in the adhesive underneath the centre of the chip compared with at the corner. Increased temperatures were also observed in the vicinity of Au bumps, due to their good thermal conductivity. This can be improved by:

— making the surface of the bonding press tool larger than the surface of the chip; this causes reduced heat losses from the corners of the chip;
— heating both the chips and the glass;
— in the case of a high conductivity metallisation on the glass, an optimum electrode design on the glass will spread the heat, thereby improving the temperature uniformity.

The size and form of the IC chip are important, along with the thermal expansion of the glass, in reducing the residual stresses on the chip-glass connection.

15.4.2 Flip Chip on Glass with Anisotropic Conductive Adhesive

The use of anisotropic conductive adhesives (films) is probably the most common method for chip on glass connections.

15.4.2.1 SEIKO: 'MAPLE METHOD'

Seiko has developed a chip on glass method using anisotropic conductive adhesives called 'The Maple Method'.[11] The driver ICs are bonded directly to a panel glass substrate using an adhesive in which the gold particles are uniformly distributed. The driver IC chips have straight wall gold bumps.

While typical COG technologies need several alignment steps, this bonding process is very simple. First the adhesive sheet is placed on the panel glass. After alignment of the chips on the glass electrodes, a temporary bonding process is carried out. During the final bonding process, no further alignment is required. The bonding needs a parallel, flat tool with precise movement, as well as high temperature and pressure. The pad pitch is 80 μm. Seiko has performed a thermal analysis of the bonding process.

15.4.2.2 CASIO: 'MICROCONNECTOR'

Casio has developed an advanced ACF[12-14] called the Microconnector for chip on glass applications. This adhesive contains conductive particles made from plastic spheres plated with a thin metal layer, and coated with an additional, 10 nm thick, insulating layer. This material can be supplied both in the form of a film or as a 'paste'. In the production process, Casio's technology behaves in exactly the same way as the conventional ACA FCOG.

The insulating layer comprises a large number of insulating micropowder particles, each finer than the plastic balls, which electrically insulate the outer surface of a corresponding metal layer. The insulation is formed by causing the insulating micropowder to adhere to the surface of the metal layer with an electrostatic effect. The base adhesive resin is a thermal type, such as thermoplastic or thermosetting, producing thermocompression when the bonding process takes place. When the bonding heat and pressure are applied, the insulating layer, which is in contact with the bump surface of the IC, is broken. However, on the particles not crushed by the bonding pads, this insulating layer remains intact. As the layer produces only z-axis electrical interconnections, lateral short circuiting is prevented. This method also requires driving ICs with bumps.

Casio's method is believed to solve most of the shortcomings of the conventional ACA FCOG method while keeping the process simple. With an additional insulating layer, a fine pitch and low contact resistance without the risk of lateral short circuiting can be realised by increasing the quantity of particles per unit volume to be mixed with the base adhesive resin or film. If the insulating layer works as well as claimed and does not increase the cost of the material significantly, Casio's method is an excellent technique. The company is manufacturing LC pocket TVs using this material.

15.4.2.3   OKI: 'ACF WITH AU BUMPS'

OKI is another manufacturer using anisotropic conductive adhesives for chip on glass applications.[15] The IC has aluminium pads with 120-μm pitch, on to which gold bumps are formed. The ITO metallisation on the glass substrate has an additional gold film in the contact area. The ACA is made from a UV-curable base resin mixed with conductive particles. The conductive particles are Au-plated resin balls with a uniform diameter of 5 μm. Two UV adhesives have been evaluated as the base resin.

OKI's ACA FCOG process is composed of three simple steps. First the ACA is printed on the glass substrate. Thereafter the ICs are aligned with the glass substrate. During the bonding process, an appropriate load is applied on to the ICs. Curing of the ACA is achieved by UV light exposure from under the substrate.

OKI found that the number of conductive particles existing on a bump increased as the content of conductive particles in the adhesive increased. The values counted almost matched those obtained by calculation. The content of the conductive particles seriously affected the connection resistance and the insulation between pads. The results showed that the most suitable amounts of conductive particles were within the range of 2.5 to 12.5 vol%. Interconnection resistance decreases as the volume content of conductive particles increases until reaching <7.5 vol%. However, in the region of >7.5 vol%, the interconnection resistance stabilises at 1.5 to 2.0 Ω. The insulation resistance of the neighbouring interconnections measured in the condition of 12.5% content of conductive particles and loaded voltage 50 V was measured to be better than $10^{12}\,\Omega$.

In addition to the preceding experiments, OKI presents the stress-strain curve per conductive particle, the relationship between resistance and current, and the dependence of contact resistance on temperature change and reliability tests.

15.4.2.4   HITACHI: 'DOUBLE-LAYER ACF'

Hitachi has developed another advanced double-layer ACF which consists of an adhesive layer and a monolayer[16] of particles. Conventional ACF has only one layer of adhesive in which the conductive particles are dispersed in a random distribution. In Hitachi's ACF, the conductive particle layer and the adhesive layer are formed separately and attached together later. The conductive particle layer is thin, similar to the diameter of a conductive particle, and has a high-viscosity thermosetting material in which conductive particles are arranged in monolayer. The adhesive layer is thick (depending on the bump height) and has a low viscosity (lower than that of the particle layer) pure thermosetting resin. The conductive particle layer contributes to electrical interconnection, while the adhesive layer contributes only to attaching and binding the two components. This material can therefore be supplied only as a film, and requires driving ICs with bumps.

The thickness of a conventional ACF is much greater than the diameter of a conductive particle. During the bonding process, the conductive particles beneath the bumps become a monolayer. The other conductive particles, which do not contribute to this monolayer, are squeezed between the bumps, thereby causing potential short circuiting. However, since Hitachi's double-layer ACF already has a monolayer of conductive particles with a much higher viscosity than the adhesive layer, the conductive particles are not squeezed out but remain in the same place, thereby preventing short circuiting. Figure 15.3 shows a schematic view of the bonding process of double-layer ACF. Hitachi claims to have successfully achieved 10-μm pitch interconnection in laboratory experiments using their double-layer ACF. They will commercialise this newly developed double-layer ACF for FCOG applications with 20-μm pitch interconnection. This double-layer ACF will be a promising FCOG material if it is cost-effective. The double-layer design is reported to increase the number of particles on the interconnection electrodes.

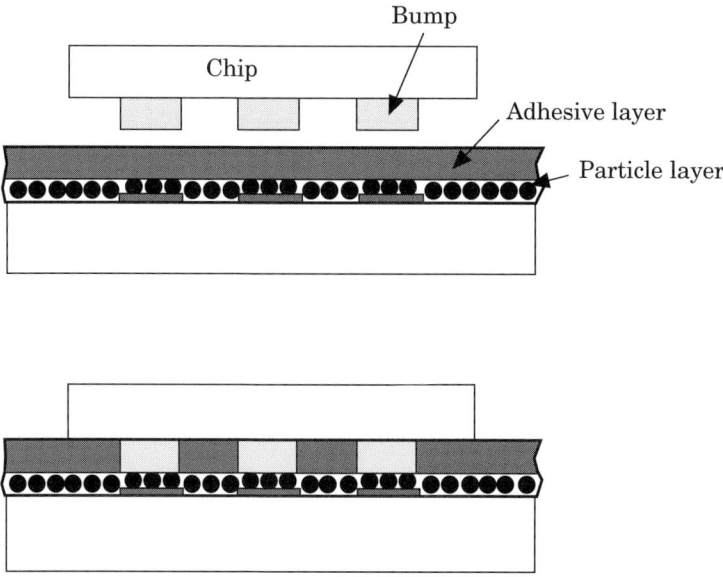

Fig. 15.3 Schematic of the Hitachi double-layer ACF process. The high viscosity in the particle layer implies that there is a very small change in the particle distribution before and after bonding.

15.4.2.5 SAMSUNG: 'DIELECTRIC DAMS'

Samsung (Samsung Display Devices) and Zymet, an American manufacturer of anistropic conductive adhesives, have co-developed a modified ACA FCOG bonding method using peak-shaped dielectric dams between the electrode pads of the glass substrate.[17] These dams are formed by a backside imaging process. The dams function as a block, insulating the two electrical interconnections on the right and left. They eliminate short circuiting by preventing any conductive particles from being positioned on top of them. This method requires driving ICs with bumps and glass substrates with opaque electrode pads, and uses a conventional ACA material.

The backside imaging process is carried out as follows:

- Application of a negative-acting photoimageable dielectric to the glass substrate by the screen printing, stencilling or syringe dispensing method.
- Projection of light from the backside of the glass substrate to expose the negative-acting photoimageable dielectric, which resides between the two opaque electrode pads.
- Removal of the negative-acting photoimageable dielectric on the electrode pads, which are not exposed to UV light, thereby forming the peak-shaped dielectric dam.

The bonding process is the same as in conventional flip-chip bonding, but the dielectric dams themselves can serve as an alignment guiding dam. The gap between the top of a dam and the passivation layer of a driving IC should be less than the diameter of a conductive particle to prevent any lateral short circuiting. The wall angle of the dam should be made to have a peak-shaped top according to the distance from the surface of a glass substrate to the passivation layer of a driving IC and the gap between two opaque electrode pads of a glass substrate.

15.4.2.6 SUMITOMO: 'VIS'

Sumitomo has developed a somewhat different style of anistropic conductive film,[18] called vertical interconnection sheet (VIS). This sheet consists of pure Au balls aligned in vertical and horizontal directions on an equally spaced matrix arrangement on a polyimide film. The balls are formed by a plating method whereby gold is plated through the holes in the film. This sheet is inserted later for electrical interconnection before bonding between a driving IC and a substrate after they have been aligned with each other. Au balls are melted and attached to the Al electrode pads of a driving IC and the electrode pads of a substrate by thermocompression when the two components are pressed with high temperature and high pressure. Sumitomo's VIS process consists of the following:

- Coating a negative-acting photoimageable polyimide, approximately 4 μm thick, to the NiCu alloy sheet, approximately 70 μm thick.
- Irradiating UV light through a mask from above.
- Developing polyimide film, thereby forming equally spaced aligned

holes in vertical and horizontal directions.
- Etching the NiCu sheet to form bowl-shaped spaces penetrating the sheet.
- Forming Au balls by plating through the holes.
- Removing the NiCu sheet from the polyimide film by etching.

This material also eliminates the problem of short circuiting. However, VIS is a difficult and complicated process and expensive. The spacing between Au balls on VIS should be decreased for finer-pitch interconnection, so the VIS process will become more difficult. Furthermore, it is difficult to handle VIS because the sheet is weak and fragile.

15.4.3 Flip Chip on Glass with Isotropic Conductive Adhesive

15.4.3.1 CITIZEN: 'PLATED BUMPS WITH ISOTROPIC ADHESIVE'

Citizen has been using COG technology for some time in their LC pocket TVs. In Citizen's process, mushroom Cu bumps with a thin Au overcoat are plated on to the chip electrodes with a pitch of 216 µm. The bumps are 50 µm high, as opposed to the conventional 25 µm. This is done to better absorb thermal strain between the chip and glass panel. Conductive silver-filled adhesive is screen printed on to the ITO bond pads of the FPD. The chip is aligned to the substrate and bonded. The adhesive is then cured to form a permanent bond.

They have also developed a small size liquid crystal display device for use in a conventional slide projector.[19] Here the driver electronics is COG bonded with a bump pitch of 150 µm and a bump (made of copper) diameter of 110 µm. The conductive adhesive is transferred on to the bumps. The driver IC chips are then pressed on to the glass substrate and the adhesive is cured. After the bonding is completed, the driver IC's are sealed with a non-conductive epoxy.

15.4.3.2 MATSUSHITA : 'STUD (WIRE) BUMPS'

Matsushita has developed a process[20] which in many respects is similar to Citizen's. The most significant difference is in the bump formation process. Matsushita uses a conventional ball bonder to form the Au ball bumps. Using a 20 µm diameter wire, the size of the pads can be reduced to 70 µm in square. An even finer wire has been tested but the result was a reduction in yield. The ball bumping speed is significantly faster than complete wire bonding. In this way the traditional sputtering and plating processes in 'normal' bump formation have been omitted.

To prevent the bond area from becoming too large, the bumps are formed in a conical shape. They are pressed level by a flat surface and the height is adjusted. The bumps are then dipped into a thin film of adhesive so the adhesive is only transferred to the tips. A specially formulated isotropically conductive adhesive is used, containing 20% palladium in a silver palladium alloy. This is chosen to avoid any problems with silver migration. An optimum amount of filler has been obtained to combine the flexibility of the adhesive with a low resistance.

Matsushita has developed an interesting approach to the problem of electrical testing of naked dies, by using a two-stage curing process. After the first stage, an electrical contact is obtained and a test can be carried out. If necessary, repairs are undertaken. In the second and final step the cure is completed. This two-stage curing has been achieved by using two different solvents with different boiling points. The minimum bonding pitch is reported to be 50 μm, and the contact resistance measured by a 4-probe technique is less than 1 Ω. An insulation resistance of better than 100 Giga ohms has been reported.

A silicone resin is used to seal the chips and bumps after the final curing process. After this process, the adhesion strength is better than 10 kg/cm².

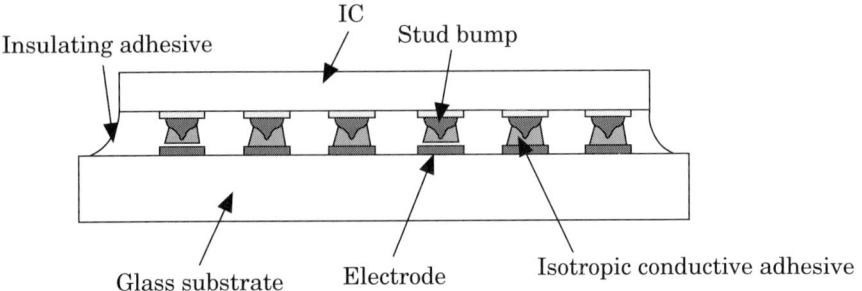

Fig. 15.4 A schematic of the Matsushita stud bump process.

15.4.3.3 PHILIPS

Philips has reported COG connections using isotropic conductive adhesive.[21] The chips are bumped with gold bumps. Before bonding, the driver IC is dipped into a very thin layer of adhesive. In this way, a thin layer of glue is transferred on to the bumps. The chip is then precisely aligned to the LCD. The adhesive used is conductive even before curing. This allows functional testing before curing, and thereby much easier replacement of defective dies. The bonding method exerts very little pressure or mechanical stress on both the chip and the LCD.

15.4.4 Flip Chip on Glass with Non-conductive Adhesive

15.4.4.1 MATSUSHITA: 'MICRO BUMP-BONDING'

Matsushita[22,23] has reported an extremely fine bonding pitch using non-conductive adhesive. In the process, the shrinkage stress in light-setting insulating resin was used to apply a compressive force. An inter-electrode spacing of 10 μm was obtained with a total of 2320 contacts of 5 microns square. The electrodes on each side are pressed together and the chip is fixed by the adhesive. The bonding connection is made by the internal shrinkage stress in the same adhesive.

The features of this method are:

- Connections with micron order pitch can be attained, as an insulating resin is used for bonding.

- High reliability, as thermal expansion mismatch between chip and substrate will not break any metallurgical bonds.
- With the use of a proper resin-solvent system the chip can easily be removed and replaced.
- Low bonding cost due to a simple process and very low material cost.
- With the use of a light curable system, there is no need to apply heat to either the substrate or the chip.

The bonding method has been successfully used in both ITO and Au metallisation and on different substrate materials. UV light from the LCD glass side is used for curing. The resin has been chosen with consideration for thermal stress, adhesive force and the internal shrinkage stress. The gap distance between the chip and the substrate is determined by the height of the bump, after deformation caused by the pressure applied during the connection process. The curing shrinkage of the acrylic adhesive was 8.8%.

Unlike the existing solder bump method, the electrodes are not bonded completely. In other words, the fixing of the chip and the bonding of the electrodes are separate processes. The attachment of the LSI chip is due to the adhesive power of the resin, while the bonding between the electrodes is accomplished by the contractile force developed under curing. A minimum pitch of 2-3 micron is envisaged using this technology.

The pressure bonding ensures a flexible structure which is more resistant to thermal and mechanical stress. The force used during bonding is set to cause a gold bump deformation of 0.5 to 1 micron, corresponding to 1.5-3 g/bump for a 5 micron square bump. The plastic deformation of Au bumps is reported[24] to be in the order of 10-20%.

An excellent V-I characteristic is obtained from 10^{-5}V and upwards. The resistance was found to be independent of the contact area, and was within a 3 to 7 milli-ohm range.

15.4.4.2 SHARP: 'ELASTIC'

Sharp has developed a new flip-chip bonding method using conductive particles,[25-28] '*Electrical interconnection using light-setting adhesive selectively cured and conductive particles*' (ELASTIC) for chip-on-glass applications. The most significant feature of Sharp's COG technology is the method of mounting electrically interconnecting material on to LSI electrode pads. This 'bumping' process can be described in four steps.

The first step is to coat the wafer with a 1-3 μm thick light-setting adhesive. The coated wafer is then irradiated with ultra-violet (UV) light in a standard photo-lithographic process, while the Al pads of the chip are optically masked. As a result of this process, the thin adhesive film above the electrodes is still uncured and remains tacky, whereas the adhesive above the other areas has been cured. Due to the tackiness of the adhesive on the electrodes, electrically conductive particles can be easily mounted on these sites only. The conductive particles are gold-plated polymer spheres with, depending on the bonding pitch, a uniform 5 or 10 μm diameter.

Light-setting adhesive is dispensed on the LSI chip before the chip is aligned with the glass substrate. While still applying pressure between the LSI chip and the glass substrate, the light-setting adhesive is irradiated with

UV light. Upon releasing the pressure, the LSI chip electrodes are electrically connected to the glass substrate electrodes by the conductive particles which are deformed plastically. As the developed COG technology does not need bump plating, the fabrication process is simplified. The bonding process can be performed by irradiating with UV light at room temperature, therefore the developed COG process does not damage other materials with heat. This packaging concept can potentially achieve a very high throughput.

4.5 mm x 15.0 mm sized test chips, with gold electrodes of 80 μm in an area array at a minimum pitch of 300 μm, have been bonded on to borosilicate glass substrates with molybdenum electrodes. The bonding pressure was about 30 N per chip. Similar chips were bonded on to glass substrates with ITO electrodes. In both cases a small change was observed in the connection resistance during the moisture resistance test. After 480 hours, the average value of the connection resistance was 0.36 Ω.

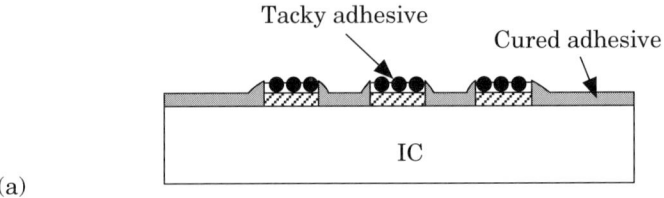

(a)

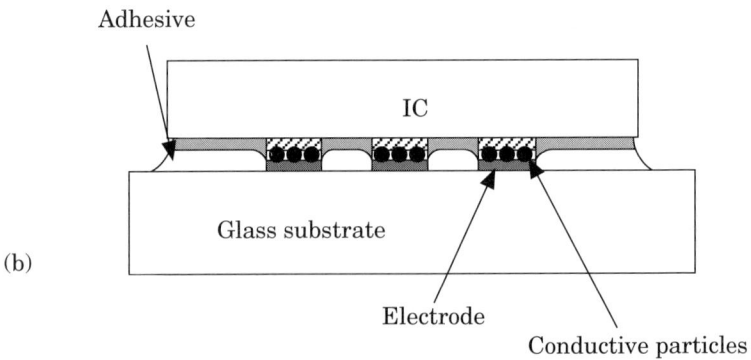

(b)

Fig. 15.5 Sharp's ELASTIC chip-on-glass process. In (a) the conductive particles are placed on top of the IC contact areas. In (b) the chip is placed on top of the glass substrate, and a UV-curable, non-conductive adhesive is used to attach the chip.

In order to verify the possibility of interconnecting at fine pitch using this COG technology, 6.00 mm x 10.00 mm sized test chips, with perimeter array electrodes of 30 μm at a minimum pitch of 50 μm, were bonded on to the same glass substrates, but with gold electrodes. In this case conductive particles of 5 μm diameter were used and the bonding pressure was about 20 N per chip. There was little change in the connection resistances during the moisture test; even after 1000 hours of testing, the average value of the connection resistances was 0.579 Ω. This confirms that this COG technology can be successfully used down to 50 μm pitch.

Sharp's method has some advantages over the conventional method. Due to the use of non-conductive adhesive, no short circuits will occur between neighbouring interconnections, therefore fine-pitch interconnections are possible. It is possible to obtain a near-maximum monolayer density of conductive particles on the IC electrode pads so that the lowest possible contact resistance can be realised. However, unless users can purchase the driving ICs with conductive particle bumps, they will have to handle the wafers to perform the conductive particle mounting process. Performing probing work for electrical die sorting (EDS) tests on the chips after the conductive particle bumps have been formed will also be difficult.

15.4.4.3 SEIKO EPSON: 'UN-BUMPED DIES', WITH CONDUCTIVE PARTICLES ON THE GLASS ELECTRODES

Seiko Epson has developed a modified FCOG bonding method using conductive particles which use standard driving ICs with aluminium pads instead of bumped driving ICs.[29,30] Unlike the previous method described, the conductive particles are printed on the electrode pads of the glass substrate in a pattern which corresponds exactly to the contact electrodes on the glass substrate. The bumpless ICs are bonded with adhesive in a face-down position. The bonding result of Seiko Epson's method is exactly the same as that of the Sharp method.

The crucial technique in Seiko Epson's method is the printing process. How this conductive particle printing is carried out, however, is not mentioned in their papers. None of the usual printing methods seem to be suitable for mass production of LCDs because the conductive particles must be printed accurately on the electrode pads on the LCD glass panel after this is assembled. However, given a reasonable, simple and practical printing process, Seiko Epson's method would eliminate the disadvantage while retaining all the advantages of the Sharp method.

15.4.4.4 MITSUBISHI: PHOTO PROCESS OF CONDUCTIVE PARTICLES

Mitsubishi's modified FCOG method[31] uses driving ICs with bumps. They use a photolithographic process to distribute the conductive particles on the electrode pads of the glass substrate before flip-chip bonding. Figure 15.6 shows the backside imaging process, which is as follows.

- Coating a positive photoresist in which the conductive particles are dispersed on to the glass substrate by a spin-coating method and prebaking the coated resist.
- Irradiating with UV light the glass substrate coated with the positive photoresist from the backside of the substrate, whereby the pattern of electrode pads which are Ni and Au plated acts as a photomask.
- Removing the positive photoresist with conductive particles on the outside of the electrode pads, which are exposed to UV light, so that the conductive particles are mounted only on the electrode pads.

The bonding process between IC and substrate is the same as in the methods described above. Although this method cannot load as many conductive particles on one electrode pad of glass substrate as the Sharp or Seiko Epson method, the backside imaging process is much simpler and eliminates the lateral short-circuit problem.

This method can scarcely be economical because many conductive particles are wasted in the spin coating and developing processes. The spin-coating process seems to be unsuitable for mass production because an LCD panel with electrode pads must be spin-coated or a COG module must be made separately from the LCD panel and interconnected to the LCD panel later.

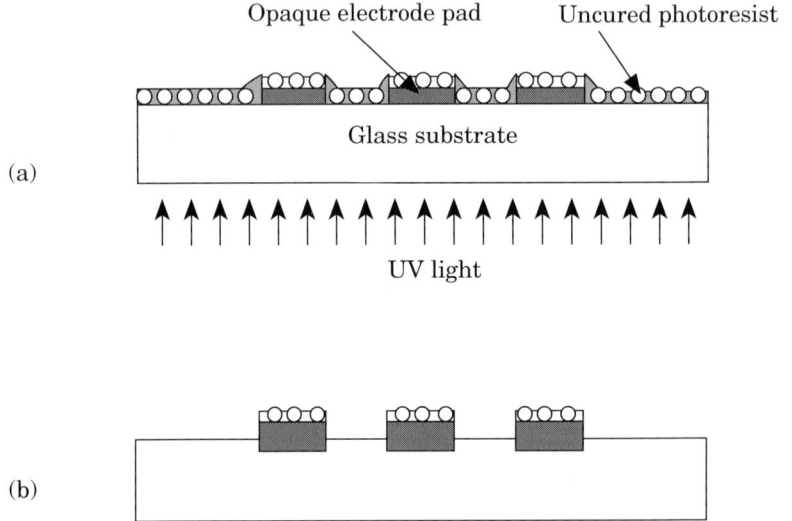

Fig. 15.6 In (a) the photo process is shown, where the opaque electrode pads are used as a mask. In (b) the final result of the photo process is shown. The electrodes on the glass substrate are covered with conductive particles, ready for the mounting of the chip.

15.4.5   Non-adhesive COG Technologies

Hitachi has for a long time used chip-on-glass technology with soldered bumps. Many other manufacturers such as Oki Electric, IBM and Toshiba have also developed metallic bond COG processes. Although materials and processing conditions vary, most are based on a low melting-temperature metal to produce the bonds. Typically, the chip is bumped with metal such as indium[32] (In) or indium-lead (InPb) solder, formed as a low-melting-point bump on top of the gold bumps of driving ICs. ITO traces on the glass are metallised with a wettable metal, and the chip is soldered to the FPD glass. Metallic bond COG assembly processes tend to provide lower joint resistances than adhesive assisted processes, and costly substrate pad metallisation is required for most processes.

15.4.6   Challenges for COG

Some problems still exist with COG technology. For example, the bond pad layout and routing for the LCD driver can become so complex that the wiring resistivity becomes high, adversely affecting the image quality of the display.

Because COG is a fairly new assembly technology, with non-standardised material and process steps, there has been little assembly equipment available on the market. Most COG processes have therefore not been fully compatible with high volume surface mount equipment. However, it is now possible to buy automatic and semi-automatic flip-chip bonders that are applicable for adhesive COG applications.

15.5   RELIABILITY

The reliability of the driver electronics connections in LCDs is an important issue. It is essential to have precise control over the bonding parameters in order to acheive high reliability. Correct curing temperature and pressure are vital parameters[33] to form a good adhesive joint. With the use of organic materials such as adhesives, bonds may be electrically unstable at either low or high temperature or in a high humidity environment, as the adhesive may swell or creep.

15.5.1   Failure Mechanisms

Since the adhesive matrix is a non-conductive material, a conductive adhesive joint will rely to some extent on pressure contacts. These contacts can either be between individual conductive particles, between particles and electrode or, in the case of non-conductive adhesive, directly between the two electrodes to be connected. The use of adhesive interconnection techniques therefore implies different failure mechanisms compared with those of traditional solder connections, where the formation of intermetallics and coarsening of grains are the main mechanisms. A considerable amount of work has been done to understand the failure mechanisms in the adhesive joints and thereby increase reliability.

There are basically two failure mechanisms that can destroy the contacts. The first is the formation of a non-conductive film either on the contact areas or on the conductive particles. The second is the loss of mechanical contact between the conductive elements. This can be due to either loss of adherence, or relaxation of the compressive force.

The compressive forces between the conductive components are partly obtained by cure shrinkage of the adhesive. With non-conductive and anisotropic conductive adhesives, an additional compressive force is applied by external pressure during the connection. Both the cohesive strength within the adhesive and the adhesion between the adhesive and the parts to be bonded must be sufficient to maintain this compressive force. On the other hand, the thermal expansion of the adhesive and its swelling due to humidity as well as mechanical stress from the environment will tend to destroy this compressive force. The result will be increased contact resistance and, occasionally, a complete loss of electrical contact.

Another effect of humidity is the oxidation of the metal on interconnecting materials. This mechanism has been studied theoretically by Liu *et al.*[33] The rate of oxide formation and the type of oxide are shown to be one mechanism, explaining the rate of resistance change in a humid environment.

15.5.2   Reliability Testing

Several different environmental tests are used to investigate the reliability of LCD driver connections based on adhesive techniques. Most of these tests are adapted from tests used for soldered connections. There is still work to be done to optimise the reliability tests with respect to the failure mechanisms present in adhesive joints and to obtain activation energies or acceleration factors.

Table 15.2

Typical Environmental Exposures used for Reliability Evaluation of LCD Connections.

Parameter Test	Temperature	Humidity
Constant humidity	60°C	95% RH
	85°C	95% RH
High temperature storage	125°C	-
Temperature cycling	-45 to 85°C	not controlled
Humidity cycling	5 to 75°C	95% RH

These environmental exposures are often combined with measurements of electrical resistance to determine the number of open joints and the daisy chain resistance. These measurements can be performed during exposure or samples can be taken at given intervals for testing. By doing *in-situ* measurements, intermittent failures can be observed. Often these electrical tests are combined with testing of the adhesion strength, typically measured by shear tests.

The humidity cycling test, where the temperature is varied between 5 and 75°C under high relative humidity, presents rigorous conditions resulting in most of the adhesive joint failures encountered.

Several different analytical tools have been used to characterise the adhesive itself or the electrical contact. These could be microscopic techniques such as optical microscopy or scanning and transmission electron microscopy. Chemical surface characterisations have been performed by Auger electron spectroscopy or X-ray photoelectron spectroscopy. Process parameters like curing time and temperature have been tested with differential scanning calorimetry (DSC).

15.6   FUTURE

LCDs have been an enabling or enhancing technology for a wide range of new products. Today, LCDs are found in practically every consumer product on the market and also in professional equipment.

Due to the increased interest in LCD technology, both economic and technical, display driver packaging technology is expected to make rapid progress during the coming years. The continual decrease in pitch and reduction in physical size will probably imply a shift in packaging technology from TAB to chip on glass. However, in order for fine-pitch COG to be taken into high-volume production, several problems must be addressed. These include inspection and test for fine-pitch drivers, high volume assembly equipment for COG, and reliability issues for some COG processes in adverse environments.

When considering a packaging method for ultra-high-definition colour LCDs for light valve applications or view finders, the high-density and fine-pitch features of COG make it the most promising technology. In addition to its expansion into high definition panel driver packaging, COG will probably be used for a wider range of applications in the near future, due to the potential low cost and the small area needed for the electronics.

In the longer term, an interesting approach is to use the glass substrate as an interconnect board for the system electronics. It is now technically possible to mount many of the required ICs directly to the LCD glass substrate, where the conductors connecting the chips are a part of the display substrate. Lawrence C. Seifert, President for global manufacturing and engineering at AT&T,[34] has said that AT&T's current concept of a multimedia terminal is an active-matrix LCD with chips around the display's periphery. These chips would not be limited to the display driver chips, but would also include the processor, support chips, memory, disk controller and local network interface. The LCD would be the chassis for the terminal, with most of the terminal's cost in the display.

As was mentioned previously, the build-up of thin-film transistors for active matrix LCDs uses the same type of photolithography processes as the manufacture of integrated circuits. It is logical then to attempt to integrate the driver electronics on the LCD glass substrate itself by constructing the IC together with the TFT drive array. This approach requires two additional lithography steps, but could save 30% of the total module cost for large area LCDs because of the substantial costs of driver IC assembly. Sanyo and others have demonstrated prototype LCDs with integrated driver ICs in a 1.5 mm wide space along the edge of the display area. This makes it possible to implement other circuitry on the glass panel such as LCD drives, support and some system electronics. Once the electronics can be integrated into the display, the display effectively becomes the chassis, the complete product. As a consequence, there will be little added value once the complete glass panel has been produced. This can make flat panel displays a key product in future commercial electronic products. This technology provides the ultimate space reduction for driver packaging, and may replace both TAB and COG for this application in the future. However, processing yield and cost are currently the limiting factors for this technology. Consequently, TAB and COG will continue to be the dominant FPD driver packaging methods for several years to come.

REFERENCES

1 Yamaguchi, Y. and Kato, M., 'Some Progress in Anisotropic Conductive Film', Proceedings Nepcon West '91, pp. 221-235 (1991).
2 Bjorneklett, A, 'LCD Driver Connection', Report No. 90 02 18, SINTEF/SI, Norway (1990).
3 Kubo, K., Touma, S., Kanazaki, M. and Ross, D., 'Chip-on-glass LCD for Automotive Application', SAE special publication SP-654, pp.115-119 (1986).
4 Erlewein, J. and Rachner, H., 'Chip-on-glass Technology for Large Scale Automotive Displays', SAE special publication SP-565, pp. 31-35 (1984).
5 Williams, D. J. and Whalley, D. C., 'The Effects of Conducting Particle Distribution on the

Behaviour of Anisotropic Conducting Adhesives: Non-uniform Conductivity and Shorting between Connections', *Journal of Electronics Manufacturing*, No. 3, p. 94 (1993).

6   Liu, J. and Rörgren, R., 'Joining of Displays using Thermo-setting Anisotropically Conductive Adhesives', *Journal of Electronics Manufacturing*, No. 3, pp. 205-214 (1993).

7   Kristiansen, H. and Bjorneklett, A., 'Fine-pitch Connection to Rigid Substrates using Non-conductive Adhesive', *Journal of Electronics Manufacturing*, No. 2, pp. 7-12 (1992).

8   Andoh, H., Yanada, Y. and Fukuda, Y., 'Fine Connection Technology Using Anisotropic Conductive Film', *Hybrids*, **Vol. 8**, No. 6, p. 19 (1993) (in Japanese).

9   Kristiansen, H. and Bjorneklett, A., 'Fine-pitch Connection to Rigid Substrates using Non-conductive Adhesive', *Journal of Electronics Manufacturing*, No. 2, pp. 7-12 (1992).

10 Lau, J. H., 'Flip Chip Technologies', McGraw-Hill, Chapter 5 (1995).

11 Endoh, K., Nozawa, K. and Hashimoto, N., 'Development of "The Maple Method"', Proceedings IEMT, pp. 187-190 (1993).

12 Casio, US Patent 4,999,460, March 12 (1991).

13 Casio, US Patent 5,123,986, June 23 (1992).

14 Casio, US Patent 5,180,888, January 19 (1993).

15 Takahashi, W., Murakoshi, K., Kanazawa, J., lkehata, M., Iguchi, Y. and Kanamori, T., 'Solderless COG Technology Using Anisotropic Conductive Adhesive', Proceedings International Microelectronics Conference, Yokohama, pp. 93-98, June (1992).

16 Hitachi Chemical, 'Connecting Materials for COG', technical report, September (1994).

17 Lau, J. H., 'Flip Chip Technologies', McGraw-Hill, Chapter 10.3.5 (1995).

18 Yasuo, N. and Tetsuo, Y., 'Micro-film Connector for High Density Interconnection', *Electric Materials*, pp. 28-35, November (1992) (in Japanese).

19 Miyajima, A., Morokawa, S., Yamada, O. and Arai, M., 'Small Liquid Crystal Display Device for Projection', SPIE, **Vol. 1255**, Large-Screen Projection Displays II, pp. 46-51 (1990).

20 Bessho, Y., Horio, Y., Tsuda, T., Ishida, T. and Sakurai, W., 'Chip-on-Glass Mounting Technology of LSIs for LCD Module', Proceedings International Microelectronics Conference, pp. 183-189, May-June (1990).

21 Stijns, W., 'Chip-on-glass — for LCD Modules with Totally Integrated Driver', *Electronic Components and Applications*, **Vol. 10**, No. 4, pp. 169-177 (1992).

22 Hatada, K. and Fujimoto, H., 'A New LSI Bonding Technology "Micron Bump Bonding Technology"', Proceedings 39th Electronic Components Conference, pp. 45-49, May (1989).

23 Hatada, K., Fujimoto, H., Kawakita, T. and Ochi, T., 'A New LSI Bonding Technology "Micron Bump Bonding" Assembly Technology', IEEE/CHMT International Electronic Manufacturing Technology Symposium, pp. 23-27, October (1988).

24 Hatada, K., Fujimoto, H., Kawakita, T. and Ochi, T., 'LED Array Modules by New Method Micron Bump Bonding Method', IEEE/CHMT International Electronic Manufacturing Technology Symposium, pp. 230-233, October (1989).

25 Nukii, T., Kakimoto, N., Atarashi, H., Matsubara, H., Yamamura, K. and Hatsui, H., 'LSI Chip Mounting Technology for Liquid Crystal Displays', Proceedings ISHM International Symposium on Microelectronics, pp. 257-262 (1990).

26 Sharp, US Patent 5,065,505, November 19 (1991).

27 Atarashi, H., Kakimoto, N., Matsubara, H., Yamamura, K., Mukii, T. and Matsui, H., 'Chip-on-Glass Technology Using Conductive Particles and Light-Setting Adhesives', Proceedings Japan International Electronic Manufacturing Technology Symposium, Tokyo, Japan, pp. 190-195, June (1990).

28 Matsubara, H., Atarashi, H., Yamamura, K., Kakimoto, N., Naitoh, K. and Nukii, T., 'Bare-Chip Face-Down Bonding Technology Using Conductive Particles and LightSetting Adhesives: ELASTIC Method', Proceedings IMC 1992, Yokohama, pp. 81-87 (1992).

29 Masuda, M., Sakuma, K., Satoh, E., Yamasaki, Y., Miyasaka, H. and Takeuchi, J., 'Chip on Glass Technology for Large Capacity and High Resolution LCD', Proceedings International Electronic Manufacturing Technology Symposium, pp. 57-60, April (1989).

30 Sakuma, K., Nozawa, K., Sato, E., Yamasaki, Y., Hanyuda, K., Miyasaka, H. and Takeuchi, J., 'Chip on Glass Technology with Standard Aluminized IC Chip', Proceedings ISHM

International Symposium on Microelectronics, pp. 250-256 (1990).

31 Otsuki, H., Kato, T., Matsukawa, F., Nunoshita, M. and Takasago, H., 'Chip-on-Glass Packaging Technology Using Conductive Particles', Proceedings IIWC 1992, Yokohama, pp. 99-103 (1992).

32 Mori, M., Saito. M., Hongu, A., Niitsuma, A. and Ohdaira, H., 'A New Face Down Bonding Technique Using A Low Melting Point Metal', Proceedings International Electronic Manufacturing Technology Symposium, pp. 114-118, April (1989).

33 Liu, J. and Rörgren, R., 'Joining of Displays using Thermo-setting Anisotropically Conductive Adhesives', Proceedings International Seminar 'Kleben mit anisotrop leitfähigen Kleben in der Mikrosytemtechnik', November (1993).

34 Werner, K., *IEEE Spectrum*, p. 65, May (1995).

Chapter 16

INTEGRATION OF MICROSYSTEMS USING FLIP-CHIP TECHNOLOGIES AND ADHESIVES

MAJA AMSKOV and HENRIK L. HVIMS
DELTA Danish Electronics, Light & Acoustics, Hørsholm, Denmark

16.1   INTRODUCTION

Standard CMOS processes can, with some modifications and with a few additional processes, be used for creating micromechanics. Micromechanics are basically mechanical devices such as sensors or actuators made entirely from silicon. One of the major advantages of micromechanics over conventional mechanics is their smaller size. However, the mechanic does not perform by itself; it has to be driven by some electronics, for instance a microelectronics chip of about the same size as the micromechanic.

This chapter will focus on the challenges of combining micro electromechanical systems (MEMS) with conventional microelectronics, thereby creating what is known as an intelligent microsystem.

Combining the two parts of a microsystem can be performed in the same way as conventional MCM solutions. Packaging density can be increased by flip-chip mounting of one or more of the parts in the microsystem. The optimal packaging density can be obtained by stacking the devices.

This chapter describes different stacking approaches and includes different bonding solutions involving both conductive and non-conductive adhesive systems.

16.2   MOTIVATION FOR STACKING

To achieve higher packaging density, the demand for smaller and cheaper devices is increasing, and creative ideas for new cost-effective solutions to assembly and interconnection problems are appearing.[1,2] The ultimate solution (with regard to the component size) is of course monolithic integration, but until this can be achieved more cost-effectively (batch processes, high yield, low cost, fast process times, etc.) other solutions must be found.

In the stacking approach the basic idea is to connect the micromechanic and the microelectronic devices directly to each other by stacking them, and then to consider this as one silicon device, that must be packed, EMC shielded, and mounted.

Stacking the silicon chips in this way before finally mounting the device has a number of advantages:

The connection from chip to chip is formed by flip-chip mounting of one chip to the other. In this first flip-chip assembly many challenges, such as mismatch of thermal expansion coefficient and stress, are avoided. If each chip is mounted on the substrate, all these challenges have to be faced for each chip. With this technology a flip-chip mounting of silicon on a substrate occurs only once.

The completed device takes up less space on the substrate. This is a tremendous advantage, especially in constrained spaces.

Parasitic loads from bonding wires are minimised, and as all the interconnections in a flip-chip assembly are the same length (whereas bonding wires may not all have the same length), the parasitic loads will also become more 'reproducible'. This is illustrated in Figure 16.1.

Conventional mounted chip

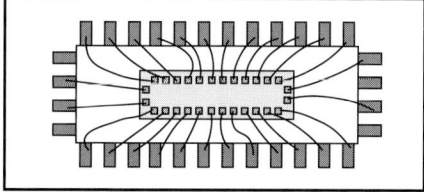

Flip chip, stack mounted chip(s)

Fig. 16.1 This shows that, when using flip-chip mounting techniques in assembly of microsystems, the parasitic loads will be, if not smaller, then at least more reproducible.

As long as the interconnection pads are kept in certain places (not necessarily on the edge of the component), the different parts of the microsystem can be custom-designed and assembled.

By selecting a feasible mounting technique, it is possible to assemble the microsystem wafer to wafer or, as a good alternative, known good die to a tested wafer. This will mean less handling and, if mounting die to wafer, an even better yield.

In spite of all the above mentioned advantages, there are of course also many challenges involved in creating microsystems.

16.3   INTERCONNECTIONS

With regard to interconnections, three levels of interconnection within a microsystem are of interest:

First level of interconnection:
Electrical connection inside the individual device, i.e., inside the micromechanical part itself. This is a problem especially if the micromechanic device itself consists of more than one wafer. This interconnection (level 1) must be embodied in the design of the micromechanic in order to produce a functional device.

Second level of interconnection:
Electrical connection from one silicon device to another, i.e., from the micromechanic part to the microelectronic part.

Third level of interconnection:
Electrical connection from the microsystem to the substrate.

In Figure 16.2 an example of an assembled and mounted microsystem is shown.

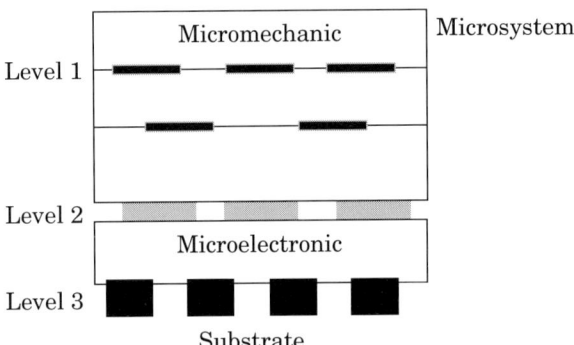

Fig. 16.2 An example of the distribution of the different interconnect levels in a microsystem.

The second and third levels of interconnection are coupled, as the complexity of the third problem depends strongly upon the solution of the second.

16.4   VARIOUS BONDING METHODS

16.4.1   Bump Processing

Adhesives combined with bumps are a new rapidly growing technology, which offers a low-cost solution for high volume production. Furthermore, the process is fluxless and leadfree. These technologies are of special interest for interconnect level 2 and interconnect level 3.

There are mainly three types of bumps:

— Mechanical stud-bumps (Au, Sn/Pb) (see Figure 16.3)
— Polymer bumps (conductive adhesive)
— Chemically plated bumps (Au/Ni).

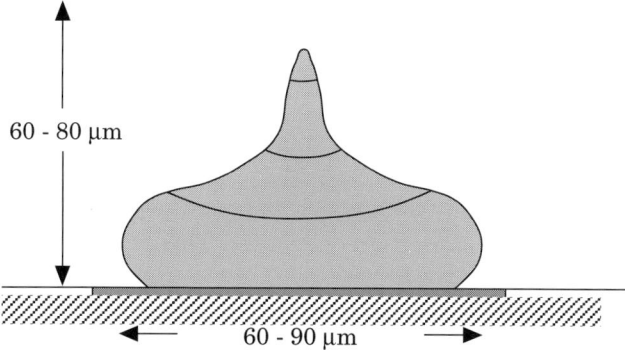

Fig. 16.3 Mechanical Au stud.

Mechanical stud-bumps (e.g., gold or tin (Sn/Pb)) are produced by a flexible low-cost bumping technique based on a conventional wirebonding procedure. The bump, called a stud-bump, is a two-step construction. First, the ball is formed on a tip of wire through the capillary and fixed on the chip part to form the bottom of the stud-bump. Then the wire is cut off by the capillary edge to form the tip on the upper surface of the bump. Thus the bump is formed with good reproducibility and has a stable shape. The sizes and geometry of stud-bumps are principally dependent on the wire diameter and the geometry of the capillary as well as on the bumping parameters.

Polymer bumps can be produced in two ways, namely stencil printing or microdispensing.

In stencil printing a stencil that has openings in the areas where adhesive is required is placed above the wafer. A squeegee is passed across the stencil and forces the conductive adhesive through the uncoated areas of the stencil and on to the substrate. Stencil printing is a batch process as all bumps are screened on the wafer in 'one go'. After screening the bumps, the polymers are fully cured.

The microdispensing technique is not a common process, but interest in this technique is growing. Furthermore, as the speed of the dispensers is increasing dramatically (>10 dots/s) it is becoming an alternative method for high volume production. A problem associated with microdispensing is the size of the silver particles, typically 25-50 µm, which tend to block the dispenser needle.

New conductive silver particles are being developed with a size of 3-5 µm. With these particles it will be possible to dispense dots with a diameter of less than 75 µm for 100 µm x 100 µm or 75 µm x 75 µm pads. Dispensing conductive adhesives is of special interest for repair. After removing the failed device (chip) it is possible to dispense new adhesive dots on a board which has already been assembled with other components.

Chemically plated bumps are of pure Au or pure Ni or a combination of Au and Ni. It is possible to make batch processing either electro or electroless.

16.4.2 Adhesives — Conductive/Non-conductive

The use of adhesives as solder replacement has recently gained importance not only due to environmental issues such as replacement of lead and fluxes, but also due to fine-pitch requirements and the possibility of polymerising at much lower temperatures for a reasonable time. This is of special interest for polymeric substrates with a low Tg. Conductive adhesive opens up the possibility of using a series of low-cost flexible substrate materials like polyester.

Adhesives will, as pointed out in the section on 'Bump processing', typically be used at second and third interconnect levels.

The adhesives can be inks (fluid), epoxy, or tapes/films. The binders can be epoxies, phenols or acrylics or a blend of these. Furthermore, as the adhesives can be conductive or non-conductive, we are dealing with four main types:

— non-conductive film, underfiller;
— non-conductive adhesive ink, underfiller;
— conductive adhesive, isotropic (ink);
— conductive film, anisotropic, (Z-axis).

Underfiller is used under the chip to stabilise it with consideration for long-term reliability.

16.4.2.1 NON-CONDUCTIVE ADHESIVE

Non-conductive adhesives are insulating thermosetting/thermoplastic blends without conductive particles and are used as underfillers. Films are delivered in dry film format of different thicknesses between 25 μm and 75 μm and with a film carrier. The film is placed on the substrate and heated so that it is possible to remove the film carrier. The gold stud-bumps on the chip and the pads on the substrates are aligned.

The chip is bonded to the substrate with an appropriate load and temperature so that the studs will penetrate the film. The IC is electrically connected to the substrate via compressed and deformed gold stud-bumps. The pressure on the chip is maintained until the melted film has cooled to room temperature.

To repair the interconnection, the entire flip-chip joint is heated to an appropriate temperature in order to debond the IC. After debonding the chip, it is possible to repeat the process without removing the film.

16.4.2.2 CONDUCTIVE ADHESIVES

Conductive adhesives are isotropically conductive, which means that they are electrically conductive in all directions, like solder joint bonding. Conductive adhesive bumps can be produced by stencil printing (batch process) or by dispensing as described above. It is possible to make holes in the stencil down to 25 μm by using a laser.

Conductive adhesive combined with gold studs is of special interest. It is well known that the interface between an aluminium pad and a wirebonded gold ball is reliable. It has been proven by several institutes (DELTA/IVF) that silver-filled conductive adhesive produces reliable bonding to gold (gold studs and/or gold pads).

One method of adding conductive adhesive to the studs is to use a stainless steel stencil. The conductive adhesive is placed on the stencil which has a full opening larger than the chip size. A stainless steel squeegee transfers the adhesive through the opening, resulting in a flat surface containing a thin-film silver conductive paste.

The IC with gold studs is then placed in the thin film of conductive paste, resulting in an equal amount of conductive paste being applied to each gold stud. The rate of transfer is controlled by changing the stencil thickness. After mounting, the conductive adhesive is post-cured. After post-curing the adhesive, the chip will be underfilled by dispensing non-conductive paste, normally along two non-parallel sides. After underfilling, the whole system will finally be cured.

Other methods are dispensing or printing conductive adhesive on the substrate/counter part.

16.5   TOPOLOGIES

When assembling microsystems by stacking, a number of requirements must be met. Regardless of the function and working principle of the micromechanic, two aspects are important:

— The system must have access to the surroundings.
— The micromechanic device must have electrical connection to the microelectronics device.

All other requirements derive from these two aspects, for example:

— A microphone must have acoustic access to the environment.
— An accelerometer must be able to sense the acceleration.
— A micropump must touch the substance which it is pumping (liquid or gas).
— Depending on the working principle of the micromechanic, the electrical connections must be kept free of unwanted parasitic parameters.

Many other examples could be cited.

It is clear that the topology for a microsystem depends strongly on the type of microsystem being discussed.

The ability to produce vertical feedthroughs in wafers[5] opens up a new range of possibilities for the stacking of components, see Figure 16.4.

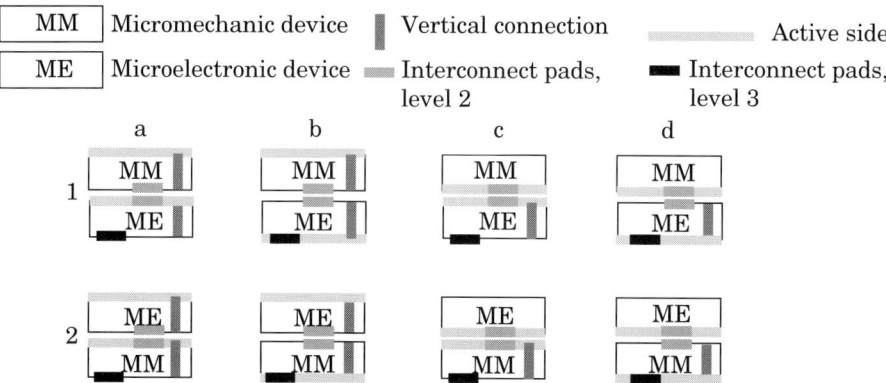

Fig. 16.4 When the microsystem is connected from the bottom (or the top), there are eight different ways of orienting the chips. These possibilities are shown in rows one and two. Vertical interconnections are used to establish the electrical connection from the top chip to the substrate. Not all of the possibilities shown are feasible. Columns a and b are practical only for specific types of microsystems; normally, vertical interconnections should be applied only on one chip. Choosing between c and d must be a matter of what is practical with respect to the physical performance of the system and the electrical noise originating from the vertical interconnection.

16.6   CONCLUSION

This chapter has demonstrated several solutions for stacking chips and thereby achieving a very dense package. An indication of different bonding solutions has been presented combining different bumps with adhesive systems. Advanced flip-chip bonding solutions using adhesive systems combined with the stacking technique are being implemented for high volume and low-cost production in the next generation of microelectronics.

16.7   ACKNOWLEDGEMENT

The authors wish to thank all contributors to this chapter working in the Mikrosystemcentret (Micro System Center, MSC) and the steering committee of the Danish project on conductive adhesives conducted in 1990-1993.

Special thanks are extended to the steering committee of the NORAD project: Nordic Adhesives 1993-1994.

REFERENCES

1   Aschenbrenner, R., Zakel, E. and Reichl, H., 'Flip Chip Assembly Using Adhesives', Proceedings Workshop on Flip Chip and Ball Grid Arrays, Berlin (1995).

2   Hvims, H. L., 'Adhesives as Solder Replacement for SMT', DELTA Danish Electronics, Lights & Acoustics, January (1994).

3   Rusannes, O. and Pennanen, V., 'Experience of Working with Thermosetting and Thermoplastic Conductive Adhesives', Proceedings Adhesives in Electronics, Stockholm (1996).

4   Ostmann, A., Azdasht, G., Kloeser, J., Aschenbrenner, R., Zakel, E. and Reichl, H., 'Flip Chip Interconnection using Chemical Wafer Bumping', Proceedings Workshop on VLSI and Microsystem Packaging Techniques and Manufacturing Technologies, Baveno (1996).

5   Christensen, C., Bouwstra, S., Petersen, J. W. and Kersten, P., 'Wafer Through-hole Interconnections for High Vertical Wiring Densities', Proceedings EuPac '96 (1996).

6   Aschenbrenner, R., Zakel, E. and Reichl, H., 'Flip Chip Assembly using Adhesives', Fraunhofer-Institut für Zuverlässigkeit und Mikrointegration (IZM), Berlin.

7   Kreutter, N. P., Grove, B. K., Hogerton, P. B. and Jensen, C. R., 'Effective Polymer Adhesives for Interconnect', 3M, Austin, Texas.

8   Aschenbrenner, R., Gwiasda, J., Eldring, J., Zakel, E. and Reichl, H., 'Flip Chip Attachment Using Non-Conductive Adhesives and Gold Ball Bumps', Technische Universität Berlin and Fraunhofer-Institut für Zuverlässigkeit und Mikrointegration (IZM), Berlin.

9   Bessho, Y., Tomura, Y., Hakotani, Y., Tsukamoto, M., Ishida, T. and Omoya, K., 'A Stud-Bump-Bonding Technique for High Density Multi-Chip-Module', Matsushita Electric Industrial Co. Ltd, Osaka.

10 Bessho, Y., Tomura, Y., Shiraishi, T., Ono, M., Ishida, T. and Omoya, K., 'Advanced Flip-Chip Bonding Technique to Organic Substrates', Matsushita Electric Industrial Co. Ltd, Osaka.

Chapter 17

ADHESIVES AND HEALTH HAZARDS

HELENE CARLSSON and ANN-BETH ANTONSSON
Swedish Environmental Research Institute, Stockholm, Sweden

17.1   INTRODUCTION

This chapter gives an overview of factors influencing chemical health hazards, how chemical substances might affect health and some advice concerning how to choose an adhesive. It is based upon the experience gained during work on a handbook dealing with occupational health aspects of constructive bonding. The handbook was compiled in cooperation between the Swedish Environmental Research Institute, IVL, and the Swedish Institute of Production Engineering Research, IVF, in 1993. Adhesives are continuously developing and the reader is advised always to check up on the latest developments.

17.2   FACTORS INFLUENCING CHEMICAL HEALTH HAZARDS

Different factors influence chemical health hazards when working with adhesives.

17.2.1   Intrinsic Health Hazardous Properties of the Adhesive

These depend on how potentially harmful or dangerous the different substances in the adhesive are, and also on their concentration in the adhesive. If an adhesive contains a very small amount of a very poisonous substance, the adhesive itself is not necessarily very poisonous. In the same way, a relatively harmless substance can make an adhesive hazardous if exposure is excessive. Allergy-forming substances are an exception; allergic persons may develop allergic reactions after contact with very small amounts.

Adhesives are based on polymers and monomers (polymers are built of monomers). The polymers are usually considered harmless whereas many monomers, from which the polymers used in structural adhesives are built, are associated with health hazards. It is, however, almost impossible to avoid having a small amount of monomers in cured adhesives. The amount of monomer is so small that it is usually considered harmless, possibly with the exception of persons already allergic to the monomer.

17.2.2   Extent of Exposure

This is influenced by the type of adhesive. A one-component adhesive is processed in a different way from a two-component adhesive. A solid adhesive is applied differently from a liquid adhesive. Enclosures, ventilation and other protective measures as well as the degree of automation also influence the exposure.

17.2.3   Duration and Frequency of Exposure

In general, the risks increase with concentration and time of exposure. Some health effects will occur only after long exposure, while others can occur after a single contact. Usually long-term exposure to low concentrations causes different injuries from short-term exposure to high concentrations.

17.3   MEANS OF EXPOSURE

The skin	contact	local effects at place of contact
	uptake	effects in other organs
The mouth	directly	unusual
	through food	adhesives on the fingers etc. can stick to the food and thereby be eaten
Inhalation of fumes	directly	when using adhesives containing volatile substances or when heating adhesives
	through smoking	adhesives on the fingers can stick to the cigarette and will be inhaled together with the smoke
Inhalation of aerosols		when using adhesives in liquid form in such a way that an aerosol is formed, for example spraying

17.4   WHAT DO WE ACTUALLY KNOW ABOUT HEALTH HAZARDS WITH DIFFERENT SUBSTANCES?

Daily we are exposed to a great many substances, during both work and leisure. The effect of exposure to one substance may be influenced by the other substances to which a person is exposed. The effect might be strengthened or weakened. It is difficult to identify those substances that are harmful from this complex exposure, but it is not impossible. Most likely, however, only the most potent substances will be discovered.

In epidemiology the relationship between illness and exposure to different substances is studied. Epidemiological studies deal with exposures in the past or over a prolonged period.

Because of the considerable time necessary for epidemiological studies a lot of toxicological information is based on animal experiments. There are always uncertainties when translating results from animal experiments to humans. The more species showing similar effects after exposure to a substance, the more likely it is that humans react in the same way. The sensitivity, that is the exposure necessary to produce adverse effects, may also vary strongly between species. The sensitivity can also vary considerably between individuals of the same species, e.g., some people become allergic whereas their colleagues under the same exposure do not. Animal studies and epidemiological studies do, however, provide valuable information. It is important to remember that many substances are insufficiently investigated concerning health impact.

A substance for which no adverse effects are known may be harmless or insufficiently studied.

17.5 HOW CAN DIFFERENT SUBSTANCES AFFECT HEALTH?

This section follows the classification in the Swedish regulation:

Irritation/corrosion

Substances that destroy tissue and cause damage after contact with skin within three minutes are classified as *strongly corrosive*. Substances needing more than three minutes but less than four hours to cause the same effect are classified as *corrosive*. Non-corrosive substances which cause a local inflammatory reaction after long-term or repeated direct contact with skin or mucous membranes are classified as *irritating*.

Acute toxicity

Substances having adverse effects, other than corrosion or irritation, immediately upon exposure are called acute toxic. The acute toxicity is graded according to the amount of substance necessary to cause adverse effects, and to some extent also according to the seriousness of the effects. A substance has *very high acute toxicity* if very small doses can cause death or very serious effects after short exposure. A substance has *medium high acute toxicity* if relatively small amounts can produce adverse effects after short exposure. A substance has *moderate acute toxicity* if only relatively high doses can give adverse effects.

LD50 values are frequently used as a measure of acute toxicity. The LD50 value is the dose necessary to kill 50% of the animals in a test. The higher the LD50 value, the lower the acute toxicity. It is important to remember that LD50 values relate to death. LD50 values may never be used to assess the total health impact of a substance since many adverse effects, acute and transient as well as permanent, can appear at a much lower dose than the one causing immediate death.

Toxicity after repeated exposure

Repeated exposure, of short or long duration, may ultimately affect health. This can be studied in animal experiments and in epidemiological surveys. Exposure may give rise to different effects upon health, some of which are described below.

Organ lesions, e.g., impaired function or more serious damage to liver, kidneys, pulmonary system or nervous system.

Some substances adversely affect *reproduction, sex cells, foetus* or *offspring*. Damage or disease that is inherited or affects the foetus or offspring is considered serious since it affects a new generation.

Cancer generally takes a long time to develop. Cancer is considered very serious. One reason is that it is difficult to discover cancer in time, i.e., when it is still possible to treat it sucessfully.

Substances that are mutagenic affect the genes. Many, but not all, substances that are mutagenic (tested in bacterial cells), or in other ways able to affect genes adversely, can also cause cancer and/or affect reproduction in a negative way. If a substance is shown to affect genes, it is wise to investigate its carcinogenic potential and effect on reproduction as well.

An *allergy* usually develops first after long-term exposure. Contact allergy can give rise to itching, redness, swelling, peeling skin and rash etc. An allergy can also manifest itself as asthma-like attacks, sneezing, clogged or running nose etc. Persons having an allergy will be allergic for the rest of their lives. An allergy should not give serious problems. It may be possible to avoid the allergenic substance or perhaps the symptoms do not give much discomfort. It could, however, also necessitate major changes in work and lifestyle for allergic subjects (in order to avoid the allergenic substance). For some people it may even be fatal (e.g., heavy 'asthmatic attacks').

Substances producing adverse effects after long-term exposure, or effects discovered a long time after the time of exposure, are particularly treacherous. It is possible to continue the exposure for much too long before receiving a warning or before the illness itself breaks out.

17.6   WHAT DO ADHESIVES CONTAIN?

Adhesives contain mainly polymers. Polymers are very large molecules built of many small, identical segments, known as monomers. A curing adhesive could be built of monomers or prepolymers or both. Prepolymers are short polymers built of a limited number of monomers and are supposed to react further to build 'real polymers' when curing. During curing the monomers and/or prepolymers are linked together into an endless network.

In curing adhesives the monomers or prepolymers have reactive end-groups. The most common reactive end-groups are:

— epoxy (in epoxy adhesives);
— acrylates and methacrylates (in acrylate and cyanoacrylate adhesives);
— isocyanates and isocyanatereactive groups (in polyurethane adhesives).

Non-curing adhesives set through evaporation (solvent or water-based adhesives) or cooling (hot-melt adhesives). The flexibility of the long polymers in the adhesive decreases as the adhesive hardens and the polymers stick to each other, building a tangled skein.

Adhesives can also contain inhibitors, stabilisers, catalysts, accelerators and retardants. In addition, there are numerous modifiers to influence the toughness, strength, conductive properties, colour, etc. of the bond.

17.7 HEALTH HAZARDS ASSOCIATED WITH EPOXY ADHESIVES

An investigation from 1987 shows that epoxy is the third most common causative agent in work-related allergy.

17.7.1 How to Choose Epoxy Adhesive — Recommendations

- Use adhesives without low-molecular epoxy, or with as low content as possible.
- Handle all epoxy adhesives as if they can cause allergy even if they are said not to contain free monomers.
- Avoid reactive diluents.
- Solid epoxy adhesives are preferred, but be careful to avoid dust problems with adhesive powder.
- Use amine adducts instead of amines as curing agents.

17.7.2 Monomers and Prepolymers

All investigated epoxy monomers and prepolymers seem capable of giving rise to contact allergy. The most potent are the low molecular monomers. Epoxy resins are not volatile. To become allergic towards epoxy, or to have problems if already allergic to epoxy, skin contact with epoxy monomers is necessary. Resins of high mean molecular weight may contain considerable amounts of free monomers. Cured resins may contain enough monomer to give epoxy-allergic subjects problems.

17.7.3 Curing Agents in Epoxy Adhesives

Aliphatic amines and acid anyhydrides irritate eyes, skin and respiratory tract. Aliphactic amines are highly volatile whereas acid anyhydrides are volatile at raised temperatures. Many amines can cause contact allergy and sometimes also allergic responses affecting the respiratory system. Various acid anhydrides are allergy forming, which manifests itself in disturbance of respiration. Several aromatic amines are suspected of causing cancer. Amine adducts are not usually considered allergy forming and are therefore recommended as a substitute for amines.

17.7.4 Reactive Diluents

Reactive diluents should be avoided, since they can cause contact allergy. They are also volatile and can evaporate from the adhesive, which increases the possibilities of exposure.

17.8   HEALTH HAZARDS ASSOCIATED WITH ACRYLIC ADHESIVES

Many adhesives are based on acrylates or methacrylates. They can be classified as:

— modified acrylates, acrylates   first generation acrylates (also called surface activated or honeymoon adhesives) and second generation acrylates (also called SGA adhesives)
— anaerobic adhesives
— UV-curing acrylates
— cyano acrylates

17.8.1   How to Choose Acrylic Adhesive — Recommendations

- Use adhesives based on methacrylates rather than on acrylates.
- Use adhesives based on monomers of higher molecular weight (less volatile).
- Avoid adhesives with separate activators if these lead to excessive exposure to solvents.
- Avoid the following substances, which have been classified as strong to extremely strong allergenic agents when tested on animals: urethane acrylates with straight carbon chain (aliphatic urethaneacrylates), some epoxy acrylates;
     tripropylene glycol diacrylate (TPGDA)
     trimethylol propane triacrylate (TMPTA)
     1,4-butanediol diacrylate (BUDA)
     1,6 hexanediol diacrylate (HDDA)

17.8.2   Monomers and Prepolymers

Acrylate and methacrylate monomers irritate mucous membranes and skin. They can also give rise to contact allergy. Methacrylates seem to be less potent sensitisers than the corresponding acrylates. Di- or triacrylated substances should be considered as allergy forming. Dimethacrylated substances are weak or not allergy forming. Methyl methacrylate has also been seen to affect peripheral nerves after extensive skin contact. Acrylic acid, ethyl acrylate and some methacrylates negatively affect the foetus. Cyanoacrylates are allergy forming and highly irritating to the respiratory passages as well as to the skin.

17.9   HEALTH HAZARDS ASSOCIATED WITH POLYURETHANE ADHESIVES

17.9.1   How to Choose Polyurethane Adhesive — Recommendations

- Use adhesive based on prepolymerised MDI (4,4´-diphenyl methane diisocyanate) or IPDI (isophoron diisocyanate). MDI and IPDI are less volatile than TDI (toluene diisocyanate) and HDI (hexamethylene diisocyanate), and prepolymerisation reduces the number of free isocyanates. Check that the MDI is free from phenyl isocyanate.

- Some amine catalysts (e.g., dianisidine, dichlorobensidine, tolidine and MOCA) should be avoided since they are carcinogenic.
- Do no heat adhesive or adhesive bonds. If heating is necessary, adequate ventilation is essential.
- Adhesives with organic solvents should be avoided or the work area must be ventilated carefully.
- If the adhesive contains blocked isocyanates, it is still necessary to ventilate carefully when the blockage is broken, i.e., on curing.

17.9.2   Monomers and Prepolymers

A high concentration of isocyanates in the workplace air is irritating. Isocyanates can give rise to impaired lung function and hypersensitivity manifested in asthmatic attacks, and in rare cases flu-like fever. Isocyanates are irritating to the skin and have in rare cases given rise to contact allergy. Toluene diisocyanate (TDI) is classified as possibly carcinogenic to humans. TDI and 1,6-hexamethylene diisocyanate (HDI) are more volatile, and hence are more easily spread in high concentrations to workplace air than 4,4´-diphenyl methane diisocyanate (MDI) and isophoron diisocyanate (IPDI).

17.9.3   Prepolymerised Isocyanates

Prepolymerised isocyanates are less volatile and contain fewer free isocyanate groups than the corresponding monomers. Prepolymers contain an excess amount of isocyanate monomer which may evaporate to the workplace air. Spray painting with lacquer based on prepolymerised isocyanates has led to sensitisation. The use of prepolymerised isocyanates results in a reduction but not a complete elimination of the risk of sensitisation. Health hazards accompanying blocked isocyanates have not been investigated widely, but it seems likely that they are less hazardous than the corresponding free isocyanates.

17.9.4   Polyurethanes

Polyurethanes are considered harmless. When heated, they can dissociate and give off free isocyanates.

17.10   ENVIRONMENTAL ASPECTS OF ADHESIVES

Resins are not usually considered hazardous for the environment.

If solvent-based adhesives are used, emissions to the air during production must be considered. (In Sweden the use of several chlorinated solvents has been banned or heavily restricted: CFC after 31/12 1992, carbon tetrachloride after 31/10 1993, methylene chloride, 1,1,1,-trichloroethane after 31/12 1994, trichloroethylene after 31/12 1995.)

Uncured adhesive (left in containers etc.) should be cured before disposal. Burning adhesives may give off undesirable gases.

During ageing of an adhesive bond additives etc. may possibly migrate and leak into the environment. This has not been widely investigated.

Environmental impact can be studied in a wide perspective. The method of evaluating environmental aspects from cradle to grave is called 'life cycle analysis'. A life cycle analysis covers the environmental effects of a certain production method from extraction of raw material, production and use to final disposal of the product.

Chapter 18

HEALTH AND ENVIRONMENTAL ASPECTS OF CONDUCTIVE ADHESIVES — THE USE OF LEAD-BASED ALLOYS COMPARED WITH ADHESIVES

H. WESTPHAL
Danish Toxicology Centre, Hoersholm, Denmark

18.1 INTRODUCTION

This chapter deals with the environmental aspects of the use of conductive adhesives compared with the traditional solder bonding technique. The objective was to assess the viability of using adhesives as alternatives to solder for surface mount technology. DTC performed the comparative environmental analysis of the use of adhesives related to solder in a typical production process with regard to occupational health and the environment. Other Danish partners in the work were DELTA Electronics, Technoconsult, Brüel & Kjær, Danfoss and Modulex. The work was supported by the Danish Environmental Ministry. The quantitative analysis of lead consumption included in this chapter was performed by Technoconsult.

Based on the information given by more than 20 manufacturers of isotropic electrically conductive adhesives, chemical constituents have been toxicologically evaluated with regard to toxicity to health and environment, and the use of solder is compared with the use of epoxy adhesives within the electronics industry. A life cycle study was performed in which adhesive technology is compared with the traditional bonding method with lead-containing solder. The work included legislative concern within the area.

The environmental evaluations comprised the following four topics:

- Ecotoxicological and toxicological profiles on substantial chemical components from a number of commercially available adhesives.
- Estimation of the amount of solder and especially lead used in electronics production in solder replacement.
- Comparison of environmental advantages and disadvantages in the use of solder and conductive adhesives, respectively.
- A partial life cycle analysis of the major steps in electronics production.

In this chapter, the substitution potential of lead by adhesives is presented together with a short environmental comparison of the two techniques.

18.2   ADHESIVES OR SOLDER?

The use of adhesives as a method of fastening or joining is becoming more and more common in industry. It is now beginning to find its place in the electronics industry, for example in the use of conductive adhesives to achieve mechanical and electrical contact between components and PCBs when using surface mount technology (SMT).

The substitution of conductive adhesive for solder is of interest from an environmental standpoint, in view of solder's tin (Sn) and lead (Pb) content. Solder commonly contains c. 40% Pb, c. 60% Sn (a eutectic alloy) and often a few percent of silver (Ag). Conductive adhesives contain no lead, but typically silver or copper (Cu). Converting from solder to conductive adhesives in electronics production could thus eliminate the use of lead and tin.

Lead is currently in focus as an environmental problem. Recent studies in the USA have identified lead as one of the greatest sources of pollution. Two initiatives have been introduced in Congress, the Reid Bill (S2637) and the Cardin/Bradley Bills (H2479, S1347); the former proposes a complete ban on lead, the latter the introduction of an environmental levy on the use of lead. None of the proposals has been passed in the USA. In Denmark, a total ban on lead in products was discussed politically in early 1997 in connection with DEPA's introduction of a product orientated environmental policy.

Lead has a number of harmful effects. It accumulates in blood and blood-rich organs (e.g., the liver and kidneys) in the human body. The mechanism for its toxic effect is the inhibition of some of the enzymes essential for the blood's capacity for transporting oxygen, for energy conversion in cells, and for the liver's detoxification processes.

The symptoms of lead poisoning are anaemia, hypertension and impairment of the central and peripheral nervous system. As far as foetuses and infants are concerned, lead is even more toxic and has an especially harmful influence on brain development. The IARC (International Agency on Research of Cancer in Lyons) considers that lead can have a carcinogenic effect in humans. In an ecotoxicological context, lead has an effect on algae and fish and on certain micro-organisms, affecting some bacteriological conversion processes. It also has a tendency to accumulate throughout the food chain.

The decision to substitute adhesive for solder can be taken on a solid basis of fact and experience of the chemistry of the adhesive, production processes and the overall environmental impact. Apart from the elimination of lead and tin, the use of adhesives has a number of technical advantages such as greater contact reliability, lower costs and simplified production processes.

At the same time, fluxes and some of the cleaning agents currently employed could be eliminated from the production process, since adhesives do not require flux or subsequent cleaning. In the future, the consumption of large quantities of lead and tin which are otherwise involved in electronics manufacture could also be avoided, as the use of adhesives does not require components to have Pb/Sn terminals, nor do PCBs have to be pre-tinned.

On the other hand, adhesives do have a number of environmentally hazardous properties. Some types, for example, give off vapours which can be harmful to humans, so air extraction has to take place in the assembly shop, just as it does today to evacuate lead and flux vapours arising from the soldering process. Adhesives can also be hazardous in other ways in their uncured state: some (particularly epoxy adhesives) are allergenic, inhalation of the fumes can cause respiratory problems, and some types can, with improper handling, cause irritation of the skin and eyes.

Adhesives may be sensitive to chemical substances, especially strongly alkaline solutions. They may be soluble in organic solvents, softeners and oils. Heating renders them plastic, so that repairs can be undertaken. Corrosion of the glued surfaces may result in the adhesive working loose from the surface if it has not been properly treated before mounting.

18.3 SCOPE OF THE PROBLEM — LEAD CONSUMPTION IN SOLDERING

A study of the literature has formed the basis for an assessment of the types and quantities of solder used in the following processes: surface mounting (SMT), through-hole mounting (THM), hot air solder levelling (HASL), component terminals, automated mounting and manual repair.

Conductive adhesives can replace solder paste for reflow soldering and will also make it possible to eliminate the use of solder for component terminals. The PbSn pre-tinning process, nowadays often employed for the surface treatment of PCBs, can also be replaced by the use of flash gold. In addition, conductive adhesives will probably be able to replace much of the lead currently used for wave soldering of through-hole mounted components.

The consumption of solders for component mounting in Sweden is estimated at 200 t/y. Surface treatment consumes c. 20 t/y, of which less than 2 t is delivered with the product; the remainder is recycled.

18.3.1 Suppliers of Soldering Materials

To obtain a picture of the consumption of solders in Denmark, the following suppliers to the Danish market were interviewed (Table 18.1).

Table 18.1

Supplier	Trademark	Market Share
Boliden Bergsøe	KOGI	≈ 35%
Holger I. Nielsen	ASAHI, Seho, Stannol	≈ 25%
JPS Ketec	Alpha	≈ 20%
Radioparts	Multicore	< 5%
Electro-Science Laboratories	ESL	< 5%
LIF Elektronik	Qualitech	< 5%

They were asked about the size of their market, their market share, how the market is growing and the proportion of pastes recycled for reflow soldering, rods for ultrasonic soldering, wire for manual soldering and surface treatment tinners. The three largest suppliers are noted to have around 80% of the market.

18.3.2 Quantitative Analysis

On the basis of the interviews, the electronic industry's consumption of solders is estimated to be 133 t/y, with 4 t being used in reflow soldering, 80 t in wave soldering, 16 t in surface treatment and 30 t in manual mounting and repair using solder wire. In addition to this are the c. 3 t contained in terminals on bought-in components. The solders consist of c. 40% lead. Only a small proportion of the 16 t used in surface treatment follows the product; the remainder is either recycled or disposed of. The results of this analysis are summarised in Table 18.2 as follows:

Table 18.2

Use	Solder Alloy/Year	Lead Content	Lead/Year	Growth	Recycling	Lead Year 2000
Reflow soldering	4 tons	36%	1,400 kg	+15%	-	3,700 kg
Wave soldering	80 tons	40%	32,000 kg	-10%	-	15,300 kg
Component	3 tons	36%	1,100 kg	-	-	1,100 kg
Surface	16 tons	40%	6,400 kg	-	80%	1,300 kg
Solder wire	30 tons	40%	12,000 kg	-5%	-	8,400 kg
Total	133 tons	-	52,900 kg	-	-	29,800 kg

The last column in the table shows the potential for substitution in the year 2000. The figures are obtained by projecting the current annual consumption of lead taking the given growth rates into account.

The total amount of lead consumed each year is distributed according to Swedish research as shown in Figure 18.1.

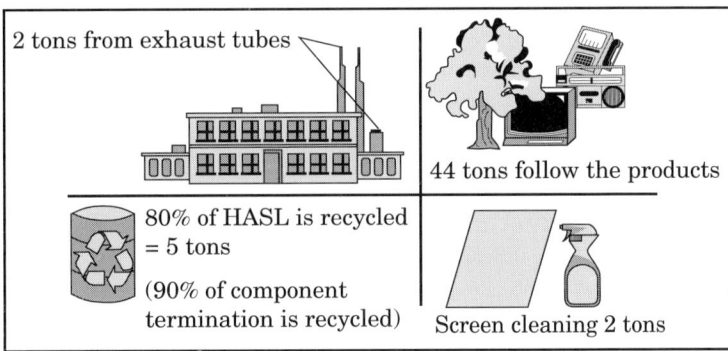

Fig. 18.1 Distribution of 53 tons of lead used in soldering electronics products in Denmark.

18.3.3 Substitution Potential

Conductive adhesives are not a realistic alternative in all of the above production methods in the short term (the next 3-5 years or so). An estimate is given below of the potential substitution in the year 2000 — in other words, how much the electronics industry's consumption of lead could be reduced by the introduction of conductive adhesives.

Introducing conductive adhesives in the electronics industry would reduce the annual consumption of lead by c. 16 t in the short term. The consumption of tin would be reduced by c. 24 t at the same time.

These quantities of lead should be viewed in the context of an overall lead balance in Denmark. One estimate has been constructed from data gathered in 1985. Since many of the sources of lead pollution have been significantly reduced in the last decade (motor fuel additives, ammunition, paints), some rough estimates have had to be made.

Using the source mentioned as a basis, the annual emission of lead to the atmosphere, to water and into the ground is currently estimated at c. 3,200 t. A reduction of 16 t in the electronics industry's consumption as a direct result of the substitution of adhesive for solder would thus reduce the total emissions of lead to the environment by 0.5%. In the longer term, the reduction could reach 1.5%, as more and more processes are converted from solder to adhesive. This evaluation also has to include an evaluation of how controllable these emissions are: it has so far proved difficult to control how electronic refuse is disposed of.

18.4   THE METHOD

Based on information on the chemical product compositions of more than 20 isotropic conductive adhesives obtained world-wide from the respective manufacturers, DTC have evaluated the environmental properties of the main types of conductive adhesives.

Each adhesive may contain up to 10 or more different chemical constituents. The constituents have been divided into groups with respect to their chemical characteristics and function.

For each substance or group of substances, a toxicological profile has been drawn up where the following factors have been described:

— Physical and chemical properties
— Classification and appearances on lists of dangerous substances
— Degradability (chemical, photochemical, biological)
— Metabolism in mammals (how chemical substances are taken up and excreted in the body)
— Acute toxicity (oral, dermal and inhalation)
— Irritation and sensitivity
— Toxicity and long-term exposure
— Acute and chronic ecotoxicity
— Assessment of environmental and health related hazards in different life cycle phases.

Based on the profiles, each substance is summarised and an evaluation is made of whether the choice of adhesive is of consequence for the environment. The polymeric part of the adhesive is probably the most significant factor for the environmental and health hazards in fully cured systems, as the binder is assumed to be crucial to the binding of single substances in the system and thereby decisive for the product risk.

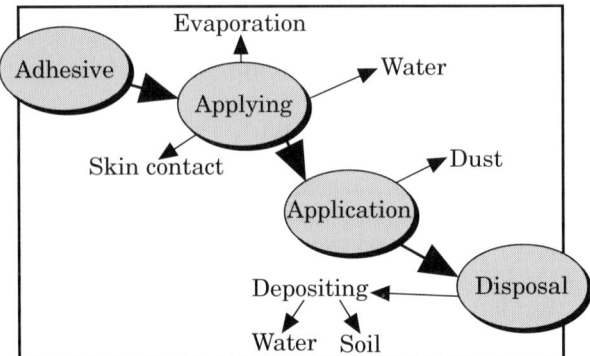

Fig. 18.2 Life cycle of an adhesive.

The advantages and disadvantages of the use of conductive adhesives and soldering are related to the state of environmental knowledge and considerations of volume.

18.5   CHEMICAL GROUPS OF ADHESIVES

Conductive adhesives are based on polymers. To the polymeric resin is added conducting metal in the form of powder or flakes and some additives. The additives may be organic solvents, hardeners and/or metal catalysts.

The polymeric binder is decisive for the splitting of adhesives into groups. The four main groups are:

1   Epoxy adhesives (1 or 2 component).
2   Silicone adhesives (1 or 2 component).
3   Polyimide adhesives.
4   Acrylate adhesives.

To elucidate the environmental investigation of the adhesives, a summary of the first group mentioned, e.g., epoxy adhesives, is given below.

18.5.1   Epoxy Adhesives

Epoxy substances are very reactive and are generally used as floor material, paints, lacquers or adhesives, or as sealants, vapour barriers or insulation foam. The base component in epoxy products is epoxy resin which may contain organic solvents. The resin may be high or low molecular and the solvents may also be epoxy substances, so-called reactive solvents.

The conducting metal (usually 40-80% w/w of the adhesive) typically consists of silver particles or flakes or silver-plated copper particles. Other metals such as nickel or gold are also found.

One-component epoxy products will generally contain a latent amine hardener which will initiate the polymerisation process after application. The hardener of a two-component product will usually contain an active amine.

The content of solvents is found within a large range. There is a wide range of organic solvents used in epoxy adhesives although information on organic solvents is not stated for every product.

18.5.2   Working with Epoxies — Hazards Identification

Epoxy products are irritating to skin and eyes and may cause allergy through contact by sensitised persons. Once an allergic reaction to these substances has been acquired, the worker will be excluded from all work with epoxy and polyurethane for life. Once cured or polymerised, the substances are neither reactive nor allergenic.

The advantages of using the products are their high adhesive properties and their formation of very strong and durable surfaces.

Some epoxy adhesives contain organic solvents, inhalation of which may cause dizziness, fatigue, headache and nausea. Frequent inhalation of even small concentrations of organic solvents may cause irritability, memory failure and in time permanent damage. Very few of the products investigated contain reactive solvents which may contain volatile epoxy components. Inhalation of such reactive volatile components may also lead to allergic reactions in the form of asthmatic breathing.

The major risk when handling epoxy resins is assessed to be skin allergy and skin and eye irritation through direct contact. Disposable gloves do not give adequate protection. Special laminate gloves are developed to resist epoxy materials. Some epoxy resins are found to be mutagenic (inducing mutation in cells) and clastogenic (inducing chromosome damage), but no epoxy resins were found to be carcinogenic or reprotoxic (reducing the ability to have healthy children).

The hardeners usually contain components of the chemical family amines. Most amines are sensitising through skin contact and are strongly irritating or even corrosive through skin and eye contact, but product types vary from irritant to poisonous. Amines may be more or less volatile. Vapours given off will have the same effect as the product. Many amines are allergenic through skin contact, and the volatile products may give off allergenic vapours. Some hardeners may also contain organic solvents.

The conductants in these products are silver, silver-plated copper or nickel. Usually, silver does not involve any further risk when handled wet. Conductants containing nickel compounds are sensitising, and metallic nickel may be carcinogenic.

Vapours emitted from the products may be flammable and can be ignited by sparks or open flames.

Fully cured products do not have any sensitising properties and will not emit any harmful vapours.

All hazards should be related to the actual use of the product before an actual risk can be evaluated. Some of the factors influencing risk through use of a specific product are:

— the amount used per work process;
— the training of the employees;
— the handling of the product;

and, of course,

— the production process, manual or automatic, whether the product is heated as part of the manufacturing process, the need for cleaning agents, generation of waste etc.

18.5.3 Epoxy Adhesives and the Environment

After polymerisation (curing) the water solubility of the resins will be low. The polymers will absorb some water from the air humidity. Some fillers in the resin may raise this absorption level. The smooth surface of the adhesive will become granulated and, on repeated exposure to humidity, the polymer may break and release some substances which will usually be bound in the polymeric matrix.

No information on the ecotoxicity of epoxy polymers has been identified. Due to the low water solubility, the bioavailability is presumed to be very low.

The essential influence on the environment from the use of epoxy adhesives is assessed to be unintended release of epoxy monomers in the organic solvent.

The conductive metals in the adhesives are more or less protected in the polymeric matrix. Little environmental effect is expected from the metals while they are encapsulated in the matrix. However, the metal is foreseen to be washed out in time. In the case of incineration, the metal will be more bioavailable in the ashes, and metal salts may be washed out to the environment from the ashes. Silver is one of the more ecotoxic metals, but most of the salts expected to be formed have very low solubility, which means that the bioavailability is limited.

The major concern regarding metals is considered to be the use of nickel, as this metal is readily taken up in a lot of plants in our food chain. As many individuals are very sensitive to nickel, increasing the possibility of nickel in plants is an undesirable outcome.

Many of the organic solvents used are undesirable in the external environment. However, these concerns should probably be taken most seriously when solvents are released during the manufacturing process. When scrapping electronics containing adhesives, the organic solvents will no longer be present.

18.6 SUBSTITUTION OF THE SOLDERING PROCESS

When substituting tin/lead containing solder with electrically conductive adhesives, more factors than direct action on the environment should be taken into account in order to evaluate the environmental impact.

For instance, an electrical joint with solder will be replaced by a smaller volume of adhesives, typically 10% of the solder volume. As the solder material weighs approximately double the adhesive material per volume, the use of electrically conductive adhesives will reduce the weight of the material to 1/20 compared with soldering in general.

Further, the process for soldering will typically involve cleaning processes, the use of fluxes etc. As the use of CFCs is already banned in Europe, the substitution of CFC-cleaning processes has not been taken into consideration.

The solder will typically be an alloy of tin/lead and the flux is usually based on colophony resin. The use of large amounts of organic solvents as cleaning agents is not necessary when using adhesives. The DTC work in the joint venture project includes a careful examination of the soldering process.

18.7   ENVIRONMENTAL COMPARISON AND RECOMMENDATIONS TO USERS OF CONDUCTIVE ADHESIVES

It is the author's view that it would be advantageous from the standpoint of the working environment to replace the many stages in the soldering process involving chemical substances with an adhesive process. Traditional electronics production suffers from not insignificant problems in the working environment, even though modern electronics firms seem to have solved some of them.

There is also the question of the considerable difference in the quantities that require to be handled in the two processes. For example, the consumption of a quantity of adhesive that is only 5% of that required of solder paste involves only a doubling of the amount of silver consumed, but at the same time a total eradication of the lead used in solder — a reduction in consumption of 16 t/a by the year 2000. Over and above this is the quantity of lead used in the PCB pre-tinning process and the application of terminals to components, amounting to not less than 2 t annually. The amount of epoxy and acrylate compounds used for the soldering mask (essential to the conventional solder technique) is several times larger than the amount of epoxy handled in the adhesive process.

The emission of silver to the environment has proved to be a critical issue, since silver is apparently much more potently ecotoxic than lead. This should, however, be considered in the light of bioaccessibility: this is low for silver, so the amount of silver absorbable in the ecosystem is also low. Thus only a small proportion of the silver compounds emitted will be accessible in the ecosystem where its toxicity becomes a real risk. The timeframe for release of the remainder of the silver compounds is presumably extended.

When replacing tin/lead solder with conductive adhesives, the following factors will be minimised:

— toxic solder fumes in the working environment;
— skin contact with fluxes which may cause irritation and allergy;
— lead poisoning of the environment from the manufacturing process and from the disposal of electronics;
— release of organic solvents due to cleaning, if necessary, in the working environment as well as their release to the external environment.

Using epoxy adhesives demands the following environmental considerations:

— training of workers in handling epoxy to avoid major allergy problems;
— changes in production processes, personal protection;
— the spread of other metals, e.g., silver, in to the general environment;
— regulatory claims;
— replacement of organic solvents, if their use is necessary.

As epoxy-based adhesives have very different environmental properties, the choice should fall on adhesives that present the lowest possible risk of damage to health. The epoxy base should therefore have the lowest possible content of reactive epoxies, and organic solvents should only be used in small quantities and should be of a type that presents the smallest possible risk of harm to the environment and to health. Adhesives based on ingredients less harmful to health should be preferred wherever technically feasible. Silicone adhesives and other materials less harmful to the external environment and the working environment are also worthy of further study.

18.8   ACKNOWLEDGEMENTS

The work represented is part of a joint project, KAMILLE, where DTC investigated the ecotoxicology and health aspects of the use of electrically conductive adhesives.

REFERENCES

1   Allenby, B.R. *et al.*, 'An Assessment of the Use of Lead in Electronics Assembly', Part 1, *Circuit World*, **Vol. 19**, No. 2, pp. 18-27 (1993) and Part 2, *ibid*, **Vol. 19**, No. 3, pp. 25-31 (1993).

2   Clayton and Clayton, 'Patty's Industrial Hygiene and Toxicology', 3rd revised edition, USA (1978).

3   'Conductive Adhesives', BPA (Technology & Management), Inc., Report No. 414, USA, July (1991).

4   Courtney, D., 'Health and Safety in Soft Soldering', *Circuit World,* **Vol. 9**, No. 4 (1993).

5   Danish working services' list of threshold limit values, July (1994).

6   Executive Order No. 199/1985 on epoxy resins and isocyanates issued by the Danish Working Environment service.

7   Fregert, S., 'Possibility of Skin Contact in the Automatic Processes', *Contact Dermatitis,* No. 6, p. 23 (1980).

8   Goh, C.L., 'Occupational Dermatitis from Soldering Flux among Workers in the Electronics Industry', *Contact Dermatitis*, No. 13, pp. 85-90 (1985).

9   Hvims, H.L., 'Adhesives as Solder Replacement for SMT', DELTA report, Danish Electronics, Light & Acoustics, January (1994).

10   Kou, D. *et al.*, 'Dermatological Hazards in the Electronics Industry', *Contact Dermatitis,* No. 22, pp. 1-7 (1990).

11   Richardson, M.L., 'The Dictionary of Substances and their Effects', The Royal Society of Chemistry, England (1992).

12   Sørensen, F. and Petersen, H. J. S., 'Substitution of Organic Solvents and Hazardous Binders by Bonding with Adhesives in the Manufacture of Fabricated Metal Products, Machinery and Equipment', *Staub-Reinhaltung der Luft,* No. 53 (1993).

Subject Index

Surface tension 23, 40, 158-159, 213, 362
Surface to volume ratio 38-39
Swelling 155, 177, 395, 410
Syringe dispensing 178, 381, 388

TAB devices 13
Taguchi method 357
Tape automated bonding 117, 256
Temperature coefficient of resistance 43, 66
Temperature cycling 177, 185, 208, 277, 279, 281, 284-285, 290, 293, 295, 343, 353, 356-357
Temperature cycling test 177, 236, 284, 328
Temperature shock 208, 277
Tensile strength 8, 361
Thermal analysis 104, 356, 385
Thermal coefficient of expansion 129
Thermal conductivity 31, 250, 319, 337, 339, 343-350, 354, 356, 362, 368, 374-375, 385
Thermal cure process 99, 112
Thermal curing 27
Thermal cycling 23, 72, 118, 129, 157, 178, 266, 277, 284, 297, 307, 315, 329, 352, 369, 373
Thermal fatigue 164, 343, 352, 354
Thermal gravimetric analysis 206
Thermal resistance 249, 251, 343, 348-350, 353-356, 362, 364, 368, 370, 374-375
Thermal shock 12, 234, 269
Thermionic emission 46, 48, 51
Thermo gravimetric analysis 104, 276
Thermodynamics 157, 159-160, 162-163
Thermomechanical analyser 132
Thermomechanical analysis 104
Thermomechanical stress 281, 343, 350, 363
Thermoplastic 3-5, 7-9, 23, 31, 33-34, 79, 91, 185-186, 213, 222, 257, 277, 295, 307, 320, 360, 363, 385, 404
Thermoplastic adhesive 4, 8, 156, 179, 185, 258, 274, 277, 315, 323, 326-327, 329, 360, 378-379
Thermoplastic binder 9, 34
Thermoplastic paste adhesive 277
Thermoset 3, 5, 7-9, 24, 102, 360
Thermosetting 17, 27, 29, 34, 79, 117, 155, 164, 179, 185, 188, 213, 222, 257-258, 315, 320, 378-379, 385, 387, 404
Thiol-olefin 18
Thixotropy 30-31

Tin-lead 3, 10, 12, 157, 163, 165, 212-213, 361-365, 374
Tolidine 413
Toluene diisocyanate 412-413
Toxicity 363, 410, 415, 419, 423
Translucent 10
Transmission electron microscopy 104, 225, 306, 331, 396
Triarylsulphonium hexafluoroantimonate 27
Triarylsulphonium salts 24
Trichloroethylene 413
Trimethylol propane 23
Trimethylol propane triacrylate 412
Triol 23
Tripropylene glycol 412
Tunnelling 10, 48, 51, 65, 67-68, 72, 74-75, 313
Two-component epoxy 333

Ultra-fine line circuitry 14
Ultrasonic microscopy 222
Ultra-violet radiation 9
Unbumped flip-chip 267, 269-270
Under bump metallurgy 153
Under-cure 106, 109, 114-115, 146-148, 150
Undercured adhesive 275
Underfill 154, 190, 201, 250-251, 259, 263, 266, 384
Unidirectional conductivity 2, 5
UV curable resin 18-19
UV cure 17, 19, 31, 34
UV cured non-conductive adhesive 6
UV curing 25-27, 29, 379
UV-curing acrylate 412
UV irradiation 17, 27, 29, 315
UV light 18, 25, 118, 185, 199-200, 379-380, 386, 388, 391-393

Vertical interconnection sheet 388
Vinylcyclohexene oxide 20
Viscoelastic fluid 87
Viscosity 7, 20-22, 30-31, 40, 72, 81, 85-87, 89, 91, 100, 111, 158-159, 199, 259, 284, 330, 332, 387
Vitrification 72, 100-101, 108, 111
Void formation 192, 276-277, 284

Work life 19

X-ray photoelectron spectroscopy 331, 396

Yield stress 94, 125